'This deeply researched and provocative study highlights the key significance of Confucian political ideas for Kyoto School thinkers while demonstrating the futility of approaching their philosophy from the standpoint of "moral history"'.

Graham Parkes, *University College Cork, Ireland*

The Philosophy of Japanese Wartime Resistance

The transcripts of the three Kyoto School roundtable discussions of the theme of 'the standpoint of world history and Japan' may now be judged to form the key source text of responsible Pacific War revisionism. Published in the pages of *Chūō Kōron*, the influential magazine of enlightened elite Japanese opinion during the twelve months after Pearl Harbor, these subversive discussions involved four of the finest minds of the second generation of the Kyoto School of philosophy. Tainted by controversy and shrouded in conspiratorial mystery, these transcripts were never republished in Japan after the war, and they have never been translated into English except in selective and often highly biased form.

David Williams has now produced the first objective, balanced and close interpretative reading of these three discussions in their entirety since 1943. This version of the wartime Kyoto School transcripts is neither a translation nor a paraphrase but a fuller rendering in reader-friendly English that is convincingly faithful to the spirit of the original texts. The result is a masterpiece of interpretation and inter-cultural understanding between the Confucian East and the liberal West. Seventy years after Tōjō came to power, these documents of the Japanese resistance to his wartime government and policies exercise a unique claim on students of Japanese history and thought today because of their unrivalled revelatory potential within the vast literature on the Pacific War. *The Philosophy of Japanese Wartime Resistance* may therefore stand as the most trenchant analysis of the political, philosophic and legal foundations of the place of the Pacific War in modern Japanese history yet to appear in any language.

David Williams is one of Europe's leading thinkers on the modern Orient. Born in Los Angeles, he was educated in Japan and at UCLA, and contributed for many years to the opinion section of the *Los Angeles Times*. He has taught at Oxford, where he took his doctorate, Sheffield and Cardiff Universities. He has worked for the Industrial Bank of Japan, Mitsui and Co., the Iran-Japan Petrochemical Co. and *Tōyō Keizai* ('The Oriental Economist'). During twelve of his twenty-five years in Japan he was an editorial writer for *The Japan Times*, before working in financial services in Tokyo, London and New York City. He is the author of *Japan: Beyond the End of History* (1994), *Japan and the Enemies of Open Political Science* (1996) and *Defending Japan's Pacific War: The Kyoto Philosophers and Post-white Power* (2004), and co-editor of *The Left in the Shaping of Japanese Democracy* (with Rikki Kersten, 2006). His work has been short-listed for the Kiriyama Pacific Rim Book Prize and the John Whitney Hall History Award. In 2009 he delivered the inaugural Master Class on Paradigm Innovation in Interdisciplinary Research at University College Cork in the Republic of Ireland, where he is now visiting fellow in philosophy.

Routledge Studies in the Modern History of Asia

1. **The Police in Occupation Japan**
   Control, corruption and resistance to reform
   Christopher Aldous

2. **Chinese Workers**
   A new history
   Jackie Sheehan

3. **The Aftermath of Partition in South Asia**
   Tai Yong Tan and Gyanesh Kudaisya

4. **The Australia–Japan Political Alignment**
   1952 to the present
   Alan Rix

5. **Japan and Singapore in the World Economy**
   Japan's economic advance into Singapore, 1870–1965
   Shimizu Hiroshi and Hirakawa Hitoshi

6. **The Triads as Business**
   Yiu Kong Chu

7. **Contemporary Taiwanese Cultural Nationalism**
   A-chin Hsiau

8. **Religion and Nationalism in India**
   The case of the Punjab
   Harnik Deol

9. **Japanese Industrialisation**
   Historical and cultural perspectives
   Ian Inkster

10. **War and Nationalism in China, 1925–45**
    Hans J. van de Ven

11. **Hong Kong in Transition**
    One country, two systems
    Edited by Robert Ash, Peter Ferdinand, Brian Hook and Robin Porter

12. **Japan's Postwar Economic Recovery and Anglo-Japanese Relations, 1948–62**
    Noriko Yokoi

13. **Japanese Army Stragglers and Memories of the War in Japan, 1950–75**
    Beatrice Trefalt

14. **Ending the Vietnam War**
    The Vietnamese communists' perspective
    Ang Cheng Guan

15. **The Development of the Japanese Nursing Profession**
    Adopting and adapting Western influences
    Aya Takahashi

16. **Women's Suffrage in Asia**
    Gender nationalism and democracy
    Louise Edwards and Mina Roces

17. **The Anglo-Japanese Alliance, 1902–22**
    Phillips Payson O'Brien

18. **The United States and Cambodia, 1870–1969**
    From curiosity to confrontation
    Kenton Clymer

19. **Capitalist Restructuring and the Pacific Rim**
    Ravi Arvind Palat

20. **The United States and Cambodia, 1969–2000**
    A troubled relationship
    Kenton Clymer

21. **British Business in Post-Colonial Malaysia, 1957–70**
    'Neo-colonialism' or 'disengagement'?
    Nicholas J. White

22. **The Rise and Decline of Thai Absolutism**
    Kullada Kesboonchoo Mead

23. **Russian Views of Japan, 1792–1913**
    An anthology of travel writing
    David N. Wells

24. **The Internment of Western Civilians under the Japanese, 1941–45**
    A patchwork of internment
    Bernice Archer

25. **The British Empire and Tibet, 1900–22**
    Wendy Palace

26. **Nationalism in Southeast Asia**
    If the people are with us
    Nicholas Tarling

27. **Women, Work and the Japanese Economic Miracle**
    The case of the cotton textile industry, 1945–75
    Helen Macnaughtan

28. **A Colonial Economy in Crisis**
    Burma's rice cultivators and the world depression of the 1930s
    Ian Brown

29. **A Vietnamese Royal Exile in Japan**
    Prince Cuong De (1882–1951)
    Tran My-Van

30. **Corruption and Good Governance in Asia**
    Nicholas Tarling

31. **US–China Cold War Collaboration, 1971–89**
    S. Mahmud Ali

32. **Rural Economic Development in Japan**
    From the nineteenth century to the Pacific War
    Penelope Francks

33. **Colonial Armies in Southeast Asia**
    Edited by Karl Hack and Tobias Rettig

34. **Intra Asian Trade and the World Market**
    A.J.H. Latham and Heita Kawakatsu

35. **Japanese–German Relations, 1895–1945**
    War, diplomacy and public opinion
    Edited by Christian W. Spang and Rolf-Harald Wippich

36. **Britain's Imperial Cornerstone in China**
    The Chinese maritime customs service, 1854–1949
    Donna Brunero

37. **Colonial Cambodia's 'Bad Frenchmen'**
    The rise of French rule and the life of Thomas Caraman, 1840–87
    Gregor Muller

38. **Japanese–American Civilian Prisoner Exchanges and Detention Camps, 1941–45**
    Bruce Elleman

39. **Regionalism in Southeast Asia**
    Nicholas Tarling

40. **Changing Visions of East Asia, 1943–93**
    Transformations and continuities
    R.B. Smith, edited by Chad J. Mitcham

41. **Christian Heretics in Late Imperial China**
    Christian inculturation and state control, 1720–1850
    Lars P. Laamann

42. **Beijing – A Concise History**
    Stephen G. Haw

43. **The Impact of the Russo–Japanese War**
    Edited by Rotem Kowner

44. **Business-Government Relations in Prewar Japan**
    Peter von Staden

45. **India's Princely States**
    People, princes and colonialism
    Edited by Waltraud Ernst and Biswamoy Pati

46. **Rethinking Gandhi and Nonviolent Relationality**
    Global perspectives
    Edited by Debjani Ganguly and John Docker

47. **The Quest for Gentility in China**
    Negotiations beyond gender and class
    Edited by Daria Berg and Chloë Starr

48. **Forgotten Captives in Japanese Occupied Asia**
    Edited by Kevin Blackburn and Karl Hack

49. **Japanese Diplomacy in the 1950s**
    From isolation to integration
    Edited by Iokibe Makoto, Caroline Rose, Tomaru Junko and John Weste

50. **The Limits of British Colonial Control in South Asia**
    Spaces of disorder in the Indian Ocean region
    Edited by Ashwini Tambe and Harald Fischer-Tiné

51. **On the Borders of State Power**
    Frontiers in the greater Mekong sub-region
    Edited by Martin Gainsborough

52. **Pre-Communist Indochina**
    R.B. Smith, edited by Beryl Williams

53. **Communist Indochina**
    R.B. Smith, edited by Beryl Williams

54. **Port Cities in Asia and Europe**
    Edited by Arndt Graf and Chua Beng Huat

55. **Moscow and the Emergence of Communist Power in China, 1925–30**
    The Nanchang Rising and the birth of the Red Army
    Bruce A. Elleman

56. **Colonialism, Violence and Muslims in Southeast Asia**
    The Maria Hertogh controversy and its aftermath
    Syed Muhd Khairudin Aljunied

57. **Japanese and Hong Kong Film Industries**
    Understanding the origins of East Asian film networks
    Kinnia Shuk-ting

58. **Provincial Life and the Military in Imperial Japan**
    The phantom samurai
    Stewart Lone

59. **Southeast Asia and the Vietnam War**
    Ang Cheng Guan

60. **Southeast Asia and the Great Powers**
    Nicholas Tarling

61. **The Cold War and National Assertion in Southeast Asia**
    Britain, the United States and Burma, 1948–62
    Matthew Foley

62. **The International History of East Asia, 1900–68**
    Trade, ideology and the quest for order
    Edited by Antony Best

63. **Journalism and Politics in Indonesia**
    A critical biography of Mochtar Lubis (1922–2004) as editor and author
    David T. Hill

64. **Atrocity and American Military Justice in Southeast Asia**
    Trial by army
    Louise Barnett

65. **The Japanese Occupation of Borneo, 1941–45**
    Ooi Keat Gin

66. **National Pasts in Europe and East Asia**
    P.W. Preston

67. **Modern China's Ethnic Frontiers**
    A journey to the West
    Hsiao-ting Lin

68. **New Perspectives on the History and Historiography of Southeast Asia**
    Continuing explorations
    Michael Aung-Thwin and Kenneth R. Hall

69. **Food Culture in Colonial Asia**
    A taste of empire
    Cecilia Leong-Salobir

70. **China's Political Economy in Modern Times**
    Changes and economic consequences, 1800–2000
    Kent Deng

71. **Science, Public Health and the State in Modern Asia**
    Edited by Liping Bu, Darwin Stapleton and Ka-che Yip

72. **Russo-Japanese Relations, 1905–17**
    From enemies to allies
    Peter Berton

73. **Reforming Public Health in Occupied Japan, 1945–52**
    Alien prescriptions?
    Christopher Aldous and Akihito Suzuki

74. **Trans-Colonial Modernities in South Asia**
    Edited by Michael S. Dodson and Brian A. Hatcher

75. **The Evolution of the Japanese Developmental State**
    Institutions locked in by ideas
    Hironori Sasada

76. **Status and Security in Southeast Asian States**
    Nicholas Tarling

77. **Lee Kuan Yew's Strategic Thought**
    Ang Cheng Guan

78. **Government, Imperialism and Nationalism in China**
    The Maritime Customs Service and its Chinese staff
    Chihyun Chang

79. **China and Japan in the Russian Imagination, 1685–1922**
    To the ends of the Orient
    Susanna Soojung Lim

80. **Chinese Complaint Systems**
    Natural resistance
    Qiang Fang

81. **Martial Arts and the Body Politic in Meiji Japan**
    Denis Gainty

82. **Gambling, the State and Society in Thailand, c.1800–1945**
    James A. Warren

83. **Post-War Borneo, 1945–50**
    Nationalism, Empire and state-building
    Ooi Keat Gin

84. **China and the First Vietnam War, 1947–54**
    Laura M. Calkins

85. **The Jesuit Missions to China and Peru, 1570–1610**
    Ana Carolina Hosne

86. **Macao – Cultural Interaction and Literary Representations**
    Edited by Katrine K. Wong and C.X. George Wei

87. **Macao – The Formation of a Global City**
    Edited by C.X. George Wei

88. **Women in Modern Burma**
    Tharaphi Than

89. **Museums in China**
    Materialized power and objectified identities
    Tracey L.-D. Lu

90. **Transcultural Encounters between Germany and India**
    Kindred spirits in the 19th and 20th centuries
    Edited by Joanne Miyang Cho, Eric Kurlander and Douglas T. McGetchin

91. **The Philosophy of Japanese Wartime Resistance**
    A reading, with commentary, of the complete texts of the Kyoto School discussions of 'The Standpoint of World History and Japan'
    David Williams

92. **A History of Alcohol and Drugs in Modern South Asia**
    Intoxicating affairs
    Edited by Harald Fischer-Tiné and Jana Tschurenev

93. **Military Force and Elite Power in the Formation of Modern China**
    Edward A. McCord

94. **Japan's Household Registration System and Citizenship**
    Koseki, identification and documentation
    Edited by David Chapman and Karl Jakob Krogness

95. **Itō Hirobumi**
    Japan's first prime minister and father of the Meiji Constitution
    Kazuhiro Takii

The Philosophy of Japanese Wartime Resistance

A reading, with commentary, of the complete texts of the Kyoto School discussions of 'The Standpoint of World History and Japan'

David Williams

Routledge
Taylor & Francis Group
LONDON AND NEW YORK

First published 2014
by Routledge
2 Park Square, Milton Park, Abingdon, Oxfordshire OX14 4RN
and by Routledge
711 Third Avenue, New York, NY 10017, USA

First issued in paperback 2016

Routledge is an imprint of the Taylor & Francis Group, an informa business

© 2014 David Williams

The right of David Williams to be identified as author of this work has been asserted by him in accordance with sections 77 and 78 of the Copyright, Designs and Patents Act 1988.

All rights reserved. No part of this book may be reprinted or reproduced or utilised in any form or by any electronic, mechanical, or other means, now known or hereafter invented, including photocopying and recording, or in any information storage or retrieval system, without permission in writing from the publishers.

Trademark notice: Product or corporate names may be trademarks or registered trademarks, and are used only for identification and explanation without intent to infringe.

British Library Cataloguing in Publication Data
A catalogue record for this book is available from the British Library

Library of Congress Cataloging in Publication Data
Williams, David, 1948 July 19
  The philosophy of Japanese wartime resistance : a reading, with commentary, of the complete texts of the Kyoto School discussions of "the standpoint of world history and Japan" / David Williams.
    pages cm. – (Routledge studies in the modern history of Asia ; 91)
  Includes bibliographical references and index.
  1. Philosophy, Japanese–20th century. 2. World War, 1939-1945–Japan. 3. War (Philosophy) 4. Nishitani, Keiji, 1900-1990. 5. Kosaka, Masaaki, 1900-1969. 6. Koyama, Iwao, 1905-1993. 7. Suzuki, Shigetaka, 1907-1988. I. Title.
  B5241.W553 2014
  181'.12–dc23
              2013025037

ISBN 13: 978-0-415-78811-3 (pbk)
ISBN 13: 978-0-415-47646-1 (hbk)

Typeset in Times New Roman
by Taylor & Francis Books

For Robin Reilly and Kenneth Jones in gratitude, and to honour the memory of Louis Massignon, one of Europe's greatest readers of Oriental texts

A lake on fire: the symbol of revolution
Thus the moral man
Renews the order of history
And makes the significance of the times manifest.
        (*The Book of Changes*, 49th Hexagram)

Contents

Prologue: the Kyoto School, Confucian revolution and the exhaustion of liberal history — xvii
The book in brief and the key research discoveries: the Kyoto School as Kuhnian anomaly — xix
Escape clause: essence vs. attribute, or how a translation became a reading — xxviii
Acknowledgements — xxxv
Japanese usage and style — xl
Dramatis personae: intellectual leaders of the Imperial Navy – Kyoto School resistance to Tōjō — xli
Essential chronology: the Confucian war of ideas between the Yonai-Kyoto School and Tōjō factions — xlv
Texts, conventions and abbreviations — liii

PART I
Introduction and commentary: the prince of our disorder and the fate of Imperial Japan — 1

1. Versailles to Pearl Harbor: Woodrow Wilson and the origin of the ethics of 'liberal imperialism' — 3

2. Ethics as power: the prince of our disorder and the fate of Imperial Japan — 8

What is the Kyoto School? — 14

3. Learning to resist imperialism: the three phases of the classic Kyoto School and the *Chūō Kōron* symposia on 'the standpoint of world history and Japan' — 15

4. Confucianism, realism and liberalism: three approaches to the *Chūō Kōron* symposia — 22

5 How East Asians argue: the Confucian form and language of the
   Chūō Kōron symposia   29

The Pacific War and the exhaustion of liberal history   34

6 The revisionism of what happens when: Parkes, Ōhashi and the
   exhaustion of liberal history   35

7 Rejecting Tōjō's decision for war: the Kyoto School rethinks the
   state, international law and globalization   52

8 Are Japan studies moral? Confucian pacifism and Kellogg-Briand
   liberalism between Voltaire and Walzer   59

The Kyoto School and the Post-Meiji Confucian Revolution   67

9 Endless Pearl Harbors? The Kyoto thinker as grand strategist   68

10 Confucian tipping points: how East Asians make up their minds   80

11 Plotting to bring Tōjō down: the Post-Meiji Confucian Revolution
   and the Kyoto School-Imperial Navy conspiracy   93

PART II
**The Standpoint of World History and Japan or a reading of the
complete texts of the three Chūō Kōron symposia**   107

I   Two weeks before Pearl Harbor: the first symposium   109
     The Standpoint of World History and Japan (26 November 1941)

II   Three days after the fall of the Dutch East Indies: the second
     symposium   182
     *The Ethical and Historical Character of the East Asian
     Co-prosperity Sphere (4 March 1942)*

III Five months after Midway: the third symposium   261
     The Philosophy of World-historical Wars (24 November 1942)

     Index   370

Prologue
The Kyoto School, Confucian revolution and the exhaustion of liberal history

This is the Rosetta Stone of the Pacific War, the text as door of perception, a threshold that once crossed, one cannot re-cross without having transformed one's understanding of the greatest conflict in human history. To decode the wartime reflections of the Kyoto School on the theme of 'the standpoint of world history and Japan' is to attempt to do for Japan studies what Champollion and Young accomplished for Egyptology. It is perhaps no accident that a knowledge of China and Chinese has proven indispensable to cracking the linguistic codes of the political culture of both modern Japan and ancient Egypt. Such is the cultural impact of the ideograph and the formalities of language.

To break a textual code is a revelatory act. It is to pass from the realm of myth and wishful speculation to the disciplines of fact and scientific objectivity. Sometimes condemned as chauvinist and authoritarian, the three transcripts on 'the standpoint of world history and Japan' that appeared in the pages of *Chūō Kōron* in 1942–43 were in fact bold public gestures by young thinkers of the Kyoto School, one that sought to defy the Tōjō ruling clique and alter the course of the Second World War. As such, these texts form what may be *the* key document of the Japanese wartime resistance to predictable repression at home and doomed expansion abroad.

This book, the first decoding and explanation in any language of the complete texts of these far-ranging discussions, shows these Kyoto thinkers to be neither obscurant fascists nor morally callous Buddhists, but rather sober patriots in the Confucian tradition who, after a sustained meditation on German ideas of history, proclaimed the dawn of Asia's renaissance. To discover the Confucianism of the Kyoto School is to expose the power of Confucian revolution in ways that reveal the Pacific War to be a rehearsal and template for any future military confrontation between the United States and China.

Enter Carl Schmitt. Once dismissed, like Heidegger, as an opportunistic Catholic sycophant of Hitler's revolution, Schmitt has emerged as one of the twentieth century's most formidable thinkers on liberal geopolitics and international law. Prophetic on the causes and logic of '9/11', Schmitt as a critic of liberal imperialism enables us to appreciate why the Kyoto School rejected the post-Versailles assault on national sovereignty and the status of the great powers in favour of East Asian autonomy and rational self-mastery.

The Kyoto School proposed a humane version of the East Asian Co-prosperity Sphere, a potential *Großraum* modelled on the Monroe Doctrine, as a successor to the Confucian cosmos. Dispelling liberal confusions about China as well as Japan, the Kyoto School illuminates the character of the first Confucian challenge to our liberal order, while preparing us for East Asian solutions for a world that can no longer afford the follies of Lehman Brothers, the 'War on Terror' or Libor rate corruption.

With the exhaustion of liberal history, Japan studies may now seek to renegotiate its relationship with Orientalism to become something greater and more rigorous than the moral handmaiden of empire. To draw this conclusion is to signal the end of the long chapter of intensely felt liberal moralism among Western students of modern Japan. This liberal hour in the writing of Oriental history traces its roots to Woodrow Wilson's 1919 counter-revolution against the Westphalian system of international law, and then assumed its unmistakable 'Whig' character after the Manchurian Incident of 1931 that opened the road to Pearl Harbor.

Crystallized into a rigid orthodoxy during the Pacific War, it achieved its greatest flowering in the work of such celebrated liberal historians as Bix and Dower, Garon and Nish in the 1980s and 1990s, and began to dissolve with the revelation of the true character of the United States empire after 9/11. Thus, a century since Versailles, the moral spectre of the contagion of judgement may now be banished, and the historian, unencumbered by ethical inferences, is once again free to resume his interrupted vocation as a student of the facts of the Oriental past.

* * *

The epigraph that begins this book and is repeated at the beginning of Chapter 5 is taken from the *I Ching*, the ancient Chinese text known as *The Book of Changes*. The moral challenge proclaimed here animates all that was serious in the Japanese factional struggle to renew the mandate of heaven after the death of the Emperor Meiji in 1912. This translation from the classical Chinese, or, more accurately, interpretative rendering of the 'image' of the 49th Hexagram, is my own.

The book in brief and the key research discoveries
The Kyoto School as Kuhnian anomaly

> Normal science ... is a highly cumulative enterprise, eminently successful in its aim, the steady extension of the scope and precision of scientific knowledge ... Yet one standard product of the scientific enterprise is missing. Normal science does not aim at novelties of fact or theory, and, when successful, finds none. New and unsuspected phenomena are, however, repeatedly uncovered by scientific research, and radical new theories have again and again been invented by scientists ... Discovery commences with the awareness of an anomaly, i.e., with the recognition that nature has somehow violated the paradigm-induced expectations that govern normal science.
>
> (Thomas Kuhn, 'Anomaly and the Emergence of Scientific Discovery'[1])

Overview of the book

This is a study of one of the most provocatively brilliant, indeed notorious, assessments of Japan's place in a Eurocentric global system, made at the very moment when that order was collapsing during the early 1940s. This statement of Japan's historical *Standpunkt* was the work of four thinkers of the Kyoto School and their theme is known in Japanese as '*Sekai-shi-teki Tachiba to Nippon*' or 'the standpoint of world history and Japan'. It took the form, as noted above, of a series of three round-table discussions or symposia held in Kyoto between November 1941 and November 1942, which were then published in the pages of the influential monthly *Chūō Kōron*.

I have divided my presentation and analysis of these Japanese texts into two parts. Part I (chapters 1–11) forms an introduction to the three round-table discussions. Part II (sections I–III) offers a 'reading' or English-friendly rendering of the entirety of the original Japanese text. The publication of this book, alongside Richard F. Calichman's translation of *Overcoming Modernity*, makes two of the most discussed Japanese intellectual interventions in the discourse of the Second World War available in English for the first time.[2]

My reading of the three transcripts that later were revised and censored before being published in book form as *Sekai-shi-teki Tachiba to Nippon* includes numerous footnotes which provide essential background information on the text. I have used these to give details about the writers cited by the participants in the symposia and concise explanations of concepts – European, East Asian and South Asian – of particular significance to the philosophical and academic climate in Japan during the Second World War. In some cases I have used them to highlight where the text achieves a certain importance, even greatness. By contrast, my commentary, that is Chapters 1–11, is devoted to making the text clear and understandable to an English reader without Japanese or specialized philosophical interest who is tackling these remarkable discussions today.

The argument

The audacious anti-Tōjō stance that these Kyoto thinkers adopted on the political and philosophical controversies of the day in the pages of the *Chūō Kōron* symposia has inspired persistent and major interest among students of modern Japan. It might be worth noting that someone coming to Japanese studies from outside the subject may be struck by how resistant some historians of philosophy have been to the application of tried and tested research methods for establishing matters of fact in the study of war. The suggestion would be that the Pacific War, at least for a few older scholars, is not over yet.

Guides to reading classic texts often urge us 'to catch on from the title'. Whether this set of three Japanese symposia and what I have made of them qualifies as a 'classic text' I leave to the reader's judgement, but the title remains a good place to begin to make sense of what this 'reading plus commentary' is about. The word 'philosophy' in my title is best understood by the Western reader as referring to post–Enlightenment ontology in which notions such as 'the people' and 'history' replaced 'God' as the central reality or demiurges. What the Western reader after Hegel must keep in mind is the key role that Buddhism and, more importantly, Confucianism played in this redefinition of reality in Japanese thought.

The word 'resistance' in the title intentionally invites comparisons with examples of European resistance to German and Italian conquest and occupation between 1939 and 1945, but the impact of Confucianism decisively colours the struggle of the Kyoto School with the Tōjō faction before Pearl Harbor and with the Tōjō government until July 1944. In short, Confucian resistance must be understood in East Asian terms.

By 'wartime' I mean the period from the Japanese occupation of Manchuria in 1931 until the Japanese surrender in 1945. Thus the expression 'The Pacific War' (which the Kyoto School did not use) is an umbrella term for the facts of the struggle waged by Imperial Japan against the United States and the British Empire between 1941 and 1945. Other powers were involved, and the road to the war has also figured prominently in the labours of the Western historian on this empirical slice of our past. As used here, the term 'Pacific War' refers strictly to what the historian means by this expression; not what it may encompass for the politician, moralist or wartime propagandist.

In the subtitle, a 'reading' refers to my interpretative rendering or close paraphrase of the whole of the Japanese original. This is not a translation because in my judgement a translation into post-Holocaust English is impossible. Indeed, I argue that no translation will ever be possible without broad recognition and acceptance of 'the exhaustion of liberal history' where the word 'liberal' is understood as denoting a *moral* approach to the study of Japanese intellectual history or, more precisely, *Geistesgeschichte* (*seishinshi*). This liberal method of doing history, sometimes called 'Whig history', has exercised overwhelming influence on how we have hitherto interpreted the events of the Pacific War. If liberalism as a method of understanding the past no longer quite works because it is threatened with exhaustion as an idea, our understanding of the Pacific War will be transformed. This book is, in essence, about that transformation.

Observe that this transformation is undergirded by two contrasting but related propositions. First, I argue that the impact of what I call the 'Moral Revolution of 1914–45' and the 'Moral Aftermath of 1946–2001' encouraged passionate support, and not just among historians, for the idea that moral history is the most compelling and worthy form of historical understanding. However, this twentieth-century liberal form of moral history must be rejected – and this is my second proposition – not only because it does not permit a persuasive reading of the *Chūō Kōron* symposia, but also because this ethical approach to the past subverts any and all attempts to understand the Pacific War or the history of modern East Asia *factually*, that is *objectively*. Indeed, such moralizing as a form of ethical absolutism is the mortal enemy of all historical research.

The factual history of the wartime Kyoto School of philosophy represents a tiny fraction of all the detail we know about the Pacific War. The content of the *Chūō Kōron* discussions involves an even smaller piece of the historical puzzle. However, the failure of successive liberal readings of this document as well as the school of thought that produced it have made these symposia into the Oriental historian's equivalent of a scientific anomaly – using the term, *mutatis mutandis*, as Thomas Kuhn defined it in *The Structure of Scientific Revolutions*: a piece of reality that threatens the foundations of previous historical assumptions about the nature of the Pacific War *as a whole*.

It is the status of the *Chūō Kōron* symposia as an Orientalist, social scientific and historical anomaly that makes this text the Rosetta Stone of the Pacific War. Decoded, these discussions demonstrate that liberalism as a moral approach to the past cannot adequately respond to the wartime Kyoto School nor produce a rigorous reading of this, the key document of the Japanese wartime intellectual resistance to the *policies* of Prime Minister Hideki Tōjō's government. Perhaps even more important, Kuhn's idiom, the plain language of natural scientific reasoning, offers a poignant reminder of how moral imperatives have – at liberal insistence – eroded the factual or research character of the historical sciences since 1914.

My subtitle – 'A reading, with commentary, of the complete texts of the Kyoto School discussions of "the standpoint of world history and Japan"' – summarizes the ambitions behind my determination to find a sounder textual approach for understanding the wartime Kyoto School. Thus, the strategy of selective quotation is consciously rejected here in favour of an analysis of the text in its entirety. The textual whole of the *Chūō Kōron* transcripts is greater than the sum of its parts, and the use of random quotes chosen for purposes of moral critique has proven inadequate to the seriousness of the task at issue. As a key but hitherto neglected factual anomaly, this text is significant for the Western moralist because it undermines the *entire* liberal interpretation of history, Asian or otherwise. In other words, this book marks the death of a *method*.

I arrive at this unsettling conclusion via a long encounter with East Asian society and thought sustained over a lifetime of observation and reflection. In my experience, no text has occasioned such intensity of reading as the *Chūō Kōron* symposia. It demands what Henry James called 'the deep-breathing fixity of total regard'. The theme of the Kyoto School, the hitherto neglected significance of Confucianism to the Kyoto School, and the revelatory importance of the ideas of Carl Schmitt for understanding this text help to signpost the great ports of the non-liberal tradition where I lowered and weighed anchor on my various archival travels and armchair expeditions. Although I began this journey of discovery in fundamental sympathy with the liberal's ethical approach to the past, my enchantment has faded with repeated revelations of the moral or Whig historian's inability to deal with the historical record of the Kyoto School *sono tori* (as it was).

As I uncovered ever more evidence of liberal exhaustion, Confucianism not only revealed the authentic structure of Kyoto School political thought but illuminated in an unrivalled way the nature of the political struggle these Japanese thinkers waged with the Tōjō faction in the unfolding drama of what I call the 'Post-Meiji Confucian Revolution'. This in turn highlighted the failure of the liberal understanding of Confucian revolutions elsewhere in modernizing East Asia, from Korea to Vietnam. In an entirely different vein, Carl Schmitt's revisionist history of international law since the Treaty of Westphalia, which concluded the Thirty Years War (1618–48), provided what liberalism has so singularly proven unable to offer: an explanation of the global outlook of the Kyoto School on something approaching genuine Japanese terms. Finally, Herbert Butterfield's brilliant 1931 dissection of Whig history furnished the outline of a critique that defeats any claim of liberal moralism to qualify as factual history.[3] This confirms the hitherto unsuspected importance of the modern Japanese gift to planetary thinking. The wartime Kyoto School was generous to a fault with its contribution. Armed with such intellectual treasure, I sailed home, like Ulysses, finally confident, for the first time in my career as a student of the Orient, that I was equipped to address the great issues of the Japanese past from the new standpoint of the post-liberal historian.

Lastly, there is a matter of faith in this text. It is the specifically moral quality of 'Whig history' and 'liberal ethics' that explains why religion forms an indispensable leitmotiv in this commentary on the three *Chūō Kōron* discussions. Confucianism as a corrective to Buddhism in Kyoto School thought is one example; the Protestantism of Whig history is another. What I call 'The Moral Revolution of 1914–45' is all but unthinkable without the stimulus of liberal Protestantism, just as Judaism may be the decisive influence on 'The Moral Aftermath of 1946–2001'. Catholicism's contribution to our liberal century since 1914 merits more study. Certainly Roman Catholicism as a classroom experience shaped me more as a liberal than family, ethnic background or sexual orientation. A predictable feature of the Catholic response to modern life is the crisis of faith that Mallarmé called his *nuits de Tournon*. Writing this book has been the occasion of my own *nuits de Tournon*, and so I ask the reader's forbearance if occasionally I conjure visions of 'the bare ruined choirs where once the sweet birds sang'.

Thesis and evidence

The dynamic relationship between thesis and proof – that is, between a proposition or theory about the nature of an aspect of reality, and the evidence gathered to demonstrate that this theory is true – unites the researcher in the humanities and most sciences; physics is in its own realm. The meaning I give to the word 'reality' may sound Newtonian or passé to students of nature after Einstein, but that is the way research works in my end of the library of human knowledge. Furthermore, while I am a great admirer of Friedrich Nietzsche, his dictum that 'there are no facts, only interpretations' has been placed to one side in what follows.

Thus in the book before you, *The Philosophy of Japanese Wartime Resistance*, I seek to *prove* the broad thesis of how philosophy, politics and the history of ideas collided during the early 1940s in Kyoto, the secret intellectual capital of the Pacific War, that I first proposed in *Defending Japan's Pacific War*.[4] I encourage the reader to make up his own mind about whether I have succeeded in doing so.

In my earlier book I sought to deconstruct the sandy foundations of Pacific War orthodoxy and defend the Kyoto School from its critics by demonstrating its liberal-minded credentials. By contrast, *The Philosophy of Japanese Wartime Resistance* offers a 'total reading' of a timely political text of enduring philosophical interest that is by its essential nature at once *pre-* and *post-liberal* in character. As a reader of Japanese, my ambition has been to meet the expectations of the finest interpreters of Asian and Islamic writings that European Orientalism has produced without falling foul of the kind of metaphysical and methodological errors of which students of the Orient have been accused. I am therefore entirely at one with French Orientalists such as Louis Massignon (1883–1962), the great expert on Shia Islam, and Paul Mus (1902–69), one of the dazzling minds of the École Française d'Extrême-Orient, in their shared conviction that if one is to penetrate the human heart of any great Oriental text, Japanese or otherwise, one must resist, as Edward Said has put it, any 'sort of inert piling up ... of sources, origins, proofs, demonstrations, and the like', which has so often characterized Orientalism at its least inspiring. Rather, one must strive to 'include as much of the context of a text or problem as possible, to animate, to surprise the reader, almost, with the glancing insights available to anyone who ... is willing to cross disciplinary and traditional boundaries'.[5]

What is required if we are to penetrate the human heart of the *Chūō Kōron* symposia? Four steps are necessary. First, we must agree that after decades of interpretive failure, the tenets of the orthodox Allied interpretation of the Pacific War, the product of the Moral Revolution of our liberal century and the propaganda needs of a wartime emergency, do not allow us to read the writings of the Kyoto School with clarity, confidence and accuracy. This orthodoxy must be treated by the serious historian of ideas as what it is: a flawed branch of Whig moralizing.

Second, we must embrace the proposition that piecemeal translations and the selection of out-of-context quotations as *methods of research* have conspired against the fulfilment of our duty as historians and heirs of Leopold von Ranke to describe the past *as it was*. Since 1945, 'the standpoint of world history' as a theme of wartime reflection has repeatedly defeated us, whatever our nationality and whatever the linguistic gifts we have brought to the task. The only practical solution, in my judgement, is to prepare a reading of this substantial text *in its entirety*, and then take up the challenge of interpreting it fairly and properly: that is, without yielding to the temptations to judge the morals of the past.

Third, we must recognize that post-war Japanese studies has been the sad victim of a revolution in European ideas about war and peace, the state and sovereignty. This revolution has a precise if almost forgotten genealogy. As an ideology and set of ideals, the liberal conscience sought in reaction to the slaughter of the Great War to banish inter-state conflict from human affairs. The monuments of inter-war pacifism include the Treaty of Versailles (1919), the League of Nations (which first met in 1920) and the Kellogg-Briand Pact of 1928. The same spirit later inspired the creation of the United Nations and the imposition of Article 9 on Japan's post-war pacifist constitution. These form key chapters in the Moral Revolution of 1914–45 that began to assume institutional form with Wilson's 1919 assault on the Westphalian state system.

Many of these ethical aspirations have now been disappointed. The War on Terror and the consolidation of the United States' global empire have, for example, encouraged growing acceptance of the view that a high-minded but now antiquated form of international liberalism has led directly and inevitably to the rise of what Benno Teschke has called a distinctly 'liberal way of war'.[6] This trajectory runs from Woodrow Wilson's 'war to end all wars', to Harry Truman's 'liberal wars of annihilation', of which the Pacific War qualifies as one of the most murderous. Always the goal is the same: the forced transformation of a 'bad' society – where the word 'bad' means 'illiberal' – into a liberal one. Nothing less will do because there can be no compromise with evil. America's War on Terror since 2001 does not, according to the new consensus, confound liberal logic; it fulfils it.

Fourth, we must acknowledge the prophetic character of the *Chūō Kōron* discussions. The wartime Kyoto School encourages us to recognize the enormous but often obscured impact of Confucian patterns of thought and behaviour not only on modern and contemporary Japanese politics but on Chinese political affairs and diplomacy as well. The suggestion would be that China's hegemonic potential will promote the cultivation of a Confucian moral world order that at many points departs from and therefore clashes with the liberal world-view that governs our international system today. In this sense, the Kyoto School may help us not only to make better sense of our recent global past but also to prepare us intellectually and ethically for a future in which Confucian East Asia may be very well able to resist the homogenization of the world into a 'liberal flatland'.[7] The suspicion must therefore be that only if we put aside or, to use Edmund Husserl's useful technique, temporarily suspend or 'bracket' liberal values will we be able to read this Kyoto School text as both historical revelation and instructive prophecy.

Principal research discoveries and interpretations

The main insights yielded by my reading of the *Chūō Kōron* transcripts may be summarized as follows:

- Demonstration of the decisive importance of Confucianism to the political reflections of the wartime Kyoto School. So crucial and influential is this Chinese code of ethics to wartime Japanese thought and conduct that I suspect the entire Western understanding of modern government and politics not only in Japan but also in China, Korea, Vietnam and Singapore may have to be rethought in the light of the enduring legacy of Confucian tradition that is so active in Kyoto philosophy.
- The introduction, definition and application of the rubric of 'Confucian revolution' as a form of regime change driven by factional struggle in order to understand the real nature of the intellectual struggle between the Kyoto School and the supporters of Tōjō's policies. In this clash of ideas as a battle for discourse hegemony, the Kyoto School provides the empirical and theoretical foundations for a more plausible understanding than any hitherto offered of the nature of Japanese wartime resistance to official attempts to suppress internal criticism and thus thwart efforts to dislodge Tōjō from power. In short, the example of the 'Post-Meiji Confucian Revolution' as a normal, legitimate and predictable form of regime change is proposed. This provides a more objective way to

interpret Japanese political history between 1912 and 1945 than any offered by the moral historian.
- The clarifying – indeed, theoretically liberating – notion that the defining narrative of international relations between the First World War and the War on Terror is not the decline of European imperialism, the rise and fall of Soviet Communism, the challenge of fascism or Japanese expansionism, but rather America's rise to the status of global hegemon.
- The overwhelming significance of the notion of subjectivity, as Hegel and Weber might have defined it, in 1941–42 to the entire thrust of wartime Kyoto thought. Subjectivity or *shutaisei* – that is, effective agency – is the ruling idea and unifying concept of all three symposia.
- The discovery of a set of compelling textual reasons for 'bracketing' the ruling ethical assumptions of the our Kantian liberal-cosmopolitan orthodoxy on the nature of the state and the law of war in order to arrive at a persuasive appreciation of the political and moral standpoint of the wartime Kyoto School.
- The indispensability of Carl Schmitt's reflections on sovereignty and international law if we are to grasp the global context of Kyoto School thought as a reaction to the eclipse of the Eurocentric system of modern states and international law after 1918. My reservations on Schmitt's insights include the relative neglect of Japan and the Confucian state system in his reflections on the ideas of Alfred T. Mahan and the concept of the *Großraum* in *Land und Meer* (1942) and *Der Nomos der Erde im Völkerrecht des Jus Publicum Europaeum*.[8]
- The prophetic nature of the Kyoto School meditation on the inequalities between nations that have become so prominent in the age of 'failed states' and 'the bottom billion'.[9] The first requirement of an emerging nation is not freedom but agency and self-mastery (*shutai*).
- The comprehensive overthrow of the conventional understanding of the wartime expressions used by the wartime Kyoto School, such as *sō ryoku sen*, *hakkō no ichi-u*, *kyōeiken*, *kindai no chōkoku* and *dōtoku-teki seimeiryoku*.
- The chapter and verse demonstration of the exhaustion of Whig history as a manifestation of liberal ethics, laying the ground for a definitive rejection of 'moral history' as a contradiction in terms.

Conclusion

The Philosophy of Japanese Wartime Resistance is a form of thought experiment that tries to prove a thesis or argument. As an experiment in empiricism, this study of the wartime Kyoto School inevitably differs in scope, structure and tone from its 2004 companion volume. In presenting a reading of and commentary on what is a very demanding Japanese text, my scope here is inevitably narrower. The structure of my exposition has been shaped by the structure of the original, and the tone aspired to is one of modest precision, punctuated by very occasional cries of 'Eureka!' when some extraordinary rupture or tear appears in the Japanese transcripts.

As an enterprise in interdisciplinary research, this book draws on four fields or domains of human knowledge: social science (particularly political science and sociology) for its rigorous approach to theory and evidence; Orientalism for its unrivalled powers of reading in depth as an act of translation; history for its factual-minded rejection of moral judgements; and the theory of international law for its systemic revisionism. Success in interdisciplinary research is achievable only if we submit to the strict protocols of reading, research and writing that govern the fields from which we propose to borrow. The wolves of academic lawlessness have no place here.

The spirit of this empirical exercise in textual depth and total reading is nicely captured by Ernest Renan, the formidable nineteenth-century philologist and Orientalist, in his observation – following Curver's nice phrase, 'Philosophy is instructing the world in theory' – that 'To do philosophy is to know things'.[10] This is what I believe the wartime Kyoto School attempted to do. Only by reading this text faithfully and scientifically, in a secular spirit, will we be able to judge for ourselves whether these Japanese thinkers succeeded.

Notes

1 Thomas Kuhn, 'Anomaly and the Emergence of Scientific Discovery', in *The Structure of Scientific Revolutions*, 2nd edn, Chicago and London: University of Chicago Press, 1970, pp. 52–53.
2 Richard F. Calichman, *Overcoming Modernity: Cultural Identity in Wartime Japan*, New York: Columbia University Press, 2008.
3 Herbert Butterfield, *The Whig Interpretation of History*, New York and London: W.W. Norton & Co., 1965.
4 David Williams, *Defending Japan's Pacific War: The Kyoto School Philosophers and Post-White Power*, London and New York: RoutledgeCurzon, 2004.
5 Edward W. Said, *Orientalism*, Harmondsworth: Peregrine Books, 1985, p. 267.
6 Benno Teschke, 'Exorcizing Schmitt', *New Left Review*, 67, Jan.–Feb. 2011, p. 66.
7 Thomas Friedman, *The World is Flat: A Brief History of the Twenty-First Century*, New York: Farrar, Straus & Giroux, 2005.
8 Berlin & Duncker, 1950; English version translated by G.L. Ulmen, *The Nomos of the Earth in the International Law of the Jus Publicum Europaeum*, New York: Telos Press, 2003/2006.
9 Paul Collier, *The Bottom Billion: Why the Poorest Countries are Failing and What Can Be Done About It*, Oxford: Oxford University Press, 2007.
10 Cited and translated by Edward W. Said in *Orientalism*, p. 132.

Escape clause
Essence vs. attribute, or how a translation became a reading

When I was eleven or so, the Sister of Divine Providence who taught my class of fifty-five or so attentive but confident pupils at my Los Angeles parochial school decided that we needed to be equipped with a more sophisticated understanding of the Transubstantiation. That doctrine holds, of course, that during the Consecration of the Mass, the bread and wine that the priest uses to celebrate the Eucharist are transformed, not symbolically but literally, into the body and blood of Christ. As was often the case, the quest for sophistication in such matters returned us, nun in hand, to the ancient Greeks. Sister's explanation pivoted on Aristotle's distinction between 'essence' and 'attribute'. After the Consecration, as before, the communion wafer looked, tasted and smelt like bread – but these were mere attributes. The bread's essence had been transformed into something else: the body of Jesus. Confronted with this Aristotelian exposition, the class wit immediately thrust up his hand and observed, 'Ah yes, Sister, bread with the bread removed'. So when is a translation that smells, tastes and looks like a translation, not a translation? Essence versus attribute. Welcome to the miraculous realm of the meta-text, where translation is a resurrection but not of the body.

Heian Chippendale

One of the supreme masterpieces of Japanese Orientalism is Arthur Waley's translation of *The Tale of the Genji*, the tenth-century novel of court life and sexual intrigue in the Heian period, one of the earliest examples of this genre and perhaps the finest ever written by a woman. Working on this very challenging text in the basement of the British Museum, Waley, who apparently never visited Japan, encountered one of those dilemmas that makes translation a byword for frustration and betrayal. Certainly from the Heian period until almost yesterday, the Japanese have lived their lives, as it were, on the floor: on *tatami* or some other form of mat or, if very poor but proper, on immaculately swept earthen floors. Waley was perfectly capable of understanding what the Japanese text said about such arrangements, but he had no confidence whatever that he could confront his Edwardian readers with the vision of aristocrats, Japanese or otherwise, slithering across the floor in one scene after another in a great novel. So he was tempted to furnish the Heian court portrayed by Shikibu Murasaki with something that would never have occurred to her. He considered altering her text in his translation to include chairs.

Note that the problem occurs not in the original novel but in the mind of the Western reader. No Japanese, then or now, would have any trouble conceiving of life unfolding on *tatami*. As the difficulty is confined to the assumptions of the reader, translation studies refers to this dilemma as an aspect of 'reception theory'. The message in the bottle is clear: the difficulty arises entirely within the mind of the person who finds and opens the bottle. More than a thousand years after Murasaki set down her ink brush, *Sekai-shi-teki Tachiba to Nippon* conjures up the reception theory equivalent to what the meteorologist terms a 'perfect storm'.

What is the moral equivalent of a chair? The very title of our second symposium poses this translation quandary in categorical terms: 'The Ethical and Historical Character of the East Asian Co-prosperity Sphere.' The orthodox liberal interpretation of the Pacific War holds that the 'Co-prosperity Sphere' was a sham, a mere pretext for Japanese imperialism. How can a sham be moral? If this is more than a mere play of words, whatever *do* our Kyoto thinkers mean by 'ethical'? Is it just a propaganda pretence to political virtue: a moral cover-up of manifest wrongdoing? Whatever it means, how is it to be translated into post-Holocaust English and still carry conviction with the Western reader? How are the words 'moral' and 'ethical' to work, as it were, on the page?

If this were not enough, such reception theory dilemmas defeat any contrived solution such as Waley proposed with his Heian Chippendale, because the problem of reception is not confined to the Western reader. Many Japanese would pose harsh objections of their own to the wartime use of the word 'ethical' to describe the nature and intent of the Greater East Asian Co-prosperity Sphere. The problematic nature of our Kyoto School message in a bottle would appear to be all but overwhelming, such as to confound *any* attempt to translate this formidable text from wartime Japanese to contemporary English.

Confronted with this conundrum, one might be tempted to close one's eyes to the intractable aspect of the problem and boldly proceed to render *rinri-teki* as 'ethical' and *dōtoku-teki* as 'moral' because these words occur so often in the text as to conspire against the frequent repetition of a complex paraphrase or gloss. However, such practicality merely shifts on to the reader the burden of the hermeneutic task of getting true meaning from one mind to another, and this is hardly a trivial concern when it involves using English words, as it were, without English meanings. Such practicality would demand that every time the reader encounters these words on the page, he translate them in his head in ways that confront him repeatedly with the uncompromising vocabulary of an alien and all but incommensurate moral cosmos. Colliding with this ethical iceberg, my enterprise as a *translation* project sank. After this, only a 'reading' would do.

The matter requires blunt statement because of the commonplace insistence by many readers that all they want from a translator is a clear and simple *verbum pro verbo* paraphrase of the original. So let us set out the challenge of a total reading with an unforgiving paradox: to 'translate' the content of the three transcripts that compose the *Chūō Kōron* symposia into credible post-Holocaust English today would have entailed, indeed required, a wilful refusal to understand it. The contemporary Western reader is, as it were, 'word-blind' to wartime Japanese texts such as our three *Chūō Kōrōn* transcripts because of a major change in liberal values and sensibility since 1919. Note that a change in Western sensibility explains why the whole meaning and import of this text – its significance – would have been lost in translation. The Moral Revolution and the Moral Aftermath have thus all but destroyed the possibility of the kind of hermeneutic success that is the normal promise of a conventional translation. Our word-blindness explains why sections I–III, much the larger part of this book, had of necessity to become a meta-text – that is, a text about another text. A literal translation was not an option.

The truth of this whole affair is that because we liberal readers, as liberals, are morally *incapable* of being faithful to the original, any translator of this text would be condemned to betray it. It may simply be the case that it is still too early to attempt to translate the three transcripts that travel under the informal flag of convenience that is the theme of 'the standpoint of world history and Japan' because we are not ready, that is, not mentally and morally prepared, for the leap of understanding required. While a translation would have faltered over the attributes of the text, my reading aims to provide only the essence of the thing.

Sō ryoku sen: from 'all-out war' to 'world-historical war'

> The expression 'world-historical war' (*sō ryoku sen*) is shorthand for the transformation of everything. And such struggles cannot be understood merely as 'wars' or matters merely of military tactics.
> (Shigetaka Suzuki, third symposium, 3)

Confucian tradition classically places great stress on the need for regular exercises in the rectification of names. Because the names we give to pieces of reality may gradually come to describe our imaginings about reality rather than what is actually there, meticulous effort must be routinely exerted to ensure the soundness of any form of truth that unites words and things. Only in this way can linguistic precision be preserved.

The rectification of names demands care at every level of a discourse. For those still clinging to their faith in *verbum pro verbo* paraphrase, it might be well to note that thus far we have wrestled just with the *titles* of our three symposia. Indeed, we have addressed but one of the formidable difficulties posed by a single word in the title of only the second symposium: the term 'ethical' as it occurs in the phrase 'The Ethical and Historical Character of the East Asian Co-prosperity Sphere'.

What about 'historical' as in the 'historical character' of the East Asian Co-prosperity Sphere? The Kyoto School's use of the word 'historical' derives from the ideas of two German thinkers: the philosopher G.W.F. Hegel and the historian Otto von Ranke. The contributors to the *Chūō Kōron* discussions have reworked the hard metaphysical soil of this complex German inheritance from two European thinkers into Japanese expressions of great contemporary plausibility and power.

For the wartime Kyoto thinker, the meaning of the word 'historical' refers to the rejection of eternal or ahistorical norms and truths. The historicist insists that man inherits no ideas from God or Nature; everything he would possess he must create himself. All truth must be derived from his experience because all of his ideas are his own alone (these Japanese readers knew their Vico). However, in a kind of *complexio oppositorum*, history itself conjures up and sustains enduring standards of communal or national achievement. This is what the Kyoto School believed defined world-historical success.

Observe that merely by using the word 'historical' in this way, the contributors to our symposia aroused the ire of Japanese ultranationalists because the truth of eternal essences was being denied in ways that called into doubt any enduring Japanese essence. The implicit message of the Kyoto School thinker was that all standards of real world success must derive from world history and not from the Japanese national experience, mythical or religious. In short, mid-twentieth-century Japan as a national success story was to be judged by standards that had their origins outside Japan. All this conceptual dynamite is compacted in the single word 'historical'.

An entirely different challenge is posed by the title of the third and longest symposium: *Sō ryoku sen no tetsugaku*, or 'the philosophy (*tetsugaku*) of total or all-out (*sō*) war (*sen*)'. Leaving aside the issue of what 'philosophy', strictly speaking, could possibly mean in this context, there is the vexed issued of determining what 'war' these Kyoto School thinkers are referring to when they use the word *sen*. The first symposium was held before the attack on Pearl Harbor, so it seems fair to ask what war anyone anywhere thought they were fighting in November 1941. Certainly these Japanese thinkers do not refer to the 'Second World War' in the pages of the *Chūō Kōron* transcripts even after the air strike against US naval forces in Hawaii.

Post-war Japanese historians regularly use the expression 'Pacific War', but in ways that distinguish that conflict both from the Second World War more broadly and also from the Second Sino–Japanese War that began in 1937. Cognisant of the resulting lacunae, some post-war Japanese historians have resorted to the expression 'Asia–Pacific War'; but this, too, distinguishes Imperial Japan's struggle with America, Britain and China from the conflict in Europe and Africa. To complicate the picture further, a small minority of Japanese historians refer to the struggle from 1931 to 1945 – that is, the period between the Japanese expulsion of Chinese forces from Manchuria and

xxxii *Escape clause*

the atomic destruction of Hiroshima and Nagasaki – as 'The Fifteen-Year War'. The implied rejection of the historical rubric of 'the Second World War' is intentional.

Within the wartime Kyoto School, the fall of France in 1940 was recognized as a major event that demonstrated the decay of French moral energy during what in the first symposium is called the 'Second European War'. Furthermore, the expression 'Pacific War' tended not to be used by the Kyoto School even after 1945. Writing in 1965, for example, Ōshima still speaks of 'The Great East Asian War'.[1] Despite the conservative taint that has been assigned to this expression since 1945, the close reader of the *Chūō Kōron* symposia will note that in grand strategic terms, the concept of a 'Great East Asian War' is the correct rubric for the wartime Kyoto School, for whom the oceanic contest with the Anglo-Saxons was a tactical means to achieve a regional goal: the independence and military security of East Asia as a whole.

The wartime Kyoto School thought that Japan was fighting 'The Great East Asian War'. The nature, significance and consequences of the Pacific War, as an object of understanding, form the substance of a *Western* liberal problem of historical interpretation. The exhaustion of liberal history is a Western problem, but naming the 'war' does not tell us about the nature of the war. What kind of war did the Kyoto School think that Imperial Japan was fighting?

As noted above, the title of the third symposium is usually rendered as either 'The philosophy of total war' or 'The philosophy of all-out war'. Given the wide acceptance of this terminology, it was disconcerting to discover that none of the standard reference dictionaries – neither bilingual reference books (English–Japanese dictionaries, for example) nor *kokugo jiten* (that is, dictionaries of the Japanese language itself) – provides a translation that can withstand a close reading of *Sekai-shi-teki Tachiba to Nippon*. Again, linguistic complications of the most taxing sort plague the would-be translator.

For one thing, the Japanese have a different expression for the German phrase *totale Krieg* or, in English, 'total war'. This is *zentai sen*, in which *sen* is, as before, the Chinese character for 'war' and the Chinese character compound *zentai* refers to 'total', as in the expression 'totalitarianism' or *zentaishugi*. *Sō ryoku sen*, on the other hand, tends to be understood as either an alternative Japanese rendering of *totale Krieg* or a home-grown expression that appears to describe the twentieth-century phenomenon of complete mobilization for war.

Over the course of these three round-table discussions, the four contributors (and their censors and editors) may have used the word 'war' perhaps 500 times, and they knew what they meant when they employed this word. These Japanese thinkers are clear and consistent. They do not conceive of their nation's titanic struggle with China, America and the British Empire as a 'total war' in the conventional English dictionary sense. They do not see it as a form of Ernst Jünger's total mobilization or as Clausewitzian absolute war. They explicitly reject Ludendorff's stress on the decisive importance of 'morale'. They dismiss Wilson's notion of a war to end all wars. They think that the liberal pacifist crusade to ban war by making it illegal because immoral is woolly and self-defeating. The war-making innovations of Napoleon, Lincoln, Bismarck, Clemenceau and Lloyd George are acknowledged, explicitly or otherwise, but serve mainly as counter-examples. Hegel's interpretation of the significance of the Battle of Jena is another matter.

The principal consequence of this terminological precision about the nature of war for the reader, translator or commentator who would address the theme of 'the standpoint of world history and Japan' is unavoidable. Neither 'total war' nor 'all-out war' will do as an English rendering of *sō ryoku sen*. Only the closest reading of the text can save the unwary liberal from compounding an unfortunate limitation of *Japanese* dictionaries: the false ethical conclusion that the expression 'a war of our all powers' must always be elided into 'all-out war' *for liberal reasons*. This lapse becomes indefensible when one encounters what the literary structuralist might call a 'tear' or 'burn hole' in the fabric of the text of the third symposium where *sōryoku* is set out on the page as not one but *two* words: *sō* and *ryoku*. One might be tempted to conclude that this is a typographical error, but such mistakes are so rare, certainly in my experience, in Japanese proofread printed texts as to make this conclusion highly implausible. Even if it was a 'typo', the point would still stand: *sō* is not an adjective but a noun. This makes *sō ryoku* into an idea on its own in which *sō* refers to the 'all' in the translation of *sō ryoku* as 'all of our powers, strengths, capabilities and capacities'. The text demonstrates that this conclusion is not a matter of opinion, moral or otherwise.

As allies of the Yonai faction of the Imperial Japanese Navy, the members of the wartime Kyoto School opposed the timing of Tōjō's decision for war, the grand strategy that guided his direction of the war and his methods of waging this conflict, particularly on the Chinese mainland and in South-East Asia. As is clear in the text and between the lines of the *Chūō Kōron* transcripts and also *The Ōshima Memos*, these philosophers thought that Tōjō's war of strategic despair would end in disaster. However, if the war was to be fought under such unfavourable conditions, the intellectual task of the moment was to make clear to the Japanese elite what was at stake in any struggle, now or later, to secure the subjectivity, security and future of East Asian civilization.

In the early 1940s, history presented the Japanese people with an unprecedented opportunity to change the world by overthrowing the European global order before either the Chinese giant woke up as an ethnic Han superpower or the emerging American empire made itself the planet's hegemon. Rejecting the European, Chinese and American commitment to global *imperia*, the Kyoto School called for a world of independent regions, beginning with East Asia, to be left to manage their own affairs without interference from outside. The creation of this world, one formed of a plurality of 'historical worlds' (*rekishi sekai*), would qualify as an epic transformation of world history that would secure Hegel's laurel as 'a world-historical people' for the Japanese nation. Imperial Japan was thus compelled to engage in a valiant and originary struggle to remake the world ethically by fighting the only kind of war truly worth waging: a world-historical war. Armed with this insight, one may finally appreciate that the titles of the three symposia are in effect three versions or statements of the same moral vision:

- The Standpoint of World History and Japan
- The Ethical and Historical Character of the East Asian Co-prosperity Sphere
- The Philosophy of World-historical Wars

Notes

1 Ōshima Yasumasa, 'Dai-tōa Sensō to Kyōto-gakuha: Chishiki-jin no Seiji Sanka ni tsuite' (The Great East Asian War and the Kyoto School: On the Political Involvement of Intellectuals), *Chūō Kōron*, 80, Aug. 1965.

Acknowledgements

This book is a celebration of reading and readers. Conceived in that *dokusho ōkoku* (kingdom of reading) that has been modern Japan, advanced during perfect-for-reading frosty nights and pristine mornings on Exmoor (the West Country is home to some of Britain's best-used public libraries), and finally brought to conclusion in Cardiff in my book-crowded study with a glass wall overlooking the Taff, this project has been aided and sustained by a legion of readers, many of them voracious, on three continents. Indeed, a hopeless weakness for reading is one quality that these readers and I share with the participants in the *Chūō Kōron* discussions.

Many of the books these Japanese thinkers cite almost casually in these extraordinary Japanese transcripts were still being passed from hand to hand, shelf to shelf, by young students when I first arrived in Tokyo in 1968. My fate as a reader of Asian texts was sealed on my first visit to Kanda, that district of the Japanese capital which at the time could probably boast the greatest concentration of bookstores in the world. It is the search for such treasures that explains why the Orientalist, as Flaubert observed, travels so much. But for my love of Europe and Europeans I would never have left Orient.

Unlike writers, readers expect to find the whole of the world to be already gathered between the covers of the books with which they spend their lives. Certainly the discovery of the North-West Passage through the moral fog that has bedevilled the Western student of East Asia for almost a century now was *never* my intention. However, with the support of my well-read colleagues and students, my bibliophile friends and those closest to me, I have managed to discover, finally, the startling moral realm, undreamt by our liberal age, that is the East. So unlikely a venture sustained over so long a period has required quiet, stimulus, patience, support and serious talk.

Special thanks are owed to Peter Sowden, the legendary RoutlegeCurzon editor who first commissioned *Japan: Beyond the End of History* back in the early 1990s. He has patiently endured my years of intellectual frustration with the conundrums raised by Japanese Confucianism and the anti-liberalism of the wartime Kyoto School. He never flagged in his support. This depth of commitment to so revisionary a project has been invaluable during the long – sometimes painful, sometimes profoundly rewarding – term of gestation.

Under the pressure of Second World War liberal orthodoxy, I first sought to demonstrate that, appearances to the contrary, the wartime Kyoto thinker was at heart a kind of *bien-pensant* liberal engaged in a form of resistance to despotic authoritarianism. By 'resistance', I meant something comparable to the 'White Rose' moment in Nazi Germany or the spirit of elite opposition to Mussolini one finds in such courageous figures as Dino Grandi. This flawed thesis influenced the original title proposed for this book: *The Kyoto School Philosophy of Wartime Resistance*. Now I realize that liberalism has been the principal barrier that has conspired against my acceptance of Asia and Asians as they are rather than as I would wish them to be.

Two exemplary products of the International Christian University in Tokyo played indispensable roles in aiding the progress of this project. At the very beginning, Eiichi Shimizu, the industrious translation-rights broker and bibliophile *extraordinaire*, arranged a meeting with Chūō Kōron-sha, the original publisher of the *Chūō Kōron* transcripts in all its printed forms. I am grateful for the useful and sober advice I received then and subsequently. As I approached completion of this book, Setsuko Aihara, the distinguished reader of Nishitani, portrait painter and polymath, was gratifyingly generous with her time in Cork checking my 'readings' of some of the more opaque turns of phrase in the text.

When deep into this project, I asked Robin Reilly, whom I met at Oxford, to read my version of the entire text of *the Chūō Kōron* discussions. As the author of *The Sixth Floor: The Danish Resistance Movement and the RAF Raid on Gestapo Headquarters, March 1945*,[1] his view mattered to me, and it was incisive. He thought that whatever struggle the Kyoto School was waging, its war with Tōjō was not comparable with the radical dissent from National Socialism or Italian Fascism or indeed to the opposition to Axis occupation that fuelled resistance movements across Europe. Something else was going on in the pages of these three Japanese symposia. However, having encouraged doubt about my *concept* of the book, Robin seized on two aspects of my research that proved decisive to the breakthrough when it came. First he insisted that my earlier critique of neo-Marxist writings about wartime Japan was more than an exercise in criticism or book reviewing: it suggested a *method* for reading texts closely. His other point was that chronology – timelines that linked texts and events in the real world – would prove uniquely illuminating. Both of these insights were sound. Thus the path was cleared for the transformation of a flawed concept into something more robust.

Pursuing this method for close reading of difficult Japanese texts, I developed an almost inexhaustible hunger for primary sources. This need was fed with unique passion and determination by Professor Kenneth Jones, another product of the International Christian University. His relentless raids on the libraries and bookstores of Tokyo proved indispensable to whatever success this book has achieved. For his tireless support over eight long years I am grateful and more. But for the method and the supply of primary sources, this book would have not been written.

The scholarship of Graham Parkes and Ryōsuke Ōhashi has been an enormous stimulus, particularly during the period of exploratory uncertainty between the appearance of *Defending Japan's Pacific War* in 2004 and my discovery of the Confucian *kosō* or the archaeology of knowledge at work in wartime Kyoto School thought. I have devoted a chapter here to their pioneering labours as a mark of respect and gratitude.

Orientalism is what Orientalists do at night. A long evening of intense discussion in Sacramento with Richard Shek, the thoughtful Ming historian and a former classmate, helped me make better sense of the Confucian dimension of Kyoto School ideas as a programme of national reform. On some future occasion, we need to spend another evening addressing the intellectually unsettling aspects of Ming loyalism. The impact of such unorthodox forms of Chinese resistance to foreign rule may stand as the most important *unaddressed* issue that East Asian tradition presents to the reader of the *Chūō Kōron* symposia. Only the cultural implications of Vietnam's millennium-old struggle against Chinese imperialism may matter as much. Both historical episodes are ripe with warnings for future relations between the West and Confucian East Asia. In an era of mounting tensions between the United States of America and the People's Republic of China, it is vital that we are mentally prepared (in ways that we were not in 1941) to assess the relevance of the Pacific War as a template and rehearsal for any Sino–American conflict tomorrow. Scholars like Richard have a unique contribution to make to the indispensable working partnership between the historians of modern and of traditional Asia.

The foundations for my discovery of the importance of Vietnamese Confucianism to wartime Japan were laid decades ago in discussions with two of my oldest friends: David Holzgang (Silicon Valley's very own classicist) and John Svitek (is this Freiburg-based Californian ever without his copy of the *New York Review of Books*?). During the most savage phase of America's war in Vietnam, we dissected Frances FitzGerald's extraordinary *Fire in the Lake: The Vietnamese and the Americans in Vietnam*.[2] Some thirty years after the fall of Saigon, I was reading late one night at home in Somerset after a day spent struggling with the ethical quandaries that trying to transpose the *Chūō Kōron* transcripts into English, particularly the second symposium, poses for the liberal-minded translator. It was then that I recalled what FitzGerald had made of Paul Mus's experience of Vietnam's most recent Confucian Revolution. My shout of 'Eureka!' woke the dog.

The example of this French Orientalist opened my eyes to my own experiences of Japanese Confucianism during my life in Japan (I have lived longer in Tokyo than any other place). My encounter with East Asia's most influential political tradition had begun in earnest with another late-night discussion, on that occasion with Nozomu Nakaoka, later to become a distinguished journalist and translator, in the poorly painted concrete cells of that hotbed of intellectual excitement that was my university dormitory in Mitaka. He was one of the first Japanese to alert me to the latent potential of *ekisei kakumei* or Confucian-contoured regime change in Japanese life, and to his own vulnerability, *as a Japanese*, to the moral demands of such ethical revolutions.

I must confess that I am at one with Camille Paglia when she observes that 'real interdisciplinary work is done at home and in the library'.[3] The Orientalist, as Flaubert reminds us, must make repeated voyages to the font of knowledge that is the East, but the demands of one discipline, let alone two or three, have made regular conference-going an unaffordable luxury. There simply has not been time. However, on my very occasional ventures away from my library at home in Wales, two superb scholarly networks – the Comparative and Continental Philosophy Circle (CCPC) and Global War Studies – have provided three opportunities for me to lecture on my research findings and enjoy that rarest fruit of the conference circuit: critical feedback, at once instructive and constructive. At the CCPC I would like to mention David Jones, Brian Schroeder, Jason M. Wirth and Bret W. Davis. These gatherings have provided occasions to spend time with such luminaries as Roger Ames, Timothy Engström, Matsukatsu Fujita, Thomas Kasulis, David Farrell Krell, Joseph Lawrence, Brad Park and John Sallis, among many others. Among the ranks of the *enfants terribles*, the conversations with young Adam Burgos and Kyle Bond have been full of interest and promise. Civilized occasions to break bread with these wine experts in Carmel and Honolulu have been a further attraction for spending time, however occasionally, with this formidable circle of philosophers.

In 2012 Robert von Maier, the impresario of Global War Studies, announced that he was organizing a major conference at King's College London on the oceanic theme of 'The Global–Regional Nexus: The Sea and the Second World War'. Robert, who lives in Oceanside in North County, near San Diego, where my late parents lived, gently badgered me into attending to present my thoughts about the Kyoto School's contribution to Pacific War grand strategy. Thanks to his invitation, I experienced once more that rarest of things, the academic conference as learning experience. The depth of expertise and the sometimes passionate commitment to the field displayed by the faculty and guests of the War Studies Department of King's College London were impressive. I had the pleasure of listening to and learning from Alan D. Zimm of the Johns Hopkins University Applied Physics Laboratory (about the technological and tactical failures that hampered the attack on Pearl Harbor), from Alessio Patalano of King's (about Japanese naval strategy), and from Rotem Kowner of the University of Haifa (about the rise of the aircraft carrier in the Pacific theatre). There were also some fruitful but not-quite-long-enough discussions with Lisle Rose and his delightful wife, historian Harriet Dashiell Schwar. Japan as a theme was not to be evaded on such an occasion, and my most persistent questioner was Hiroki Katō of the Japanese National Defense Academy, who pressed me with a certain vigour about my interest in Carl Schmitt. As if this were not enough, the redoubtable Nigel West stimulated and unsettled with his presence, while the occasion was graced by an eloquent and thoughtful conference dinner lecture by Richard Overy (University of Exeter).

Regular attendance at Japan studies guest lectures at Cardiff University with Mr Masakazu Kudara, and our discussions afterwards, helped prepare me more than he realized for appreciating the strengths and weaknesses of the orthodox liberal critique of modern East Asian life. We also shared responsibilities over a decade for preparing the fourth-year students of Japanese for their final language examinations. That presented me with opportunities to lecture on Carl Schmitt and Japanese sovereignty for our Law and Japanese course on comparative German and Japanese constitutional law, as well as allowing me to prepare one of the first examination papers ever set outside Japan on the work of Hajime Tanabe in our Advanced Japanese Studies and Texts course. I am grateful to my fourth-year victims for their keenness to rise to the occasion, and particularly to Thomas Rhydwen, who made his own contribution to the background biographical information exploited in this text.

Then there has been the pleasure of working with Gillian Somerscales, the finest editor of demanding texts I have yet to encounter. She has made an enormous difference to the readability of this very difficult book, and I am the grateful beneficiary of her patience, skill and intelligence.

Finally, on the home front in Cardiff, Stephen Condon has never known me when I was not writing this book, and so will be delighted when the task is finally completed. He has been greeted on his return home from work more often than he would wish by the sound of computer keyboard-pounding competing with a chorus from Puccini or Wagner, or, more recently, the *Missa Solemnis*. Without his support, and Robin's, I would have never completed this salt-in-the-eyes and occasionally *mal de mer* provoking journey of moral trial and factual revelation. This grateful Ulysses is home to stay.

David Williams
Cardiff Bay, Wales, May 2013

Japanese usage and style

Throughout this book, I have followed the style employed at *The Japan Times*, in which Japanese names are given in English order: that is, personal name followed by family name. This departs from the conventions of Japan studies, and my reasons for doing so are as follows. First, attempting to reproduce the Japanese convention of giving family name first and personal name second works against the natural order of English, thus producing horrors such as 'Mishima Yukio's novels', where Yukio is the Japanese novelist's personal name. Second, confronted with Nishida Kitarō, Western readers without Japanese often mistakenly and quite understandably conclude that this great Japanese philosopher's family name is Kitarō. Third, and even more disconcerting, one discovers that undergraduate students of the Japanese language often make the same error well into their courses. Finally, the attempt to reproduce Japanese usage in English is largely to blame for the typographical nightmare that is the English side of the Japanese business card, where one confronts a chaos of font sizes and typefaces. All this trouble could be eliminated if we would use the sensible style of *The Japan Times*.

Macrons have been reluctantly employed for all Japanese words except for a few place names, such as Tokyo, Osaka and Kyoto, and a few Japanese expressions that have been naturalized in English, such as 'bushido'. I was persuaded to keep the macrons in 'Tōjō', although I still think it looks like a caricature of Groucho Marx.

Notes

1 Robin Reilly, *The Sixth Floor: The Danish Resistance Movement and the RAF Raid on Gestapo Headquarters, March 1945*, London: Cassell Military Paperbacks, 1969.
2 Frances FitzGerald, *Fire in the Lake: The Vietnamese and the Americans in Vietnam*, Boston and Toronto: Little, Brown and Co., 1972.
3 Camille Paglia, 'Junk Bonds and Corporate Raiders: Academe in the Hour of the Wolf', in *Sex, Art and American Culture*, New York: Random House, 1992, p. 221.

Dramatis personae
Intellectual leaders of the Imperial Navy – Kyoto School resistance to Tōjō

This book is an attempt to provide a detailed sketch of the complex network of lives and works that tell the story of the Kyoto School of philosophy from the Japanese expulsion of Chinese forces from Manchuria to the end of the Pacific War. As such, it aims to contribute to a comprehensive picture of a large, diverse and complex set of Japanese academic allegiances and intellectual tensions, all complicated by that mysterious bond that is the relationship between teacher and student. We still need a more realistic and nuanced appreciation of the institutional dynamics that shaped and were shaped by these personal relationships within the larger setting of inter-war Japanese politics. Despite the voluminous writings of these philosophers, major retrospective assessments such as Michiko Yusa's *Zen and Philosophy: An Intellectual Biography of Nishida Kitarō*,[1] and the biographical information published in connection with the translations of some of the principal writings of the Kyoto School, an extraordinary amount of research and writing remains to be done, in all the languages concerned, including Japanese.

While Nishida, Tanabe and Nishitani have well-earned places in such classic Western publications as *The Encyclopaedia of Philosophy*, there are remarkable biographical gaps in the reception of the Kyoto School, both in Japan and abroad. Thus when I purchased Tanabe's complete works for posting to Britain in the late 1990s, the manager of one of the largest academic bookstores in Kanda scratched his head in near-astonishment, confessing that he could not remember ever being asked before to send a collection of this importance to the UK. Perhaps more revealing was the puzzlement that the young owner of one of the most serious academic bookstores in all of western Tokyo could not hide when I asked him about books by or about Kōsaka and Kōyama. His response was: 'Who are they? I have never heard of them.' He certainly did not know how to write the admittedly unusual rendering of their names correctly.

Here I will confine this brief biographical summary to nine Japanese thinkers understood as policy intellectuals: two from the Imperial Navy (Admirals Mitsumasa Yonai and Sōkichi Takagi), and seven of the most important figures of the wartime Kyoto School: the philosophers Kitarō Nishida, Hajime

Tanabe, Iwao Kōyama, Masaaki Kōsaka, Keiji Nishitani and Yasumasa Ōshima, and the historian Shigetaka Suzuki.

Imperial Navy

Mitsumasa Yonai (1880–1948). Japanese prime minister, Navy minister and admiral; leader of one of the most important factions opposed to Tōjō. A moderate, rational patriot, Yonai has often been misunderstood as an appeaser of liberal imperialism. Quite the contrary: he believed in Japanese sovereignty and supported the defence of its hard-won status as a regional great power. He opposed the Axis alliance on practical grounds: it could do nothing to enhance Japan's maritime insecurity vis-à-vis the United States. He fought an often brilliant tactical campaign with few cards and even fewer allies within the Imperial Navy against those who insisted on a precipitate war against Britain and America that Japan had no chance of winning. He did his best to prevent Japan's slide into the Pacific War and, once Tōjō was brought down, he sought a prompt negotiated settlement.

Not a conventional intellectual, Yonai respected and protected the brilliant minds around him, including Admirals Isoroku Yamamoto and Sōkichi Takagi. When he returned to a position of power within the Japanese government after the fall of Tōjō, Yonai helped to break the grip of the Army Faction or *Gunbatsu* over national policy making. However, Yonai struggled unsuccessfully to bring the war to a prompt close because his efforts were handicapped by the Allied insistence on unconditional surrender. The conflicting motives of Tōjō's opponents within the new Koiso cabinet and the anti-Tōjō army high command (think of Field Marshall Sugiyama, for example) were another stumbling block. Finally, the so-called 'peace faction' was in the end defeated by the underlying coherence of Imperial Army grand strategy and the way it mitigated the impact of MacArthur's otherwise stunningly triumphant Confucian Revolution after 1945.

Sōkichi Takagi (1893–1979). One of Japan's most energetic military intellectuals and political networkers of the inter-war and war years. Restless and brilliant to a fault, he reminds one of the young Theodore Roosevelt in his refusal to observe the limits of any job specification, his voracious reading habits and his almost inexhaustible urge to understand the facts and true situation of his beloved country. The wartime figure he perhaps most closely resembles is the Italian Dino Grandi, who carried two grenades into the Fascist Grand Council that overthrew Mussolini in July 1943 just in case Il Duce resisted. More than anyone else, Takagi courted and cultivated the leadership of the Kyoto School and helped to rally these Japanese thinkers to the aid of their nation at its hour of greatest need. Commissioned by Admiral Shimada, Takagi's grim assessment of Japan's strategic options in early 1944 may have helped to provoke the final showdown between Tōjō and his opponents in the Imperial Court, among the elder statesmen who composed the

Jūshin, and within the embittered ranks of the Army and Navy high commands.

Kyoto School

Kitarō Nishida (1870–1945). Japan's most celebrated modern philosopher was more than a figurehead during the final phase of his life. Although beset with illness and domestic tragedy as well as terrible anxieties about the fate of his country and his students (two of the most famous would die in prison), he prepared the way for the Kyoto School's alliance with the Yonai faction. His involvement in wartime politics was grounded in his rooted opposition to what he believed to be the risky policies first promised and then delivered by the Imperial Army faction led by Tōjō. He had no time for the ultra-nationalist obscurantism of the political extremists who have regularly visited violent blows on the practical leaders who have tried to make Japanese society work over the centuries. The semi-literate fanatics of wartime Japan were among his bitterest critics.

Hajime Tanabe (1885–1962). The second great figure of the Kyoto School played a more active role than Nishida in his risky wartime resistance to the rise of the Tōjō faction and the government it dominated in 1941. Although he published little during the Pacific War, Tanabe delivered a major lecture – 'On the Logic of Co-prosperity Spheres' – to the secret Imperial Navy-Kyoto School seminar on 29 September 1942. As recorded in *The Ōshima Memos*, this lecture offers a revealing gloss on the man as a thinker and political actor. There is no doubt that his active involvement sustained the morale and energy of the younger generation in both the Kyoto School and the Yonai faction.

Iwao Kōyama (1905–93). Perhaps the pivotal figure in the 'gang of four' Kyoto thinkers involved in the *Chūō Kōron* symposia. As an adviser to the Navy Ministry, Kōyama served as the indispensable point of liaison between the Imperial Navy and the Kyoto School.

Masaaki Kōsaka (1900–69). Possibly the best-known of these four Kyoto thinkers, because of the success of his best-seller *Historical Worlds*, and possibly the one with the most sophisticated understanding of war as an idea. This was particularly important when the Yonai faction was in 'internal exile' during the first year of the Pacific War.

Keiji Nishitani (1900–90). The most brilliant (and most talkative) of the contributors to the *Chūō Kōron* discussions, Nishitani was worldly and politically astute in ways that challenge the well-advertised notion of him as a religious-minded scholar utterly focused on everything but the real world. Quite the contrary: Nishitani was an engaged intellectual who brought his formidable intelligence to bear on the ideological and practical needs of wartime Japan.

Yasumasa Ōshima (1917–89). Student of Tanabe and compiler of *The Ōshima Memos*, and the youngest of all our intellectual leaders, Ōshima played an indispensable role as editor, meeting planner and liaison coordinator. He also qualifies as one of the incisive post-war commentators on the significance of the wartime Kyoto School's conspiracy with the Yonai faction against the Tōjō government.

Shigetaka Suzuki (1907–88). An economic historian and European specialist who may have substituted for Kiyoshi Miki among the contributors to the *Chūō Kōron* discussions. This may have been intentional so as to allow Miki, with his reputation as a left-wing sympathiser, to draw the fire of the censors with his own contribution to the January 1942 issue of *Chūō Kōron*. In that case, the choice of Suzuki may have been particularly clever for he was a man of forceful but un-reactionary nationalist opinions. His contribution to our three symposia may, therefore, have made these discussions just that less vulnerable to the censor during the course of 1942. As a master of the incisive sound-bite, Suzuki's vigorous attack on the liberal world order in his interventions in the *Literary World's* 'Overcoming Modernity' roundtable discussion in July 1942 may have played a similar protective role. The game of cat and mouse with the wartime censor was a subtle one.

Essential chronology
The Confucian war of ideas between the Yonai-Kyoto School and Tōjō factions

Patterns and factions

Confucian-style regime change involves struggles over how political reality is defined. Factions must contend for intellectual domination. Networking, intense public argument and secret conspiracies all figure prominently in such wars of ideas. The seizure and defence of positions of power and influence within the political system provide the most important stakes for these intellectual struggles. The following are some of the key developments in this battle for discourse hegemony during the period in question. Names in **bold type** refer to the 'intellectual leaders' of the Yonai-Kyoto School faction introduced in the Dramatis personae section of this book.

In post-Meiji Japan, factions made their way to power by winning arguments over policy. Resort to violence was rare. Having won the argument, the winning faction then enforced the new consensus with Confucian-style purges of the intellectual losers. In the wake of the 'fleet faction' victory over the pro-Washington-Geneva-system 'treaty faction', the Ōsumi purges in 1933–34 targeted naval officers who continued to insist that Japan was not threatened by the growth of American naval power. Spared by Ōsumi, Admiral **Yonai** eventually became Navy minister, but only after the powers of this position had been much weakened by the new ascendancy of the Naval General Staff. Thereafter, **Yonai** and his allies (including Isoroku Yamamoto and **Takagi**) were on the losing side in two new debates within the Navy: whether Japan should ally itself with Germany, and then whether Tokyo should go to war to resist American hegemony in the Pacific. The **Yonai** faction was eventually purged from positions of decisive authority for refusing to *tenkō* (affirm its support for a new consensus about political reality). Nevertheless, its residual influence conspired with the rooted Confucian urge to remain open to the potential emergence of unorthodox truths to keep the faction politically in play for four further years. Defeated by the Tōjō faction in 1941, the **Yonai** faction turned to **Nishida** and the Kyoto School for support.

Phase I: the rise of the Tōjō faction and the origins of the Yonai-Kyoto School 'brains trust' (1937–41)

1937

June: Representing a weaker faction, **Yonai** becomes Navy minister. He serves in this post until August 1939. At the behest of **Yonai** in this capacity, **Takagi** becomes chief of the Navy Ministry's Research Section. Using this position as a platform for networking, **Takagi** nurtures links with such influential political figures as Fumimaro Konoe (**Nishida**'s former student and intimate), Kōichi Kido and Kinmochi Saionji.

1938

August: In response to moves towards the formation of a new consensus within the Imperial Navy on the German question, the **Yonai**-Yamamoto-(Shigeyoshi) Inoue triumvirate wages a senior rear-guard effort (the 'Y-Y-I line') to delay official Navy endorsement of a Japanese alliance with Germany.

1939

18 February: **Nishida** meets **Takagi** (among others, including Finance Minister Shigeaki Ikeda). It may have been in reaction to the escalation of the Army's struggle against China that provoked the **Yonai** faction to reach out to the Kyoto School.

3 September: Britain and France declare war on Germany after Hitler attacks Poland. During the same month, **Takagi** visits **Nishida** at his home in Kamakura. The Navy's proposal for cooperation in resisting the Army is made and apparently accepted.

November: **Takagi** organizes his own think tank.

1940

6 January: **Yonai** leaves active duty and becomes prime minister: this destroys the 'Y-Y-I line' within Navy policy making, as the pro-war faction intended. Intellectually, his appointment reflects stubborn doubts (Emperor Hirohito's included) about the view of geopolitical reality proposed by the Tōjō faction. All factions are playing for time, each hoping that events will prove its worldview to be sound. As prime minister, **Yonai** is able to block any official embrace of the Tōjō line, but is vulnerable to being brought down by the resignation of either the Navy or the Army minister.

It is also during 1940 that **Nishida** approves of **Takagi**'s plan to approach **Tanabe** and **Kōyama** to ask for active cooperation in resisting the Army in general and the Tōjō faction in particular. **Ōshima** confirms that **Tanabe** and **Kōyama** responded enthusiastically to **Takagi**'s proposal when he visited them in Kyoto that year. Subsequently, **Kōyama** receives commitments of active support for the Navy's plans from **Kōsaka**, **Nishitani** and **Suzuki**.

21 July: **Yonai** is forced to resign as prime minister over his anti-German stance.

22 July: Prince Konoe becomes prime minister. Tōjō becomes Army minister in the second Konoe cabinet.

August: **Takagi** organizes and staffs his **Yonai** 'brains trust' which mobilizes a broad group of Japanese intellectuals including members of the soon to be closed Shōwa Research Society as well as the Kyoto School.

27 September: Japan concludes the Tripartite Pact with Germany and Italy: a major defeat for the **Yonai** faction.

1941

23 January: **Nishida** lectures before the Emperor. Later in the year, at **Nishida**'s urging, **Kōyama** accepts an invitation from **Takagi** to join his Research Section in the Navy Ministry. Hidefumi Hanazawa notes that during 1941 **Tanabe** continued his campaign of moral support for Karl Jaspers, the celebrated German philosopher who had been dismissed from Heidelberg at least in part because he was married to a Jew.

1 August: Washington imposes economic sanctions on Japan and a total embargo on its exports of oil and gasoline. This provokes 'sanctions panic' in senior ranks of the Imperial Navy.

9 October: **Yonai** is unable to meet **Nishida** at a seminar in Fushimi. The entry in Nishida's diary entry offers no explanation for the former prime minister's failure to appear. Given **Yonai**'s rather desperate position in a tottering cabinet that fell a week later only to bring Tōjō to power, one might reasonably assume that **Yonai** was rather busy.

16 October: Fall of third Konoe cabinet.

17 October: Tōjō becomes prime minister.

Phase II: resisting Tōjō's policies – the Yonai faction and the genesis of the *Chūō Kōron* transcripts and *The Ōshima Memos* (November 1941–June 1942)

The endorsement of the decision for war by the Japanese cabinet and the imperial court created a new intellectual and political consensus that sharply narrowed the scope for *legitimate* public dissent from official policy. This feature of Confucian wars of ideas for the mandate of heaven (however defined) gave impetus to the institutionalization of that new consensus. An earlier example of this phenomenon may be found in the creation on 12 October 1940 of the Imperial Rule Assistance Society (*Taisei Yokusankai*), of which Tōjō was one of the leaders, and the simultaneous closing of certain organs of dissent, a notable example being the disbanding of the Shōwa Research Society (so named in 1933) in November 1940. Refusing to subscribe to the new national consensus signalled by the formation of the Tōjō government, the Kyoto School escalated its programme of resistance by going underground (with activities such as the secret lectures and seminars recorded in *The Ōshima Memos*), while also courting public support with, for example, the three high-profile, if cautious, round-table discussions that became the *Chūō Kōron* symposia, and appeared in print *after* the attack on Pearl Harbor.

1941 (continued)

26 November: The First Symposium of the *Chūō Kōron* discussions (the one entitled 'The Standpoint of World History and Japan') is held, with **Kōyama**, **Kōsaka**, **Nishitani** and **Suzuki** as participants. The original dictations of these transcripts have yet to come to light but Ōshima insisted that the quasi protocol version contained clear objections to the decision to go to war with the United States, Britain and the Netherlands. These objections may have been censored by the publisher, Chūō Kōron-sha, because in Confucian terms they jarred with the new definition of political reality created by the imperial endorsement of the decision for war and the opening of hostilities in the Pacific.

8 December (Japan time): Japanese forces attack Pearl Harbor.

1942

1 January: The first symposium, 'The Standpoint of World History and Japan', is published in the periodical *Chūō Kōron*. This issue of the magazine may have appeared in bookstores as early as late December 1941. In an era of wartime paper rationing, **Takagi** or someone acting for the **Yonai** faction of the Imperial Navy approached the editors of *Chūō Kōron* to ensure there was space in the January issue for the transcript of the first symposium. Originally intended to make the case for not going to war with the United States and the British Empire, the first symposium was edited to shift its focus after Pearl Harbor to the stakes in the conflict, the need for reason to trump emotion, and the instinct to caution the Japanese public about underestimating American power.

Essential chronology xlix

8 January: Special Higher Police visit the editors of *Chūō Kōron* to complain about the content of the January 1942 issue. On that visit, the police objected to Miki's contribution to the same issue and the editors were informed that **Nishida**'s favourite student was under police supervision. Miki was henceforth barred from contributing to magazines of 'general opinion' (*sōgō zasshi*) such as *Chūō Kōron*. He was drafted and sent to Manila to 'improve' his outlook by serving with the Army's information unit (*senden-han*).

22 February: Secret meeting 1: the first of the underground lecture-seminars held by the Imperial Navy-Kyoto School between February 1942 and November 1943, marking the birth of *The Ōshima Memos*. **Kōyama, Kōsaka, Suzuki** and **Nishitani** are present.

2 March: Secret meeting 2 (**Tanabe, Kōyama, Suzuki, Nishitani, Ōshima**).

4 March: The second symposium of the *Chūō Kōron* discussions, 'The Ethical and Historical Character of the East Asian Co-prosperity Sphere', is held. Participants are **Kōyama, Kōsaka, Nishitani** and **Suzuki**.

1 April: The second symposium is published in the April edition of *Chūō Kōron*. Appearing as Japanese arms carried all before them in the South Pacific and South-East Asia, the contributors hammer away at the necessity for a humane version of Japanese leadership in the region in ways that would address the needs of East Asia as a whole.

Date unknown: Secret meeting 3 (**Takagi, Tanabe, Nishitani, Suzuki**). By the time of this meeting, **Takagi** had been purged from the Navy Ministry's Research Section because of his opposition to Tōjō's decision for war.

11 April: Secret meeting 4 (**Kōyama, Kōsaka, Nishitani, Ōshima**).

24 May: Secret meeting 5 (**Kōyama, Nishitani, Suzuki**).

Phase III: the Yonai-Kyoto School faction and the decline of the Tōjō government (June 1942–July 1944)

If Confucian factional struggles turn finally on the understanding of reality, there are intellectual and practical consequences for the side that loses the argument. The repeated defeats suffered by the **Yonai** faction from 1937 onwards called into doubt the soundness of its understanding of the realities of Japan's geopolitical position after the start of the Second Sino–Japanese War in 1937. Purged from power by the Tōjō faction after Pearl Harbor, **Yonai** and his followers had turned with renewed energy and need to the Kyoto School for intellectual assurance, both to clarify their ideas and to strengthen them. This was to prepare the **Yonai** faction for the moment when reality itself would confirm the power of their insights into the truth of Japan's strategic situation. This moment came with the defeat of Japanese forces at Midway in June 1942.

1   *Essential chronology*

1942 (continued)

3–5 June: Imperial Navy decisively defeated by US forces at Midway.

15 June: Secret meeting 6 (**Takagi, Kōyama**). First obvious opportunity for the **Yonai** faction to inform the Kyoto School about the results of the Battle of Midway.

July: **Kōyama** is invited with two other professors to join the Committee on the Imperial Navy within the *Sō Ryokusen Kenkyūjo* with responsibilities for the war of ideas.

12 July: Secret meeting 7 (**Kōyama, Kōsaka, Nishitani, Ōshima**).

26–27 July: 'Overcoming Modernity' symposium (participants include **Nishitani, Suzuki**).

19 September: Secret meeting 8 (**Kōyama, Suzuki, Kōsaka, Suzuki, Ōshima**).

29 September: Secret meeting 9 (**Tanabe, Kōyama, Kōsaka, Suzuki, Ōshima**): **Tanabe** gives his lecture 'On the logic of Co-prosperity Spheres'.

4 November: Secret meeting 10 (**Takagi, Kōyama, Suzuki, Nishitani**).

9 November: Secret meeting 11 (**Tanabe, Kōyama, Kōsaka, Nishitani, Suzuki, Ōshima**).

24 November: The third symposium of the *Chūō Kōron* discussions, 'The Philosophy of World-historical Wars', is held. Participants are **Kōyama, Kōsaka, Nishitani** and **Suzuki**. A carefully judged appeal for a more rational approach to war strategy on the part of the government while arguing for a long view of the struggle because, as the contributors make quietly clear, almost as a matter of mood, that the Great East Asia War is likely to be lost.

1943

The most perplexing year of this factional struggle. One might reasonably conclude that the right hand of the Tōjō government did not know what the left was doing about the Yonai-Kyoto School posture (but see note for 19 May).

1 January: The third symposium is published in the January edition of *Chūō Kōron*.

16 February: Secret meeting 12 (**Tanabe, Kōyama, Kōsaka, Suzuki, Ōshima**).

2 March: Secret meeting 13 (**Nishitani, Tanabe, Kōyama**).

25 March: The three symposia are published as a book under the title *The Standpoint of World History and Japan* (1943), with an initial print run of 15,000 copies. Another 1,000 copies are printed because the book proves to be a wartime best-seller, only to have Army censors block further publication by refusing to allocate more paper to the publisher.

17–18 April: **Kōyama**, **Nishitani** and **Suzuki** travel to Tokyo to make a formal report to the Navy Ministry's Research Section (Research Group on the War of Ideas).

1 May: **Takagi** becomes rear-admiral.

19 May: **Nishida** is approached by Kazuo Yatsugi (rival of **Takagi** and his equivalent within the Tōjō ruling faction) to help to draft the 'Proclamation of the Great East Asian Nations' at a meeting of the National Policy Research Society, a think tank founded by Yatsugi in 1937. Within the context of a Confucian war of ideas, this gesture may be seen as an attempt to bolster the government's intellectual position by suggesting that even its critics support it, or as a way of co-opting the opposition, or as a signal of a crisis of confidence in the government's intellectual position, or as an effort to divide the opposition, or as all of the above. Nishida prepares a draft that is revised by others.

1 June: **Kōyama**'s final contribution to *Chūō Kōron* is published.

4 June: Secret meeting 14 (**Kōyama, Nishitani, Suzuki, Kōsaka, Ōshima**).

July 1943: The issue of *Chūō Kōron* is voluntarily withheld and the editorial staff purged at Imperial Army insistence.

19 August: Secret meeting 15 (no list of those present).

September: **Takagi** ordered to prepare an official analysis of the causes of the Imperial Navy's defeats in the 1942 Pacific campaign by Navy Minister Shigetarō Shimada. After gathering and analysing the data, **Takagi** proceeds to expand the scope of his inquiry, only to reach the conclusion, it has been suggested, that Tōjō had to be assassinated if Japan was to negotiate a truce with the Allies and thus end the Pacific War.

On the subject of Tōjō as a potential target of assassination, a Confucian gloss may be useful. Murder is of course a crime in East Asia, but the leader who attempts to resist obvious and irreversible evidence of his declining grip on the mandate of heaven exposes himself to quasi-legitimate acts of violence. This truism applied to Tōjō in 1944 no less than it applied with more brutal effect to the political and business leaders who sought so ineffectually to shore up a dying Japanese establishment during, for example, the 1930s. The once famous expression 'government by assassination' misleads. Such killings are not acts of government but rather ways of accelerating regime change to order to ensure a fresh beginning for a Confucian society in radical need of renewal.

26 September: Secret meeting 16 (**Kōsaka, Kōyama, Suzuki, Nishitani, Ōshima**).

23–4 October: Secret meeting 17 (**Kōyama**, **Kōsaka**, **Nishitani**, **Suzuki**, **Ōshima**).

2 November: Secret meeting 18 (**Kōyama**, **Nishitani**, **Suzuki**, **Ōshima**).

5–6 November: Tōjō delivers his address at the international conference formally inaugurating the Greater East Asian Co-prosperity Sphere. Neither his speech nor 'The Greater East Asian Declaration' suggest **Nishida**'s draft or intentions have been respected.

1944

January onwards: anti-Tōjō factions within the Japanese elite, including the **Yonai**-Kyoto School faction, launch a campaign to bring down the war cabinet.

2 May: **Nishida**'s farewell philosophical gathering (*Tetsugaku-kai*). Attended by **Kōyama**, **Kōsaka**, **Nishitani**, **Suzuki** and perhaps Motomori Kimura.

31 May: Civilian advisers to the Navy Ministry, including **Kōyama**, gather in Tokyo to discuss how to bring down the Tōjō cabinet. Kyoto School hopes are invested in the promise of new government headed by **Yonai**.

9 July: Saipan captured by US forces. Mortal blow to the Tōjō government, but when war party refuses to yield to mounting pressures for the cabinet to resign, a conspiracy takes shape to plan the assassination of Prime Minister Tōjō. **Takagi** appears to have been involved in the planning.

10 July: Chūō Kōron-sha closed down as a publisher as a voluntary act consistent with expectations of the censors within the Second Division of the Cabinet Information Bureau.

18 July: Tōjō resigns premiership.

22 July: **Yonai** becomes deputy prime minister and Navy minister in the Koiso cabinet. He remains Navy minister in the Kantarō Suzuki cabinet until April 1945 and continues in this post until its abolition in December 1945. For the next months, the pro-peace faction led by **Yonai** and his allies struggles to win a ceasefire with the Allies but is frustrated by divisions among the anti-Tōjō factions, the continued influence of the war party, the growing chaos caused by the fire bombings of Tokyo and other cities, and the fears of what the Allies will insist on as their conditions for ending the war. However, the larger issue is the uncertain outcome of the inevitable Confucian Revolution that will be encouraged by the spectre of defeat and consummated by the reality of surrender.

1945

19 May: **Tanabe** writes to **Nishida** and Konoe seeking their help to preserve the imperial throne after Japan's defeat.

7 June: **Nishida** dies.

Texts, conventions and abbreviations

The round-table discussion edited for publication, known in Japanese as *zadankai*, has been an enormously popular and influential genre of the print media in modern Japan. Our three *zadankai* were held on 26 November 1941, 4 March 1942 and 24 November 1942. Transcripts of these discussions were then published in *Chūō Korōn* (sometimes referred to elsewhere in English as *The Central Review*), the Japanese magazine of general opinion and serious fiction (*sōgō zassi*), in the January 1942, April 1942 and January 1943 issues. The participants in all three symposia were the same: Masaaki Kōsaka, Iwao Kōyama and Keiji Nishitani, three of the brightest lights of the second generation of the Kyoto School of philosophy, along with Shigetaka Suzuki, an economic historian and fellow traveller of the Kyoto School.

These *zadankai* were later edited for publication as a book under the title *The Standpoint of World History and Japan* (the overall title being taken, as noted above, from the first round-table discussion) by the magazine's publisher, Chūō Korōn-sha, in the spring of 1943. The volume became a wartime best-seller (the first of 15,000 copies, and another 1,000 followed) and a celebrated text. University draftees apparently carried it off to war in their backpacks. However, the nature of the content was judged subversive to the war effort, and so the state censors banned further publication. This scandal contributed to the closing of the publisher on state authority in July 1944.

The book before you provides a commentary on and a reading of these three texts as they appeared in the pages of the magazine, not the later book. The editorial changes made between publication in the magazine and in book form are not large but do suggest that the pressures of censorship had grown stronger three months after the publication of the third symposia, 'The philosophy of world historical wars', in January 1943. This led me to conclude that the magazine version is a more genuine representation of both the views and the tone of argument of the four contributors.

The first symposium and the book of 1943 bear the same title in Japanese, but for our purposes *in English* the three transcripts of the symposia will be distinguished from the first symposium and the book in the following way:

The first symposium will be referred to in roman type in quotation marks, thus:

'The Standpoint of World History and Japan'

The three symposia that appeared in *Chūō Kōron* will be referred to as the *Chūō Kōron* 'transcripts', 'symposia' or 'discussions', but the symposia taken as a whole *in my reading* in English will be referred to in italics, thus:

The Standpoint of World History and Japan

The later book will be designated in italics, with the addition of the year of publication, thus:

The Standpoint of World History and Japan (1943)

To ease the burden on the reader of keeping the three titles clear, I have ensured, without strain, that there are no more than a handful of references to the book of 1943. In italics without the date, *The Standpoint of World History and Japan* will *always* refer to my English version of the three symposia collectively as they appeared in the magazine version. If the title appears between single quotation marks without italics, *only* the first symposium is being referred to.

Notes

1 Michiko Yusa, *Zen and Philosophy: An Intellectual Biography of Nishida Kitarō*, Honolulu: University of Hawai'i Press, 2002.

Part I
Introduction and commentary
The prince of our disorder and the fate of Imperial Japan

1 Versailles to Pearl Harbor

Woodrow Wilson and the origin of the ethics of 'liberal imperialism'

> The isolation of the United States is at an end, not because we chose to go into the politics of the world, but because, by the sheer genius of this people and the growth of our power, we have become the determining factor in the history of mankind.
>
> (Woodrow Wilson, 1919[1])

On 24 August, St Bartholomew's Day, 1572, a massacre of French Protestant leaders began in Paris. The ensuing slaughter of thousands of Protestants across France ignited yet another brutal round in the infamous Wars of Religion. Of more lasting consequence, these events called into question the use of religious morality to justify the sectarian butchery of one people by another. Such doubts would issue in an ethical revolution in European civilization: the gradual but comprehensive rejection of the medieval theory and Reformation practice of 'just war' or *justa causa belli* in favour of the more humane philosophy of the 'just enemy' (*justus hostis*). This refusal to indulge in endless crusades of annihilation, at least within Christendom (*republica Christiana*), transformed how Europeans defined not only war and peace, but also state sovereignty and the rights of the subject as well as the role of religion and ethics in public life between the Treaty of Westphalia (1648) and the Treaty of Versailles (1919).

Under the impact of President Woodrow Wilson's 'counter-revolution' of 1919, the theory of just war was revived and became the mainstay of the Western liberal approach to international law. The impact of this revival on global civilization was manifested more clearly in the Pacific War than in any other twentieth-century conflict. As a philosophical meditation on the attack on Pearl Harbor and the war of annihilation that followed, the *Chūō Kōron* transcripts offer us a textual aid in a fresh effort to rethink the ethical dimension of international law in ways that would once again divorce morality from politics, and thus constrain the violent passions of destructive moral absolutism with a more benign form of moral relativism. This reanimation of some of the cardinal insights of European public law – and the ethical 'bracketing' of war's worst excesses by the acceptance of the moral worth of one's opponent – was one of the finest achievements of the

Westphalian system, and may someday soon help to moderate relations between states and peoples for centuries to come.

Recent world events lend strength and plausibility to this proposal to formulate a new version of early modern *jus publicum europaeum*. On 11 September 2001, religiously inspired morality was, in the pre-1648 mode, once again invoked to justify the murder of thousands of New Yorkers. This in turn provoked, in the post-1919 manner, the slaughter of tens of thousands of Muslims in Afghanistan and Iraq in the name of democratic revenge and moral justice. However, like St Bartholomew's bitter feast day, the horrors of '9/11' may have heralded not just further episodes in the murderous abuse of ethics, but the beginning of the end of humanity's most recent relapse into the rhetoric and practice of just wars to end all wars fought in the name of morality, religious or liberal.

How to read this text

This is the first of eleven brief chapters of commentary on the *Chūō Kōron* symposia. This commentary has a clear and specific relationship to the 'reading' or fuller rendering of the Japanese original than a mere translation that forms the larger and concluding part of this study of the wartime Kyoto School. The goal of this commentary as an exercise in textual exegesis is threefold.

First, the ambition is to read this dense and resistant Japanese text properly. By 'properly', I mean in such a way as to generate an interpretation that would be recognizable and persuasive to the authors of the Japanese original. Many able Asian and Western scholars have attempted to explain or comment on this classic text, but few have been willing to produce a reading that meets the required standard of objectivity because the ethical traditions – Confucianism or liberalism – within which they work will not permit it. The decisive consequence of post-1919 liberal international law theory for the study of the Pacific War has been the temptation to trump reality with morality. This explains the Western failure to develop a suitable conceptual framework for soundly interpreting this Japanese text. Discovering such a framework is, therefore, the second exegetical goal. While I have abandoned my intention to produce a definitive translation for the reasons set out previously, in the 'Escape clause', I do believe that I have identified a reliable framework of interpretation, one that is impartial in a way that is true of none of its rivals.

The third ambition is textual rigour, or the Orientalist's counterpart to the rational certainty of the mathematician. The quest for such rigour motivates the pursuit of our first and second goals, but rigour is also one of the rewards of achieving these goals.

This strategy of intercultural communication forms a virtuous circle: textual rigour is achieved through, and demonstrated by, proper reading guided by a reliable conceptual framework. The necessity for such rigour is absolute, because the opposite of rigour is interpretive defeat. It is the pursuit of such rigour, via the application of a suitable framework to ensure a proper reading, as an integrated act of reflection, that has given birth to this commentary.

Understanding the overarching title of the three symposia

The title of the first symposium, 'The Standpoint of World History and Japan', sets out the philosophical fundamentals of a programme of political action to secure East Asian regional autonomy. The Kyoto School draws simultaneously on the philosophy of history, of politics and of war, while criticizing the traditional assumptions of these three branches of thought, as part of a project to reform these ideas in order to influence the outcome of a contemporary Confucian revolution in East Asian affairs. The key words in the title have been chosen with particular care by the four participants in this symposium, and if one is to understand what the wartime Kyoto School was about, one must be aware of how the specific meaning assigned to the terms 'Japan', 'world history' and 'standpoint' sets these thinkers apart from their critics and opponents just before the attack on Pearl Harbor.

Risking the intervention of the wartime censor, the four participants in the symposium – Keiji Nishitani, Masaaki Kōsaka, Iwao Kōyama and Shigetaka Suzuki – reject traditional Japanese exceptionalism. Thus 'Japan' is conceived in secular terms, not as a divine meteorite arriving from the heavens on the alien surface of an accidental planet called 'the world'. For the Kyoto School, Japan is not only in the world but of it. It is this secular Japan that, having broken free of the squalor of underdevelopment, has proceeded to force its way into the ranks of the great powers of the earth. This gathering of strength, coupled with the rapid decay of Europe's global hegemony during the first half of the twentieth century, presented the Japanese people with a previously undreamt opportunity to make world history, at the same time as the growth of Chinese nationalism and American imperialism threatened to deny Japan its place in the sun. For the Kyoto thinker, therefore, 'world history' is a unique arena, a zone of action and thought, offering Japan the opportunity to demonstrate regional leadership in East Asia and the Western Pacific through trials of strength with other great powers. As a Hegelian, the Kyoto philosopher believed that Japan's unprecedented ambitions and accomplishments had to be judged by the most testing of standards, and as a result the bar of world-historical success had to be elevated to a new level.

The Kyoto School brought a kind of tough-mindedness to its interpretation of history. It was not enough that Japan had defended its independence, broken the shackles of the unequal treaties imposed by the West, carved out an overseas empire by humbling Imperial China (the region's traditional hegemon) and then ousted Russian and German power from Japan's 'near abroad' in East Asia and the Western Pacific. No: if Japan was to play for the highest stakes, it must seek to win the crown that Hegel accorded to 'a world-historical people'. Nothing else was adequate to the nation's hopes, potential and capabilities. G.W.F. Hegel and Leopold von Ranke were the two German thinkers most valued by the Kyoto School in its search for a recognized 'standpoint' from which Japanese worldly success could be measured and judged; in the eyes of the ultranationalists, according so decisive a role in the assessment of the significance of Japan's modern trajectory as a nation to two Germans was itself a traitorous blasphemy.

The Kyoto School perspective on history ensured that whatever doubts these philosophers may have entertained about the timing of the attack on Pearl Harbor and the strategic intent behind the assault, they were fully alert to the enormous historical significance of the events of December 1941. The success of Japanese modernization was dramatically demonstrated by the vast distances and complicated logistical obstacles overcome by the Imperial Navy in mounting this operation. The air strikes on the US Pacific Fleet in Hawaii qualified not only as the greatest naval defeat in American history but also as the most effective act of Oriental resistance to Western expansion since the high tide of Ottoman power almost captured Vienna in 1683.

This weight of significance explains why the expression 'the standpoint of world history and Japan' not only had to serve as the heading for the first symposium, but has become, in my Reading of the text, the overarching title for all three symposia. Observe also that the title captures the essence of Kyoto School hopes and ambitions for East Asia as one regional totality or 'world' in 'a world of worlds' (Kōsaka). This East Asian 'world' was to be secured and developed by rational and humane Japanese leadership.

One may reasonably conclude that the wartime Kyoto School implicitly endorsed 'a functioning system of legal norms, regulating the excesses of inter-state anarchy in a geopolitical pluriverse without erasing the essence of sovereign statehood: the public and sovereign decision to conduct war'.[2] This Japanese project rejected, in principle, any global hegemon as a universal sovereign in favour of a world composed of independent regions. The new world order inaugurated by Wilson at Versailles would not permit this form of regional autonomy. Imperial Japan would therefore have to be disciplined, or, failing that, destroyed.

Imperial Japan and the fate of the great powers

In the history of relations between nations since the late nineteenth century, a single narrative is primary in global affairs: the ascent of the United States to its contemporary status as *hyper-puissance* and global dominator. All rival narratives – the decline of European imperialism, the rise and fall of Soviet Communism, the challenge of fascism or Japanese expansionism – are secondary to that primary narrative, which may also be expressed as the triumph of liberal imperialism. Thus in a standard orthodox work such as *The Pacific War Papers: Japanese Documents of World War II*, the historical thesis is proposed that 'the Japanese military – particularly the Army – was not interested in peace; it was interested in conquest and power'.[3] This assertion can tell us nothing significant about the diplomatic and military events of 1941–42 *if* any secondary narrative is confused with our primary narrative. Liberal imperialism, not Japanese expansionism, qualifies as the primary narrative of the Pacific War because liberal imperialism won.

As America's rise doomed the other great powers, their fate forms a crucial chapter in our primary narrative. The whole planet could not be made subservient to a single global hegemon without the decline, demotion, defeat or dismemberment of seven of the eight great powers of 1914 (the two Central and four Allied European powers of consequence plus Japan) and the military eclipse of all of them by the United States. True, after 1919, some of the former or fading great powers sought to resist, sometimes violently, the consequences of their decline and demotion, but all in the end were made to conform to America's 'empire of right'.

For the student of Japan's fate in the unfolding of our primary narrative, the *Chūō Kōron* transcripts are important on two counts: first as a clear and considered Japanese response to the mounting provocation of *universal* liberal imperialism, and second as a set of insights into the Confucian way of war as it defined Japanese geopolitical aspirations in the 1940s (and shapes Chinese geopolitical ambitions today). By contrast, many of the most frequently quoted documents that form the canonical historical record of the Pacific War, Allied and Japanese alike, suggest that the authors are frequently unclear or self-deceiving about geopolitical reality or so constrained by policy and politics as to render their remarks inadmissible as statements of genuine intent. They affirm little more than the banally obvious about the state of affairs at issue. The result is the documentary equivalent of the fog of war or the preparation for war. The *Chūō Kōron* discussions help us to dispel such fog.

Notes

1. Quoted in Anders Stephanson, *Manifest Destiny: American Expansion and the Empire of Right*, New York: Hill & Wang, 1995, p. 117.
2. Carl Schmitt's position as summarized in Benno Teschke, 'Exorcizing Schmitt', *New Left Review*, 67, Jan.–Feb. 2011, pp. 63–64.
3. Donald M. Goldstein and Katherine V. Dillon, eds, *The Pacific War Papers: Japanese Documents of World War II*, Washington, DC: Potomac Books, 2006, p. 113.

2 Ethics as power
The prince of our disorder and the fate of Imperial Japan

> President Wilson introduced the problem of a discriminatory concept of war – a 'just war' – into international law when he declared war on Germany in 1917. Whereas 'holy wars' were long gone, the war mobilization against Germany had become a crusade. Since the League of Nations was in a position to decide what constituted a 'just war', it also became the arbiter of the 'discriminatory concept of war'. Since, by definition, a 'just war' is a 'total war', the League thus became the agency of supra-state and supra-national 'just' wars.
> (Carl Schmitt, 1950[1])

Liberal unease

In 1926, George Macaulay Trevelyan confessed in a private letter: 'I do not understand the age we live in, and what I do understand I do not like.'[2] This influential historian was one of the enlightened figures of his times and a giant of the English liberal camp. Trevelyan's unease seems surprising because at that moment liberals were vigorously engaged in consolidating what President Wilson called his 'new world order'. In fact, between 1919 and 1928, between the Treaty of Versailles and the Kellogg-Briand Pact renouncing war as a means of resolving international disputes, liberal thinkers, old and young, devised institutions to arbitrate the peace while recasting the philosophy of international law to keep this new world order secure. Sweeping all before it, this was the liberal hour in full spate.

So why Trevelyan's note of discontent then, and why might we share it now? The question commands attention because of the impact of the values mobilized and put into effect during the first decade of the twenty-year ceasefire of 1919–39. Between the imposition of the Treaty of Versailles on Germany and the de-legitimation of war with the Kellogg-Briand Pact, liberal thinkers transformed international law by dismantling the moral relativism of the Westphalian system of great powers and state sovereignty. The ideas and assumptions behind this resurrection of medieval concepts of just war and the moral absolutism of the Wars of Religion would later be marshalled to justify what, after Thomas Friedman, we might call the liberal 'flattening' of Imperial Japan.

The post-Versailles goal was to transform the Japanese people into liberal subjects who would be made to conform to the values of the post-1919 American global order, and therefore no longer pose a threat to it. Such liberal ideological notions would also come to form the ethical bedrock of modern Japan studies in the West and thus preclude for decades the objective study of the wartime Kyoto School. In the name of objective history, the new historian of the Pacific War must learn to follow the twists and turns of the unbroken road that leads from Wilson's 'war to end all war' to the destruction of Hiroshima and Nagasaki.

If we are to appreciate the intellectual and moral world-view of the wartime Kyoto School in a truthful manner, a revisionist eye needs to be cast over the first decade of the liberal transformation of international law after Versailles. The immediate explanation for the disappointments of Trevelyan and other liberal reformers of the world system was that many of their hopes proved difficult to realize. A confused and inefficient system of global governance, in self-proclaimed possession of the moral high ground but hardly in charge, created more problems than it was ever able to solve.

After the sometimes impressive successes of the 1920s, liberal cosmopolitan orthodoxy was battered by geopolitical reality and legal incoherence until pacifism as a faith, the League of Nations as an institution, and the treaties that embodied the new liberal order – Versailles, Locarno, Kellogg-Briand and the rest – were compromised by the Japanese occupation of the bulk of Manchuria in 1931, Italy's conquest of Abyssinia in 1935, Hitler's reoccupation of the Rhine in 1936 and the dismemberment of Czechoslovakia in 1938. The year after that, Britain and France would go to war with Germany to defend Poland, a country they could not protect. With the fall of Warsaw and the opening of the door on hell that would later become the Final Solution, the whole liberal experiment lay in ruins – or would have done but for the enduring project inspired by the ideas and determination of President Wilson, the most influential liberal statesman of his age.

A new world order

The ill-informed idealism of Wilson's Fourteen Points and his insistence on the imposition of the doctrine of national self-determination on the fragmented ethnic mosaic of Central and Eastern Europe make him the author and prince of our post-1919 disorder. However, he also had a remedy in mind for the chaos engendered by his Versailles counter-revolution: a new world order in which all resistance to a single sovereign with global policing powers would be de-legitimated. This son of a legendary Presbyterian preacher envisioned a liberal cosmopolitan order ultimately guaranteed by US might and moral authority. He may have been derided by satirist H.L. Mencken at home as 'the Archangel Woodrow' for his self-serving moralism, and his negotiating skills and ignorance of European political realities may have been belittled in print by no less a figure than John Maynard Keynes, but it was the genius of

Wilson to unite the thrust of America towards global hegemony with the liberal urge to forge one's ideals into a hammer the better to bludgeon reality into a more ideal shape. The diplomatic, legal and moral programme that Wilson set in motion would result in a formidable alliance of principle and force: the liberal way of war.

Having insisted on devising an unstable world system in need of endless remedy and intervention, the liberal conscience, inspired by Wilson's vision, became ever more ambitious in its goals, just as the liberal way of war became ever more destructive in its means. Capturing the spirit of the aggressive liberalism that underlay this new making-war-for-peace ethos and stiffened the sinews of its adherents, Michael Howard observes of Trevelyan: 'He had none of our contemporary inhibitions about writing "drum and trumpet history". War was for him the very stuff of history, and he found no difficulty in reconciling it with his Liberalism. How have men gained and preserved their liberties, he would have asked, except by fighting?'[3]

In the name of ethical universalism, international public law was transformed into a version of private criminal jurisprudence, requiring not only laws, courts and jails but also policemen and executioners to enforce an uncompromising set of ethical absolutes. Accordingly, *bien pensant* orthodoxy – call it 'world public opinion' – yielded, more or less completely, to the practical need for a muscular global hegemon to enforce the morality embedded in the new form of international law conceived and instituted in the decades after the counter-revolution of 1919. It was this transformation of the ethical-legal order of the world that the Kyoto School was determined to resist.

The rights and privileges that the United States had exerted over Latin America since the proclamation of the Monroe Doctrine in 1823 were incorporated into the text of the Versailles Treaty, and thus came to apply to the whole world. After 1919, Washington issued a series of policy declarations, culminating in the Stimson Doctrine of 1938 and the Hull Note of 1941 (Roosevelt's final ultimatum to Tōjō), which made international law and diplomatic practice more congenial to the fostering of a cosmopolitan order in which the United States alone exercised true sovereignty. After the Pacific War, the San Francisco Peace Treaty and the Tokyo War Crimes Tribunal would consolidate these hegemonic ambitions and give them moral and quasi-legal force.

This partnership of moral universalism and liberal imperialism explains why our *Pax Americana* admits of no political exterior: the whole world without exception will eventually be subject, as it must be, to the sole legitimate *universal* authority. As this nascent world order came to dominate more and more of the globe, it had, of necessity, to develop a pan-oceanic strategy. American global naval hegemony posed a mortal threat not only to the status of the Empire of Japan as a great power but also to Japanese independence and sovereignty. This threat gave impetus to the Kyoto School's search for anti-Tōjō allies within the Imperial Navy, and suggests why the contributors to the *Chūō Kōron* discussions developed, in outline, a navy-based grand strategy for a Japanese Empire reinvented as a co-prosperity sphere or an East Asian *Großraum* (see Chapter 9).

Until the advent of still newer technologies of warfare (strategic bombers, land-based intercontinental ballistic missiles, or ICBMs, satellite weapons and cyber attacks), a credible oceanic strategy was wholly dependent on naval power, and what began as an expensive vehicle to demonstrate America's capability to project its influence beyond the waters of the New World (Teddy Roosevelt's 'Great White Fleet') became over subsequent decades (naval budgets permitting) an ever more potent instrument for confronting, containing and, ideally, eliminating all and any remnants of a political exterior capable of resisting American will. The People's Republic of China is the most important of these 'remnants' today.

The strategic imperative of pan-oceanic domination inevitably shaped America's negotiating stance in the great naval arms control conferences of the inter-war period: Washington (1921–22), Geneva (1927) and London (1930). The main targets of this diplomatic offensive were Britain and Japan. In the name of American national security, London and Tokyo were pressed to accept naval theatre parity and then yield to US global naval superiority. By 1945, this ambition was achieved. This success belies one of the rooted difficulties faced by American naval strategists: namely, how to convert the manifestly pre-1919 Westphalian great power 'navalism' of Alfred Thayer Mahan – so influential on the grand strategist, and not only in the United States – into something consistent with the moral-minded liberal imperialism of Wilson's global vision.

Liberal navalism

The unreconstructed pre-1919 spirit that characterized the pronouncements of the US Navy's General Board from Versailles to Pearl Harbor draws attention to the conundrum at issue. Inter-war treaty limitations on naval construction as well as restrictions on fortifying American possessions in the Western Pacific made it more difficult for the US Navy to meet its operational objectives. These included recapturing Guam and the Philippines in anticipation of a blockade of Japan's home islands to starve the country into submission. This strategy was fixed before the Wilsonian era and these naval objectives remained largely unaltered from the first version of 'Operation Orange' in 1907 up to the Pacific War, but they were consistent with the kind of great power logic that pricked the liberal conscience. So how was one to guarantee that the 'empire of right' remained 'right' as it became an empire?

The problem could be solved by making the supposedly conflicting approaches to fostering American hegemonic power found in the ideas of Theodore Roosevelt and Woodrow Wilson work in tandem. The ideal solution would not only affirm the ethical character of America's emerging global role but also close the door on the legitimate exploitation of Mahan's theories by the Imperial Japanese Navy, which had been so deeply influenced by his philosophy. Liberal imperialism as an ideology solved this dilemma. Later, after the elimination of the Imperial Japanese Navy, US naval rivalry with the Soviet Union contributed formidably to a deeper synthesis of Teddy Roosevelt's great power aggressiveness and Wilson's moral-minded imperialism. The language of recent US Navy assessments of the new Chinese naval menace suggests an almost seamless integration of muscular navalism with affirmation of America's rights as the supreme but benevolent guarantor of the world's sea lanes.

For Asia's only great power, the implications of this new world order became steadily more uncomfortable after 1919. As the nation most endangered by American naval expansionism, Japan steadily invested in the Imperial Navy, only to find time and again that it lacked the financial resources to compete with the United States. However, if the Imperial Navy could not secure the Western Pacific, it would be unable to secure military or commercial success on the Asian continent. Furthermore, the ghost of Wilson's universal moral vision would not rest. The Versailles settlement quickly congealed into a legal endorsement of the territorial status quo even though the boundaries of East Asia in 1920s and 1930s were in many cases the unsustainable legacy of Manchu and Western imperialism. Asian nationalists, Japanese and others, were determined to revamp these often arbitrary frontiers, made still more porous by the impact of modern technology. In a world of carelessly drawn borders and shifting geopolitical realities, however, liberal statesmen after Wilson insisted that the map of the world could be altered only by local consent, international agreement and American acquiescence. Furthermore, war, the pre-1919 remedy for intolerable frontiers, was condemned as illegal and unconscionable by the moral legislators of this new liberal world order.

Equally gravely, the United States insisted on the territorial status quo in East Asia while denying Japan the very security arrangements, notably the Anglo-Japanese alliance and more generous capital ship ratios, that might have made the status quo more bearable. When Japan had sought to win emigration rights for its excess population in the 1920s, Americans greeted such proposals with hostility; California politicians and voters gave voice to the nation's fears and prejudices on this subject. After the First World War, any previous sympathy for Japan's plight yielded to alarm in Washington and London over Japanese moves to win access to new export markets and reliable supplies of strategic resources, particularly after the crash of 1929 that would usher in the Great Depression. At the same time, Japan's efforts to expand its influence on the Asian mainland by threats and force stimulated the growth of Chinese nationalism.

Only slowly did it dawn on Japanese awareness in general and Kyoto School thinking in particular that America's transcendent role as the nascent policeman of this new order – a role in which it became ever more assuredly embedded over time – meant that any form of armed resistance to US authority was by definition illegal because immoral (not the other way around). For Latin Americans, this was an old story that began with the unilateral declaration of the Monroe Doctrine, but for the remainder of the non-Western world, the decisive denouement was reached with America's assertion of its hegemony over the Western Pacific and its right to arbitrate the affairs of East Asia during the 1930s.

The Pacific War was the watershed. Policy makers in Washington and financial leaders in New York City, the twin capitals of the new American century, were supremely confident, and with good reason, that Imperial Japan would be compelled to yield.[4] Pearl Harbor was a blow, but even the Nazi threat only delayed the inevitable because the ultimate outcome was never in doubt. American might and morals were in unique and irresistible accord. The ethics of liberal imperialism fed a relentless logic. Roosevelt's oil embargo, the crushing of the Imperial Navy, the terror bombing of Tokyo and other Japanese cities, the destruction of Hiroshima and Nagasaki, no less than the enforced transformation of the Japanese into liberal subjects during the post-war US occupation, and the subsequent reduction of Asia's first modern great power into an American protectorate achieved the aim willed from the outset.

Read in the light of our primary narrative, the key foreign policy statements of Franklin D. Roosevelt, his Secretary of State Cordell Hull and his Secretary of War Henry Lewis Stimson (who had been Herbert Hoover's secretary of state) can be soberly interpreted, without strain, to be consistent with the liberal goal of American global hegemony. Thus after Pearl Harbor the liberal way of war reached its apogee of power and effect. In a triumph of ethical cunning and muscular Christianity, the liberal learned to lay waste to his enemies in good conscience.

Notes

1 Carl Schmitt, *The Nomos of the Earth in the International Law of the Jus Publicum Europaeum*, trans. and ann. G. L. Ulmen, New York: Telos Press, 2006, p. 21.
2 Quoted in Michael Howard, *War and the Liberal Conscience*, London: Temple Smith, 1978, p. 9.
3 Howard, *War and the Liberal Conscience*, p.10.
4 If anything, middle-ranking officials and their private-sector counterparts within the American financial elite were even more convinced that Japan could be bankrupted into submission to the liberal global order by US banking controls on international trade and capital movements alone. On this vital subject, see the detailed labours of Edward S. Miller, *Bankrupting the Enemy: The US Financial Siege of Japan before Pearl Harbor*, Annapolis, MD: Naval Institute Press, 2007.

What is the Kyoto School?

3 Learning to resist imperialism

The three phases of the classic Kyoto School and the *Chūō Kōron* symposia on 'the standpoint of world history and Japan'

> The world of history is the world of ethics.
> (Masaaki Kōsaka[1])

> In the political field, Mencius was even more insistent than Confucius that government was primarily an exercise in ethics.
> (Edwin O. Reischauer and John K. Fairbank[2])

To the reader coming fresh to the *Chūō Kōron* symposia, it may seem obvious that this is a philosophical text about the world of politics, history and war. And so it is. However, in that branch of Japanese studies that is heir to religious-minded Orientalism, the Kyoto School has been identified almost entirely with Zen Buddhism. Contrary to the obvious facts at issue, the religious-minded Orientalist insists on portraying the Kyoto School as a group of naïve apolitical philosophers who in the 1930s and early 1940s happened to wander into the real world by accident. This Romantic vision of the wartime Kyoto School as a flight from political and social reality is an evasion. What is obvious to the new reader of the wartime Kyoto School is the truth of the matter.

The Kyoto School and geopolitics

The planet experiences no greater form of geopolitical revolution than when one world order yields to another. Just now our global society is caught in such a moment. It is beyond our powers to predict the precise consequences of either the West's current financial crisis or the rise of new emerging powers such as China, India and Brazil. The sudden and irresistible shift from European to American hegemony at the end of the Great War was another world-order crisis. Does the first year of the Pacific War also qualify as such a liquid moment? Certainly, during the first five months of the Pacific War, the fruits of five centuries of European conquest, commercial penetration and imperialism in East and South-East Asia were swept away, never to return in a sustainable way. It is also a fact that after June 1942 the irresistible assertion of American hegemony over the Western Pacific blotted out Japan's moment in the sun and set back the cause of East Asian regional autonomy for nearly a century.

The Kyoto School had its own reasons for believing that it might be able to give direction to the new world order that seemed to be emerging from late 1941. In their three meetings during that tumultuous twelve months just before and then after Japan went to war with the United States and the British Empire, Kōsaka, Kōyama, Nishitani and Suzuki collectively produced an incisive response to this revolution in the political life of our planetary system. The expression 'world order' occurs more than fifty times in the *Chūō Kōron* transcripts, and therefore this term merits a special place alongside 'standpoint', 'world history transcripts' and 'Japan' in any serious framework of interpretation of the wartime deliberations of the Kyoto School.

Whatever we may think now and whatever a liberal universalist may have thought at the time, the wartime Kyoto School understood itself as an intellectual movement and school of geopolitical philosophy with two vocations. First, these Japanese thinkers sought to deconstruct the post-1919 ideology in which the demands of conscience that so obsessed the liberal pacifist were united with the cosmopolitan goal of creating Friedman's liberal 'flatland'. The Kyoto School believed that the post-1919 redefinition of war was at once unrealistic and dangerous, while hopes for the League of Nations had been dashed as it became clearer that the new organization was an instrument for sustaining the status quo in the form of a liberal world order. Second, these Japanese grand strategists sought to design a more realistic and sturdier *regional* order to replace Wilson's liberal *global* order, which was at once unstable and menacing. Rightly or wrongly, the Kyoto School concluded that Woodrow Wilson's vision of endless war to end war threatened both Japan's status as a great power and its saner hopes to construct a form of regional unity and autonomy consistent with the aspirations of East Asia as an autonomous civilization.

Geopolitical necessity encouraged creative engagement with some of the fundamental problems of the philosophy and theory of politics, history and war. Thus in the *Chūō Kōron* symposia, we find that these Kyoto philosophers formulated a specifically Japanese response to the classic themes of Hegelian subjectivity and world-historical peoples; to Ranke's meditation on the great powers and the role of moral energy in the making of world history; to the key political topics that concerned Plato, Machiavelli and Hobbes (the nature of sovereignty, the legitimacy of the state and the duties of the citizen); to the nature of war in thinkers from Clausewitz to Ludendorff; and to the dilemmas facing designers of world orders from Woodrow Wilson to Carl Schmitt.

The *Chūō Kōron* symposia are neither benighted works of off-piste religious philosophy, nor are they a surrender to wartime propaganda. Quite the contrary: it is part of an impressive outpouring of books, articles, lectures and discussions by the Kyoto School between 1928 and 1945 on the philosophy of history, war and the state. Taken as a whole, this body of writing qualifies as a remarkable chapter in modern Asian thought. Conscious of this substantial corpus and the pivotal status of the *Chūō Kōron* symposia within it, we are now in a position to retell the story of the genesis of the Kyoto School in a manner that grants due importance to this hitherto neglected revolution. This entire enterprise falls under the rubric of what Ōhashi calls the 'potential' of the Kyoto School.[3] It was formidable then and it remains formidable now.

The provocation of European excellence

Throughout the classic age of the Kyoto School, from the publication of Nishida's *Zen no Kenkyū* in 1911 to the death of Keiji Nishitani in 1990, these philosophers were given purpose and focus by the conclusion reached during the preceding half-century that the European mind had opened the door on human and natural reality in a way matched by no Asian science or school, ancient or modern. The resulting Japanese assimilation and mastery of the language and logic of Western philosophy should be judged as one of the most arresting examples of enlightened exchange, of the confident assimilation of the fruits of one civilization by another, in history.

The kind of mental power necessary to meet this European challenge was manifest as soon as the daunting scale of the task was recognized, between the first lecture of Amane Nishi in 1862 on *Kitetsugaku* (Greek philosophy) and the early philosophical maturity impressively demonstrated by Hajime Tanabe in his inaugural essays on Kant and 'the philosophy of society', which appeared between 1932 and 1935 – essays that would form the foundation for *The Logic of the Species*. This energetic Japanese appropriation of a taxing body of alien ideas over eight decades represents one of the great chapters in the modern history of ideas.

Behind this supreme effort and achievement lay a double refusal. There could be no simple surrender to Europe's manifest superiority, but neither could the power of European civilization be ignored or comfortably wished away in some ultranationalist daydream. This unyielding perception gave a distinctive voice and poise to the Kyoto philosopher in the *Geistesgeschichte* of pre-war Japan. The Kyoto School's ambition to meet the philosophic standards of the classic European tradition required mastery of the broad sweep of Western civilization.

Recognition that Europeans had invented the modern world led to a voracious bookish hunger for things European. Hence the almost insatiable appetite demonstrated by Kōsaka, Kōyama, Nishitani and Suzuki for Greek, Latin, English, German, French, Italian, Russian, Danish and Dutch texts, read in the original or in translation. The result was a perhaps unrivalled command of a large and representative sample of the outpourings of the European mind, from classical antiquity through the key texts of medieval and Renaissance civilization down to the age of Kant and Hegel, thence to arrive at the masters of the intellectual powerhouse that was Weimar Germany. The evidence of these tireless armchair labours is obvious on almost every page of *the Chūō Kōron* symposia.

The task of this chapter is, therefore, to explain the importance and scope of the innovative labours and creative achievements of the wartime Kyoto School thinkers, as manifested in the *Chūō Kōron* symposia, which have hitherto been ignored or denigrated in the Western reception of Japanese philosophy. A schema of interpretation will be stipulated that places this textual mountain range within the wider typology of the Kyoto philosophical tradition. In this manner we may begin to assess properly – *seriously* – the philosophical significance of the 'middle' phase (1928–45) of the classic Kyoto School. One surprising conclusion may be drawn from this close perusal of the first large wartime text to be so intensely examined: the depth of these Japanese insights, both practical and metaphysical, into geopolitical reality suggests that the Kyoto School meditation on history, politics and war *as objects of philosophical reflection* may be without peer in modern Asian thought.

Hence my principal conclusion: this formidable Japanese response, so subtly and incisively at work in the *Chūō Kōron* symposia, to the crisis of the modern state, the triumph of liberal universalism, the emergence of American unipolar domination and the enduring powers of Confucian revolution, along with the challenge of Asian subjectivity and regional integration, may be set with confidence alongside any of the earlier or later examples of celebrated Kyoto School success in the fields of the philosophy of religion, aesthetics and the like. We must open our minds to the ideas of the four contributors to *the Chūō Kōron* symposia if we are to trace the development and to judge the *quality and timeliness* of the young Nishida's political ideas, predating even his pioneering masterpiece, *Zen no Kenkyū*. This in turn may allow us finally to gauge the true significance of Tanabe's *The Logic of the Species*. Here, as elsewhere, one rule must apply: first understand, then judge.

The genesis of the classic Kyoto School: a schema

The scale of the literary output of the Kyoto School since 1911 has been extraordinary. The published works alone form a considerable mass. Given the impact of the wartime fire-bombing of Japan's great cities, the variety of natural disasters to which this nation is prone and indeed the losses inflicted by the wear and tear of everyday life, one can only speculate about what hidden treasures – diaries, manuscripts and lecture notes – have been lost or, more hopefully, remain to be discovered in private collections, university archives and library basements in provincial Japan.

It is not obvious, however, that we are *mentally* prepared to make more than a tentative appraisal of the large textual corpus of classic Kyoto School thought that we already have in hand, much of it still unread or untranslated. The ideological battlements and moats built by the academics of both liberal imperialist and Confucian pacifist convictions have yet to be stormed and rendered harmless. In other words, we are far from producing a persuasive overview of the classic Kyoto School as a whole because we are still inhibited by the minatory whisperings of morality. Unlike Bluebeard in his castle, liberals remain unconvinced that we should *want* to open the door on the truth, but given what we already know now, a preliminary assessment of the philosophical success of the Kyoto School is possible. To assist the reader in getting his bearings among the sea of texts, the vast labour of the giants of the Kyoto School and their students, the following schema is offered.

The classic age of the Kyoto School (1911–90)

Phase I: the founding of the Kyoto School (1911–27)

- Principal Kyoto thinker: Kitarō Nishida
- Textual monument: *An Inquiry into the Good* (Nishida)
- Dominant Asian philosophical tradition: Buddhism
- Most influential European philosopher: Kant

Phase II: the wartime Kyoto School (1928–45)

- Principal Kyoto thinker: Hajime Tanabe
- Textual monument: *The Logic of the Species* (Tanabe)
- Popular manifesto: the *Chūō Kōron* symposia (Kōsaka, Kōyama, Nishitani, Suzuki)
- Dominant Asian philosophical tradition: Confucianism
- Most influential European philosopher: Hegel

Phase III: the post-war Kyoto School (1946–90)

- Principal Kyoto thinker: Keiji Nishitani
- Textual monument: *Religion and Nothingness* (Nishitani)
- Popular manifesto: *Nihilism* (Nishitani)
- Dominant Asian philosophic tradition: Buddhism
- Most influential European philosopher: Nietzsche

This schema is provisional. It is premised on a triangulation among Nishida, Tanabe and Nishitani at the expense of the contributions of the other, often brilliant, members of the Kyoto School. Attempting to factor in the writings of Kiyoshi Miki – say, his 1932 book *The Philosophy of History* – alone disturbs these neat conclusions based on our 'three-gods-in-one' perspective. Imagine trying to integrate the divergent ideas of Jun Tōsaka, the Kyoto School's radical Marxist, or Tetsurō Watsuji, its most formidable outlier, or Toratarō Shimomura, the philosopher and historian of science, or Shigetaka Suzuki, the economic historian and one of the contributors to the *Chūō Kōron* symposia, and it becomes clear that any tidy summary is likely to be commensurately implausible.

Other judgements essential to our schema also invite potential revision. Confucianism, for example, almost certainly underwrites most of the *political* writings of the first phase, while Hegel may well prove to be more influential than Kant *before* as well as after 1928. Nishitani's domination of the third phase may well turn out to be less impressive as we learn more about the huge post-war output of the growing membership of the Kyoto School after the Pacific War. Similarly, the educational, ethical and political themes that dominate the post-war period will almost certainly call into doubt the apparent primary influence of Nietzsche and Buddhism after 1945.

What do the *Chūō Kōron* discussions tell us about the Kyoto School?

Tanabe's complicated intellectual trajectory over the period requires more detailed examination, as does the precise measure of his influence on his successors as well as on Nishida. Only when such revisionary research is well under way will we be able to judge whether my assessment of Nishida's role in the final phase of his school and his life to be more that of a public intellectual and political impresario than *maître de pensée* will stand or not.

What makes the *Chūō Kōron* symposia the popular manifesto of the revolution of Kyoto School thought between 1928 and 1945 is its role as a vortex, drawing in a prodigious output of books, articles, lectures and unpublished writings by a phalanx of Japanese philosophers, historians and political thinkers. This refocus of the energies of the Kyoto intellectual on the political-social sphere in all its varied faces, from history to ethics, from politics to the economy, and from metaphysics to international relations, gave direction and scope to this eruption of textual productivity.

Even a selective list of the literary harvest of the wartime Kyoto School in the wake of Tanabe's 'turn to society' and Nishida's deepening historical-mindedness during the late 1920s and early 1930s includes a substantial number of both full-length books and celebrated essays. A representative sample includes Kiyoshi Miki, *The Philosophy of History* (1932); Tanabe, 'The Logic of Social Ontology' (1934/35); Tanabe, 'The Logic of the Species and the World Schema' (1935); Kōyama, *Hegel* (1936); Tanabe, 'The Social Ontological Structure of Logic' (1936); Kōsaka, *The Historical World* (1937); Risaku Mutai, *Fichte* (1938); Tanabe, 'The Logic of National Ontology' (1938); Kōsaka, *The Philosophy of History and Political Philosophy* (1939); Kōyama, *Classifications of Culture* (1939); Kōyama, *Philosophic Anthropology* (1939); Risaku Mutai, *The Theory of Social Ontology* (1939); Suzuki, *Ranke and the Study of World History* (1939); Shinsaku Aihara, *The Great Powers*, a translation of Ranke (1940); Kōsaka, *Myth* (1940); Kōyama, 'The Idea of World History' (1940); Nishida, *The Problem of Japanese Culture* (1940); Nishitani, *The Philosophy of Primordial Subjectivity* (1940); Tanabe, 'Eternity, History, Action' (1940); Nishida, 'On the Philosophy of History', a lecture before the Emperor (1941); Nishida, 'On *Staatsräson*' (1941); Nishitani, *Worldviews and Views of the State* (1941); Suzuki, *The Idea of the Historical*

State (1941); Suzuki and Aihara, *The Idea of World History*, a translation of Ranke, 1941; Tanabe, 'Ethics and Logic' (1941); Kōsaka, *The Philosophy of the Nation* (1942); Kōyama, *The Philosophy of World History* (1942); Kōsaka, *Introduction to the Philosophy of History* (1943); Kōyama, *Japan's Agenda and World History* (1943); Kōyama, 'On the Spirit of *Hakkō no Ichiu*' (1943); Kōyama, *The Dynamic of World History* (1944); Risaku Mutai, 'The Genealogy of World History' (1944); Nishitani, 'The Philosophy of World History' (1944); Suzuki, 'The World Historical View of History' (1944).

To this impressive but far from exhaustive catalogue one might add interventions by members of the Kyoto School in symposia such as that on 'Overcoming Modernity' (*Kindai no chōkoku*) in July 1942, in which Nishitani, Suzuki and Shimomura took part. Hundreds of articles were written by these scholars in response to developments in international affairs after the Japanese occupation of the bulk of Manchuria in 1931. *The Ōshima Memos*, which came to light in 2000, have proven uniquely valuable to understanding the wartime Kyoto School's conspiracy with the Imperial Navy against the Tōjō faction. More political and philosophical texts may yet be found. Finally, no list of the output of the wartime Kyoto School will be complete without reference to the much-discussed wartime interventions and political reflections of Nishida himself.

This profusion of material, much of which we are only beginning to examine and digest, overthrows the hoary orthodox assumption that the Kyoto School is a meditation on Mahāyāna Buddhism, and nothing more. This is simply not true. The Kyoto School was a broad church that should attract a wide variety of readers and researchers: the Zen enthusiast and the Confucian ethicist, the political theorist and the metaphysician with a gift for abstraction, the ecologist and the geopolitical strategist, the historian of ideas and the East Asian aesthetician. The proposed schema of the classic Kyoto School lends itself to the growing interest in Japanese mathematics, propositional logic and the natural sciences. This 'broad church' characterization anticipates the varied and unpredictable research discoveries and interpretative revisions that tomorrow may bring, and it is with this open stance that we may best answer our question: What is the Kyoto School?

Notes

1 Masaaki Kōsaka, *Sekai-shi no Tetsugaku to Seiji no Tetsugaku* (The Philosophy of World History and Political Philosophy), Tokyo: Kōbundō-shobō, 1939, p. 1.
2 Edwin O. Reischauer and John K. Fairbank, *East Asia: The Great Tradition*, Boston: Houghton Mifflin; Tokyo: Charles E. Tuttle, 1960, p. 1969.
3 Ryōsuke Ōhashi, *Kyoto Gakuha no Shisō: Irorio no Zō to Shisō no Potensharu* (The Mind of the Kyoto School: A Variety of Portraits and Reflections on its Intellectual Potential), Kyoto: Jinbushoin, 2004.

4 Confucianism, realism and liberalism
Three approaches to the *Chūō Kōron* symposia

> The only revolutions that Vietnamese political wisdom considers authentic are those that effect complete change. The main proof of a party's right to power is a programme that provides new solutions for everything, and in East Asia this conception has forever been familiar to the simplest countryman.
>
> (John T. McAlister and Paul Mus[1])

> The Schmittian vocabulary – the concepts of the political, friend–enemy, state of exception, decisionism, executive government, *nomos*, pan-regions, pan-interventionism and non-discriminatory concept of war – presents not only an important rediscovery and addition to the mainstream international-relations lexicon, but has become a significant idiom for the social sciences at large; presenting a powerful counter-narrative to conventional imperialist liberalism.
>
> (Benno Teschke[2])

The *Chūō Kōron* symposia present us with a single task, at once simple and exact: to clear our minds of any interpretive scheme that prevents us from reading what is on the page. To keep our minds focused on this exacting task, we must know how liberalism, Confucianism and realism, as strategies of reading, may help or hinder us in attaining our goal.

Bracketing liberalism

This commentary departs from almost all writing on the wartime Kyoto School in one significant way: my refusal to engage in moral criticism. To read the *Chūō Kōron* transcripts as the participants spoke them, it is essential to avoid all forms of what Roland Barthes acutely called 'the contagion of judgment'.[3] This commentary is an experiment in textual exactitude, painstaking hermeneutics and Orientalist science, not moral dissection. Objectivity is the goal because our sole motive is to decode the message in the barnacled bottle that has taken some seventy years to wash across the sea to Europe from Japan.

When I use expressions such as 'liberal imperialism' or 'hegemonic domination', they are intended as realistic descriptions, and therefore carry no weight of ethical censure. In the first phase of a proper reading, certainly while we are preparing to test the soundness of our framework of interpretation, the task is to distinguish not right from wrong, but truth from falsehood. No moral inventory is taken here of the virtues or demerits, successes or failings of European, American or Japanese imperialism. Our mantra remains: understand, not judge.

As a descriptive idea or umbrella concept, liberal imperialism has three pillars:

1 Moral universalism, or a code of ethical beliefs held to apply at all times and in every culture. The absolute character of this ethical system demands legal enforcement, because to violate this code is to reduce oneself or one's nation to the outlaw status of a criminal.
2 American hegemony, or the assumption by the United States after 1919 of the right to exercise global sovereignty and enforce the legal code elaborated by moral universalists in the Kantian tradition. As the policeman of this ethical-legal order of global domination, the United States may legitimately treat armed opposition to its status as global hegemon to be at once illegal and immoral. There is no effective limit on the exercise of this power over the international system other than the opposition offered by the rare nation that refuses to bow to American will and authority. Imperial Japan and revolutionary Vietnam are the two most important Confucian examples of such resistance. Thus, by moral and legal inference, the liberal way of war must include, as its supreme expression, wars of annihilation, the Pacific War being the *exemplum* that figures most prominently in these pages.
3 Neo-liberalism, or the doctrine of market perfection embodied in the ideology of the Wall Street system of global finance. The assumption of market perfection, always true in theory and enforced as if true in practice, means that resistance to the Washington or International Monetary Fund (IMF) Consensus, or any of its earlier incarnations, is held to be economically irrational and politically indefensible. Like Kantian moral cosmopolitanism, this economic doctrine admits no compromise or empirical exceptions. As a form of universalism, it acknowledges no economic exterior. Varieties of capitalism do not, by definition, exist. They are unthinkable.

The wartime Kyoto School rejects liberal imperialism so defined, and the *Chūō Kōron* discussions set out the reasons for this rejection. This fact means that liberalism cannot provide an objective reading of our text. Liberalism cannot work as *an approach* because conscience does not permit the luxury of objectivity. This is why textual rigour so frequently eludes the liberal reader of Asian political texts. Thus there is but one recourse for the liberal who would read this text properly: he must bracket his liberalism *à la Husserl*, that is to place an idea or concept to one side in our deliberations without abandoning it because it may be needed in the future. The suggestion would be that liberalism as an interpretative strategy or method of reading falls short of the needs of the serious student of the wartime Kyoto School. In this chapter, two such alternatives will be proposed: Confucianism and realism.

The Confucian approach

The liberal imperialist, as the practical proponent of Kantian moral universalism, denies any validity to East Asian ethics. It is beyond the scope of this commentary to trace the story of how Kant's notion that his ethics should apply to all societies, Western or otherwise, evolved into Woodrow Wilson's attempt to impose such an ethical system on the whole world via the criminalization of war.[4] However, when the German philosopher famously declared that even God would have to obey the dicta of a universally valid set of morals, a formidable *Denkverbot* or ban on thinking was erected against the objective understanding of the non-liberal world. If morality was what Kant said it was (to the exclusion of all else), what was the Western student of Asia to make of Confucian ethics? Specifically, how was one either to translate or explain the title of the second symposium: 'The Ethical and Historical Character of the East Asian Co-prosperity Sphere'?

The status of the Greater East Asian Co-prosperity Sphere in the modern history of Japan is unambiguous. Allied Pacific War orthodoxy insists that from the invention of the term, whether or not by Prince Konoe's brains trust in 1941, to the official proclamation of the creation of this sphere by the Tōjō government in 1943, this notion was always a sham. It served as an illicit justification for Japanese aggression and imperialism. It was nothing more than an ideological pretence cynically concocted to mask the brutal exploitation of subject peoples from China and Korea to Burma and the Dutch East Indies. Beyond the malign intent lurking in this perverse slogan, the expression 'Greater East Asian Co-prosperity Sphere' meant nothing. As critics of the wartime Kyoto School, Japanese pacifists often share this assessment, but for Confucian, not Kantian, reasons.

So why did the Kyoto School thinker insist on the ethical character of the Greater East Asian Co-prosperity Sphere as a Confucian-inspired *Großraum* or *kōiki-ken*? To answer this question we must revisit the cardinal failure of liberal scholarship on the Pacific War: the inability to explain how the Japanese moved during the course of 1945 from fierce, indeed suicidal, resistance to the American assault on the Japanese homeland, to prompt and complete surrender, and then to ready and enthusiastic cooperation with the US occupation.

The answer lies in the Confucian ideas of *tenkō, tenmei* and *toku*. Sometimes rendered as 'apostasy' or 'forced conversion', *tenkō* is a shortened form of *hōkō tenkan*, which means 'change of direction or orientation'. *Tenkō* is the predictable and necessary 'change of mind' by all members of a Confucian society in response to the transition from one political regime to another. The more familiar doctrine of *tenmei* or the 'mandate of heaven' refers to the crown of legitimacy conferred on the successful originator of a new political regime. The defining elements of *tenmei* include destiny, moral authority, practical effectiveness and raw power. Might makes right in Confucian Asia because for might to succeed it must be right; and, having triumphed, might is assumed to be right until proven otherwise. Managers of America's Japanese protectorate, critics of the crushing of the Tiananmen Square uprising, and proponents of Tibetan as well as Taiwanese independence, please note.

Radical novelty is what defines such Confucian revolutions. The leader of a movement who seeks *tenmei* will demonstrate his suitability for power by proclaiming and then instituting a complete departure from the practices and policies of the previous regime (the Co-prosperity Sphere, for example, as a revolutionary successor to European colonialism). Success comes with the assertion of *toku*, a conventional term for 'morality' or 'virtue' that in fact includes the ideas of 'political system' and 'political effectiveness'. Thus, when *toku* begins to slip from the hands of the current holder of the mandate, dynastic or otherwise, his hold on *tenmei* is threatened, and the population he governs will begin to contemplate a mass *tenkō* – just as the Japanese people did in the 1860s and at the end of the Pacific War. For the elite loyalist of the old regime, the only Confucian options are suicide, illegitimate underground resistance or sincere *tenkō*, because one is *morally obliged* to embrace the new regime. This was the point of the prison interrogation scenes in Bertolucci's film *The Last Emperor*.

Liberal moral universalism after Kant is unable to cope with such ethical doctrines, and this is why liberals so frequently fail to grasp the nature of political change across Confucian East Asia. This ethical handicap may have condemned thousands of Westerners and millions of Asians to unnecessary horrors. Certainly the decision to drop atom bombs on Japanese cities might have been judged unnecessary if the Truman Administration had done its Confucian homework. Similarly, we must do our Confucian homework today if we are to understand the Kyoto School's support for a Greater East Asian Co-prosperity Sphere with a human face or China's contemporary response to similar liberal imperialist pressures.

Realism and the three global orders

Japan's emergence into the modern world as a great power was conditioned by three mutually exclusive visions of global political order. First there was the Confucian cosmos, effectively an enclosed regional order composed of a hierarchical system of tributaries and barbarians caught in the moral orbit of Imperial China. No state was equal to China and none qualified as a modern state in the Weberian sense. Second, there was the first genuinely global order, created and sustained by the great powers of Europe between 1492 and 1918. Five fundamental assumptions came to govern this system and keep it vital after 1648:

1 the state as the sole legitimate maker of war and peace;
2 secularized and absolute state sovereignty;
3 the executive branch of government as the sovereign and supreme authority in all extreme emergencies that threaten the survival of a political order. This state of exception is what Carl Schmitt had in mind when he declared 'the sovereign is he who decides on the exception (*Political Theology*)';
4 the idea of *justus hostis* or the 'just enemy' as the ruling norm of warfare; and
5 the idea of war as a morally neutral exercise (non-discriminatory war).

A third world order began to take shape with the Versailles Treaty, based on the alliance of moral universalism and American unipolar domination that I call 'liberal imperialism'. As a reaction to the 1648–1918 order, the post-Wilsonian Versailles-Geneva-Washington world order between 1919 and 1939 and the *Pax Americana* after 1945 rejected all the premises of the previous system in favour of the following new principles:

1 no wars permitted but just wars (those of self-defence, or international police actions sanctioned or executed by the United States);
2 the end of absolute national sovereignty and the demotion of all but the United States from the status of great power;
3 executive authority subject to international sanction and pan-intervention, with the United States as ultimate practical and moral arbiter over any state of exception in any nation;
4 delegitimation of all opponents of liberal imperialism as unjust foes, rogue states, criminals or terrorists; and
5 punishment and prevention of war crimes by the ultimate sanction of liberal wars of annihilation.

These axioms formed the principles of the Versailles counter-revolution. Without reference to them, the causes of the Pacific War, the logic of the Tokyo War Crimes Tribunal and the 'liberal flattening' objectives of the post-war occupation of Japan cannot be understood. This truth applies with particular force to the rejection of Christian moral absolutes and the doctrine of just wars that characterized the pre-Versailles world order. The abandonment of such moral universalism was essential if non-Christian powers, such as the Ottoman Empire and Imperial Japan, were to be admitted as full members of the Concert of the Great Powers.

With the crushing of Japan in 1945, a form of universal moralism not seen since the Crusades and the Wars of Religion was resurrected with martial vigour (only to be challenged by the rise of Chinese power six decades later). Thus the Pacific War may be viewed as a moral clash of civilizations between Imperial Japan and Wilson's Versailles counter-revolution. The clash was provoked by the liberal West's revival of the theological concept of just war. The conflicts that have shaped the world since 1919 have, more often than not, been forms of pan-interventionism. The liberal assertion of the global hegemon's right to intervene in the internal affairs of all other states forms a predictable corollary of any form of international law based on Kantian moral universalism.

For the student of the wartime Kyoto School in particular and the Pacific War in general, the list of changes wrought by Wilson's liberal revolution merits close scrutiny. The moral revolution in international law set in motion by the Versailles Treaty includes not only the previously noted resurrection of the medieval idea of discriminatory or just war, but also the international criminalization of aggressive war, including an unprecedented legal culpability not only of states but of rulers, and the abrogation of the right to make war as the highest expression of state sovereignty, as exemplified in Article 9 of the 1946 'peace' constitution imposed on Japan.

The treatment of post-Imperial Germany after Versailles prefigured the fate of post-Imperial Japan after Hiroshima and Nagasaki. Carl Schmitt placed particular emphasis on the reduction of Germany to an externally administered albeit still supposedly sovereign state through the internationalization of German canals, mines and factories.[5] Nominally part of Germany, the Rhineland became the toy of France after 1918, just as Okinawa, nominally part of Japan, became – as it remains – the toy of America after 1945. All these changes were subsequently legitimated by a relentless rebalancing of rights and powers away from the sovereign state in favour of the individual and the liberal imperium (moral universalism, American hegemony, and globalization). This was the great labour of liberal legal thinkers such as the influential French jurist Maurice Hauriou, who struggled tirelessly to deconstruct the state to ensure the triumph of the individual and the universal interest after 1919. It was this form of liberalism that the Kyoto School would oppose in the *Chūō Kōron* discussions.

Contradictions of principle plagued Wilson's counter-revolution from the beginning. For example, how was one to square the national right to self-determination with Western colonialism, or the prerogatives of a liberal global hegemony, or the claims of liberal public opinion? The Kyoto School thinker pounced on such confusions. Wilson fanned the insistence by liberals of conscience that national self-determination be treated as an inalienable right for all European peoples otherwise bereft of statehood. However, as an American Southerner, with a racial attitude to match, Wilson also sought to secure the vested interests of the European colonial powers, and thus he ruled against Japan's call at Versailles for international recognition of racial equality. In this, the American president clearly acted out of deference to America's white allies. Wilson's successors in the White House began to conspire actively against the colonial power base of America's European rivals only after its own strength became irresistible. At every twist and turn in the logic of pan-interventionism, Japanese interests would suffer.

With defeat in 1945, Japan became the first important non-Western victim of liberal flattening, and thus experienced the blunt end of the New World's distinctive approach to international law. The liberal imperialist commitment to 'legal norms' drew less on legal precedent than on moral compulsion, raw power and the weakness of the common law for the immediately obvious – as witness the impact of 'legal common sense' in the proceedings of the Tokyo War Crime Tribunal. The liberal imperialist assumption appears to be that international law is to be applied by the global hegemon to other nations, but that it is a matter of hegemonic discretion when and if such legal constraints apply to the United States.

In extremis, the liberal imperialist *as a liberal* will not submit to the law because he is the embodiment of cosmopolitan virtue. It is those who resist the liberal imperium who must surrender to the law because they embody immorality and evil ('the evil empire', 'the Axis of evil', 'the original Axis of evil', etc.). It is they who must be flattened liberally as part of a universal programme of punishment and reform in order to convert the offender into a *contrite* subject who willingly submits to the empire of liberal righteousness. In this manner, ethics as power scatters all before it. This is how the moral universalist squares his conscience with the logical necessity for victor's justice. Rightly or wrongly, the ethics of liberal imperialism comes to depend on the liberal's confidence in his inward sense of his own moral rectitude, and its predictable fruit: moral ferocity.

Notes

1 John T. McAlister, Jr and Paul Mus, *The Vietnamese and their Revolution*, New York, Evanston and London: Harper & Row, 1970, p. 63.
2 Benno Teschke, 'Exorcizing Schmitt', *New Left Review*, Jan.–Feb. 2011, p. 61.
3 Roland Barthes, *The Pleasure of the Text*, trans. Richard Miller, Oxford: Basil Blackwell, 1990, p. 32.
4 Lest the accusation of false clarity be raised, Kant's long essay on 'Eternal Peace' sometimes pulls towards Westphalia, sometimes towards Versailles, and sometimes falls between these polar positions. In international relations theory, the term 'Kantian liberal-cosmopolitan mainstream' appears to rely on the internal coherence and manifest comparability of these two 'liberals' rather than evidence that President Wilson knew his Kant.
5 Carl Schmitt, *Writings on War*, trans. and ed. Timothy Nunan, Cambridge, UK: Polity, 2011, p. 156.

5 How East Asians argue
The Confucian form and language of the *Chūō Kōron* symposia

A lake on fire: the symbol of revolution
Thus the moral man
Renews the order of history
And makes the significance of the times manifest.
  (*The Book of Changes*, 49th Hexagram[1])

In her beautifully judged collection of interviews with some of the most influential American philosophers of the late twentieth century, Giovanna Borradori echoes Nietzsche's observation that there are no philosophies, only philosophers when she suggests that 'the very format of the literary conversation' as well as the 'belief in the existence of a person-philosopher behind every theory' are 'distinctly European' responses to the humanity and charm of this most ancient form of philosophical exchange.[2]

In a comparable way, the *Chūō Kōron* symposia conjure up characteristically Japanese notions of how one gives shape to occasions when thoughtful human beings seek shared enlightenment. There is the same palpable sense of an enclosed civilized space that so attracted the samurai generals of the strife-torn Japan of an earlier age, men who exploited the meditative hush of the tea ceremony, as our Japanese thinkers remind us, not to escape from the world but as a calm occasion for gathering one's thoughts in order to make the world a better place.[3] Inevitably, there are Confucian touches to such occasions. Certainly the refusal to seek pride of place among one's colleagues no less than the ritual depreciation of one's own opinions was quietly at work during these three evenings of long discussion held in the very capital of Japanese tradition.

This youngish 'gang of four' intellectuals comprised Keiji Nishitani, destined to become a major figure in modern Japanese thought, two now neglected but brilliant philosophers introduced earlier – Iwao Kōyama and Masaaki Kōsaka – plus the always shrewd and often provocative Shigetaka Suzuki, economic historian and fellow traveller of this academic circle. These four witty, engaging and intellectually generous scholars, together with the absent and slightly older Kiyoshi Miki, richly represent the flower of the second generation of the Kyoto School. These Kyoto thinkers sought to make the world new, and the struggle they set in motion has yet to reach its conclusion.

A meeting of minds

In the *Chūō Kōron* discussions, the four participants demonstrate the surprisingly satisfying powers of a form of human intellectual interaction for which the Western mind traditionally has had little respect: group-think. These symposia do not represent a clash of egoists jockeying for advantage or superiority. No one is showing off. Rather, they are gatherings of like-minded thinkers attempting to flesh out a collective position, in competition with other groups of intellectuals, on a set of themes at once politically sensitive and of immense interest to the makers and shapers of national opinion within the Japanese elite. The tension, anxieties and sense of urgency on display reflect the unmistakable atmosphere of crisis that colours these otherwise confident and unruffled discussions as the storm gathered and broke over the Pacific during the winter of 1941–42.

Colleagues for decades, intellectually *simpatico*, students of the same great philosophical masters – Nishida and Tanabe – these are public intellectuals who were fearlessly willing to contest, in print, the policies of the powers that be as represented in the Tōjō clique, as well as the army censors and the noisier extremists among the country's better-read ultranationalists. They took their stand together just as Japan was plunging into a war they were not confident it could win. They share a vision, a language and a profound sense of mutual commitment to each other and to the humane political passions of the Kyoto School. No wonder Nishitani, Kōsaka, Kōyama and Suzuki can complete each other's sentences.

All born during the first decade of the twentieth century, that is, the final decade of the Meiji era, these four thinkers bring to their discussions something more than a rigorous philosophical tradition. They are intimate with a vast corpus of European writing on a huge array of topics, from literature, anthropology and history to politics, military strategy and technology. Their shared horizon allows them to rehearse established lines of argument with economy while developing new ones almost as they speak. They can discourse at length, confident that they will be patiently listened to. They gracefully cut across each other's remarks (despite their differences in age; differences that require sensitive navigation in Confucian East Asia) and tease each other's intellectual pretensions. They share a sense of humour. One would invite all of them cheerfully to a dinner party because they appear to be such good company – and that includes Suzuki, notwithstanding his crusty moments. Even Nishitani's often remarked weakness for repetitiveness is indulged here; but then, he is the oldest and most brilliant among them. Difficult to render into English, the linguistic markings of the hierarchies of age are exact: they are reflected in Japanese nouns, pronouns, honorifics and verb endings. They are silently at work beneath the surface of any translation into a non-Confucian language.

The total effect of the transcription of these discussions is an extraordinary tour of the wartime horizon of the Kyoto philosopher in which an elaborate and sophisticated argument is developed as part of a cogent plea for Japan to gather its powers (*sō ryoku*) and remake the order of the world. Their instincts are sound and, despite their reactionary reputations, their opinions will unsettle the prejudiced liberal critic. They treat arguments for the importance of blood purity with well-judged scepticism at a time when black soldiers were apparently not allowed to give blood transfusions to white solders in the US armed forces. These Japanese thinkers celebrate the place of women in history, praising the demise of polygamy while upholding the domestic decencies of the monogamous family and the dignity of women within it. They draw a firm line around what lessons Japan could learn from Fascist Italy and Nazi Germany. They admire William James.

Ryōsuke Ōhashi calls them 'the anti-establishment establishment' (*hantai-sei-teki*).[4] Other Japanese commentators have praised the fruitful exchange of views that gives their talks a greater fluency, depth, direction and coherence than the other celebrated symposium of 1942, 'Overcoming Modernity'.[5] For the Western student of Japanese society, these discussions are an education in how a Japanese thinker may skilfully navigate cultural rules and taboo themes, and still challenge authority. Or, to put the matter more positively, they present a case study in East Asian reason. This offers the contemporary Western reader a set of rare insights into something that may influence the future of our entire planet: the manner in which East Asians argue and how they exploit even now the powers of the millennia-old discourse of the mind that is Confucianism.

The Confucianism of the Kyoto School

Among Western students of Kyoto philosophy, one often finds a serious personal commitment to Buddhism as a well-worn path to a more contemplative relationship between the self and the cosmos. The motives for such commitments are quite varied, ranging from the quest for an appreciation of nature that fosters ecological gentleness to the anxious, and rather un-Zen-like, hankering after cures for the private pathologies of the soul. This stance is fundamentally inconsistent with the social-scientific posture of students of modern area studies; they will have none of it.

The urge to understand Confucianism among Western students of East Asia does not arise from personal need; *The Analects* almost never performs daily service as a breviary in the way that Nishida's meditative writings apparently have done for some Western devotees of the Kyoto School. No, the reason why Orientalists immerse themselves in the Chinese classics is to transcend the moral barrier that separates the ethically incommensurate. The task is as demanding as that posed by any Zen *kōan*: to recognize and accept the patterns of behaviour that gave birth to the Chinese classics only to become still more rooted and fixed because of these texts. The key dialectical moves are thus sequential: from moral conduct to moral text, and then from moral text to moral conduct, and so on.

In his persistent crossing of frontiers between civilizations, the Orientalist seeks to puzzle out the ways in which Vietnamese, Koreans, Chinese and Japanese act out, on the quotidian stage, the binding character of ethics and the family, the constraints of society and politics, and the duties of war and peace. At root, this commentary seeks to take the reader on a voyage of discovery in search of footnotes and glosses to illuminate the otherwise mysterious and alien maxims and insights employed by individuals in Confucian societies better to position themselves in conformity with the larger truths of collective life. As Confucianism is the very air the East Asian breathes, and the Kyoto thinker is unmistakably an East Asian, the student of the Kyoto School will need to demonstrate a confident grasp of East Asian ethics and social psychology. *Pace* the frequent Japanese criticism found in the pages of our symposia of Chinese tradition in general and Confucianism in particular, the Orientalist must learn to breathe this air, simultaneously bracingly fresh and as strange as if from another planet. However, because area studies are a branch of the science of empire – America's empire – this is one breathing exercise that the area expert will not submit to because he thinks Confucianism is immoral.[6]

The four Japanese participants in these symposia do think in Buddhist categories – Nishida's fundamental metaphysical notions have a natural place in these deliberations – but Confucian ideas about politics, history and war are vastly more important. As a recoil against the weaknesses of East Asian tradition and a vigorous settling of accounts with Buddhist otherworldliness, the *Chūō Kōron* transcripts are best understood as a sustained defence of verbal precision and philosophical clarity in an act of rational resistance to the cultivated Zen weaknesses for suggestive nuance, poetic vagueness, the emptiness of language and the flight from reality. Roland Barthes famously defined *satori* or Buddhist enlightenment as 'the loss' or the abandonment of meaning.[7] The wartime Kyoto School offers no quarter to proponents of the 'loss of meaning'. Japan's great historical task is ripe with significance and meaning.

In these discussions, Nishida's keystone concept, 'the logic of place', takes on a geopolitical cast. Nishida uses the term 'self-identity of absolute contradiction' to describe the fact that while independent individuals may also be points or places in which the world manifests itself, in this time of the breaking of nations states and civilizations may also play this role. Most striking of all, there is an almost tireless stress on the imperative of lucidity and self-transparency (*tōmei*), to adapt an expression of Lacan, for the purposes of capturing something of the wartime Kyoto School's insistence that policies and programmes be clearly stated and that words be used in the public sphere with respect for their innate potential for precision as guides for world-historical action.

How East Asians argue, or perhaps, more gently, discuss in groups, or, better still, collectively search for the truth, depends finally on an ancient approach to the power of words that was given canonical formulation in two famous passages from *The Analects*. The first is a marvel of Chinese common sense: 'The Master said: "There is no point in people taking counsel together who follow different ways"' (XV, 40); and the second is an affirmation of the high seriousness and the moral worth of the individual: 'Heaven is the author of the virtue that is in me' (VII, 23). The trick is to see how the two quotations, and the patterns of behaviour that stand behind such wisdom, are necessary for any *shared* pursuit of the truth. Every time East Asians argue thoughtfully and effectively, both insights will be found at work.

Notes

1 This translation from the ancient Chinese is my own. Wang-ming Ng offers this incisive and relevant summary of this most ancient of Chinese texts. 'The character *I* literally means "change", and the *I Ching* elucidates the philosophy of change. According to the text, the wise man should follow the changes of the times, not because this is a moral law that one is constrained to obey, but because by following the new developments, he will survive and flourish.' *The I Ching in Tokugawa Thought and Culture*, Honolulu: Association of Asian Studies and the University of Hawai'i Press, 2000, p. 214.
2 Giovanni Borradori, *The American Philosopher: Conservations with Quine, Davidson, Putnam, Nozick, Danto, Rorty, Cavell, MacIntyre, and Kuhn*, trans. Rosanna Crocitto, Chicago and London: University of Chicago Press, 1994, p. ix.
3 See Part II, p. 160–61.
4 Ryōsuke Ōhashi, *Kyoto Gakuha to Nippon Kaigun: Shin Shinryō 'Ōshima Memos' o Megutte* (The Kyoto School and the Japanese Navy: On the New Historical Documents: 'The Ōshima Memos'), Tokyo: PHP, 2001, p. 22.
5 For a translation of the 'Overcoming Modernity' symposium, albeit from a liberal orthodox standpoint, see Richard F. Calichman, *Overcoming Modernity: Cultural Identity in Wartime Japan*, New York: Columbia University Press, 2008. It may be worth noting that in Confucian terms the question of cultural identity did not define the role and function of this round-table discussion or *zadankai* in 1942. That question only roared into life after 1945.
6 For the problem presented by Asian thought, including Confucianism, to the Western social scientist and philosopher, see my *Japan and the Enemies of Open Political Science*, London and New York: Routledge, 1996, esp. chs 3 and 4.
7 Roland Barthes, *Empire of Signs*, trans. Richard Howard, London: Jonathan Cape, 1983, p. xi.

The Pacific War and the exhaustion of liberal history

6 The revisionism of what happens when

Parkes, Ōhashi and the exhaustion of liberal history

> Has ideology so permeated historical scholarship [on the wartime Kyoto School] that reasoned argument on the basis of textual evidence has become *passé*?
>
> (Graham Parkes[1])

> By the very finality and absoluteness with which [the moral historian] has endowed the present he has heightened his own position. For him the voice of posterity is the voice of God and the historian is the voice of posterity. And it is typical of him that he tends to regard himself as the judge when by his methods and his equipment he is fitted only to be the detective.
>
> (Herbert Butterfield[2])

> All energy goes toward show, pretence, posing. Twenty years ago, I hoped for a bright future for interdisciplinary research. Now I see that the space opened up between disciplines is outside the law, a wasteland where wolves run free.
>
> (Camille Paglia[3])

How fact trumps opinion: moral history and post-liberal history

Orientalism as a rigorous science begins with the quest to master a single text before moving to other texts. The student of the Pacific War must, I argue, master the significance of the *Chūō Kōron* transcripts before he moves on to other texts or indeed to the facts of the war itself. Such mastery must precede any conclusion he may eventually reach about the world within which the war unfolded and which the war changed. This is the essence of the scientific approach to texts. Strict fidelity to this method is what makes philology the exact science of mental objects ('La philology est la science exacte des choses de l'espirit' – Renan[4]). In this way, philology and the disciplines of reading become one of the pillars of the science of humanity.

Rejecting the scientific approach of philology, Pacific War orthodoxy as a method subverts this science of humanity by reversing the intellectual priorities in our encounter with Asian reality. Orthodoxy begins with a world-view (perhaps completely unexamined in the doctoral research seminar), and then effortlessly shifts to the war (in respect of which one already has a completely settled opinion and moral valuation). The orthodox researcher then turns to a body of texts, large or small, upon which he selectively draws in the pursuit of a blanket of evidence to confirm the moral opinion of the world and the war to which he subscribed *before* he initiated his research. Orientalist rigour tends to be more faithful to Asian reality; the orthodox approach is loyal to liberal values (imperialist or pacific or both).

One might be tempted to seek a sensible compromise between these two approaches. Surely the difference can be split here, methodologically speaking? Unfortunately, liberal orthodoxy treats this compromising spirit as a form of moral relativism that cannot be tolerated; the rights and feelings of the victims of the enemies of the liberal order trump the need for objectivity. The facts that confirm liberal orthodoxy are privileged, while facts that unsettle or challenge liberal orthodoxy are treated with suspicion or ignored. This highly selective approach to the historical record governs the orthodox interpretation of the Pacific War as a form of Whig or moral history. This approach does *not* therefore encourage us to read the text of the *Chūō Kōron* transcripts correctly, because such orthodoxy will not admit any facts inconsistent with liberal morality.

So what is the precise relationship between moral or liberal history and factual or research history? The factual historian, as a historian, accepts all facts – old and new, good or bad, soothing or upsetting – of the historical record; moral or liberal history excludes or ignores any facts inconsistent with its moral purpose. At best, moral history is a form of general history that generalizes or abridges selectively from the historical record. Research history is the custodian of the historical record in its entirety; its fundamental method is the commitment to detail, not to generalization.

When the empirical historian generalizes, he seeks to mirror as closely as possible the facts of the case. With empirical history, one accepts the generalizations from the historical record with confidence because the facts inform the general conclusions drawn. With moral or liberal history, one is subject to a series of surprises or shocks because the ethical generalization is ultimately *never* confirmed by the historical record. While I accept the convention according to which reference is made to the 'Whig historian', and likewise to the 'liberal historian' or 'moral historian', strictly speaking only the empirical historian is a historian because the moral historian rejects the historical record.

Strictly speaking, *moral history is not history.* As a Whig historian, for example, Lord Acton insisted that the historian's conclusions always serve a higher moral cause, and his school maintained this insistence, but such service requires the historian to distort the historical record in order to advance liberal ends. No facts that call liberal orthodoxy into question are permitted. Thus when a moral historian addresses a subject like the wartime conduct of Emperor Hirohito, the ethical imperative is to discover even more facts that prove that the Japanese emperor was worse than previously thought. But any facts that suggest that a Japanese wartime leader might have been less bad are rejected out of hand because such facts encourage the approval of evil.

In the mind of the liberal moralist, the balanced assessment of a historical figure is ethically tainted in such a way as to invite suspicion of the empirical historian's motives for seeking to be objective. In truth, historical facts are entirely neutral because objectivity has nothing to do with moral judgements. Thus liberalism wants to trump historical fact with moral opinion, but history as a branch of empirical study cannot withstand such moralism. Ethical judgements applied in this manner spell the death of objectivity, and therefore the death of history itself.

Indeed, the threat posed to history as history by the liberal moralist is so perverse that a stark choice must honestly be faced. Either the historian who regards himself as a liberal must bracket his liberalism in order to read his Japanese text with authority, or he must agree to abandon the quest for objective knowledge about the subject and refuse to read the text, in order to cling more securely to Allied orthodoxy. Starker still is the prospect for which the liberal as a liberal may have to brace himself: that of the crisis of faith that will inevitably ensue the moment he begins to suspect that liberal moralism as a mode of understanding and acting on the world may yet prove to be another twentieth-century god that has failed.

When we say that the liberalism of the Asian specialist must be bracketed, two difficulties are involved. First, the liberal-minded researcher's urge to deny and ignore the facts on the page must be overcome. Second, Confucianism has to be acknowledged by our self-bracketing liberal as a respectable form of ethics. If liberalism is exhausted, the post-liberal historian must seek out and then elaborate convincing East Asian schemas of interpretation to organize his data. Only then will he be able to mobilize the full powers of the revisionism of what happened when: that is, the precise dating and determination of the significance of the wartime text and the other texts with which it forms a discourse.

Close examination of the *Chūō Kōron* transcripts has repeatedly uncovered factual anomalies that led me to conclude that the members of the wartime Kyoto School were intellectual *and* ideological combatants in a moral and political struggle (*tenkō toshite kakushin*). Led by the evidence, I concluded that this struggle is best understood under the rubric of a 'Post-Meiji Confucian Revolution', a schema of interpretation that encourages one to mine the historical record of the Pacific War as intellectual history with greater confidence and authority.

Confucian tipping points and the Kyoto School's view of history

For the thinkers of the Kyoto School, the three *Chūō Kōron* discussions as publications provided a public occasion for settling accounts with the idea and practice of history, as a field of action as well as of study, in the two great civilizations to which modern Japan was heir: China and Europe. The Kyoto

School's endorsement of German empirical and philosophical history signalled a break with many of the traditional ideas of history found in the East, Chinese as well as Japanese. Thus the four contributors to the *Chūō Kōron* transcripts were united in the view that ancient Chinese historiography had little to contribute to the modernization of contemporary Asia. Nevertheless, one aspect of the Confucian approach to understanding the past – the framework of interpretation provided by the triplet of *tenkō*, *tenmei* and *toku* – proved almost fatal to the reception of wartime Kyoto philosophy in Japan and elsewhere after 1945.

In the *Chūō Kōron* transcripts, the Chinese philosophy of history is rejected because it contains no principle of development. Quite the contrary: there was a frozen quality to traditional Confucian reflection on historical change. Dynasties came and went, the seasons altered, names were rectified, but the moral framework that governed this apparently circular process was untouched by time. This vision of the Chinese past was the eternal dance of the same, and historians such as Suzuki therefore concluded that this apparent intellectual dead end had nothing to offer to the contemporary Japanese reformer who knew his East Asian history.

Another view might be that such Japanese criticism of China was a product of wartime chauvinism. This was manifestly not the case. These Kyoto thinkers were unstinting in their praise of the glory that was the civilization of traditional China. Furthermore, they were critical of the nationalist excesses of contemporary Japanese education. Kōsaka in particular was dismissive both of the exaggerated status of Japanese history in the secondary school curriculum (the pass mark was significantly higher for history than for mathematics and the natural sciences) and of the manifest bias against critical thinking about the past embedded in teaching and testing methods. For example, he disagreed forcefully with how the controversy over the Anglo-Japanese alliance was treated in the national curriculum. He did not approve of the way debate and discussion of this major historical theme had been banished from Japanese classrooms by the time of the Pacific War. The imposition of educational orthodoxy at work in such pedagogy was consistent with the Confucian belief that reality teaches that there is only one practical answer to any important question.

Although perfectly aware of the urge to foster national consensus that underlay this approach, Kōsaka favoured a strategy in which the student was exposed to the historical evidence in order to make up his own mind – not as an end in itself, but rather as a way of ensuring that the consensus eventually reached does in fact reflect a truthful understanding of the past, and is not just a form of lip-service to orthodox teaching. However, whatever the merits or assumptions of the curriculum and its critics, it is interesting to observe that the censor did not prevent such public opposition to the policies of the Ministry of Education from being published only weeks after Japan went to war with Great Britain and the United States. Perhaps the ministry had some enemies among the public censors.

As for the successes and limitations of Chinese historiography, a more generous assessment of the traditional approach to dynastic change might conclude that it represented the process as not circular so much as cyclical – that is, an unbroken pattern of rise and fall – and acknowledge that this philosophy of history encouraged extraordinary attention to and reverence for documenting the past. However, orthodoxy permitted no standpoint outside the Confucian framework, and this effectively conspired against the kind of benchmarks of comparison that are indispensable to fostering the competitive drive to innovate. While Chinese tradition did not deny the need for political reform and policy remedies, it sought such amelioration not in progress towards a better future but rather in the return to an ideal past.

Whatever their criticisms, the participants in the *Chūō Kōron* discussions never broke free of the Confucian moral framework. This final point about the staying power of Confucian revolution is cardinal. However much the Kyoto School favoured the philosophy of history found in the works of Hegel, Ranke and Weber over traditional Chinese historiography, there was no escaping the influence of the *practice* of Confucian revolutions, understood as exercises in the wholesale rejection of the immediate past so that one may shift from one form of complete unanimity to another. Here is Kōyama's gloss on the Meiji Restoration:

> After 1868, the Edo Shogunate was decisively rejected, and rejecting the Shogunate meant turning one's back on Edo culture as a whole. Overnight everything about the Edo period was condemned as a form of medieval darkness. This was the fundamental undercurrent of post-Meiji thought and feeling, and it explains why 1868 marked such a radical break with the past.[5]

What happened in the 1860s would happen again in the early 1940s and yet again in 1945. With the surrender of the Japanese government to the Allies, Confucian expectations fuelled a mixture of enthusiasm for total change and a paroxysm of anger against the old order. This phase of radical and unsparing criticism of a now *passé* regime is as Confucian as the Old Master himself. Riding this wave of bitter denunciation of wartime ideas and personalities, a few Japanese Marxist intellectuals took an early opportunity to single out the wartime Kyoto School for special opprobrium. One of the bitter fruits of this Confucian-inspired criticism of the intellectual discourse of wartime Japan was a handful of articles published during the decade after the surrender that laid the foundations for the American neo-Marxist critique of Kyoto School 'fascism' nearly half a century later.

Facts on the page and the textual historian

The methodological rigour of the textual historian of the Pacific War derives from two canonical sources: textual criticism and historical empiricism. Some of the basic assumptions of the textual criticism were set out in Chapter 1, while the principles for dealing with the facts of history were treated in Chapter 4. These two approaches must be made to work in tandem.

Here our understanding of the basics of proper empirical history will be deepened by careful attention to chronology. For the textual historian, dates matter. If we are to start to make any sense, to cite a key example, of the claim by Yasumasa Ōshima (the stenographer-editor and preserver of *The Ōshima Memos*) that the contributors to our three symposia hoped first to delay and then to deflect Tōjō's decision for war, it is essential to know that the first symposium, 'The Standpoint of World History and Japan' took place on 26 November 1941, that is, twelve days *before* the attack on Pearl Harbor on 8 December (Japan time), but was published in the January issue of *Chūō Kōron* and thus appeared in bookstores probably at the end of December 1941.[6] Already the historian is faced with issues of timing.

For the strategic reasons set out in Chapter 9, the Kyoto School opposed Japan's decision for war, and this opposition provides the main motivation behind their deliberations on 26 November 1941, conceived as a form of public intervention in this national debate. By the time this symposium appeared in print, Pearl Harbor had been attacked, so the focus of Kyoto School effort shifted to the search for a ceasefire and a negotiated settlement. As this could be achieved only by removing Tōjō as prime minister, the Kyoto School conspired with the Imperial Navy for his replacement by Admiral Mitsumasa Yonai.

Again, if one is to appreciate the timing and logic of the second symposium, 'The Ethical and Historical Character of the East Asian Co-prosperity Sphere', one needs to know that this discussion took place on 4 March 1942 (three days after the dissolution of the American, British, Dutch and Australian Command or the ABDA in the Dutch East Indies), just as the high tide of Japan's southern thrust into the tropics started to crest. In other words, if a Greater Asian Co-prosperity Sphere was to be erected on a genuinely cooperative basis, governed by the shared pursuit of national subjectivity for all the member countries, this policy needed to be recognized, proclaimed and implemented before it was too late (the sorry state of Sino-Japanese relations served the decisive warning here).

In Chapter 9, the Imperial Navy's three war options are elaborated. They consisted of: 1 an early strike to reduce the capital ship advantage of the United States and the British Empire; 2 protection of a ring of Pacific island defences to delay the American counter-offensive in the slight hope of a forcing a ceasefire; and 3 a decisive battle in Japanese waters. The many mood swings between desperate urgency and calm resignation that colour the final symposium, 'The Philosophy of World-historical Wars' (24 November 1942), are impossible to get into perspective unless one factors in the impact of the Japanese defeat at Midway (3–6 June 1942), which called into question the viability of all three strategies. Given the intimate ties between the Kyoto School and the Yonai faction of the Imperial Navy, it seems reasonable to conclude that Kōyama almost certainly knew that the fortunes of battle were shifting against Japan during the second half of 1942. After all, he held an official position as an adviser to the Navy Ministry in Tokyo.

Further evidence of the close links between the Imperial Navy and the Kyoto School may be found in the pages of *The Ōshima Memos*. Careful attention to dating allows one to relate the public statements contained in the *Chūō Kōron* discussions to the content and timing of the eighteen secret lectures, transcribed by Ōshima, that were delivered by members of the Kyoto School (including all the participants of our three symposia) to a small group of individuals, most of them Imperial Navy officers, between 12 February 1942 and 2 November 1943. It is thus possible to trace the development of the arguments and insights in the interplay between the various Chūō Kōron-sha publications and *The Ōshima Memos*.[7]

Respect for chronology is fundamental to rigorous textual research, but to assign proper *significance* to the dates at issue in the historical record requires a credible schema of interpretation. Close examination of the historical record of the Pacific War draws attention to the price the field has paid for the liberal moralist's hostility or indifference to Confucian ethics. Despite its illiberal character, Confucian revolution gives the historian a formidable interpretive framework for making sense of our empirical findings. Neither the Kyoto School nor its opponents within the Japanese elite sought a return to the Meiji settlement; nor was Taishō democracy regarded as a viable alternative, because history had demonstrated its flawed character. Consistent with Japanese reformist common sense on the subject, some form of Post-Meiji Confucian Revolution was at once inevitable, necessary and moral. To be comprehensible to one's fellow Japanese, one had to conjure up a vision of the national future that marked an unqualified rejection of the now fraying status quo.

This thesis is developed in more detail in Chapter 9, but I will outline my argument here to strengthen the case for the importance of dating the relevant primary sources at issue. The Kyoto School and the reformists in the Imperial Navy endorsed this grand strategy of resistance to American imperialism because the Versailles-Geneva-Washington world order was so threatening to Japanese national sovereignty and great power prerogatives. In other words, the argument by Baron Kijūrō Shidehara, Japanese foreign minister between 1924 and 1927, and again between 1929 and 1931, that Japan had to 'go along to get along' in a liberal world dominated by the United States, was false. No amount of compromise or conciliation or diplomatic good behaviour on Japan's part would satisfy the American hunger for global hegemony. There was no place in this emerging liberal order for Japanese sovereignty (or British sovereignty, for that matter), except on American terms. To insist that Imperial Japan could successful appease Washington, and this formed the central premise of 'Shidehara diplomacy', was to misread geopolitical reality.

Yonai's apparent support for 'Shidehara appeasement' of Washington was tactical, aimed at gaining time for Japan to strengthen its defences. There was no safe version of the status quo for Japan to make its own, because American diplomacy from the Versailles Treaty to the Hull Note ultimatum sought to undermine systematically Imperial Japan's place in the world.[8] As navy minister in the late 1930s, Yonai sought to contain the pressures from junior naval officers to take more forceful action not because they had misread the geopolitical challenge (they had not), but because of *what* they wanted to do about the American threat and *when* they wanted to act. Unless one is clear about this situation, one can make no sense of the grand strategy developed by the Kyoto School in alliance with the Yonai faction.

What does all this mean for the historian of the Pacific War today? Armed with the rubric of Confucian revolution, we can now affirm that God is very much in the detail. Take the crucial year of 1943. At the beginning of the year, Japanese forces were still resisting on Papua and Guadalcanal. By the end of year, Burma and the Philippines had been declared independent and the Allies had invaded New Britain. Between Japan's withdrawal from Guadalcanal in February 1943 and the American landings on Makin and Tarawa in November 1943, the war began to run against Japan in ways that even the Tōjō loyalists had to concede.

During this crucial year, the wartime Kyoto School's contest with the Tōjō regime took several sharp turns. After the publication of the last of our symposia in the January 1943 issue of *Chūō Kōron*, the book version of all three symposia appeared in the spring of the same year, only to provoke the censors into eventually banning further print runs. Interestingly, in March that same year, the Tōjō government approached Nishida with the commission to prepare a text through which the prime minister could announce 'The Principles of a New World War' before the end of the year. This episode has resulted in a tissue of confusions and misperceptions, none of which can be clarified unless one draws on a suitable conceptual framework such as 'Confucian revolution' and then examines the facts with a mind open to the possibility that the historical record may demand a radical revision of one's hitherto most closely held opinions. This is something that the liberal historian of the Pacific War has often been unwilling to contemplate. Perhaps Tōjō was reaching out to his critics in hope of strengthening his government's hand as defeat loomed; perhaps the Kyoto School thought they could at once influence and undermine Tōjō's position by publicly advertising his weakness; perhaps this exercise ended in predictable failure *because* each of the two sides was aware of what the other was up to. Only empirical research can give us the answer.

It matters whether Kōyama's lecture on the controversial wartime slogan of *Hakkō no Ichiu* (literally, 'a marquee for the palace' but often translated as 'the world under one roof') was delivered early or late in that momentous year of 1943. Tetsurō Mori tells us only that Kōyama gave his talk at the Japanese Naval Academy in 1943,[9] but Hidefumi Hanazawa informs us that the lecture was published in January 1944, Kōyama having joined a combined Imperial Army-Imperial Navy *Sō-ryoku-sen* research group at the Naval Academy the month before.[10]

So did the bloody events on the strategic island of Tarawa, for example, have any impact on Kōyama's lecture? This is a question to which the orthodox liberal historian cannot assume the answer without examining Kōyama's text. Without reference to the evidence, one cannot blithely conclude that this would-be propaganda slogan lent justification for Japanese expansionism in the minds of the group of officers that were Kōyama's audience. After all, these officers and intellectuals were supposedly considering ways of sustaining some form of *sō ryoku sen* or the 'total war/resistance' in a struggle that Japan was manifestly losing. Once again the dateline of texts and events on the battlefield is of decisively interpretative importance. What could the expression *Hakkō no Ichiu* plausibly mean in the winter of 1943–44? The suggestion must be that the text in question needs to be read rather more closely before one leaps to any moral judgements based on ideology.

Comparing dates allows one to weigh the evidence about the likely sources of the expression *kōiki-ken* (literally, a wide or large area or region) used by the Kyoto School as a generic classification for co-prosperity spheres. There is a linguistic twist involved here. Japanese, like Chinese, suffers from a built-in ambiguity about whether nouns are singular or plural, proper nouns or common nouns – one cannot tell which is intended by looking at a Chinese character in isolation – and this makes context indispensable for determining how to render the word or phrase into a language that does not employ Chinese characters. Similarly, only careful examination of the context and background of wartime ideas allows one to conclude whether the Kyoto thinker is talking about co-prosperity spheres as a generic idea or the Co-Prosperity Sphere as a specific institution.

Borrowings from German complicate this discussion. Does, for example, the appearance of the term *koiki-ken* in the *Chūō Kōron* transcripts derive from Carl Schmitt's use of the expression *Großraum*? The Japanese text cites *Großraum* as the source of the expression *koiki-ken*, but should *Großraum* be given a Schmittian gloss? The dates in question suggest that it might derive, directly or otherwise, from Carl Schmitt's 1939 lecture entitled 'Völkerrechtliche Großraumordnung'.[11] In a subsequent note that appears in the 1941 version of the lecture, Schmitt observes not only that an Italian and a Spanish translation were already in print, but also that 'a French, Japanese and Bulgarian translation have also appeared or are in preparation'.[12]

All this forms the grist for further research, but no such dating controversy is more tantalizing than the suspicion aroused by the publication of Kiyoshi Miki's essay 'Senji Ninshiki no Kichō' in January 1942, in the same prestigious New Year's issue of *Chūō Kōron* as the first symposium, 'The Standpoint of World History and Japan'.[13] We know for a fact that the Army censors pounced on the magazine's editors for letting a controversial philosopher with suspected communist sympathies contribute to the pages of *Chūō Kōron*, especially with the country now at war. The whole business is particularly intriguing because of the possibility that Miki, rather than Suzuki, was supposed to be the fourth participant in the *Chūō Kōron* discussions.

Only further archival research will allow us to determine whether Miki's intervention was the equivalent of what in baseball is called a 'sacrifice fly', drawing the censor's fire and thereby ensuring that Kōyama, Kōsaka, Nishitani and Suzuki got into print.

Half of the story about this episode is already known from research on wartime censorship. Thus we have eyewitness testimony that when Kenjirō Nakamura, chief of the Second Section, Special Higher Police, Metropolitan Police Board, called on Shigeo Hatanaka, chief editor of *Chūō Kōron*, on 8 January 1942, he brought a copy of the January issue in which the first symposium appeared.[14] Nakamura proceeded to read through the list of contributors in the table of contents, reeling off names of leftists, real or suspected, who had no place in this magazine in wartime. Miki, Hatanaka was informed, was under 'supervision by the thought police', but apparently no official objections were made about Nishitani and the other contributors to the symposium, which was the most prominent piece in the January issue.[15]

The mind reels at the possibilities. As it is inconceivable that Nakamura was ignorant of Miki's links with the Kyoto School, the suggestion may be that Miki's essay was planted to draw fire from the censor or that the *Tokkō* (the higher branch of the police that dealt with political crimes) might be warning Nishitani and his fellow symposium participants to be more careful in the next symposium, planned for the spring – or, most intriguing of all, that Nakamura may have agreed, if only in part, with some of the sentiments expressed in 'The Standpoint of World History and Japan'. That possibility in turn raises the question of the tactics of *Chūō Kōron* and the Kyoto School in this game of 'cat and mouse'. Finally, the episode with all its murky intrigue seems to illustrate to perfection Yoshimi Takeuchi's celebrated remark to the effect that in wartime Japan, the difference between support and opposition to the war was often no more than the thickness of a single page. In this case, the 'page' was published by *Chūō Kōron*.

Ōhashi's discovery: the file at the back of the drawer

If the genius of the physicist and the mathematician peaks all too early, the historian is one of nature's marathon runners, often breasting the tape of high achievement very late in life. The archive hunter may spend decades breathing the dust of ancient libraries in the often fruitless pursuit of a lost or forgotten text that will transform our understanding of some great episode of our past. It was Ranke who canonized this passion for documentary evidence among historians in whatever field of endeavour, from the realms of diplomacy and war to those of ideas and philosophy. To recount one of the more rewarding episodes of 'seek and find' in recent research on the wartime labours of the Kyoto School is to consider once more the true price the moralist pays for the conscience-inspired neglect of such major wartime texts such *The Ōshima Memos* and the *Chūō Kōron* transcripts.

The story begins with one of the more mysterious figures of the Kyoto School, Yasumasa Ōshima. Decades after Japan's defeat, Ōshima published one of the most suggestive of all the post-war assessments of the wartime Kyoto School. Appearing in 1965 in the pages of *Chūō Kōron*, the same journal that had published the transcripts almost twenty-five years before, Ōshima's article claimed that the anti-Tōjō message of our three symposia had had to be wrapped in 'several layers of cloth' to get past the censor and into print in *Chūō Kōron* – then as now a *sōgō zassi*, or journal of broad but educated Japanese opinion.[16] Ōshima was the official commentator on Tanabe's masterpiece, *The Logic of the Species*, in Tanabe's collected works, as well as the young amanuensis and meeting coordinator for some of the most sensitive of the wartime lectures and discussions of the Kyoto School. In his 1965 essay in *Chūō Kōron*, Ōshima opaquely alluded to what was still a secret text that had been produced by the Kyoto School in alliance with a faction of the Imperial Navy. He was certainly as well placed as anyone living to know the relevant facts of the case.

For the distinguished Heideggerian Ryōsuke Ōhashi, one of the more openminded of recent Kyoto thinkers, this hint set off a niggle in the mind that he was unable to ignore. Spurred on by Ōshima's hints of textual treasure, Ōhashi began his search in the late 1990s. The result was a major discovery without which this study of the *Chūō Kōron* transcripts might never have been written.

The fact that the text that eventually surfaced had remained hidden for half a century cannot be explained without reference to the obstacles that history and ideology had placed in the way of the archival researcher. Among the many readers of Ōshima's article, few potential researchers appear to have been tempted by the rather vague reference. Then there was the Confucian blight on the wartime reputation of the second generation of Kyoto School philosophers (Nishida and Tanabe, the founding first generation, were both dead by now), including Ōshima and all the contributors to the *Chūō Kōron* symposia. On this subject, Allied Pacific War orthodoxy and Confucian pacifism performed their obscuring work in parallel.

Furthermore, Ōshima was rumoured to have had personal problems that might have impaired his scholarly judgement, and even among Kyoto School insiders this may have discouraged potential investigators from taking his suggestion seriously. However, Ōhashi apparently could not quite bring himself to forget Ōshima's intriguing intimation.[17] So he began his search. In his retelling of the story, Ōhashi wondered if Ōshima had hidden this dangerous wartime text among his papers, but his family were adamant that there was no such document to be found. They allowed Ōhashi access to Ōshima's old library in the family home, but a thorough search yielded nothing. Nor did any other investigations prove fruitful. At this point, even the most determined researcher might have abandoned the chase, but Ōhashi asked for one more opportunity to examine Ōshima's old study, with its desk from the war period that was now being used by the younger members of the family to do schoolwork.

With a member of the Ōshima family at his side, Ōhashi pulled out the drawers from the desk, and in the last drawer he opened, at the very back, there was an aged paper file with the word 'Navy' written on a tab in English. Hoping against hope, Ōhashi carefully lifted the file – and thus *The Ōshima Memos* were discovered, some fifty-five years after Ōshima had made his final entry. The documents he had found contained evidence of a web of conspiracy to stiffen the resolve of the Kyoto philosopher as well as the Imperial Navy officer to resist the hegemonic discourse of the Tōjō clique and the ruling establishment in the search for a negotiated peace with the Allies, as well as forward planning for post-war reconstruction. Observe once again that it is the interpretive framework provided by the idea of Confucian revolution that allows us to exploit such material with unrivalled confidence and precision.

The truth will finally make us free, but only if we let it. Risking arrest and imprisonment, Yonai and his Kyoto co-conspirators did not realize that the Roosevelt and Truman Administrations were set on a war of liberal annihilation against Imperial Japan, and that therefore a compromise end to the Pacific War was never on the cards, but Ōshima and his colleagues did more than any other group of thinkers to reveal the historical potential of Japan's Pacific War. This makes them among the greatest of all Second World War revisionists. Their confidence that their truth would win out has finally confounded their opponents, the liberal imperialist and the Confucian pacifist alike. The facts of the page have thus now triumphed – but only among those who have embraced their own version of Derrida's watchword: *Il n'y a pas de hors-texte.*[18]

The exhaustion of liberal history: the revelation

The 'bracketing' of one's liberal values in order to read a resistant Asian text is preferable to the wholesale abandonment of liberalism. Nevertheless, the neglect of scholarly objectivity and textual rigour has become so pervasive among liberal historians of modern East Asia, especially in Japan studies, that I have been all but compelled to contemplate the possibility that liberalism is now caught in what may prove to be a final crisis of confidence. The fatal blow to my faith in liberal history has been delivered not by the neo-Marxist scandal about the wartime Kyoto School that set my revisionism in motion but rather by the complacent and disgraceful response of the academic establishment to the evidence that this scandal has brought to light.

In essence, this is a crisis of the advanced research seminar and doctoral supervision in the field of Asian or, if you prefer, Axis intellectual history. Fundamental standards of documentary research are not being maintained *for moral reasons*. Even where the liberal approach appears to be exhaustive in its ambitions and energies – think of Goldhagen or Bix – one suspects that the whole endeavour is driven by a psychological relentlessness and moral ferocity, verging on rage in some cases, that has become oblivious to Max Weber's classic warning about the 'inconvenient facts' that threaten any and all political party or ideological position, no matter how tightly embraced. Perhaps Weber did not go far enough, for 'inconvenient facts' ultimately threaten all moral positions because ethics are finally anti-empirical. At the highest level of academic research training, the Western study of modern Japanese history as a form of moralism has evolved a rigid, closed-minded set of dogmas that the graduate student ignores at his peril because these dogmas are institutionally enforced. The single best proof for this damning conclusion can be found in the 'kill-with-silence' response to the Japanese publication of *The Ōshima Memos*.

The decay of research standards is only half the problem. To set it in its broadest context, the Asian doubts first aired in the early 1940s by the Kyoto School have returned today to call into question the liberal's grip on political and economic reality. The contemporary trials of the post-Wilsonian world order, the ideas of the wartime Kyoto School as an anticipation of a Sino-centric Confucian global alternative to neo-liberalism in the economic and ethical spheres, and the rediscovery of the principles governing the pre-1919 *ancien régime* as a more practical form of international law suggest that moral history *à la Acton* may have a limited and declining place in the intellectual life of the twenty-first century.

As historians, we must objectively weigh the pre- and post-liberal facts found on these pages of Japanese in order to arrive with due and sober respect at the scrupulous truths that only the revisionism of 'what happens when' can reveal. Thus, when we retrace the road from Versailles to Hiroshima, we discover a direct link, something approaching cause and effect, between the revelation that the Pacific War is the classic example and 'ideal type' of the liberal war of annihilation and the discovery of 'the exhaustion of liberal history'.

President Wilson's revival of the theory of just war and its transmutation into the liberal way of war as the ultimate weapon for enforcing a liberal world order is a better explanation of the causes of the Pacific War than the orthodox alternative, whether liberal or Confucian, because it is more honest and truer – that is, more faithful to the facts. The realist historian's principal advantage over his liberal rival rests in the fact that the realist is fair-minded: he is less vulnerable to 'the contagion of moral judgement', and thus more deeply committed to history 'as it really was'.

The realist historian can tell us in ways that the liberal historian cannot why America demanded unconditional surrender so early in the conflict, why the invasion and occupation of Japan was deemed essential, why 'terror bombing' of civilian populations in Asia became the preferred military strategy for the liberal imperial enforcer not only during but *after* the Pacific War (in Korea, Vietnam, Cambodia and Laos), why the struggle against Imperial Japan concluded so violently in the world's first and only atomic war, and finally, why the liberal historian insists that the Japanese themselves were to blame for the Pacific War's moral ferocity: 'They made us do it.'

The cultivated susceptibility of modern liberalism since Manchuria to the contagion of moral judgement is the root cause of the liberal historian's *déformation professionnelle*. This is the price he has paid for the predictable but ultimately self-defeating ethical compulsions he inherits from Lord Acton and Whig moral history. None of these deformations has been made more pernicious by the workings of the liberal conscience than the dogma of political correctness, which insists that the 'bad word' is inevitably the mother of 'bad conduct'.

This explains the strange form of dread that forces a minority of liberal historians into a state of rancour without plausible purpose: unless I berate the Japanese on a daily basis – in the lecture hall, in print and on the web – for their bad conduct between 1931 and 1945, they may someday soon lapse again into illiberal 'badness'. Although the past is manifestly never a prologue because history never repeats itself in any exact way, the liberal historian has managed to trap himself into 'the most useless and unproductive form of reflection – the dispensing of moral judgments upon people or upon actions in retrospect'.[19]

Why the Kyoto School now?

This confronts us with the mystery of why, of all the branches of Second World War studies, it was 'the Pacific War as intellectual history' that first fired the suspicion that something was profoundly amiss in the liberal historian's treatment of the facts of the Pacific War. This hitherto neglected chapter in the flowering of Kyoto School philosophy has handed the post-liberal historian the touch paper for setting off an explosion of controversy that may eventually bring down not only the entire temple of Pacific War orthodoxy but also the whole liberal cult of moral history with it.

In its first phase, this interpretive revolution may be reduced to the story of three books and three essays, and how the modern academy has failed to respond to them. Graham Parkes first aired his revisionist doubts about neo-Marxist dogma with his pioneering 1997 essay, 'The Putative Fascism of the Kyoto School and the Political Correctness of the Modern Academy'.[20] Ryōsuke Ōhashi, having discovered the manuscript of *The Ōshima Memos*, transformed the debate by publishing them in book form, with a brilliant commentary, as *The Kyoto School and the Japanese Navy* in 2000.[21] My own first rather gentle probing of the interpretive weaknesses of Pacific War orthodoxy took the form of a piece for *Japan Forum*, also in 2000, entitled 'In Defence of the Kyoto School'.[22]

My tentative expression of doubt was rewarded not only by a comically rude question-and-answer plus door-slamming session at the Association of Asian Studies conference in Chicago that year but also, and far more valuably, with a place in Ōhashi's second book on the subject, *The Ideas of the Kyoto School*, published in 2004.[23] Having been admonished by Ōhashi for not having made 'much of a defence of the Kyoto School' the first time around, by the time that volume appeared I had published my second piece, an unsparing review essay, again in *Japan Forum*, which the book editor (I think at the time it was Christopher Goto-Jones) titled 'Modernity, Harootunian and the Demands of Scholarship'.[24] Ōhashi did not complain this time. With the publication of my *Defending Japan's Pacific War* in 2004, the last of the three books that make up the story of this first phase, the cycle of revisionist scepticism that Parkes had set in motion achieved its primary ambition: to discredit the books and articles that elaborated the pseudo-Marxist critique of Kyoto School 'fascism'.

Evidence of exhaustion

Parkes's 2008 essay on the internationalization of the Kyoto School helped to rally the forces of scholarly rigour with a fresh critique of neo-Marxists such as Leslie Pincus. At a stroke, the idle labelling of outstanding figures such as Shūzū Kuki as 'a fascist' became still more implausible.[25] In 2011 Parkes returned to the battle once again. In 'Heidegger and Japanese Fascism', he asked how the neo-Marxist and his politically correct allies had answered the criticism of their work since 1997.[26] Some fifteen years after the appearance of 'The Putative Fascism of the Kyoto School and the Political Correctness of the Modern Academy', Parkes catalogued a dispiriting list of flawed research, much of it consisting of jargon-ridden exercises in what Camille Paglia would call 'show, pretence, and posing' by neo-Marxists and their ideological defenders. With the controversies over the politics of Heidegger during the 1980s eventually provoking a groundswell of interest in the politics of the Kyoto School, Parkes renewed his attack on the tendentious determination in some quarters to smear both this giant of German thought and the brilliant Japanese philosophers of the Kyoto School with accusations of fascism. Parkes calls attention also to the feeble response of the scholarly community to the groundless criticism of the neo-Marxist. Citing examples from both sides of the Atlantic, Parkes highlights disturbing evidence of the erosion of proper standards of research among intellectual historians and philosophers working on the Kyoto School.

Reflecting on the entire episode, Parkes summarized his exasperation with one grim question: 'Has ideology so permeated historical scholarship [on the wartime Kyoto School] that reasoned argument on the basis of textual evidence has become *passé*?'[27] My own view is that the failure of the community to put its academic house in order is a measure of the exhaustion of liberal history itself. In essence, it is the price the field has paid since the inter-war period for its abandonment of objectivity, historical reality and the claims of science in order 'to make judgments of value, and to count them as the verdict of history'.[28]

Notes

1 Graham Parkes, 'Heidegger and Japanese Fascism', in Bret W. Davis, Brian Schroeder and Jason M. Wirth, eds, *Japanese and Continental Philosophy: Conversations with the Kyoto School*, Bloomington and Indianapolis: Indiana University Press, 2011, p. 257.
2 Herbert Butterfield, *The Whig Interpretation of History*, New York and London: W.W. Norton & Co., 1965 [1931], p. 107.
3 Camille Paglia, *Sex, Art, and American Culture: Essays*, New York: Vintage Books, 1992, p. 191.
4 Quoted in Edward W. Said, *Orientalism*, Harmondsworth: Peregrine Books, 1985, p. 132.
5 *The Standpoint of World History and Japan*, first symposium, 7 (see p. 125).
6 The importance of 'beginnings' and 'endings' in Japanese culture is at least in part Confucian in origin. Thus, the January issues of magazines and other publications are particularly prestigious, and no January publication schedule in the history of modern Japan was more fraught, more prestigious and more laden with historical anticipation than that of January 1942.
7 Ryōsuke Ōhashi, *Kyōto-gakuha to Nippon Kaigun: Shin Shinryō 'Ōshima Memos' o Megutte* (The Kyoto School and the Japanese Navy: On the New Historical Documents: 'The Ōshima Memos'), Tokyo: PHP, 2001.
8 Shinji Sudō, *Huru Nooto o Kaita Otoko: Nichibei Kaisen Gaikō to 'Yuki' Sakusen* (The Man Who Wrote the Hull Note: The Final Stage of Japan–US Diplomacy before the Pacific War and Operation 'Snow'), Tokyo: Bungei Shunjū, 1999.
9 Keiji Nishitani *et al.*, *Sekai-shi no Riron* (Theories of World History), *Kyoto Tetsugaku Sensho Dai Jūichi Kan* (Vol. 11 of Selected Texts in Kyoto Philosophy), Kyoto: Tōei-sha, 2000, p. 455.
10 Hidefumi Hanazawa, *Kōyama Iwaō: Kyōto-gakuha Tetsugaku no Kisō-teki Kenkyū* (Iwaō Kōyama: Fundamental Research on the Philosophy of the Kyoto School), Kyoto: Jinbunshoin, 1999, p. 396.
11 Carl Schmitt, *Völkerrechtliche Großraumordnung mit Interventionsverbot für raumfremde Mächte: Ein Beitrag zum Reichsbegriff in Völkerrecht, Dritte, unveränderte Auflage der Ausgabe von 1941*, Berlin: Duncker & Humbolt, 1991. See also Carl Schmitt, *Writings on War*, trans. and ed. Timothy Nunan, Cambridge: Polity, 2011, pp. 75–124. Note also that Nunan's commentary is something of a curate's egg: sometimes brilliant, but often hostile and occasionally uncomprehending because of its unexamined and therefore unquestioned liberal imperialist assumptions.
12 Schmitt, *Völkerrechtliche Großraumordnung*, p. 5.
13 Kiyoshi Miki, *Senji Ninshiki no Kichō* (What Matters Now that We Are at War). For the text, see Miki Kiyoshi Hihyō Senshu, *Tōa Kyōdōtai no Tetsugaku: Sekai-shi-teki Tachiba to Kindai Tō Ajia* (Essays in Criticism by Kiyoshi Miki: Philosophy of East Asian Integration: The Standpoint of World History and Modern East Asia), Tokyo: Shoshi Shinsui, 2007, pp. 337–50.
14 I am relying on the account in Richard H. Mitchell, *Censorship in Imperial Japan*, Princeton, NJ: Princeton University Press, 1983, pp. 326–27.
15 In the more or less official chronicle of the publisher, the timeline for the magazine *Chūō Kōron* mentions only 'The Standpoint of World History and Japan' for the momentous January 1942 issue. See *Chūō Kōron-sha no Hachi-jū nen* (A History of Chūō Kōron-sha), Tokyo: Chūō Kōron-sha, 1965, p. 442.
16 Yasumasa Ōshima, 'Dai-tōa Sensō to Kyōto-gakuha – Chishikijin no Seiji Sanka ni Tsuite' (The Great East Asian War and the Kyoto School: The Political Involvement of Intellectuals), *Chūō Kōron*, 80, Aug. 1965. The text is reproduced in Keiji Nishitani *et al.*, *Sekaishi no Riron* (Theories of World History), *Kyoto*

Tetsugaku Sensho Dai Jūichi Kan (Vol. 11 of Selected Texts in Kyoto Philosophy), Kyoto: Tōei-sha, 2000, pp. 274–304.
17 This retelling of the story of Ōhashi's textual treasure hunt is a perhaps imperfect recollection of a delightful discussion I had with this distinguished Japanese philosopher in Kyoto some years ago. Given the more recent effort to 'kill' Ōhashi's findings with silence (*mokusatsu*) by a few Western students of the Kyoto School who should know better, I thought it was imperative that the tale be told. It serves as an apt example of the dictum that 'Scholarship should be fun' (a *bon mot* usually ascribed to the famous essayist, literary critic and all-purpose man of letters Takeo Kuwahara).
18 Jacques Derrida, *De la grammatologie*, Paris: Les editions de Minuit, 1967, pp. 158–59. Extra-textual facts come after. Experience is external to the text, and therefore comes into its own only when it serves to illuminate the significance or meaning of the text.
19 Butterfield, 'Moral Judgments in History', in *The Whig Interpretation of History*, op. cit., p. 108.
20 Graham Parkes, 'The Putative Fascism of the Kyoto School and the Political Correctness of the Modern Academy', *Philosophy East and West*, 47(3), July 1997.
21 Ōhashi, *Kyōto-gakuha to Nippon Kaigun* (The Kyoto School and the Japanese Navy), op. cit.
22 David Williams, 'In Defence of the Kyoto School: Reflections on Philosophy, the Pacific War and the Making of a Post-White World', *Japan Forum*, 12(2), 2000, pp. 143–56.
23 David Williams, 'Ō-Bei no "Kyōto Gakuha" Zō' (Explaining the Kyoto School in Europe and America), in *Kyōto Gakuha no Shisō: Irorio no Zō to Shisō no Potensharu* (The Ideas of the Kyoto School: A Selection of Interpretations and Reflections of the School's Intellectual Potential), ed. Ryōsuke Ōhashi, Kyoto: Jinbunshoin, 2004, pp. 91–119.
24 David Williams, 'Modernity, Harootunian and the Demands of Scholarship', *Japan Forum*, 15(1), 2003, pp. 147–62.
25 Graham Parkes, 'The Definite Internationalization of the Kyoto School: Changing Attitudes in the Contemporary Academy', in *Re-politicising the Kyoto School as Philosophy*, ed. Christopher Goto-Jones, London and New York/ Leiden: RoutledgeCurzon/Universiteit Leiden, 2008, pp. 161–82.
26 Graham Parkes, 'Heidegger and Japanese Fascism: An Unsubstantiated Connection', in *Japanese and Continental Philosophy: Conversations with the Kyoto School*, ed. Bret W. Davis, Brian Schroeder and Jason M. Wirth, Bloomington and Indianapolis: Indiana University Press, 2011, pp. 247–65.
27 Parkes, 'Heidegger and Japanese Fascism', op. cit., p. 257.
28 Butterfield, *The Whig Interpretation of History*, op. cit., p. 107.

7 Rejecting Tōjō's decision for war

The Kyoto School rethinks the state, international law and globalization

> A state's sovereignty is indivisible; no denial of this principle is permitted if the state is to survive as a state. It also follows that given this type of [political] order, the state's sovereignty must be recognized by its horizontal peers [i.e. other states] if the state's stability is to be maintained in the face of [domestic] pressures of a vertical nature.
>
> How might a genuine sphere of shared prosperity – one that has mobilised the full potential of the nation state – be achieved? One option might be for the individual members of the co-prosperity sphere to resolve to limit or dilute their own individual national sovereignty not by force but voluntarily.
>
> Burdens fall on both parties in this equation. The more dominant partner – the leading nation – occupying a position of relatively greater power in our circular schema – does not rest on its laurels but actively takes the lead in helping the more dependent members of the co-prosperity sphere to secure genuine sovereignty and national development. For their part, the junior partners of the sphere do not wait passively to be led but rather seize the initiative, in keeping with national self-awakening, in order to meet their responsibilities as full partners in the co-prosperity sphere. In short, the led should pursue their own development as part of a programme to achieve true national autonomy.
>
> (Tanabe Hajime[1])

In the previous six chapters of this commentary, a number of concepts, including 'world history', 'standpoint', 'Japan' and 'world order', have been assigned special significance in the pursuit of our goal of a proper reading of this wartime text. In this seventh chapter, Kyoto School ideas of the 'state', 'international law' and 'economic regionalism' as a substitute for 'globalization' will be added to this list. As before, the text confronts the liberal reader with a twofold challenge. First, we must try to grasp what the Kyoto thinker meant by these concepts; and second, we must learn to bracket our working liberal definitions of the same or similar notions, because for our Japanese thinker these ideas spoke to the need to resist, rightly or wrongly, the imposition of a post-Wilsonian liberal hegemony on East Asia.

Great power status and the modern Japanese state

Between the final phase of the Tokugawa Shogunate (c.1850s–60s) and the Versailles Treaty, Japan's new political elite reformed the country by discarding feudal institutions and reinventing the native political tradition, a complex amalgam of historical experience informed by Confucianism, Buddhism and Shintoism, in the light of the insights of European public law, the 'Westphalian system' providing a working model of how Europe defined modern international legality. The result was a sovereign state with a mixed constitution: a monarchy absolute in letter, but limited in practice; a law-bound civilian and military bureaucracy in charge, but with imperial and parliamentary constraints.

These constitutional complexities did not prevent Japan from achieving the status of a great power by the first decade of the twentieth century. Quite the contrary: the Japanese modernizing programme was pre-eminently successful in fulfilling the expectations captured in the Meiji era call for the building of a rich economy to sustain strong armed forces or *fukoku kyōhei*. However, the dispersal of authority across a varied elite composed of court officials, senior military officers, higher bureaucrats, cabinet ministers and parliamentary power brokers produced a formal decision-making system that required a broad and deep consensus to work well. This truth became more evident after the shared ambitions for the Meiji project were achieved, and the Japanese elite discovered that this achievement was inadequate to cope with the new and ever more severe pressures on its national sovereignty and imperial defence state (*kokubō kokka*) between Versailles and the final crisis of the early 1940s.

Japan was not alone in trying to respond to the arrival of a hostile liberal world order. Seven of the eight great powers of 1914 (Britain, France, Italy, Russia, Germany, Austria-Hungary and Japan) came under severe stress as the liberal imperialist counter-revolution took hold after 1919. None was to retain its empire; the Habsburg Empire would be dismembered, and none of the remaining six powers would keep its national sovereignty unimpaired. Looming over the broken edifice of Westphalian international law and the wrecked 'balance of power' diplomacy of national sovereignty was, and is, the United States. Contrast a world map from 1914 with one roughly a century later, and then take the newer one and populate it with America's global network of military bases, and no other conclusion is credible. This is a matter not of criticism but of fact.

As the agent of moral-universalist enforcement and unipolar global order, America with its ever swelling quiver of powers and prerogatives fatefully eroded Japan's hegemonic status in East Asia. This pressure exacerbated the fundamental differences between the Imperial Army and Navy over grand strategy and exposed and then squeezed Japan's resource dependency on unsecured sea lanes, while driving home the hard truth that the economy developed to sustain Japan's status as a great power was incapable of competing with the United States Navy in capital ship building. However, just as Tōjō prepared to act on his assumption that the winter of 1941–42 presented Imperial Japan with the final choice between a war of honourable resistance and unresisting submission to American will, the Kyoto School proposed an alternative programme of reform.

The goal was to complete the process of rationally modernizing the Japanese government from within while reinventing the state and economy from without as a *Großraum* capable of defending East Asia's regional autonomy. In other words, the Kyoto School rejected the notion that Japan had to act precipitately. Indeed there was every reason, as Admiral Yonai insisted, for a still weak Japan not to risk a war it could not win with the United States in December 1941.

Transcending the nation-state

Like Hegel and Marx before them, the Kyoto philosophers believed that the truths and insights of philosophy had practical application. In this spirit, the wartime Kyoto School as a group of *philosophers* began its labours by focusing on a classic analysis of social and political reality first formulated by Aristotle. The triumph of Kantian moral universalism, liberal imperialism and American hegemony (including 'Open Door'-style globalization) in effect reweighted the traditional Aristotelian categories of universal, species and individual in ways that strengthened the universal and the individual at the expense of the species.

In an act of philosophical revisionism, Hajime Tanabe set the wartime phase of the classic Kyoto School in motion with *The Logic of the Species*. In this monumental study, he argued that the Western philosophical tradition demonstrated a perennial bias in favour of the individual and the universal over the claims and rights of the community as species. For the Kyoto School, the Japanese state was the natural, legitimate and indispensable shield of national life. Without an effective species or national community as a state (*kokka shakai*), individual Japanese were helpless before the forces of a rampant and overwhelming globalization and liberal universalism, but the Meiji state could not serve as such a shield once the effects of Wilson's counter-revolution began to chip away at Japan's rights and privileges as a great power.

It was not that the individual was ignored or devalued in this Kyoto meditation on Aristotle's famous schema; rather, as the *Chūō Kōron* symposia demonstrate, a new approach to the state as a political community was developed that might be called 'domestic modernization and regional leadership by consent'. The key concept here is subjectivity (*shutaisei*). The Japanese nation could not achieve its full potential as a world-historical people unless each and every subject of the Japanese empire was empowered and motivated to contribute his or her best in pursuit of the greater good. Such levels of subjectivity could not be achieved by compulsion. Japan's elite had to inspire, lead, support and listen if the requisite measure of public cooperation and economic effectiveness, at the level of the individual member of society, was to be attained. Confucian moral suasion underwrote the logic of consent because it kept the individual predisposed to the need for consensus.

The contributors to the *Chūō Kōron* discussions applied the same philosophical approach to constructing a Greater East Asian Co-prosperity Sphere as a *Großraum* or *kōiki-ken*. Any and all potential members of a successful East Asian *Großraum*, be they states, ex-colonies or still stateless peoples, had to display the capability to contribute to the viability of the co-prosperity sphere. They had to possess the essential qualities of subjectivity, actual or potential.

As the leader of the co-prosperity sphere, Japan had to assume, as a duty, the responsibility to enhance the subjectivity of all the members of the sphere. Subjectivity could not be imposed because the very attempt to enforce such subjectivity would stifle all sense of initiative and self-motivation. The powers of subjectivity are autonomous; they come from within. They are burdens freely assumed. However, such potential abilities, in the Confucian worldview, had to be shaped, guided and encouraged. This was Japan's *mission civilisatrice*.

Perhaps even more striking was the Confucian notion that hegemonic leadership was subject to the organic inevitabilities of rise and fall. As Tanabe's secret lecture to the Yonai faction of the Imperial Navy on 29 September 1942 makes clear, Kyoto political philosophy fully anticipated the inevitable arrival of the day when Japan would have to yield its leadership role to its hegemonic successor.[2] It might be Korea, Indonesia or, most likely, China. This is the message between the lines of Tanabe's lecture as preserved in *The Ōshima Memos* and it forms the unstated but nevertheless implicit axiom of the *Chūō Kōron* transcripts.

The Kyoto School believed that Japan had to expand to survive, but such expansion required the complete rethinking of the Japanese state as a part of a regional bloc composed of all East Asia. As a regional hegemon, Japan would orchestrate this collective enterprise but sovereignty would be shared by all the constitute nations and communities in the collective pursuit of the interest of all. Certainly the 'open door' of globalization advocated by the proponents of Wall Street free-market neo-liberalism had to be closed if East Asian autonomy was to be secured. However, in a remarkable departure from much Japanese elite thinking on the subject, the contributors to the *Chūō Kōron* transcripts took the long view. The only permanent solution to Japan's global vulnerability lay in the sustained improvement of its capacity to wage a protracted defence of its regional base in East Asia and the Western Pacific. This imperative doomed the structures of the Meiji state because a new kind of state formation was required: a *Großraum* to match the United States and the Soviet Union with their large and growing populations, vast economies, huge reserves of secure strategic resources and extensive territorial hinterlands.

This geostrategic remedy for the now obsolete modern nation-state was what the wartime Kyoto School called the 'Greater East Asian Co-prosperity Sphere'. This East Asian *Großraum* was both end and means. Only such hegemonic regionalism could secure that size of population, economic scale, variety of resources and geostrategic depth of territory necessary to protect East Asia as an autonomous civilization, but the defence of such autonomy was impossible unless the naval approaches to East Asia were secure from external attack. Only a united East Asia could provide the means to fight or, better still, convincingly threaten to sustain a protracted war of economic attrition, but because the Kyoto School was convinced that a regional bastion of this scale could not be created by force, Tōjō-style imperialism was rejected as wholly counterproductive in its violent means and its resort to the *passé* forms of nineteenth-century colonialism.

In the light of this vision of a subjective *Großraum*, one may finally appreciate why the Kyoto School was, rightly or wrongly, unswerving in its rejection of the League of Nations and the post-1919 liberal assault on the essential privilege of state sovereignty confirmed by the Westphalian system: the right to make war. Consistent with concepts such as the balance of power and conflicts between just enemies, war was accepted as the sole legal and legitimate means for a nation to transform itself into a great power in the pre-1919 state system. The logic of Japan's Manchuria occupation made perfect 'great power' sense under the Westphalian system, while Lord Leyton's report to the League of Nations with its call for Japanese withdrawal was entirely consistent with the new era of liberal imperialism. Unhappy with the hostile stance of the League of Nations, the Kyoto School sought to confer these old Westphalian privileges and rights on the new agency of a *Großraum* as part of a multipolar world composed of what Kōsaka famously called 'historical worlds'.

There is an uncanny fit between these Kyoto School ideas and the elaboration of the principles of the Westphalian system one finds in the writings of Carl Schmitt. The text of the *Chūō Kōron* transcripts suggests that the German jurist may have been an influence, but the precise measure of any impact is difficult to assess. The parallel demotion of Imperial Germany and Imperial Japan from the status of great powers after 1919 gave ample grounds for the political philosopher, theorist of international law and grand strategist to draw arresting comparisons.

One might reasonably infer that both Schmitt and the wartime Kyoto School drew on the heritage of strategic insights that circulated in the 1930s and 1940s under the flag of economic regionalism or the *Großraumwirtschaft*. However, one may also argue that the political philosophy of the Kyoto School as a response to the consolidation of a liberal global order has contemporary resonance because the Western critique of the defence and commercial policies of the People's Republic of China repeats all of the same liberal ideological moves.

In the 1940s, America sometimes sounded as if it were willing to accept Japan's peaceful rise, just as today it seems prepared to live with China's peaceful rise. The geopolitical question was the same then as now: who will dominate the Pacific militarily? Just before the Pacific War the Japanese elite concluded, reasonably in my view, that the United States would not finally tolerate Japan's status as a great power or accept the fact of Japanese empire. If China's leadership comes to the same conclusion in the next decades, a Sino–American replay of the Pacific War may follow.

What is revealing about the Obama Administration's attempts to refocus American strategic interest away from the Middle East in favour of the Pacific is how much difference it appears to make that China is economically more powerful than Imperial Japan was in 1941, and that in relative terms, America is that much weaker (in certain categories of financial health). Australia is the bellwether now, as it was in the 1930s. It was Canberra that encouraged America to extend its protective shield across the Pacific to counterbalance Japan earlier; now Australia's offer to provide a staging base for American ground troops, e-warfare, strategic bombers and naval supply reflects similar fears, but this time of the People's Republic. The difference today is that Australia is economically dependent on Chinese investment and is more fearful of alienating China than it was of provoking Imperial Japan.

In naval terms, Japan was relatively stronger then, but China today is already economically more powerful than Imperial Japan ever was. This and America's financial problems explain why Washington and Canberra are more cautious now. Recent military think tank proposals in Washington that would pave the way for a Sino-American 'co-dominion' of the Pacific reflect this logic.[3] Konoe and Tōjō would have welcomed co-dominion in 1941, but the Roosevelt Administration never would have dreamed of striking such a deal. Such calculations explain the motives behind the grand strategic ideas of the wartime Kyoto School and why the creation of a regional power base seemed so important.

Carl Schmitt argued that after 1919 Germany was too strong to be ignored in world affairs but too weak on its own to shape a new international order. The same could be said of Imperial Japan. Thus both former great powers sought enhanced security in *Großräume*. Unless China replaces the United States as global hegemon, Beijing will have to embrace some form of the *Großraum* strategy. Note that this geopolitical calculation has nothing to do with morality. Any lapse into genocidal racism, the slaughter of prisoners of war and other battlefield atrocities, or the exploitation of slave labour would undermine the potential success of a multi-ethnic and multi-national *Großraum* based on pooled sovereignty. So the wartime Kyoto School argued. There can be no ethical objections to such a mode of thinking; only liberal imperialist ones based on the Wilsonian denial of national sovereignty and its Westphalian privileges.

Notes

1 Tanabe Hajime, 'On the Logic of Co-prosperity Spheres: Towards a Philosophy of Regional Blocs', trans. David Williams as an appendix to *Defending Japan's Pacific War: The Kyoto School Philosophers and Post-White Power*, London and New York: RoutledgeCurzon, 2004, pp. 196–97; the ninth lecture in *The Ōshima Memos*, delivered on 29 September 1942. The Japanese text can be found in Ōhashi Ryōsuke, *Kyoto Gakuha to Nippon Kaigun: Shin Shiryō 'Ōshima Memos' o Megutte* (The Kyoto School and the Japanese Navy: On the New Historical Materials: The 'Ōshima Memos'), Tokyo: PHP, 2001, pp. 227–44.
2 See Note 1.
3 Quotations from interviews with US military officers at the National Defense University in Washington are found in Edward Luce, 'The Number One Threat Facing America is its Debt Burden', *New Statesman*, 23 April 2012, pp. 28–31.

8 Are Japan studies moral?
Confucian pacifism and Kellogg-Briand liberalism between Voltaire and Walzer

> During the Holocaust, Germans extinguished the lives of six million Jews and, had Germany not been defeated, would have annihilated millions more. The Holocaust was also the defining feature of German politics and political culture during the Nazi period, the most shocking event of the twentieth century, and the most difficult to understand in all of German history.
>
> (Daniel Jonah Goldhagen[1])

> When the city fell on December 13, 1937, Japanese soldiers began an orgy of cruelty seldom if ever matched in world history. Tens of thousands of young men were rounded up and herded to the outer areas of the city, where they mowed down by machine guns, used for bayonet practice, or soaked with gasoline and burned alive ... Years later the International Military Tribunal of the Far East (IMTFE) estimated that more than 260,000 noncombatants died at the hands of Japanese soldiers at Nanking in late 1937 and early 1938, though some experts have placed the figure at well over 350,000.
>
> (Iris Chang[2])

The inflamed conscience

The raw horror conjured up by these two quotations goes a long way to explaining why post-war Japan studies has so often seemed to be a moral discourse in which factual research has normally (in both senses) been mobilized to meet the imperatives of the pacific liberal conscience. The wartime alliance between Germany and Japan reinforced the sense of revulsion because the atrocities committed in Poland, China and beyond became morally linked in our minds as the integral and defining feature of the original 'axis of evil'.

This intense reaction to the Moral Revolution of 1914–45, in which the Second World War was the decisive phase, has made the revisionary impulse that is so natural to the historian seem at best callous and at worse reprehensible. To query the motive behind Goldhagen's ambush of Albert Speer, Hitler's munitions minister, officially responsible for the administration of a vast army of slave labourers, but perhaps also the saviour of the Ruhr, Holland and Berlin, arouses unease in the liberal mind.[3] To question the casualty statistics of the Second Sino–Japanese War, as Ian Buruma gently did in *Wages of Guilt*, was one thing, but to ask whether Iris Chang, especially after her suicide, had exaggerated her death count for Nanking verged on indecency.[4] Indeed, every revisionist doubt has been confronted by accusations of a moral relativism which is seen as dishonouring the victim by diminishing the crimes of the perpetrator. The Kellogg-Briand liberal and the Confucian pacifist are united in their insistence that mere facts do not, and cannot be allowed to, outweigh the claims of conscience.

Two questions capture two contrasting moral double binds. Is genuine empirical research ever immoral? Is the anti-war liberal inevitably complicit in liberal imperialism? These moral dilemmas must be addressed, honestly and squarely, by the Kellogg-Briand liberal and the Confucian pacifist alike, because 'it depends' is not an answer to either. By 'Kellogg-Briand liberal' I mean someone who subscribes to the conviction that there should be 'no recourse to war for the solution of international controversies', to quote from the text of the Kellogg-Briand Pact, which, named after Aristide Briand, the French foreign minister, and Frank B. Kellogg, the US secretary of state, was signed by thirteen nations, including Japan, in August 1928. The 'Confucian pacifist' refers to the post-war Japanese who opposes his nation's right to make war for Confucian reasons. I have focused singularly on the pacifist dimension to this argument because the public and sovereign decision to make war figured so prominently in the Westphalian system as a means of restraining the violence and destructiveness of conflicts within and between nations.

Pacifism in academe has served to undermine the objectivity of the human sciences and their capacity to tell the truth about the world as it is. When Tetsuya Takahashi, the celebrated pacifist historian, presented a talk on Hajime Tanabe's controversial wartime address on 'Life and Death' to newly drafted Kyoto University students, I asked him what he made of Tanabe's text because I could not square the content of the original lecture with Takahashi's uncompromising assault on this Japanese philosopher.[5] When Takahashi reiterated his moral judgement, I became suspicious. So I asked him whether he had actually read 'Life and Death', because it ranges from Marcus Aurelius and his *Meditations* on death and last things to Buddhism and Martin Heidegger.

Takahashi was entirely unrepentant. He said it did not matter what the content was. Tanabe was sending these young students off to war, and that was a crime. After the talk, I enquired after Takahashi's health, because he looked exhausted. He said his international lecture tour was punishing (I think he had just come from Paris), but the struggle against reactionary anti-pacifism was his cause.[6] Takahashi's stance is not unique, but it does raise important textual and ethical issues.

First, observe that his approach to Tanabe's wartime lecture effectively reverses Derrida's famous dictum that 'there is nothing outside the text'. Takahashi is insisting that 'there is nothing *in* the text', certainly nothing that calls into question his moral indictment of the wartime Kyoto School.

Second, Takahashi exposes himself to counter-critique because he refuses to examine the context of Tanabe's address. For example, did the soon-to-be-drafted students of Kyoto University *ask* Tanabe to give a talk on death? Finally, there are the complications of Takahashi's standpoint as a *Confucian* pacifist. In a way that the Western liberal will find very disturbing, Takahashi's assault on the wartime Kyoto School is a product of the great national *tenkō* of 1945. In other words, his moral stance would very likely alter beyond recognition if Japan were to experience another Confucian tipping point tomorrow. More interesting still, to be ethically consistent, the suggestion would be that Takahashi would have applauded Tanabe's talk of 19 May 1943 if he had been in the audience because he would have been *morally* obliged to do so.

As was true of Iris Chang, Takahashi is a moral historian by ethical conviction. Such a standpoint permits no disagreement under the post-1945 Japanese dispensation. 'War is wrong,' says Hiroko Takeda, 'and that is the end of the matter.'[7] Where, though, does such moral certainty, so uncompromisingly advocated, leave the truth? Can we live in a world where morality always lies in wait to ambush the truth-sayer in this way? What happens when we move from the safe sphere of ethical judgement to that much more testing arena that is human conduct? Where does the matter end in the realm not of words but of actions?

The wages of conscience

Was Tōjō a just foe (*justus hostis*)? If Tōjō was an unjust foe, the Pacific War becomes a just war. If just wars are waged against an unjust enemy, do any moral restraints apply when we make war against such an enemy?[8] May we slaughter, torture and obliterate the enemies of freedom in good conscience? 'Yes' is the emphatic answer of the liberal imperialist and, over time, every Democratic president since Wilson has affirmed this answer, wholly or in part, in practice – whatever he said in public.

Reviving the medieval theory of wars of annihilation, Wilson replaced the label 'infidel' with that of 'illiberal', thus making all unjust foes into the legitimate target of liberal war as a form of total war. Less about blood lust than about prudent calculation and moral purpose, the liberal way of war is a form of total war that seeks not only to defeat evil but also, as noted above, to make the perpetrator of evil into a liberal subject materially and morally incapable of resisting America's world order. Thus the enemy must surrender unconditionally. To compel him to surrender, he must be confronted with a realistic threat of annihilation; he must taste it and bear its wounds. So wars of annihilation admit no moral limits in *practice*. The ends *do* just justify the means in a liberal war of annihilation because this is a war to end all wars. So worthy a goal, for many Western students of Japan, justifies any number of Hiroshimas.

For Wilson and his liberal imperialist successors in the White House, the forces of righteousness never act against conscience; that is, by definition, what makes us righteous. Franklin Roosevelt and Harry Truman applied scripture's 'swift terrible sword' without restraint against Japan, its civilian population no less than its armed forces, because moral error has no rights. To ensure the complete triumph of Wilson's world order, the full weight of America's nuclear arsenal would have been brought to bear against the rest of Confucian Asia – in the Korean and Vietnamese conflicts – but for the threat of a matching response from the Soviet Union. After the Cold War, the same moral certainties have been at work in the treatment of 'prisoners' at Abu Ghraib and Guantanamo Bay no less than the Central Intelligence Agency's (CIA) programme of rendition kidnappings and outsourced torture. After 9/11, George W. Bush was not violating the logic of Wilsonian liberalism; he was fulfilling it.[9]

Was Tōjō a war criminal?

As an unjust enemy, was Tōjō also a criminal? Were the members of his cabinet at the time of Pearl Harbor criminals? They were all arrested by the Americans after Japan's surrender and some were later executed by order of the Tokyo War Crimes Tribunal, but many of the charges against them had no basis in law: neither Japanese nor American nor international statute. Most of the accused were not personally culpable for atrocities, except in the sense of 'strict liability', a legal doctrine judged by Michael Walzer as 'radically inappropriate in cases of criminal justice'. Walzer goes on to comment on the Japanese commander hanged by the Allies for the 1945 'Rape of Manila':

> Yamashita was convicted without reference to any acts he committed or even to any omissions that he might have avoided. He was convicted of having held an office, because of the duties said to inhere in that office, even though the duties were in fact undo-able under the conditions in which he found himself.[10]

Yamashita's case stands as a striking example of what changed in international law with Wilson's counter-revolution. Before 1919, Yamashita would not have been subject to criminal prosecution because such commingling of international public law and private criminal law was inconsistent with the *jus publicum europaeum*. Under the Westphalian system, war was an evil but not a crime. The horrors of war were restrained by reducing the stakes at issue in war, and by moderating its violent fury with the assumption that one's opponent was a 'just foe'.

After Versailles, international public law was criminalized as part of a programme of moral reform judged essential to delegitimizing resistance to America's global hegemony. Thus the Tokyo War Crimes Tribunal tried, convicted and executed 'war criminals' even when they had violated no laws. The principle of *nullum crimen, nulla poena sine lege* so central to European positive law was replaced by a kind of quasi-legal moralism. Walzer's *Just and Unjust Wars* signals a partial return to the canonical commentators on *jus publicum europaeum* that Carl Schmitt so celebrated, but this American ethicist remains a prisoner of some aspects of post-Wilsonian moral reasoning:

> When I talk of the rules of war, I am referring to the more particular code that governs our judgments of combat behaviour, and that is only partially articulated in The Hague and Geneva conventions. And when I talk of crimes, I am describing violations of the general principles or of the particular code: so men and women can be called criminals even when they cannot be charged before a legal tribunal.[11]

Or, to put the matter plainly, a criminal is not someone who has violated the law; a criminal is someone who has offended the liberal's sense of humanity and moral self-worth by harming others. This violation would be practically meaningless unless the liberal whose moral sense has been violated also has the power to punish such violations. The Kellogg-Briand liberal is united with the Confucian pacifist in his easy resort to the rhetoric of war criminality, but the liberal pacifist has often been reluctant to acknowledge the logic of enforcement that this need to punish entails. So, as is true of so many ramifications of the ethics of liberal imperialism, the moral judgement (and sometimes destruction) of non-liberals comes ultimately to depend neither on the law nor on ethics but on the ability of liberal societies to dominate, reduce and reconstruct illiberal societies. This explains why the expression 'the ethics of liberal imperialism' is not a criticism; it is a factual description. It is how illiberal societies are 'flattened' ethically.

Confucian pacifism

To the degree that contemporary Japan studies is liberal, the advocate of Pacific War orthodoxy falls naturally into the ethical orbit of Wilsonian liberal imperialism. The axioms, the conventions and indeed the very spirit of the Westphalian system and its 'wars of form' are lost on such liberals, as is the awareness of how novel their philosophy of ethics is. The year 1919 easily qualifies as the most important in the moral history of modern Orientalism and Asian studies, yet few students of Japan demonstrate any awareness of this immense turning point in human affairs. It is not surprising, therefore, that the Japan expert who concerns himself with such questions draws neither on international law nor on the field of applied ethics as elaborated by scholars such as Walzer but rather on the claims of conscience and its corollary, the abhorrence of 'moral relativism' as classically expounded in Herbert Marcuse's last letter to Martin Heidegger.[12] To understand just how particular, even idiosyncratic, this moral vantage is, let us compare it to its supposed Japanese ally: Confucian pacifism.

On reflection, the dissatisfactions that George Macaulay Trevelyan entertained about the post-Versailles liberal order might be seen as the inevitable outcome of the unsettling truth that liberal ideals could not be enforced without illiberal means – that is, acts of compulsion and violence that discomfort the liberal conscience. Today this conscience is fearful that the path from Wilson's high-minded Fourteen Points and the League of Nations has led inevitably and tragically, via Hiroshima and Nagasaki, to the 'War on Terror' (full-spectrum domination, CIA rendition, Abu Ghraib and Guantanamo Bay, etc.). Confucian pacifism undermines the liberal conscience in an entirely different way.

The liberal's anti-war stance is grounded in what he sees as unchanging eternal principles, but this is not true of the Confucian pacifist. He objects to war because he is obliged ethically to embrace this doctrine at the behest of Japan's moral master and the title-holder of a secularized version of the mandate of heaven – the United States – but only as long as Americans convincingly exercise their *toku* or their moral right to exercise sovereignty over Japan. The day Washington loses its *toku*, the moral justification for Confucian pacifism will effectively disappear. The viability of Article 9 of Japan's peace constitution, certainly in the minds of most Japanese, depends wholly on this assumption. In other words, pacifism is not an embedded norm, nor could it ever be. Pacifism could no more be an embedded norm than the Manchu dynasty. Like militarism and communism, pacifism and Manchu rule are what come and go under the rules of Confucian regime change. The embedded norm at work here is the mechanism of Confucian revolution: how power is sought, won, maintained and lost. This truth may take on a particularly sensitive and subtle character when a Kellogg-Briand liberal is married to a Confucian pacifist.

Voltaire's Westphalian reticence

Confronted with a serious and well-reasoned philosophy of East Asian wartime resistance, why is the task of bracketing our liberalism in order better to understand such forms of Japanese thought so taxing? In this chapter of my commentary, the difficulty liberalism poses for the Western reader of the *Chūō Kōron* discussions has turned on three explanations: the nature of Wilsonian liberalism itself, Western confusions over the nature and influence of Confucian pacifism, and the psychological double-binds that arise for the liberal conscience from the need to enforce liberal norms with violence.

The last two conundrums have rarely been examined, certainly not in courses on social science methodology or the conceptual tools of the humanist student of Asian civilization. Yet the internal mental workings of the conscience as a process of moral introspection and self-examination conspire as powerfully as any other factor against the necessary bracketing of liberal moral assumptions. However, such bracketing is essential if we are to appreciate the moral framework of Imperial Japan or any other Confucian society. Even if the Western student of Japanese ideas felt no need to submit his research findings to an examination of conscience, the discourse of moral universalism, the relatively recent 'invention' of peace, and the linked ideas of liberal imperialism and the liberal way of war will continue to pose obstacles to the sound understanding of the wartime Kyoto School.

None of the exegetical ambitions set out in Chapter 1 – a proper reading, an appropriate scheme of interpretation and interpretive rigour – can be met unless the precise impact on Japan studies since Pearl Harbor of moral universalism after Kant, and American hegemony after Woodrow Wilson, and international law after, say, Maurice Hauriou, Hersch Lauterpacht and George Scelle, is assessed in a clear, calm, objective manner: one as free as possible from moral judgements and Eurocentric cultural assumptions about how Japan *should* work as a society rather than how it *does* work as a society. Consistent with our assumption that the rise of the United States to the role of global dominatrix forms our primary or ruling narrative, one conclusion now appears to be irresistible. 'Japanese resistance' must be regarded, rightly or wrongly, as a predictable, rational and human response to the enforcement of global suzerainty by post-Wilsonian liberalism.

Before 1919, the proponent of the Westphalian system of European public law would not have raised this issue as a matter of morality; the history of the sectarian strife of the Wars of Religion had taught him not to pose it. Thus, in *The Age of Louis XIV,* Voltaire describes the rape of the Palatinate in 1688 as a 'horror' but not a crime.[13] The product of the pre-1648 ethical cosmos, the medieval scholastic, would have resorted to the rhetoric of moral absolutes in framing his objections. Seven hundred years after St Aquinas, Wilson and his ethical heirs are not troubled by such dilemmas because they have the power to cure illiberality by force. This is what the liberal means by 'international law'.

The liberal imperialist wants to apply the theory of moral war without the complications. He feels no need to recall St Augustine's classic doubts in *The City of God* about the challenge of delineating friend and foe or the sheer difficulties of keeping a just war just.[14] Nevertheless, it might be prudent for us to proceed more cautiously when we are tempted to dismiss Tōjō as a *hostis humani generes,* because of the moral consequences of our answer for liberal conduct. In other words, how we respond to this question of Tōjō's criminality will determine whether Japan studies are moral or not.

Notes

1 Daniel Jonah Goldhagen, *Hitler's Willing Executioners: Ordinary Germans and the Holocaust,* London: Abacus, 1997, p. 4.
2 Iris Chang, *The Rape of Nanking: The Forgotten Holocaust of World War II,* New York: Basic Books, 1997, p. 4.
3 For the details of the ambush as well as Speer's actions in 1945 to prevent mass deaths in the Ruhr, Holland and Berlin, see Gitta Sereny, *Albert Speer: His Battle with Truth,* London: Picador, 1996.

4 Ian Buruma, *Wages of Guilt: Memories of War in Germany and Japan*, London: Jonathan Cape, 1994, p. 112. For Chang's statistics, see *The Rape of Nanking*, op. cit.
5 Hajime Tanabe, *THZ* 8 (Volume 8 of Tanabe's Complete Works), Tokyo: Chikuma Shobō, 1964, pp. 245–62.
6 Taking the measure of the man, I asked whether he was suffering from *jisa-boke* or *heiwa boke*. A play on words, impossible to reproduce in English, between 'jet lag' and the 'intellectual detachment from reality caused by pacifist thinking'.
7 Personal communication. Dr Takeda was my delightful colleague for three years at Cardiff University. The place was never the same after she left.
8 Despite being frequently evoked by just war theorists, certainly since America's war against Vietnam, Aquinas is strict in his definition of the conditions that must govern just wars in a way that is rarely true of the liberal imperialist who acknowledges the truth that maintaining an empire always necessitates illiberal means.
9 I have criticized the treatment of Iraqi prisoners in print in *The Left in the Shaping of Japanese Democracy: Essays in Honour of J. A. A. Stockwin*, ed. with Rikki Kersten, London and New York: Routledge, 2006. Here, by contrast, I seek only to make clear the nature of the moral thinking that has underwritten American diplomatic and military policy since the Treaty of Versailles without recourse to the obscurant and self-serving language in which such policy analysis is so often wrapped.
10 Michael Walzer, *Just and Unjust Wars: A Moral Argument with Historical Illustrations*, 4th edn, New York: Basic Books, 1977, p. 320.
11 Walzer, *Just and Unjust Wars*, op. cit., p. xxii.
12 For a detailed analysis of the Heidegger–Marcuse correspondence, see my *Defending Japan's Pacific War: The Kyoto School Philosophers and Post-White Power*, London and New York: RoutledgeCurzon, 2004, pp. 117–26.
13 Jean François Marie Arouet de Voltaire, *The Age of Louis XIV*, trans. Martyn P. Pollack, London: Dent/Dutton; New York: Everyman's Library, 1961, pp. 148–49. Originally published in 1751, the text had taken Voltaire over twenty years to complete.
14 Book XIX. Carl Schmitt seizes on this point in *The Nomos of the Earth in the International Law of the Jus Publicum Europaeum*, trans. and ann. G.L. Ulmen, New York: Telos Press, 2006, p. 155.

The Kyoto School and the Post-Meiji Confucian Revolution

9 Endless Pearl Harbors?
The Kyoto thinker as grand strategist

> If national mobilization was taken to mean that the Japanese home islands should attempt to mobilize vast quantities of men and munitions on the scale expended from 1914 to 1918 by France, for example, then the effort would bankrupt Japan, no matter what the outcome.
> (Major Kanji Ishikawa, 1927[1])

> If by any chance the coming naval conference should recognise the traditional discriminatory ratios, our Empire will forever be ordered around by the Anglo-American powers, and it is obvious that our Empire will go to ruin. This is the reason why the coming conference has far greater consequences for our Empire than the Washington and London Naval conferences.
> (Japanese Navy Ministry memorandum, 1934[2])

Among the varied portraits of the Kyoto School thinker of the period between 1930 and 1945, none presents him as a grand strategist; a philosopher, propagandist, fascist, enlightened dissident or politically muddled Buddhist perhaps, but not an intellectual with a distinctive feel for the potential of naval power or an innovative perspective on the oceanic dimension of a renewed global order. Such strategic insights draw on a set of truths about Japan's geopolitical position in the Western Pacific that obtained from the Russo–Japanese War to the atomic destruction of Hiroshima and Nagasaki. For the historian of ideas and military affairs who would tease out the Kyoto School's response to these truths, the creative anticipation of the fruits of future research involves something between connecting the dots as in the child's game and completing an oil painting based upon a particularly fine artist's sketch of these Japanese philosophers as grand strategists.

One might begin this historical reconstruction with a question. Why did the Kyoto School settle on the Navy as its ally of choice in the struggle to shape the strategic discourse of Imperial Japan as it slid wretchedly down the road to Pearl Harbor? The factual record suggests three pegs upon which the historian may hang his coat: 1 the geographical assumptions that the Kyoto School brought to its reflections on politics, history and the nature of war; 2 the obvious military and economic constraints that American naval and industrial might imposed on Imperial Japan; and 3 the search for a grand strategic remedy for Japan's vulnerability that drew simultaneously on the incisive labours of Japan's more realistic naval researchers, the vision and chess player's patience of Admiral Mitsumasa Yonai, and the gift of the Kyoto School for the long view that informed its anticipation of the world as it might be. This is why I conclude that the imperatives of the grand strategist have left their mark on the pages of the *Chūō Kōron* transcripts and *The Ōshima Memos*.

Building a grand strategy

The ideas and institutions upon which the Kyoto School erected its philosophy of world history and political subjectivity may be conceived as the building blocks of a grand strategy. The motivation for such thinking included creating an alternative to European suzerainty over Asia, deflecting the thrust of American power across the Pacific, and blunting Chinese nationalism so that this surge of ethnic energy might advance the cause of regional integration under Japanese leadership. The Kyoto thinker thus rejected Wilson's new world order while seeking to preserve the most practical features of the Westphalian system. A multipolar world as an act of creation was the prime strategic objective.

To achieve these goals, the programme of modernization undertaken after the Meiji Restoration had to be rethought. In essence, Japan was not wealthy or productive enough to meet the burdens of its world-historical role or the grand strategy that this role demanded. Economically, it needed to grow much more. Its industries still required more rationalization (*gōri-ka*). At the level of the shop floor, everyday logistics and the home front, life was not efficient enough. The Japanese elite responded to this dilemma in a variety of ways. In *MITI and the Japanese Miracle*, Chalmers Johnson gives us a snapshot portrait of the thinking of reform-minded politicians, military officers and bureaucrats who helped to create the Ministry of Commerce and Industry in 1925, which later evolved into Ministry of Munitions, Ministry of Greater East Asia, and, after the war, the Ministry of International Trade and Industry (MITI).[3] It is not difficult to image what a pre-war grand strategist would have made of this effort.

Taking the economics of scale in its grossest sense, the Japanese Empire had to be transformed into a much larger and more powerful co-prosperity sphere. At the level of the private firm and the individual worker, greater efficiency, responsibility and autonomous self-development had to be pursued across East Asia as a whole. Nishitani repeatedly argues for the importance of 'stable' or 'sure-footed' dynamism within the public and private sectors.[4] One also senses that the Kyoto School's grasp of the autarkic logic of the economic *Großraum* was informed, via Suzuki's interventions, by an awareness of the same kind of economic lessons that Carl Schmitt drew from the transnational development of energy and other supply chain networks and infrastructures that German economists dubbed *Großräume*.[5]

This plan, at once patriotic, practical and humane, for the reorganization of Japan and the relaunch of its regional and global role, required a powerful political player capable of influencing policies and perceptions at the highest level of government and the armed forces. Here the Kyoto School rejected Tōjō's continental expansionist dream (was the Japanese war leader a student of Hannibal's defeat-a-naval-power-without-a-navy strategy in the Second Punic War?) and seized upon the Imperial Navy as the national saviour. In return, the faction led by Admiral Yonai embraced the Kyoto School as a brains trust and source of strategic advice and analysis. However, the Kyoto School's choice of the Navy was grounded not only in practical political need but also in grand strategic necessity. Why this was the case may be explained by a closer look at the stark realities that defined Imperial Japan's geopolitical place in the increasingly hostile world that came into being after the birth of Wilson's counter-revolution.

The realities of Japan's strategic position

Whatever the claims of Allied Pacific War orthodoxy, the sober Japanese grand strategist *never* envisioned a campaign of global conquest, if for no other reason than that Japan lacked the means.[6] On this subject, naval historians report a remarkable uniformity of opinion among Japanese Navy ministers, senior commanders and tactical planners between 1907 and 1941.[7] Driven by often astonishing technological innovations, the expense of capital ship construction even before 1914 had become all but crippling. Even Great Britain found it difficult financially to sustain the pre-eminence of its powerful navy.

With the lapse of the Anglo-Japanese Alliance, effectively in 1921 and formally in 1923, Japan was exposed to the prospect of a warship-building construction competition with the world's largest economy. Japan could not win this contest with the United States, and the senior command of the Imperial Navy knew it. Briefly in the 1920s, Japan tried to keep the gap from growing still wider with heavier armaments for fewer ships, more submarines, and superior numbers of smaller (and cheaper) warships, but this could not alter the imbalance. Even island fortifications in the South Pacific proved futile. In any case, the completion of the Panama Canal in 1914 sealed Imperial Japan's fate. Seizure of Germany's South Pacific colonies was, in strategic terms, neither here nor there, but the American capacity to move its Atlantic fleet quickly to the Pacific decisively improved its advantage in theatre operations.

The upshot was that Japanese war planning focused on the least unlikely of all its strategic options: the small chance of a victory over America in the waters of the Japanese home islands (China's contemporary effort to control the Taiwan Straits offers a relevant parallel). Domination of the Western Pacific in the face of such American power was not possible, and this fact governed Japanese naval thinking from the era of Heihachirō Tōgō to that of Isoroku Yamamoto.

US Navy thinking exhibited a parallel consistency. Thus successive versions of War Plan Orange were more or less constant in its assumed scenarios; campaign durations varied, but objectives and battle planning were all but fixed from 1907. The original Plan Orange, and all of its successors, anticipated the initial loss of the Philippines and maybe Guam (an attack on Hawaii was sometimes factored in), but their prompt recapture by the main US fleet thrust across the Pacific using either the 'central' or the shorter 'northern' route was predicted with equal confidence. Even the US occupation of Amani-Oshima just beyond Tokyo Bay was assumed as early as 1908. The American plan foresaw (as the Japanese war planners also did) a Tsushima-type final battle off the Japanese home islands. An American victory would open the way for the blockade of Japanese ports and the eventual surrender of Japan to avert starvation.

Only two subsequent innovations on the American side deserve attention here. First, the potential of air bombardment slowly began to influence the American way of war. Navy tradition and the difficulties of air strikes launched from aircraft carriers posed formidable barriers to such ideas, so the breakthrough in strategic thinking occurred elsewhere, most notably with Plan Red against the British Empire. The controversial 1935 version is particularly instructive because it initiated the building of forward air bases in northern Atlantic states to facilitate the 'terror bombing' of Canadian cities. Less than ten years later, the fate that had been planned for Toronto and Ottawa was inflicted on Tokyo and Osaka.[8] This alternation of war strategy melded perfectly with another change: the liberal imperialist revival of just wars of annihilation to force the illiberal opponent into unconditional surrender. This was essential if the unjust foe was to be punished, broken and reborn as a compliant liberal subject.

Asymmetric warfare: Masaichi Niimi and the three war scenarios

The measure of Japan's economic weakness was reflected in the three types of war that defined the range of options for any naval conflict with the United States, as noted above: 1 an early Tsushima-style 'quick and decisive battle' in home waters; 2 an interceptive offensive to delay the arrival of the American fleet off Japan; or 3 a protracted war. From 1907 onwards, the magic figure of a 70 per cent fleet ratio vis-à-vis the United States in capital ships or the equivalent was judged by Japanese Navy planners as the essential minimum to give the country a fighting chance in its own waters. This ratio was never met, neither in dreadnought class battleships nor in armoured battle cruisers. Observe also that even 70 per cent secured only sufficient forces for Japan to try to defend the waters around Honshū; even this never achieved figure was judged by naval planners in both countries as wholly insufficient for Japan to defend its island possessions in the Western Pacific. Even if captured by Japanese forces, Hawaii, Guam and the Philippines could not be held.

In 1909, in *The Valor of Ignorance*, Homer Lee warned that the Japanese Navy might occupy and hold Los Angeles and San Francisco, but this was nothing more than an alarmist fantasy.[9] Between 1907 and 1941, Japan had a slight chance of winning a decisive battle in a very short war, no chance of defending any extended region of the Western Pacific, and no capability whatever of sustaining a protracted war. The naval commands on both sides of the Pacific were in fundamental accord about Japan's weakness, whatever they may have said in public to encourage higher naval spending.

Realists such as Commander Masaichi Niimi called even the Tsushima strategy into doubt. Basing his findings on research he had conducted in Britain after the Great War, Niimi prophesied that a clash of massed capital ships off Shizuoka might well prove as inconclusive as the titanic Anglo–German battle at Jutland in 1917.[10] He therefore argued that the only way for Japan to secure its maritime defences was to build the industrial and military capacity to sustain a protracted war. As the threat of a confrontation with the United States drew closer after the outbreak of a second European war in 1939, Admiral Yonai and his supporters appear to have drawn a similar conclusion. Certainly the Yonai faction concluded it was wiser to play the game 'long' rather than to rush into a war that Japan could not win. The country had to be patient and husband its strength to the point where the United States would accept rather than contest Japanese hegemony over the seas immediately off East Asia. The relevant comparison may be with the Soviet Navy during the height of the Cold War, when Soviet naval control of the Baltic and Black Seas was effectively conceded.

The strategic remedy that the Kyoto School endorsed in print transcends the normal contest between 'land' and 'sea' in grand strategic design. Only the Navy could secure the western approaches to their island nation, but only a co-prosperity sphere could provide the resources, productive capacity and manpower necessary to make the threat of a protracted naval war credible. The choice between land and sea as strategic options was therefore a false one. The naval option was essential to secure the continental option, and vice versa. This wartime Kyoto School double embrace of Imperial Navy and the Greater East Asian Co-prosperity Sphere also explains why the Kyoto thinker rejected Tōjō's strategy of battlefield brutality and *passé* colonialism as flawed 'land-only' strategies.

The panic and despair of 1941

Japanese strategic naval thinking between the world wars was dominated by the contrasting ideas and perspectives represented by the two Katōs: Admiral Tomosaburō Katō and Admiral Kanji Katō, respectively Navy minister and chief of the Naval General Staff at the time of the 1920 Washington Conference. In the liberal literature on naval diplomacy during the inter-war years, Tomosaburō Katō tends to be viewed as the hero of the times, Kanji Katō as the insubordinate villain. The revisionist position rebalances this judgement, seeing the senior of the two, Tomosaburō Katō, as a cautious appeaser committed to Japan's 'peaceful rise' on American terms; an advocate of the doomed diplomacy of accommodation and compromise in the face of America's growing naval power and global reach. The improbable but hitherto largely unexamined assumption of his approach was that the post-1919 Versailles-Geneva-Washington liberal world order might allow Japan to keep its smallish empire provided it abandoned the path of forceful expansion and submitted to American leadership. History shows that this assumption was false.

In contrast, Kanji Katō opposed appeasement and therefore has been dismissed as mindless and reckless. Some of his supporters refused to yield quietly to the advance of liberal imperialism, preferring in the end to go down fighting rather than take the path of voluntary surrender. In retrospect, both Katōs and their supporters failed to appreciate the strategic wisdom of Niimi and the Kyoto School.

This neglected wisdom might have eased the moment of panic that engulfed the middle and higher ranks of the Imperial Navy in response to the imposition of an oil embargo by the Roosevelt Administration after the Japanese occupation of the southern half of French Indochina in the summer of 1941. Washington's decision set off the 'barrel count' emergency. As the embargo was only slowly and less than strictly imposed on the American side, the fear that the Japanese Navy had really begun to run down its reserves of oil was probably premature, but the decision for war was taken all the more hastily because the impact of the embargo was perceived to be so damaging.

Another view might argue that the crisis of summer and autumn 1941 is better understood as the culmination of a decade of insubordination and rebelliousness on the part of middle-ranking Japanese officers against the old school accommodative logic that still prevailed in some senior circles of the naval high command. This logic of appeasement also commanded loyalty among many older members of the political, diplomatic and court elite. Orthodox historians have tended to be very critical of these various rebellions and upsets, condemning them as irresponsible and wilful violations of the chain of command by 'hot-headed' malcontents and pro-German fanatics.

As this interpretation is widely endorsed in the academic literature on the subject, there is probably a great deal to this view, but sometimes experience of the society one is trying to understand can provide an alternative perspective on a slippery issue like military discipline under stress. Drawing on a peacetime example to illuminate a wartime issue may not be ideal, but when I encounter comments on Japanese group dynamics by liberal-minded historians of the Pacific War, my mind is cast back to the headquarters of an important Japanese bank in Tokyo that I knew well in the 1980s.

If one wandered into a major department of the bank in Ōtemachi after 6.30p.m. or so on a working day, one almost never encountered a senior manager. If one enquired, 'Who is running the show tonight?' the middle-manager response was, 'We are. As we do every night'. Asked to explain, the answer was always the same: 'We cannot get anything done until they go home. We know it, and they know it.' Senior managers took responsibility when things went wrong; gave strategic direction to company policy; took the broad view; read widely and thought deeply about the bank's future. They represented the firm at home and abroad; arbitrated factional tensions; and kept the ship in shape. However, middle managers ran the bank. American and British scholars familiar with the rigid top-down system of managerial control that prevails in military and business life in Anglo-America find this kind of middle-management assertiveness and confidence a bit unnerving. So do Japanese academics who know about this very Japanese organizational dynamic only at second hand.

Did middle-ranking officers run the Imperial Navy in the same way? Do we need to think ourselves free of Western assumptions about how East Asian organizations and institutions go about their collective tasks in the light of practical experience and Confucian psychology? Few organizations, Japanese or otherwise, cultivate a weakness for hotheads or fanatics of any kind, but consensus-based organizations only flourish when the group consensus is grounded in reality. As was noted in Chapter 5, in the Confucian scheme of things it is the responsibility of every member of a decision-making unit to cultivate a well-honed appreciation of reality. This is a Confucian moral duty.

Harmony rests on a solid consensus about what is truly real – which means that reality must be feasible. When the virtue of harmony is valued as much as it is in East Asian cultures, the one thing that must not happen is for the consensus about what is 'real' to break down from the top. So what was the diplomatic reality that these middle-ranking naval officers were reacting to between the humiliation of the Washington Naval Treaty of 1930 and Secretary of State Hull's ultimatum of November 1941? The clue may be deduced from the often remarked 'anguish' of the emperor. Court officials were appalled by the prospect of Japan plunging into a war with the United States that it had no chance of winning. At home, in the quiet of the night, everyone, hothead or otherwise, knew this was true. Japan was not tricked into going to war in 1941; it was trapped into fighting.

The lessons gleaned from practical experience of Japanese organizational reality, coupled with Confucian insights into the morality at work in East Asian behaviour during wartime, are still more powerful when assessed in the light of comparative grand strategies, East and West. From the standpoint of the ethics of liberal imperialism, Hirohito's empire was intolerable regardless of whether Japan cooperated with the Versailles-Washington order and abided by international public opinion or not. After 1853, the Japan that was dragged involuntarily into the international system by the United States sought to play its part in the global order. It joined the Allied cause during the Great War, only to find that its hard-won status as a great power was relentlessly eroded under the Versailles-Geneva-Washington system. After

Wilson, Japanese cooperation with the United States won Tokyo little, standing apart won it nothing, and resistance brought calamity.

In *The Cambridge History of Japan*, Ikuhiko Hata draws up the grim table of loss that resulted from Japanese support for the Allied cause in the First World War and its post-1919 embrace of Shidehara's pro-liberal diplomacy of appeasement:

> Why did Japan eventually break away from the Versailles-Washington system? The main reason was the rollback begun by the United States and Great Britain at the war's end which forced Japan to give up most of the wartime gains it had made in the Asia-Pacific area [as an Allied power]. The rollback included the abolition of the Anglo-Japanese Alliance, the withdrawal of Japanese troops from Siberia, the 5:5:3 ratio in capital ships in a naval arms limitation treaty that left the Japanese fleet inferior in strength to those of the United States and Great Britain, the return of the Shantung concession to Chinese sovereignty, and the suspension of the Lansing-Ishii agreement.[11]

Pacific War orthodoxy insists that it was Japanese expansionism that caused the Pacific War, but not even during the Axis high tide of 1942 did Japan have the material means to consolidate any gains of consequence against the Western powers; it could not even defeat China. As history shows, the power that mattered to the future of the Pacific was the United States, and colonialism was not acceptable to the world's new liberal hegemon. The Roosevelt who badgered Churchill to give up India and who adamantly refused even to contemplate the return of French authority to Indochina – and these were America's principal liberal allies – would never have permitted Japan to retain its rule over Korea, Taiwan or Manchuria. This was the bitter truth revealed by Eisenhower's decision to enforce American hegemonic discipline against British Prime Minister Eden for his Suez intervention in 1956.

Under the Westphalian system, the right to make war was the essential condition of national sovereignty. Britain lost that right in 1956. Twenty-six years later, the measure of the change to Britain's status since its days as a pre-1919 great power was uncomfortably confirmed when, in 1982, Margaret Thatcher had to press Ronald Reagan to acquiesce in her invasion of the Falklands. If Reagan had said 'no', that would have been the end of the matter, and the Falklands would have become the Malvinas. This is how the liberal world order has come to work since 1919. This is a demonstrable fact.

Sooner or later, Washington would have compelled Japan to renounce the right to make war, and thus renounce its national sovereignty. It therefore did not finally matter to Wilson's successors in the White House whether Imperial Japan assumed a high posture or low, was led by Tōjō or Shidehara, stood its ground or abased itself by appeasing Washington. Japan was a great power, and demoted, demolished, dismembered or dispatched it would be. The full implications of American global hegemony did not register immediately on

Japanese Navy thinking – but with time they did, especially on the younger members of the officer corps. Eventually the true scale of the threat became clear to all, including the Kyoto School. This may explain the despair of 1941 when a loosely imposed oil embargo seemed to bring Japan almost to its knees without America firing a shot. Has history witnessed a purer act of hegemonic power?

Endless Pearl Harbors?

It may not be true that military leaders always fight the last war, but victors find the temptation almost irresistible. For American grand strategists, the Civil War of 1861–65 has had almost paradigmatic importance for the Pacific War, from the expected intensity of total war as demonstrated in Sherman's brutal march across Georgia (burnt-out Atlanta as a rehearsal for firebombed Tokyo), the naval strangulation of Confederate imports echoed in the intention to blockade Japan into surrender as set out in successive versions of Plan Orange, and the Japanese Occupation as a version of the 'Reconstruction' of the post-bellum South. The historian Richard Slotkin sees the Northern victory at Antietam in 1862 and Lincoln's Emancipation Proclamation the same year as not only advancing the cause of securing 'a new birth of freedom' for the United States, but also signalling on the Northern side 'a shift from the strategy of conciliation to a war of subjugation'.[12] A template of moral expectations for twentieth-century wars of liberal annihilation was thus prepared.

The Japanese brought their own vision of victory at sea to their struggle with American naval power. For Japanese optimists and realists alike, the battle paradigm that counted was the Russo–Japanese War. The great Japanese naval triumph at Tsushima in 1905 held out the hope of a victory against an obviously superior foe. The Imperial Navy's only chance was to draw the American fleet across the Pacific into Japanese home waters, thus stretching the enemy's supply lines to the maximum. Vis-à-vis the United States, Japanese 'expansionism' was always governed by this narrow ambition to secure a minimum of naval superiority just beyond Tokyo Bay. Note the similarities with China's effort today to secure naval advantage over the United States only in the Taiwan Straits.

Such naval minimalism obscures an important pre-cyber war paradox: no ocean was secure if any ocean was insecure; no single ocean was secure if any part of that ocean was insecure. The Pacific War demonstrated comprehensively that American naval invincibility off San Diego translated seamlessly into irresistible power off Hawaii or Shizuoka. Such universal reach is still the stuff of Chinese security nightmares. Long before the forthright American insistence on full-spectrum military supremacy, the oceans as an integrated object of naval superiority required more or less total control. This explains the true significance of Nelson's victory over French naval power at Trafalgar and why the Monroe Doctrine is so arresting an example of grand strategy for the naval thinker. It also suggests a practical naval interpretation of the expression *Hakkō no Ichiu* as a slogan for the prudent grand strategist.

The struggle for oceanic supremacy informs the American rivalry with Great Britain no less than the five most recent major challenges to British and American domination of the oceans: Germany in the First and Second World Wars, Japan in the Pacific War, the Soviet Union during the Cold War, and emerging Chinese naval power today. For the seven seas to be dominated, the oceans had to be imagined as a global system. On this subject, Carl Schmitt made some penetrating observations about the genesis and development of this global system as the embodiment of a set of legal concepts and conventions.[13] Like the story of Christopher Columbus and the egg, once illustrated, the necessity for total oceanic domination seems compelling and obvious, but in fact this vision has proven remarkably difficult for the strategist to realize. This may explain why none of our five naval challenges but the Soviet Navy came even close to contesting the oceanic control of American power.

The lesson for the Japanese grand strategist was that while sufficient military and economic power might strengthen the position of the empire in the Western Pacific, truly effective control over half an ocean translates almost automatically into mastery of all oceanic theatres of potential conflict (near land defences and chains of supply being the principal constraints). China's recent identification of the South China Sea as an 'area of core interest' and the development of its naval, air and cyber powers to 'deny access' to foreign naval power (i.e. the US Navy) has precise parallels in Japanese naval thinking during the first half of the twentieth century. The two East Asian regimes are manifestly different in many ways but the constraints at the heart of their grand strategic dilemmas bear close resemblance.[14]

In practice, Imperial Japan in the 1930s and 1940s discovered this truth just as China may rediscover it tomorrow. In other words, effective control of the Sea of Japan or the South China Sea demands the capability to dominate all sea lanes as the United States does today. Cyber-warfare against command and control centres hints at the mode of war implied. Otherwise one is forced into fighting asymmetric struggles in which some form of surprise attack to improve the odds at least temporarily becomes the predictable and repetitive threat to the global hegemon. Hence the logic of Admiral Nagumo's 'join the navy and see the world' air-raid tour of Hawaii, North Australia, Ceylon and south India in 1941–42. All practical Japanese considerations of what was involved in global domination found their touchstone in Nagumo's all-but-hopeless wartime exercise in defence as offence.

To the degree that al-Qaeda was acting strategically rather than symbolically, the 9/11 attacks on the command centres of American empire in New York and Washington reflect a similar logic and need. American power is so great that all warfare against it is inevitably 'asymmetric', and this makes 'surprise attacks' such as Pearl Harbor an endless temptation. Only overwhelming military power allows a nation threatened strategically to dismiss the 'sneak attack' as a morally dubious option, as the Kennedy Administration concluded during the Cuban Missile Crisis of 1962. To put the matter concisely, a successful programme of liberal hegemonic rule on a global scale solicits Pearl Harbors. It is the only option the weaker enemy has as long as global domination remains invulnerable to any other form of serious threat. The exception that proves this historical rule *in terms of grand strategy* is the unique triumph of Vietnam over the United States in 1975.

Notes

1 Quoted in Chalmers Johnson, *MITI and the Japanese Miracle*, Stanford, CA: Stanford University Press, 1982. Ishiwara later became a general, and Johnson calls him 'the chief economic architect of Manchukuo' (pp. 117–18).
2 Quoted in Sadao Asada, *From Mahan to Pearl Harbor: The Imperial Japanese Navy and the United States*, Annapolis, MD: Naval Institute Press, 2006, p. 197.
3 Johnson, *MITI and the Japanese Miracle*, op. cit.
4 For Nishitani's remarks, see Section III of *The Standpoint of World History and Japan*, p. 294–98.
5 Carl Schmitt, *Writings on War*, trans. and ed. Timothy Nunan, Cambridge, UK: Polity, 2011, pp. 77–78.
6 The orthodox position is based on some official records, some produced at a very high level, but some at best wishful thinking or designed for bureaucratic infighting over budgets, etc. Certainly the often cited documents of IMTFE or the Tokyo War Crimes Tribunal suggesting that *Sō-ryoku Kenkyū-kai* was envisaged as a sphere of Japanese influence that included India and Australia was entirely fanciful because the Navy never had the means or intent of achieving such a defence perimeter. Strategic calculations in naval circles in Tokyo and Washington were remarkably consistent on this point from 1907 onwards. See Sadao Asada, *From Mahan to Pearl Harbor: The Imperial Japanese Navy and the United States*, Annapolis, MD: Naval Institute Press, 2006.
7 For example, the documents on naval strategic planning found in the safe of the burnt-out office of Naval General Staff after the war are best read against the historical record as we find it in American and Japanese naval thinking from the Russo–Japanese War. On this subject, again, Asada is clear. One might also observe that first-hand experience of Japanese elite thinking and planning even after the war can be enormously helpful in understanding the import of official documents.
8 The relevant document is apparently titled 'Joint Army and Navy Basic War Plan – Red', and figures prominently in Floyd W. Rudmin, *Bordering on Aggression: Evidence of U.S. Military Preparations against Canada*, Bristol: Voyageur Publications, 1993.
9 For more about Lee's analysis, see David Williams, *Defending Japan's Pacific War: The Kyoto School Philosophers and Post-White Power*, London and New York: RoutledgeCurzon, 2004, p. 174.
10 In his *From Mahan to Pearl Harbor*, op. cit., Asada mentions two reports on p. 56: 'Economic Warfare and the Navy' and 'Preparations for a Protracted War'.
11 Ikuhiko Hata, 'Continental Expansion, 1905–41', in *The Cambridge History of Japan*, vol. 6, *The Twentieth Century*, ed. Peter Duus, Cambridge: Cambridge University Press, 1998, pp. 282–83.
12 The quotations from Richard Slotkin's *The Long War to Antietam: How the Civil War Became a Revolution* (Liveright, 2012) are taken from James M. McPherson's article 'A Bombshell on the American Public', *The New York Review of Books*, 22 November 2012, p. 20.

13 Poetically and mythically evoked in his *Land und Meer* of 1942. The conclusion of this book-length essay yields to a more realistic treatment of British naval power and the ideas of Mahon. Many of these insights are given more conventional expression in his *Der Nomos der Erde* of 1950.
14 See Ronald O'Rourke, 'China Naval Modernization: Implications for U.S. Navy Capabilities – Background and Issues', Kindle e-book edition. O'Rourke's text is dated 1 October 2010, and is issued by the Congressional Research Service, 7-5700 (www.crs.gov R33153).

10 Confucian tipping points
How East Asians make up their minds

> Ideas and products and messages and behaviours spread like viruses do.
> (Malcolm Gladwell[1])

> If Europeans have grown fearful of change, Japanese consciousness of world history reflects a formidable desire for change, that is the will to reform (*kakushin*), and thus remake the world.
> (Shigetaka Suzuki[2])

> In culture and at a given moment, there is never more than one episteme which defines the conditions of possibility of all knowledge.
> (Michel Foucault[3])

> Since present evils resulted from neglect of the Confucian model, their cure lay not in innovation but in the return to the ideal. Knowledge as technique was pure conformism.
> (John T. McAlister and Paul Mus[4])

The involvement of the Kyoto School in the factional struggles that so influenced wartime Japan is best understood within the context of a Confucian revolution: an act of elite insurgency or foreign occupation that recasts the life of the nation irreversibly by culminating in a Confucian tipping point.[5] Indeed, such Confucian revolutions are predictable and necessary features of the story of the peoples of East Asia – Japan's 1945 tipping point being a classic example – in ways that call the orthodox moral views of the liberal historian into rational doubt.

The East Asian way

In Chapter 9, the wartime Kyoto School thinker was reconceived as a grand strategist in order to present a more realistic picture of how the Japanese elite made sense of its defence options in the face of mounting US domination of the Pacific. Such domination is reasonably judged to be only part of Washington's pan-global consolidation of a liberal world order. In this chapter, the form and dynamic of Confucian revolution – as a pragmatic blend of political action, cultural psychology and traditional morality – will be examined more closely in order better to assess the kind of factional contest that the Kyoto School was waging. The Kyoto School's battle with the Tōjō clique as an episode in the unfolding of the Post-Meiji Confucian Revolution will be treated in the next chapter.

Two earlier Confucian tipping points inaugurated and gave direction to the Japanese encounter with modernity: the establishment of the Tokugawa regime after the battle of Sekigahara in 1600 and its replacement at the Meiji Restoration of 1868. A similar pattern of regime or mandatory change can be seen in other Confucian societies: China in 1644 and 1949, Vietnam in 1885 and 1975, and Korea in 1392, 1910, 1945, 1950 and 1951. As these examples show, sometimes the resulting alteration of regime is immediately and comprehensively successful; sometimes nationalist reaction to foreign conquest issues in a simmering calm punctuated by regular and often violent efforts to test the *toku* of the new mandate. Vietnam under French rule offers a useful example.

Examined more closely, two contrasting stages, the peaks and the valleys, define these contours of political change in Confucian societies: the peaceful and assured stability of the regime in the fullest possession of its *toku* versus the decisive, often brutal, interregnums between such moments of satisfying order and moral unanimity. Such an interregnum is a kind of domestic struggle or civil war that ends with a revolution that overthrows the previous regime. These civil wars are concluded in a practical and morally satisfying way only when one side wins conclusively.

All of America's wars with Confucian Asia have involved the liberal imperialist in taking sides in such civil wars: the Chinese Civil War, particularly in its final mainland phase between 1945 and 1949; the Korean Civil War that lay at the heart of the Korean conflict between 1950 and 1953; and the Vietnam Civil War, particularly during its final phase between 1965 and 1975. Only the Pacific War, the earliest of these US wars to transform the domestic circumstances of a Confucian society, saw success for American intervention, in this case in Japan's Post-Meiji Confucian Revolution. In none of these examples did the Orientalist or policy intellectual who sought to explain Asian politics to successive White House administrations demonstrate an appreciation of the true nature of Confucian revolutions because their expert powers of perception were blunted by moralism, patriotism or an American version of Eurocentrism.

The geopolitical consequences of this Orientalist and area studies failure colour regional politics to this day. Thus the United States continues to prevent the morally satisfactory conclusion to the Chinese Civil War by maintaining its defence commitments to Taiwan; frustrates the Korean hunger for national unity and moral consensus by refusing to allow this civil war to reach a natural, if geopolitically fraught, outcome; daydreams in defiance of the Japanese confidence that heaven's mandate will eventually issue in a regime controlled not by Americans today or the Chinese tomorrow but by the Japanese themselves. However, on the subject of Japan, no liberal illusions must be entertained. Post-war Japanese constitutional pacifism is the fruit of American conquest but also a hostage to America's staying regional staying power – or so Confucianism tells us.[6]

Just as the significance of these peaks and valleys in the dynastic or factional cycles has tended to elude us, so Westerners have repeatedly been caught off guard when these Confucian revolutions have taken their classic shape of a sudden, complete and unifying shift in public judgement at an obvious 'tipping point'. Such *tenkō* occurred in Japan in 1945, China in 1949, Korea in 1950 and Vietnam in 1975. It was a Confucian tipping point that was at work in the factional triumph that elevated Tōjō to premiership in 1941, that exploded in revolutionary anticipation with Ho Chi Minh's declaration of Vietnamese independence in 1945, and that might have redefined China in 1989 if the Tiananmen uprising had succeeded. One day it will happen in Korea when either the North or the South finally triumphs. It will happen when the People's Republic of China finally assumes control of Taiwan. It will happen in Japan on the day after the last US base is closed down. It is the way of the East Asian world.

Consistent with the East Asian pattern, political revolution in modern Japan is a struggle for national consensus in the Confucian mode. Two such revolutions are of particular importance to the ideas and politics of the wartime Kyoto School: the Meiji Restoration of 1868 and the Post-Meiji Confucian Revolution that unfolded between 1912 and the false dawn of 1940–42, only to be consummated in 1945. The Meiji Restoration has been studied in great detail, while the notion of a 'Post-Meiji Revolution' is an attempt to make sense of the eclipse of the Meiji consensus, the conflicting alternatives developed during the Taishō era (1912–26), and the final struggles to consolidate a new national consensus during the early Shōwa period (1926–42). A new harmony of opinion (although not a nationalist one) was finally achieved with the American war effort to make Japan a part of a new global liberal order by defeating, occupying and remaking aspects of the country in order to convert the Japanese into liberal subjects. In the process, Americans, again unbeknown to themselves, repeated many of the moral gestures of Confucianism when they imposed the corrective disciplines that characterize post-interregnum re-education campaigns.

Post-Meiji Confucian Revolution, as an inevitable struggle to establish a new consensus about the values, institutions and goals necessary for Japanese society to modernize further while retaining some plausible form of ethnic and cultural identity, forms the indispensable political context for any authoritative reading of the *Chūō Kōron* discussions. This was a nationalist Confucian quest (the contradiction is noted). Ethically, it is the Confucianism of this Confucian Revolution that allows us to interpret this context in Japanese terms. Area studies, and not just in the American imperialist mode, tend to be too vulnerable to the pressures of liberal moralism to be useful. Indeed, no Western method of philosophy or science may be rigorous enough to address the formidable difficulties at issue. Only the deep textualism of

Orientalism at its most rigorous reality can begin to cope with the scale of the task, and even here a leaven of experience of Asian life is required to achieve the depth of intellectual mastery demanded. So, pre-eminently, Asia must be our method because it is to Asian reality that we must *submit* intellectually if we are to appreciate what was Confucian about Confucian Japan.

Regime change in Confucian societies reflects the influence of shared non-Western values as manifested in non-Western patterns of behaviour. These repetitions have arisen through a subtle interplay of behaviour and text, so much so that one might conclude that in East Asia, 'society is the content of its own literature'.[7] The first step towards making sense of such patterns in order to test their empirical validity is, here as before, the bracketing of one's liberalism.

First-hand experience vs. arm-chair moralism

One of the first Europeans to recognize and make initial sense of what I call 'Confucian revolutions' was the great French Orientalist Paul Mus. He elaborated a Chinese context for his singular focus on political change in Vietnam, as manifested in that society's civil wars, which were also struggles of resistance and national liberation against French colonialism and American liberal imperialism. However, Mus's pioneering discovery was the product not of archival research nor yet of ethnological fieldwork but of wartime *experience*.

Indeed, it was only when encouraged by Mus's writings to draw on my own long experience of living among the Japanese that I was able to see the unmistakably Confucian logic at work in the *Chūō Kōron* symposia. What needs to be understood by the Western observer of Asian affairs is not just the timing of and stakes involved in one event or another but also, and more importantly, the form or pattern of moral conduct. Mus was transfixed by the sudden evaporation of French colonial legitimacy in Vietnamese eyes as manifested in the tumultuous events that unfolded in Hanoi in August–September 1945. The perverse but nevertheless telling Japanese analogy may be the role of the attack on Pearl Harbor in *confirming* Tōjō's hold on his mandate to rule. Ironically, it was the Imperial Navy success in Hawaii that all but sealed the new Japanese consensus, emotionally if not quite rationally. Different as Vietnam and Japan as societies are, the central methodological lesson remains that the Western observer's experience of living in East Asia rather than library research or armchair study has proven decisive to putting Confucianism in its proper context. Of all the Western sciences, anthropology comes closest to providing the proper orientation for such experience, but involvement in the life of the East Asian community may finally be more conclusive than mere observation.

It is experience that taught Mus that the East Asian peasant is almost instantly alert to any sign of 'regime death' signalled by battlefield defeat or drastic administrative failure, just as my experience of Japanese student struggle in the late 1960s educated me in the psychology and morality of Confucian conformism as a response to shifts in political power. Whenever the ruling faction of a state or organization falters in any fundamental way, doubts immediately arise about the soundness of the mandate holder's insight into reality. This also explains the pattern of secrecy and denial of uncomfortable facts that characterize organizations across East Asia.

How is such logic relevant to the Pacific War? When Tōjō assumed the premiership and won official confirmation from court and cabinet for the decision for war, he demonstrated his hold on the secularized, non-dynastic version of the mandate of heaven. He therefore exercised his office legitimately, confident that the great bulk of the population accepted his position within the structure of governance of Imperial Japan as proper. Retrospective doubts about Tōjō from the vantage of liberal moralism or Confucian pacifism must not be allowed to obscure the fact that Tōjō's exercise of power as prime minister between 1941 and 1944 was legitimate. His authority only came into serious question when his policies began obviously to fail.

At the same time, however, Tōjō's position remained vulnerable to *elite* challenge despite the legitimate nature of his government because of persistent doubts about the soundness of his factional programme for national renewal. Too many members of the Japanese establishment continued to doubt whether the Pacific War was winnable (in any sense). The original unpublished transcripts of the discussions that became the *Chūō Kōron* symposia apparently aired such scepticism in overt form. The edited version that appeared in print in January 1942 made the same case but by indirection. Tōjō's legitimacy mandated such caution because open dissent became even more illegitimate after official endorsement of the decision for war.

Such intellectual resistance explains the Tōjō government's sometimes desperate efforts to bully, cajole and seduce sceptical members of the Japanese elite into toeing the official line or risk arrest or imprisonment. However, the greater threat was posed not by elite criticism but by the danger that the non-elite majority of Japanese society might shift, en masse, from enthusiastic support for the war effort to the 'wait and see' posture (the default Confucian stance when things begin to go wrong). The elaborate and finally futile efforts to disguise the scale of the chain of military reversals that began with Midway issued from the same fear. From the end of 1944 until the summer of 1945, 'wait and see' became the predictable response of broad sections of Japanese society to the American bombing campaign and the mounting threat of foreign invasion. Once the emperor signalled that some form of regime change was now unavoidable, the entire nation began to move to the new embrace, not of defeat, but of the new order of foreign rule.

Confucian tipping points are often so sudden and definitive that one is tempted to ignore the fact that mandatory change is often long in the making. We need a more detailed understanding of the process of gestation that prepares the ground for the sudden transformations of Confucian politics in Vietnam or, more interesting still, the 'zigzag' pattern displayed by public attitudes as repeated *tenkō* is performed. In the Japanese case, the consequences of the unravelling of the Meiji consensus were not resolved for three decades, but the larger point remains the revelatory character of experience. Mus's experience of Asian reality enabled him to see beyond the limits of seminar theorizing and Whig history as an exercise in counterfactual moral judgements.

'Après moi, le teenager'

Any *mission civilisatrice* offers a method to finesse the problems that arise when one culture dominates another. The superior culture erases the discrepancies between the metropolitan civilization and the target culture by a programme of value assimilation, often carried out with missionary zeal. How much easier the proposition of invading, controlling and administrating Vietnam from Paris became when the local population started converting from Buddhism to Catholicism.

Today, consumer capitalism as a form of 'soft power' plays a comparable role in the shaping of a liberal imperialist global order. 'Soft power' is the perfect complement to 'hard power' because liberal imperialism needs to exercise both forms of influence to secure America's global hegemony. Strangely, Joseph S. Nye, the originator of the term 'soft power', is manifestly uncomfortable with the fact of American empire;[8] however, soft power and hard power cannot, in Martin Jacques's phrase, 'be treated as separate compartments as Nye argues'.[9] Clearer on the subject in his famous essay on 'the end of history', Francis Fukuyama acknowledged that the victory of liberal capitalism over communism was facilitated as much by America's gift for the design, production and distribution of mass-market high technology as by the attractiveness of certain forms of liberty or the demonstrated effectiveness of democratic institutions.[10]

Certainly the crisis in financial markets and state borrowing (sovereign debt) that broke with the collapse of Lehman Brothers in 2008 has made every thoughtful East Asian more aware of the stakes involved in the debt-driven economics of mass consumption for the future of our neo-liberal economic order. Thus, the 'liberal flattening' of Japan and the rest of East Asia requires that the formerly illiberal subject help legitimate the new liberal order not only via positive participation in the processes and institutions of democracy, but also as consumers of a form of modernity informed by liberal or quasi-liberal values and notions of economic activity.

This imperative feeds the grand strategic significance of web-based virtual hobbies such as 'Second Life' or 'Spanx' shapeware in South Korea. Western advertising provides other striking examples of how our cultural assumptions inform the way such 'soft power' exercises its marketing magic. The post-Confucian subversion at work in contemporary promotion-video *chinoiserie* provides us with a kind of virtual experience of the contemporary clash of civilizations that informs the latest chapter in the cross-cultural struggle for 'hearts and minds'. And wallets.

In 2005 Alberto-Culver, more recently part of the Unilever Group, produced a television and web advertisement with a Chinese theme for one of its hair gel products. The tale unfolds in a grimly spartan secondary school, apparently in the People's Republic, where a frowning uniformed female teacher of a certain age monitors and lectures a group of Chinese teenagers, also dressed in uniform grey. While the harridan holds forth, a handsome Chinese male student opens his folding desk-top and signals to an equally good-looking female student that he has brought his secret cache of hair gel to class (he has hidden some for her in her desk). He proceeds to apply it, and the female student follows suit. The new hair shape comes with a hint of surly attitude. Trouble is inevitable. In the final scene, the outraged teacher is shown pursuing the trendily coiffured students from the school as they run laughingly to freedom, the triumph of fashionable Western consumerism complete. The ad's slogan: 'Break the mould.'

The happy ending, with its embrace of Western individualism at the expense of Chinese communist regimentation, is predictable because so attractive to the liberal-minded Westerner, but how would a Confucian conclude the ad? Only two scenarios are likely. If Western values are judged to be the more practically powerful, the final scene would show the teacher back in her classroom but with her hair gelled, and all her students similarly transformed. The second scenario would conclude where we began in a repeat of the original classroom scene, with the teacher in charge but no offending hair gel in sight.

Confucian happy endings celebrate the restoration of moral unanimity because 'the Way is one'. The very last thing that can be contemplated, let alone embraced, is 'breaking the mould'. This would be to turn one's back on everything that is moral and decent, rational and practical. Given the Confucian veneration of age, it is predictable which of the two Confucian versions of this hair gel ad is likely to prove to be the more morally satisfying to the thoughtful East Asian. If one wants to understand how East Asians make up their minds, there are worse places to begin than to return once more to the dynamics of group decision-making.

Turning on a sixpence

EAST Asians are human beings, and argue much like the rest of us, but Confucianism at once shapes and restrains how they comport themselves in the social realm. The outward signs of this shaping and restraint include formalized respect for the sensitivities of self and others, a moral weakness for the practical, deference to maturity and the urge to reach a shared view or consensus. At its most demanding, it makes consensus relatively easier to achieve in East Asian societies because the pursuit of truth is entirely practical (never abstract or utopian or morally absolutist). This is a search for what is manifestly the best and therefore the preferred way of achieving one goal or another. In this way, Confucians trump the liberal's obsession with formalistic pluralism; however much individuals may differ in the preferences about how things should be done, there is finally only one best way to which all Confucians will subscribe because it is the most practical.

The only major exception to this Confucian obligation to comply with a manifestly good consensus is found in the defence of ethnic identity and national sovereignty, but here too collective identity is conceived as community in which best practice must prevail. Otherwise all forms of dissent are a kind of symbolic or literal death: silence, exile or suicide. In other words, the architecture of Confucian thought consists of a set of pillars or rhetorical strategies that aim not so much to convince East Asians how they should behave as to educate them in the reasons why they behave in a certain way.

So what happens in a Confucian society when the consensus about what faction should exercise legitimate authority is called into question? This represents the core dilemma in the Japanese inter-war debate over national defence, particularly within the middle ranks of the Imperial Army and Navy. As Confucian communities and organizations move from one agreed form of unanimity to another, the ruling discourse exhibits a consistent character, one that bears an uncanny resemblance to Western discourses as Michel Foucault defined them: 'In culture and at a given moment, there is never more than one episteme which defines the conditions of possibility of all knowledge.' This applies in Confucian societies, where there is in practice never more than one episteme that legitimates the power and morality of a system of rule (*toku*) at any one time because one and only one episteme is supremely practical. However, should the episteme be legitimate in this way, if it succeeds, then everyone will willingly submit to its authority. Such compliance will be, in the unfolding of the ideal type, total and immediate (*tadachi ni*): 'The moment the wind shifts, and if it all goes for the best, the whole society changes from unanimity to unanimity.'[11] The entire nation turns, as it were, on a sixpence. Or a dime.

Pace Karl Löwith's famous objection that 'The Orient does not endure the kind of inconsiderate critique, either of itself or of others, in which all European progress is grounded'; criticism plays a cardinal role in the build-up to such moments of revolutionary change as well as in the immediate aftermath of the passing of heaven's mandate into fresh hands.[12] The job of criticism is to reveal that virtue has departed from a system of governance. Language becomes a form of political action because *toku* and the 'system of rule' are so tightly interwoven by the Confucian mind as to be tautological. After the moment of regime change, the role of the critic is to expose the errors of the old regime in a manner that prevents any return to the mistaken beliefs of the past. When the wind to which the small man intuitively bends begins to blow, every East Asian becomes a critic.

What Foucault calls 'the conditions of the possibility of all knowledge' are never at stake at such moments. These conditions are at once universal and unchanging, the very substance of Confucian moral order, which lays down the tramlines for regime change but stands above all such change. This complex dynamic is what sets East Asia apart from the world's other great civilizations. It provides the indispensable trope for understanding the discourse of Confucian criticism and the indispensable role such criticism plays in the drama of violent regime change. The irony is that Löwith did not perceive that he was in fact, while in Sendai during the latter half of the 1930s, witnessing the moment of pending consolidation of power by a new factional mandate holder in Japanese life, the key phase of a Confucian revolution in which the criticism falls mute and a new consensus is being proclaimed. It was at this crucial phase in the process of building and enforcing a national consensus that the Kyoto School decided to act against Tōjō.

To intervene as late in this struggle as the Kyoto School did meant that it had to accept the emerging broad consensus on the country's strategic plight and its ever-shortening list of remedies. This was the only route to moral credibility for a potential rival to an ascendant faction within the dominant force of Japanese politics that was the Imperial Army. So, in ways that confound the liberal critic, the Kyoto School's late battle was confined to tactics and constrained by timing. In short, by the late 1930s it was too late to make an effective ideological challenge to the moral consensus that bolstered the cause of what became the ruling Tōjō clique.

The Marxist *tenkō*

This sharp narrowing of the ideological horizon of early Shōwa Japan also explains why the class-based ideological offensive of Marxism crumbled so quickly. In essence, 'progressive politicians' allowed themselves to fall behind the tide of ideological change; they appeared to the Japanese public to have lost touch with reality. Perhaps they ignored the pressures to comply with the new consensus longer than was prudent out of loyalty to the Comintern and foreign philosophies such as Marxism. Such 'dangerous ideas' (*kiken shisō*) were harmful, in the first instance, not to the *kokutai* or national polity but to the individual himself as part of a Confucian society where each and every thinking adult is obliged to attend to changes in the country's real circumstances.

To embrace foreign ideas as unquestionably sound was in practical terms potentially immoral because such ideas made left-wing politicians less sensitive to the rapid pace of ideological consolidation that is the characteristic feature of all Confucian Revolutions in their final phase. Certainly after the failure of the 1936 coup attempt, the apparent success of more moderate factions within the Imperial Army prepared the ground for the final version of the new mandatory (in both senses) national consensus. Events were overtaking potential opponents of the nascent new regime: liberal, Marxist, Kyoto School, Imperial Navy, Konoe's elite faction or any other. Therefore, the more astute members of so-called left in Japan opted for prompt, total and sincere *tenkō* to demonstrate their renewed responsiveness to public moral expectations lest they cease to be credible participants in wartime Japan's unfolding Confucian Revolution.

The very narrowness of the new rules of political engagement inevitably coloured all resistance to Tōjō's assumption of the premiership. This is why Ōhashi describes the Kyoto School's status within the Japanese elite during the final phase of the Post-Meiji Confucian Revolution as an anti-establishment branch of the establishment that pursued a subversive form of war cooperation (*hantai-sei-teki na sensō kyōku*).[13] The Kyoto School was subversive because in this struggle it lent its energies and ideas to the anti-Tōjō peace faction. This was a practical if personally risky political option; Marxist insurgency was not.

Having turned on a sixpence: Kōji Eizawa criticizes the Kyoto School

Reluctantly or otherwise, Tōjō effectively seized the mandate of legitimate rule during the course of 1941. He forced through the decision for war (the wisdom of which was confirmed by the content of the Hull Ultimatum), pressed the Navy into executing a logistical miracle at Pearl Harbor, and presided over the greatest ever triumph of Japanese arms in the spring of 1942. Tōjō thus achieved a kind of resolution of the Japanese domestic impasse with what appeared, on more than one front, to be a genuine Confucian revolution. This brought an end to the long interregnum that traced its roots back to the last years of the Meiji era. However, Tōjō's moment of glory was short-lived, its end heralded by the military reverses that began in June 1942. Less than three and a half years later, Japan was compelled to turn on a sixpence when the United States assumed the new mandate of heaven by triumphing in the Pacific War.

With this dramatic transformation in Japan's place in the world, from the status of great power to that of an American protectorate, all the values identified with the previous regime (if not the framework of change itself) were called into severe question. The new orthodoxy – Confucian pacifism – had no time for the old verities. War was renounced at the behest at Japan's new masters. Only the residual claims of national identity and the faith that Japan would not be ruled forever by foreigners linked the new dispensation with old in Japanese minds. The new dispensation and the regime based on it has survived despite a variety of challenges since 1945.

In the field of national history, Confucian pacifists have since the end of the Pacific War produced a rich vein in Asian moral history or history as moral narrative and critique. In *'Dai Tōa Kyōeiken' no Shisō* ('The Great East Asian Co-prosperity Sphere' as Thought), Kōji Eizawa provides an instructive case study in how such moral critiques redefine the labours of the professional historian. Indeed, his book could not be more germane, because he takes as his target the wartime Kyoto School, particularly the contribution of Iwao

90   Kyoto School and Post-Meiji Confucian Revolution

Kōyama to the *Chūō Kōron* discussions.[14] The contagion of judgement that so colours Eizawa's book is wholly dependent on the Confucian notion, nowhere mentioned in his text, that Japan turned on its axis in 1945, moving dramatically from one form of intellectual and moral unanimity to another with a very different character as a result of American conquest.

This Confucian version of what might be called a type of paradigm revolution imposes an exact but very un-Western interpretive schema on Eizawa. This schema encourages him to understand Kōyama's writings – and, for that matter, the entire wartime output of the Kyoto School – as part and parcel of a larger discourse in which a uniformity of ideology and vocabulary can be assumed for purposes of moral critique. Consistent with the notion that 'the Way is one', Eizawa takes his reader abruptly from the moral unanimity of the wartime era, now judged irreversibly *passé* and immoral because impractical, to post-war renegotiation of moral unanimity as a form of pacifism (America, the indispensable deus ex machina or agent of this change, is never mentioned). For Eizawa, as for any other Confucian, only the content of the mandate alters, the completeness of the difference between 'before' and 'after' being *de rigueur* if it is to qualify as a total and therefore persuasive rupture with what has gone before.

In Eizawa's view, the wartime ideology of his country was composed of a set of ideas and ideological slogans. His list is long but not exhaustive, ranging from predictable notions such as *Dai Tōa* (Greater East Asia), linked to *Kyōeiken* (Co-prosperity Sphere), *sōryoku sen* (total war), *ijōki* (state of emergency), *sōdōin* (general mobilization), *Ajia kaihō* (the liberation of Asia), *kaizō* (the restructuring of society) and *shinchitsujō genri* (the new order and its principles), to such apparently specifically Japanese concerns as *Hakkō Ichiu* (the whole world under one roof), the *ie* (the family, both Confucian and the State Shinto versions), *genjō dapa* (breaking out of the present) and *shisō-sen* (wars of ideas). Eizawa also considers ideas and slogans that have been less prominent in Western interpretations of the Pacific War, such as *uchinaru eibei* (the Anglo-America within, that is, internalized values of liberal modernity). Finally, Eizawa's list includes some notions that are particularly important to the *Chūō Kōron* symposia: the Hegelian idea of *rekishiteki ishiki* (historical consciousness), *shidō genri* (principles of Japanese leadership of others) and *sono tokoro o eshimeru* (a place in the sun and each people knowing its own place, something to be jealously guarded).

What guarantees the coherence and seamless character of so large and diverse a list? In Eizawa's mind all these ideas and slogans firmly hang together, so much so that the use of any one by an intellectual, a politician and a bureaucrat allows him to conclude that the three figures share the same ideological outlook. Eizawa nowhere explains how this system holds together, but he takes it as axiomatic that it does. He therefore feels no need to engage in an examination of first principles or methodology. There is no necessity for such critical apparatus because the coherence of this ideology is manifest and beyond question morally. Eizawa's critique of the Kyoto School is an exercise in Confucian common sense. This in turn makes it all but impossible for someone working within the moral paradigm to make sense of the ideas of the old order except as an object of denunciation.

Before we attempt to explain why Eizawa believes so firmly that the coherence of ideas is obvious, let us attempt to explain how this approach to Japanese intellectual history might convince. For Eizawa's moral critique to succeed as a schema of interpretation, each of the ideas is taken to be univocal – that is, each idea has one and only one meaning. So each time this wartime academic or that journalist uses the expression 'Greater East Asian Co-prosperity Sphere' or 'the war of ideas' or 'the family', Eizawa takes it for granted that the writers or speakers in question mean the same thing.

Taken as a whole, this constellation of ideas functions much like the spokes of a wheel. They form a flawed totality that qualifies as a totality not because Japan embraced some form of fascism or totalitarianism but because politics, ancient and modern, is governed by the pursuit of moral unanimities. It is not the moral-minded conscience that performs that act of ethical judgement, as in Whig history, but the spirit of the age. Any historian who attempts to understand the ideas of the wartime Kyoto School *objectively* is engaged, therefore, in a futile and suspect effort to resurrect a *passé* ideology that by definition cannot tell us anything worth knowing about the past. However, it also follows that the Confucian pacifist as a historian has *nothing* to contribute to the objective understanding of the history of ideas in Japan between 1931 and 1945. Quite the contrary: the very notion of reconstructing the viewpoint of the wartime period is, from a Confucian vantage, not so much stupid or evil as pointless. Eizawa's standpoint is therefore entirely consistent with Confucian need and purpose, but it prompts one crucial question: is such moral history, history?

Notes

1 Malcolm Gladwell, *The Tipping Point: How Little Things Can Make a Big Difference*, London: Abacus, 2000, p. 7.
2 See 'A reading of the complete text of the *Chūō Kōron* symposia', first symposium, 1, 'Why world history has become the problem of our era', p. 110–14.
3 Michel Foucault, *Les Mots et Les Choses*, Paris: Gallimard, 1966, p. 179. Quoted in David Macey, *The Lives of Michel Foucault*, London: Vintage, 1994, p. 163.
4 John T. McAlister, Jr and Paul Mus, *The Vietnamese and their Revolution*, New York, Evanston and London: Harper Torchbooks, 1970, p. 36.
5 Confucian 'tipping points' are culturally contoured canonically inflected modes of behaviour, whereas Gladwell's 'tipping points' are spontaneous forms of conformist behaviour understood by reference to scientific analogies such as the spread of infectious diseases.
6 These conclusions follow on two articles that I contributed to *The Left in the Shaping of Japanese Democracy: Essays in Honour of J. A. A. Stockwin*, ed. with Rikki Kersten, London and New York: Routledge, 2006: 'The Japanese Evasion of Sovereignty: Article 9 and the European Canon – Hobbes, Carl Schmitt, Foucault,' and 'After Abu Ghraib: American Empire, the Left-Wing Intellectual and Japan Studies.'

7 McAlister and Mus, *The Vietnamese and their Revolution*, op. cit., p. 32.
8 Joseph F. Nye, *Soft Power: The Means to Success in World Politics*, New York: Public Affairs, 2004.
9 Martin Jacques, 'The Beginning of a New World Order', *New Statesman*, 23 April 2012, p. 24.
10 Francis Fukuyama, 'The End of History?' *The National Interest*, Summer 1989, pp. 3–18.
11 Frances FitzGerald, *Fire in the Lake: The Vietnamese and the Americans in Vietnam*, Boston & Toronto: Atlantic Little Brown, 1972, p. 28.
12 Karl Löwith, 'Afterword to the Japanese Reader', in *Martin Heidegger and European Nihilism*, ed. Richard Wolin, trans. Gary Steiner, New York and Chichester, West Sussex: Columbia University Press, 1995, pp. 228–34, quotation on p. 233.
13 Ryōsuke Ōhashi, *Kyōto-gakuha to Nippon Kaigun: Shin Shinryō 'Ōshima Memos' o Megutte* (The Kyoto School and the Japanese Navy: On the New Historical Documents: The 'Ōshima Memos'), Tokyo: PHP, 2001, p. 21.
14 Kōji Eizawa, *'Dai Tōa Kyōeiken' no Shisō* ('The Greater East Asian Co-prosperity Sphere' as Thought), Tokyo: Kōdan-sha, 1995.

11 Plotting to bring Tōjō down
The Post-Meiji Confucian Revolution and the Kyoto School-Imperial Navy conspiracy

> The principles and vocabulary of China's history are centred on the idea of a rivalry for power with Heaven as the arbiter ... This was a game of destiny. The stakes are territorial power, and each one placed his bet on a dynastic faction.
>
> (John T. McAlister and Paul Mus[1])

> There was a large area of agreement between the ultranationalists and others who were less willing to resort to extremist measures. And internally the ultranationalist movement represented a complicated picture of personal and regional cliques whose standards and objectives shifted frequently in response to the dictates of opportunism.
>
> (Ryusaku Tsunoda, William de Bary and Donald Keene[2])

> To understand Japanese history and culture, it is essential to realize that no government ever united the whole country until the Meiji Restoration of 1868. The imperial government had always ruled the whole of the land in theory, but never in fact. The imperial house had never really been more than a centre of powerful factions.
>
> (Thomas Cleary[3])

> Vietnam's traditional values have been inadequate to organize the power to sustain a modern government unifying all Vietnamese within one nation. Unity by itself, of course, carries no certainty that there will be an end to factional struggles for power.
>
> (John T. McAlister and Paul Mus[4])

Between the death of the Meiji emperor in 1912 and the beginning of the American Occupation in 1945, Japan found itself trapped in an interregnum during which a factional struggle for power was fought over what kind of society it should be and how it should be governed. Although Japan was more modern and advanced than other Confucian societies, the issues that defined this interregnum were common across East Asia: how to balance the aspirations of the mainly poor and rural majority with the expectations of the wealthier urban minority; how to overcome the manifest limits of an influential set of traditional values with an effective form of modernity that was recognizably Asian; and how the nation was to assume a proper place in international society that preserved Japanese autonomy and its ability to act independently on the regional stage. This struggle came closest to conclusive Confucian resolution with the triumph of the faction of the Imperial Army and its civilian allies associated with Hideki Tōjō, only for this revolutionary mandate to be overturned by American intervention in what in reality was a domestic Japanese conflict.

Such Confucian interregna are battles of ideas (*shisō-sen*), and the Kyoto School played its part in this struggle. Coming to national prominence at the very end of the Meiji period, Nishida and his handful of philosophy students initially adhered to the Meiji paradigm of intellectual Westernization, but as the Taishō mandate was inherited, not won (and therefore not secure because not legitimated), the Kyoto School became involved in the examination of new values to renew Japanese society in preparation for a fresh mandate. As this factional struggle drew to its close at the end of the 1930s, the more violent episodes of factional strife were replaced by a narrow but increasingly pervasive consensus within the Japanese elite about who would rule and why.

During the final phase of this struggle before Tōjō's triumph, the Kyoto School bolstered the camp of Prime Minister Konoe, for example by supporting the Shōwa Kenkyū-kai (Shōwa Research Association), in an effort to prevent Tōjō's faction from coming to power. When Tōjō secured the premiership to pursue his programme of domestic reform and resistance to America, his authority became legitimate in ways that forced the Kyoto philosopher as an intellectual in the public sphere to take his struggle partially underground. The Kyoto School remained confident that Tōjō's grand strategy would ultimately fail because it was fatally flawed. It was an inadequate reading of reality. This judgement explains why these thinkers opted to support a faction of the Imperial Navy, in public ways as well as covertly, in conspiratorial anticipation of a further chapter of factional struggle that would issue in a lasting national settlement. This chapter examines the form and timing of such Confucian revolutions while explaining why liberal historians have had such difficulty in accepting how such factional struggles are fought and why these contests are *normal, legitimate* and *moral*.

The text of texts

The archive presents the researcher with a historical record composed of texts. The Orientalist, political scientist, historian of ideas and literary scholar may seek different things from their textual explorations, but one feature of this *exercise of will* tends to colour all the rest: the intentions and outlook of the researcher. It is the researcher who animates the process of gathering and selecting texts which are otherwise judged to be inert and voiceless. The text thus tends to serve the interpretive purpose of the researcher, freeing the scholar to ignore the unethical, incomprehensible or merely uncomfortable messages that text may present. This is the predictable consequence when the priorities of the Western researcher, our world-view and our interpretive needs, give direction to these explorations of the realm of fact at the expense of Asian reality.

The resistant quality of the *Chūō Kōron* transcripts figures so prominently in the discourse of the Pacific War because they force the Western reader to confront the impact of Confucianism on *modern* Japanese life. This text also functioned as a vortex for the literary output of the Kyoto School while dramatizing the world-order conflicts that dominated its wartime horizon. All these factors tend to reverse the flow of influence from the Western researcher to the Oriental text. Thus these symposia come to leave their stamp on us, and not – as in liberal history – the other way around. In the Orient, the text leads the historian because the truth of the text comes into being at the precise moment when the text pursues its own ideas – for the Oriental text does not have the same ideas as I do. The consequence is the triumph of Asian reality over Western interpretive expectations. As the mental world of the Asian thinker comes to the fore, we begin to hear the authentic voice of the individual Asian as a person and a political actor. In this manner, Asia becomes our method.

Armed with the truth of this Japanese text, we may proceed to peel away the mystifying fictions of Marxist, liberal and pacifist prejudice and propaganda about other Kyoto School texts. This in turn encourages revisionism about the major interpretive statements concerning the ideological character of the wartime Kyoto School, not only as politics but also as philosophy. Thus this tiny tear or burn in the fabric of the vast textual discourse generated by the Pacific War, this otherwise small scorch hole, spreads, threatening to consume the entire material substance of the interpretive and moral judgements of the liberal imperialist and Confucian pacifist alike. In this way the true nature of the clash of wills between the Kyoto School and the Tōjō clique, between the Imperial Navy and the Imperial Army, is revealed. The claims of moral judgement begin to falter *empirically* before the hitherto neglected or belittled arguments of the Asian participants in the *Chūō Kōron* symposia and its best-informed Asian interpreters, the people such as Ōshima who transcribed and edited some of our texts, and then commented upon them with an eye to posterity.

Men on horseback and the Post-Meiji Confucian Revolution

Why were the Tōjō clique and the Kyoto School at loggerheads over grand strategy? Policy formed, as we saw in Chapter 9, the substance of the dispute: how to develop the Greater East Asian Co-prosperity Sphere, when and how to resist pressure to submit to the new liberal global order, and how to push through the next stage of Japanese modernization. The stakes in this contest of political wills included control of policy making, achieved by influencing the intellectual assumptions behind these policies. The ensuing battle for discourse hegemony sought to clarify and reinforce these choices.

The way the Kyoto School sought to prevail in this contest was to make every effort to ensure the victory, after Tōjō's seizure of power, of the Yonai faction and its allies over their rivals within the Japanese elite. This is what the Kyoto School sought to achieve, as a 'brains trust', by providing these Imperial Naval officers with practical policy advice and grand strategy wrapped in a visionary narrative of Japanese national greatness achieved via a programme of cooperation and integration with East Asia as a whole. In this way, the Kyoto School played for the highest stakes in what was in fact an unfolding revolution in Japanese society: a struggle governed by the logic and conventions of dynastic succession to the mandate of heaven in the traditional Confucian manner, but one also influenced by modern institutions, needs and dangers.

When we attempt to understand revolutions and regime change in East Asian societies, we must begin with a precise grasp of the traditional patterns of faction-driven dynastic change as well as a nuanced appreciation of how these often largely agricultural societies responded to these political campaigns to spark revolution. What is the nature of the logic of Confucian expectations? The canonical master statements of the ethical psychology at work in such struggles are found in *The Analects* and *Mencius*:

> The virtue of the gentleman is like the wind; the virtue of the small man like the grass. Let the wind blow over the grass and it is sure to bend.
> (*The Analects*, XII, 19)

For our purposes, the 'gentlemen' in this quote refer to the Japanese elite. It is the burden and glory of the elite to govern; the peasant's role in Confucian politics is not to make policy or revolution but to signal distress, bear witness to the impact of changes in social reality, benefit from good government and affirm the new order when it arrives. The gentleman acts; the peasant mirrors reality, and then waits and judges. Elite factions struggle for the crown of legitimacy that will reduce their rivals to illegitimate insurgents. The spirit of the Peace Preservation Law of 1925 drew on this Confucian heritage and logic. Although indispensable to any Confucian system of governance, dissent has no *final* legal rights. In this tradition, rights are a matter of demonstrated power rather than legal form because Confucian authority as authority is legitimate *by its very nature*.

When counter-elites mount a challenge to legitimate authority, they knowingly wager against the odds, hoping that fortune will favour them because they know something vital about reality to which the powers that be have proven blind. Tōjō and his clique misconstrued Japan's strategic options, but so did quasi-liberals such as Shidehara, as well as the likes of 'moderate' appeasers such as Admiral Tomosaburō Katō. The Tōjō government as a Confucian regime proposed an unworkable mix of policies to address Japan's strategic plight. This failure explains why the Kyoto School supported Admiral Yonai and the Imperial Navy in the struggle to force Prime Minister Tōjō to relinquish his hold on the levers of *legitimate* authority.

Making sense of Confucian revolutions

What does the Orientalist bring to the social scientific effort to understand such revolutions? The answer is an unrivalled philological and practical awareness of the interaction of Confucian canonical texts and patterns of East Asian behaviour. Teasing out the interplay between traditional values and the demands of modern life in the Vietnamese struggle for independence and a modern state, McAlister makes clear that Paul Mus traced the development of the patterns of behaviour involved in these struggles to force regime change back to the Chou dynasty. In East Asian tradition, factional struggles for power predate both Confucianism and the establishment of imperial dynastic rule. The behavioural facts precede the genesis of the canon, but the canon confirms and fixes the pre-existing habits of conduct, thus helping them to persist and become habitual: hence the pattern. The mandate of heaven as a doctrine seeks to tame the violence of these struggles by strengthening the legitimacy of the victor with expectations of benevolent rule.

A variant of this tradition of war-as-revolution factionalism has continued to shape patterns of political struggle for ultimate power in East Asia even after the passing of the monarchy in China, Korea and Vietnam. The interaction of the peasant mass and the revolutionary elite is the central dynamic. Peasant support was indispensable to the Confucian revolutions orchestrated by Ho Chi Minh and Mao Ze Dong in 1945 and 1949. Douglas MacArthur benefited from the same dynamic in 1945, although he appears to have had little idea why the Japanese people *as a whole* yielded so completely and unresistingly. In all three cases, revolution marks a total symbolic and programmatic break with the failed past, but nevertheless such regime change unfolds within the Confucian framework, as society moves from one unanimity to another.

The suggestion that the Japanese would shift almost instantly from the military compulsions that obsessed national life from Perry's intrusion in 1853 to Truman's liberal war of annihilation only to swing to a passionate embrace of pacific democracy surprises no one in East Asia who accepts that Confucianism normally trumps nationalism when a tipping point is reached. Or, to put the matter more carefully, the content of the change was cause for surprise; the form and the timing of the change were entirely predictable. The only people caught completely off guard by this revolutionary transformation were Western liberal observers of the Japanese scene.

Liberal scholarship on modern history has consistently failed to grasp the nature of the sometimes violent transformation of Japanese politics from the late 1920s onwards because it has neglected to consider Confucian patterns of behaviour. The Taishō experiment ended in failure because it had manifestly lost its *toku*. In any case, its grasp was never that secure. Therefore a new vision of society that would serve as the basis for a programme of political reform and renewal was essential. Taking the longer view, it can be argued that the Taishō period fulfilled its transient role as a time for testing many of the ideologies proposed for reordering Japanese national life. Both interpretations assume that a programme of change embodying a symbolic and substantive departure from the immediate past must appear to be 'total' to be comprehensible to Japan's peasant mass. The programme had to be sufficiently analogous in scale and potential effectiveness to be plausibly compared to the Meiji Restoration rejection of Tokugawa values, proclaimed as a complete rejection of the feudal past. It also had to inspire the kind of revolutionary upsurge that drove Japanese politics until this Confucian revolution lost its *toku* by defeat in war.

Pace liberal sympathies and pacifist ethics, violence has a natural and predictable role in Confucian revolutions, which inevitably produce winners and losers. Those whose interests are threatened often stand and fight. Thus the old guard may struggle to defend the decaying order. Over and over again in East Asian history, cliques or dynastic loyalists have proven recalcitrant, obtuse or uncomprehending in the face of the realities of a new political order, and when they do, these loyalists expose themselves to physical attack from the mandatory challenger. The old regime will return the favour as long as it is able, but the rising force knows that this opposition must be deflected, marginalized or crushed if its claim as a new mandate holder is to win legitimacy.

Persuasion as the goal and force is only a means, because the final objective is the birth of broad harmony of opinion. This is best achieved by elite and mass *tenkō*, but in the dynamics of political transformations such as the Post-Meiji Confucian Revolution, the forces of dynastic renovation must demonstrate their *powers of compulsion* if they are to be plausible holders and protectors of a new mandate. Confucian societies will not readily yield to the obviously weak, indecisive or cowardly mandate seeker, but even when the challenger who seeks to seize the mandate from its current holder is manifestly courageous and committed, he must exhibit the qualities of resolution and determination to fight, win and rule. The weak cannot rule, and this Confucian insight may explain the 'wait-and-see' stance on the part of the Chinese public that contributed to the failure of the Tiananmen Square uprising.

Despite the traditional Confucian suspicion of warriors, regime change in Japan has frequently involved what S.E. Finer called 'a man on horseback'.[5] The most important names of mandatory revolutionaries include Ieyasu Tokugawa, Hideki Tōjō and Douglas MacArthur. Given Japan's long martial tradition of fighting rulers, the prominent role of military men in the leadership of Imperial Japan should not have surprised any informed observer of the modern Japanese scene. However, only Confucianism could have shaped a mandatory revolution that resulted in the complete disappearance of such military figures from Japanese political life after 1952.

Timing and form in Confucian revolutions

The orthodox interpretation of Japanese politics from the death of the Meiji emperor in 1912 to the imposition of the American Occupation in 1945 has tended to focus on the *content* of the contending ideologies in question at the expense of the issues of the *form* and *timing* of such Confucian revolutions. The rubric of 'the rise of revolutionary nationalism' in *The Sources of Japanese Tradition* is a worthy and influential example of this liberal stress on the content of political ideas as programmes of radical change.[6]

Granted, the Western historian of Japanese government has to start somewhere, but the three words 'rise', 'revolutionary' and 'nationalism' pose almost intractable difficulties. The Japanese were 'nationalist' before 1912, so why the 'rise'? Was the political instability after Meiji fed by nationalism or ultranationalism? Should the expression be 'The rise of revolutionary ultranationalism'? If so, how are we to explain that the 'ultranationalist' was defeated in the mid-1930s by the 'nationalist'? Or is the conflict between the 'Imperial faction' (*Kōdo-ha*), which was vanquished by Tōjō's more ideologically pluralistic 'control faction' (*Tōsei-ha*), better understood as normal, that is predictable and legitimate, political groupings of such complexity as to transcend the simplistic language of liberal and Confucian pacifist criticism?[7]

Based on European and North American experience and values, the concepts of liberal political analysis rarely suit East Asian political realities. Westerners intellectually map things differently. Not only do we tend to dismiss what Asians say is important to them, but we insert our own internal controversies on our consideration of Asia in unhelpful ways. The very notion of right-wing 'revolution' offends against progressive, Marxist and American ideals of popular revolutions against authoritarian governments, while the expression 'conservative revolution' appears to unite Margaret Thatcher and Benito Mussolini, George W. Bush and Adolf Hitler. Concepts such as 'fascist revolution' (George L. Mosse) strain the French Revolutionary categories of left and right almost to breaking point, and have trouble coping with the differences between Italian Fascism and Nazism, to say nothing of the gap between 'European fascism' and Japanese 'ultranationalism'.[8] Ernst Nolte has a point here.[9]

Despite the domestication of the language of 'right' and 'left' in Japanese political analysis, Western use of these categories regularly invites confusion about the Confucian realities that still determine how the Japanese and other East Asians are governed. As if such conceptual difficulties were not enough, there is the persistent but troublesome legacy of the Tokyo War Crimes Tribunal. This exercise in 'victors' history' has left its stamp on the selection of readings on 'The Rise of Revolutionary Nationalism' in *The Sources of Japanese Tradition*. This is not a criticism but a statement of fact.

That anthology reflects the cultivated weakness of Pacific War orthodoxy for conspiracy theories. This is where the focus of interest lies in the collection, from the labours of the Amur Society, through Ikki Kita's programme for reorganizing Japan, to Shūmei Ōkawa's 'The Way of Japan and the Japanese', understood in the *Sources of Japanese Tradition* as a 'justification for war' in 1941.[10] All of this, as we shall see, has particular relevance for any attempt to arrive at a sober and rigorous grasp of the place of the wartime Kyoto School and the *Chūō Kōron* transcripts in the struggle for discourse hegemony as Imperial Japan made its way along what Chihiro Hosoya taught me to call 'the road to the Pacific War'.[11]

The Tokyo War Crimes Tribunal as a laboured exercise in victors' history is at once heir and perpetuator of this conspiracy theory. Count 1 of the Allied Powers' indictment against the Japanese accused states:

> All of the accused together with other persons, between the 1st of January, 1928, and the 2nd September, 1945, participated as leaders, organizers, instigators, or accomplices in the formulation or execution of a common plan or conspiracy, and are responsible for all acts performed by any person in execution of such plan.[12]

In the judgments of the Tokyo Tribunal, the nature and goal of this conspiracy were elaborated:

> These far-reaching plans for waging wars of aggression, and the prolonged and intricate preparation for and waging of these wars of aggression, were not the work of one man. They were the work of many leaders acting in pursuance of a common plan for the achievement of a common object. That common object, that they should secure Japan's domination by preparing and waging wars of aggression, was a criminal object.[13]
>
> This conspiracy had as its object the domination of East Asia, the Pacific and Indian Oceans, and all the countries bordering on them.[14]

These statements are a dense and twisted forest of legal difficulties. How is one to define a 'conspiracy', let alone prove one? Are individuals responsible for actions of the state? What precisely is a 'war of aggression' and was this a crime in 1941? None of these issues would have been raised in court proceedings of this significance before the impact of Wilson's counter-revolution of 1919. Yet despite the failure of the Tokyo War Crimes Tribunal as a proper example of international legal justice or of the establishment of the definitive historical truth about pre-war Japanese politics, these proceedings have had a lingering impact on the liberal interpretation of the Pacific War. The reason is that the tribunal was motivated, as Pacific War orthodoxy has been ever since, by the conviction that between 1912 and 1945 the sometimes violent cast and illiberal outcome of this chapter in Japanese politics forces one to ask: 'What went wrong?'[15] This liberal question, with a predictably liberal answer, is misconceived. To appreciate why it is misconceived is to grasp finally why our preferred rubric in these deliberations should be the idea of a 'Post-Meiji Confucian Revolution'.

The hour of the blade

Between 1912 and 1945, Japan found itself, as we have noted, in an interregnum between two periods of manifest political *toku*: the reign of the Meiji Emperor and the reign of Douglas MacArthur. Three decades of factional struggle ensued during which a variety of programmes of total change were proposed, only to be found wanting and thus discarded. This civil war of ideas and cliques finally concluded in what I have labelled the 'false dawn' that was the triumph of the Tōjō clique, which in turn was crushed and replaced by the Pax Americana. Why the question 'What went wrong?' is flawed is best explained by keeping in mind that Confucian revolution is first and foremost not about people or content, strong men or robust ideas, but about form and timing – that is, patterns of political behaviour. The priority of form and timing over content is absolute.

Traditionally the Japanese sense of time and its cultural evolution has tended to be appreciated as a response to the natural world, particularly the change of seasons, but a profound responsiveness to and mindfulness of temporal 'beginnings' and 'endings' are motifs that merit close attention, particularly as they relate to politics, administration and the spiritual realm embodied in the life of the imperial court. The death of General Nogi, hero of the Russo–Japanese War, provides a salient parable. In 1912, three days after the passing of the Meiji emperor, Nogi and his wife committed double suicide. The day before their deaths, individual photographs were taken of the aged couple – he in uniform, she in formal dress – looking at the camera with blank unflinching dignity: the very embodiment of Meiji virtue. In *L'Empire de signe*, Roland Barthes reproduced the pair of photos, giving them one of the most arresting captions in all Japan studies: 'They are going to die, they know it, and this is not seen.'[16]

Why did Nogi commit suicide? Out of loyalty and solidarity with his liege lord, of course. Indeed, in part 20 of the final symposium, Kōyama speaks movingly of this sense of an ending: 'I mean [the intensity of] the sentiment that arises from absolute loyalty such as one might experience with particular force when one is with one's lord facing death, and finds oneself overcome with the emotion that one would freely sacrifice oneself in his place.'[17] However, there is also a sense of an age coming to its inevitable finish, of time reaching its end. To have gambled on this faction or another, on this leader or another, gives a shape, a trajectory, an organic arch of rise and fall, to one's fate as an individual. Once one's time is done, there is no desire to live under the alien sky of a new and therefore different era or dynasty. The old dispensation has fled. In the Confucian tradition, this signals to those most intensely involved in the now dead regime that it is time to depart because the *toku* one struggled so assiduously to maintain and keep vibrant is now, in every sense, *passé*. Thus the hour of the blade arrives.

After the Russo–Japanese War, there was a darkening of the national mood. Natsumei Soseki, the greatest and, by tradition, the most loved of modern Japanese novelists, was one of the earliest to register the new atmosphere as his country approached a momentous tipping point. In this realm of a dying era, Japan began to prepare for the renewal of national life in a different key. Despite the promise of continuity affirmed in the transition from one imperial era to another, and despite the formidable power of institutional inertia, the storm cloud of Confucian revolution was visible on the national horizon. By 1912 the question of who would rule Japan and in what manner inevitably loomed. It only required the hopes for the post-1912 imperial transition to be disappointed (as they were) and the prisoners of institutional inertia to lose touch with reality (as they did) for the question of the mandate of heaven to reassert itself, thus forcing the whole nation once again to gird itself for the Confucian interregnum of factional conflict. The violent phase of this contest of will and ideas was not resolved until after the crushing of the 1936 coup attempt.

To ask 'What went wrong?' from Meiji onwards is to pose the wrong question. Nothing went 'wrong' with the ending of Meiji; it just happened. However, the gates were thus inevitably open to radical change. Before any consideration of the 'content' of this programme or another for reorganizing Japan, Confucian form demands the very thing that the liberal historian rejects: a complete break with the past, even if that past is liberal. Conventionally, such breaks require not the inauguration of a 'year zero' but something sufficiently radical and comprehensive to mark a genuine new beginning for the state and society.[18] The call for *kaizō*, or reconstruction, coheres perfectly with the mandatory form of a Confucian revolution. When Ikki Kita produced his 'Plan for the Reorganization of Japan' in 1919, he was being radical, but only in a predictable Confucian sense. The police suppressed the distribution of his text because of institutional inertia and something more: heaven had yet to disclose a plausible new mandate holder. Or, to put the matter squarely, the day the police would know that Kita's text was not banned was the day when the holder of the new mandate forbade the police to ban it.

Liberalism and the failure to 'win hearts and minds'

In the *Chūō Kōron* discussions, there are frequent references to *shisō-sen* or 'the battle of ideas'. These Kyoto thinkers were in effect responding to the end game of the domestic struggle in 1941–42, when Japan's options for national reformation had sharply narrowed. This was inevitable given the approach of a more or less settled national moral consensus that the birth of a new regime demands. At the beginning of this process, however, a hundred flowers may bloom as a whole world of programmatic options appears on the horizon of a modernizing East Asian society (think of China today).[19] This was the Taishō moment as it unfolded after the death of the Meiji emperor. Almost all these blooms – liberalism, parliamentary party government, European high culture and cosmopolitanism, Marxism, American consumerism, liberal capitalism, socialism and Wilson's new liberal order, as well as anarchism, 'return-to-the soil' agrarianism, Asianism, xenophobia, Heigo Asahi's call for a 'Taishō Restoration' (echoed in the later demand for a 'Shōwa Restoration') – would inevitably wither because 'the Way is one'.

The 'one Way' had to be sound and correct. The end of the Meiji era meant that names had to be rectified, the nature of social reality had to be clarified. That required that any and all plausible world-views and schemes of effective action had to be examined in the vigorous search for a convincing 'reading' of reality around which Japanese society could be reorganized and renewed. The marketplace of ideas was ruled by creative destruction. An idea or programme or faction was tested and tried, sometimes more than once, in a relentless experiment in trial and error. In this unsparing intellectual version of survival of the fittest, liberalism as a form of economic, political and cultural organization, as tested on Japanese home ground by the Japanese themselves, failed after 1929. It failed as capitalism, as a philosophy of *effective* government (rather than a set of modern legitimating organs) and, finally, as a global order and system of values.

As Suzuki said on the first day of the 'Overcoming Modernity' symposium in July 1942, 'The struggle to overcome modernity requires the overcoming of democracy in the sphere of politics, liberalism in the sphere of thought, and capitalism in the sphere of economics'.[20] Almost seven months after Pearl Harbor, this symposium played its double role of airing a wide and varied set of positions and arguments while helping to consolidate a national consensus. Agreed, the views presented are so diverse and the interests at issue so at variance that a 'one-Way' consensus about detail, let alone the general harmony of opinion that East Asians find so satisfying, was all but impossible to achieve.

The manifest failure to foster such a harmony of intellectual opinion was not a disappointment so much as a message. It was the literary world's word of warning to the powers that be about the thinness of the national consensus that had taken shape in the wake of Tōjō's assumption of the premiership. This may explain why three members of the Kyoto School participated in this famous discussion sponsored by the Japanese magazine *Bungakkai* (Literary World). However, for the liberal student of Japan it is also essential to see that in the deliberations of the 'Overcoming Modernity' symposium, there is a broad agreement that Japan has moved well beyond the 'let a hundred flowers bloom' pluralism of Taishō.

That is as it should be. Japan as a society had by the summer of 1942 dispensed with most of the options examined and tested since Taishō. Indeed, Tōjō's assumption of the premiership signalled the end of public debate over the war decision, the formal unity of command, and the need for a significant degree of 'total' mobilization that was as close as Imperial Japan came to consummating the Post-Meiji Confucian Revolution. Note that liberalism as a national option was long dead. It could only be revived and imposed by a foreign power.

True, at the beginning of this intellectual struggle, liberalism displayed many of the features necessary to break completely with the Meiji era. It was so untraditional, so un-feudal and so un-Japanese, and seemed to be so ripe with the future. It suggested a programme for the further modernization of Japan in a manner that seemed uniquely consistent with the way of the wider world: it offered egalitarianism, party politics, improved status for women, high cultural modernity, free market capitalism, popular culture *à la* Hollywood, technological progress and consumer novelty, made all the more attractive in the 1920s by an unsettling air of decadence. However, these were urban ideas with limited appeal to the large majority of Japanese society that was more or less trapped in rural poverty.

The Westerner's uncritical enthusiasm for 'Taishō democracy' is another example of the liberal backing the wrong horse because of the comprehensive failure to 'win the hearts and minds of the people'. The root of this failure may be traced to our fundamental ignorance of what animates the hearts and minds of the peoples of East Asia. This ignorance has its source in our profound indifference to the genuine concerns and values of the evolving peasant mass.[21]

Whatever the cause of this ignorance, the consequences have been unmistakable. By consistently backing urban minorities, with their liberal sympathies, Western tastes, and a gift for English and French, at the expense of the incomprehensible peasant mass, liberals have repeatedly supported the losers in modern Confucian politics: Taishō democracy, Chiang Kai-shek and Madam Nhu.[22] Even the Dalai Lama as a moral agent is caught up in these Western ethical confusions. For the scholar no less than the managers of our neo-liberal global order today, one epistemological truth has proven fatal. Certainly since 1931, we have allowed liberal moralism to serve as our master narrative for understanding the traumatic movement from 'the great tradition' to 'the modern transformation' in East Asia. This has contributed to a century of Western defeats – military, economic and intellectual – while obscuring the true nature of our occasional would-be victory. This is what has gone wrong.

Notes

1 John T. McAlister, Jr and Paul Mus, *The Vietnamese and their Revolution*, New York, Evanston and London: Harper Torchbooks, 1970, p. 113.
2 Ryusaku Tsunoda, William Theodore de Bary and Donald Keene, eds, *Sources of Japanese Tradition*, vol. 2, New York and London: Columbia University Press, 1964, p. 253.
3 Thomas Cleary, 'Translator's Introduction', in Miyamoto Musashi, *The Book of the Five Rings: A Classic Text on the Japanese Way of the Sword*, Boston and London: Shambhala, 1994, p. xiii.

4 McAlister and Mus, *The Vietnamese and their Revolution*, op. cit., p. 1.
5 S.E. Finer, *A Man on Horseback: The Role of the Military in Politics*, London: Pall Mall Press, 1965.
6 Tsunoda *et al.*, *Sources of Japanese Tradition*, vol. 2, p. 252.
7 Herbert P. Bix, *Hirohito and the Making of Modern Japan*, New York: Perennial, 2001, p. 244.
8 George L. Mosse, *The Fascist Revolution: Towards a General Theory of Fascism*, New York: Howard Fertig, 1999.
9 Ernst Nolte, *Three Faces of Fascism*, Dublin: Mentor, 1969.
10 Tsunoda *et al.*, *The Sources of Japanese Tradition*, vol. 2, p. 288.
11 Personal communication. The distinguished historian Hosoya was co-author of volume 5 of *Taiheiyō Sensō e no Michi*, published in 1953.
12 Quoted in Richard H. Minear, *Victors' Justice: The Tokyo War Crimes Trial*, Tokyo: Charles E. Tuttle, 1971, pp. 127–28.
13 Ibid.
14 Ibid.
15 'What Went Wrong?' is of course the title of the famous article that Edwin O. Reischauer contributed to James W. Morley, ed., *Dilemmas of Growth in Prewar Japan*, Princeton, NJ: Princeton University Press, 1971. Reischauer's 'answer' was in response to the question posed in the article in the same book by Ron Dore and Tsutomu Ōuchi, entitled 'Rural Origins of Japanese Fascism'.
16 Roland Barthes, *Empire of Signs*, trans. Richard Howard, London: Jonathan Cape, 1983, pp. 92–93.
17 See third symposium, 20, p. 323–27.
18 The Western liberal student of Asia is tempted to explain Pol Pot's resort to the language of 'year zero' by reference to 'Year One' of the French Revolutionary calendar, but the deeper question is how much this Cambodian revolution owed to Confucianism and why this Chinese tradition did not prevent the 'killing fields'. Is there a more profound issue in contemporary global governance?
19 This conceit, using the term in the stylistic sense, allows for a suitably rich way of reading a book such as Mark Leonard's *What Does China Think?* London: Fourth Estate, 2008.
20 David Williams, *Defending Japan's Pacific War: The Kyoto School Philosophers and Post-White Power*, London and New York: RoutledgeCurzon, 2004, p. 58.
21 See McAlister and Mus, *The Vietnamese and their Revolution*, op. cit., p. 6.
22 To say nothing of the strangely parallel defeat of Soviet power in Afghanistan, destroyed in the end by its 'we know better' programme of modernization, education and post-feudal politics that depended on the triumph of urban forces over a rural mass that refused to be crushed.

Part II
The Standpoint of World History and Japan or a reading of the complete texts of the three Chūō Kōron symposia

I Two weeks before Pearl Harbor

The first symposium

THE STANDPOINT OF WORLD HISTORY AND JAPAN

A round-table discussion held on the evening of 26 November 1941 at Sa-aimi Maruyama, Kyoto

Participants: Masaaki Kōsaka, Iwao Kōyama, Keiji Nishitani and Shigetaka Suzuki

Table of contents[1]

1 Why world history has become the problem of our era
2 The world history of philosophers vs. the world history of historians
3 The European sense of crisis and Japanese world-historical consciousness
4 European reflections on the unity of Europe
5 The European sense of superiority
6 The defining qualities of European civilization
7 The notion that Japan has experienced two kinds of modernity
8 The concept of history in the East (*Tōyō*)
9 Criticizing the theory of stages of development
10 The problem of mechanized civilization
11 The problem of historicism
12 The problem of our awareness as individuals
13 The European Renaissance and modern history
14 Historicism and the challenges of teaching Japanese history
15 Viewing Japanese history from the standpoint of world history
16 World history as a method
17 Philosophy and reality
18 World history and morality (*moraru*)
19 Race, nation, people (*shuzoku, minzoku, kokumin*)

---

1 This table of contents is an editorial convenience. The original dictation of these round-table discussions appears to be seamless, the headings evidently being added afterwards.

20 The problems of urban life
21 Explaining America
22 Contemporary Japan and the world

1 Why world history has become the problem of our era

KŌSAKA: Recently someone asked me, with some exasperation, 'What does the philosophy of history actually mean, and how has it developed in Japan?' Caught off guard, I was at a loss to offer an immediate reply, but upon reflection I think one may conclude that there have been three stages in the growth of [serious][2] Japanese interest in the philosophy of history. The first stage saw Rickert's ideas about historical meaning or epistemology becoming popular.[3] This interest now belongs irrevocably to the past. In its place a style of historical-minded philosophical reflection that drew on the 'life philosophy' and 'hermeneutics' of Dilthey came to the fore.[4] These ideas dominated what I call the second stage of the rise of the philosophy of history in Japan. Today we have entered a new phase, one that represents a further advance over the two previous phases. This third phase is characterized by an insistence that the philosophy of history must specifically become a philosophy of world history, thus reflecting the stage that self-consciousness has arrived at today. This in my view defines the third of our three stages.

Why has this path been taken in Japan?[5] The fundamental answer is that we have embraced the philosophy of world history because we are compelled to do so by the place that contemporary Japan has achieved in world history. Of course, to think in this way is to acknowledge how much we have learned

---

2 All interpolations within [] are mine (DW). They reflect elements of meaning which I believe are implied or suggested by the writers but which do not appear literally in the original Japanese. The four participants are intimately familiar with each other's ideas, and therefore tend to speak to one another in a kind of shorthand that may not be transparent to the reader.
3 Heinrich Rickert (1863–1936): German neo-Kantian philosopher who explored the logical and epistemological foundations of the natural and historical sciences. For the wartime Kyoto School, Rickert's speculation on how universal history might be underwritten by a system of values served as a point of departure for developing a distinctly Japanese idea of the philosophy of world history.
4 Wilhelm Dilthey (1833–1911): German philosopher, a student of the great historian Leopold von Ranke (see Note 7); influenced by Kant, Hegel and the British empiricists in his notion of *Philosophie des Lebens* (philosophy of life), and by Schelling and Schleiermacher in his study of hermeneutics (the philosophy of reading, translation and interpretation). Dilthey's reflections on the idea of *Weltanschauung* or world-view and on the nature of historicism attracted sustained attention from the Kyoto School.
5 This question, I believe, implies two constituent questions and one conclusion: Why have these three stages evolved in this particular order? Most importantly, why have we arrived now at this precise form of world-historical consciousness? The answers lie not in academic reflection but in the facts of the world.

from two great thinkers: Hegel[6] and Ranke.[7] But today we pose for ourselves a particular set of quite specific questions: What is to become of our country? What significance is Japan set to assume in the new age that is taking shape even as we speak? What meaning does Japan need to realize in history (and we with it)? In other words, the [overriding] question becomes: What is Japan's mission in the unfolding of world history? When we confront these questions, we have no reason to expect answers from Western thinkers, however great. We have to find the answers ourselves as thinking Japanese. It is these kinds of questions and the pressing need to answer them that explain why the development of a philosophy of world history has become an urgent quest for contemporary Japan.

SUZUKI: I am very much in agreement with these sentiments. As Kōyama recently observed, our consciousness of world history is exceedingly strong today. And this is as it should be because, after all is said and done, this consciousness determines the direction and shape of contemporary analysis. In other words, the 'contemporary' as a phase of human experience is founded on [national] self-criticism and self-examination.[8] Isn't this the case? I suspect that consciousness of world history now governs human awareness everywhere on the planet, but it is felt with particular force in Japan – so much so that one might say it is the defining characteristic of contemporary thought here.

In Europe the idea of world history has an ancient lineage. There the term 'world history' is very old. But this longevity has acquired a special poignancy today because one can conclude that the contemporary crisis of ideas in Europe is decisively connected with the idea of world history itself. If Europeans see a natural link in their own circumstances between the concept of world history and the idea of a crisis in their affairs, Japan paints a striking contrast,

---

6 Georg Wilhelm Friedrich Hegel (1770–1831): German idealist philosopher who, of all Europeans, exerted by far the greatest influence on the intellectual thrust of *The Standpoint of World History and Japan*.
7 Leopold von Ranke (1795–1886): German historian and, as the father of 'historicism', the second most influential European figure in the wartime discourse of the Kyoto School. Ranke's reflections on universal history or *Weltgeschichte*, and on the character of the great powers in history, left a profound mark on *The Standpoint of World History and Japan*. Shigetaka Suzuki, for example, published a short but thoughtful study of Ranke under the title of *Ranke to Sekaishigaku* (Ranke and the Study of World History) in 1939, and co-translated (with Shinsaku Aihara) Ranke's *Über die Epochen der neueren Geschichte* as *Shikaishi Gaikan* (The Concept of World History), which appeared in 1941.
8 The stress on self-criticism and self-examination distinguishes the Kyoto School from the militant discourse of Japanese nationalism. Informed by Hegelian rationalism, this stance in turn influences the Kyoto School's application of Confucian assumptions to the solution of the problems facing contemporary Japan. Consciousness is therefore a specifically philosophic term referring to rational grasp of reality in a complex interplay of objectivity and subjectivity. As this is the language of German idealism, conventional use of the terms 'consciousness' or 'self-consciousness' in normal English is irrelevant.

because the awareness of recent world history has taken a radically different form here. If Europeans have grown fearful of change, Japanese consciousness of world history reflects a formidable desire for change, that is the will to reform (*kakushin*) and thus remake the world.[9]

Genuine reform (*kakushin*) involves more than the mere subjective (*shukanteki*) urge or desire for change; it must be grounded, to a decisive degree, in objective reality if it is to succeed. And it is vital that Japan now should be acutely aware (*jikaku*) of this objective necessity.[10] But this is, I would think, precisely what world-historical consciousness involves, doesn't it? It might be noted in this context, however, that thinkers such as Troeltsch insist that there is an academic motive behind all this because the tasks set by world-historical consciousness today turn on the need to overcome historicism.[11]

KŌSAKA: The way we now think about these ideas is changing significantly. Unfolding as it does in the moving current of history, philosophy as a discipline has become a method of establishing where one finds oneself in this historical flux while also suggesting in which direction one should move on. Thus it is essential that philosophy analyse the 'contemporary'. This analysis must begin with the present moment or 'instant', as defined by world history, and nowhere else. This is what 'analysis of the contemporary' means. Philosophy is not just the discipline that secures the foundations of existence; rather, it is a form of study that provides a compass enabling us to confront historical change as it inches forward. Philosophy orientates us.[12]

I suspect that the direction of world history appears very differently when viewed from an Eastern rather than a Western perspective. As distinct 'worlds', these two civilizations have pursued different ways of thinking from the start.[13] Indeed, I think the problem today is grounded in the different ways in

---

9 Suzuki uses the expression *kakushin iyoku*, which in this context can quite naturally take on a Hegelian (desire) or Nietzschean (will to change) gloss. This is indeed how a philosophically literate Japanese *reading at speed* might well have understood this remark in 1942.

10 As we will find repeatedly in this text, *jikaku* does not mean what the English 'aware' (having something in mind) implies. Rather, it suggests a full mastery of self (self-transparency of intent and the unsparing assessment of one's capabilities), as well as the (near) total grasp of objective circumstance.

11 Ernst Troeltsch (1865–1923): German theologian and social scientist, best known for his oppositional ideas of 'community' versus 'society' or *Gemeinschaft* vs. *Gesellschaft*, but also important here for his writings on historicism and its problems.

12 It makes us practical, in the Confucian mode. The word 'orientating' is set out in *furigana* from the German. *Furigana* is a Japanese subscript that can written alongside a foreign term in order to suggest how the word may be pronounced in Japanese. It is a form of transliteration.

13 A 'world', according to the wartime Kyoto School, is more than a geographical region of the globe; it is a civilization. Before the emergence of modern Europe as the global hegemon, there were several regions or 'worlds' that were superseded when Europe became, as it were, 'the world'; however, in the 1940s the old pattern re-emerges with Europe's decline and the simultaneous rise of new regions that display the full panoply of civilized powers.

which East and West define 'the world'. From a European perspective, as Suzuki has noted, the present is viewed as a time of crisis, while we Japanese tend to see the present differently. These differences rest, to stress the point, on contrasting approaches to the idea of 'the world'.

KŌYAMA: I agree. The notion of world history held by contemporary Europeans differs sharply from that embraced by us.

KŌSAKA: I suspect that this indeed is the case. The difference being?

KŌYAMA: That there should be a difference. World history is something one must feel with one's whole body. This and this alone qualifies as the genuine article. And I believe that it is not the contemporary European but we Japanese who feel the force of history in this way. But when I say that here is to be found the truth of the matter, I am not referring to some subjective Japanese conception of the problem (*shukan-teki na kannen*) but rather to something [objectively] grounded in world history itself. This anyway is my opinion.[14]

KŌSAKA AND SUZUKI: We agree with you.

KŌSAKA: Despite the recent example of Spengler and others who have seized on the theme of the decline of the West, I must confess I do not know of many other countries where the philosophy of world history is being taken as seriously as it is in Japan.[15]

SUZUKI: In that case, it represents a specific form of Japan's reform-minded world consciousness.

KŌYAMA: Brandenberg, the German historian, has written a book titled *Europe and the World* which presents a Western version of the world consciousness committed to change that we find in Japan today.[16] His view is that an authentic version of world history has begun only in the twentieth century. He also argues that the world outside the West has gradually assumed a confrontational stance towards Europe, suggesting that the European domination over the rest of the world may be becoming less easy to sustain than has hitherto been the case. Nations outside Europe such as Japan and Arabia, and indeed some colonized societies, are demonstrating a new unwillingness to do what they are told by the European powers. The

---

14 Kōyama is criticizing the impracticality of Hegelian idealism (*kannen*), but note that what he is dismissing is *shukan-teki* (passive subjective observation), not *shutai-teki* (the subjectivity of empowered agency).

15 Oswald Spengler (1880–1936): German writer and philosopher of history whose *Der Untergang des Abendlande* (The Decline of the West), which appeared in two volumes in 1918 and 1922, may qualify as the most influential speculation on the fate of global civilization to appear during the past century. It left a profound stamp on the themes and motives that inspired *The Standpoint of World History and Japan*.

16 Literally, 'change-minded'. The major works of Arnold Otto Erich Brandenberg (1868–1946) include *Die Reichsgründung* (1916), *Die materialistische Geschichtsauffassung* (1920) and *Von Bismarck zum Weltkriege* (1924), all of which thematically would have attracted the interest of the middle or wartime phase of the Kyoto School (1928–45).

creation of institutions such as the League of Nations suggests that all its members share the same rights. And in a way even Europe is finally becoming [merely] one world [among others]. Thus, Brandenberg seems to be suggesting that as a result of all these developments, and as a very recent phenomenon, a genuine world history is taking shape.

In looking back at the past, Brandenberg cites several examples – I cannot remember them all, but I think he includes the interrelationships between Europe, East Asia and the Middle East as cultural regions. In a similar manner, one can debate whether Russia is part of Europe or belongs to the non-European world. What really alarms Brandenberg is his fear that Europe is in danger of splitting apart, and it is this [potential] crisis that he warns about. But in any case his way of thinking is extraordinarily suggestive.

2 The world history of philosophers vs. the world history of historians

SUZUKI: This is what I thought as well but I do wonder about the difference between history and philosophy, between the philosophy of world history and the world produced by the historian.[17]

KŌSAKA: That's right. There is a problem here.

SUZUKI: A historian's version of world history is very much needed. This involves something different from the philosophy of world history. One might say that the world history of the historian may be regarded as reflecting an 'internal' need. For example, the current tensions in the Pacific are among the central issues of world politics. But if one asks oneself why these tensions are so pressing, one cannot dismiss this crisis as a mere blip in world affairs: on the contrary, this problem is profoundly historical in character. Its importance does not arise from temporary pressures.

But note that if one really wants to grasp the importance of this crisis in the Pacific, traditional Western notions of world history are useless. This is not a question of knowledge; it is a question of standpoint. Quite simply, the standpoint offered by conventional Western practitioners of conventional empirical history (*rekishigaku*) is inadequate to grasp the new realities emerging in the world. But note further that traditional Japanese and Oriental (*Tōa*) historiography is not any better. On this point what is needed is a

---

17 In the text, the contrast is drawn between *rekishi no tetsugaku* (the philosophy of history) and *rekishigaku* (literally, 'the study of history', or conventionally 'historiography'). However, as historiography tends, certainly in an academic context, to refer to the study of historical methodologies, I have chosen to recast the two sides of this debate as 'world history from a philosopher's point of view' opposed to the strictly empirical labours of the conventional historian who does not rely on philosophy for an interpretative schema.

history [of the whole of humanity] from a world-historical standpoint. Without such a historical approach, problems such as current troubles in the Pacific cannot be comprehended. I feel strongly about this issue.

KŌYAMA: I fear that the relationship between the world history of the historian and the world history of the philosopher is problematic. I wonder if it is really possible to create an effective approach to world history [exclusively] from the methods of positivistic historiography or, for that matter, to foster a philosophy of world history from the husks of traditional philosophy?[18] Fatal limitations can be found not only in historiography but also [in the gap] between philosophy and [empirical] scholarship, fields that have gone their separate ways since the nineteenth century. Today the two approaches appear to be drawing closer together, or so it seems to me. But unless some common ground between philosophy and the so-called 'special sciences' can be found, the special sciences will not advance, and of course this applies to the study of world history by the historian as well.[19] This is the point at which I think we have arrived today. As this need is being increasingly recognized among historians, the solution is to be found in the philosophy of world history. Isn't this the case? If so, this means that an interdisciplinary frontier or zone, or the like, is taking shape where the [rigid] distinction between the historian's understanding of world history and the philosopher's approach to world history will not apply. What do you think, Nishitani?

NISHITANI: I feel the same way. In general Europeans, even now, seem to be me to be unable to shake their habit of always viewing the world from a European perspective.

KŌSAKA: Everything is seen as an extension of Europe. This is their standpoint.

KŌYAMA: The crisis is Europe's crisis.

SUZUKI: The European understanding of this new world situation is not informed by a genuine form of world-historical consciousness; rather, they have seized on the concept of crisis [to explain the world]. Their outlook is dominated by a consciousness defined by crisis (*kiki ishiki*).

3 The European sense of crisis and Japanese world-historical consciousness

NISHITANI: For Europeans, Asia has never been a matter of intense personal concern or uncomfortable deliberation, but for us, Europe has always

---

18 Here 'positivist history' refers to empirical or factual approaches to the study of the past, not the elaboration of positivist laws. The exact analogy would be with the use of the word 'positivism' among practitioners of literary criticism rather than by students of the natural sciences or economics.

19 In Japanese, *tokushu-kagaku*. Philosophy is not a science. It deals with 'the whole', while a science deals with a specific field.

been a matter of pressing concern and painful reflection; that is what distinguishes Europe from Japan. Asia has been for Europeans something to act upon, and it is from that viewpoint alone that they have viewed this part of the world.[20] Europe has acted upon Asia, which has served as the object of its action; not the other way around. It is an 'I' and 'Thou' relationship, and Europe has assumed the role of the 'I': this is its standpoint. But this also explains why the transformation now under way is the stuff of crisis for Europeans, while here it takes the form of a new world order. And when we discover that we are able to conceive of new concepts of world history and the philosophy of world history here in Japan now, this ability arises, I suspect, from the [very] gap in consciousness about which I have been speaking.

SUZUKI: I have just remembered Henri Massis, the formidable French ultra-nationalist intellectual who belongs to Action française.[21] He is the author of *Défense de l'Occident*, and his work reflects a kind of world-historical consciousness. In his thinking, Massis particularly stresses how the new situation in East Asia has become an issue deserving attention and reflection among Europeans. Somehow I think that Massis's views can be seen to reflect a form of crisis consciousness. That is to say that the world-historical changes unfolding in contemporary East Asia may be perceived as a kind of threat to Europe. I wonder if this reaction does not derive [directly] from the European view of world history.

KŌYAMA: Near the end of *The Future of Capitalism*, Sombart asserts that the new power of East Asia should be viewed as something to fear.[22] Brandenberg holds a similar view. The suspicion must be that writers such as Brandenberg do indeed think in world-historical terms but take the European view (that is, the view that was common before the outbreak of the Second European War in 1939) that the struggle between the former Allies and the German side was a dangerous folly. Such perceptions define his world-historical consciousness. From this viewpoint, Russia poses a distinct set of problems because writers such as Brandenberg perceive Russia as part of the non-European world, rather than as a part of Europe, and place particular emphasis on Russia's apartness.

---

20 An early elaboration of the problem more recently brought into controversial focus by Edward W. Said in *Orientalism*, Harmondsworth: Peregrine Books, 1985 [1978], p. 267.
21 Henri Massis (1886–1970): French Catholic literary critic and supporter of the Vichy regime. Member of the Académie française. Suzuki mentions Massis's 1927 work *Défense de l'Occident* in his study of Ranke, where he gives it the English title *Defence of the West*, a translation published in 1928. See Shigetaka Suzuki, *Ranke to Sekai-shi-gaku*, Tokyo: Kōbundo, 1939, p. 66.
22 Werner Sombart (1863–1941): German economic and social theorist; author of *Die Zukunft des Kapitalismus* (1934). His work was widely read in Japan before, during and after the Pacific War. The influential economic historian Hisao Ōtsuka was still enthusiastically lecturing on Sombart in the early 1970s at the International Christian University, having left the University of Tokyo.

SUZUKI: This is the same Massis who made the provocative observation that Russia, rather than falling into the orbit of Europe, actually embodies a form of Asianism. Bolshevism may have wrapped itself up in Marxism, that is, a West European veil, but it is only a form of Asianism in European dress ...

NISHITANI: This is the opinion that is generally held in Europe.

SUZUKI: If this were not enough, Massis thinks that Germany, too, represents a form of Asianism, and therefore a threat, indeed a danger, to Europe. Coming from a French ultranationalist, this may appear to be an unexpected, even ironic (*omoshiroi*) opinion, but French ultranationalism holds that [Europe's] true tradition derives from Rome and Latinity, that is from Europe west of the Rhine. This reduces Germany to an Eastern outsider, a manifestation of the Oriental.[23] The implication would be that a suspect Easternism (*Tōyōshugi*), a neither-one-nor-the-other form of pseudo-Orientalism, German and Russian alike, is lurking inside Europe's walls.

There are implications to be drawn from such views when we consider the national awakening now taking place in Asia itself. Note, for example, that the intellectuals who have given expression to this awakening, whether in Japan, China or India (particularly the last in connection with the ethnic question), have tended to come from the classes educated in the European manner. [The profoundest truth is that] there can be no revival of classical or traditional Asia, and this truth means that only a pseudo-[or hybrid] Orientalism offers itself.[24] We may therefore conclude that today Europe has begun to come under attack from a form of pseudo-[Westernized] Orientalism. The new notion of 'Fortress Europe' captures the essence of the European response to this challenge.

To defend Europe requires that Europeans themselves must once more rediscover and reaffirm their authentic tradition. This is Massis's broad contention. In any case, Europeans appear to feel under pressure from the East: this has given currency to the idea of a 'crisis', and at the same time the new global situation is one that Europeans feel they are unable to evade. But the new world-historical situation means, at least to me, that the idea of world history qualifies as one of the ruling ideas of our times. In Japan, world-historical consciousness is becoming stronger and stronger, and the reason is that the facts themselves are world-historical in character.

---

23 The expression is transliterated from English. 'Oriental[ism]' as used here does not refer to the often biased Western understanding of the Orient as criticized by writers such as Edward Said, but serves as an alternative term for 'Asianism' as used above. Both 'Orientalism' and 'Asianism' appear to be translations of *Tōyōshugi*, literally, 'Easternism'. Note that the term 'Asianism' may also refer to calls for regional integration in Asia in general and within East Asia in particular.

24 An Asia that is not traditional because it has been so influenced by Western modernity.

NISHITANI: Listening to you I have remembered an episode from my journey back to Japan from Germany. On my ship there was a man from Switzerland, and he lent me a huge book with the title *The Battlefront of the Coloured Races*.[25] The book was a German translation of a work originally written in English. I have forgotten who the publisher (*nanpan*) was, but I read it carefully. In essence it is about the emergence of the coloured races (*jinshu*). According to the book, the most problematic manifestation of this development is the emergence of Japan. Strangely enough, Saionji makes an appearance in the book.[26] Indeed, the author claims to have met Saionji. It is that sort of book and it appears to have sold widely. But one of the most important consequences of this change [in reality] is that Europe is becoming merely one region among others instead of the region that dominates the rest.[27] Europe is ceasing to be the world. The reason for this [relative] decline in global status is the emergence of the coloured races. This development appears to have cast a great shadow over the West. There is a sense that the East is projecting itself as a vast shadow on the horizon of Europe.

KŌYAMA: This is the source of Europe's new consciousness of a crisis. Do you not all agree?

KŌSAKA: Yes, in effect, that appears to be the case.

KŌYAMA: What this doesn't mean is that our world-historical consciousness is the same as Europe's. Isn't that the point?

NISHITANI: Of course it is different. In any case, hardly anyone in Europe knows anything about the East. The scholarly specialist aside, the average member of the public there still thinks of the East as utterly remote. By contrast, Europe for us is terribly close at hand.

KŌYAMA: For Japan, Europe is nearer than China ...

KŌSAKA: Yes, I think that one can say that.

KŌYAMA: In terms of actual physical distance, Europe is much further away but ...

KŌSAKA: For Europeans, the East is so far removed it seems to be barely on the same planet ...

SUZUKI: Yes, quite so. That is an interesting way of putting the matter. That's the idea ...

KŌSAKA: For a European, it appears to be an attack from the outside on the very heart of civilization ...

SUZUKI: Yes, that is the European view of the world.

---

25 *Yūshoku Jinshu no Sensen*.
26 Baron Kimmochi Saionji (1849–1940): scion of an ancient aristocratic family, twice prime minister and the last *genrō* or elder statesman from the Meiji era (1868–1912).
27 Nishitani's remark predates Dipesh Chakrabarty's *Provincializing Europe: Postcolonial Thought and Historical Difference* (Princeton: Princeton University Press, 2000) by six decades, and offers further evidence of the ways in which the wartime Kyoto School anticipated many ideas now associated with French theory and post-structuralism.

KŌYAMA: Alongside the determination to resist Europe that one finds in Japan, and for that matter in East Asia as a whole, there has been another form of consciousness (*ishiki*), one that has sought to repudiate from within Japan itself the legacies of the early modern (*kinsei*) as well as the Meiji and Taishō periods.[28] Note further that these two forms of consciousness have been at work simultaneously in the Japanese mind.

4 European reflections on the unity of Europe

SUZUKI: In Christopher Dawson's ideas about the historical consciousness of European unity, there is a form of world-historical reflection.[29] The question is: how should Europe understand the new circumstances with which world history confronts it? Faced with this change, Europe needs once more to become aware of what unites it. Because Europe is threatened by the forces of disunity and division, one must judge nineteenth-century European nationalism to have been a folly. In short, Europeans must reflect on why they have fallen into disunity. Dawson believes that if nineteenth-century liberal nationalism is the main cause of Europe's divisions, then its salvation lies in a deeper awareness of the profundity of its cultural unity. It should also be noted that Dawson has nothing to propose beyond this remedy.

KŌSAKA: He is calling for Europe to return to the Middle Ages?

SUZUKI: Yes, that is the case.

NISHITANI: 'Cultural unity' I take to be grounded in a 'spiritual unity'. This is what the term really means. Europeans repeatedly manifest a deep pride in their culture. Driven by such pride, Europeans could demonstrate an awesome degree of historical power if they could but make themselves aware of the depths of their spiritual unity. I make no claim to professional expertise on the subject, but I wonder if the trend towards European unity will not someday make it [once again] a force to reckon with. Yet, having said as much, there is the complicating factor of the unifying tendencies of the Anglo-Saxon world. This, in my opinion, represents a very awkward challenge [for European unity].[30]

SUZUKI: That's right. The Anglo-Saxons themselves are a major problem. Yet the consciousness of unity in contemporary Europe displays a singular sense of superiority. Isn't this always the case?

---

28 In other words, the urge to transcend the Meiji achievement and thus make Japan 'postmodern' is grounded in the genuine failings and limitations of the project initiated in 1868. This perception united the critics of the Meiji-style 'Enlightenment and Civilization' (*Bunmei Kaikai*) project across much of the political spectrum of early Shōwa Japan (*c.*1926–41).

29 Christopher Dawson (1889–1970): influential English historian and Catholic intellectual. His first book, *The Age of the Gods*, appeared in 1928; *The Making of Europe: An Introduction to the History of European Unity* was published in 1932.

30 Again, Nishitani is prophetic on the subject of Britain's or, more precisely, England's dilemmas about its place in Europe and its problematic dependence on the United States.

KŌSAKA: Why might that be so?

SUZUKI: Because this is inevitably how Europeans view their own culture. When we consider European civilization, we see it as just one regional culture among many. Don't you wonder if the facts will eventually compel Europe to recognize the truth of its reduced situation?

5 The European sense of superiority

NISHITANI: The problem is more deeply rooted. Europeans do not believe that they need to protect themselves [or that their global role is over]. Quite the contrary: they think that they still have something to contribute to the world – if I interpret the matter generously – that is, they entertain the notion deep inside themselves that they can shape the emerging new world order.[31] Isn't that what they really feel? One can see an extreme version of this sentiment in Hitler's book.[32] There he observes that the Aryan race alone is creative in the cultural sense. The Japanese, by contrast, are ranked below the Aryans as 'preservers of culture' rather than 'originators of culture'. Vast numbers of Europeans subscribe to that broad view. It is, in short, a superiority complex. Hitler is only giving extreme expression to this widespread opinion.

At the same time there is alarm among Europeans about the Japanese. This nervousness has assumed the form of something approaching a phobia – the Japanese are nimble, quick and shrewd, and thus it is impossible to predict what we will do! One finds this attitude ridiculously widespread. But aren't the two views basically intertwined?

SUZUKI: The new forms of consciousness that characterize contemporary Europe are the product of the new order taking shape in the world, and the new culture that is informing this new order. This new 'world' consciousness, using the term in the broadest sense, expresses itself, as we have discussed, in two ways. First, there is the painful awareness of a crisis arising from the new assertiveness of the world beyond the immediate European sphere. It appears that this new assertiveness has provoked a vague fear, one that both triggers and perpetuates this new extreme nervousness, this state-of-siege mentality, on the part of Europe. On the other hand, Europeans appear [still] to be convinced that their culture is the best – indeed, they seem unable to shake themselves free of this confident belief.

KŌYAMA: A European version of the Chinese conviction that culturally they are the centre of the world.

NISHITANI: As a result, Europeans look down on East Asia as a culture of inferior rank – although it should be noted that among researchers who

---

31 This insight speaks directly to the ambitious efforts of the French poet, mathematician and intellectual statesman Paul Valéry during the interwar period.
32 *Mein Kampf*, published in two volumes in 1925–26.

know East Asian culture well there exists a shared perception that East Asia is the one culture in the world capable of rivalling Europe. To that degree [the greatness of] East Asia is acknowledged. This perception draws on a wide range of features of East Asian civilization, but is held only by those Europeans with a profound grasp of our culture. Ordinary Europeans do not share this view. One consequence is that Hitler's insistence on the relative inferiority of East Asians strikes a chord with the general public.

SUZUKI: Yes, of course, that very much appears to be the case. It is therefore important – in my view – that we recognize just how much Europeans themselves continue to assume that their culture is the best. Of course, we Japanese extended this recognition to Europe long ago. Furthermore, this was not a mistaken perception. [But now,] provoked by the new assertiveness of non-Westerners, Europeans have leaped to the conclusion that the whole world is caught in a crisis – or, to put it another way, that the whole world is going wrong. And this, of course, is a very problematic, indeed wrongheaded, perception.

It is true that until now Europeans have been the unmistakable leaders of the world. This is a fact. Furthermore, this domination has not been only political or economic; Europe's manifest superiority over the rest of the world has extended beyond these spheres. Culture has been the decisive factor. European culture has demonstrated universal validity of the highest order, and it is through this cultural superiority that Europe has exercised its power over the rest of the world. It is this that made a European global order possible. Furthermore, it is utter nonsense to believe that a global culture, a culture that exercises global domination, can be sustained without such universal validity. By contrast, [an effective Japanese form of] politics by itself does not offer the means to meet this challenge. This point is, I think, of enormous importance.

KŌYAMA: Culture exercises that kind of power. But don't we have to ask ourselves how this situation arose, how Europe came to this position of superiority through the fundamental role played by capitalism in the expansion of its civilization across the world? Isn't this the central issue? The roots of Europe's sense of superiority arose not directly from European culture but rather from its economic, technological and finally political domination ...

SUZUKI: No, I beg to differ here because I think the fundamental source is culture. Why do I think this is the case? Because capitalism turns on [the development of] new methods of production.[33] Technology is what gives birth to a genuinely modern civilization. For example, science in Europe is not a [static] body of knowledge. Rather, this knowledge is used to

---

33 Suzuki uses the German word *Methode*, transliterated into Japanese.

transform society and civilization. In other words, scholarship is not just knowledge. Or, it does not exist simply as knowledge. Rather, knowledge serves as the foundation of scientific civilization in that it determines the very kind of civilization that comes into being. The resulting type of civilization – let's call it 'rational civilization' – provides the indispensable foundation for capitalism itself. And this conclusion compels us to ask whether capitalism itself is a wholly European invention.[34]

NISHITANI: Capitalism may, as it were, be importable: lock, stock and barrel. Not only that, the importing culture may make innovations that surpass the quality of the original.[35] But this suggests that the Japanese intelligentsia, taking the term in its broadest sense, is being kept off balance not by capitalism as such but by the superiority of European culture.[36]

SUZUKI: But if Europe had the ability, that is the technology, [to exploit] natural resources, it lacked [many of] the natural resources themselves. Furthermore, I suspect that to a degree this drove Europe down the path to imperialism. Capitalism, mechanized civilization, if you will, gave birth to imperialistic struggles such as the Great War [the First World War]. But it has also produced Europe's crisis. What perhaps, I think, should not have happened has happened: European civilization has become mechanized. This means that the crisis of civilization is indistinguishable from the crisis of European civilization; they are the same thing.

6 The defining qualities of European civilization

KŌYAMA: This suggests that it is extremely difficult to determine the relative superiority or inferiority of a civilization … [The temptation] to conclude that one civilization is superior when in fact it is merely different only arises when that civilization exerts its powers outside its natural sphere or homeland. The values at work in judging the relative superiority or inferiority of civilizations are created from the encounter between civilizations. The sense of being overwhelmed, militarily and economically, that we Japanese must have felt during the final phase of the Tokugawa Shogunate [c.1850s–1860s], gave currency to the conceit that we were being overwhelmed [not just by gunboat diplomacy but] by another civilization …

NISHITANI: I think, in general terms, one can draw that conclusion. But as Japan has shown itself able to catch up with the West to a significant

---

[34] Suzuki appears to be advocating an inquiry comparable with Max Weber's pioneering examination of the question why rational capitalism arose only in Europe after the Reformation.

[35] The implication is that Japanese capitalism may one day outperform European capitalism.

[36] This entire section of the discussion can be read as a footnote or response to Karl Löwith's treatment of the issue of Japan's response to the challenge of European civilization in his 'Afterword to the Japanese Reader', in *Martin Heidegger and European Nihilism*, ed. Richard Wolin, trans. Gary Steiner, New York: Columbia University Press, 1995, pp. 228–34.

degree, both militarily and economically, one may also conclude that we possess some of those [superior] characteristics as well. I suspect that if one had asked the Japanese people how they perceived the matter at the time of the Meiji Restoration [1868], they would probably have identified the sources of Western strength with what we now call 'science'. Astronomy, medicine and so forth had largely come to Japan from China; but it was Europeans who seemed to have grasped the true facts of reality, call it positivism or science in the broadest sense. I think this was the contemporary impression.

In a way it was the same with European arts and letters. When we ask ourselves why the arts and letters of Europe were superior to our own, the answer can be found, I think, in the empirical approach, taking the term 'empirical', as we must, in its widest sense. In other words, Europeans pursued the facts of human life or psychology in shaping their artistic forms. Wasn't this in a broad sense empirical? In other words, the arts and letters in Europe also involved the search for 'truth'. And in this quest for 'truth' something was found that could be relied upon, could be trusted. It was this, I think, that gave the arts and letters in Europe their impressive power.

KŌYAMA: Certainly, the gap between Edo culture [1600–1868] and the empirical spirit of European culture was enormous. While it is true that the rational spirit penetrated numerous aspects of Edo culture, one rarely finds anything one could describe as the empirical spirit. This fact has to be acknowledged. For contemporary Japanese, I suspect, the most painful aspect of their encounter with European civilization was not the rationalism of Europe but the spirit of empiricism.

KŌSAKA: I agree. It depends upon one's point of view, but when one considers modern European literature it seems to exhibit a more serious approach than one finds, for example, in the light Japanese fiction of the Edo period. This difference can probably be traced to the spirit of empiricism, and I think one can draw this conclusion regardless of the relative merits or demerits of the works at issue.

7 The notion that Japan has experienced two kinds of modernity

KŌYAMA: It is my opinion that Saikaku displays, to some degree, the qualities of naturalism or empiricism.[37] But I have long suspected that two kinds of modernity have been at work in the making of modern Japan: one unfolded before the Meiji Restoration, and the other after 1868. This is, as far as I know, a new departure in the interpretation of Japan's recent past, and I invite criticism of my thesis.

---

37 Saikaku Ihara (1642–93): Popular Edo period poet and novelist, known in Japan by his personal name, Saikaku.

Japan's experience of modernity began roughly at the same time as Europe's. When Europeans began to expand overseas, the Japanese started to do so as well. The background for such expansion was the same in both cases: the development of individualism and commerce. Hence the suspicion that if Japan had not withdrawn into self-imposed isolation, its development as a country would probably have been entirely different. In fact, however, because of its isolated condition, the spirit of modern development in Edo Japan contrasted sharply with that in Europe. From this different path a much altered national character seems to have resulted.

The long Tokugawa peace transformed the samurai class. Samurai were still called 'samurai', but in reality the warrior became a kind of bureaucrat. At the same time, the growing merchant class – which left unhindered might naturally have expanded its activities abroad – found its efforts in Edo Japan confined to the home market. The result was that over time the samurai acquired something of the spirit of modernity while the merchant class became, if anything, *more* feudal in character. For example, the individual never became the focus of business activity: rather, the family or its near equivalent assumed that role, and became the core of most businesses. Such conditions allowed the development of a modern spirit with a pronounced feudal character. I think this was the defining characteristic of society, civilization and the human spirit in the Edo period.

In contrast with the religious spirit of the feudal period, [secular] ethical concerns dominated the spirit of Edo modernity. In short, Confucianism ousted Buddhism from its hitherto pre-eminent role. Confucianism also had the effect of curbing the speculative strain in the National School of Shinto. This encouraged the advocates of the National Learning Movement (*Kokugakusha*) to focus on the 'sadness of things' (*mono no aware*), fostering a cult of feeling and thus transforming Shinto sensibility in an entirely humanistic direction. The Tokugawa period – culturally, intellectually and economically – reflects these trends. In this sense, the Edo period can be said to display an impressive degree of modernity. After the Meiji Restoration, this modern spirit continued to influence the country at the same time as European modernity was having its impact; but there is no question that from 1868 onwards our modernity was gradually recast in a European direction, and that this spirit helped to build Japan. One is forced to conclude that Europeans have sustained a wonderful degree of development over a long period; but the whole business was not as wonderful as these Europeans claimed. On this point, I think that Japanese intellectuals have misconstrued the import of the European view.

So why have the Japanese since the Meiji Restoration regarded the culture and spirit of Europe as utterly different from our own? I think there are various reasons. One is that European customs and conventions were obviously alien. The spirit of modernity may have been the same but customs were a great divide. For example, there is something very Japanese about the notion that as a result of a blast from the cannons of a few warships a whole culture decided overnight to embrace the spirit of a completely alien civilization.[38]

When the Japanese decided to begin revolutionizing their culture with the Meiji Restoration, this meant a total change of politics and society. After 1868, the Edo Shogunate was decisively rejected, and rejecting the Shogunate meant turning one's back on Edo culture as a whole. Overnight everything about the Edo period was condemned as a form of medieval darkness. This was the fundamental undercurrent of post-Meiji thought and feeling, and it explains why 1868 marked such a radical break with the past. But this view of the past, with its [enthusiastic and singular] embrace of modernity, was itself a product of the modern mood. Today, we see the transition from feudalism to modernity as more complicated and nuanced, and we view the feudal past with less hostility. For example, we can recognize that the Edo period also displayed a marvellous kind of modern spirit. Hence my conclusion that Japan has experienced two phases or kinds of modernity, and this, I think, implies a mixture of continuities and discontinuities in the recent Japanese past.

NISHITANI: In general, might one conclude that before the self-imposed isolation of the Edo period, the merchant classes were on the rise, and after Japan became isolated, the warrior class, the samurai, became the focal group of society ... ?

KŌYAMA: I think the situation was a little different. Before the closure of the country under the Tokugawa, the merchants and the samurai could be said to belong, very roughly speaking, to the same social group. When Japan expanded overseas before the Tokugawa isolation, it was this 'group', for the most part, that was active in trade and commerce. The people who engaged in this trade were merchants who possessed a certain samurai spirit – people like the merchants of Sakai [near Osaka] and the daimyo of the West Country (*Nishi kuni*). But when Japan entered the Tokugawa period, the merchants and samurai were officially designated as separate classes. And what began as a government imposition ended up changing how the merchants and samurai regarded themselves. They began to see themselves as distinct groups. One consequence [of this changed self-perception] is that the distinctions between farmers, manufacturers and merchants became rigid caste divisions reflecting the relative status of occupations within Japanese society as a whole. As for the samurai, although still officially warriors, they now lived in a country at peace: thus they became a class of quasi-bureaucrats, as noted above, and it was merchants, rather than samurai,

---

38 What is described as 'Japanese' here is in reality Confucian to the core. The phenomenon of sudden total changes in the direction of a society is universal across East Asia. The next two sentences reinforce the point while avoiding the 'Confucian' label.

who came to dominate the economic activity of Japanese society during the Edo period.

KŌSAKA: I think that is basically what happened.

SUZUKI: Thus, in the East, there was a rational spirit but not an experimental one. In essence, Eastern rationality was 'metaphysical'.

KŌYAMA: We had a kind of metaphysical rationality but not experimental or scientific rationality. And thus in the East the indispensable link between rationality and experimentalism did not develop.

SUZUKI: In astronomy, the constellations and solar eclipses were observed but such observations were not grounded in mathematics. In medicine, there was plenty of clinical observation but no experimentation. The foundations of Oriental science were rooted in such metaphysical ideas as the Five Fates, the Six Energies, or the Five Actions of Yin and Yang. This tradition did not include physiology or anatomical dissections. This discrepancy [between Eastern and Western rationality] reflected not only a relative lack of development in Eastern scholarship and science but also a fundamental difference between the civilizations.

8 The concept of history in the East (*Tōyō*)

KŌSAKA: We have drawn a distinction between the positivistic or experimental and the metaphysical, but I wonder if there isn't also a fundamental difference in logic as practised in the East and the West. After all, China developed its own Chinese form of positivism.

SUZUKI: Well, yes, I guess that might be right. Indeed, we might very well eventually reach that sort of conclusion.

KŌSAKA: I have been looking at the ways in which recent European and Chinese historians have addressed their work. It is my impression that Europeans and Chinese take radically different approaches to the study of the past. European historians develop a steady stream of different ideas and themes. This pattern is very evident in their writings. But when one turns to books by Chinese historians, there appears to be comparatively little development of ideas or themes. Rather, one topic after another is raised only suddenly to disappear. An era ends, and so does the story. Rulers come and go, and there the discussion ends. Developmental explanations are extremely rare. The fundamental method appears to be that some principle or other is adopted, and the relevant historical material, in its various forms, is arranged and set out according to a governing principle. Examples of this approach are numerous. By contrast, instances where principles are developed are rare. There is no or little reflection on one's ruling assumptions. For example, the principle or rubric of 'Wood, Fire, Earth, Metal and Water' is taken up and applied to historical material in order to make comparisons or to draw contrasts with alternative principles or rubrics such as 'North, South, East and West' or 'Spring, Summer, Autumn and Winter' or 'Anger, Happiness, Desire,

Sorrow, Fear'.[39] The changes in the 'Three Kingdoms', for example, are explained by reference to the three colours 'Black, White and Red'.

Reflecting on such examples, we might concede that there are mutual relationships of a kind between 'Wood, Fire, Earth, Metal and Water' – but it is not obvious what any of these elements have to do with 'North, South, East and West'. While acknowledging that there may be a comparative or contrastive relationship between such groups of ideas or notions, or even that they can serve as methods for arranging or presenting historical material, it is equally clear that they lack a developmental or cause-and-effect dimension. This is the source of their conceptual poverty. They display a kind of discontinuity rather than the continuity characteristic of developmental ideas. Chinese historians have an undeniable interest in applying and sorting historical materials in accordance with such overarching principles, and they often do so with much skill. But they do not display the ability to explain history using such approaches. Or at least so it seems to me. I guess this might serve as an example of Chinese 'logic'.

NISHITANI: It's cyclical, isn't it?

KŌSAKA: And therefore it does not progress. There is no attempt to achieve conceptual depth. It is just a system of classifications. In terms of time, it is merely cyclical. Isn't that right?

KŌYAMA: We should probably accept that the concept of developmental progress is unique to European modernity. After all, we had no equivalent of the idea of progress in Japan. From the middle of the Heian period we had the eschatological notion of 'the end of the world', the idea that Japan was approaching some kind of demise. This feeling was particularly strong when the spread of warrior clans throughout the country suggested that evil times were at hand. This was the view embraced by the old aristocracy. But curiously, the emerging warrior clans did not themselves develop a progressive notion of the changes they were effecting, and therefore they too lacked a view of history based on progressive development. Then, later, the Edo period saw the rise of the view that Japan had to return to the past (*fukkō*) – rejecting any idea that the Edo period, or what we regard as early modernity, represented a developmental improvement over the Japanese Middle Ages. In either case, no idea of progress resulted.

NISHITANI: The West was in many ways the same. Religion in the West was traditionally susceptible to calls to return to the past. This made it necessary to develop a form of religion that could accept the modern idea of progress as well as a kind of idealism based on experience, while not

---

39 The Chinese grouping of these five emotions is significant in classical Chinese thought, but there appears to be no agreed translation in English.

SUZUKI: I am in broad general agreement with Kōyama's thesis that Japan has experienced two forms of modernity. But I am even more in accord with some of the ideas that Kōsaka proposed, for example, in this collection of essays *The Philosophy of History and Political Philosophy*.[40] In fact I have been in secret agreement with Kōsaka for two long years now. (*All laugh.*) In particular, I am attracted by his idea that the East has had a classical phase (*kodai*). Not only did the East experience a classical age, it was an age of particular splendour. But however excellent the East's period of classical greatness was, and however fine our antiquity was, this great age was not [followed by] the triumph of modernity. My conclusion is that Eastern antiquity was a superb achievement, rivalling anything produced by Greco-Roman antiquity; but in no sense can we say that the East produced the revolution that we call 'the modern'. However, this general Eastern failure does not include Japan. Japan has produced its own version of modernity, and this fact has revolutionary implications for East Asia. It announces the arrival of a new age in the history of the East. And this event is of the greatest world-historical significance; exactly as Kōsaka has argued in the set of essays I have just mentioned.

KŌYAMA: There is a tendency to think of the prehistoric (*genshi*) as soon as one mentions antiquity (*kodai*). [But] thinking only of Japan, one cannot conclude that our ancient age consisted of nothing more than the prehistoric.[41] For example, Japan developed a kind of genuine state during the Nara [646–794 CE] and early Heian [794–898 CE] periods. This is a bit of an overstatement but the point will stand. These were literate states (*bunka no kokka*). They had sophisticated systems of law (*Ritsuryō*). They had currency as a means of exchange. There is some doubt about how widespread the use of money was, but the development of money as a medium of exchange preceded the development of [a large-scale] barter economy, and continued to develop even when barter became the prevalent form of exchange. The Edo period is the great classic example of a dual-medium exchange economy, one that may offer the best example of the theories of Dopsch and others.[42]

9 Criticizing the theory of stages of development[43]

SUZUKI: The thesis of stages of development is a [theoretical] formula concocted by modern man. Given my specialization as a historian, I have

---

40 Masaaki Kōsaka, *Rekishi Tetsugaku to Seiji Tetsugaku*, Tokyo: Kōbundō, 1939.
41 'Prehistoric' here means 'pre-literate'. The absence of writing shuts the door on the research methods of the historian working in the Rankean tradition.
42 Alfons Dopsch (1868–1953): Austrian historian and medievalist.
43 *Hatten Dankai-setsu*.

had the opportunity to examine this argument from time to time. Historians everywhere have long debated whether this thesis fits with the facts or not. For myself, I have recently come to hold a more sceptical position. My doubts centre less on whether the thesis does justice to the facts and more on questions of historical method and outlook. I have come to feel that however many facts one brings to the task, and however one revises one's thesis to reflect the facts, the theory always falls short of the facts. And this fatally impairs the stages of development thesis. Or at least that is what I think. Perhaps it is better to conclude that this thesis merely reflects a stage in the development of the study of history.

KŌYAMA: I completely agree. I suspect that it is probably a mistake to assume that the stages-of-development theory is consistent with the facts of history or facts in general. The empirical weaknesses of the thesis are serious. Rather, it is better appreciated as a kind of middle-range [heuristic] generalization or standard to be used in understanding the special, sometimes unique, features of various national histories.[44]

SUZUKI: It is a classification system based on types.[45]

KŌSAKA: Yes, 'type' is the right term. But the theory of cultural stages of development does not even pretend to offer in any sense a way of identifying the direction of history, and this is particularly obvious when it comes to delineating that stage of history we call the 'contemporary'. Traditionally a type has been not simply a theoretical concept but something with considerable practical implications in giving direction to attempts to guide history. In short, it has a leadership dimension.[46] But this in itself is insufficient. Types have to be linked to other types to form a system of comparisons or genealogy. This is essential. Thus the theory of stages of cultural development as it stands is incomplete. A more world-historical approach is essential: one characterized by greater dynamism, one that is open to the idea of radical change. Without such features, this system of cultural classifications cannot stand as it is. The validity of the interpretations arising from it cannot be accepted.

KŌYAMA: But the belief that such systems of classification have scientific validity is a particular feature of modern European culture. This says a lot about European scholarship.

SUZUKI: The process of trying to think about the theory of stages of development in various ways has made me sceptical about this thesis on methodological grounds. This is the conclusion at which I have arrived. In any case, there is no limit to how much one may argue about whether the facts of the case fit or don't fit the theory.

---

44 That is, something between what we might today call 'grand theory' and 'micro-empiricism'.
45 Suzuki uses the German term *Typus*, transliterated into Japanese.
46 The implication is that if Japan or any other world-historical power is going to lead the world, it must have a confident grasp of the direction in which history is moving or should move.

KŌYAMA: The final manifestation of this approach may be found in the application of the historical materialist approach to [the study of] Japan and China.

10 The problem of mechanized civilization

SUZUKI: Taking mechanization as a defining feature of civilization allows us to treat the problem of civilization more broadly. Just because civilization may be in crisis, as we argue, does not mean that material or scientific progress has stopped. This crisis is unfolding on a [quite] different level. In other words, it is possible to conclude that modern civilization remains a scientific civilization, in which the core sciences function effectively. But, at the same time, this scientific civilization may be obstructed on another level and thus find itself in crisis. [Despite such emergencies,] the sciences will continue to advance, and the necessity for this kind of progress will only grow in the future.[47]

In other words, modernity has no end point. This much is obvious. Anyone who believes that civilization is about to disappear, or that material civilization is [fatally] obstructed, or that that civilization is caught in [a fatal] crisis, is dreaming. Or so the optimist would seemingly have us believe.

My view is that while, of course, scientific civilization will continue to advance, there is a genuine problem in the relationship between the progress of civilization and the spirit of mankind, [by which I mean] the spirit within.[48] This is the relationship that I think is out of phase. Mechanization is the civilization of man's external environment. [Mechanized] civilization is about making the impossible possible, but a civilization that is anchored in the external world is not one likely to address what we really are inside. Furthermore, alienation between what we are inside and outside, a fundamental disharmony [between 'spirit' and 'material'], has grown exceedingly strong in the contemporary world. And it is this disharmony that fuels what has been called 'the crisis of contemporary life'.

NISHITANI: I wonder if the problem does not arise because the standpoint of the scientific disciplines, what we may call the sciences of externality, of the external world, is finally the standpoint of man himself.[49] We are

---

47 Here Suzuki breaks entirely with the 'reactionary' or 'humanist' thrust of the Japan Romantic School, which rejected modernity and all its works.
48 Before the nineteenth century, most Europeans might have used the word 'soul' to highlight the point Suzuki is making.
49 Such doubts invite comparisons with Heidegger's critique of material or subjectivist philosophy. The objectivist character of Nishida's philosophy may also be relevant here. Both fall under the rubric of what Heidegger would later call 'humanist philosophy'.

divided within ourselves. The result is the rupture between what we are outside and what we are inside. Doesn't this seem to be the case?

SUZUKI: But isn't there what one might call a philosophy of happiness at work here? This is the kind of thing that Nishitani has described recently as the philosophy of practicality or effective action or utilitarianism (*kōrishugi*).[50] The external environment (*kankyō*) is a source of human happiness. Improve the external world, and the result is progress; this makes a better society possible. Human happiness is thus increased. [But] I must confess that I find the contradictory nature of this world-view very unsettling.

NISHITANI: The impact of the sciences or what I called earlier the empirical or positivist spirit casts an irresistible shadow over human existence. Once one has awakened to its powers, one is changed for ever.

SUZUKI: We cannot go back; the transformation is irreversible. I believe that, furthermore, the development of the sciences will continue their uninterrupted advance. And this scientific advance means that something must be done to restore the harmony between the sciences and the inner spirit of man.

KŌYAMA: That's right. Since technology has come to govern the horizon of humanity, this problem has decisively shaped the debate over the 'philosophy of technology'.

NISHITANI: This challenge, the conflict between religion and science, is the most radical problem facing contemporary Europe. Christianity stands at the heart of Europe's difficulties [over science], but the struggle [with scientific truth] is also the great problem for us in Japan as well.[51]

SUZUKI: In any case, in order to save a civilization that is mechanized, such as ours, does one simply proceed with further development or not? That is the issue. Will more progress really save us?

KŌYAMA: A similar view is taken in Dessauer's recently translated *The Philosophy of Technology*.[52] According to Dessauer, who evokes the language of Kant, the categorical imperative of technology, its supreme goal and obligation, is the abolition of war. Rather than seeing modern technology as the source of greater darkness, Dessauer believes that progress can rescue modern civilization from its current unhappy state.

NISHITANI: He thinks that conventional religion's role has been superseded in modern life, to the point where it has become powerless. Technology has

---

50 The three terms are an attempt to suggest the range of meanings that Suzuki is suggesting. In the Japanese text he uses only the term *kōrishugi*.
51 An anticipation of the ideas to which Nishitani would later give influential form in his work *Nihilism*.
52 Friedrich Dessauer published a book in 1908 that was translated into Japanese as *Gijutsuteki Bunka* (Technological Culture); Eberhard Zschimmer wrote a book with the title *The Philosophy of Technology* that appeared in 1914. The two texts may have been confused here.

replaced it. The world-view of technology's advocates tends to assert its power to save the world. The very notion that technology can save the world is an extraordinary idea, and a terrifyingly modern one at that. But I suspect that salvation via technology will not be easy. The whole standpoint reflects an excessive faith in the powers of technology.[53]

SUZUKI: Such trust itself is problematic.

KŌYAMA: I do not believe that civilization's problems can be solved so easily.

KŌSAKA: I agree with that. As Suzuki has explained, technology has emerged as a problem because, as the world has progressed, contradictions have arisen between our inner natures and our external circumstances. This contradictory condition is most obvious in Europe. There, as Nishitani noted, the struggle between Christianity and technology or mechanized civilization is fundamental.

So how has this problem come to obstruct mankind's path? The answer lies in the basic orientation of Western civilization or, to express the issue even more broadly, the European spirit. This spirit is thoroughly penetrated by mechanistic civilization, but this is only one side of the coin. At the same time, the European spirit displays a profound degree of interiority, of internal depth. The mechanistic dimension of the European spirit must not be allowed to obscure the importance of this interiority.[54] On the contrary, it is precisely the way in which this interiority radically distinguishes itself from the externality of technology that gives this inner quality its unique profundity. Surely this is the lesson of Kierkegaard and Dostoevsky.[55] But the price of this inner rejection of the factual world is to project us into a bottomless pit. And this is the source of the crisis of the European spirit.

This crisis explains why the current fascination among young [Japanese] readers for Pascal and Montaigne qualifies as something more profound than just a passing fad.[56] It reflects the impact of a radically divided civilization. This obsession among young Japanese suggests a degree of fascination with interiority, as an intensely individual experience, almost entirely unknown to our ancestors. What, then, is to be done? The problem posed is deeply disturbing. But might not the depth of the individual spirit be mediated by the depth of the historical spirit of the nation (*minzoku*)?

---

53 Nishitani here offers a Japanese version of 'the question of technology' to which Heidegger gave celebrated expression.
54 For a forceful and influential as well as witty treatment of this issue, see Matthew Arnold's *Culture and Anarchy* (1869).
55 Søren Kierkegaard (1813–55): Danish philosopher and major influence on Existentialism. Fyodor Dostoevsky (1821–81): Russian novelist who, alongside Leo Tolstoy, was regarded in Japan as the pre-eminent master of the novel of the modern age.
56 Blaise Pascal (1623–62): French philosopher, mathematician and physicist, in great vogue in inter-war Japan, as was Michel Montaigne (1533–92), traditionally the most admired of all French writers.

This may sound somewhat paradoxical, but one can say that the modern phenomenon of total war is itself the product of mechanistic civilization.[57] This insight yields a painful dilemma in which national subjectivity (*minzoku-teki shutaisei*) allows itself to be dominated by mechanistic structures and organizations. If we agree to follow this line of argument, might it be conceivable that the agency of the individual ethos could find expression in the nation's historical practice, thus enabling it to transcend the divisions of mechanistic civilization? As contemporary wars are total wars, would a kind of dialectic not apply?

This is no more than a speculative idea. But to push this notion or conceit a bit further, history is not the product of the individual spirit. History is a product of the species: peoples make history.[58] If we think about the problem posed by the spirit of the individual within the context of the nation's history, these divisions may be transcendable. The vantage point of historicism offers an effective way of looking at the problem of the spirit of individualism. I would like to call this mode of interpretation 'historical symbolism', an approach that takes as its point of departure the fact that the idea of Eastern nothingness (*Tōyō-teki na mu*) is itself a product of history.[59]

11 The problem of historicism

SUZUKI: Earlier Kōyama referred to differences between Chinese accounts of history and European ones. I wondered what everyone thought of Troeltsch's observation that while it is true that the East has understood [the problems of] historiography, Europe alone has grasped the full implications of historicism.[60]

---

57 Kōsaka's remark is paradoxical because the idea of total war was viewed by many Japanese at this time as a psychological state or condition rather than a degree of material mobilization or rationalized production. The meaning and significance of the term 'total war' is treated at length in the commentary on the third round-table discussion (November 1942), in section III.
58 The reference to species (as in Aristotle's logic of universals, species and the individual) would have been taken by many literate Japanese readers of 1942 as referring to Hajime Tanabe's masterwork, *The Logic of the Species*, of which the twelfth of what would be eventually thirteen sections was published in October and December 1941. For details of the order of publication and Tanabe's argument, see David Williams, *Defending Japan's Pacific War: The Kyoto School Philosophers and Post-White Power*, London & New York: RoutledgeCurzon, 2004, ch. 7. Note also Kōsaka's insistence that 'peoples (*minzoku*) make history'. This can be seen to echo Vico's remark that man makes history. Hegel's insistence that peoples or nations make world history is probably the decisive influence here.
59 Having evoked the labours of one founder of the Kyoto School, Hajime Tanabe, Kōsaka almost immediately brings into play the key idea of the other founder: Kitarō Nishida (1870–1945). Kōsaka's deliberate historicizing of one of the great trans-historical categories of Eastern thought – nothingness or *mu* – is typical of this young thinker during the early days of the Pacific War.
60 Suzuki may well be referring to Troeltsch's much-discussed *Der Historismus und seine Probleme* (Historical Relativism and its Problems), published in 1922.

KŌSAKA: I think Troeltsch is correct.

KŌYAMA: Yes, but that also explains why the East has not been suffering from a crisis of historicism. We talk about the idea of historicism in contemporary Japan but our sense of the past is different from Europe's, not least because Christianity and Buddhism are so dissimilar.[61]

KŌSAKA: Quite right. Chinese and European historians approach their subjects differently, as was said, but this is because their historical consciousness is fundamentally different. Furthermore, if one looks at the problem more closely still, it is obvious, at least to me, that the sense of historical motion or movement is not the same for the West and China, or for that matter, for China and Japan. There is a difference of dynamic. This is fundamental. In Japan one does not see the kind of fierce confrontations and struggles that characterize the West. But one does find in Japan a sense of forward motion, of reform and change, and that one does not find in any way in China. [Overall] one may conclude that the rhythm of history, the way it moves through time, distinguishes East from West.

SUZUKI: I feel the same. I think this gap in historical consciousness explains why the Western idea of 'development' did not appear in the East. But, to try to move our discussion back a bit, this situation also means that Japan has not experienced the crisis of historicism as it has affected Europe. Instead, our approach to history is full of desire for change and the will to change.

KŌYAMA: Also, we don't draw a rigid distinction between the historical and trans-historical realms, and this means that we are less likely to engage in decisive struggles with clear outcomes. And, furthermore, because we approach history with a relativist mindset, we tend not to experience a sense of 'depth'. We consistently reduce history to the trans-historical sphere, the realm of the eternal and undying. One may conclude therefore that in East Asia one does not generally witness the kind of historical consciousness that produces phenomena such as the crisis of historicism.

NISHITANI: For my part, I remain in doubt about whether it is a good thing or not for Japan that our current [world-historical] situation arose before we had, as a nation, fully absorbed [the lessons and significance of] historicism. When all is said and done, the overcoming of historicism itself can only be achieved by working our way through historicism, by making historicism our own, before we seek to overcome it. At least that is what I think.[62]

---

61 It would be interesting to know what was going through Nishitani's mind when he heard these views, because at the end of the war he would assert that the trial of Nihilism, the bastard child of historicism, was unavoidable in Japan despite the cultural differences between East and West.

62 Keiji Nishitani, *Nihirizumu*, Tokyo: Kōbundō, 1949; pub. in English as *The Self-Overcoming of Nihilism*, trans. Graham Parkes with Setsuko Aihara, Albany, NY: State University of New York Press, 1990.

KŌYAMA: That is a point very much worth discussing. There are a great number of ahistorical ideas in circulation here [in Japan] at the moment. These ideas are flawed. They suggest that we have failed to ground our self-understanding rigorously enough in an authentic consciousness of the past. I think this kind of grounding is essential. Take, for example, the observations one hears nowadays that liberalism is not suited to our national polity or that individualism offends against the Japanese spirit. If one examines carefully what these critics are saying, one discovers that they are thinking in completely unhistorical ways. Liberalism and individualism are products of social and historical reality.

To say that these ideas are not to be permitted today suggests a drastic failure to grasp the role such ideas have played [in the making of the modern world]. Such arguments are not persuasive. How can one say that the meritorious retainers of the Meiji period were really traitors and thieves? There is nothing constructive at work in such criticism. If one refuses to place the ideas of liberalism and individualism in their proper historical context, if one distorts them into ahistorical abstractions or clichés, one departs completely from the facts of the case, from reality, and descends into empty speculation about the past. One result is that if one denounces modern individualism and liberalism, one ends up denouncing all forms of individual self-awareness as wrong. This is a major error. It effectively denies the foundations for any and all forms of individual responsibility.

Why? Because a strong sense of responsibility is inevitably the product of the genuine development of individual consciousness. The idea that individuals are responsible for their lives completely vanishes if one assumes that individuals are merely to be ordered about or that they are just cogs in a mindless machine. Without the sense of individual responsibility, the feeling of obligation that the contemporary heirs of 2,600 years of Japanese history owe to our society is unthinkable. Indeed, the urge to eliminate this profound sense of responsibility has become a kind of disease in contemporary Japan.

12 The problem of our awareness as individuals

KŌYAMA: I have always thought that Japan could boast a long history of individual awareness or consciousness. Take, for example, Japan's topsy-turvy Era of the Warring States, the late medieval period, when retainers overthrew their lords, and a destitute peasant could become master of the whole country. When those wielding power could never be confident of their hold on authority, a kind of anarchy erupted in which the thrust of individual self-assertion came to the fore. The same phenomenon can be seen in Japan's advance abroad, in which individual consciousness burst the narrow confines of the nation. Of course, with the consolidation of Tokugawa rule after 1600, individuals were subjected to a rigid caste or status system in which one spent the whole of one's working life in a single occupation. But even this encouraged the flowering of a very strong sense of individual, that is, subjective (*shutai*) responsibility. And this was not confined to the Edo period. Samurai, for example, displayed what was in fact an extraordinary kind of individual consciousness and discipline, indeed freedom, of the will in being prepared to take final responsibility for their grave mistakes by committing very bloody suicides. Of course, this kind of 'freedom' and 'individualism' had little to do with the unrestrained pursuit of individual wealth or profit, or with the modern bourgeois freedoms of a society of city-dwellers.

Nevertheless, I believe that pre-modern Japan does offer examples of genuine individual consciousness and freedom. To neglect this Japanese tradition of individualism is to deny an important aspect of the lives of our ancestors. In other words, I think it is a mistake to assume that the master-retainer relationships of pre-modern Japan were undiluted expressions of totalitarianism or feudal absolutism. Such interpretations should be regarded as *passé*, as examples of modern prejudice and ignorance. This kind of thinking is not empirical: it is not based on an examination of the facts, but is rather a flawed exercise in deductive reasoning which takes modern individualism as its premise and concludes that the past was the opposite.

Feudal warrior society was grounded in relationships of personal trust between individuals. The master or social superior trusted his retainers or social inferiors absolutely, and he was trusted accordingly. Feudal society would not have lasted without such relationships of mutual trust. Why were such relationships possible? The answer is because the samurai lived, as it were, constantly on the frontier between life and death. Among samurai who confronted the absolute fact of life or death on a daily basis, lies and deception would in principle never occur.[63] In such a situation, where honesty was always judged to be the best policy, it was unthinkable that the virtue of honesty would be prostituted to the pursuit of monetary advantage or profit. Such conduct was not permitted because it was inconsistent with the founding principles of the society in which the samurai lived. In other words, the original or defining principles that underwrote the conduct of [respectively] the samurai and the merchant, were fundamentally at odds. 'Honesty is the best policy' [is a principle that] could have never governed bourgeois society because, if anything, the fundamental premise of modern society is mutual distrust. This system of moral conduct, [which prevails] because everything is designed to advance personal profit, arises from an unspoken premise that everyone tacitly subscribes to it. Such silence of assent is unthinkable among samurai. Their ethics were explicit.

---

63 'Absolute' in the sense of being unconditional, that is, not dependent on other factors within the scope of human freedom.

Now, while it is certainly true that individualism and liberty in modern Europe are of an entirely different character, Japanese feudalism did produce moral agents capable of taking total responsibility for their conduct. This kind of self-aware subjectivity was enormously strong among the samurai class. Indeed, without such subjectivity Japanese feudal society as we know it was all but unthinkable. Trust and loyalty formed the foundation of social relations, and this was as true of relationships between social equals, whether colleagues or friends, as it was of the ties between masters and retainers. In such a society, to betray a trust was about as sensible as cutting off one's hand. And people recognized this view as sound. Thus the suggestion that one might betray one's friends or peers was ethically eliminated [as inconceivable] lest it weaken the thrust of the samurai ethos.

Nevertheless, it is true that modern society has crushed its feudal predecessor, and the view that feudal life lacked both liberty and individualism is grounded in the facts of the case. The realities of modern society compel one to accept this interpretation. And this means that nowadays we must significantly rethink our ethical ideas about what is to be expected of human conduct. Blind obedience will no longer do. We have to devise ways of rethinking the notion of trust if it is to serve as the foundation for a more progressive form of self-actualizing subjectivity (*shutaisei no jihatsusei*).

SUZUKI: We talk of the 'modern individual', but isn't his self-awareness confined to an atomistic singularity? Does modern man really have an authentic interior life? Is he a real 'person'? If the modern individual singularity lacks this kind of personality then this reduces democracy, organizationally speaking, to a collection of atoms, of individual voters. Whatever one says about our current politics of strong leaders, one can at least argue that they have personalities.[64] But the larger point is that modern individualism has diminished the 'person' [as the nexus of a set of human relationships] and his interior life. By contrast, feudal-style loyalty provided a personal ethical orientation, uniting one person to another in a powerfully human way. The human ties of today's modern individual are mechanistic, thus reducing the human person to a unity of abstractions.

KŌYAMA: In medieval Japan, human relations were mediated by something absolute. Without this absolute mediation, a samurai would have been asked to throw his life away for some idiotic unfeeling ruler.[65] Was this likely? Of course it wasn't. In the Era of the Warring States, masters

---

64 A back-handed compliment to Hideki Tōjō?
65 This analysis of samurai conduct is underpinned by an exercise in dialectical reasoning. Like a catalyst in chemistry, the samurai and his master were mutually transformed by their relationship while remaining distinct individuals capable of making moral choices. Their relationship, grounded in a death pact, is thus made absolute, unconditioned by their separate existence as individuals. It is the relationship that matters because, in a way that it is true of neither the samurai nor his master individually, it defines what they are together in death.

could be chosen. If a samurai felt that he was in the service of some benighted ruler, he would find a more enlightened lord to serve, one who would reciprocate the trust the samurai was prepared to invest in him. This bond of trust rested on the willingness of the samurai to sacrifice his life for his lord, but such sacrifices were subject to absolute mediation. The act itself had absolute significance and thus was of an entirely different character from contemporary individualism, which is mediated by practical reason. The motivations of the medieval samurai were utterly different from conduct mediated by selfish desire and greed for material gain.[66]

SUZUKI: I agree.

NISHITANI: But, at the same time, we must not forget the limitations of the medieval spirit. In my opinion, yes, the Middle Ages saw the development of a profoundly self-aware personality. One finds this particularly true of the period's religious consciousness. Furthermore, it is also true that this self-awareness flowered within the context of absolute [mediated] relationships between people as persons. This spirit underwrote the relationship between lord and retainer. With this conclusion I am in full accord. But the modern period saw the shift from the 'person' mediated by an absolute relationship to one grounded in the absolute individual. And the significance of this transformation can be found in the way the individual is unable to separate himself from the existing public order, no matter what political complexion that order may take. In other words, if public order collapses, the individual goes down with it. At the same time, if there is progress in the public sphere – even, to put the point somewhat negatively, if this progress is of the most modest sort – the individual benefits. The individual is unbounded; he can go as far as he allows himself to go.

My choice of expression may be a bit odd, but I have come to conclude that human life in the modern era is, if you will, 'adventurous'. The activity undertaken may be the founding of a new business or the discovery of a new continent, but taken in the widest sense – and there is a link here to our discussion earlier of the empirical spirit – the life of the individual is conceived of as self-made.[67] The focus of this life is the event or the experience. It is this that makes the endeavour of modern life an adventure.

One of the defining features of modern man is found in what he seeks from experience. One must see and touch things; otherwise one is not persuaded of their existence. Experience offers a kind of proof without which one will not give one's assent. The flourishing of modern science and philosophy is a direct reflection of this spirit, which extends to the arts and letters as well. Great progress has been made in all these fields of endeavour in the modern era.

---

66 A brief encomium to the purity of purpose that characterized a lost age of Japanese feeling.
67 Nishitani uses the German word *Leben*, transliterated into Japanese.

Any attempt to move beyond modern individualism must return to this truth. We must make this return to our starting point if we are to have any chance of success. In this context it is pointless to evoke the nation (*kokka*) or see Japanese-ness as the gifts of the gods, as we have done until now. This is hopelessly ineffective (*dame da*).[68] At least this is what I think.

KŌYAMA: I am not very familiar with things in Europe, but in the case of Japan there was a splendid kind of individual consciousness in the medieval period. After the Era of the Warring States, the Edo period saw a rigid class system imposed on Japanese consciousness. When taking final leave from parents or wife or children in order to confront the absolute finality of death, one had to give expression to a marvellously singular or individual consciousness of an absolute character. At that time, something not unlike what philosophy today calls 'existence' (*jitsuzon*) or *Existenz* prevailed.[69] The intensity of this form of consciousness gradually relaxed during the Edo period. The spirit of Bushido could be still found in this or that individual, but in society as a whole the samurai spirit was extinguished. And the cause of this change was the imposition of the caste system – warrior, farmer, craftsman and merchant – based on Confucian ethics. In the detail of its prescriptions, this system evolved into an extreme kind of formalism. Later this caste hierarchy was undermined as merchants, the group supposedly at the bottom of the Confucian social scale, began to exercise more and more social influence. Inevitably this change produced a confused mixing of the classes. In such circumstances, rigid distinctions of class status became blurred while notions of individualism gained influence. This type of individualism was different from the kind of absolute individual consciousness of the Middle Ages. It was not religious. It was ethical and secular.

This means that the kind of individual consciousness that appeared in Japan after 1868 was not a direct descendant of medieval individualism but did have a close relationship with modern individualism. This type of modern Japanese individualism, which was something distinctive and new, involved borrowing Europe's clothes.[70]

KŌSAKA: That is interesting.
KŌYAMA: Something suddenly appeared in the Meiji period that was entirely out of keeping with previous Japanese experience. What is striking is that in the medieval period the rights of the first-born daughter were

---

68 From a Confucian perspective, this standpoint is the source of the Kyoto School's uncompromising resistance to the Tōjō clique in particular and aggressive militarism in general.
69 Graham Parkes confirms that Nishitani's source for this idea is Karl Jaspers.
70 This may be compared with Löwith's remark on the irreversible impact of Western values on the non-Westerner who adopts them, in 'Afterword to the Japanese Reader', Note 36.

recognized. That was the time when the status of wives, women and daughters was enhanced.

KŌSAKA: On that count, Masako displayed a kind of decency, even greatness?[71]

KŌYAMA: What was called for was the marriage of one man to one woman. The sympathy displayed by Masako towards Shizuka (*Gozen*) reflected such feelings.[72] In fact this was not an example of [strict] monogamy; but the notion of marriage defined as one man united with one woman did reflect an improved status for women, and this represented a splendid revolution, given the mores of the Heian period.

In this period, individuals had absolute significance. One has only to recall the battle of Ujigawa to illustrate the point.[73] If each and every individual had taken on full responsibility for his part in the struggle, such battles would have been unthinkable. But it is also worth noting how things changed during the Edo period. Take the siege of Osaka Castle, when the forces of the Tōyōtomi clan were destroyed. The front-line fighters wanted to take the battle to the enemy, but were accused of refusing to obey orders and were punished. Battle strategies, of course, change over time, but the fall of Osaka Castle can be taken as symbolic of the new order that emerged during the Edo period.

That new order would eventually be destroyed by the form of new individual consciousness that has come into being with the rise of modern Japan. True, it appears possible to trace back a link between this new individual consciousness and that of the distant medieval period, and indeed, the individual consciousness of the Edo period, if it had been allowed to advance a bit more, might have evolved into something not unlike that of Europe. But what is sometimes negatively described as modern individualism was very different from the individualism of the medieval warrior.

KŌSAKA: If one pursues that line of interpretation, one might also say that we can find a kind of individual self-awareness in ancient Japan, as reflected in the *Manyōshū*, although one somewhat different from the kind we have been discussing.[74] How can one describe this? It is different from both modern individualism and the medieval personality. I think the individual consciousness of that period approaches the rich life of natural man. I find in it a kind of [attractive] innocence.

---

71 Hōjō Masako was the wife of Yoritomo, the first Kamakura shogun.
72 The two women are two of the great romantic figures of early medieval Japan. The stories told about them vary: in the version referred to by Kōsaka and Kōyama, Masako saves Shizuka, then the concubine of Yoshitsune, Yoritomo's brother and rival, from imprisonment.
73 There were three historically significant battles at the Ujigawa River near Kyoto: Kōyama seems to be referring to the one in 1180 involving what may have been the first ritual suicide or battlefield *seppuku*. Strictly speaking the '*hara-kiri*' took place at the nearby temple of Byōdō-in.
74 Japan's oldest collection of poetry, complied by Tachibana no Moroe around 750 CE.

KŌYAMA: Doesn't the structure of the Kegon universe, with its concept of harmony between the individual and the totality, of the one in the all, of all in the one, offer an effective expression of the individual consciousness of the Nara period?[75] Furthermore, one might ask whether the Kegon world-view does in fact nicely capture the relationship between the individual and the state in the same period. In this philosophy, neither the totality nor the individual had a prior status; they stand in a *qua* relationship of mutuality.[76] To live for the state is to live for oneself; to live for oneself is to live for the state. In other words, there is no division, no conflict of consciousness between the individual and the state. They are united in harmony, directly and seamlessly. This is what I think is new about the Nara period's national consciousness; and it came about precisely because the Kegon universe was a living force in Japanese life during this period. But this sense of harmony between the individual and the whole proved impossible to sustain. The destruction began with the arrival of the Heian court, certainly by the middle of the Heian period or thereabouts. The new emerging clan system inserted itself between the individual and the whole, thus destroying the relationship.

NISHITANI (*TURNING TO SUZUKI*): How were things in the West?

13 The European Renaissance and modern history

SUZUKI: You are asking, 'How did the individual manifest itself in Western consciousness?' On the subject of the individual and the totality in Europe, it is difficult for me [to reply]. I don't really know [very much about this]. But when one mentions the equivalence or unity of the individual and the whole, the self and the totality, I am reminded of Nishida's recent essay, 'The Problem of *raison d'état*'.[77] There he observes that in the ethics of the ancient Greek *polis* there is no fundamental contradiction between the state and the individual.[78] I think that was actually the case. In medieval German law, a kind of totalitarianism prevailed, at least in spirit, and this offers a complete contrast to the individualism of the modern period. The principle that mattered here was the indivisibility of public and private law. Neither was judged to have precedence over the other. The ideas of public and private law had their origins in Roman law.

---

75 Kegon-shū was a Buddhist sect brought to Japan by Dōzen in 735.
76 The Latin word *qua* or 'as' is conventionally used to render the Japanese term *soku*, so crucial to the language of Japanese dialectics, in which the transcendent unity of apparently contrasting ideas – life and death, individual and cosmos, state and individual – are recast as equivalent unities: the state as the individual, life as death, etc.
77 Kitarō Nishida's essay 'Kokka no Riyū' appeared in 1941. The text may be found in *Nishida Kitarō Zenshū, Dai-Kyū-Kan*, Tokyo: Iwanami Shoten, 2004, pp. 301–56.
78 The theme was important for contemporary Japanese philosophy. Cf. Tetsurō Watsuji's *Porisuteki Ningen no Rinrigaku* (The Ethics of the Greek *Polis*), Tokyo: Shironichi Shoin, 1948.

In the modern period, a radical contradiction between public and private, the whole and the individual, has been assumed.

It is conventionally believed that the individual was given new status in Western life with the coming of the Renaissance. On the other hand, the issue of whether there was a genuine sense of the individual before the Renaissance has been, certainly in the past, the object of considerable debate. Indeed, this controversy inflicted considerable damage on our field, and nowadays we tend to neglect the issue. But in response to what I suspect Nishitani is asking about, I might say that all the meanings assigned to the name 'Renaissance' – new birth, rebirth, renewal of life, making life new, etc. – have roots in occult notions of the religious life of the late Middle Ages. The Renaissance, as an occult idea, thus shares roots with the Protestant Reformation. Both the Renaissance and the Reformation were, as it were, in search of a new 'Adam', and thus sought to return to a form of 'original man', and all these notions are occult in origin.

NISHITANI: Isn't this the viewpoint of historians such as Burckhardt?[79] When I read Burckhardt I thought, 'Yes, of course, this is a dimension of the story. But the history of the Middle Ages itself has its foundations in an emerging secularity. This is what links the Middle Ages to the Renaissance. And I suspect that secularization may be closer to the real essence of the story.

SUZUKI: That is of course right. But the Renaissance was more than just the secularization of a culture or even the birth of a secular civilization. The ambition was to identify the sources for the [total] renewal of humanity (*ningen no kaizō*). From this perspective, the new man or view of man that was sought had less to do with the revival of the classical Greek view of man than with a Christian idea. Anyway, this is the interpretation now in vogue. I suspect that Burckhardt's idea of the rediscovery of man should probably be regarded as a nineteenth-century notion.

NISHITANI: It sounds as if the kind of historical movement identified by Burckhardt within the direction of history as a whole might be a tributary rather than the mainstream.

SUZUKI: Are you perhaps closer to the interpretation developed by the French historian Gilson?[80]

NISHITANI: Yes. I see antiquity as being transcended [in the Hegelian sense] by the Middle Ages, but continuing as an underground current that

---

79 Jacob Burckhardt (1818–97): Swiss historian of art and culture, author of *The Civilization of the Renaissance in Italy* (1860). This book was one of the most influential products of the nineteenth-century European mind, and was well known in Japan even before the 1940s.
80 Etienne Gilson (1884–1978): French historian of the medieval period who argued, to great effect, that St Thomas Aquinas deserved serious attention from the twentieth-century mind.

gradually reappeared during the twelfth century. And this is how the continuity between antiquity and the Renaissance was achieved.

SUZUKI: Yes, of course. However, the view of contemporary historians, including myself, is that Gilson and Burckhardt are proponents of the continuity between antiquity and the Renaissance, and therefore in that sense belong to the same school of interpretation in that they support the idea that there is one fundamental trend at work here.

Gilson and Burckhardt are representative figures in contemporary Renaissance studies, as is Huizinga.[81] There are, of course, others. Broadly, they share the same perspective. The previous view stressed the discontinuities of world history. In other words, the revival of antiquity in the Renaissance suggested a break with the Middle Ages. From the standpoint of the advocate of classicism, first there was the classical age; this was followed by an age without the classical inheritance, which in turn was followed by the revival of the classics. A schema of three ages of world history was, of course, suggested.

By contrast, Gilson argues for continuity, insisting that the Middle Ages took possession of the classical inheritance, and that this inheritance was a core element of their makeup as a historical period; not something alien or exceptional to the medieval spirit, but rather something that naturally unfolded in modern times. In other words, there was something Renaissance-like within medieval culture.

NISHITANI: My suspicion is that, in fact, there are discontinuities within the continuities, and vice versa. The development of the individual during the Middle Ages continues in both the Renaissance and the Reformation. That is anyway my view. But from about the twelfth century Europe starts absorbing influences from everywhere – Jewish, Arab, Greek and Roman – while German and Celtic culture comes to the fore as well. And the result is that a kind of 'world' – integrated and whole – takes shape. Would you say this is the case? And all these currents appear to have influenced the Renaissance …

SUZUKI: That is, naturally, all fine and good; but the mode in which human beings became aware of themselves as individuals, the new form of self-awareness that characterizes modern man, is mediated by something profoundly religious, and that is the important point here. But having said as much, it must be acknowledged that this current of religiosity receded by the fifteenth century, during the High Renaissance. This was when the Renaissance became a secular culture, using the term in its strict narrow sense. Here one can locate the strict parting of the ways between the Renaissance and the Reformation, the latter best regarded as a wholly

---

81 Johan Huizinga (1872–1945): Dutch historian of enormous influence, best known for *The Waning of the Middle Ages* (1919), which was still being widely read in Japan in the late 1960s.

144 *The Standpoint of World History and Japan*

religious programme of reform. Therefore, to a degree, the two movements eventually become polar opposites. This is the final outcome of two contrasting movements in history that shared a single common origin or point of departure. This appears to be Burckhardt's view ...

NISHITANI: Take the examples of Staufen and Frederick II. Does it not seem that the primary motive of each was to recreate a version of pagan antiquity rather than respond to some depth of Christian feeling? But the fundamental orientation of the Renaissance was towards the modern. This is how I interpret this 'rebirth'. In other words, the stated aim of a return to antiquity in fact turned out to be an advance from the Middle Ages to the modern era. This crucial transformation is the historical trend that matters. The movement towards the modern world is of a piece with the secularization of medieval culture. This secularizing tendency has its source in the inheritance from antiquity that was transcended during the Middle Ages. Isn't that the true form of the historical phenomenon we are examining? In other words, the march towards something entirely new, that is the trend towards modernity, had of necessity to arise from something that only slightly earlier had been an effort to resurrect antiquity. The reason for this was fundamental: European culture presented no viable alternative to the resort to antiquity. But this effort to return to the classic past did not last very long. It couldn't have. Or, to put it another way, within the movement that we know as the Renaissance the necessity for the modern, for something that transcended the Renaissance, had to emerge. I think this is what Burckhardt means when he says that this movement was about the rebirth of man himself.

In some sense, the same can be said about the Reformation. What began as a return to primitive Christianity turned out in reality to be a movement towards something entirely new. This conflict may explain the deadlock that prevented the movement's ultimate success. I wonder if history is pushed forward, especially during eras of great transition, by generating maelstroms of conflicting pressures and directions. Or, to put it another way, history moves forward by initially retreating. It is this 'retreat' that generates the thrust forward. Thus, in the Renaissance, an act of 'rebirth' contains powerful elements of a future modernity. Thus, too, the Reformation produced extreme movements such as the Münzer uprising.[82] These powerfully illustrate the conflicting impulses at work in the Renaissance and the Reformation, confirming the thesis of continuity within discontinuity, and vice versa.

KŌSAKA: Standing aside from these more specialized arguments, doesn't there appear to be a great number of political issues at stake in the

---

82 Thomas Münzer (*c.*1489–1525): radical leader of the Peasants' Revolt in Germany. Advocated the violent overthrow of established authority in favour of a communistic theocracy. Beheaded.

Renaissance?[83] For example, the Ottomans were beginning to bring great pressure to bear on Constantinople. Growing calls for cooperation between Eastern Orthodox and Western Christianity reflect the impact of this Turkish pressure. This was why Nicholas of Cusa was dispatched to the Byzantine Church, or at least I remember reading something like this about him.[84] Here we have some of the underlying reasons why the Renaissance arose first in Italy. On the one hand, there was the pressure of Turkish power; on the other, there was Spain. In other words, Italy was caught between two forces, and thus trapped at the centre of a world-historical transformation. This is what stands behind the sudden appearance of a new Italian politics and ethnic (*kokuminteki*) consciousness. Doesn't this help explain, to some degree, developments such as the patriotic feelings expressed in Petrarch's writings?[85]

Thus there were nostalgic feelings for ancient Rome at work in Renaissance thought, particularly in response to the sheer scope of the world empire of the ancient Romans. Yes, of course, as the discussion between Nishitani and Suzuki makes clear, the Renaissance was a cultural movement. And it is also true that religious and occult influences can be identified at numerous points in this movement. But the political dimension of the Renaissance should not be overlooked. One has only to think of the appearance during the Renaissance of figures such as Caesar Borgia or Machiavelli. The ideas of *virtù*, morality and power, not just *virtù*, were prominent in the Renaissance, and all three can be seen to have political meaning.[86] On the basis of such evidence, I conclude that today it is important that the Renaissance be viewed no longer – as it has been up to now – as principally or only an idea in cultural history, but as a key concept and phase in political history. The link between Renaissance ideas and Western colonialism, for example, offers grounds for this political interpretation.[87] Burckhardt asserts that the Renaissance involved the discovery of the world and of man: any notion of the 'world' surely includes a political dimension, and similarly, doesn't the idea of 'man' necessarily include reference to 'political man'?

83 Kōsaka uses the German term *politisch*.
84 Nicholas of Cusa (1401–64): German cardinal, mathematician and philosopher. He served as member of a papal delegation to the Eastern Church that negotiated a temporary union of the two churches in 1439 at the Council of Florence.
85 Francisco Petrarca (1304–74): Italian poet, known in English as Petrarch. One cannot help wondering whether, in his musings here, Kōsaka is implicitly drawing a comparison between Renaissance Italy and 1940s Japan, the latter caught between the rising tide of Chinese nationalism and America's emerging global hegemony.
86 Kōsaka's broad point is salient and incontestable, but one wonders if there is a misperception that Machiavelli's term *virtù* refers to ethical virtue rather than to 'vitality' or, if you will, moral energy.
87 This link serves a crucial theoretical move in Carl Schmitt's rethinking of the modern history of war and international law from the 1940s onward.

As for the 'world', viewed in the light of the expansion of the 'European world' during the period, the 'world' of the Renaissance obviously relates to the medieval notion of the Christian world or Christendom. In this sense, there is continuity between the two eras in their senses of 'the world'. But at the same time, in the movement from the Middle Ages to the modern era, there is also a discontinuity at work because one is moving from a religious conception of the world to a political one.

SUZUKI: What is to be made of this idea of 'the world'? The Italian consciousness mentioned by Kōsaka refers to ethnic or national consciousness. This is one of the most fundamental aspects of Renaissance thinking. The Renaissance is something Italian, and outside Italy there was no Renaissance. This probably qualifies as the orthodox view. In contrast, historians such as Huizinga insist that the Renaissance should be interpreted as a pan-European phenomenon. Huizinga and those who agree with him consider the notion of the Renaissance as an entirely Italian affair distinctly flawed.

The orthodox view also conspires against thinking about 'the world'. For example, take the Crusades as they occurred at the conclusion of the Middle Ages. The Crusades were an important stage in the development of Europe as a world, or a European global consciousness. The consciousness of European unity only became clear from the time of the Crusades. Through the sense of struggle with and resistance against the non-Christian infidel and the world beyond the boundaries of Europe, Europeans became clear about what it meant to be European. This revolution of consciousness accompanied all the other changes, profoundly novel in character, that accompanied the Renaissance. Is this what you mean? Or do you have something else in mind?

NISHITANI: I think that is broadly what I mean. There is a connection with the discovery of the New World and the acquisition of overseas colonies …

KŌSAKA: Hence the obvious attention that Spain has attracted, particularly in the light of its success in global conquest. Hegel once referred to the 'truth' of the Renaissance, and I think it is the example of Spain that reveals this truth. Whatever else it may have been, the Renaissance as we know it was redolent of religion. This is what distinguishes it from the modern. Even so, the truth of the Renaissance contains a secular and political dimension. But Spain did not display this kind of secular consciousness. Quite the contrary: Spain made itself the very heartland of the Counter-Reformation. Isn't this the characteristic of the Renaissance in Spain? This is also the reason why Spain failed in this project: religion was too prominent in Spain's conception of its role as global conqueror. By contrast, the success of Britain can be traced to its purely secular and political approach to devising its strategy to global policy making and [imperial] administration.

SUZUKI: That is true. This is an important theme in any [genuine form of] world-historical reflection. Spain was very much as you describe it. And yet this appears to be the working out of a kind of historical necessity. Among modernizing nations, Spain's path of modern state building was very much its own. This was the country born of the spirit of the Crusades, as wars of religion. The Iberian Peninsula had no place in the Middle Ages or in Europe. How could a country ruled by Saracens, that is Arabs, be part of Europe? As a state and a nation, Spain was a creation of the global Christian struggle, the Crusades, the battles against the Arab world. The spirit of Spain is the spirit of the Crusades, the spirit of the wars of religion.

The impact of this distinctive Spanish history becomes apparent when one turns to the sixteenth century and the beginning of Europe's age of religious war. In this struggle, Spain took up the colours of the old religion, and as the representative power of this reactionary cause, oppressed Protestants across Europe. Another thing that must be remembered here is that the discovery of new lands beyond Europe, of the New World itself, all had what might be called a 'pre history'.[88] And that naturally links with what we have been saying.

The voyages of discovery before Columbus, such as those of Portugal's Henry the Navigator, aimed to discover Christian nations outside Europe, whose existence had been suggested by famous stories such as the legend of Prester John.[89] The idea appears to have been to find previously unknown Christian peoples who might serve as allies in a pincer strategy against the Saracens.

The result was the discovery of various islands in the Atlantic, reaching down to Cape Verde and eventually the Cape of Good Hope. In the beginning these efforts were conducted in the uncompromising Crusader spirit, and not motivated by the search for gain. In this way, Portugal and Spain seized the initiative in the discovery of the New World and the achievement of global hegemony while at the same time serving as the chief Catholic powers in the wars of religion, the discoveries and the struggle being two sides of the same coin. Both reflect the workings of historical necessity. The Spaniards who came to Japan in the sixteenth century converted the 'Kiristhan', an intrusion that eventually provoked Japan's retreat into isolationism.[90] For the Spanish [themselves], the world path they took was the result of necessity.[91]

---

88 Suzuki uses the English term.
89 A mythical Christian priest and monarch who was supposed to have reigned over a vast empire in Asia or Africa. The legend first appears in the late twelfth century and was influential down to the beginning of the Age of Exploration.
90 Japanese version of the Portuguese 'Cristan'. Christianity was brought to Japan by St Francis Xavier, the great Jesuit missionary, who first landed in August 1549.
91 In the Hegelian sense of intellectual or *geistig*, as opposed to material, necessity.

148   *The Standpoint of World History and Japan*

KŌSAKA: To this 'necessity' one more factor needs to be added: the issue of geographical position. The shift from the Mediterranean-centred Middle Ages to Atlantic-centred modernity is conventionally, and somewhat precipitately, viewed as a shift [of centrality] from Rome to the nations of the Atlantic. But this is to leap over the middle phase in this historical process, embodied in a self-denying mediator (*jiko hitei-teki baikai sha*), that is, Spain.[92]

Spain's role as mediator is premised on its geographical position. In other words, in the transition from Mediterranean civilization to Atlantic civilization, Spain was indispensable by virtue of its being at once a Mediterranean power and an Atlantic one. Without Spain's mediating role, there would have been no transfer of geographical leadership within Western civilization. Ranke indirectly acknowledges this. For Western historians, the direction of world history has a particular meaning. Again and again, the West has had to confront a challenge from the East, and as a result a new world has been created in the West.[93]

The example of the Ottomans was mentioned earlier. The Turks were a formidable power and repeatedly clashed with Spain in the seas off the coast of Italy. But in the end it was the Spanish who established control of the seas, just as, centuries earlier, the Greeks had routed the Persians and, later, Rome crushed Carthage. The great turning points of history involve clashes between East and West, in which the West is always the victor. I suspect this is where Westerners have acquired their belief that the main current of history favours them.[94]

14   Historicism and the challenges of teaching Japanese history

NISHITANI: We previously touched on the issue of historicism, and the question why historicism has not registered in this country as a serious intellectual challenge. [On the other hand], one cannot help but notice how vociferous arguments about Japanese history have recently become. In one sense this is a good thing, but does anyone here think there is something problematic about this trend?

KŌSAKA: There are many different arguments about historicism. In its purest or ideal form, historicism holds that all phenomena should be judged

---

92 A conventional move in dialectical logic is suggested. Translating the point into practical terms, one might say that Spain allowed its 'new Atlantic' path to be defined by the historical logic of its 'old Catholic Mediterranean' path.
93 Many readers might see in Spain's historical role a reflection of Japan's hybrid status as an advanced nation but also an Asian one.
94 The stark suggestion appears that Japan may now be about to add its name to the long list of the defeated powers of the East. Kōsaka's remark also gives ironic pathos to the concluding passage of the third and final round-table discussion when Japan is identified with the heroic but doomed resistance of the Spartan '300' against the Persian Empire at Thermopylae in 480 BCE.

[solely] from a historical standpoint, that is from within time or history. In other words, phenomena outside history, things that would transcend the historical, principles such as nature or the *logos* [the term is transliterated from the Greek], anything that assumes the existence of trans-historical principles – all these things are excluded by definition from historicist consideration. But the historicist does not leave the matter there. On the contrary, the historicist insists that anything that moves history, that orchestrates the historical process, must by definition be a product of the historical process, and this includes the *logos*, nature, reason and the form of being we call 'human'. In this way history takes the fabric of its thought from history itself. Following this logic, historicism as we know it is a product of the modern European experience of history. While it is true that there is an element of historical thinking within medieval Christianity, that was history with a fixed course from Adam and Eve to the Last Judgement. Such a determinist view of history is not historicist.

To exploit the full potential of historicism, to domesticate it to [our] national need, we must make these fundamental ideas our own. This forms the essential requirement if we are to grasp the momentous significance of Japanese history. Without such mastery, the successive phases in Japan's past development cannot be thought through. A fixed past is a dead past; it precludes life itself.

I am not advocating a simple surrender to historicism as it is. That path will inevitably end in relativism and scepticism. And these [failings] are Europe's inheritance. But the East can transcend such relativism and scepticism, and thus it can hold out the possibility of a different kind of historicism based on a new principle: absolute nothingness (*zettai mu*). This presents the East with a new way of understanding the past, one different from that of the West. Of course, there is the example of the Chinese approach to history based on the concept of 'heaven'. This does not offer a practical option for an Eastern historicism but it does emphasize the differences in principle that distinguish East from West.

SUZUKI: I see. The idea of 'heaven' offers a distinct concept of the past.
KŌSAKA: But if the idea of 'heaven' is made the mainstay of an Eastern understanding of the past, it returns us to the same dilemma that we discussed before in our treatment of Chinese logic: it conspires against understanding history as it really is. Therefore, for the East to give birth to a new kind of historicism, a very different kind of new principle must be sought from within the history of the East.[95]

---

95 Here the wartime Kyoto School appears to be abandoning yet another pillar of Confucian orthodoxy while continuing to think and act within the Confucian ethical framework.

As Nishitani just concluded, historicism has to be taken very much more seriously in Japan. Unless we do so, this thing we may call 'Japanese history' will not be able to seize on the great moments in the history of our nation as they unfold in reality.[96] I do not want people to memorize history; I want them to appreciate thoroughly the problems generated by historical reality, and to recognize the complications that attend these problems. Unless this is achieved, historical education will have neither purpose nor influence.

NISHITANI: In general, leaving aside the specialist in history, ordinary people are made to study history to equip them with an understanding of historical reality and thus to enhance their ability to judge the soundness of their understanding. If this is the case, one is left wondering why educational policy makers would have us concentrate so singularly on teaching only Japanese history. To put the point critically, this narrow focus will produce a generation of students whose understanding of the world is no better than that of an insect stuck in the bottom of a well.[97] As for the supposed goal of inculcating a sense of patriotism in young people, all I can say is that I wonder whether historical instruction is the proper means to achieve such an end. A patriotism erected on such sandy foundations will not provide a solid basis for anything, or at least so it seems to me.

Speaking from personal experience, I can only say that the kind of historical education I was provided with in school provoked within me a fiercely hostile reaction to what I was taught. If I love Japan now, it is not because of what I was taught in school about Japanese history. Rather, it was the understanding I nurtured for myself. Formal education has nothing to do with it. What I have achieved has been achieved despite the education I received ...

KŌSAKA: The way Japanese history is taught needs to be completely rethought. It should be more international in its scope and more politically minded. Without such changes, the teaching of Japanese history will continue to be ineffective.[98]

SUZUKI: Listening to this discussion, I have just had a thought about what we mean by 'national history'. Nowadays, Japanese history is a required subject in university entrance examinations. Looking over the students' answer sheets, it appears that the quality of the answers has improved

---

96 This passage can be read as fruitfully against the essay on subjectivity that is Daniel Defoe's *Robinson Crusoe* as against the chapter on 'Masters and Slaves' in Hegel's *Phenomenology of Spirit*.
97 Japanese proverb.
98 Without being provocative, Kōsaka is calling for a genuinely politically minded study of history, as opposed to religious, mythical or ideological interpretations of the Japanese past.

conspicuously over the past two or three years. This is all very well, but this year things changed. The pass mark in Japanese history is 85%. That is a very respectable standard. But compared to this, the pass mark for foreign languages, mathematics, physics, etc., is only 70%. This is a level not worth talking about. I discovered this discrepancy quite by chance, and was so astonished that I wanted to examine the pass marks in other subjects but never found the time to do so.

But how in the world has this situation come about? The cause is the overemphasis being placed on the study of Japanese history in schools. This in itself is not a bad thing. But if high schools concentrate on the teaching of Japanese history at the expense of every other subject, as tends to happen in junior high schools, the [following] kinds of geniuses result. Last year I took time to look at how the issue of the Anglo-Japanese alliance was treated in history entrance examinations [for university]. As the alliance was revised several times and expanded in scope, it provides an excellent vehicle for an examination of changes in Japan's position in international affairs in the broadest context. But when one examines the answer papers, one finds that in the overwhelming majority of cases the student has concluded that the Anglo-Japanese alliance was merely a product of the idolization of all things British during the Meiji period. Having been taught that the question has only one answer, the students gave that one answer back. This is a terrible way to teach history. There is no purpose in studying history in this way. In effect, this suggests that we are teaching history in this country in a way that entirely contradicts and undermines the student's ability to think intelligently about the past. Does it not?

NISHITANI: Teaching history will not be effective unless we do something like they do in Europe, where the detailed examination of the complex diplomatic relations of various rival nations is commonplace.

KŌSAKA: That's right. This suggests that new history textbooks are needed, as I have argued before on another occasion. What are practice answers to questions doing in a textbook? It is not even appropriate in mathematics textbooks. For the study of history, the most important thing is to be aware of the problems raised by historical reality. The ability to think through such problems is the skill that needs to be inculcated. This was the way people in the past studied history, and this is how it should be taught now.

In the history of art, new [artistic] forms are created as answers to problems that have to be solved. But when addressing the kind of historical questions we are discussing here, one needs a political approach to history, one grounded in the horizon of world history, if one is really to understand historical reality. This, I believe, will give us a convincing form of our history of the Japanese, both as a people (*minzoku*) and as a nation (*kokka*), but I expect some disagreement with this view.

15 Viewing Japanese history from the standpoint of world history

KŌYAMA: I have no disagreement with any of that. Quite the contrary: I have come to believe that it is essential that Japanese history be radically rethought from exactly that perspective. Take, for example, Nishitani's insistence that ancient Japanese history has its roots in the complex international relations of the period. If one carefully reads the *Nihon Shoki* from the time of Emperor Ōjin [270–310 CE], but particularly during the reign of the Emperor Kimmei [539–71], it seems sensible to conclude that at that time Japanese historical consciousness was very internationally aware.[99] There is not enough time to go into detail about this [here], but in general one can say that if one examines Japanese history from the time before Prince Shōtoku to the inauguration of the Taika reforms [645 CE] and the beginning of the Nara period [646–794], one discovers that, in contrast with us Japanese today, the nation had a superb grasp of national history and at the same time could boast a world-historical method of thinking about the times. The reason why this was so was grounded in reality. It was simply impossible to make Japan work [as a state and a society] by concentrating only on domestic affairs. Japan was deeply affected by its relationship with the three Korean kingdoms (*Sankan*) as well as by China. Indeed, it was confidently assumed then that Japan's development as a nation could only be properly assessed within the web of these international relationships. If Japan exercises the role of the stabilizing regional power in relationship to the Korean peninsula today, the same may be said of ancient Japan's relationship with the three Korean kingdoms from the reign of the Empress Suiko [599–628].

Gradually this degree of international historical consciousness began to fade. Then catastrophe struck: Japanese authority in Minama [Gaya] was destroyed. There were various causes of this disaster, but one factor was the rise of formidable [Korean] states such as Shiragi [Silla]. These became powers of consequence eventually rivalling Japan itself. Diplomatic relationships became at once subtle and fraught, but the main result was the transformation of Japanese politics from without.

These external pressures were rendered even more influential by concurrent changes in Japan's domestic situation. These domestic changes were set in motion by the rise of the military clans. This contributed to the decay of national unity, making an effective form of [domestic] politics increasingly difficult to sustain. The resulting power struggle had a dramatic impact on Japan's international position. Unity of command between domestic authority and Japan's outpost in Korea broke down. There were grave mistakes of

---

99 After the *Kojiki*, the *Nihon Shoki* or *Nihongi* is the second oldest of the ancient foundation texts of Japan. Compiled in 720 CE, it is known in English as *The Chronicles of Japan*.

administration, on the part of both the military and the civilian officials (*kankōri*). As these failures compounded one another and the crisis deepened, national prestige collapsed, and the Japanese administration in Minama with it.

The destruction of Minama was a serious blow. In response to the edicts of the Emperor Kimmei, the recovery of Japan's position in Minama became the central goal of contemporary government policy. However, the stronger Shiragi became, the less it was willing to be bossed around by Japan. How this situation arose had less to do with Japan's growing weakness than with the consequences of the Shiragi embrace of Buddhism and the development of a new system of laws. This contributed to a series of reforms that resulted in the creation of an impressive new system of government. Genuine Korean progress was the real story here.

It became obvious that if Japan were to maintain national prestige and sustain its established position as a force for regional stability, it had to create a new form of state, one that outshone and outstripped its Korean rivals. The real challenge came not from outside but from within. And the greatest difficulty was that of nurturing internal unity. This anyway was the opinion of the leading and most progressive-minded of the Japanese political elite at the time. For example, in a report to the Throne, Nichira proposed that Japan abandon its system of three-year [forced] conscription and with the resulting savings build a fleet. This force could then be used to demonstrate the nation's power to the leaders of Korea (*Sankoku*). He believed that this [show of strength] would of necessity compel them to submit to Japanese power.[100]

Nichira had been stationed for a long time in Kudara [Baekje]. I suspect that Shōtoku Taishi's ideas about such proposals were influenced by an attempt that had been made earlier to dispatch troops to Shiragi, an action that had not gone according to plan. From that time forward, national energy was focused on the cultivation of inner unity, what today we call a new system (*shintaisei*). In the effort to build a new system of centralized government, of one kind or another, a hierarchical bureaucratic system (*kan'i*) was introduced along with a [written] constitution.[101] At the same time, every effort was made to introduce, as Shiragi and other Korean kingdoms had already done, the benefits of the world culture of the age.[102] Until that time, Japan had imported Chinese culture via Korea (*Sankan*), but henceforth it was decided that direct contact should be made with the centres of Chinese civilization in order to select what was judged desirable for Japan to absorb.

---

100 Nichira (d. December 583) was a Japanese-born official who served for many years in the court of Kudara.

101 The *kan'i* bureaucracy was modelled on Chinese practice and was noted for its ranking system, in which gradations were indicated by the colour of the bureaucrat's court hat.

102 The reference here is to China, but Kōyama's phrase *tōji no sekai bunka* (what was then contemporary world culture), reasserts the Kyoto School's insistence that it is European or Western culture that has played that central role in the modern world in which Japan still found itself during the 1940s. Note that the *world*, not the narrowly national, is the stage that counts.

This, I take it, was why Japan dispatched people to China in the Sui dynasty (c. 581–618).

This amounted to an excellent strategy for completing the process of building internal unity while raising Japan's prestige abroad by demonstrating its superior political system and its claims to civilization. Unfortunately, the goal proved beyond the reach of Shōtoku's Japan. The increasingly extreme despotism of the Soga and other clans was a major factor. At the same time, the students dispatched to China were eyewitnesses to the destruction of the Sui dynasty and the consolidation of the Tong. When they returned to Japan, their experiences fed criticism of the existing order as inadequate to national need, and thus helped to spark the Taika reforms.

KŌSAKA: The introduction of Buddhism also contributed to the enhancement of domestic unity. There was a relationship between the two developments, wasn't there?

KŌYAMA: But this was ultimately related to the conflict between the clans. The complex nature of this struggle posed the greatest danger to internal unity. At the heart of the problem was a dilemma: if the struggle between the clans ended [with the Soga victorious], the country would have been faced with arbitrary rule by the Soga. But the ultimate triumph of clan politics would have called into question the very survival of the Japanese state as the pinnacle [and embodiment] of national life itself. Therefore it was necessary to find a set of principles that stood apart from the clans, one that transcended, if you will, the idea of clannishness, and through which the priority of the state and national unity could be affirmed. Buddhism met this need uniquely well. At the heart of the difficulty of achieving internal unity was the pervasive character or spirit of clan politics. It demonstrated a weakness for arbitrary domination. There was no way the traditional worship of our ancestors alone was going to be able to bring clan conflict to a satisfactory conclusion or overcome the implicit susceptibility of the clans to rampant tyranny. It was essential, therefore, that the spirit of state supremacy and 'national unity' [transliterated from the English] be grounded in a set of universal principles that transcended the limitations of clan politics. It is my speculation that such profound considerations were at work in the mind of Prince Shōtoku when he promoted Buddhism to the centre of national life. The scope of such a vision was beyond the grasp of ordinary men and women [then or now].

Some have taken the view that Buddhism was introduced into this country on a whim; but in fact it was used to enhance national unity. Buddhism was embraced in the name of pacifying and preserving the state (*chingo kokka*). The commitment may have been shallow or it may have been profound, but it was made, and it left its mark on Buddhism as it has been practised in this country. In short, I think the aim was to attempt to create something that broke with Japan's previous experience of civilization, a [new model] in which domestic conditions were linked with international ones, in which a fundamental unity between outside and inside was assumed.

This, in my view, provided the deepest motivation for the introduction into Japan of the fruits of what was then contemporary world civilization. This [line of thought] also suggests that unless one adopts some variety of [what we have called here] a world-historical perspective, it will prove impossible to understand Japan's history during the period in question. I suspect that, given Japan's current circumstances, the same argument can be persuasively made today. But to argue that [Chinese] civilization was imported in the seventh century for implausible or unserious reasons is wilfully to misunderstand the nature of the period and the motivations of the people involved.

[There is another dimension to this argument.] One hears the observation that the Japanese have a gift for imitation, or that Japanese culture tends to be receptive to [the influence of] foreign civilizations: such ideas are unable to explain adequately what they purport to describe. They reflect a posture that rejects the scientific (*gakumonteki*) analysis [in favour] of ideas such as mentalities (*soshitsu*) or instinct. For example, [consider the question]: Why do wars occur? Because, we are told, human beings have an instinct to fight. This hardly qualifies as a serious explanation of anything.

As soon as one simply assumes a narrow nationalist reading of history, one exposes oneself to unscientific ideas such as 'mentalities'. If one seeks to explain such phenomena in a scientific way, one must assume a world-historical standpoint. At least, that is what I think. But in any case, when the ancient Japanese thought about his country, he did so in an internationally aware way. Thus one can conclude that the Nara period produced a cultured state (*bunka kokka*) in which the foreign and domestic, the inside and the out, were one and the same sphere.

16 World history as a method

KŌSAKA: To some it may seem that for a country to possess genuine international awareness (*sekaisei*) is to offend against the spirit of 'nationality' (transliterated from the English), but there is in fact no contradiction here. International awareness strengthens the state rather than weakening or betraying it. There is certainly no need to assume a contradiction here. In the case of Korea, its Buddhism became, in the end, the Buddhism of the State Defended (*Chin Koku no Bukkyo*). Thus one may conclude that both Japan and Korea embraced the call 'to pacify and preserve the state by the power of the Buddha' (*Kokka Chingo*), although conflicts between the two societies persisted.[103]

---

103 In other words, in both societies national identity was unimpaired and there was no diminishment in the will to defend the national interest, however defined.

NISHITANI: The same can probably be said of China (by this I mean that Chinese Buddhism also included the idea of its being a national protection cult).[104]

KŌYAMA: Perhaps one has to think about this problem in this way. There are those who regard as ridiculous the very notion that international or trans-national Buddhism was necessary to the unity of the Japanese state and nation. How, such critics contend, did something international [that is, foreign] become indispensable to the formation of Japan's internal unity? How could it be that national unity was achieved with borrowings from abroad? Such scepticism defines the outlook of us Japanese today. That is to say, those of us who have received the baptism of modern thought tend to be prejudiced when we examine the [supposed] link between individualism and internationalism. Or, to put it another way, when confronted with the notion of the individual as someone who is able to look at his nation without resorting to nationalist-tinted spectacles, we immediately associate such a posture with what we regard as [*passé*] international-minded cosmopolitanism.[105] We therefore tend to conclude that to be patriotic is to be anti-internationalist, and to be internationalist is to be unpatriotic. Doesn't this kind of thinking define our condition today? But this approach is [fundamentally] flawed. It is wrong to attack the path Japan took in the time of Prince Shōtoku and the Nara period from this perspective. To criticize the past in such a matter is to confess to being totally ignorant about the historical conditions that prevailed at that time. This view of the past is completely ahistorical.

NISHITANI: But given that, how about this? [We have been discussing] the international relationships between and among Japan, Korea and China – what, to borrow your expression, for the Japanese at the time was the 'world': if this was the world of Japanese history, it was inevitable that this world was viewed from a Japanese perspective or horizon. But in Europe, there is a history that stands beyond the individual national histories, for example, of Germany or Italy,[106] and that is the history of Europe, a history that begins with ancient Egypt and classical Greece. In other words, beyond individual national histories there is a world history that is a European history. In a similar way, Japan, Korea and China, taken together, formed such a world, a world with a history, an East Asian 'world' history. And I think that this is the most important

---

104 The gloss added by Nishitani in this remark appears to be a post-symposium but prepublication clarification. It is written uniquely in *katakana* and is the only example of such an editorial insertion in the entire text.

105 Cosmopolitan individualism was an influential cultural and political trend in Japan in the 1920s, but it was later fatally associated with the failures of liberal capitalism, the incompetence of parliamentary parties and the decline of moral cohesion in Japanese society.

106 The book version of these symposia, *The Standpoint of World History and Japan* (1943), cites the examples of Germany and Britain.

historical insight that can be learned from this kind of world history.[107] What do the rest of you think?

KŌYAMA: Viewed as a single 'world', Japan, Korea and China had not achieved the same degree of unity or awareness of being part of the same civilization as we find in Europe. The gap between East Asia then and the degree of unity that characterizes the 'world' of Europe reflects, I suspect, fundamental differences in the histories of the two regions.

NISHITANI: That being the case, this perspective is even more one-sided.

KŌYAMA: As the Chinese regarded the rest of us as 'Eastern barbarians', the whole idea of trans-civilization solidarity was spoiled from the start.

NISHITANI: But one can feel nothing but disappointment in our search for a genuine way of thinking (*Denken*) about the truest form of history if we conclude that it is wrong to say that Europe offers us the best example of such an approach.[108]

KŌSAKA: I think along with that point one further issue might be noted. If contemporary world history is a version of European history, the dynamic of previous Eastern history is somewhat different from its Western equivalent. In the West's modern phase, one can observe numerous quarrels between various peoples (*minzoku*) and states (*kokka*), and the West is characterized by more than one centre. The changing relationships between these various centres drive the history of change in the West. By contrast, Eastern civilization has had a single centre: China. This centre orders our 'world'. According to the Chinese view of our 'world', there is China, the centre, and there is a variety of other countries that complement it, forming the margins of Eastern civilization. Today, however, one has to recognize that the world has many centres.

NISHITANI: The Middle Ages may offer the closest Western approximation to the classic Eastern model. In Europe, it was ancient Greece and the modern age that saw conflicts between numerous states.[109] In a general sense, our history today is driven by a similar dynamic. It takes its shape from that dynamic.

SUZUKI: That seems to be a reasonable conclusion to me.

KŌSAKA: These periods of conflict are when history experiences its greatest changes.

NISHITANI: The contemporary world is characterized by a plurality of centres. This framework of understanding allows us to see that Japan has broken

---

107 For 'insight', Nishitani uses the German word *Denken*, transliterated into Japanese.
108 As above, Nishitani uses the German word *Denken* to supply the precise nuance of what he means by thought or intellectual method.
109 This would appear to understate the endless strife between kings and princes that characterized the Middle Ages, conflicts of which all the participants in this symposium were well aware. The emphasis is instead on the influence of systems of governance that embodied in fact or ideal the claims of universal monarchy: Imperial Rome, the Roman Catholic Church and the Holy Roman Empire.

into the ranks of civilization as one of these 'centres'. And it follows, for example, that generalists – people like me who are not specialists in the study of history but want to acquire a genuine appreciation of Japan's place in the world – must spend some time carefully studying the history of places such as modern Europe. Similarly, when we read about the history of classical Greece, there is something about it that is immediately recognizable and comprehensible to us today. And I think this is really interesting.

KŌYAMA: The Eastern analogies are Japan during the Era of the Warring States [1482–1558] or the struggles that beset China during the Age of Spring and Autumn Annals [722–481 BCE] as well as its own Warring States period [lasting until 214 BCE].

NISHITANI: That's right. I think one could learn a lot from the political developments during the Era of the Warring States.

KŌSAKA: Once the Qin dynasty [221–206 BCE] establishes in its dominance, the history of China becomes rather boring (*omoshiroku nai*). There is little to learn from this phase of Chinese history that has any direct contemporary relevance.

KŌYAMA: I think that's probably right ... the concept of the 'historical world' (*rekishi-teki sekai*) was never fully grasped in China.[110] One reason has been the Chinese insistence on the unique position of their country as the unchallengeable centre of the world. This assumption conspired against thinking about history in the proper sense because dynasties could come and go without altering the idea of the mandate of heaven. When the nation underwent change, the stress was placed on continuity rather than on what had become different. This approach (*mi-kata*) preserved the framework inherited from the past, but it also meant there was no sense of progress.

KŌSAKA: That's certainly right. To the degree that one gives the 'world' [as it is] proper attention, one finds that a single principle tends to underpin this world in all its manifestations. For Christianity, examples of such transcendent ideas include 'God' and 'humanity'. For China, I suspect that the transcendent idea has been 'heaven' or the 'mandate of heaven' (*ekisei kakumei*). But it was a mistake to reduce the history of China merely to a series of [unprogressive] changes of regime in accordance with the shifting fortunes of the mandate of heaven.[111] One thinks of such revolutions as the effect of the mandate of heaven. However, the 'mandate' conception of the past crystallizes the Chinese idea of history, and therefore freezes it. It makes it impossible to understand the dynamic nature of universal

---

110 The 'historical world' was an idea developed by Kōsaka in two best-sellers, *Rekishi-teki Sekai* (The Historical World) and *Zoku, Rekishi-teki Sekai* (The Historical World: The Sequel), published in 1937 and 1950, respectively. Both are found in volume one of *Kōsaka Chosaku shu, Dai Ikkan* (The Collected Works of Masaaki Kōsaka), Tokyo: Risō-sho, 1964.

111 Another crucial example of the Confucian template that underwrites the Kyoto School's world-view, despite its overt hostility to many Confucian ideas.

history and the world it shapes. It is Japan's task, therefore, to bring that dynamic of change to bear on the Eastern experience. In broad terms, Prince Shōtoku was responsible for the first history of Japan, although the text itself was destroyed by fire. It is my belief that the editing of Japanese histories, and the consciousness of history itself that was so evident at that time, occurred then because history was on the move across East Asia in that period. Curiously, and perhaps not accidentally, Japanese architecture also flowered during that age. In any case, Japanese culture flourished during a time when it is said that one could think out a Japanese approach to things, through ideas such as *sabi*.[112] We must not dismiss the achievements of periods such as the Nara and Momoyama, however gaudy and ostentatious. It is furthermore worth noting that these periods saw Japan's most energetic engagement with the outside world. A young friend of mine recently wrote to me while visiting Nara and he forcefully confirmed this view. I think such impressions contain an element of truth. This was an age awash with creativity in architecture and building. Today we need another age of innovation in architecture and construction in a Japanese mode.

KŌYAMA: Mention has been made of Prince Shōtoku as a historical editor. He was spurred on by an awareness of Japan's place in the world. The author of the *Tennō-ki* unambiguously affirms the imperial household as an unbroken lineage, therefore he could hardly be a clan retainer. But would such texts have been written had our domestic and foreign affairs not been so influenced by the challenges posed by our relations with Korea and China? The text makes explicit reference to the country of the setting sun and the country of the rising sun, to the *Tennō* of the East and the Emperor of the West. The composition of this country's first national history took place in the context of a rich awareness of Japan's place in the wider international context. International conditions fostered a national response of a kind that suggests that the dynamic [such as cause and effect] was at work here.

KŌSAKA: I think that was very much the case. Furthermore, one can argue that, in a way untrue before in Chinese history, the culture of the Tong dynasty manifested a much broader and unprecedented notion of itself as a genuine world, a totality unto itself. And gradually this grand idea influenced Japan as well. What unfolded then is very much like what is happening in East Asia today: a genuine world or totality has taken shape before our eyes as a practical manifestation of something new.

NISHITANI: I felt very much the same when reading *Spring in Ch'ang* by Mikinosuke Ishida.[113]

---

112 Frequently rendered into not entirely satisfactory English as a quiet or antique simplicity of design or mode.
113 Mikinosuke Ishida (1891–1974): popular Japanese writer and historian. *Cho-an no Haru* was published in 1941, and appears to be still in print today.

KŌYAMA: We speak of 'Tong culture' but in fact there were Persian and Arabian influences [at work] in China at the time, suggesting an international world culture. In other words, what entered Japan from the continent was something more than just Chinese culture. Buddhism, for example, was more than just either Indian or Chinese Buddhism; it was an international form of Buddhism.

NISHITANI: Architecture (*kenchikuteki*) and *sabi* were mentioned earlier, but I think I have taken a slightly different view of these subjects. *Sabi*, for example, as a way of viewing [the world], contains elements not just of Buddhism in general but Zen in particular. In this sense, it reached beyond the architectural. True, architecture can leave something majestic behind, but the taste for haiku and the tea ceremony, the pure spiritually ... if someone asked where I thought the international or global character of ancient Japan was expressed architecturally ... I would answer that it is to be found in an intensive internationalism, in the universal claims of Zen.

KŌSAKA: That's right. One might one add that as far as the tea ceremony is concerned, the notion of the tea master receiving guests or the very idea of the tea ceremony as a formal gathering suggests the distinctly social character of these practices. I do not know much about the history of the tea ceremony, but my impression is that during the age of Hideyoshi and Nobunaga the tea ceremony could assume a political character. It was an encounter between a host and his guests. Thus one samurai would prepare the tea for the others, but he was never vulnerable to the swords of another because the space was too confined [and everyone accepted this constraint]. There was an [unmistakable] seriousness to these occasions, but nevertheless wasn't it really in the end a form of escape? Perhaps this judgement is a bit severe?

SUZUKI: I don't know about saying it was in the end a form of escape. There was a determination at work in the way commanders of the Warring States period pursued Zen and the tea ceremony amid the demands of their military lives as constantly active mounted soldiers. Perhaps an activity devoid of purpose was exactly what was required.

KŌYAMA: It may have been refreshing precisely because it was empty of purpose.

KŌSAKA: That is a nice way of putting it. Nevertheless I would like to register a note of opposition to the idea that Japanese culture consists entirely of *sabi*. Even in the case of the tea ceremony, as conceived by Rikyū and others, there was more involved than just *sabi*.[114] There was another dimension that does not quite fit under this rubric, something full of life, at once ferocious and vital. At least I think so. The political dimension [of the tea ceremony at the time] we touched on earlier is consistent with this view. In other words the political, the mere facts of existence, was trumped by something transcendental. Isn't this suggested by the way

---

114 Sen no Rikyū (1522–91): legendary master of the tea ceremony.

Rikyū loved the young flowers just nudging their blossoms through a thin layer of the snow?

NISHITANI: I would like to turn this around and think about it in another way. Even if these practices were exploited for political ends, there are things that cannot be solved by politics [as a process] alone. Resolution of some disputes can begin only when one human being spends time with another. Zen and the tea ceremony brought combatants together, and these cultural diversions acquired a certain kind of political usefulness ...

KŌSAKA: Yes, of course. But these forms were gradually subverted as decadent and vulgar temptations began to violate the narrow [purity] of the four-and-a-half-mat room.[115]

KŌYAMA: Like the chambers of assignation that the politics of the Middle Ages so loved. (*All laugh.*)

17 Philosophy and reality

SUZUKI: The question of whether philosophy has the power to help shape (*shidōsei*) the contemporary world has been raised.[116] In other words, the suggestion is that if the special sciences dominated the nineteenth century, these same sciences are now approaching a kind of limit. When the businessman thinks about economics or the lawyer about the law, such thinking is confined to the bargain they have struck with their particular special science. The very narrowness of such sciences means that they lack a global vision of sufficient power to orchestrate change. These sciences reduce genuine change to a mere trend, and thus foster the domination of our intellectual horizon by subjective narrow-mindedness. Only philosophy allows us to break free from such domination.

We talked about this last evening. The politics of the philosopher, no less than his idea of economics, even his notion of war, may be regarded at first glance as hopelessly removed from real life by virtue of their idealism.[117] But such ideas are in fact more realistic and practical than any other. This truth is one of the [great] discoveries of the contemporary mind.[118]

KŌYAMA: Philosophy is elevating. It has the power to remove us from our immediate circumstances. It inspires wonder.[119] This is the traditional

115 In Japanese architecture and interior design, a mat is a standard measure of floor size. A four and a half-*tatami* mat room is the standard size of a small traditional room.
116 Martin Heidegger was the one thinker who gave the problem classic form.
117 Suzuki uses the expression *tetsujin*, meaning 'sage' or 'philosopher', instead of philosophy, but as one reads on, one realizes that it makes more sense to refer to 'political philosophy', etc.
118 The notion of what is apparently far distant in fact being closest to us bears uncanny resemblance to Heidegger's contrasting ideas of 'things ready to hand' and 'ready at hand'.
119 Perhaps an echo of the Greek idea of *thaumazin*, rendered by George Steiner as 'radical astonishment'.

view. For example, legal philosophy or economic philosophy reduces philosophy to the status of a mere servant of the law and economics, to aid the economist or the lawyer in his wrestling with methodology and epistemology. But this is like using a hammer to open a window. Unless one abandons this approach, no genuine philosophy of law or philosophy of economics – that is, a philosophy that can give direction and shape to the special sciences [rather than just follow in their wake] – will be possible. Only by burying the idea of philosophy as the servant of the special sciences can we renew the bond between the special sciences and their foundations in philosophy. These foundations need to be constantly strengthened. This is the thing that most needs doing now.

KŌSAKA: If I might be allowed to digress to a slightly embarrassing topic, I must admit that I gave my family something of a shock when I announced my intention to study philosophy. They were terribly worried that I was proposing to leap over a waterfall. It might have been a good Buddhist waterfall but it was a waterfall nevertheless.

KŌYAMA: My mother said much the same sort of thing.

KŌSAKA: It is because they all saw philosophy as something hopelessly remote from practical life. But most people have forgotten that philosophy makes its home inside each and every person ... And therefore, a new philosophy – a philosophy of national and global renewal (*kakushin-teki*) – is taking root today precisely because of the stalled nature of the project of historicism.

Viewed historically, philosophy can help guide a society, and thus help to set in motion a programme of reform. Such a programme should represent a rupture with previous traditions and orientations in favour of a body of ideas founded entirely on a new world-view. This potential suggests that a contemporary struggle with and against historicism is only to be welcomed. A new world is being born, one that breaks with both the Eastern and Western worlds of the past. Nay, better than a new world, a new power [to reshape the world] is coming into being. While the worlds of East and West are cracking [under the weight of change], while historicism remains trapped in its obstructed path, the absolute foundation that lies behind such a new force is beginning to show itself. I think that this deeper foundation, in all its newness, should be called 'absolute nothingness'. This will give it practical expression and thus not only transcend mere historicism but also confer genuine significance on the so-called special sciences. I think philosophy has to mediate historical reality. Historical reality and ...

SUZUKI: There is one more thing that I believe historical consciousness must achieve: the effort to formulate a profounder kind of historicism. If, on the one hand, we are beginning to think through a world-historical philosophy, then we also need to think through a new set of methods and approaches, a new historiography of world history. Granted, history is not historiography. The study of history is not the same as the study of how history is studied. But these two things are patently related. In order for world historiography to overcome the limitations of conventional historiography, it is necessary for it to develop a [new] set of philosophical motifs and insights. The flawed aspects of historicism have to be overcome ...

NISHITANI: This is what contemporary philosophy has to do. But I might add that I think that it is a good thing that our own philosophies have a Kegon dimension, that is a Kegon waterfall dimension ... [120]

SUZUKI: What?! Kegon what?

NISHITANI: Yes, Kegonist. Not the Kegon sutras. My Kegon is more like the waterfall. (*All laugh.*)

KŌSAKA: That's right. Without something like that, philosophy will never be authentic (*hon-mono*). It will fall short of true seriousness.[121]

KŌYAMA: Hmm. More like the Kegon Waterfall. Thinking about ways to join the individual and the absolute, it would be better if the content of the historical world came to resemble that Kegon Waterfall. Yes, it would be a good thing if we could leap from the highest rock of the Japanese spirit into that Kegon Waterfall, taking world history with us.[122]

SUZUKI: Nevertheless, on the one hand, yes, we do have to take this approach. We have to think about things in this way. As was mentioned just now, in reality the things we feel most keenly appear to be the things most removed from us, and it is these things we must glean from philosophy. This imperative arises from our search for fundamental principles. At present, it is these principles that we seek, but this pursuit has conjured up an aspect of philosophy that is distinctly off-putting (*osore*) [because it appears to depart from common sense]. There is something excessive about the very need for such bold creativity. This feeling has intensified just as the world confronts a historic turning point. This is always a danger when one squares off with something [at once] extremely clear [but entirely novel]. Here lies a threat to scholarship. Granted, we must pursue something radically new; but we must not lose sight of the clear truths previously uncovered. On the one hand, it is scholarship's mission to make what is clear ever clearer. Ages may come and go, but this mission is unchanging. While accepting the challenges of the present, it is vitally important to protect this spirit of academic inquiry.

---

120 Nishitani is ironically referring less to the Kegon School than the waterfall near Nikkō, which was named after the school, but was also a famous leap for suicides.
121 A clichéd but rather moving relapse into the Daoist and Zen spirit in which the total absence of seriousness is often its highest expression.
122 Kōyama is suggesting something like Kierkegaard's leap of faith, but the Japanese leap is more rational because Kōyama is profoundly committed to the advance of the secular world and spirit.

KŌYAMA: There may be a fear that things that were obvious have now become obscure.

NISHITANI: Do you think we have failed in this way?

SUZUKI: Well, no, actually. I do not think we have really.

KŌSAKA: Ah, the spectre of the esoteric mystery cult (*shinpishugi*).

NISHITANI: At least the content of a mystery cult is consistent.[123]

KŌYAMA: I think what Suzuki is hinting at is basically right. On the one hand, it is right to be dismayed by the idea that anyone and everyone can and should become a philosopher. But the stance of the [pure] philosopher can be problematic. For example, the special sciences have produced outstanding philosophers.

SUZUKI: That was what I was trying to say. We have to defend what common sense tells us is clear and obvious.

NISHITANI: I for one, and I say this in light of my own standpoint in all of this, would like to see students of the special sciences become more philosophical in their approach. I mean philosophical in a way that arises from the precise content of these various special sciences. This holds even if the first fruits of such efforts turn out to be less than satisfactory. One must be resigned to this prospect from the outset. But the point is to make a genuine start in the struggle to bring about a rapprochement between the two sides, so that gradually the gap between them is narrowed, while at the same time, and in the process, improving the quality of our work on both sides of the divide.

KŌYAMA: That would be a sounder approach.

NISHITANI: And that means that the process must be governed by mutual criticism. Priority should be given to that goal. Otherwise there will be resentments on both sides that will eventually have to be vented.

SUZUKI: That's right. Dogma has no place in philosophy. The dogmatic and philosophical approaches to reality are polar opposites.

KŌSAKA: Can you imagine the incomprehensible intellectual monstrosity that would result if a science such as biology tried to tackle the problem of 'the phenomenon of life'?

KŌYAMA: That was Hölderlin's problem, wasn't it?[124]

KŌSAKA: Hölderlin was sober compared to some of the others. Then there is the question of how to respond to the issue raised by Suzuki … the business just mentioned of the relationship between empirical world history and the philosophy of history … I have given some thought to this issue.

SUZUKI: This is a complex question and I really don't understand it all that well, but, simply put, I suspect that the gap between the two approaches can finally be reduced to the difference between history and philosophy. Because the empirical study of world history has yet to shed the methods of [conventional] historiography, it takes as its basic [unexamined] assumptions

---

123 Its meaning may be hidden but its message is clear.
124 Johann Christian Friedrich Hölderlin (1770–1843): German poet, novelist and dramatist, famous for his almost religious veneration of nature.

the fundamental ideas of the positivist historian, and proceeds from there. This sets up a conflict, in my view, between empirical world history and the metaphysics of the philosophy of world history. The contemporary philosophy of world history tends to be much more empirical in its approach but philosophy is in the end still philosophy.

KŌYAMA: We must try, in our effort to develop the kind of philosophy of world history we are seeking, to incorporate or mediate (*baikai*), at least to some degree, the more advanced insights achieved by the empirical student of world history since the age of Hegel. To fail to do so will reduce the philosophy of world history to a branch of metaphysical speculation.

SUZUKI: The standpoint of the empirical world historian is rather different. He is less interested in the metaphysics of the thing. But this is not true of the work of the contemporary philosopher of world history. Here by contrast there is a profound link with the labours of the empirical historian. The difference lies in the methodology …

KŌYAMA: I am in no doubt that there must be a rapprochement between philosophy and the special sciences, but we must be careful how we try to achieve this goal. In this context, it may seem a strange thing to observe, and I think it is strange, that from time to time I have without doubt placed a kind of absolute but rarely declared faith in philosophy, a kind of conviction that would astonish people who are unfamiliar with my craft. My point becomes clearer when one recalls the way we are all regularly urged to get on with the job of constructing and promoting a specifically 'national school of philosophy' (*Nippon Tetsugaku*). If a Japanese version of any and every discipline, including philosophy, were possible, so the argument goes, we would have a specifically Japanese form of economics and a specifically Japanese form of constitutional science [jurisprudence] as well. This is the [nationalist] assumption being pressed upon us. There is something to this argument, but it does not strike me as very philosophical. Whatever it is, it contradicts the nature of philosophy. The idea seems to be that as soon as one delimits one's notion of the universal, then out pops the specific/particular (*tokushu*). Such an idea has to be completely rethought. The suggestion by people who have no real understanding of philosophy seems to be fatally simplistic: all one has to do is to embrace a principle or two, and the great thing that is Japanese philosophy suddenly appears from nowhere. Such conjuring tricks can produce nothing that qualifies as genuine philosophy.

Things are much as Nishitani has noted earlier. What is essential is that the special sciences themselves should attempt to delineate their defining principles, and then and only then, so armed, can they embark on the engagement with philosophy proper. This is the task of which the proponents of the special sciences must make themselves sufficiently aware, of which they must be properly conscious. The belief that philosophy is a kind of first aid kit for the mind is neither serious nor helpful. Such thin 'science' offers no hope. People

166 *The Standpoint of World History and Japan*

who entertain such beliefs in effect want philosophers to do their work for them. They would impose the entire burden on us. But what is really needed is for the special sciences to do the essential metaphysical spadework themselves; they must unearth their own particular principles. Furthermore, having identified the problems that these principles present to the special sciences, the workers in these fields should then try to devise solutions from the standpoint of the special sciences. From this process, I believe a genuine form of philosophy can take root and flower.

18   World history and morality (*moraru*)

KŌYAMA: Then there is the problem of '*potence*' (power/*potestas*). Yes, France was defeated [in 1940], but why? What was the cause? I think one may say, borrowing from the language of Ranke, that France faltered from a lack of *moralische Energie* or *dōtoku-teki seimei ryoku*.[125] A gap or divide developed between France's culture and politics, and thus the country's political culture fell to pieces.[126] Both spheres lost their healthy vitality, and therefore France experienced a collapse of moral energy.[127] And this is the cause, in my view, of its defeat. In other words, the focus of our hopes [for France] is not, therefore, the culture of Paris's past but rather a new French culture that can generate a new moral energy, one that would defend Paris even if it meant reducing the French capital in all its beauty to ash. The larger point is that moral energy is the force that moves world history; that is true not only today but always.[128] Furthermore, I suspect that this force assumes the shape of a [defining] political principle at historic turning points.[129] To put the point in its proper context, what we must hope for from the youth of Japan today is such moral energy, such a feeling of healthy morality and fresh energy.[130]

---

125 If the Third Republic had genuinely embodied effective legitimacy, it should have defended itself even if this had meant the destruction of Paris. But in any case, if the Third Republic proved unable to stave off defeat in 1940, this meant – for the Confucian – that it was time for France to turn its back on this flawed regime and reinvent itself. Only a genuine national renewal, in this sense, could create a new France capable of defending itself. Behind this interpretation stands the notion of *toku* or the virtue of a regime. Here virtue refers to spiritual and material capability (*potense*).
126 See Note 21 for a gloss.
127 Note that in Kōyama's mind animal 'vitality' is not the same thing as 'moral energy'.
128 This sentence artfully states Ranke's ruling assumption in a way that renders it readily intelligible in a Confucian light, despite the earlier criticism of Chinese historiography in general and the Confucian commitment to the ideal of the mandate of heaven. The suggestion would be that just as Ho Chi Minh recast Confucian ideals in ways that legitimized a Communist Marxist revolutionary movement in Vietnam, so the Kyoto School more or less consciously did the same for Japan at the start of the Pacific War.
129 The idea of 'turning points' or tipping points is rightly understood here in Confucian terms.
130 The language of biological vitality was a product of the nineteenth century. Social Darwinism, which was so influential in Japan, is one of the most studied of these discourses in vitality.

KŌSAKA: A feeling of genuine vitality is indispensable. This sense of bursting with health ... It may be an old way of thinking, but what moves history in reality is not only the economy or academic ideas but something more *subjektiv* [transliterated from the German] or subjective (*shutaiteki*),[131] or, to put it still more concretely, something that captures the life force of the nation (*minzoku no seimeiryoku*). Of course, this has to be part and parcel of the culture. When the contest of making world history becomes decisive, the vitality of the nation, and to an even greater extent moral energy, become the factors that count.

KŌYAMA: When one talks of war, one immediately assumes that war is the opposite of ethics, the notion being that war and ethical conduct stand eternally apart. But to think in this way is to reduce ethics to simplistic formalism. Such formalism already spells the death of genuine moral energy. As Ranke and others have noted, there is a moral energy to be found in war. In any case, formal ethics tends to be self-serving; it tends to justify the injustices of the old order in its defence of the status quo at the expense of the promise of the new. This is why such ethical formalism is criticized by the healthy forces of change. This is what I think 'moral energy' means. In the face of the trend to break up short of reaching the objective realm, healthy moral energy gives subjectivity the power to overcome these fractures, to bind them together and make them whole.[132]

NISHITANI: I, too, think this is the case. In this context, I must confess that I really detest the word *rogaraka*.[133] I know that it was a kind of catchphrase until quite recently, but I really can't bear hearing it, regardless of the idea that this expression is supposed to conjure up suggestions of health or wholesomeness. I am not an expert in etymology but *rogaraka* evokes in me something hollow or empty. It seems to me to be the slogan of an age deficient in energy, élan and strength [rather than the reverse].[134]

KŌSAKA: The strained rhetoric of health is proof of its unhealthy character. Granted, it is not entirely a bad idea to be sensitive to the need for genuine [as opposed to pretended] vitality. Nor is it too late to address this challenge. On this point, I might observe that in terms of philosophy we have tended to neglect approaches that allow us to grasp life as it really is. This is a failure. Methods such as those of 'value philosophy' are in fact attempts only to define the essence of life rather than to grasp it

---

131 At once more personal, more effective and more communal than the colder logic of the so-called 'marketplace' of things or ideas.
132 The argument appears to travel entirely on Germanic tracks, but a Confucian gloss digs deep even here.
133 Often rendered as 'cheerful' or 'bright'. Given Nishitani's infatuation with Nietzsche, I think the Japanese thinker regarded the national weakness for relentless cheerfulness as vulgar sentimentality, a false form of unearned emotion. Like Voltaire, Nishitani was no Pollyanna. I suspect Nietzsche's insistence on genuine healthiness appealed to him enormously.
134 The chiding of popular sentiment as war clouds gathered in the Pacific is striking.

practically.[135] I think this mistakenly narrow, because we need a quantitative approach rather than something merely qualitative. We need a philosophical approach that can respond with some confidence to such questions as: What are the true measures of a nation's greatness? How large must a region become to survive and be viable [in world affairs]? What are the best ways to calculate our capability to mobilize our powers? The striking thing here is that the philosophy of subjectivity provides a means for thinking about such quantitative valuations and calculations. We must ask of philosophy not how to purify our souls (*kokoro*) but rather how we can give breath to our greatness of spirit (*kokoro no ookisa*) and thus strengthen our ability to act decisively (*ketsudanryoku*). We have just talked about 'moral energy' and I think this is what it is.

KŌYAMA: If you ask me why Germany triumphed in its recent struggle with France, I would conclude that the Germans as a people (*minzoku*) had the moral energy to win. One often hears of world history described as the court of the world (*sekai saiban*).[136] But this court of judgment does not stand outside history in order to judge it with the eyes of God. The court of the world is the criticism that a nation (*kokumin*) makes collectively of itself. In effect, we judge ourselves. In the end, countries (*kuni*) are not destroyed by external factors such as foreign invasion. External pressures are just one cause. Rather, national decline is the result of the inner decay of moral energy. In other words, a nation may collapse even when an enemy nation poses no external threat. The challenge lies not without but within. The same dynamic applies to the economic and cultural spheres, because the ultimate reason for national decline is always to be found in the loss of moral energy, of healthy morale or vigour at its freshest and most compelling.[137] This dynamic should not be reduced to external factors. We neglect this truth at our peril.

NISHITANI: [It is a curious thing but] somehow when we talk about morality we neglect the vital dimension that is energy, and vice versa. Moral energy is a very good term [precisely because it helps prevent such neglect].

KŌYAMA: To bind ΚΡΑΤΟΣ (might) with ΈΘΟΣ (ethos: moral principle)[138] we require a method for linking and binding these two ideas, as in expressions such as *Staats-raison*,[139] but this is not enough. To create a genuine bond, one needs mediation, and I think moral energy serves this purpose.

---

135 Perhaps a reference to Rickert, who sought to give a more objective cast to the historical sciences by addressing universal objective values.
136 'Die Weltgeschichte ist das Weltgericht' ('The world's history is the world's court'): German poet Friedrich Schiller (1759–1805), in 'Resignation', 1786.
137 From a Confucian perspective, it would appear that Kōyama is evoking not 'springtime for Hitler' but the highest point in the arch of virtue that governs a freshly confirmed mandate of heaven in it all its moral assurance and freshness. Dylan Thomas's 'green fuse' comes to mind.
138 Both terms transliterated from the ancient Greek.
139 Transliterated from the German for *raison d'état*, literally 'reason of state'.

NISHITANI: You mean what Kōsaka called 'subjectivity' ...
KŌSAKA (*NODDING TOWARDS NISHITANI*): You're the one who has talked about subjectivity.
KŌYAMA: You're the one who wrote the book with 'Primordial Subjectivity' in the title.[140] (*Laughter.*)
KŌSAKA: As an idea, moral energy works here.

19   Race, nation, people (*shuzoku, minzoku, kokumin*)[141]

KŌSAKA: While acknowledging Gobineau's dismal reputation, I think some of his ideas may be worth considering in this context despite his disturbing thesis, based on the ideas of blood purity and *Rasse*,[142] that Aryans are born to dominate the world. Nevertheless, there is something suggestive here if we entertain the notion that a race (*shuzoku*) or nation/people (*minzoku*) might be one of the prime movers of world history. Gobineau tries to explain the rise and fall of culture in terms of the purity of the blood of the people (*minzoku*) that sustains the culture in question. He insists that when the blood is contaminated the vital energy (*seimeiryoku*) of a people (*minzoku*) is sapped.[143]

The point is to think through the idea of blood purity via the philosophy of subjectivity. Or, better still, one should replace the notion of blood purity with the idea of *moralische Energie*.[144] Then, and only then, does the suggestiveness of the idea of blood purity become something worth slightly more than nothing.

KŌYAMA: For me, the agency (*shutai*) of *moralische Energie* is a nation (*kokumin*). The idea of a 'people' is a product of nineteenth-century [European] cultural history.[145] But whatever one may say about the past, today mere peoples lack the power to alter the course of world history.[146] The solution to the problems of the world is to be found in the nation

---

140 Keiji Nishitani, *Chosaku Shu, Dai Ikken, Kongen-teki Shutaisei no Tetsugaku* (The Philosophy of Primordial Subjectivity), *Sei*, Tokyo: Sōbun Shuppan, 1986; Keiji Nishitani, *Chosaku Shu, Dai Ni Ken, Kongen-teki Shutaisei no Tetsugaku, Zoki*, Tokyo: Sōbun Shuppan, 1987.
141 The title of this section is less than straightforward. In Japanese, the terms used are, in order, *shuzoku* (race or tribe or species), *minzoku* (nation, people, tribe on a very large scale and, anachronistically, race), and *kokumin* (literally, national people).
142 Kōsaka uses the German word for 'race', transliterated into Japanese.
143 This entire paragraph can be rendered into English only by blurring fine distinctions in both languages. The German word *Rasse* alone retains its unambiguous meaning.
144 Kōsaka uses the German term, transliterated into Japanese.
145 The assumption is that Kōyama is talking about Herder's idea of *das Volk* or 'the people', where the emphasis on culture, language and religion squeezes out almost all nuances of race.
146 Here Kōyama's argument draws on Hegel's notion of 'world-historical peoples', that is, nations or civilizations (for example, the Persians or Chinese or ancient Greeks) who altered the course of history by having a great and enduring impact on global civilization.

(*kokumin*), in the true sense of the term, and nowhere else. Moral energy achieves its true home neither in ethical individualism nor in moral character, and nor, for that matter, does it have anything to do with how pure one's blood is. Rather, the focus of moral energy now is to be found in the nation as a cultural and political phenomenon. Isn't that right?

KŌSAKA: I agree. A people (*minzoku*) in and of itself is meaningless. When a people acquire subjectivity, it becomes a nation-state. A people without subjectivity, a people that has not transformed itself into a nation (*kokumin*), is powerless. The proof of this proposition can be found in the fate of peoples such as the Ainu. Fail in your struggle to achieve national self-determination, and you are condemned to be absorbed into the fabric of a genuine nation-state. Does a similar fate await the Jewish people (*minzoku*)? Such examples explain why one is forced to conclude that the true agency or subject (*shutai*) of world history is to be found only in a people that has formed itself into a state (*kokka-teki minzoku*).

SUZUKI: When contemplating the ebb and flow of national energy, is it possible to think in terms of whether a country is young or old? Is a country, in this sense, a living organism?

NISHITANI: I think that is unscientific. Isn't that right? The problems arising from the issue of blood purity cannot be totally ignored, however. I am not suggesting that (*addressing Suzuki*). Italians, for example, are said to have lots of African blood in them.

SUZUKI: That is what the well-known Italian anthropologist Sergi is studying.[147] Apparently there has been so much mixing that even African blood is involved.

NISHITANI: Having seen many Italians, I must say that is very much my impression.

KŌYAMA: There is little of the ancient Romans about them.

NISHITANI: The Romans of classical times were, in essence, a very different stock. But what exactly has been the impact of the subsequent interracial mixing? It is really hard to say with confidence what the influence has been. In general terms, it seems that racial mixing can be a healthy thing. But sometimes it is not so good. The whole business of blood is extremely complicated.

KŌSAKA: Can we think about it in this way? Take examples of obvious mixing of blood such as Spain or Hungary. Note that such assimilation is not confined to blood; cultural mixing is also involved. Note furthermore that such mixing takes place not in the centre of the culture but at its margins. After all, culture spreads from a centre [where it is strongest because densest] and it is thus thinner at its frontiers. As a result, I think

---

147 Giuseppe Sergi (1841–1936): a biological anthropologist who ridiculed Nordic or Aryan theories of racial superiority in favour of what he called 'the races of the Mediterranean'. He traced the origins of the Italian nation to the Horn of Africa and stressed the importance of cranial morphology.

we might conclude as follows. The commingling of blood does not weaken a culture. From the outset it affects it only when it is still in bud on its least developed frontiers. On such frontiers, a culture is not pure; it is naturally mixed.

The same logic may be applied to the question of whether a culture is young or old. This question cannot be cast in terms of blood alone. Quite the contrary: one must frame it in terms of the creativity of a culture. Setting aside the matter of moral energy, raised earlier, my own view is that notions of blood purity, as one finds them in writers such as Gobineau, quite simply don't work.

KŌYAMA: I have previously given this issue some attention but quite frankly have never found a way to answer it plausibly. To say that blood merely as blood can determine the superiority or inferiority of a people or culture is not a persuasive idea. It cannot explain why this nation or that is strong or weak. So the question is: where does blood lead us? And the answer is to be found in factors beyond blood. It is these factors that will determine the fate of a blood line. In any case, closeness of blood ties is no guarantee of harmony. Blood battles make brothers strangers to one another, and such conflicts are much more common within families than between distant relations.

NISHITANI: The problem is challenging, isn't it?

KŌYAMA: Frobenius regarded culture as something alive, a product not of the times but of its [own] age.[148] He judged age to be a relative notion: some may be young, others are mature; others are old and thus face decline. He applied the same logic to peoples (*minzoku*).

KŌSAKA: There is something to that.

SUZUKI: But can't one imagine a people recovering the vigour of its youth? Take, for instance, the ancient peoples of Europe. However advanced in years, these nations were rejuvenated by their arrival in the Americas. This seems, at least to me, to be a possibility. But, as Nishitani says, there are of course no scientific grounds for speaking of the 'age' of a people, and we should, as far as possible, avoid such language.[149]

KŌSAKA: In the case of the rejuvenation of the ancient Latin peoples in America, I interpret this development as the emergence of a new 'American nation' and a burst of new moral energy.[150] In any event, to argue that nations (*minzoku*) age is unscientific.[151]

---

148 Leo Frobenius (1873–1938): German archaeologist and ethnologist of Africa. Although he was regarded as an intellectual hero in much of Africa, Wole Soyinka felt compelled to denounce him in his 1986 speech in acceptance of the Nobel Prize in Literature.
149 Racial thinking is also effectively covered by this ban.
150 The words 'American nation' are in English.
151 Kōsaka is blurring the distinction in Japanese between *minzoku* (roughly, 'people') and *kokumin* (roughly, 'nation' in the political sense).

NISHITANI: May there not be some connection here with class (*kaikyū*), political or otherwise, in the sense that a new class can come to the fore as the embodiment of a historical force?[152]

KŌYAMA: In Japan the governing class has constantly changed. In the past, the aristocracy has given way to the warrior class, and in turn the samurai have yielded to an emerging urban middle class (*chomin*) ... maybe we are in a period of stable consolidation now. Isn't this what is happening in China?

KŌSAKA: Yes, a ruling class of officers and officials is taking shape. Under the pressure of invasion from without, China is facing the arrival of a new age.

KŌYAMA: Changes in class and social status are very important phenomena, especially when viewed as *sub specie aeternitatis* (*eien*) of the nation. They demand the most careful reflection.

NISHITANI: I don't put this forward as any more than a tentative suggestion, but might there not be some connection between the development of cities and the supposed youth of a culture?

KŌYAMA: There may be some sort of link, and it is worth noting that Edo and Osaka [the principal cities of Tokugawa Japan] were well developed when compared with the Western cities of the same period.

NISHITANI: Somehow I feel that the nation as a whole seems very urban in character, and at other times it seems very rural. For a definite answer about contemporary Japan, we may need to turn to the sociologist.

20 The problems of urban life

NISHITANI: Well, as a matter of fact last year I returned for the first time in a long time to my home town. It is a tiny and very remote fishing village. It is interesting to see how much it has been influenced by urban tastes. At some point in the recent past, young women began to dress in modish Western clothes and wear makeup and lipstick ... the kind of Western shoes which might startle the horses have not yet appeared, but there are coffee houses now as well as bars – the changes have been tremendous.[153] And I cannot help wondering if there is not a connection [between these developments and] what we have been describing as the moral energy of the nation, be it ours or any other.

KŌYAMA: You mean a way to rejuvenate ...

---

152 One of the most important neglected topics in the rise of the Kyoto School is the explosive impact of Marxism on Japanese political thinking from the 1920s onward.

153 At various times and places in modern Japan, coffee shops have offered polite cover for sexual encounters, sometimes including prostitution. Not entirely unlike their post-Victorian counterparts in the West, women wearing makeup such as lipstick were viewed as evidence of fast living and social decadence.

NISHITANI: No, I do not mean rejuvenation. Rather, I feel that in the process of being more sophisticated (*bunka-teki ni*), we have somehow lost something vital.

KŌYAMA: The healthy brutality or vitality – perhaps this is what has been lost? ... There are old folks in my home town who resent the fact that today's young people ride their bicycles to the rice paddies instead of walking ...

NISHITANI: Things in Tokyo now are so different from the city I grew up in.

KŌYAMA: In what way?

NISHITANI: It feels so much more like ... a city. (*General laughter.*)

KŌSAKA: Old Tokyo was a city of farmers or ex-farmers. But today, I don't know. It seems so different. (*Laughter.*)

KŌYAMA: Cities are not places where one readily encounters sincerity and seriousness. People tend to be thrusting and dismissive.

NISHITANI: Hmmm. If everyone was like that, society would be awful ... but on the other hand one often finds townies are open and welcoming.[154] That's cultural in a good sense.

KŌYAMA: Thinking about the cities of the future, what kind of places should they be?

KŌSAKA: We need a programme of mixed development so that urban areas include farmland and rice paddies.

KŌYAMA: We need a development plan for the whole nation. If we don't properly prepare for the future, there will be trouble. Take cities such as Tokyo, Osaka and Kobe. With some effort, these conurbations are either being divided or their expansion somehow limited, as they must be from the standpoint of the nation as a whole. If these large cities are allowed to go on expanding at their current rate, the result could be dire.

NISHITANI: This is only my personal impression [from living there], but comparing Germany and Japan, Germans have fewer very large cities than we do but their small and medium-sized cities are much more developed. One result is that in Japan we have a culture that can manifest itself only in mega-cities partly because alone they have the scope to provide it.

SUZUKI: This is going to lead to problems here. Great cities, that is *Regionstadt*,[155] come with their own unique problems. They are world-historical in their epoch scale. Their huge populations explain their dominant place in our times and culture [to a great extent] but not entirely. From the standpoint of world history, the age of the *Regionstadt* (the mega-city) has been of two kinds. One can be illustrated by the example of Alexandria as the culmination of the Hellenistic age and the climax of classical antiquity. The other finds representative examples in New York and Chicago. Both embody the age of the *Regionstadt*. And, interestingly, both types are

---

154 In contrast to the notorious closed character of the typical Japanese village. Within living memory, outsiders even in towns in Aomori, for example, were still called *tabibito* even after years of residence.
155 Suzuki uses the German word, transliterated into Japanese.

products of civilizations that share many characteristics. A distinction drawn by Spengler to explain the role of cities in civilization can be used to reinforce this view. Maybe that is what cities are all about. It is not entirely an issue of size. Osaka during the Tokugawa period was, it is said, larger than its contemporaries in the West, but it does not follow that Osaka was therefore more advanced. Rather, this may illustrate the different stages of cultural development in East and West respectively at the time.

KŌYAMA: If we accept Spengler's understanding of how a civilization declines, we somehow need to find a way now of returning civilization to a state of youthful renewal. I suspect that we therefore need to bring something else to our [critical] analysis of contemporary urban life. The development of our cities is [inevitably] linked with modern capitalism. And if we propose to improve on capitalism [as it has come to us from abroad], it is entirely predictable that society will be transformed to some degree by these reforms.

SUZUKI: Politics today depends on cities.

KŌYAMA: On the other hand, my thought is that although there is no question that cities can be counted among the phenomena produced by modern civilizations, the challenge posed by today's total wars serves to self-deconstruct (*bunkai*) the modern form of the city as it were from within, because the organizations necessary to wage total war are unthinkable without altering these urban spaces. In contrast with the traditional approach, at once unthinking and unplanned, to urban expansion, we have become extremely plan-minded: developments such as the breaking up of mega-cities into small and medium-sized cities and towns have become almost automatic, and indeed such action is indispensable.

SUZUKI: But this also raises the possibility that the decentralization of large urban populations to rural areas may result in the urbanization of the countryside. This will reduce rural communities to the status of minor players in a vast urban network. There is a contrast to be made here with the cities of feudal Japan, which were not by nature mega-cities, but where urban spaces were supportive of the contribution that rural life made to the strength of the nation. Or at least that is my impression.

KŌYAMA: While their nature as modern cities almost certainly contributed to the growth of Edo and Osaka during the Tokugawa period, Edo's expansion was sustained by the unique impact of the *sankin-kōtai* system.[156] And this suggests a different path of development from that taken by the great cities of modern Europe.

---

156 The compulsory 'alternate attendance' of vassals at the shogun's court. The daimyo 'were obliged to contribute heavily to great public undertakings; and so that they should not hatch mischief in their domains there was evolved a system of hostages, ultimately taking the form of *sankin-kōtai*, or "alternate attendance" at the Shōgun's Court, under which each important *daimyō* was compelled to spend several months every year in Edo, and to leave his wife and family behind when he returned to his fief'. G.B. Sansom, *Japan: A Short Cultural History*, London: Cresset Press, 1946, p. 447.

SUZUKI: The legacy of our medieval towns can be found today in Japan's castle towns. They are models of smallness. German cities are small cities in this sense. Historically they are the heirs of German's medieval cities.

NISHITANI: One can still find them in contemporary Germany. These are sources of what is healthy and vital in German culture.

KŌYAMA: Because this medieval legacy survives in Germany, it is less vulnerable in some ways to the effects of total war. France, by contrast, keeps its heart and soul in Paris, and only there. This makes France that much more vulnerable. Occupy Paris and you deliver a fatal blow to France.

SUZUKI: Britain from the Industrial Revolution onwards has experienced a massive wave of urbanization across the breadth and length of the country. The whole nation has, as it were, become the factory of the world. But what about the United States today? Extreme versions of urbanization and ruralism seem to exist there simultaneously.

KŌSAKA: America has a great number of cities, but, as someone has observed, it has no true metropolis. Its cities are the foci of commerce and manufacturing or political administration. But none of them qualifies as a true metropolis. At least that is how it appears.

SUZUKI: The American landscape is still dotted by the vestiges of frontier expansion. There is a huge number of rural hamlets and villages.

KŌSAKA: As one of our junior colleagues has observed, America manifests an impressive stylishness and an unmistakable barbarism.

SUZUKI: Let me share with you my perception. Americans sometimes appear to be prehistoric men blessed with the gifts of civilization. On the one hand, a civilized sophistication has developed there; on the other, there is a culture of extraordinary simplicity and primitiveness.

KŌSAKA: A conceited child but an innocent one.

21 Explaining America

SUZUKI: According to one scholar, America is better understood as a continent than as one nation among many (*kokusai-teki seikaku*); continents stand apart from the equality of nations. In the economic sphere, America does not exercise the British role of being the trading intermediary, the commercial go-between, for the world economy. The port of New York's capacity to absorb the output of the world reflects precisely the capacity of the American inland empire, understood as a region of continental proportions, to absorb these products. What New York imports, it almost never re-exports. Everything is consumed by the continent that is America. Everywhere one looks, one discovers a continent that is a new world. Recalling the frequently made observation that America is defined not by history but by geography, I cannot help wondering if America is less a geographical phenomenon than an invention of sociology. By that I mean America is at once a sociological experiment and an exhibit in a museum of sociology. Why sociology? Because I think both sociology and America display a remarkable sense of superiority, while also suffering from the limitations of their origins. But having said as much, I believe we need to think about America properly [and that this involves] resisting the temptation, noted by one professor, to dismiss the country out of hand. This reflects our habitual tendency to disregard [inflated] claims for America as soon as we hear the expression 'Americanism'.

KŌSAKA: I have tried to be very careful not to do that.

SUZUKI: Is that right? I have not been so careful.

KŌSAKA: I like Americans such as [William] James very much. He has a wonderful feel for nature.

SUZUKI: Europeans habitually belittle the United States, and I think we here in Japan have been influenced by this. I think this is unquestionably true. We might long to believe that our judgements and criticisms of America are based on observation and experience, but this is by no means always the case ...

KŌYAMA: America has not been properly introduced or explained here. What we have been exposed to is the America of the movies ... [One of the problems is that] America is not an ancient country; it is a new creation. It was born not long after modern civilization came into being. It is from these special circumstances that America has been formed. Isn't this the case?

KŌSAKA: One way of looking at the problem is to say that modern history begins with America.

NISHITANI: In *The Philosophy of the History of Science*, Shimomura has recently written that America has been an experiment in reducing European civilization to pure potential.[157] I find this a rather striking observation.

KŌSAKA: When, in his analysis of Puritanism, Max Weber sought to explain the spirit of capitalism, he described America as the catalyst for the capitalistic spirit and the true home of its birth. As for the state, in America it is actually the society; this is a society that has taken on the form of a state. And that is why I called it a sociological invention ... the country is like one of those stiff boaters. If you wear it long enough, it fits perfectly. Whether it fits from the start is not an issue. Everybody there [eventually] becomes a full member of the society. In the end, they all fit perfectly. And that is how society's unity has been achieved there. The country is united to the root.

SUZUKI: In thinking about this issue of national unity, that is, the state (*kokka*), one has to accept that America's existence as a country is both special and unusual. For one thing, the individual states that compose America [in some cases] predate the founding of the country, and exercise state-like functions [not unlike those of the central government]. Out of

---

157 Toratarō Shimamura, *Kagaku-shi no Tetsugaku*, 1941.

necessity, the structure of the United States of America has been erected on this pre-existing set of institutions. In other words, the states are prior to the nation, and are more fundamental in their importance. The resulting form of government is extremely rare and counter-intuitive to the point of eccentricity (*myō ni*). Hence the conclusion the USA is better understood as a society rather than as a state.

KŌSAKA: That is certainly the case. I think it was Tocqueville or someone who observed that America has developed in a pattern entirely the reverse of that of Britain. For their part, the British have seized a great number of colonies and unified them into a British universe (*igirisu-teki sekai*). But over time, these colonies have gradually gone their own way. The reasons behind this phenomenon are complicated and require more detailed explanation. But in the case of America, the thirteen original colonies first united themselves into a single whole, and then proceeded to develop autonomously into a deeper union that has greatly expanded over time. America followed this path until it seized the Philippines from Spain. Since then it has set off down the imperialist path, suggesting that it has reversed course and has taken the route pioneered by the British. But the original point stands. Driven by a powerful force, America has used this model of society to expand enormously. The social impact of America on China reflects the working of the same process. Clearly the United States needs to be much more thoroughly researched.

NISHITANI: Which raises the question of why Japanese historians have devoted so little time to studying America.

SUZUKI: The fundamental reason for this neglect can be traced to the impact of traditional European historiography on Japan. Isn't this the reason? And this limitation is illustrated by the fact that the recent enormous growth in interest in the United States derives from that country's new world-historical significance. More than [historical] research on America, we need to understand it [philosophically]. Certainly this is the argument that André Siegfried has put forward.[158]

On this subject there is an interesting comparison to be made between America and China. Both nations need to be understood [philosophically] before they can be studied empirically [that is, understanding must precede research, and underwrite it] because of their special significance. Neither is a nation or country [in the conventional sense]; both are continents with vast geographical divisions of east, west, north and south. It is in their profound continental character that China and America most resemble each other.

---

158 André Siegfried (1875–1959): French geographer and political writer well known in Japan at the time for his commentaries on American, British and Canadian politics.

22 Contemporary Japan and the world

KŌSAKA: Having ranged over so many topics during our discussions, and in the light of the current turmoil that grips the globe, what, we might ask, are the key issues and challenges facing Japan today? My feelings on this subject are as follows. Although the Meiji and Taishō periods have become the targets of a variety of criticisms nowadays, no one disputes the fact that Japan's world-historical significance became manifest during those periods. Japan has now to launch itself onto the sea that is the world (*sekai no naka ni noridashita*). The [prevailing] idea was that a synthesis of East and West was taking place, and although it may sound old-fashioned, I think there was a point to this perception. But a synthesis was not enough; Japan regarded the West with suspicion and unease [and rightly so]. A new Japanese culture had to be created, one capable of making this country part of the world (*sekai-teki Nihon bunka*).

The term 'culture' may lead one to imagine something that transcends the confines of Japan's geographical reality, something apolitical; a flower with no roots – in short, a culture without subjectivity. But that will not do. A narrow insularity of mind confined by the limited geographical reality of these islands is hopeless. By contrast, consider the authentic form of moral energy that could arise from the vast territory that lies to our west, the huge expanse of geography that forms the whole of East Asia, stretching as it does from China to the [tropical] islands of South-East Asia and the South Pacific. Even this geographical potential is not enough; we must have new 'principles'.[159] But having said that, there is no point merely denigrating what was achieved during the Meiji and Taishō periods; we must build on what has been accomplished in the past. A new order must be created [from this beginning]. Hence we arrive at this demand for a new set of principles. Germany, Russia, China: all these nations are struggling to create a new set of world-historical principles.

In our world that has been torn asunder, which country will emerge as the new world-historical centre? To achieve this status, economic and military might are of course necessary, but such power must be informed by principles that embody a new world-view and moral energy. The future direction of world history hangs on whether a new world-view or new morality is born or not. This will decide our future. This creative act will give leadership to world history. Under [great] pressure, given the kind of world-historical significance we have been discussing, Japan must develop this kind of principle. This imperative arises not only from within. It is also being urged upon us from without, as it were, by world-historical necessity itself. That anyway is what I believe.

World-historical necessity does not refer to a kind of God-given progress that will unfold regardless of the capriciousness or stupidity of human actions. It will not save us from the effects of human ignorance or the limitations on

---

159 Kōsaka uses the English word, transliterated into Japanese.

our ability to act (*muryoku*). World-historical necessity, as I noted earlier, is that form of necessity that arises between the problem and its solution, where to solve something is a [supreme] act of creation, both imaginative (*sōzō*) and practical (*kensetsu*). The number of follies that mar human history is legion. But can we not, through tireless human effort, help put things right by curbing something of the impact of the stupidities that might otherwise derail human history? The mysterious or secret promise (*himitsu*) of our humanity manifests itself within the course of human history. It is our task to strive to bring this promise to fruition, whether we succeed to a greater or lesser degree. Hence the call for us to bring a world-view to bear on our circumscribed island condition [and thus transform both].

SUZUKI: Thus the matter is as Nishitani has described it in his essay *Worldviews and Views of the State*.[160] The ideas that will give direction to East Asia as a region can be conceptualized because the process of regional creation is still unfolding. But we must not think of the ideas as philosophically complete (*kannen-teki*),[161] because the structure itself remains incomplete. The fact that the struggle (*jihen*) is still being waged must not be overlooked.[162] And I agree. I think this is the case.

KŌSAKA: In the truest sense, it marks the awakening (*hatsugen*) of the Japanese people. From that point, the construction of a [proper] Japanese state can begin to take shape step by step.

SUZUKI: It is coming into being. Its meaning is becoming clear as the thing itself takes shape, as it puts itself into practice. This significance has become strikingly apparent even from the time of the Manchuria Incident [1931], and certainly now since the China Incident [from 1937] has unfolded.

KŌYAMA: The significance of these incidents, as well as their conceptualization, becomes clear only afterwards.[163] This is always true of history. Genuine significance is created as the struggle proceeds. Meaning is created by our actions. The creative potential of our struggle in China is for us to cultivate or destroy. There is a quotation from the *Jinnō Shōtōki* which I like to quote at such junctures: 'We recreate the universe each day.'[164] This captures the importance of the act of creation we are talking about. The creation of heaven and earth is not something that occurred once upon a time, a long time ago. It is something we create each and every morning.

---

160 *Sekai-kan to Kokka-kan*, 1941. Frequently the title is translated to preserve the parallelism of the original, at the price of a certain awkwardness in English.
161 Idealistic in the Hegelian sense as prior to and determinate of experience.
162 *Jihen* ('struggle' or 'incident') refers to the Japanese conflict with China.
163 A reference to Hegel's remark that Athena's owl or understanding 'takes wing at dusk'.
164 Literally, 'the beginning of the world starts from today'. The quotation comes from *The Chronicle of the Direct Descent of Divine Sovereigns*, an ancient Japanese text which sought to demonstrate the legitimate succession of the imperial household.

180 *The Standpoint of World History and Japan*

Every day must be made afresh. A new order must be created from the destruction of the old. In other words, to make a new world somehow we must break out of the ABCD encirclement.[165] Thus are new heavens and earths created.

KŌSAKA: Behold the making of the world.

KŌYAMA: But one swallow does not make a spring. Ordinarily only the physical manifestation [of a transformation of nature] counts as 'the creation of heaven and earth'. Anything short of that, according to this way of thinking, falls short of the full meaning of the expression. Rather than assume that the meaning of these incidents was present from the beginning, we should give this meaning to the new creations that arise from our future actions. In the conduct of a war, it is by pursuing our course of action that we give genuine meaning to our actions, those things created through struggle. The import of the past lives or dies in our actions in the present. It is here that the creation of the universe has meaning. That is because today is the beginning of the world. Or, to put the matter another way, this is the impact of the eternal consequence of the founding act of the nation on the present.

KŌSAKA: Of course, the problems of history are not discovered at random, but are mediated through the past. But the meaning of history lies in advancing towards a solution to the problems [posed by history] that forms part of the process of constructing a new world. A people armed with a state (*kokka-teki minzoku*) is the subject that solves these challenges. New worlds are created by nations (*kuni*). It is as Kōyama says: the beginnings of heaven and earth are found in the present, in the morning of creation. The insight is crucial [and suggestive].

NISHITANI: Kōyama's expression is very apt.

SUZUKI: To think through the problems of East Asia involves more than just concepts; one must be constantly alert to [the changing realities of] what is historically significant now. This is the most important challenge for me.[166]

NISHITANI: When we were talking yesterday, the matter of historical necessity came up. This necessity is intrinsically connected to our actions. Necessity becomes an object of our awareness; we awaken to it only when we act.

KŌSAKA: Only when you try to do something does necessity manifest itself clearly.

NISHITANI: The question 'What must be done?' can be answered, that is, thought through, only by reference to the requirements of practical and

---

165 The ABCD encirclement refers to the working alliance among America, Britain, China and the Dutch East Indies (the Netherlands proper having been occupied by Nazi Germany in 1940), which sought to curb Japanese overseas expansion and hegemony over East and South-East Asia.

166 The ambivalence over the term 'concept' derives from Marx's assault on what he saw as the unrealism of Hegelian idealism. Marx accused Hegel of believing that to conceptualize a problem is to solve it.

realistic national action. Ignore the problem of national action and necessity is reduced to a version of fate. Isn't this the inevitable consequence of not thinking about the nation as an actor in the world? But historical necessity is not fate.

KŌYAMA: It is sometimes said that world history is the realm of guilt, but this is the comment of somebody who thinks he stands alone outside world history. This stance [is so unrealistic that it] does not merit attention.

KŌSAKA: If it is the realm of guilt, it is also the realm of absolution. It can purify us.

KŌYAMA: That's right. World history can cleanse the world of sin. History stands on the frontier between heaven and hell. Standing in time, history is our link to eternity.

KŌSAKA: How about we recast the problem in this way: rather than confining the matter to the salvation of the spirit of the small man, we assume the attitude that sees it as a hard-fought struggle to liberate mankind itself.[167] As Professor Nishida observed recently, world history is the purgatory of the human spirit. It's the realm of purgation.[168] War also has that significance (*imi*). Dante in his *Purgatorio* describes an individual's experience of purgatory. But if a great poet today made purgation his theme, he would compose his song in verse about the profound experience of purgatory that is the history of the world. In their day of wrath, human beings are gripped by anger that possesses their whole bodies. Their wrath is one with their spirit. War offers us such a day. Heaven and earth are united in shared anger. And this is how the human spirit purifies itself. This is because the outcome of war determines how the turning points of world history turn. And it is this that makes world history our purgatory.

---

167 Another twist in the millennial meditation of successive East Asian elites on Book XII of *The Analects*: 'The virtue of the gentleman is like the wind; the virtue of the small man is like the grass. Let the wind blow over the grass and it is sure to bend.'

168 From the Latin *pūrgātōrium*: literally, place of cleansing.

II Three days after the fall of the Dutch East Indies
The second symposium

THE ETHICAL AND HISTORICAL CHARACTER OF THE EAST ASIAN CO-PROSPERITY SPHERE

A round-table discussion held on the evening of 4 March 1942 at Sa-aimi Maruyama, Kyoto

Participants: Masaaki Kōsaka, Iwao Kōyama, Keiji Nishitani and Shigetaka Suzuki

Table of contents

1 History and ethics
2 Ranke or Hegel: empirical world history vs. the philosophy of world history
3 Two methodological approaches to world history (*sekai-shi no hōhō*)
4 The ethics (*rinri*) of historical turning points and the birth of world-historical consciousness (*jikaku*)
5 World-historical peoples (*minzoku*) and the ethical (*rinrisei*)
6 Japan and China (*Nippon to Shina*)
7 World history and *Großräume* (*kōiki ken*)
8 The ethics of the nation (*minzoku*) and the ethics of the world
9 Greater East Asia as a region of nations (*minzoku ken*)
10 Western ethics and Eastern ethics
11 The ethics of war and ethical wars
12 The politics of philosopher-kings/sages (*kentetsu*)
13 The ethics of the family (*ie*)
14 Politics and the spirit of the family
15 Ethics as the fundamental problem of co-prosperity spheres (*Großräume*)
16 Towards a new kind of Japanese

1 History and ethics

KŌSAKA: The other day in Tokyo I met Yūzō Yamamoto, and he told me that he had read the previous symposium in this series.[1] Among the various ideas treated there, he noted that we had taken up Ranke's notion of *moralische Energie*[2] or *dōtokuteki seimeiryoku* in Japanese. This he found extremely interesting. But he also wished to know how one is to cultivate such *moralische Energie* and what it involves ... He wanted to hear more about our views. I feel that we have a responsibility, indeed a great deal of responsibility, to make our opinions still easier to understand.

Earlier I was asked by someone else how the Chinese Incident might be resolved, and I responded by saying the whole business was subject to a variety of extreme complications but in the end the struggle would probably be decided by which nation could demonstrate superior morale (*moraaru*) or morality (*dōtoku*). Inevitably we need to make a great deal of political and cultural effort, but our moral posture (*taidō*) towards China is, in my view, tremendously important. For example, if we dispatch a large number of morally superior people [to the mainland], the Chinese will instantly and convincingly be persuaded, in the light of this display of *moralische Energie*, that we possess the ethically better character [as a political movement, state and people], and they will be won over by such a posture. This is why it is crucial that we demonstrate it. In other words, there is a dimension of morale or moral conviction to our struggle with China. With the outbreak of the Great East Asian War [against Britain and America], this aspect of the struggle has taken on a still wider significance because it sets Eastern and Western morality in conflict. Or, to put it in a way that is perhaps even better, the issue hangs on which form of morale will prove more effective, and thus more significant, in the light of world history and the future of the planet. Until now the question has been: how can we keep Eastern civilization vital in the face of [the provocation of] European civilization? But today, in my view, the more fundamental challenge is [the task of sustaining] the power of a new Eastern morality. What form, then, should this new Eastern morality take? It should be obvious from our previous discussion of 'The Standpoint of World History and Japan' that we should be able to identify the specific character of this morality.[3]

---

1 Yūzō Yamamoto (1887–1974): Japanese novelist and playwright; public critic of Japanese government wartime policy. Yamamoto is referring to the previous round-table discussion, 'The Standpoint of World History and Japan', published in the January 1942 issue of *Chūō Kōron*.
2 Kōsaka uses the German term, transliterated into Japanese.
3 The experiment is once again double-edged. If the Japanese empire can demonstrate that it possesses a superior morality, it should and will, in the eyes of the Kyoto School thinkers, triumph. On the other hand, obviously barbarous conduct may undermine this claim if the Chinese masses perceive Japanese violence not as the inevitable part of the cruel shift from one *toku* to another *toku* but as a fatal flaw in Japan's claim to assume the equivalent of the Confucian cosmology described conventionally as 'the mandate of heaven'.

If one examines the traditional approach to morality, one finds a pronounced disinclination to combine morality with history. Even in the case of Kant, morality is conceived from the outset as a form of transcendental ethics. But in reality there is an extremely important relationship between peoples and states as they move through history, on the one hand, and ethics[4] and morality on the other. This relationship tends to be entirely forgotten [nowadays], first because of the view that ethics are unchanging and therefore untouched by history, and second because of the flawed perception that ethics can be safely ignored when judging the actions of the state. But nation building and the processes involved in forming (*keisei*) the state do not transcend the ethical realm. History and ethics always have to be united. This is especially true in our current circumstances, when a new stage in history has become possible, so now this connection has to be thought through even more thoroughly. The history of the world confronts us with a set of problems that have to be solved. One of the tasks that has to be addressed is of particular importance: the problem of ethics. We must recognize the world-historical significance of the strength of our morale as we find it at the moment. Or, to reverse the argument, the substance (*naiyō*) of any new form of East Asian ethics must be derived from our place and status within world history. The crisis of contemporary world history is to an unexpected degree a crisis of ethics, and this explains why *moralische Energie* matters so much.

If this discussion appears to be a bit circumlocutory, one must remember that when history turns on its axis, things that seem most removed from our immediate circumstances often turn out to be precisely those things that are most readily to hand, and therefore the most open to ready solution.[5] This I suspect is frequently the case, and it is along these lines that I want to respond to Yūzō Yamamoto's concerns.

A new form of ethics for East Asia: this is what world history is calling for. This will be determined by the ethical mission of the philosophy of world history.[6] As was noted in our earlier discussion when we dwelled on this topic at some length, this issue had become the most pressing of concerns even before the events of 8 December 1941. But, in the light of recent developments, the question of what form our [moral] posture towards the peoples of the Asian and Pacific tropics (*Nanpō*) should take has now assumed an immediate and unavoidable seriousness.[7] Furthermore, as our treatment of

---

4 More often than not, the four thinkers appear to use the words 'ethics' and 'morality' as more or less equivalent, but *rinri* or 'ethics' in Japanese more than hints at academic or abstract usage, as in expressions such as 'the philosophy of ethics', and carries Western associations.

5 A parallel with, rather than a borrowing from, Heidegger's notions of 'readiness to hand' and 'present to hand' is suggested. Kōsaka uses the term *tejika*, meaning literally 'at hand' or 'near to hand', both suggesting something familiar, in contrast to the term *uen-na* (circuitous or once removed).

6 Where 'determine' (*kettei*) refers both to the identification of the content of such an ethics and to its implementation by assuming the posture required by historical reality.

7 As noted above, the key word is *taidō*, 'moral posture' or 'attitude', and the same instantaneous recognition of genuine virtue as the occasion for a revolution in *toku* is implied.

this topic in our previous symposium provoked a certain degree of comment among those who read it, we must now set out our views in detail. Thus, while we touched on the tensions between the world history of the historian and the philosophy of world history in our earlier discussions, that topic was of secondary significance; it now requires closer attention, especially in connection with the new ethical concerns we have just identified.

SUZUKI: On the subject of *moralische Energie*, 8 December ('8.12') was the day when I think that we as a nation (*kokumin*) felt the power of the *moralische Energie* we possess in a most vigorous and moving way.[8] But if we spoke of historical necessity during our previous symposium, we did not mean something for which one [merely] waits with folded arms but rather the kind of inevitable consequence which results when one acts subjectively [on the world].[9] In other words, historical necessity is subjective necessity, the necessity of praxis or practical necessity, if you will.[10] This truth was brought home to me by what happened on '8.12'. At the time, our feelings pulled in two different directions. On the one hand, there was a sense that what had to happen had finally happened.[11] The clarity of necessity had [finally] possessed us. But at the same time there was an overwhelming feeling of astonishment because we had achieved what we had hitherto regarded as impossible.[12] Here, after having fought a great war [against China] for so long, we had taken on the burden of a still greater struggle. But I think there were also serious doubts across the country about our ability to meet this challenge. Nevertheless, despite such uncertainty, it was widely accepted that this conflict had become increasingly difficult to avoid. The pressure came from outside Japan, that is, from history itself. But necessity of this kind only began to take on genuine greatness when

---

8 The dateline in mid-Pacific made it 7 December 1941 in Hawaii and the continental United States.
9 'In the beginning was the deed' (Goethe's *Faust*, Part I, Act 1).
10 Suzuki says nothing more than '*jissenteki hitsuzensei*' (literally, 'practical necessity'), but the literal translation is insufficient. The word 'practical' in English normally suggests something that can be done or demonstrates a realistic prospect of completion, in contrast to the 'theoretical'. But practical necessity for Suzuki is part of a triplet of meanings: something is practically necessary because one can do something; does do something; and is driven to do something in the face of whatever the historical situation demands. In the language of Althusserian Marxism, the kind of necessity at issue is over-determined, not only from without but also from within. Such subjective necessity is worlds away from the essentially private personalism of the early Nishida.
11 Compare this with the relief and excitement that swept Europe on the outbreak of the First World War.
12 Here, again, the meaning is so forceful, so replete with significance, as to be over-determined. The Japanese military successes of the winter of 1941/42 signalled the simultaneous triumphant manifestation at home of Japanese subjectivity, in the Hegelian sense, and sweeping victory abroad in the contest of comparative moralities with the West.

the Japanese people rose to this challenge on '8.12'. At this point, our *moralische Energie* came into play, the kind of *moralische Energie* that has the power to shape world history.

2 Ranke or Hegel: empirical world history vs. the philosophy of world history[13]

SUZUKI: How does the philosophy of history relate to the study of history by historians? As Kōsaka has raised the topic, and I believe I had a bit more to add to my remarks in the previous symposium, I suspect we may have to give more thought to why the significance of world history today needs to be understood, of necessity, as a form of world-historical consciousness. Various approaches are possible. For example, as is frequently observed, the world [or world history] was regarded formerly as only an idea and has now become a reality.[14] Or, to put it another way, the world has hitherto been regarded as a movement in space, whereas today we understand it as unfolding in time.[15] Or, previously the world was mono-dimensional but today it has taken on its current [plural] structure (*tagensei*).[16] Such changes have given rise to world-historical consciousness. These concepts do not differ that radically from each other, but there is another aspect of the problem – one that figures with special prominence in contemporary world-historical consciousness – that we have to address practically: the theoretical challenge of overcoming historicism.

The traditional study of history consisted of – how should one put it? – resurrecting or reconstructing (*fukugenshugi*) the past.[17] The duty of the historian was to conjure up, one more time as it were, the past as it really was (*sono*

---

13 The title of this section in Japanese can be literally translated as 'The philosophy of world history and the study of world history'.
14 A bridging moment between Hegelian idealism and Marxism realism, curiously argued from the Marxist point of view. Previously Europe was the world but now the world had become a global totality of which Europe was only a part. Or, to continue the analogy, Japan had now become a totality, a world in itself, where previously only Europe qualified as a world in the proper sense.
15 As noted in the first symposium, a contrast is drawn between the modern spread of Western imperialism and the sudden reversal of the imbalance of forces between East and West in the Asia-Pacific region that occurred in the middle of the twentieth century.
16 Here, ideas of the mono-dimensional refer to the West's singular domination of the modern world, while today the world has become multidimensional, or in Kōsaka's language 'a plurality of worlds'.
17 This argument unfolds on two levels: the conscious and the semi-conscious. On the conscious level of authorial intent, Suzuki is attacking Ranke's famous argument that the prime duty of the historian is the exact reconstruction of the past 'as it really was'. On the semi-conscious level, however, reconstructionism hints at the Confucian stress on the ideal past of the ancient sages to which the best kind of governments seek to return. Suzuki dissents from both viewpoints.

tori). But the problem is that [strictly speaking] *someone from one age cannot understand the past in the way a person of that age could*.[18] Or, to put it another way, by far the greatest form of history demands that one understand *another age in terms of the assumptions of that age*.[19] Or, to put it still another way, history becomes history only by being historical about the past.[20]

History must be conceived from within history [not from the standpoint of eternity]. But we have to be clearer than our predecessors about what exactly this phrase 'from within history' signifies. The proper understanding of the expression 'from within history' requires, I think, that we add something practical to the equation.[21] This suggests that when we think about the contemporary world 'from within history', our awakening to world-historical consciousness must include addressing the challenge of overcoming historicism. I am therefore not entirely convinced, for example, by the arguments that Kōyama makes in his theory of the plurality of worlds within world history. If you are arguing only that the world has had more than one centre, this merely highlights something previous historians have been well aware of. There is no need, in this sense, to stress the obvious. Which is why I have trouble with this argument.

Nevertheless, it is equally evident that Japan has today assumed the burden of creating a new world order. Moreover, Japan's new place in the world is being confirmed in a variety of ways. We thus are actually creating a world with more than one centre. But it is only when we will the creation of a new world order that we can be said to be assuming the standpoint of world history.[22] It is then [and only then] that the issue of the plurality of worlds takes on the colour of genuine innovation [making it new] and originality as an issue or problem (*mondai*), and should be so understood. This is why world-historical consciousness will not be revived in the Rankean form today; it does not provide a convincing way of understanding contemporary world history (*sekaishi-gaku*). Note further that what is at issue is not the breadth or narrowness of the historical vision.[23] Contemporary world-historical understanding reflects a different form of consciousness or awareness. It wants to understand how to create a new world, and therefore it is of an entirely different character from that of the historian as a passive observer that characterizes

18 Italics in the original.
19 Italics in the original.
20 I interpret this to mean that history becomes history, that is, a genuine understanding of the past, only when it attempts to transcend the limits of its own time without recourse, for example, to eternal unchanging metaphysical concepts. Suzuki's exact words are *rekishi wa rekishi ni tai suru koto in yotte hajimete rekishi de aru*. The conflict with Confucianism is noted.
21 Another surprising evocation of Marx's practical assertion that the point of philosophy is not to understand the world but to change it.
22 This use of the verb 'to will' harks back to Nietzsche and Heidegger but has specifically Hegelian implications because the members of the wartime Kyoto School refuse to surrender to a Western form of nihilism. Their commitments are resolutely Hegelian or subjectivist.
23 Suzuki is not echoing the clichéd criticism of Ranke as being myopically Eurocentric.

the contemplative stance of the Rankean approach to history. This is what has made the understanding of world history the issue of the hour that it has become in Japan today, and it is our approach to world history that to my mind distinguishes it radically from world history in the Rankean mode. This fact is, in my view, of overwhelming importance now.

KŌSAKA: On this point, let me give you my impression of what I take to be your position, more or less. As Suzuki notes, and I have no doubt that this is right, the present heightening of world-historical consciousness generally has been strongly influenced by the constructive/creative urges that have fed our desire to build a new world order. This, I believe, is a fact. But let us for the moment draw a distinction between the study of world history by the positivist historian and the philosophy of world history as the philosopher understands it. If we do this, conventional academic history has [necessarily] to be positivist or empirical to be history. And, in a parallel way, the philosophy of world history will, to the degree that it is philosophy, have to deal in absolutes [the unconditioned foundations of existence]. And this raises the important question: how does the absolute, the ultimate truth of the world, manifest itself in history? The eternal against the temporal; ultimate truths against [the facts of] history: how are we to connect these things? This is the task that faces the philosopher of world history. There is no need for the [exclusively empirical] student of world history to grapple with such metaphysical concerns. Indeed, the particular strength of such historians arises from the fact that they don't attempt to do so.

And won't this distinction manifest itself even more as we build the future, our future? Granted, the past, present and future must necessarily mediate each other, but I suspect that the burden of past fact weighs heavily on the historian when he addresses world history. On the other hand, the philosophy of world history is necessarily ruled by an *Idee* of the future.[24] Such ideas don't necessarily come to the fore in the labours of the [empirical] historian, who can work without them. This forms its distinctive inner foundation. Indeed, without it, the world history of the empirical historian would [collapse into and] be one with the philosophy of world history. Thus we set one against the other: the historian is empirical where the philosopher is idealistic [in the Hegelian sense]; the historian's task is to place the past in order, the philosopher's is to construct the future. These differences are more or less inevitable, but the two approaches can only be sustained by mutual mediation.

---

24 *Idee* is transliterated from the German as a translation of *rinen*. It may be prudent to acknowledge that for the German Idealist and the Kyoto philosopher alike, 'Ideas are concepts of reason' (Michael Inwood, *A Hegel Dictionary*, Oxford: Basil Blackwell, 1992). Ideas are thus embedded in reality and drive history. These two schools of thought differ at many points, but on this subject they speak, more or less, the same language.

3 Two methodological approaches to world history (*sekai-shi no hōhō*)

SUZUKI: That is of course true. Indeed, this distinction may be the most important point of all. The remarkable thing is that today these two contrasting approaches – the world history of the empirical historian and the world history of the philosopher – have drawn so close despite their methodological differences. There are unmistakable junctures where they mediate each other. Nevertheless, fundamental contrasts remain, and should remain. At root, such differences can probably be traced back, to put the matter a bit simplistically, to the rooted incongruity between the study of history and philosophy. History is an empirical science, and this is not going to change. A scientific method defines its character. Nevertheless, and this may sound strange coming from a historian, this method has some significant limitations, and we are aware of them because of our consciousness of world history.[25]

The nineteenth century witnessed the greatest flowering of history in the empirical mode, but this approach fell into difficulty because its practitioners were overconfident. As Croce himself observed at the end of this impressive period, the more complex and exacting a method becomes, the less it is able to speak about achieving the absolute truth about this or that aspect of the past.[26] Or, to rephrase the point, the historical record serves as the means of the historian, not as his object. Therefore, to the degree we take this means to be our object, the substance of history will be lost. Pushed to an extreme, the excessive confidence of the nineteenth-century empirical historian results, in the view of thinkers such as Croce, in an ironic reversal: the question ceases to be 'How certain is what I know?' and becomes 'Among all the fictions (*uso*) of the historian, which is the least untrue?' This is the kind of scepticism that has arisen in response to the nineteenth-century approach.

Let us restate the issue by returning to something noted earlier. According to the nineteenth-century empiricist, the historian achieves objectivity by judging the past from the same perspective as the people he is studying. But there are problems with the notion of objectivity being taken as uncontested in this formulation. These problems lie not in the method itself, but in the fundamentally flawed assumptions that underwrite the method before it is applied. Furthermore, in addition to these foundational concerns [*Grundprobleme*], and the very condition of a discipline in which such problems are so significant, the resistant character of world history also poses grave obstacles

---

25 The sentence is pivotal. Suzuki's recognition of the power of philosophical conceptualization to explain history, that is, his acknowledgement of an implicit superiority of Hegel over Ranke, explains why the Japanese historian has a secure place in this round-table discussion.
26 Benedetto Croce (1866–1952): Italian philosopher and historian who during his long life dominated the intellectual milieu of the new Italy to a perhaps even greater degree than John Dewey or Kitarō Nishida in their respective countries.

for the scholar. Therefore one must conclude that while it is true that history must be an empirical discipline and therefore it must approach the study of world history from an empirical standpoint, one will nevertheless be wise to be sceptical about the empirical approach because of the doubts that have been raised since the nineteenth century.

KŌSAKA: Such scepticism is warranted.

NISHITANI: On this question, I think we can argue that the empirical historian and the philosopher of world history shoulder different responsibilities arising from their different fields of study. But there is a place where their approaches mutually mediate one another, although we must simultaneously acknowledge the contrast between them as distinct branches of scholarship.

KŌSAKA: I agree.

NISHITANI: I wonder if we might provisionally consider the matter in this way. Ethics has traditionally been regarded as something distinct from history [or historical change].[27] But practically (*gutaiteki ni*) speaking, ethics does not stand apart from the historical process but is rather something shaped by history, that is by historical necessity. In this sense, ethics is bound, on the one hand, in a fundamental or foundational way to what we are calling the philosophy of world history ...

KŌSAKA: That, in my view, is the case.

NISHITANI: ... by all of which I mean that ethics as a standpoint involves more than one process. On the one hand it can serve as a starting point from which we can proceed deeper into philosophy itself, while on the other hand ethics cannot be understood if it stands apart from historical understanding (*ninshiki*), from the insights into the movements and trends of the historical process that can be garnered from the empirical standpoint. Any form of ethics that is not informed by historical understanding (*ninshiki*) is inevitably abstract.[28] In other words, I believe that there is a place in all of this where ethics can be made to work in tandem with the positivist understanding of the pure historian, mentioned earlier.[29] But observe further that the historical understanding we are talking about refers to more than just historical data about the past. It must seek to do more than [merely] reconstruct (*fukugen*) the truth about this or that

---

27 This remark turns, at least in part, on the classical notion that philosophy, metaphysics and ethics are all about eternal, unchanging verities, while history is about transitory alterations in the human situation.

28 One might dismiss this as a merely tautological insight. Classically ethics and philosophy are inevitably abstract in the sense that neither experiences change; they deal in the eternal. But when viewed from the standpoint of human action, the abstract conception of philosophy becomes literally useless because it cannot respond to the ever shifting demands of human subjectivity. Furthermore, when Nishitani's remarks are read at speed, this attack on abstraction resonates immediately with the traditional Japanese suspicion of all abstractions.

29 Nishitani uses the German word *positivistisch*, transliterated into Japanese: this term refers to the empirical or factual understanding of the past, not to positive laws.

historical event. Rather, it must aim at transcending the [local] significance of such happenings into order to pierce the [vital core of the] movements of the great current of history so as to accelerate the tide of world history, thus enhancing its impact. It is this process which must be made ethical. In this way also ethics can be grounded in our understanding of the past.

SUZUKI: So it must be.

KŌSAKA: Absolutely.

NISHITANI: This means that ethics mediates the interpretations of the [empirical] student of world history as well as the philosophy of world history; but it also follows that unless mediated by these two approaches to history, ethics itself cannot be made to work. This, I suspect, is the fundamental truth of the matter ... the voice that guides us to do what is ethically right comes to us from the depths of what is genuine in the past.[30] We can hear it in the great movements of history.

KŌSAKA: I think you may have a point.

NISHITANI: Yes, and therefore I think we can conclude that at some profound level (*fukai tokoro*) human *Existenz* (*jitsuzon*) as it unfolds in the real (*genjitsu*) world of history is mediated by the factual history of the world and the philosophy of world history.

SUZUKI: I hold that the empirical approach to the study of the past is indispensable, but I am unable to free myself from the suspicion that the traditional methodology of the historian needs to be radically reconceived (*tatenaosu*). Conventionally, the historian as observer of the historical process is said to stand radically (*hijō ni*) apart from the object of his study, that is from history in its [strictly] factual guise. This distance between the observer and what is observed is axiomatic to the conventional study of the past. This assumption, I believe, is mistaken. Note, furthermore, that it follows that any study of the past, no matter how systematic or careful, will be fatally compromised if its methodological assumptions are flawed. It will be beyond salvation. The thinking subject (*shutai*) which studies history and the objective history which is studied are both located within the historical process; they are inescapably bound together. We therefore need to devise a methodological approach that recognizes this unity and accepts it as its axiomatic foundation. This I believe to be indispensable. Are we clear here?

In his recent writings, Meinecke has defined history as the synthesis of the past and the present.[31] He appears to be suggesting that we must have a new

---

30 Again Nishitani uses the German term *Das Sollen* or *sollen*, from Kant's German for 'what we ought to do or correct behaviour', transliterated into Japanese as *furigana*.

31 Friedrich Meinecke (1862–1954): German historian whose major works – *Weltbürgertum und Nationalstaat* (1908), *Die Idee der Staatsräson* (1924) and *Die Entstehung des Historimus* (1936) – all have enormous resonance in the wartime deliberations of the Kyoto School. But it is his minor classic of 1946, *Die Deutsche Katastrophe*, that in my view uniquely captures the intellectual climate of opinion in the 1930s and early 1940s in Japan and continental Europe.

approach to the study of history. Doesn't this confirm the suspicion that a certain degree of scepticism (*gimmi*) about empiricism itself is in order?

KŌSAKA: Yes, I think that is what is being called for.

KŌYAMA: That's an awkward one. I have written about this issue in a variety of places, and I have concluded that the point of departure in the relationship between the empirical history of the world and the philosophy of world history first becomes explicit in the selection of evidence or data from the historical record (*shiryō*). Even the daily news is the object of selection and editing. So, obviously, is the world-historical record. In the case of the latter, the data must be subjected to empirical scrutiny. But the facts from which the historical record is composed do not choose themselves. All selections are made from the standpoint of the person doing the selecting: the thinking subject (*shutai*). It is this subject who then brings this record of the past to bear on contemporary historical reality.

Furthermore, we will think how world history 'comes into being' (*seiritsu*): the same process of selection is involved, only this time the selection is made from the standpoint of the subject that is caught up in the enterprise of writing a new chapter in the contemporary history of the world. But observe that this task, that of writing a new chapter in the history of the world, is assigned to the philosopher of world history (*sekai-shi tetsugaku*). In other words, the process of selection or editing from the historical record is governed by the interface between empirical world history and the philosophy of world history. This encourages us to anticipate a fit or compatibility between the detailed understanding generated by empirical world history and by the philosophy of history. For example, when we consider how contemporary world history is coming into being, certain events take on very great significance. The list of such events includes the Meiji Restoration and the Russo–Japanese War as well as the Japanese occupation of Manchuria and our country's departure from the League of Nations. Viewed from the [narrow] standpoint of national history (*kokushi*) alone, these events may not seem that much more important in relative terms [than many others]; but judged as developments in the 'coming into being' (*seiritsu*) of contemporary world history, assessed from this singular standpoint, their degree of relative importance increases enormously.

Why, then, should such prominence be assigned to events such as the Russo–Japanese War or our abandonment of the League of Nations? The answer is straightforward: we are not talking about routine events in the 'making' (*seiritsu*) of world history as conventionally understood. Routine does not offer us the relevant 'standpoint'. No, the birth of contemporary world history provides a superior vantage or standpoint for judging the [relative] significance of these events, and this vantage is defined by the act of historical 'creation' or 'construction' (*kensetsu*). This is history judged from the standpoint of the subject or the historical agent who edits or selects from the historical record because he is in the act of making world history. The result is that we are caught in a temporal zone in which empirical world history and the philosophy of world history are neither rigorously distinct nor near equivalents but rather two mutually informing processes [of understanding and action].

NISHITANI: Not only that, the stance of the acting subject (*shutai*)[32] includes the awareness (for judging the relative relevance of individual parts of the historical record) of the apparent relative insignificance and importance of other events [in contrast with conclusions from a conventional point of view] ...

SUZUKI: That is of course right. Events both less and more significant are weighed up ...

NISHITANI: Objectivity is at work here. As for subjective goals themselves ...

SUZUKI: Yes, that kind of objectivity exists. Or at least I believe it does.

NISHITANI: In a sense that departs from what we [conventionally] term the objectivity of the historical record, we have to imagine a form of objectivity that gives rise to genuine insights, both profound and [apparently] superficial, into world history.

SUZUKI: That is correct. I think that Meinecke has said much the same thing. This implies that there is a kind of subjectivity (*shukan*) that transcends the limited vision of the individual, a subjectivity (*shukan*) with the egotist (*shukan*) removed.[33]

NISHITANI: All of this reminds me of my time in Germany. I was listening to a lecture by Heidegger, and Burckhardt's name came up in connection with the problem of historical consciousness. I think, no I am sure, that this was the occasion. In any case, Burckhardt was judged to have got many things wrong. Indeed, from Heidegger's perspective, the Swiss historian was mistaken on all counts. Be that as it may, it was argued that what Burckhardt had to say was still of value because there was something compelling about the kind of consciousness or attitude (*taido*) that he brought to the study of the past.

4 The ethics (*rinri*) of historical turning points and the birth of world-historical consciousness (*jikaku*)

KŌYAMA: The expansion of Europe overseas has been frequently discussed but I believe insufficient attention has been paid to the main consequence of this expansion: the growing dependence of Europe on the non-European

---

32 Nishitani says only *shutai*, but I have rendered this as 'acting subject' because the notion of agency is so important to the contrast that is being developed among the participants between understanding history passively but objectively, and acting on history and thus making it.

33 The reference here is to the individual who is incapable of seeing the larger picture because consumed by self-limiting selfish desires and aspirations, and thus lacking in self-transparency as well as a vision of totality.

world. While Europe may have possessed sufficient reserves of coal and iron ore to sustain the Industrial Revolution and its aftermath, the arrival of the age of oil has forced Europe to seek natural resources beyond its borders. This is just one example of the growing and irresistible dependence of Europe on the rest of the world, in terms of both markets and resources, that has been the ironic result of its global hegemony. In other words, the nature and impact of the extension of Europe's power overseas during the age of late capitalism marks a fundamental break with the Age of Mercantilism and the earliest phases of market capitalism. This new world history [that Europe has created] has provoked (*yōin*) Asian resistance. If such resistance is to be effective, it will seize on the vulnerabilities that have resulted from the trend of Europe's deepening dependence on the non-European world. Furthermore, I think it is worth arguing that the gap between the assessments of Europe's global rise offered by empirical historians and the insights produced by philosophers of world history explains why this growing European vulnerability has hitherto not figured prominently enough in Japanese thinking on this crucial subject.

SUZUKI: Perhaps we can reformulate the issue in this way. The philosophy of world history has hitherto focused on the universal, on [positivist] laws of historical development. This was the kind of understanding that was pursued in the past by the philosopher of history. But now things are different. Today the student of world history views our times through the prism provided by the *Individualität* that defines the contemporary era.[34] Isn't this the way we now grasp the historical ...

KŌSAKA: I, too, am convinced that this enterprise we call 'the philosophy of world history' has to be fundamentally rethought. In the broadest terms, Fichte[35] and Hegel believed that the philosophy of world history had first to be erected on *a priori* foundations. They focused on theory, and almost immediately this approach was criticized by people such as Ranke for being more about theory than history. This explains why the Fichtean and Hegelian stress on *a priori* foundations was dismissed as a speculative exercise that had nothing to do with history. And if it did not qualify as history then, by definition, it did not qualify as world history. This is exactly the kind of conclusion that one would expect from historians ... Which means that if we are to devise a proper philosophy of history, we must break with the tradition of Fichte and Hegel. For the philosophy of history to be credible it must be credible as history, and thus win the respect of historians as historians. Of course, such a philosophy of history

---

34 That is, seeing individual facts as opposed to overarching scientific laws. Suzuki uses the German word, transliterated into Japanese.
35 Johann Gottlieb Fichte (1762–1814): German philosopher who was important to the Kyoto School because of his insistence that any authentic grasp of the everyday real world or of world history must be grounded in metaphysics.

must still [seek to] demonstrate the ability to grasp ultimate reality, but to attempt to uncover [a local version of] ultimate reality within the endless altering flow of time is extremely difficult. For us, the only way forward is to face up to the task of grasping ultimate truths without being defeated by the transient. This test is unavoidable when we attempt to be creative by leaping from the present into the future.

I do not mind calling this philosophy or metaphysics or butting up against 'the unflinching pursuit of the ultimate' [undeterred by the claims of the transient]. This must serve as our point of departure. The task is formidable because we are trying to foster something worthy of the name of the philosophy of history as a genuine form of philosophy but at the same time something continually mediated by empirical world history. Both aspects would need to be mediated by ethics. This is what I would propose. Isn't this close to what you are arguing, Nishitani? The issue turns on the relationship between creative action (*kensetsu*) and ethics: history and ethics. I see history as determining (*kettei sareru*) both the concrete content of the ethical and the direction of the creative process.

NISHITANI: It is at historical turning points that our consciousness of history becomes sharpest and clearest. This is because such turning points occur precisely when historical continuity breaks down. As the historical process unfolds, it is on these occasions that, as Kōsaka has noted, ultimate truths (*kyukyokuteki na mono*), metaphysical truths (*keijō-teki na mono*), emerge from the historical world in all their uniqueness (*yuinaka*). In other words, as gaps or breaks appear in continuities of the historical process … the depths of the historical world come into view.[36] And notice that these breaks are characteristic of history as history itself (*rekishi jishin*). Such breaks are historical ruptures, and at the same time they can be convincingly understood as opportunities to transcend the historical [as the routine or ordinary or merely empirical]. In other words, such ruptures are at once historical and final [as the exception]. Because they are once historical and metaphysical, such disruptions must be grasped philosophically. Today we stand on the brink of such a rupture.

KŌSAKA: That is my feeling as well.

5 World-historical peoples (*minzoku*) and the ethical (*rinrisei*)

SUZUKI: Another way of looking at the problem is to stress the importance of the gap between the traditional philosophy of history and contemporary empirical history. In connection with this gap, I have been brooding on

---

36 The parallels with the ideas of the French philosopher and dialectician Alain Badiou (b. 1937) and of the post-Marxist Slovene thinker Slavoj Žižek (b. 1949) are striking.

the notion of world-historical peoples as one finds it in the work of thinkers such as Hegel, and I think there are significant *lacunae* between the traditional idea and what we think of world-historical peoples today. When Hegel talked about assuming the burden of world history, of accepting this mission, he had in mind the examples of the ancient Romans and West European peoples.[37] And in a similar vein, contemporary Japan has awakened to this world-historical opportunity and the *mission* that it confers. At various points, there appear to be similarities between Hegel's concept and what we have been arguing, but in fact there are major differences at issue here.[38] It is our recognition of our world-historical mission that underwrites our right and ability to lead and guide East Asia today. Our consciousness defines our position. The burden is not imposed by objective circumstance [but assumed voluntarily] because we have subjectively awakened to it [by and through ourselves].[39] And isn't this precisely what we mean by *moralische Energie*? Isn't this Japan's historical sense of the ethical (*rekishi-teki rinri-kan*)? Our moral life force (*dōtoku-teki-na seimeiryoku*)?[40]

NISHITANI: Yes, I agree that this is the decisive point. The defining characteristic of a world-historical people, taking contemporary Japan as the case in point, is that such peoples are historically self-aware. Whatever the achievements in former times of even the Greeks or the Romans, I don't think one can credit them with being moved to make history from a practical or constructively conscious attempt to create a new world order. Rather, they were driven to become world-historical peoples by what in some sense can be regarded as a form of historical necessity, but was not self-consciousness. Granted, this form of consciousness was present among the ancient Israelites, but in ways that contradicted genuine subjectivity; this consciousness was not informed by historical reality. Rather than displaying that form of consciousness that rises from the depths of history, the Israelites viewed their mission as something handed down from heaven.

---

37 In Hegel's *The Philosophy of History*, as translated by J. Sibree, the following passage occurs: 'The Orient knew and knows that only one is free, the Greek and Roman world that some are free: the Germanic world knows that all are free.' For 'West European' Suzuki uses a transliteration of 'German'.
38 There is a curious irony at work in Suzuki's critique of Hegel's notion of world-historical peoples as set out in the German philosopher's *Lectures on World History*. If Japan's subjective character is understood in terms of the arguments developed by Hegel in his *Phenomenology of Spirit*, Suzuki must also qualify as a closet Hegelian, whatever his criticism of the German thinker.
39 To borrow from the language of Heidegger, it has been an act of self-assertion.
40 As *dōtoku-teki-na seimeiryoku* can be read as a Japanese variation of *moralische Energie*, it may appear that Suzuki is merely repeating himself; but if we assign a specifically Confucian nuance to the term *dōtoku*, then Suzuki is recasting the German expression in the language of East Asian Confucian ethics.

For a nation to qualify today as a genuine world-historical people, as judged from the standpoint of world history, it must cultivate a self-conscious synthesis that both recognizes the nature of historical necessity and embodies an ethically informed subjectivity that is simultaneously practical and creative [because these are all but synonymous]. These characteristics define, I believe, any world-historical people worthy of the name today. There is no question that both the Romans and their European successors were world-historical peoples. But they lacked the self-awareness of being world-historical peoples, that specifically constructive stance towards the world that we find in Japan today; and it is this quality which defines a genuinely world-historical people in the strict sense. This strikes me as a highly significant distinction.

KŌSAKA: I agree.

NISHITANI: Returning to the topic of *moralische Energie*, the greatest challenge appears to me to be: how can such energy be given practical expression, ethically and morally, in East Asia? This question is fundamental to any attempt to resolve our current struggle with China. Here the core root of the difficulty lies in the Chinese insistence, their consciousness if you will, that China is the centre of the world. The notion that China, and it alone, is the [moral] centre of East Asia encourages the view that Japan is nothing more than a step-child to be educated, the [humble] one-sided beneficiary of the blessings of Chinese civilization.[41] In these circumstances, it is absolutely essential that the Chinese be persuaded – that is, convinced in their consciousness – that in addressing the task of building a Greater East Asia, Japanese leadership (including an appreciation of why our leadership is indispensable) reflects the workings of nothing less than historical necessity itself.[42] It therefore follows that in this clash with Chinese consciousness as just described, it is for the Chinese themselves to awaken to a central truth: Japan's rise to the status of a great power has, practically speaking, prevented the colonization and carve-up of China by the Western powers. Japanese modernization, and all the effort implied in that process, should serve as a spur to the self-awakening of the Chinese people to their own world-historical role. This recognition should also include the idea that the essential way forward lies in Chinese cooperation with Japan in the building of a Greater East Asia, thus

---

41 Nishitani's argument is wholly Confucian. If the mandate of heaven has unambiguously passed from China to Japan, the Chinese as Confucians are morally obliged to yield to Japanese leadership and guidance. To fail to do so is impractical and immoral: impractical because Japanese civilization is manifestly superior in subjectivity and material strength, and immoral because Confucianism insists that the moral is infused with the practical. In this context, Chinese condescension towards the Japanese is at once incomprehensible and intolerable. This is what underwrites Nishitani's manifest irritation and frustration here.

42 I have slightly strengthened Nishitani's language to convey the emotional force of what he is stating and how he states it.

allowing the *moralische Energie* of the whole region to manifest its immense [potential] powers. One aspect of this new Chinese openness to the future must be the abandonment of any claim by the Chinese people to be the centre of the universe (*Chūgoku ishiki*).[43] Does history offer another way? The only effective force that has stood in the way of the reduction to the status of a Western colony is Japanese *moralische Energie* and it alone. From these truths I conclude, guided by a still more profound historical understanding from the standpoint of world history, that two things need to be achieved. First, the Japanese nation itself must fully appreciate its own position [and responsibilities] through a proper awareness of [the burdens of] world history. Second, this message has to be brought home, with conviction, to the Chinese people. Awakened in this manner, East Asian *moralische Energie* can be newly mobilized to unleash the basic strength or fundamental power (*kihon-teki na chikara*) needed to build a Greater East Asia.

KŌSAKA: I would like to add a bit about this subject of conflicts won or lost by morale (*moraaru*) or moral conviction. The Chinese have an overwhelming sense of their centrality in the world. This superiority complex is a direct consequence of the prestige of Chinese civilization. China is the Athens of the Orient. The Chinese tend to dismiss Japan as little more than an extension of their civilization. All Japanese must recognize that we owe an enormous debt to Chinese culture, which has had such a profound impact on our own. From a cultural standpoint, one must acknowledge that there are many fine things about China. This argument is beyond question. But there is one point that it is essential that the Chinese appreciate about us, and that is the quality of [contemporary] Japan morale or moral confidence. This is not part of our Chinese inheritance.[44]

Morality in China has become more like what the Germans call *Sitte* [custom or tradition] or the Chinese 'propriety' [courtesy, ceremony and rites]. The Japanese sense of morality has rarely manifested itself in such a way. Maybe an example can explain the contrast. When faced with the culture of Europe, Chinese culture made no effort to resist and just collapsed. The Chinese obviously lacked the *moralische Energie* to resist. The presence or absence of *moralische Energie* explains, in my view, the sharply contrasting responses of China and Japan to the provocation of European power.

---

43 Note that the Kyoto School thinkers almost always refer to China by the Sanskrit-Latinate term *Shina*, not *Chūgoku*. But the origin of both words – 'China' and 'Shina' – is conventionally traced back to the name of the Ch'in or Qin dynasty (221–207 BCE).

44 Note how the Western vocabulary of 'morale', moral energy and subjectivity allows Kōyama to explicate the problem of morality in ways that can accommodate the reality of Japanese power and capacity and yet still remain within the framework of the Confucian moral order. The key bridging concept that cannot be invoked because of Shinto is the 'mandate of heaven'. However, though it remains unnamed, it is the idea that counts throughout this Kyoto School discourse.

SUZUKI: Chinese conceit can explain what happened. Because the Chinese regard themselves as the only civilized people worthy of the name, their sense of centrality is overwhelming. Equally strong is their absolute conviction that they can absorb any other culture and Sinify it. This attitude arose because, throughout their long history, the Chinese have had to contend only with primitive cultures, many of them nomadic peoples from beyond the Great Wall. But this experience has left the Chinese utterly unprepared to withstand an encounter with a superior culture. This explains why the Chinese promptly abandoned their sense of superiority when the Europeans arrived. If anything, the Chinese displayed the completely opposite reaction, and the result was a new kind of Europeanized Chinese.

KŌSAKA: That's right.

SUZUKI: It is as we have already noted: China has had a form of morality, but has lacked *moralische Energie*.

NISHITANI: At least this appears to be the case today.

KŌYAMA: Perhaps we can argue that this is one of the defining features of the Chinese understanding of the past. On one level, it seems that the Chinese concept (*gainen*) of history is extremely ahistorical. There are various examples of this, one of which is the notion of Chinese centrality and superiority ... On the other hand, I think it is safe to conclude that the contribution of *moralische Energie* to Japanese history derives from our consciousness of world history; *moralische Energie* informs our understanding. We do not regard the defining trends of world history as random events of marginal importance (*yosoji*) or even things to be judged solely in an objective [passive] manner. In other words, [the reality of] the world is not dismissed out of hand. On the contrary, one at once identifies these trends and identifies with them subjectively, as an act of self-assertion, and seeks to shape them according to the demands of one's own awareness and consciousness. It is not evident that the Chinese people have awakened to these global realities in the same way. True, they identify collectively (*shukanteki ni*) with the notion of China as the core and substance of the world, as the only meaningful reality, thus rejecting the claims of the 'world' as it is. The latter forms no part of their consciousness. The resulting notion of history is therefore extremely passive and radically ahistorical. The tidal movements of history themselves contribute to the Chinese view of the past as a series of historical calamities immune to the shaping forces of human subjectivity. The Japanese response is very different. On each occasion when we encounter 'the other', we adopt a course of action that at once recognizes [the external or non-Japanese character of] global trends and at the same time attempts to harness such trends to our purposes. The result is a spirit that respects the facts (*koto*) [of history]. The Japanese spirit is at once constructive, historical and vital. And this is why I feel we can conclude that while the Chinese indeed have a [profound] moral (*moraaru*) sense, they lack the *moralische Energie* of the Japanese.[45]

KŌSAKA: At root, as discussed earlier, the Chinese approach to history is decisively and excessively influenced by the notion of something like 'heaven' (*ten*). Such concepts conspire against openness to change, to say nothing of the idea of shaping history [subjectively, for human ends]. Again Japan highlights the contrasting approach: because our sense of subjectivity is so strong we seek to live history, to make history. China has the moral conviction or morale (*moraaru*) without the energy. And the reason is that its sense of morality lacks any notion of historical progress.

KŌYAMA: This has all the makings of a huge problem. Today Japan is manifestly the only regional power capable of giving a lead to East Asia, and we alone are struggling to create a new world order. Of course it is true that the nations of the region – China since the Opium Wars, for example – have tried in a variety of ways to counter the intrusion of the West; but, by and large, these efforts at resistance were rather feeble attempts merely to keep Western power out of the region. Japan's response has obviously been completely different. If we were caught up in the collective (*shukanteki*) xenophobic urge 'to expel the barbarians' (*jōi*), we also reformed our nation with the Meiji Restoration. It was the Restoration that began to transform Japan into a great power in the modern mode. This project gave us the ability to resist Europe's domination of the planet and the order that it has imposed on the world. In that goal we have now succeeded.

To achieve this aim, Japan imported European science and technology. The contrast with the Chinese determination to cling to their traditions was decisive. So were the consequences. One was our conclusive triumph over China in the Sino–Japanese War of 1894–95. It should also be noted in this connection that the Europeanization of the world, as a phenomenon, has meant something entirely different for Japan when compared to the experience of the typical Western colony. Unlike peoples who lacked a cohesive culture or the spirit of independence (*jishuteki-na seishin*), Japan was determined to maintain its autonomy, and indeed it was able to borrow confidently and freely from the products of European civilization precisely because of its spirit of national independence. Japan's unique success in this regard has bewildered many Europeans. The response of China has been very different. In thrall to the greatness of its own civilization and as a result indifferent to the claims of history, the Chinese have traditionally tended to belittle the achievements of

---

45 Read at speed, this use of 'morale' strikes one as either very subtle or an error, unless this is a transliteration of the word *moral* from the French; but, as noted above, the Kyoto School effectively elides 'moral' and 'morale' into a single word, *moraaru*, that includes both notions. In this context, the elided word is 'moral'.

European civilization. In contrast, Japan freely chose to import the fruits of European civilization. The self-assertive response of Japan could hardly have been more different from that of China. Japanese élan, our life force, put the energy into our *moralische Energie*. While the will and strength to resist Europe's encroachment gradually dissipated among the Chinese, Japan has grown powerful enough to challenge Britain and America in a contest that signals a turning point in world history. This is the most important consequence, in my view, of the contrasting responses of our country and China to recent historical developments.

6 Japan and China (*Nippon to Shina*)

NISHITANI: All the same, it is important also to keep in mind that from the standpoint of Chinese sensibility (*kimochi*), Japan has become strong because it has embraced the culture and technology of Europe. In other words, Japan's power is European power. This is the way, I suspect, the Chinese consider the matter. As someone has observed, for a Chinese to study in Europe is a gold-plated experience but to study in Japan is merely silver-plated. This is because the foundations of modern Japanese culture originate in Europe. If one can study Europe directly, there is no point in bothering with Japan. This perception stands at the root of the Chinese tendency to dismiss Japan. In the past, the source of Japan's strength was China; now it is Europe. Hence the impression that Japan always has to rely on others for its borrowed strength. Viewed in this manner, Europe is ranked above Japan in Chinese eyes. This may be the result of a lack of awareness of ...

KŌYAMA: This is also the deepest source of a fundamental Chinese misunderstanding [of Japan].

NISHITANI: As Kōyama noted earlier, Japanese *moralische Energie* has been decisive to our collective ability as a nation to acquire European culture and technology subjectively (*shukanteki ni*), to master it as it were on our own.[46] The cardinal nature of this insight cannot be overstated. Culture and technology are obviously important in themselves, but in the case of Japan we had the confidence, the spirit if you will, to take these foreign things and make them our own. The truth of the matter is that we proved ourselves able to absorb European culture and technology over a relatively short period of time, and this confidence was indispensable to our success. But the awareness of the spiritual/cultural (*seishin*) dimension of the process is precisely what is missing from the Chinese appreciation of Japan. This fact has to be recognized [by the Chinese people] without qualification if

---

46 Nishitani's use of the term *shukanteki* here requires some explanation, as above the word has been rendered as 'collective'. In the previous examples, *shukanteki* has meant 'subjective' in the normal un-philosophical English sense, as in the sentence, 'Taste is always subjective'. But here Nishitani effectively elides the term *shutaiteki* into *shukanteki*, thus altering its sense.

everyone is to be clear about what is required in order to modernize successfully.

KŌSAKA: This is the point I think that the Chinese have failed to accept. On the subject of Japan becoming great because it has been able skilfully to adopt the fruits of European civilization, one might observe that the translation (*honyaku*) of the ideas of European culture into Chinese has often been not direct but via a Japanese version of the original. Japan has not been troubled by the spiritual/cultural (*seishin*) gap between Europe and itself but rather has just set about importing European things in an uncomplicated manner. At least, that has been the intention. But this radically contrasting approach to Europe is what decisively distinguishes Japan from China.

NISHITANI: Listening to all this, I have just recalled a conversation I had on my last trip to Europe. At Shanghai, a Filipino boarded ship and we fell into conversation. He was full of admiration for what Japan has achieved, and declared his hope that the Philippines might become like this country, saying that his nation had to make more effort to absorb the products and lessons of Western civilization. At the time I kept my counsel, but I thought to myself that the problem is more complicated than that. Over the course of its long history, Japan has fostered a [sober and disciplined] culture, and therefore we have completed the apprenticeship of civilization.[47] In other words, well before the arrival of European civilization on these shores, Japan could boast a highly developed culture, one animated by an active life force. The Philippines lacks such foundations. Therefore, even if the Philippines absorbed the products of European civilization on a Japanese scale, the results would be very different.

KŌSAKA: I share that view. The idea that successful imitation by one human being of another requires a minimum degree of subjectivity is a paradox that merits close examination. Successful imitation requires subjectivity, but subjectivity does not arise from imitation.

SUZUKI: The distinction between imitation and subjectivity is fundamental.

KŌYAMA: Unless one keeps this difference firmly in mind, one might conclude that Japan has achieved national greatness by mere imitation. This is complete nonsense. When the imitation thesis is evoked, even many Japanese take it seriously but ... [48]

KŌSAKA: Japan did not modernize by imitation alone. Modernization was just one step in the development of our subjectivity.

---

47 The word 'spiritual' is used here in a double sense. Conventionally *seishin* refers to an ethos or set of spiritual but not necessarily religious values, or to the psychology of motivation. But there is also an echo of Hegel's meaning for the word 'spirit' that draws on the German distinction between matter and spirit (*Geist*) while defining spirit as a form of agency at its most motivated and effective: an actor equipped with subjectivity. I have resorted to the word 'psychology' because it lacks the largely religious overtones that 'spiritual' has in English, but this is an English problem, not a Japanese one.

48 Here Kōyama appears to have suddenly lost his nerve; or perhaps his remarks were censored or, less dramatically, someone just talked across him.

KŌYAMA: This negative Chinese view of Japanese success [and the implied failure to grasp the significance of the Japanese moment] has decisively coloured the unfolding of the Manchurian and the Sino–Japanese Incidents.[49] Who prevented the partition of China? It was Japan. But, at the same time, if Japan thwarted the break-up of China, why didn't a genuine partnership between China and Japan result? If we look further back, it was Japan that blocked the expansion of Russia into East Asia with our victory in the Russo–Japanese War. From that time forward, Japan and China should have developed, as quickly as possible, ties of close cooperation. This was essential. It was written in our collective stars. Things turned out differently, but for what reason? Why has an effective partnership eluded the two countries? I think this failure has been a tragedy for East Asia. As a result we are left with what is in reality one of the great conundrums of world history. From a Chinese perspective, Japan's conduct on mainland Asia is no different from European and American imperialism.

I may think that the Chinese are mistaken but this is how they view our actions. I am absolutely convinced that this is not the case. Furthermore, if one takes a step back in an attempt to see the broader picture, there remain a host of issues that cannot in any way be interpreted as imperialist aggression. If Japan were set only on imperialist expansion, why labour to prevent the partition of China by the Western powers? The dual nature of Japan's behaviour – why has this very ambiguous duality been allowed to come into play? – has been fuelled by a variety of factors, but among them is our place in world history. This matter demands much closer examination (*kenkyū*). Indeed without mutual clarity [about East Asia's world-historical moment], it is difficult to see how China and Japan can foster the kind of partnership mentioned above. In the current difficult situation there is more at work than imperialism. It must be said that China's stubborn failure to appreciate the importance of the unfolding of world history represents the principal mental barrier standing in the way of resolving this problem ... they lack a proper form of world-historical consciousness.[50]

KŌSAKA: We have to get them to understand.
NISHITANI: Yes, and at the same time, the Japanese people themselves must become fully conscious [of their world-historical responsibilities].

---

49 The bracketed comment is implied if the rest of Kōyama's remarks is to make sense (DW). The Manchurian Incident refers to the Japanese occupation of the non-Japanese-controlled areas of the Manchu ancestral lands and the forced expulsion of Chinese nationalist forces from the region.
50 The word *ishiki* or 'consciousness' sets off the shuttlecock discussion over clarity and opacity in the next few sentences that is resolved only when Nishitani brings the apparently distinct dimensions to the debate together again in the expression *futōmei no ishiki*, referring to a kind of 'false consciousness'. This is an idea usually identified with Marxism, but as both the German revolutionary and the Kyoto School nationalists are heirs of Hegelianism, the family resemblance of their discourse is entirely predictable, although rarely remarked either in Japan or elsewhere.

KŌSAKA: Yes. The Japanese must wake up [to their responsibilities].

NISHITANI: Japanese conduct on the Chinese mainland has probably, it must be said, taken a form that appears to be imperialistic. The Chinese are no doubt mistaken in their perceptions but this is how it looks. Official Japanese policies have also assumed a form that probably seems to be imperialistic [to the Chinese people] ... [51]

SUZUKI: In other words, things have not been clear [or self-transparent] (*futōmei*).[52]

NISHITANI: Yes, the whole business has become befogged. Although, to be fair, one cannot help wondering if the tragic dimension in all this was inevitable because of world conditions and the current stage of historical development in which we find ourselves today. And yet, to an outsider today looking back at what has been mistakenly described as [our] imperialistic conduct, one is left thinking about possible continuities between then and now. Perhaps there is a level of deeper significance at work here. When we talk about our current stage of historical progress, it is probably arguable that the Japanese themselves need a clearer appreciation about where this country stands in developmental terms. Such false consciousness (*futōmei no ishiki*) about the past must be swept away.[53]

KŌSAKA: Yes, it our false consciousness about the past that must be uprooted.

SUZUKI: That's right.

NISHITANI: Japanese conduct vis-à-vis China has taken a form that has provoked mistaken judgements about our intentions. This may be a consequence of the historical limitations of the world order prevailing at the time, but this pattern of conduct must change to a course consistent with the building of a new East Asia, one grounded in action [*praxis*] that conceptually overcomes imperialism (*teikokushugi no kokufuku*).[54] One might thus

---

51 Not exactly the kind of comment that either the Tōjō cabinet or the government censors wanted to hear. Given the context, the timing and the rules governing wartime censorship in the spring of 1942, this apparent criticism of Japan's military conduct and government policy was a bold gesture on the part of both the contributors and the publisher.

52 What I believe Suzuki actually meant can be stated thus: 'In other words, the good we have tried to do has not been obvious. Or been made obvious.' However, there is a temptation, given the background of the speakers, to borrow from a Hegelian-Lacanian thinker such as Žižek when he talks about 'self-transparency'. The cultural background to this issue is that Japanese culture has a love-hate relationship with ambiguity and indirectness that combines all the unspoken codes of an ancient island people such as the English with the rooted prejudice that the Japanese tend to share with, say, (northern) Italians against stating the obvious. The trouble arises when the layers of ambiguity and unclarity become so numerous that no one involved in making a collective decision, for example, knows what is really going on in anyone else's mind. Anxieties about this kind of cultural fog feed these Kyoto School concerns about clarity.

53 See Note 50 above.

54 Thus restoring the unity of practice and theory, action and ideas, that is not only the goal of classical Marxism but an imperative in all European political thought since Plato and Aristotle. At these pure Hegelian moments, Confucianism takes a back seat, however important it is elsewhere.

conclude, looking back now, that our past conduct has harboured an obscured significance that permitted no [other] explanation and therefore has been regarded as imperialism [and nothing more].[55]

KŌYAMA: I myself think very much along the same lines. We can justify past Japanese conduct by reference to the *Idee* behind the Greater East Asia War.[56] Let us take this as so. By which I mean Japanese conduct was a product of necessity; we had to do what we had to do. And when one speaks of necessity, one has to recall Japan's relative late development vis-à-vis the West and the dependence of the Japanese economy on Europe and America. The tragic fact is that if Japan had not pursued the course it has, and had not become a global power, it would not have had the strength to prevent the dismemberment of China. In other words, the conditions that allowed Japan to block China's partition are the same conditions that have caused China to misunderstand Japan [because of the latter's perceived aggressive and imperialistic conduct].[57]

This dynamic reflects the constraints placed on Japan by contemporary world history, and the consequences have been the painful situation that the country finds itself in today. All the obscurities (*fumeiryō*) that plague Sino-Japanese relations arise from this dynamic. One result is that Japan is now in a position to justify its international position in admirably convincing terms. Therefore, from the standpoint of the study of the facts of world history,[58] if Japanese conduct [towards China] appears, as a phenomenon [on the empirical surface], to be imperialist conduct, that means that our conduct is not genuinely world-historical (*sekai-shi gaku*): that is, it cannot be located with confidence in the realm of empirical fact [as essential truth].[59] As long this remains the case, the fact that we stand on the verge of a creative turning point [in world history] will be lost from view; it simply won't be recognized.

---

55 The dialectical assumption here being that if Japanese imperialism did not harbour the potential to overcome brute imperialism it would be nothing but imperialism. At the same time, any Japanese conduct that is merely imperialistic betrays the national potential and historical necessity to transcend imperialism.
56 Kōyama uses the English term 'justify' and the German *Idee*, both translated into Japanese. The term 'idea' as used here has a very complex history. See Note 24 above.
57 The word 'perceived' is used here because although in another context Kōyama would have been more brutally frank, I do not believe that in early 1942 he could have gone further and still been published. The larger point is that subjectivity genuinely achieved gives one the power to act on the world for good or evil.
58 Kōyama uses the expression 'world historiography' (*sekaishi-gaku*) but he is clearly not referring to methodological issues here, so I was tempted to render the phrase as 'world-historical' or 'world history'. However, if Kōyama means what he says, he is addressing the facts of the case.
59 From the standpoint of the Kyoto School's own metaphysical position, no more damning assessment is possible than to say that Japanese conduct in China has not been 'world-historical'. Nowhere in these three symposia is the weight of the expression 'the standpoint of world history' felt with greater discomfort and unease than here.

To appreciate the epic scale of this contemporary transition in human affairs, we must accept the arrival of the Great East Asian War as one inevitable stage in this process, and furthermore we must seek to justify our role in the struggle in the light of the *Idee* of the Great East Asian War.[60] This is the essence of what makes history today. This is the point where I think the world history of fact interfaces with the philosophy of world history [as a horizon event].[61] But in any case this event provides a theme that I hope will spark the fullest mobilization of our creative powers and insights (*kenkyū, giron*).

KŌSAKA: Japan's experience of the initial stages of imperialism and the misunderstandings that arose from these beginnings were in some sense the consequence of this country's fate as determined by its world-historical status at the time. In the first phase of Japan's experience of imperialism, we lacked [self-transparent] consciousness of our [destined] strategic centrality within world history; we were unaware of our potential to become a world-historical people that had the capacity to create a new world. Instead of leading the world in a new direction, we were being pushed about by the world. We were passive [victims]. Because Japan had yet to become, in this sense, Japanese, misunderstandings predictably arose. We had yet to reach the stage [of development] we have today where we have achieved a clear idea of what Japan is all about.

NISHITANI: This being the case, there is no necessity to idealize (*bika*) or cover up this past.[62]

KŌSAKA: None in my view.

NISHITANI: Given this, we must acknowledge it; we must be honest about the facts. But, even so, there is no imperative to depreciate what we have achieved. In any case, there was a certain inevitability about what has happened, given Japan's approach to the world and contemporary conditions in that world. There has also been the matter of the defence of the nation. The world was caught in a certain phase (*isō*),[63] and the constellations[64] [of world power] were very different from those applying now.

KŌSAKA: In particular, imperialism was shaping the globe.

SUZUKI: On the subject of imperialism, I have something quite particular to say. The Japanese attitude towards China continues to be misunderstood

---

60 Again, the word 'justify' is transliterated from the English. Note that the word as used here and above is neither cynical nor mendacious in intent but rather carries, admittedly in a Confucian vein, the English meaning 'to show the justice or rightness of a cause'.
61 As in physics, where a surface forms a common boundary between two regions.
62 That is, to falsify past events or wartime conduct.
63 The term is conventionally taken from astronomy or electrical engineering, where it has a more complex and precise meaning than simply one stage in a series: the appropriate connotation here is less 'phases of the moon' and more a 'phase shift' or the rebalancing of alternating voltages.
64 The word 'constellation' is transliterated from the English.

by the Chinese, although to be fair some points of fact remain uncertain. From a Japanese point of view, this phase in our history reflects the workings of a necessary stage of historical development ... or, to look at the matter in yet another way, Japan had to attempt to begin all over again in order to build a new order in East Asia, and having started down this [world-historically aware] path, the hope is and remains that the best fruits of this effort would eventually be obvious for all to see.[65] I think it is possible to look at the matter in this way. But it is also true that because of this conflict between ends and means, Japanese policy during the entire period we are discussing has not been self-transparent [to us and the Chinese] in either intention or effect. Nevertheless, in my view at least, Japanese policy towards China has not been, at root, imperialistic. Japan's contemporary status (*ichi*) in East Asia has presented our region with a unique opportunity. But this has also been true of [the potential of] the singularly important relationship between Japan and China. This unique moment has been insufficiently appreciated in both countries.[66] To assert that Japan has had a privileged position of power over East Asia has been to invite, from most ordinary observers, the charge of imperialism. That is the impression that has been given.

Imperialism has been transformed by nationalism into a system in which one nation rules another, but the more fundamental issue is economic.[67] Modern capitalism marks the arrival of an irresistible stage of historical development. This has transformed the acquisition of overseas markets and resources into the defining theme of modern imperialism. The expansion of Europe overseas has been motivated by these two needs, which in turn reflect

---

65 The suggestion is of a global phenomenon that is clear and compelling in its implications and significance to all and every observer. It also returns to the decisive tear, in the structuralist sense, we find in the text of this second symposium we encountered at the beginning where the word *naruhodo* announces the decisive impact of Confucianism on 'The Standpoint of World History and Japan' as a whole and indeed on the entire wartime corpus of the Kyoto School.
66 Hegel's use of the term *Anerkennung* or recognition hovers over this entire section. In *A Hegel Dictionary*, Inwood notes that '*Anerkennung* involves not simply the intellectual identification of a thing or person (though it characteristically presupposes such intellectual recognition), but the assignment to it of a positive value and the explicit expression of this assignment' (p. 245). More tellingly still, Inwood goes on to observe that the relevant sections of the *Phenomenology of Spirit* are attempts to deal not with the problem of 'other minds' but rather 'with the problem of how one becomes a fully-fledged person by securing the acknowledgment of others'.
67 The use of the English term 'nationalism' (here in transliteration) hints at a traditional Japanese, indeed more widely East Asian, problem of how to render the Western idea of 'nationalism' into the relevant East Asian tongue, given the culturally alien as well as negative associations ascribed to the term, certainly since Versailles. *Kokkashugi* or statism emphasizes the role of the state at the expense of the popular dimension, while *minzokushugi* reverses the problem. The issue is made more complicated by the fact that the Latin origins of the term stressed the organic nature of the national union while *kokumin* still lacks the emotional attractions of expressions such as 'we the people'.

[the pressures of] that region's great density of population. But when one penetrates (*shinshutsu*) a [heavily populated] country such as China, there is no obvious room for new immigrant populations to settle, and this defeats one of the objectives of earlier forms of imperialism: the establishment of settler colonies. Contemporary imperialism, however, has different ambitions, ones that transcend the seizure of overseas markets for goods and resources because it is driven by what economists call 'excess capital'. Such capital must be exported or reinvested abroad because it has been concluded that investing it in the home market will not be as profitable as taking advantage of opportunities abroad. The result has been that overseas investment and the acquisition of commercial rights have become one of the defining phenomena of contemporary imperialism. Indeed, this development may qualify as the nineteenth century's distinctive contribution to the history of imperialism.

Western concessions in China – the leasing of settlements, the acquisition of rights to develop rail lines and to exploit [natural resources through] mining – all stand as the hallmarks of imperialism at its most economically intrusive and aggressive. This conduct is driven by the defining need of contemporary Europe to export its excess capital: hence the loans granted to China and companies created there by Europeans who have arrived with their pockets bulging with money to invest. All this qualifies it [i.e. European activity in China] as among the purest forms of imperialism. The whole purpose of this enterprise has been to create investment rights or interests in China. To this end, the Europeans and Americans involved have not sought to make their lives or build their homes in the heart of Chinese society. They have sought only treaty ports such as Shanghai and Hong Kong. Commerce is conducted indirectly with Chinese markets via local commercial agents who serve as economic go-betweens. This is the manner in which the West has pursed its interests in China.

In contrast, Japan has followed a different path. According to Professor Konan Naitō in his study *On China*, Japan's great capitalist *zaibatsu* (*dai shihon*) have not played a comparable role in the country.[68] Viewed from the standpoint of capital investment, the Anglo-American penetration of China has been huge, and the result has been that Britain and the United States have vastly larger investments and other economic interests in China than Japan does. I think the relevant statistics will bear out this conclusion. In other words, Japan's economic involvement on the mainland is different from that of the principal Western powers. Furthermore, this involvement does not lend itself to statistical demonstration. As Professor Naitō has concluded, Japanese trade relations with China are the work of micro-enterprises and small traders who make the rounds of the Chinese interior and frontiers. Naitō also notes that this kind of commercial relationship with China originated during the

---

68 Konan Naitō (1866–1934), also known as Torajirō Naitō: a highly regarded Sinologist who taught at Kyoto University. The work referred to here is entitled *Shina Ron*.

Meiji period, the suggestion being that in practical terms trade, that is the business of importing and exporting, has not played and is not likely to play a defining role in the economic ties between the two countries. But the survival of the Japanese people is linked to the survival of the Chinese people. This special bond is not an imperialistic one.

What connects our two peoples, to use the language in vogue among us today, is the need for a [shared] living space (*Lebensraum*), and this imperative is emerging, albeit in an extremely primitive form.[69] This is the trend that has been identified. It has grown in importance with the Sino–Japanese War (1895–96) and the Russo–Japanese War (1904–05), and our current situation does much to confirm the earlier picture, reflecting the particular nature of the relationship between Japan and China as well as the principles that govern this relationship and the privileges of [superior] status when it is genuinely earned. To call a spade a spade, neither war was fought to provide opportunities for Japanese capitalists to win privileges on the mainland because Japan did not have any capital to invest. This is the fact of the matter.[70] Furthermore, the purpose of the Japanese administration of Manchuria and the creation of Manchukuo is not simply to protect our economic interests there. It is necessary to preserve the [independence of the] East. This [purpose] gives Japan, according to scholars such as Professor Jinichi Yanō, its unique role and special status.[71] It is vital to stress the singular nature of this role, although one must admit that from a Western perspective this kind of argument for Japan's privileged status in East Asia is a manifest contradiction.

KŌSAKA: They will not accept it because they cannot understand it.
SUZUKI: The Lansing-Ishii Accord of 1917 recognized Japan's special status in East Asia for the first time, but the subsequent Nine-Power Treaty ignored the Japanese claim. Whether that denial was rooted in abstract principles or not may be debated, but Japan's claim to special regional status was judged to be inconsistent with the push for recognition of the formal (*kikaiteki na*) equality of nations as a general principle. Or, to put

---

69 Suzuki uses the expression *seikatsuken*, followed by the German *Lebensraum* in transliteration. Echoing the point about population density noted above, potential 'living spaces' were to be found in the lightly populated areas of Manchuria and Mongolia. The borrowing of the German expression here has nothing to do with the policies of the 'Final Solution' which were adopted by Hitler's Germany the same year at the Wannsee Conference.
70 There was, of course, vast Japanese public investment in the infrastructure of Manchuria, notably the Manchurian Railway (*Mantetsu*), so the argument is unconvincing unless one sees that a line is being drawn between types of capitalism and where the penetration is taking place and when the various kinds of investment took place: for example, the Anglo-American focus is on China proper, while Japan is concentrating on the marginal region of Manchuria. But the rising tide of peasant nationalism across East Asia meant that Japanese 'leadership' on the mainland had to be pursued in the manner recommended by the Kyoto School if it was not to be doomed to failure.
71 Jinichi Yanō (1872–1970): Japanese expert on East Asia whose works include *Kinsei Mōkoshi Kenkyū* (Studies in Modern Mongolian History), published in 1925.

it another way, there was an insistence that the world be governed, come what may, by abstract universal ideals. In short, a contradiction arose between historical reality and abstract theories, between Japan's claim to special status and [the imperative of] universal ideals.[72]

As Kōsaka has observed in a recent essay, it is a fact that the current struggle with China, which began with the Marco Polo Bridge Incident [1937], was caused by a fundamental misunderstanding between the two sides. But the principal reason why mutual understanding has proved so elusive can be found in world history itself. I am fairly certain that this was your argument. The reasons for this failure involved more than just condescending interference from the British and Americans. World history itself was at work in these events. The gap between the two forces was a contradiction of giant proportions [between] those who have insisted on the special status of East Asia [and Japan's place in the region] and those who would deny it. [I would suggest,] taking a different line from Kōyama's thesis, [that] the resolution of this contradiction will stand as the fundamental challenge to be met by any *Idee* of the world (*sekai rinen*) that takes as its basic premise the multipolar or plural character of the global community.

KŌSAKA: As for me, what I call 'the philosophy of world history' is that branch of scholarship which develops the very notion of the *Idee* itself or, if you will, reveals the genealogy of the *Idee*.[73] I think Kōyama's definition of *Genealogie* has its place here.[74] Until now the only things worth comparing with world history were the histories of individual nations (*minzoku*), most of which interpreted these narratives in an unconnected way. The rare exceptions were theories of stages of development, as found in writers such as Comte.[75] In the case of the national histories, one found demonstrations of subjectivity but without worldliness (*sekaisei*), while with world histories, the importance of the global context was demonstrated without reference to the importance of [national] subjectivity. But unless the two elements mediate each other, no genuine version of world history can come into

---

72 From a British-American-French perspective, Japan appeared to be keen to throw its new weight around in the pursuit of regional hegemony. From a Japanese expansionist perspective, international law merely endorsed the status quo established by imperial Britain and France, while ignoring the hypocrisy of the US position, given its history of intervention in Latin American affairs.
73 Kōyama's *Sekai-shi no Tetsugaku* sets out a detailed elaboration of the idea of genealogy or *keifu* as used to refer to the historical trajectory from the Oriental to the classical Mediterranean world, medieval Europe and modern Europe. Kōyama believes that the world history of the early 1940s marks a rupture with the traditional genealogy, with its continuous development through Hegel's four worlds – the Oriental, the Greek, the Roman and the German or West European – that heralds a new, plural post-European universal history.
74 Kōsaka uses the German word, transliterated into Japanese.
75 Auguste Comte (1798–1857): French philosopher and sociologist.

being. The creative genealogical leap from one stage of history to another cannot be achieved without subjectivity. Similarly, without these two elements no [persuasive] *Idee* of the 'world' as a concrete or practical notion is possible ...

Although the problem has been tackled previously, no one yet has succeeded in developing a convincing understanding of what we mean by the 'world'. But in my view a sufficient grasp [of the concept] for all practical purposes can be achieved via the philosophy of world history. The key force is a form of subjectivity that can solve the riddle of the world by learning to make history, and thus move, shape and remake the world in the process. This form of subjectivity needs to become one with the world, and thus bind, in a powerfully practical way, world history with philosophy. I believe that this is possible. What do you think, Kōyama?

KŌYAMA: I am with you here.

SUZUKI: What you have just described as the privileges of [subjective] status genuinely achieved (*tokushu ichi*), that is, the status appropriate to the character of a specific region of the world, enables us to proceed to consider what we have called the plural or multipolar structure of world history.[76] That is the standpoint at which we have arrived. Taking this as our point of departure, we can finally begin to grasp the real meaning of regional *Geopolitik*.[77]

7 World history and *Großräume* (*kōiki ken*)

KŌSAKA: It is dangerous to yield to rough and ready generalizations, but I am prepared to risk the conclusion that until now thinking about history has tended to be rather susceptible to the claims of periodization and other temporal distinctions, while a similar concentration has been lacking in respect of spatial divisions. But geography merits the closest attention. In our current stage of world history, the test of building and sustaining *Großräume* or continental-sized supranational regions has come to the fore.[78]

---

76 This argument proceeds from the general to the specific. If Latin America is incapable of managing its own affairs and the United States has achieved subjective self-mastery, the resulting power imbalance may be unfortunate but is entirely predictable. Unavoidable consequences follow. Confucianism makes the Kyoto School realistic enough to recognize that power as a fact carries with it a duty of care and responsibility by the stronger nation for the weaker. In the Kyoto School view, this includes fostering the subjective power of the relatively weak and a willingness to fall into line with a former weak power once it has achieved a still greater degree of subjective power than, say, Japan holds today.

77 Suzuki uses the German word, transliterated into Japanese.

78 Kōsaka translates *kōiki* as *Großraum* but transliterates *Großraum* as two words, *kōiki ken*. In German, *Großraum* (pl. *Großräume*) literally means 'large (or big) space(s)'. Kyoto School usage derives in part, I believe, from this expression as used by economists as well as from the text of Carl Schmitt's 1939 lecture 'Volkerrechtliche Großraumordung'.

212 The Standpoint of World History and Japan

How might we think about this issue? In the broadest terms, the question of national destinies and their functions has figured very prominently in considerations of the trials facing East Asia [as a supranational region]. China offers the key example. Traditionally, peoples and nations (*minzoku*) have served as history's subjective movers and shapers, as the historical subject (*rekishi-teki shutai*), with the expectation that different nations at different times can meet and have met the challenges of world history. The supreme illustration of this is the way many peoples and nations have learned to master their own circumstances well enough to solve their specific problems by creating states of their own. But today our difficulties are beyond the scope of any popular nation-state (*kokka-teki minzoku*) to resolve on its own. Our troubles demand a profound (*fukai*) degree of mutual mediation between different peoples. Obviously different kinds of opportunities (*keiki*) will present themselves,[79] and this will mean new quandaries will manifest themselves. This is why *Großräume* or large [supranational] regions have taken on an air of inevitability today. That anyway is what I suspect.

KŌYAMA: Might you clarify something here? Does the historical necessity that makes the creation of supranational regions or co-prosperity spheres so indispensable derive from [solely] economic causes?

KŌSAKA: Not solely economic. But economic pressures do provide very important opportunities or moments (*keiki*). If this were not the case, the historical subject would blur into insignificance.

SUZUKI: It may be asserted with some confidence that the concept (*kannen*) of *Großräume* (*kōiki*) derives from economics, the idea of an economic or economically self-sufficient region being an example of the economic theory of autarky as opposed to free trade ... *Großräume* as an idea first came into prominence in connection with the notion of zones of economic self-sufficiency. Historically speaking, it was a product of necessity. Liberal economics has trapped itself in a blind alley because of its singular focus on self-interest [to the exclusion of collective need], and the result is that between 1929 and 1931 the Great World Depression took hold. In response, economic blocs have been conceived as policy remedies to save capitalism or at least strengthen it [in the face of what have been perceived as its obvious and growing weaknesses]. The British were the first to embrace this idea with the Ottawa Accord of 1932.[80] The closing of the markets of the British Empire and its dependencies to trade with the outside world delivered a massive blow to global economic trade, given the vast resources and huge expanses of territory involved. This British move provoked (*shigeki*

---

79 *Keiki* is usually translated as 'an opportunity' or 'chance', but in Japanese Hegelian philosophy refers to the idea of 'moment'.
80 Formally known as the British Empire Economic Conference, this agreement imposed modest tariffs between members of the British Empire and very high tariffs on imports from outside the Empire.

shite) a wide debate, particularly in 1935–36, on whether this country or that should act to create its own autarkic region or self-sufficiency zone. I believe this response was all but inevitable, given the circumstances of the time. But the consequence was the unleashing of a great tide of historical necessity. In the case of Japan, proposals were made for an economic bloc allying this country with Manchukuo and China. As this seemed unlikely to secure economic self-sufficiency for these three economies, the question whether South-East Asia and the South Pacific (*Nanpō ken*) would have to be included in this economic zone gained considerable prominence. In any case, it was at this time that the idea of *Großräume* acquired a fundamentally economic orientation, and this was probably inevitable for the reasons stated.

It might also be noted, however, that this approach has resulted in the neglect of something vital: what *Großräume* might mean to the peoples of our region in terms of ideas of the nation (*minzoku kannen*) and the ethical (*rinri kannen*). In other words, it was not enough to consider the nature of a Greater East Asian Co-prosperity Sphere solely in the light of the need for natural resources. The pressing claims of ethics and national self-definition should not have been ignored. The whole idea of securing one's place [wherever that is in the hierarchy of demonstrated subjectivity] is reduced to an empty theory if these concerns are not met. Indeed, they *must* be met. This double task merits a job of intellectual work (*kenkyū*) that can generate a body of ethical theory respected by the scholar and comprehensible to the man in the street, indeed to the public as a whole in the countries concerned. Don't you think this is essential?

KŌSAKA: Absolutely. But while I completely understand what Kōyama is arguing, I would like to examine further this idea of economic self-sufficiency, and ask Suzuki whether the term 'self-sufficiency' becomes hopelessly ambiguous unless we are sure what or who is to be self-sufficient. Where is the subject (*shutai*) in all this? What kind of subjectivity is involved in self-sufficiency? Isn't there a strongly nationalistic (*minzoku-teki*) cast to the question? Considered rationally, this issue would appear to require an acceptance that the very notion of the 'nation' (*minzoku*) will be transformed by the process of achieving self-sufficiency.

8 The ethics of the nation (*minzoku*) and the ethics of the world

NISHITANI: Apologies for interrupting here, but may I interject a comment? The point Suzuki made about the privileged position that Japan holds in East Asia is hugely important. The relationship of Britain and the United States with China ultimately turns on commercial interests, but for Japan

214 *The Standpoint of World History and Japan*

our relationship with China reaches beyond the economic to include matters of national security, indeed our survival [as a great power]. Japanese national defence is directly involved. The failure of the British and Americans to recognize the economic and security imperatives at issue in our relationship with China has now become, in my view, a world-historical problem. This gap (*zure*) in understanding between the two sides – particularly between those nations that seek to erect a new world order and those that still support the *passé* old order – is rooted in differences in world-historical consciousness, indeed in how the very idea of the 'world' is defined.[81]

Granting all that, one may further observe that in addition to the economic and national security issues in question, there is a populist (*minzoku*) dimension to the problem as well. As I have observed elsewhere, the states that are seeking to establish a new world order – countries such as Germany and Italy, or, for that matter, Japan – have clearly and self-consciously appreciated the importance of proper nationalist foundations (*minzoku no kisō no ue*) in any effort to erect such a new order.[82] If one asks why this is the case, the reason appears to arise from the fact that all three of these nations share a degree of economic backwardness, a status as nations 'coming from behind' (*kōshinkoku*). In order to assert themselves in the sort of world that exists at present, countries of this kind must possess a strong degree of internal unity as states. These bonds of unity rest on popular national (*minzoku*) feeling. Thus, when the time came for the creation of a state in Germany or Italy, the foundations of these new states were laid by nationalist movements (*minzoku undō*) committed to the unity of the state and inspired by a self-consciously national spirit.[83] After the Meiji Restoration, the Japanese people themselves played a significant role *as a people* [in the affairs of the state] because they provided the foundation upon which the state was reorganized.[84] The domains or *han* of the *daimyō* were abolished, as was the occupational caste system, thus signalling the destruction of society in its feudal form. The slogan 'Revere the Emperor, Expel the Barbarians' (*Sonnō Jōi*) was one manifestation of a broader process of reflective national self-definition and affirmation of a nation (*minzoku*) committed to enhancing the bonds of inner unity.

---

81 In Paul Mus's reading of the Confucian tradition, support for a *passé* world order is at once irrational and immoral. There may be something dignified and very human at work in one's loyalty to the old regime or one's nation, but ethically such a position is difficult to defend because it defies the claims of the manifestly practical and true. Suicide is the frequent response.
82 In Confucian terms this nationalist solution resolves the classic dilemma at issue in the choice between loyalty to one's sovereign or nation and the demands of the mandate of heaven, which alone can confer ethical legitimacy in the political sphere.
83 The formula is ambiguous but it does lend itself to a Hegelian interpretation.
84 Italics added.

It is also my view that Germany, Italy and Japan continue to feel the impact of the movements that created their modern states. They all share the same self-conscious insistence on the importance of national unanimity. Indeed, any people bent on seeking to assert itself and affirm the fact of its existence as a new arrival in a pre-existing world order must be a nation possessed of *moralische Energie*. The demonstration of this assertiveness and this energy will begin, as a matter of necessity, with the creation of a state based on the nation itself. For this people, the state will find its meaning in the manifestation of such *moralische Energie*. One may also conclude that such nationalism and statism, while judged as flawed (*warui*) by the democracies, does in fact possess a great ethical significance. The kind of ethics involved is not a formalistic ethics but an ethics of self-consciousness and the embodiment of *moralische Energie*. This form of ethics first becomes apparent only when it can sustain a state within history, and therefore this *Energie* will drain from our hands if we attempt to grasp it 'academically' [theoretically], that is ahistorically, as one finds the theme addressed in pure law or other formalistic approaches.[85] But in any case when this new state, embodying the *moralische Energie* of a nation and grounded in the unity of a people, finds its future development thwarted by the pre-existing global order, this situation will of necessity encourage a movement to overthrow (*yaburu*) the old order.

The formation of a closed economic zone among the nations of the British Empire is, as Suzuki noted earlier, an example of such a provocation (*boppatsu*), and it was inevitable that such moves would spark attempts to create a new order of *Großräume* (*kōiki-ken*). It therefore follows that building *Großräume* (*kōiki-ken*) involves the pursuit of economic self-sufficiency or autarky as well as the protection of the *elementar* or basic existence [of a country] that gives the term 'national defence' its fundamental rationale.[86] These linked objectives point to the deeper truth that the prime agency at issue – that is, the state erected on the popular foundations noted above – is sustained by *moralische Energie*. This is the source of the demand for a new world order. So there is an economic and security dimension to this equation as well as a nationalist or popular (*minzoku-teki*) dimension. Also, as such national self-assertion is a demonstration of *moralische Energie*, there is an ethical dimension involved, and it is this that gives the whole process its moral weight. This is the stage at which we have arrived today. These various dimensions, including that of moral significance, taken together are what I call

---

85 Probably a reference to the ideas of 'pure law' associated with the Austrian jurist Hans Kelsen (1881–1973), who argued for a legal code whose content was 'pure' in the sense that it was 'immune to ethical, political, sociological, historical and other extraneous considerations' (David Walker, in his article on Hans Kelsen in Alan Bullock, R.B. Woodings and John Cumming (eds), *The Fontana Biographical Companion to Modern Thought*, London: Collins, 1983, p. 386).
86 Nishitani uses the German word *elementar*, transliterated into Japanese.

'world ethics'. In a dialectical sense, world ethics at its most authentic embodies progress in its truest sense. It stands as that great good place (*tokoro*) where a people (*minzoku*) affirms itself by simultaneously negating itself (*jikō hitei soku kōtei*) [in the pursuit of national transcendence].

KŌSAKA: As for myself, I have thought along lines very similar to those of Nishitani, but the thing that I would like to hear from Suzuki is why Germany and Italy were so late in developing as modern states. They were very late ... countries like Germany and Italy remained, at least in relative terms, products of the medieval mind for an extremely long time. I wonder if the influence of this medieval consciousness persisted so long that neither country was able to devise a modern-style state with any alacrity. Speaking in the most general terms, Italy and Germany had both been rather active players on the medieval stage. Perhaps this alone explains why this type of country lacked something crucial when Britain and France began to develop as modern states. And one consequence was that both countries fell behind economically, particularly in the race to acquire natural resources [overseas]. Yet it should also be noted that this also explains why both nations have rejected the existing international order and have moved to endorse the principles of the new world order now emerging. Their position is, in that sense, very similar to that of Japan. The Tokugawa Era achieved many wonderful things, but it was very late in creating the structures (*keitai*) of the modern state. And because of this – including the inevitable economic implications – Japan, too, was presented with an opportunity to shift direction towards this new world order.

SUZUKI: The delayed unification of Germany and Italy as modern states stands as one of the great controversies of modern history. One may reasonably conclude that this explains why they were late in the competition to acquire overseas colonies, thus becoming, in current parlance, 'have-not' countries. Various theses have been proposed to explain why, among all the nations of Europe, these two alone failed to unite until the nineteenth century, and I am in broad agreement with the summary explanation that Kōsaka has given us. One theory stresses economic factors, assuming that capitalism was, in some sense, indispensable to the rise of the modern state. In other words, a country had to have a bourgeois class to overturn the medieval order in order to organize the concentration of capital. It follows from this line of thinking that in the struggle against the pluralistic decentralizing tendencies of medieval feudalism, mercantile capitalism (*shōgyō shihonshugi*) was indispensable to the concentration of royal power and vice versa. As such forms of mercantile capitalism appeared early in England [and later Britain] and France, the centralization of state powers therefore followed suit. Spain developed on the strength of the benefits that flowed from its discovery of the New World. Germany, by contrast, played no role in this discovery and what followed. The resulting economic backwardness played a major role in obstructing the creation of a modern German state. That is the argument. I for one do not believe that this theory explains the whole picture. Not decisively. For one thing, it appears to apply better to Germany than to Italy, where an early form of mercantilism did develop. Nevertheless, I think Kōsaka's point about the impact of medieval principles (*chūsei-teki genri*) on Germany and Italy will stand.

KŌSAKA: Well, that is my impression.

SUZUKI: As the [core of the] Holy Roman Empire, medieval Germany could claim a unique status among nations. It sought to embody the ideal of Rome, and the concept of a unified universal government. Blinded by this high ideal, it lost sight of political 'reality'. As a country, Germany was burdened with the concept of itself as the supranational Holy Roman Empire. This ideal conspired against any form of effective national self-awakening and self-consciousness. The German people suffered as a consequence because policies to serve their interests were neglected as a result of this supranational focus. Take, for example, the involvement of the Emperor Henry I in the affairs of Italy. He conducted some half-dozen military campaigns in Italy, and Germany, thus ignored, fell into disorder. But how does one explain this simultaneous neglect of the domestic and involvement in Italy? Both were the result of the assumption that it was the duty of the Holy Roman Emperor, as a matter of necessity, to unify Italy. The ideal dictated the imperative. Minds dominated by this supranational ideal tended to neglect domestic affairs. This raised obstacles to the creation of an effective [German] nation-state. The same problem affected Italy because the Holy See in Rome also saw itself as a universal institution that transcended the borders and concerns of individual nations, including Italy itself.

More recent history teaches us that a quite specific set of historical circumstances has influenced Germany and Italy in Europe, and outside Europe the United States – and, for that matter, Japan. All four countries emerged as nation-states on the world-historical stage at roughly the same time in the middle of the nineteenth century. As great powers they were all late developers (*kōshinkoku*), and this has continued to be of historical significance down to the present day. To some degree, the same may be said about Russia. The Meiji Restoration and the American Civil War both occurred in the same decade.

America as a nation-state was shaped by the struggle between the states. The Civil War influenced the United States in three ways. First, it helped to shift its external focus away from the Atlantic and towards the Pacific Ocean. This change of orientation defined the subsequent direction of American expansion. Second, the victory of the capitalist North over the agrarian-settler South gave birth to the capitalist power that America is today. Third, the implicit contradiction between federal authority and the rights of the individual states was resolved with the victory of the centralizers. In other words, the Civil War marks the creation of the United States as a genuinely modern nation-state. There are similarities between this American transition and the abolition of the feudal domains or *han* and the creation of a unified state in Japan [after 1868]. Nevertheless, there remain significance differences between the two countries.

NISHITANI: May this question be answered by thinking about the contrasting motivations that drove these varied projects of national unification? In the case of Japan, Germany and Italy, there was the conviction that only an uncompromisingly rigorous programme of state and nation building would enable these countries to contend with their powerful neighbours. In this context, populist unity (*minzoku teki na tōitsu*) was judged to be indispensable because national survival was at stake. The result was a kind of national mobilization (*jikō shūchū*). As a single great power isolated from the Old World in the New, the United States had no need for this kind of mobilization. Quite the contrary: America was free to expand at will. Such self-aggrandizement resulted in an ever larger national territory ... In the case of Japan, Germany and Italy, it was judged essential that every effort be made to form and strengthen each subject or citizen almost individually. Each member of society had to be cultivated as it were from zero if the nation's *moralische Energie* was to be mobilized. It also follows that any nation that attempts to help construct a new world order will seek, as a matter of necessity, to link the imperatives of world ethics with cultivation of new levels of morale in each and every one of its subjects or citizens (*kokumin*).

Moralische Energie is a programme of action. If the leading powers of an age are to cultivate the kind of energy essential to their role, *moralische Energie* must be made an integral part of the country's subjectivity. This will take unsparing effort. At the same time, the national spirit must then acquire a kind of a global character that will allow the country in question to contribute to the construction of a genuinely new [world] order. The point is that both tasks must be made to work in tandem in a reinforcing way. *Moralische Energie*, in a way slightly different from that suggested earlier by Kōsaka, becomes the fundamental problem.

KŌSAKA: If there is to be an attempt to put Nishitani's 'worldly ethics' into practice (*gutaika suru*) – for example, as the ethical system for a Greater East Asian region – it seems reasonable to suggest that we need an appropriate concept. I am not sure that this will do, but how about 'world-historical morality' (*tōi*)?
SUZUKI: What? *Tōi*?

KŌSAKA: *Sollen*.[87] World-historical morality. What we are called to do by history ...
SUZUKI: I think that term works in this context.
KŌSAKA: I think that in the end this is the kind of language we will settle on. Our task today is to make it clear how the content of this world-historical morality is to be put into practice. That's the problem.
KŌYAMA: I think Nishitani is right about the link between the right to national survival of the German and Italian nations (*minzoku*) and a world order. This is very much the case. But the Japanese situation differs somewhat from that of Germany and Italy, and I suspect it may be worth spending a little more time exploring this contrast. In the case of the Nazi and Italian Fascist movements, the principal focus of attention has, in some sense, been the fostering of internal national unity. Much as with Chiang Kai-shek's nationalist movement,[88] the main emphasis has been on the domestic scene rather than on foreign affairs; on the inside rather than the outside. This is the first priority (*dai ichi-shugi*) of these movements. To confront communism, they have taken on a totalitarian cast, and all three movements are therefore extremely ideological in their orientation. In consequence, these particular ideologies have not made world-historical awakening or consciousness their primary point of departure – or rather, it is fairly difficult to claim this characteristic for them. And it is this emphasis on domestic concerns that sets them apart from the Japanese case.

Take the example we have just been discussing: *Großräume* (*kōiki-ken*). All these movements assign fundamental importance to the question of national survival. Nevertheless, faced with the task of how to build a *Großraum* (*kōiki-ken*), and viewing this project in the light of the existing historical situation, they finally stress the importance of the link between the economic and national defence, one dimension leading naturally to the other. In practical terms, this involves a shift in attention from a *Großraum-Wirtschaft* (*kōiki keizai ken*) [economic *Großraum*] to a national defence *Großraum* (*kokubō kōiki-ken*): one in effect progresses [yet again] from one concern to the other. The motivation for this interest in *Großräume* derives directly, and predictably, from objections to the unfairness of the settlement imposed under the terms of the Versailles Treaty, and to the international order produced by it.[89]

---

87 Kōsaka used the term *tōi*, which is the Japanese rendering of the Kantian concept of *Sollen*, 'that which ought to be or exist'. But this, I suspect, does not imply the endorsement of any transcendental aspirations at the expense of a more Hegelian or historicist definition of the term.
88 Chiang Kai-shek (1887–1975): Chinese nationalist leader. Also known as Jiang Jie Shi.
89 German resentment after Versailles focused on the territorial settlement as well as the punishing post-war reparations regime, while Italy, although a victor, was left extremely discontented with some of the border changes after 1918 that the rightists felt had been imposed on the country.

220 *The Standpoint of World History and Japan*

To put right or relieve such [perceived] unfairness, the Italian and German movements chose to concentrate their efforts on creating a new order within their [respective] countries. This explains their stress on ideological uniformity (*shisō-teki tōitsu*) as well as the emphasis on building a command economy (*tōsei*). But in any case the centre of attention has been the domestic ordering of society. This priority has been, in my view, crucial to their strategy. And one consequence of this fundamental focus was an emphasis on nationality (*minzoku*) and/or race (*jinshu*). In other words, because the economy and national security have been judged to be issues of the highest urgency, the search for solutions had to begin with the implementation of ideological control (*shisō tōsei*) [over the population]. But it is also follows that such priorities precluded according priority to world history or the creation of a new world order.

These issues have certainly not qualified as matters of particular urgency. Even when they had a place on the national agenda, they were not made the object of proper intellectual concern or effort (*shisō*). This [focus on internal order] opened the door for the rise of [aspects of] these ideologies such as totalitarianism and an apparent racism (*jinshushugi mitai*) in Germany and Italy.[90] Both of these ideologies have [therefore] fallen short (*fujūbun*) philosophically (*shisō*) of what is required to sustain the contemporary enterprise of building a new world order. On this subject one may conclude that neither Germany nor Italy is intellectually prepared to address the task of conceptualizing the great challenge posed by world history. As a result, my conclusion is that Germany and Italy will have to rethink the entire ideological approach that they have inherited from the past if they are to face up to the demands of erecting a new order within Europe redefined as a *Großraum*.

In Japan the situation is, in my view, wholly different. In the case of the East Asian Co-prosperity Sphere, the economic and defence aspects of the problem provide a natural and predictable angle of attack. But since the Manchurian Incident, Japan has found itself confronting the [external] world [as the most fundamental reality]. From the outset, the new realities of world history have exerted a prior claim on our attentions over that of domestic reform. In our attitude towards world history, that is towards the project of [re]ordering the world – and here the contrast with the intellectual situation in Germany or Italy has been profound – Japan has exhibited the kind of rooted awareness of world history as the fundamental problem [of our time], a kind of awareness that one does not see elsewhere.

---

90 This qualification of the term 'racism' passes without comment in the text, but may be explained by the tendency of the Kyoto School, here and elsewhere, to be fairly strict about the word *jinshu*, using it to refer only to what the dictionary defines as races: white, yellow and black. In Kyoto School thought, Germans and Jews, to take the most sensitive pairing, might be termed *minzoku* rather than *jinshu*. Significantly, Italian fascism was often not racially minded in the way that Nazis such as Hitler were. Note, furthermore, that there is no evidence in the text that these Kyoto School thinkers were aware of the full horror of the mounting intent to extinguish European Jewry that took genocidal shape from 1942 onwards.

Our relationship with Manchuria has no precedent in world history, and thus we were faced with new problems to which traditional ideas (*kannen*) provide no answers.[91] Our withdrawal from the League of Nations was inevitable. Thus, as a matter of fact, Japan was the first country to face up to the conceptual challenges posed by the *Ideen* (*rinen*) [ideas as concepts] of world history and a world order. To repeat, Japan arrived at this decisive juncture before either Italy or Germany. In the effort to address the many difficulties posed by [the struggle for] ideological (*shisō*) unity on the home front – an effort in which totalitarianism, fascism and the Japanese spirit are all cited as unifying principles – it has not been totalitarianism or fascism that has managed to give shape to Japanese consciousness but the world-historical *Horizont*.[92] It is this fact of mind, if I may repeat myself, that distinguishes Japan from Germany and Italy. Today, ideas (*kangae*) such as nationalism and racism are not up to the job of either building a *Großraum* or devising a new world. To this end, one may declare that Japan has girded its loins [intellectually] and achieved a place in the sun among all the nations of the earth. This position is pregnant with the profoundest ethical significance.[93]

KŌSAKA: I like to think about the issue in this way. In order to solve the problem posed by world history, there is no point in arguing for racism or nationalism (*minzokushugi*). This is only a recipe for getting things wrong. Nevertheless, it is also true that when a nation seeks to tackle the problems of the economy or defence, the nation/people (*minzoku*) provides the only vehicle for coping with these difficulties. This is because the nation embodies our subjectivity. We have to give serious thought to what it actually means to be a world-historical people precisely because nationalism is not the answer. The Germans and Italians regard themselves as nations (*minzoku*) exclusively.[94] But this mode of thinking suggests that neither country has understood the true nature of the world. Will this conclusion stand up?

NISHITANI: Well, I think there is a slight problem with Kōyama's formulation. While I am in broad agreement with the argument that there are significant intellectual differences between Japan, on the one hand, and Germany and Italy on the other, the suggestion that the nationalist

---

91 Japan's situation is unprecedented because the pre-1919 world order rested on the concept of the nation-state, which was no longer respected, while the Versailles-Geneva order and liberal imperialism stood in the way of the only viable post-state form of sovereignty, that is, some form of East Asian *Großraum*. Hence, in the Kyoto perspective, the necessity for Japan's departure from the League of Nations, and hence, too, the necessity for the Manchurian experiment.
92 Kōyama uses the German word, transliterated into Japanese.
93 Ethically in the Confucian sense.
94 Their expansion abroad is essentially selfish; it serves nothing but the interests of Germany and Italy. Implicit in this observation is a rejection of any temptation to follow the same selfish path. It can therefore be read as an indirect criticism of Tōjō's policies in China and the Asian tropics.

movement in Germany, for example, was primarily a struggle to unify domestic national opinion makes me wonder a bit. I suspect that such movements – and this was certainly true in the case of Germany – arose out of discontent with the terms and conditions of the Versailles Treaty. There is a fundamental connection between the urge to overthrow the Versailles system and the struggle to hammer out a domestic consensus on the direction of the nation. Looked at historically, the Social Democratic Party's effort to preserve Germany by signing the Versailles Treaty ended in failure. Exploiting this failure, the Nazis made their mark nationally with their campaign to overturn the Versailles settlement. The suddenness of their forceful emergence was the result of this campaign. As the net economic effect of the treaty was to make the whole of Germany hungry, the accusation became that it was the intention of the treaty to starve the country to death. This gave impetus to the rise of the Nazis. Hence the suggestion of an obvious link between foreign policy and the drive to unify German opinion and institute a dictatorship (*kokunai no tōsei*) based on nationalist feeling. I do not believe that one can explain the rise of [this kind of] nationalism in Germany by reference to domestic conditions alone.

The principal ideological divergence between Japan and Germany is to be found in the German embrace of racism (*jinshushugi*). Philosophically, Germany lacked, as Kōyama has noted, an equivalent of the horizon of world history. This absence decisively shaped the Germans' ideological orientation [as a people]. But if one asks why the Germans did not make this horizon (*kenchi*) their own, I think the answer can be found in their failure to break with the world-historical standpoint traditionally assumed by all Europeans: the standpoint that holds there is no [real] world beyond the reach of Europe, that Europe *is* the world. This may explain, for example, why the Germans called for the redistribution of Europe's colonial spoils when they first proposed the creation of a new world order. Japan's plea for a new world order based on achieving a place for each and every nation of the world is of an entirely different character.[95] The *Idee* (*rinen*) at work breaks with all previous ideas about the subject.

SUZUKI: I, too, must confess that I am unpersuaded by the notion that the new German nationalism arose entirely in response to domestic conditions. The German Empire was created in 1871, and at the time one can say that, compared to their more advanced neighbours, both Germany and Italy were extremely late arrivals on the global scene as modern

---

[95] The suggestion that these places in the global order are to be hierarchically assigned is not mentioned here but is assumed elsewhere. Recall also Tanabe's argument that national fortunes inevitably rise and fall, and that therefore the respective places of all nations (including Japan) within the hierarchy will alter over time.

nation-states. But it is equally true that, having become modern nations, they rapidly achieved the status of powers of the first rank. Indeed, by this advance they unsettled the [European] balance of power that had existed up to that time. And yet, if you ask what Bismarck sought to accomplish, the one thing that comes to mind is his relentless determination to restrain the German urge to expand abroad. His strategy was to win security for Germany with policies focused singularly on Europe; the world outside Europe did not figure prominently in Bismarck's thinking. When the Kaiser assumed the direction of German foreign policy after Bismarck's resignation, he pursued a vigorous global policy and the result was the tragedy of the Great War. The Nazis, for their part, made revision of the Versailles Treaty their main policy, and when the German burden of reparations proved unsustainable, German capitalists, trapped as they were in the Great Depression, rallied to support the Nazis. At the same time, there was a determination to fend off the threat of communist revolution ...

NISHITANI: Both factors were involved.

KŌYAMA: German nationalism was obviously a form of resistance to the Versailles Treaty, and sought to remove Germany from the system of international controls that became outdated in the years after 1918. But I think it can be reasonably argued that the solution of Germany's international position followed on the efforts to resolve its domestic troubles. One proceeded from the other. Japan also created a new domestically unified system [of government] after 1868, but we did not begin with the domestic and move to the international. Rather, the domestic changes were forced on this country by external pressures. The domestic and foreign challenges emerged, as it were, simultaneously. In Europe, the new internal order and the new world order were fundamentally otherwise. They did not appear at the same time; they were separate phenomena. In the case of Japan, what matters to us is the essential continuity (*dōitsu sei*) between our new Asian order and the new world order. Furthermore, our place in the new global order has set us apart. Certainly, at the earlier stages [of our breakthrough into modernity] there was a huge gap between Japan, on the one hand, and Germany and Italy on the other. This gap can be traced back to domestic circumstances. I believe that such discrepancies were real and important, at least to some degree.

KŌSAKA: I agree with that. Germany's emergence is a mere extension of the old pattern of [Eurocentric] world history. This is a credible argument. Japan's ascent signals a revolution (*kakushin*) in the pattern of world history. There is a kind of break (*chigai*) here ...

NISHITANI: I have no quarrel with the proposition that Japan's rise marks a major development, but I also believe that the relationship between internal and external conditions was similar in Japan and Germany from the beginning. With the Nazis, the crusade for domestic consensus or ideological uniformity was contemporaneous with the effort to reorganize the country's national defences. But in Germany it was essential to address the domestic agenda before the foreign problem could be tackled. For Japan, the sequence was reversed. Problems in Japan's foreign relations made the country conscious of the need for domestic change ... This distinction I am drawing turns first on the interplay of domestic and external circumstances. A comparison of Japan with Germany suggests that we did not feel the same urgency to alter how we ordered our domestic life. We were not experiencing the kind of crisis that Germany found itself in. But there was a connection between domestic and external conditions in both countries.

On other hand, I think one can suggest that political awareness was more sophisticated in Germany. The need to overhaul [rationalize] the domestic system was clearer in the minds of politicians such as Hitler than in the minds of their Japanese counterparts. Home truths may have contributed to this German clarity, but one has the feeling that Japan seems to have been somewhat late off the mark. Even now the organization (*taisei*) of Japan's domestic life does not have the same degree of [self-]transparency (*futōmei na*) as Germany's.[96] As for our new system of organization (*shin taisei*) ...

KŌSAKA: But, at the time, the vocation (*yobikake*) impressed on us by world history was different from Germany's. Our world-historical consciousness was also distinctive. One can also concede that Nishitani's point on lack of clarity about our domestic governance will stand.

NISHITANI: Somehow I cannot help but feel that to tackle [the great issues of the day] we have to have a new system that is full of energy and *lebendig*.[97] This applies to a variety of areas of [state] control. Surrounded as they are by a host of nations in the very heart of Europe, the Germans have been more politically aware than people here. There has been a major disparity in political consciousness between the two nations. Things may have changed here significantly since the events of '8.12' but until then Japan was a little ...

KŌSAKA: Complacent ... As we focus on building a new world order for the future, we are going to have to think beyond the direction that Germany is taking when we consider the shape of this new order. The pressure is on us.

NISHITANI: I think that is right.

KŌYAMA: On the issue of world ethics, the kind of principles that Japan has been advocating today offers the perspective with the longer vantage.

---

96 Whatever one thinks of Hitler's policies, he was clearly in charge almost to the end of the Reich, while in Japan, even in wartime, the age-old preference for the diffusion of power and responsibility continued to hold sway throughout the Great East Asian War.

97 Literally 'alive': Nishitani transliterates from the German for 'vitality', itself derived from the verb *leben*, 'to live'.

9 Greater East Asia as a region of nations (*minzoku ken*)

SUZUKI: Finally, one is left brooding on the question of ethics. The more one conceives any form of Greater East Asian collectivity (*ken*) as a region of nations (*minzoku ken*), the more important it becomes to think this issue through: indeed, it is essential to do so. There is an unmistakable sense in which the quest for an economically self-sufficient zone necessarily comes to the fore within the context of *Großräume* (*kōiki ken*). I believe therefore that any consideration of the nature of co-prosperity spheres will inevitably have to start with the notion of an economic region (*keizai ken*). Indeed, the entire idea of co-prosperity spheres or *Großräume* (*kōiki ken*) takes on special meaning as a reaction against the principle of the self-determination of peoples that informs the spirit of the Versailles Treaty,[98] as well as the atomistic idea of the national popular state (*minzoku kokka*).[99] The latter concept (*rinen*) is at once abstract and universalistic (*sekaishugi teki*), and therefore must be overcome.[100] This imperative provides the rationale for thinking about the ideal of regions of peoples as well as *Großräume*. It is my conviction that we must give particular attention to this question. Indeed, there is no way of evading it. One speaks of this concept as an idea, with the aim of benefiting all, but there are practical considerations involved at the level of policy making. For example, in an East Asian context, it seems reasonable that the Philippines and Thailand should become autonomous or independent. Certainly their security should be guaranteed. Other peoples may not yet be ready for independence, and will not be recognized as such. This highlights the necessity for developing a theory that bridges the gap between the idea or concept (*rinen*) [being advocated] and [the practical pressures of] policy making. Previous theories do not strike me as adequate to our present needs. Thus some nations (*minzoku*) such as the Thais and Malays may be prepared for some form of independence while other peoples (*minzoku*) may not. This is the formula suggested.

Viewed from without, the structure of the British Empire seems to involve two types of government: self-governing dominions and crown colonies. As a set of ideals, two principles seem to be involved: partnership, and direct rule

---

98 This comment is not quite as self-serving as it might appear. *Pace* Woodrow Wilson's illusions on the subject, minority rights flatly contradict the principle of national self-determination for most conventional states, all empires and any notion of a *Großraum*.

99 So-called conservative philosophies, including Confucianism, have tended to subscribe to some form of anti-individualism. During the mid-twentieth century, such hostility centred on the rootless masses of the modern urban centre, understood as atoms bereft of organic, communal or familial roots and attachments. Here Suzuki extends this atomic critique to the individual nation-state, including Japan.

100 Here it would appear that the term *rinen*, which has been normally rendered as *Idee*, has lost any Hegelian associations and thus means 'concept' in a plausibly normal English sense.

by compulsion or necessity (*kyōsei*).[101] Both principles are applied simultaneously and made to work in tandem. Our own requirements may need to be met by something like this two-tiered formula. But at the same time, because any adoption of the British approach may invite criticism that there is no difference, certainly in appearance, between our strategy and British colonialism, it will be essential in the case of the Co-prosperity Sphere to generate a new body of theory, [incorporating] both a philosophy of the nation (*minzoku no riron*) and a set of ethical ideas (*kannen*), as well as [to construct] a systematic set of ideas of government (*seiji riron*) and to put them into practice.

NISHITANI: Isn't this the real problem? The defining characteristics of Western colonial policy until now, whether British in Malaya or Dutch in the East Indies or American in the Philippines, have been, on the one hand, the provision of reasonably stable economic conditions together with guarantees of security, and on the other, systematic exploitation [of resources and markets]. These are all versions of the original British 'opium' strategy. This is not a path that Japan should follow. When we compare our situation with that of America or Europe, it becomes obvious that the core difficulty posed by an [integrated] Greater East Asian region is the test of how to treat the human beings (*ningen*) who populate it.

Take Europe, for example. The nations and peoples that compose Europe have, one by one, developed to an extremely advanced level. But in East Asia there is, when all is said and done, only one advanced nation that matches the level of Europe: Japan. Elsewhere underdevelopment generally reigns. We have to try to lift East Asians up, educate and train them, and stimulate their national self-awakening. It is my conviction that Japan's unique mission within the Greater East Asian region is to enhance the strength of subjectivity and autonomy in all the peoples of this region. As a result we will display towards the peoples of this Greater East Asian region a posture (*taido*) in fundamental contrast to that of the West because we proceed from a wholly independent spirit. This we must do. As a result, the peoples of the region will experience their own national self-awakenings and grow in autonomy and strength, while preserving Japan's special leadership role and status. But common sense tells us that this is an attempt to square a circle, and thus will inevitably fall foul of the law of contradictions. So how can we overcome the implied contradiction [between leaders and led]? This is the fundamental challenge that stands before us.

---

101 *Kyōsei* is polysemic but it tends more frequently than not to refer to some form of force or compulsion. Crown colonies, whether originally acquired by conquest or treaty, would probably fall into this category. But some colonies and territories were governed from necessity, where hostile neighbours threatened their existence (Belize) or internal divisions conspired against internal unity (Iraq).

KŌSAKA: To follow up on a point made earlier, the devising of a link between the historical and the *Idee* (*rinen*) is a challenge that accompanies the kind of great historical leap that we are witnessing in the present age. Is it not reasonable to expect that this process will present us with the key to resolving these issues (*mondai o kaiketsu suru kagi*)?[102] As each nation strives to find its place [in the global order], a new form of world history must come into being. This *Idee* is already taking shape in the flow of contemporary history. This prospect requires that we pay the closest possible attention to the present stage of history so that this new form of reality may manifest itself. For example, we must not adopt the same posture towards China as we should towards the Philippines. Indeed, each and every nation must be approached individually on the basis of its relative degree of potential to match the stage of genuine achievement that we have reached. And, of course, in every case we must aim to achieve the ideal; but the degree to which this can be accomplished will depend on how much 'self-awareness' of historical reality has been attained [by the various peoples concerned]. If one goes on to ask what will qualify as the content of the national self-consciousness that should be inculcated, the answer is world-historical consciousness. The truths of historical reality are the ones that we [collectively and regionally] must make our own ...

SUZUKI: That is what I think as well.

KŌSAKA: ... There is no alternative. Today a new world is unquestionably emerging. They [ordinary East Asians] have to become conscious of this development. They have been deficient in anything that deserves to be called history; and even when there has been some sense of the past as history [as a narrative of change], it has been little more than as a bit part in the story of some other people.[103] East Asians have lacked a history of themselves (*jibun no rekishi*). But henceforth they must learn to make their own history with their own hands. Isn't the acquisition of this form of self-consciousness the most important thing of all? Until now Britain and America have pursued what might be called an 'opium strategy' in order to rob these East Asians blind by drugging them into quiescence. The resulting stupor has made colonial exploitation seem comparatively painless. It is Japan's world-historical responsibility to put a stop to such exploitation. We must arouse these downtrodden peoples from their

---

102 In this sentence, Kōsaka uses only the term *rinen*, but almost immediately below he returns to the German word *Idee*, which I have tried consistently to employ to contrast the conventional imprecision of the word 'idea' in English with the Hegelian thrust that the word *Idee* gives to the similarly polysemic Japanese word *rinen*.

103 The 'other people' in question have been, for the Japanese, either Chinese or Europeans, but it is also implicit in the context of the Hegelian-Kyoto School interpretation elaborated here that while (for East Asians) the 'universal' narratives of the past have centred on China, the birth of the Han Chinese as a national self-conscious self-organizing people has only just begun.

drug-induced stupor. Once awakened, they can proceed to build a new world for themselves. They must. They can begin by mastering the language of the new kind of [subjective] history, and it is our responsibility to help them acquire it. The substance of this world-historical responsibility is to be found, in truth, in the collective decision of the peoples of East Asia to awaken to this opportunity, and then to construct a new history by and for themselves.

KŌYAMA: I feel entirely the same about all that you propose, but in such circumstances there remains the ideological/intellectual problem (*shisō-teki mondai*) just noted by Suzuki. A tremendous effort is going to be required, in my view, to achieve the depth of illuminating penetration demanded by this problem. The journey I have made in my own thoughts on the subject leads me to believe that the fundamental principle at work in international tensions between nations (*kokumin*) and peoples (*minzoku*) derives from the same source. This principle is the atomistic explanation (*shisō*) of social behaviour, noted earlier by Suzuki, that tends to govern how we understand relations between nations today.

Note how in international bodies each people or nation is assigned a single vote. Regardless of whether large or small, strong or weak, every state is formally regarded, in the ethical sense, as the equal of any other in terms of their respective rights. This obviously represents a wider application of the atomistic theory of modern society: the extension of the theory of individualism to the field of international rights. But this is in fact a mere formality. In reality, strong nations dominate weaker ones. The doctrine of the survival of the fittest dominates international relations. It is only the moderating impact of the balance of power among the strong that keeps the system in check. The practical sources of this system of great power hegemony derive from the doctrine of laissez-faire liberalism. In a society where free competition prevails, strong individuals compete and gain power over the losers. The result is the system of class rule. A single overarching principle defines the nature of imperialism in international relations and the struggles that characterize domestic life within nations.

The principle that Japan has proclaimed to the world paints a formidable contrast [to this picture]. We call for all nations to achieve their rightful places in the hierarchy of the global community. This standpoint is totally at odds with the ideas of the old order. This new principle (*genri*) is at once a fresh way of organizing both international relations and the internal affairs of a single nation. And precisely because this principle is contemporary [or postmodern] in the way it breaks with the modern principles created by Europe, we must seek, I believe, to give this insight still greater intellectual (*gakumon-teki*) depth. The principle [advocated here] is radically at odds with the ethics of 'the person' that grounds individualism, and which in turn assumes that individuals are born free and equal. Indeed, in the Western tradition, an immediate and close link between ideas such as freedom and equality has been assumed. But, in reality, freedom and equality are not the same things. They certainly do not hang together naturally. The inevitable consequence of free competition, for example, is inequality; the greater stress one places on equality, the greater the restrictions one must inevitably put on freedom.

Herein lies the fundamental contradiction of the concept of individual freedom: one that leaves modern societies preaching ethical ideals such as personal freedom while in reality the strong are left to devour the weak. In the end, this can hardly be termed a satisfactory solution: it prevents this system of ethics from providing moral leadership and guidance to any society that regards itself as modern in this sense. [Indeed,] such guidance becomes all but impossible because there is no effective link between ethics and power, ideals and reality. This means that henceforth we must strive to conceive of a system of ethics that can give proper guidance and shape to conduct in the real world (*genjitsu*), a new system that derives from very different principles. We must have not so-called individualism, which is a form of *moralische Energie* without the *Energie*, but rather a system of ethics that takes *moralische Energie* as its foundation, and thus gives us proper moral leadership and direction (*shidō-teki*). Such principles would, I hope, give all the people and nations of the world an ethical way of assuming their proper places in the world. The principles that would provide the moral foundations for a new world order would at the same time underwrite the building of a new social order at home (*kokunai ni*). To achieve this we must break radically with modern ethics. This break would, without question, have to speak to the ethics of subjective responsibility (*sekinin shutaisei*). In contrast with the ethics of the person, which assumes everyone everywhere is born free and equal, the ethics that should be applied to our condition seeks to assure a [proper/appropriate] place in the world, including the place aspired to, for every person. That is why it should be called the ethics of 'humanity' (*jirin*). We intend to grapple a little more with this innovation, as this kind of ethical system has been a living force in traditional East Asian thought.

NISHITANI: In other words, the ethics of humanity that has been part of Eastern tradition can be made vital [once again] by allying it with history.
KŌSAKA: That's the lesson. What Nishitani rightly calls 'world ethics' (*sekai rinri*) is what I label 'world-historical ethics'.
NISHITANI: The world-historical and the worldly (*sekai-teki*). We need both.

10 Western ethics and Eastern ethics

KŌSAKA: Whatever we call it, this is a form of ethics that allows us to respond to the voice of world history because it is consistent, in its very essence (*kosei*), with the nature of the world as it is; indeed, it underwrites the creation of that world. We must have a form of ethics that is at one with reality at its most practical and historical. But this project has two dimensions. In contrast with the ethics of the individual person, we must foster a form of national ethics (*minzoku rinri*) to regulate conduct between nations (*minzoku*). The matter of what [moral] posture or position (*taido*) one people should adopt vis-à-vis another has not figured prominently enough in what has been conventionally regarded as the ethics of a particular people or nation. If this approach is not factored into our notions of morality or benevolence (*hakuai*),[104] exploitation, domination and conquest will go unrestrained. Such incomplete and therefore flawed morals cannot therefore serve as ethical ideals to guide human conduct in the new East Asia. We need a style of ethics that mediates conduct between peoples. This is one aspect of the problem.

The other dimension involves a question: how can we validate (*urazukeru*) this new ethics historically by reference to the ethics of the East that we inherit from antiquity? This question of course raises the prior question of how the ethics of the West differs from the ethics of the Orient. Western ethics is emphatically not a wholly modern creation; it has been subject to a variety of developments (*ugoki*) since ancient times. But ancient or modern, how are we to distinguish Eastern ethics from its Western counterpart? The essential test is practical impact as apparent from the standpoint of world-historical significance. Furthermore, thinking only about the nature of Oriental ethics, one must concede there are important differences between the ethics of China and Japan, and between different ages within the Eastern tradition. But [having acknowledged this], what can be borrowed from this tradition that can be employed to best effect in the present? How can such ethics illuminate the kind of *moralische Energie* that will clear the path for East Asia as it moves towards the world of the future? It is widely held that this tradition is a living force of great relevance to contemporary Japan, but even more important in my view is the way history has conclusively demonstrated the truth of this insight. If these dimensions can be practically combined, an ethics of world-historical responsibility can be shaped from the synthesis – or, to put the point in the language of our philosophy, a form of the ethics of subjective responsibility must come to the fore. This is the kind of ethics we must pursue.

KŌYAMA: This new form of ethics has come alive in the Orient, but what is distinctive in my view is the way this ethical system has manifested itself in Japan throughout the historical process.
KŌSAKA: How has this type of ethics taken practical form here? Historically speaking? As a creative act?
KŌYAMA: Those are the questions!
NISHITANI: First of all, one must accept that the ethics of the individual and the ethics of totalitarianism are different, and we must seek to transcend both kinds of ethics. Reality demands this of us, judged either from the

---

104 *Hakuai* might also be rendered as love of humanity.

vantage of Japan as one country among others or from the standpoint of East Asia as a whole. Take, for example, the situation when the independence of a particular people (*minzoku*) is recognized. Viewed from the ethical perspective we are advocating here, the meaning of this state of independence is entirely different from the meaning conventionally assigned to this state of affairs. When a nation achieves independence within Greater East Asia, it must be prepared to take collective responsibility as part of its place within the region, as one nation co-existing with others. This inevitably takes the form of solidarity-in-independence (*rentaiteki dokuritsu*).[105]

11 The ethics of war and ethical wars

SUZUKI: I am not that knowledgeable about ethics, but I would like to touch on what I believe to be the pivotal issue raised in Nishitani's remarks. I want to hear more about the relationship between the ethics of humanity (*jinrin no rinri*), the ethics of the nation (*minzoku no rinri*) and world ethics (*sekai no rinri*). My query may seem to depart slightly from the discussion thus far, but the Great East Asian War currently being waged has made me acutely aware of the issue raised by the question: What are the ethics of war (*sensō no rinri*)? The term *moralische Energie* has frequently been mentioned in our discussions, but I myself feel that I have only become acutely aware of the vital nature, not only of the *moralische Energie* of the nation but also of the *moralische Energie* of war itself, with the outbreak of present conflict in Greater East Asia. I have come to believe that only wars decided by *moralische Energie* truly qualify as world-historical conflicts.[106] Since the outbreak of the present Sino–Japanese struggle (*Shina Jihen*), this conflict has been labelled the East's Hundred Years War. The suggestion appears to be that this conflict will drag on with no end in sight. I think this prospect is intolerable. When I try to imagine a conflict from the past that can be plausibly compared with the Great East Asian War, the only examples that seem worth mentioning are the struggle of the ancient Greeks against Persia or the Punic Wars between Carthage and Rome. The character of the Hundred Years War [1337–1453], or the Thirty Years War [1618–48], for that matter, was very different. Even the Seven Years War [1756–63], as a struggle over distant colonial possessions, seems very different. But none of these seems to qualify, at least to me, as ethical wars.

KŌSAKA: You mean struggles decided by morale (*moraaru*) [or moral conviction].[107]

---

105 This is not a euphemism for one-sided colonial domination but an uncompromising form of pooled sovereignty. A phase of Japanese hegemony is assumed, but only a temporary one.
106 In the context of the larger argument, I suspect that Suzuki actually believes that world-historical conflicts must be wars not just decided by, but fought with, moral energy.
107 It is conceivable that Kōsaka means morale, but the Confucian subtext of this entire discussion suggests that the *moraau* here refers to morality or ethics.

SUZUKI: I guess, finally, I mean a war that falls into that small group of conflicts in which the fate of world history as a whole has been decided. The Persian Wars can claim to be struggles that altered the world (*sekai sensō*). They were not just conflicts between the Persians and the Greeks, but a struggle between East and West. They set the ethos of the Orient against the *ethos* of the Occident.[108] In a similar way the Punic Wars set East against West, with Carthage representing Eastern civilization and the Romans fighting for Western civilization. Today Japan's struggle aims to give birth to a new Eastern ethos. That is what is at stake in this war.

KŌYAMA: I think that this is very much the case, and therefore when we turn to the matter of *ethos* – this forms an aspect of what Kōsaka above termed 'ethical wars' – there are, nevertheless, unethical conflicts as well as ethical ones. Unethical wars seek to destroy the *moralische Energie* of a people. Such wars seek to remove history from that to which it gives life and meaning. They drain the life from that form of [a people's] history that is moved by *moralische Energie*. Such unethical conflicts bracket, as it were, the *moralische Energie*, that is the power of historical reality, by freezing it or denying its historical character [thus putting a roadblock in the path of progress].[109] Such activity, in my view, defines the [debilitating] impact of the unethical on the unfolding of the historical process. This is a de-temporalizing (*hijikan-ka*) phenomenon within the historical process, and it exercises its influence by evoking the eternal. This defines the power of the unethical, and it always has unethical implications [for humanity]. Wars, as a manifestation of the ethical, affirm their significance by confronting the anti-ethical with the ethical. In this sense one may conclude that history itself as a process would be nothing without manifestations of *moralische Energie*. This also explains why, in the previous round-table discussion in this series, it was noted that wars may be occasions when such *moralische Energie* manifests itself, and that is why *moralische Energie* can characterize war. So at least in one sense our present struggle is an ethical war. It sets the ethics of Europe against the ethics of the East. But this struggle is also significant in the other way we have identified: it is the battle between the ethical and the anti-ethical. Amidst the realities of history, only the Anglo-Saxon world order seeks to transcend history. This *passé* world order thinks of itself as eternal. What is alive and vital in history must, I believe, resist this anti-historical power. I further hold that this struggle must not be understood either as war between the 'haves' and the 'have nots' among nations or as a battle over natural resources: its fundamental significance is moral in nature,

---

108 In this sentence Suzuki uses first the Japanese word for 'ethos' and then the Greek word *ethos* in transliteration.
109 Perhaps a clever exploitation of Husserl's notion of bracketing.

and in the course of fighting this war, that moral significance must be sustained.[110]

SUZUKI: This is what I wanted to say.

KŌSAKA: What we have been calling Western ethics did indeed once experience an age when it was creative historically, when it made history. But today it has become anti-historical. It clearly stands in the way of the advance of history as a creative or originary force (*rekishi keisei teki*). This fact is now overwhelmingly obvious. It is the function (*yakuwari*) of war to make the *Wahrheit* about the unethical character [of an existing order] obvious and undeniable.[111] The current struggle not only reveals how Western ethics has been stamped by the unethical, but also offers a way to make the world aware of this truth.

NISHITANI: I agree with that. It is also worth noting that the other side of the coin requires us to recognize how important it is that Japan assumes the standpoint from which the historical *qua* ethical and the ethical *qua* historical is brought to consciousness and sustained into the future.

SUZUKI: And this is where our consciousness of world history comes into play.

NISHITANI: Take Rome's victory and the destruction of Carthage. In order for Japan to avoid this fate, it is essential that the Japanese people awaken to their world-historical mission and pursue it relentlessly. Should we fail in this regard, if we win the war but forget our mission, our historical advance will falter, and the consequences will not be confined to the decline (*tairaku*) of Japan and Greater East Asia with it. Furthermore, and this consideration ties up with the point just made, it is imperative that we seek more than just the economic development of East Asia as a region. This project is about more than natural resources. The development of human potential (*ningen kaihatsu*) must be pursued simultaneously. I am talking about the intellectual, moral and spiritual improvement (*seishin teki kaihatsu*) of all the nations that make up the Greater East Asian region. The only nation in the region that can meet this challenge is Japan. It is our burden and mission. If the humanity of the region proves unable to lift itself up, if there is no other advanced nation (*yūshū na minzoku*) that can sustain the region [because Japan cannot do it all alone], it is entirely rational to expect that in the future Europe or some other power will attempt to impose its power on East Asia.[112]

At the same time, one must not forget that the human development of one person by another hangs wholly on the qualities of the teacher. If the Japanese

---

110 That is, it must not be frittered away by immoral conduct or the loss of subjective self-control. There may be an oblique reference here to Japanese military atrocities on the Chinese mainland and elsewhere.
111 Kōsaka uses the German word for 'truth', *Wahrheit*, in transliteration.
112 Does this prospect anticipate the future domination of East Asia by the United States through its overseas empire of bases?

nation is to fulfil such a role, this means that the moral and intellectual quality of individual Japanese must be of the highest level, and we must train each other to reach this standard. It is therefore vital that all Japanese are morally nurtured if the metaphysical ideals captured in the formula 'the ethical *qua* historical, the historical *qua* ethical' is to be realized.

KŌSAKA: In the case of both ancient Greece and Rome, victory marked the end of the enterprise. The job of work had been completed. One was now free to enjoy the undemanding fruits of peace. But this option is not open to Japan. Great tasks await this country after the war. For our nation to become the country that pursues these future projects, we must undergo the baptism of *moralische Energie*. It takes nothing away from Nishitani to say that we must make the mantra 'ethics *qua* history, history *qua* ethics' unmistakably our own. This is the case precisely because [authentic] world history must not be conceived as something unethical. I believe that history and ethics must be bound together practically. We have talked about this issue before, but all this makes clear what Nishida, our teacher, meant when he declared that world history was the *Purgatorio* of mankind.[113]

12 The politics of philosopher-kings/sages (*kentetsu*)[114]

KŌYAMA: The source of this new ethics also requires a philosophical foundation ... Ah, something has suddenly come back to me. If one looks at Shotoku Taishi's Seventeen-Article Constitution in the light of the notion I mentioned earlier of an ethics of humanity (*jinri no rinri*), I believe that it takes on a profound meaning.[115] The fundamental *Idee* is that of government by philosopher-kings or sages. While Article One endorses the importance of harmony as the cardinal principle of [sound] government, Article Two focuses on the three Buddhist treasures [the Buddha, the Law and the Priesthood]. Article Ten asserts the universal brotherhood of man. These are the kinds of idea (*kannen*) contained in the Constitution. Finally, Article Seventeen sets out the principles of government by consensus and consultation, and suggests a kind of majority rule (*shū*). At first glance, one might take this as

---

113 The term *Purgatorio* is transliterated from the Italian.
114 As the text makes clear, the term *kentetsu* recalls the philosopher-kings of Platonic tradition as well as the sage-rulers of ancient Confucianism. It lends itself to Japanese claims of a leadership role in East Asia and suggests that this role comes with strict ethical restraints. Alternatively, one may reverse the logic and argue that the Seventeen-Article Constitution demonstrates that the notion of moral guidance of unsuccessful societies by more successful ones is an ancient East Asia ideal.
115 Promulgated in CE 604 and inspired by Chinese examples, this was Japan's first constitution predominantly influenced by Han Confucianism, despite a pronounced focus on Buddhist values and practices.

advocating a form of democracy. Of course, it is not what we call democracy today but rather a kind of ideology centred on enlightened rule by a sage or a philosopher-king. [Nevertheless], bringing the ideas of popular and enlightened government into fruitful proximity, however temporary the alignment, was a remarkable idea. Before the Buddhist absolute, all men are brothers; our humanity is shared by all because there can be no discrimination between us [as human beings]. It is the same idea as the principle that in the face of the limitless possibilities of life, all distinctions between what is great and what is small disappear. Nevertheless, between men in our limited [human] condition, there exist enormous gaps and distinctions. This realm of discrimination between great and small must be governed by a kind of morality which allows a place for both the wise and the foolish, and this imperative provides a basis and justification (*konkyō*) for enlightened rule by sages or philosopher-kings. Rule by the wise secures a world composed of both the wise and the foolish, and thus genuine harmony between men and women becomes possible (*genjitsu sareru*). This will stand as the cardinal insight of Shotoku Taishi.

The Seventeen-Article Constitution represents a synthesis of the standpoint of religion (*shūkyō teki tachiba*) and a form of ethics that can and should moderate (*shihai subeki*) the differences that pertain between people in the real world (*genjitsu*). These two vantage points are here united. This is the source of the *Idee* of philosopher-kings [in the Eastern version]. Securing a moral space (*tokoro o eru*) for both the wise and the foolish, the slogan '*kengu*' (wise and foolish) would later figure in imperial proclamations (*shōchoku*) as well as in a wide variety of august imperial statements (*haiken saseru no O-kotoba*). As a result, I think one can trace a precise link from the moral space for all implied in the notion of enlightened rule by sages to the ethical ideal of subjective responsibility and the responsible subject (*sekinin shutai*). I believe that the application of this principle, as it stands, may be extended, *mutatis mutandis*, to the wider world of the relationship between nations (*minzoku*) on the world-historical stage, and that, by so doing, a form of genuine harmony among nations may be realized. Today, examples of inequality [between peoples] are manifestations of [undeniable] reality; but even so, judged from the standpoint of the overall structure of a [regional] order (*sōshiki*), the apparent inequalities between this [country] and that disappear, and the fundamental equality of this order – the freedom of this world from inequalities – is thus preserved for the future.[116] What are termed 'philosopher-kings' are those who give guidance and leadership as morally responsible agents or subjects. As individual nations awaken to the [demands

---

116 The self-worth of all nations is thus asserted on the basis of their potential for rational self-mastery and growth.

of] moral-minded subjectivity, and thus develop each along its own path, the order of the world is determined not by force, nor by the pretensions of formal equality, but in accordance with the countries that exercise leadership given global conditions as they truly are. And these countries are there to provide an order in which nations that still lack this capacity can acquire it [in the future]. In this way, an order characterized by a truly profound degree of ethical significance [and moral worth] can come into being. If this kind of thinking can be assigned to the rubric of enlightened ruler, the principle of this kind of government merits the most careful scrutiny. What do you think of this argument?

Has this been too much of a digression? I have tried to draw on the traditional Buddhist discourse of factual dialectics (*jitsusōron*). Doesn't this qualify as a kind of metaphysical approach? Striving for a harmonic synthesis between equality and discrimination along, as it were, the frontier between the two positions ...

NISHITANI: I think that in the end this problem is connected to the issue of religion inside the Great East Asia region. Within our region one can find Muslims, Christians and Buddhists. One might add Daoists and Confucians to the list as well. Almost every religion of the world lives in communities across East Asia. And this means that, in contrast to most other regions, we have a mountain of issues to address in connection with religion. How to maintain harmony between these many and varied religious groups poses a major challenge, perhaps the greatest of all. The question requires close attention.

KŌSAKA: I am very much in sympathy with the feelings you have expressed, but I do wonder, in the first instance, just how receptive Muslims may be to the idea of philosopher-kings? I think this might pose severe difficulties.

KŌYAMA: Religious differences are [by their nature] resistant to easy solution.

KŌSAKA: At this stage, all I think we can do is to offer an ethics that includes a world-historical dimension. This provides a practical approach. If we can offer a set of workable principles, these ideas may win acceptance over time. If you will allow me to digress a bit, there is a danger that in offering the Chinese one of their own ideals, the notion of rule by sages, they might become perfectly contented [so as to lose the urge to modernize].[117]

KŌYAMA: This would defeat the whole purpose of rule by sages.

KŌSAKA: This kind of relapse would weaken [a people's] *moralische Energie*. Therefore the point on which I am a little uncertain is whether there can be

---

117 How is one to introduce the idea of progress and rational but national self-improvement into the structure of Confucian ethical thought, which endorses the necessity for endless revolutions (*kakushin*) but not subjectivity, *shutai-sei*, technological revolution or the moral pluralism and hedonism of modernity? The scope of the Kyoto School's mission is revealed in this sudden tear in the text.

a precise fit (*pittari*) between some form of governance by philosopher-kings and the practical needs of a Greater East Asian sphere as it exists today.[118] I am keenly aware of problems that may arise later.

KŌYAMA: The essence of the matter is what we mean (*naiyō*) practically by the idea of governance by sages or philosopher-kings. Because we understand this idea in terms of world-historical consciousness (*jikaku*), our formal definition refers to someone who, as an agent (*jibun*), actively and freely assumes the burden of subjectivity in response to the challenges of world history. It therefore follows that because enlightened governance is enlightened, it can provide guidance to ordinary people and thus encourage their development, personal and collective. It also follows that to act from the vantage of world history and help previously undeveloped peoples (*mikahatsu minzoku*) and the like to achieve a higher stage [of development] is to underwrite the moral content of the leadership that the dominant power in any decent regional grouping should give. Here is to be found the resolution (*kichaku*) of our problem.

KŌSAKA: There is nothing with which I can take issue in all of that.

NISHITANI (TURNING TO KŌYAMA): How does all this relate to the notion of '*hakkō ichi-u*' ['a marquee for the palace']?[119]

13 The ethics of the family (*ie*)

KŌYAMA: Well now, that is a difficult one. I do not know if people like me really understand it. In contemporary terms the suggestion would be that 'a marquee for the palace' refers to the something that symbolizes new life, as the idea appears in the *Chronicle of the Emperor Jimmu*, and is therefore extremely suggestive. This issue returns us to the rubric of the 'family'. The parental guidance and instruction of the child defines the ethical structure of the family in its most fundamental sense. This represents the most fundamental model in all human ethics. Using this classical form as our point of departure, we can link three ideas: achieving one's place in the world, enlightened governance and the moral needs/unity of the world (*hakkō ichi-u*). Recognizing the mutually reinforcing nature of these ideas in a manner consistent with the idea of the family offers a compelling way of understanding the ethical universe we are

---

118 Perhaps the supreme moment of the play of language in the entire symposium. Kōsaka at once obscures and reveals the vast scale of the challenge of trying to make two apparently incommensurate moral universes work in tandem by raising doubts about how well a seamless and emotionally satisfying synthesis can be achieved. Lacan would have a field day, because the one thing that this fit cannot be is *pittari*.

119 'A marquee for the palace' – and a symbolic marquee at that – is a literal rendering of the phrase *hakkō ichi-u* as it appears in *The Chronicle of Japan* (*Nihonshoki* or *Nihongi*), which has come to be conventionally translated, predictably but misleadingly in my view, as 'the world under one roof'.

discussing ... [*gap in original text*[120]] ... I shall speak of 'the spirit of the family' to distinguish the idea of the family that I am discussing from the family as a unit of society. But even put this way, this notion of 'the spirit of the family' remains beset by problems. There are difficulties here, although it is obvious that when one speaks of the spirit of the family, one is referring to a phenomenon that unfolds within families. We are talking about something that extends beyond the boundaries of the conventional family unit. This spirit helps to define the Japanese national character (*kokugara*). Its manifestations can be found across this society and throughout its history: for example, in samurai society (*buke shakai*), the merchant classes and farming communities. The spirit of the family defines how life has been lived in such collectivities. I think we can prove that this is true empirically because it is obvious at so many points.

What we call the state is not merely an extension of the family.[121] The state works according to principles that are different from those of the family. Nevertheless, despite this fact, it is also clear that the spirit of the family has, without question, animated the Japanese state (*naka ni gen ni ikiteru*). One can make the same point about samurai society. It is organized around a distinctive set of principles that set it apart from the family. Samurai society is not a family. In fact, the principles that secure samurai society are emphatically anti-familial. [Likewise,] what unites merchants and allows them to function as a group is the pursuit of profit: here again, the principles that bind merchant society are not those of the family. But despite these truths, I believe one may conclude that the family that pre-exists all such associations, as it may be of samurai or merchants, has shaped these groupings, and in that sense one can say that such bodies are extensions of the spirit of the family. This is certainly the case in Japan. And, to repeat, this argument can be sustained on numerous fronts. It carries empirical weight.

Let us focus on just one example of this phenomenon. In the Edo period, it was common for the business equivalent of family retainers (*bantō* and *tedai*) to rise from positions such as clerks in the family business, and in the process to accumulate sufficient capital to open their own branches or enterprises (*noren o wakeru*). Such examples suggest that although such employees had no blood ties whatever with the families that employed them, they achieved

---

120 The gap is noted in the printed text. This is so rare an eventuality in these discussions that one is left wondering what it implies. The discussions were, one assumes, taken down by hand, so it is conceivable the stenographer briefly left the room. There is also the possibility that the remarks were thought to be so controversial that the editor of the text removed them. We may have here a publisher's sop to the censor.
121 See Hajime Tanabe, 'On the Logic of Co-prosperity Spheres: Towards a Philosophy of Regional Blocs', in David Williams, *Defending Japan's Pacific War: The Kyoto School Philosophers and Post-White Power*, London & New York: RoutledgeCurzon, 2004, pp. 189–99.

the status of members of what was in effect an extended household. In this manner, the spirit of the family became a feature of merchant life in Japan by virtue of this extension of the 'family'. In effect, the spirit of the family came to colour [and thus alter] the traditional relationship between employer and employee.[122] The impact of such a spirit of kinship is ubiquitous. And one can therefore conclude that while the family serves as the model here, this spirit of the family has penetrated a variety of groups outside the family in the manner of a numerical coefficient or constant.[123] I believe this general thesis can be applied with confidence to Japanese society as a whole. In exactly the same sense, Gierke believed that *Genossenschaft* could be found to be at work in German society, [at all levels] from the formation of the state to the life of the village.[124] Thus one can conclude that the ideal of the 'family' has exerted influence over Japanese society in ways that can be empirically demonstrated. This 'family' can unambiguously be located in the realm of fact; it is not a phantom of the theoretician. Note, furthermore, that this 'family' forms the factual foundation of human ethics: the family by tradition is not a collective of individuals, nor does the 'person' precede it in fundamental importance. At the same time, it is simultaneously both a fact and a Japanese social ideal. Japan is home to the 'family' that has become the spirit of the family. I hold that this position may be argued with conviction. As a result, I also think that, given the foundational character of the spirit of the family, it forms the foundations of our ethical world and should therefore edify and enlighten. Here we have both the ethics of the family and the ethics of extra-familial social institutions. Any conception of enlightened governance as an *Idee* will proceed from this notion of the ethical. Furthermore, by a natural extension of these ethical norms, the same logic can be applied to the conduct and mission of the leading powers in the contemporary world. In this way, I believe that the Japanese spirit can serve as the basis for a new set of principles and [give definition to the] spirit of our emerging world order. Having asserted as much, I will qualify these remarks by also observing that the notion of the 'family' is by no means unproblematic, and its application as a principle to human conduct will be neither easy nor straightforward.

---

122 Note that the pair of terms in question, *shujū/shūjū*, also refers to 'master/servant' and 'lord/retainer'.
123 A metaphor that draws on the definition of a numerical coefficient as 'a symbol representing an unspecified number that remains invariable throughout a particular series of operations'.
124 Otto Friedrich von Gierke (1841–1921): German legal scholar and author of *Die Deutsche Genossenschaftrecht* (1868–1913). Kōyama here uses the German term *Genossenschaft* ([spirit of] 'cooperation') in transliteration. Japanese commentators have stressed Gierke's commitment to an approach to law that viewed human association in the light of a belief in the organic nature of collectivities and cooperative bodies. He was a critic of what he saw as the overly Latinate or Roman stress on individualism, as reflected in the impact of Roman law on German legal thinking, in favour of a more collective or Germanic philosophy of *Germanistum*.

NISHITANI: Yes, but if that is the case, does this not make the business of defining what we mean by 'family', in some fundamental sense, even more difficult when we attempt to think through the relationship between the new ethics of the Great East Asian sphere and the idea of '*hakkō no ichi-u*'? Let us assume that, among other things, the 'family' in Japan has been a form of patriarchal association. This type of family stands in extreme contrast to [the prevailing norm] in contemporary Europe, where the 'person' is, to put it as positively as possible, privileged – or, to put it more negatively, where the selfish individual is given full rein. In other words, one may take as proven (*jisshō teki ni*) that the family there is conceived in the light of the absolute priority of the individual. Let us put the matter still another way. One may conceive one's idea of the individual in the light of patriarchal authority, and the resulting supremacy of the family over the individual. There are differing views of the matter, and therefore we are not obliged to accept the notion that the priority of the individual is a fact of nature. To do so would, by definition, reduce the family to a [voluntary] association of individuals [without permanent obligations to other family members].

KŌYAMA: In other words, instead of the defining axis being the relationship of parent and child, the ruling axis becomes the relationship between adults: husbands and wives.

NISHITANI: That's right. The family as a social form may be organized in such as a way that the governing principle is either fatherly authority or individualism. Note that the same dilemma or choice applies to the organization of the state as well. Confronted by this contrast, one is forced to ask oneself: what exactly is the essence of the family, in its original sense? This is problematic (*mondai*), and therefore it follows that one must ask: when one brings the whole world (*hakkō*) under one roof/covering (*ji*), into one symbolic household, exactly what form or structure must the *ie* [family] necessarily take? Merely to evoke the notion of 'the world under one roof' with any degree of seriousness is to plunge into the greatest of difficulties. One can conceivably argue that this expression, interpreted in the most serious way, applies to Japan alone, and therefore can be understood as implying that this nation is to crush its neighbours in a programme of national territorial expansion. But the opposing argument sees Japan's mission, in the light of even the slightest [rational] reflection, as consisting of giving a lead and providing guidance to our neighbours by embracing the literal and substantive meaning of the expressions 'co-existence' and 'co-prosperity'. Our ability to live together is conjured up in the very word *heizon* [co-existence] in all its literal force. There is, at least in my view, a formidable practicality at work in the notion of intercommunity relationship governed by *Genossenheit*.[125] And

---

125 Here and below, the term *Genossenheit* is transliterated from the German.

caught up in all this is the question of what leadership means to Japan. What does the expression 'the world under one roof' mean for how our relations with the rest of the region should be structured? This is the most arresting question of all. At least, that is what I think.

KŌSAKA: In considering an arrangement such as an East Asian Co-prosperity Sphere, perhaps we can find the beginnings of an answer to your question by recognizing the radically historical nature of the challenge facing us. How can I put it? There are our historical obligations (*tōi*) to the world.[126] There is also the concept of history or the *Idee* of history. Furthermore, there are the unique foundations for all these concerns in world-historical necessity. This, too, must be acknowledged. But when we attempt to give the issue a proper theoretical or abstract (*chūshō-teki*) foundation, including the possibility of uniting the whole world under one roof, the relationship between parent and child will not serve as an effective model. In historical terms, the parent precedes the child in time. True, the parent and child exist together at the same time, but history confers a different status on them. The parent leads and guides; the child is led and is guided. The distinction is cardinal and undeniable. In other words, the notion of uniting the whole world under one roof assumes that each nation or people achieves its own place in the sun or the shade, but the resulting 'place' will reflect the impact of the hierarchy among peoples imposed by historical reality. Of course, the term 'place' is probably best interpreted in spatial terms, but at the same time, any notion of 'place' also signifies world-historical rank or status. Thus major significance must be assigned to the 'place' or rank a people has achieved on the stage of world history.

The thrust of this dialectical relationship is obvious in the effort to construct an East Asian Co-prosperity Sphere, as it must be if this project is to succeed. It therefore follows that there are no grounds for Japan to indulge in wilful and self-aggrandizing national expansion; and, on the other hand, it does not follow that all the members of such an East Asian Co-prosperity Sphere are equal in status and real power as, in this case, is misleadingly suggested by the term *hitosu no u* (*ji* or *ichi*) or 'one household' in the expression '*hakkō ichi-u*'. Only if we acknowledge this will it be possible to design an order or an organization in which the whole of East Asia can find a home. On the basis of this new concept or ideal (*rinen*) it may be possible to devise a form for a unified co-prosperity sphere that would accommodate the extremely numerous and diverse peoples of our region under a single roof in a manner previously unattempted, let alone achieved, in all of world history.[127]

126 As noted elsewhere (see Note 87 above), this is the Japanese term for *Sollen*, German for 'what one ought to do'.
127 The European Union offers a striking example of such an organization – one that began to take shape during the two decades after Kōsaka's prescient remarks, and one that illustrates the difficulties of any such attempt.

Of course, the notion of [formal] equality between individuals has been embraced as an ideal, but even the West has never succeeded in the attempt to secure a place [geographically and historically] for [each of many] different nations and peoples. This failure highlights, in my view, the importance of this new concept of East Asian regionalism, which draws heavily on the example of the family and the thinking (*kangaekata*) behind it.

KŌYAMA: I entertain the view that regionalism conceived in a formally abstract manner that departs from the realities of world history is wholly impractical. However, it is my belief that any theory that would [suffice to] guide the establishment of a new regional order in East Asia would have to serve, certainly in principle, as the guiding ethical framework for the domestic life of the nation as well. There can be only one ethical foundation (*gensoku ni oite wa hitosu mono da*). And in order for such a foundation to qualify as genuine, it is essential that it qualify as a considered form of ethics (*rinri gaku*). Isn't this an obvious truth? For example, a form of ethics (*rinri*) or a definition of humanity (*jirin*) that takes the individual person as its keystone, to the degree that has hitherto characterized the prevailing view, cannot provide the foundation for the new order embodied in a co-prosperity sphere. How could it be otherwise when world history itself calls for something entirely novel, and, by virtue of this novelty, more appropriate to the demands of our new age? I am entirely in accord with this argument and therefore pose no objections. But, to repeat, if this condition of genuine renovation or novelty is not met today, a practical (*gutaiteki na*) new world order will not be achieved. As a necessary condition that should help to satisfy the requirements of a sufficient condition, it is right to seek to give a universal character to any fundamental ethical principles.[128]

Here we should be able to conceive of a set of ethical rules that would apply in a consistent manner, as principles, to a world-historical or social order, and vice versa. While the challenge of devising such a set of principles will be a demanding task for students of ethics in the future, a provisional model can, in my view, be sought in a new conceptualization of the idea of the 'family' (*ie*), in some form or another, rather than in that of the modern citizen [of the West] or the clans (*shizoku*) of ancient Japan. Of course, throughout history, the family as a social form has experienced a variety of changes, and because of these changes one cannot declare with conviction that the family of any particular age, even the family of the feudal ages, qualifies as the generalized ideal type of the family for all time. As Nishitani just mentioned, the European family, viewed from the standpoint of individualism, has been very

---

128 In other words, Kōyama is arguing that, given the relevant form of ethics, a universal foundation is necessary but in itself is not enough to qualify as a sufficient condition to establish such an ethical system. The contrast with conventional liberal thinking, in which one proceeds from the universal, which is judged as all-powerful, is striking and definitive.

different from the family as we find it in Japan. With individualism, the focus of the family tends to shift from the relationship between parent and child to the relationship between husband and wife. But there is a danger that if this trend towards individualism takes still greater hold, the family itself will break down and begin to disappear. Men and women will take up with whomever they find attractive, and the state rather than the parent will end up raising those children that the society manages to produce. In such circumstances one would be forced to conclude that this spelled the end of the 'family' however defined. Humanity as a species would probably persist but the 'family' would face extinction. This is not a form of society that anyone should find desirable. We may call to mind the expression 'at home' that one hears in Europe.[129] Certainly in countries such as Britain one can probably find what we could call a 'family'. And it follows, given that this [family structure] can probably be found anywhere among human beings simply because they are human beings, this is probably the inevitable consequence of the form of love that unites all human beings. It is something we all share.

Burdened by the false clarity of rationality, civilized nations have managed to lose their way [by departing from common sense and instinct]. The result is a puzzling, if not absurd, dead end. This suggests that as long as it avoids dissolution, the 'family' as an ideal type will remain the bedrock of human society. In place of the 'kingdom of ends' (*mokuteki no ōkoku*), it becomes possible to conceive of an idealized type of the family.[130] From this new concept of the family, the [core] relationship between parent and child cannot be eliminated. The family is shaped, indeed arises from, the difference in generations implied in the relationship between parent and child. This family structure gives rise to the differences in age that set siblings apart as well. There is also the distinction between the sexes: husbands and wives have different functions within the family. Our abilities, duties and talents also vary with the individual; differences arise in what any one of us can contribute [to the meeting of our shared goals]. This means that we should strive to foster a harmonious totality (*zentai*) that complements and supplements our differences by drawing us together in a perfect unity of purpose, rather than surrendering to the notion that everybody is the same, and therefore qualifies as nothing more than an incremental atom to be added as merely one more in a pile of numbers (*kansan teki no sōtai*). By assuming that this meaning of the family

---

129 The expression 'at home' is transliterated from the English.
130 Kant's *Reich der Zwecke*. In *A Kant Dictionary* (Oxford: Blackwell, 1995) Howard Caygill explains: 'The kingdom of ends is introduced in the *Grounding for the Metaphysics of Morals* as a consequence of the concept "of every rational being as one who must regard himself as legislating universal law by all his will's maxims". By "kingdom" is understood "a systematic union of different rational beings through common laws", each of which determines ends according to "universal validity"' (p. 273). Kōyama is objecting to this classic form of the European commitment to individualism and universalism as a threat to the unity of the family, just as Kant's essay on 'Eternal Peace' (1795) threatens the viability of the nation-state in favour of individualism and the cosmos.

alone carries conviction and should therefore serve as the keystone of our principles, I think a genuine kind of harmony can be fostered, don't you?

With this form of the 'family', we transcend the choice between husband and wife versus parent and child, and thus achieve something not unlike Gierke's idea of *Genossenshaft*. I suspect that it is probably the case that Gierke's *Genossenshaft* is a model based on the relationship of siblings. Because my notion of the 'family' also includes what Gierke might term a *Genossenschaft*-like dimension, the membership of my 'family' consists entirely of 'singularities' (*ichi*) who respect the independent character of every other person (*dokuritsu no jinkaku*) in the family.[131] With this point in mind it becomes obvious that the 'family' conceived in this way boasts a remarkable degree of complexity, even richness, that can be neither matched nor explained by either individualism or totalitarianism.[132] In any case, I believe that it is possible to realize such a notion of the family as simultaneously fact and ideal.

Assuming as much as has already been said, I would like to focus, with apologies, on a more abstract aspect of the problem: how we might cast our idea of the family as a universal principle of ethics, as something true in essence. In this way, we could develop a set of principles to be used to regulate contemporary society in a practical manner by extending the reach of universal principles that are at the same time sensitive and responsive to [the needs of] particular societies and local principles and values (*genri*).[133] Furthermore, because one can also imagine (*kangaeru*) the wider application of such principles (*genri*) to inform the ideas (*genri*) that govern relations between peoples (*minzoku*) in any new world order, we can expect to arrive at a set of principles that will have practical (*gutaiteki na*) import for the task of building this new world order today, ones that will stand as an effective (*hontō*) synthesis of fundamental ethical principles and world-historical conditions, and therefore meet the requirements of both aspects of the problem with the precision required. Isn't this possible? And this means that the [ideal of] '*hakkō ich-u*' can be achieved as we simultaneously keep our minds attuned to world-historical realities and take some version of the 'family' as we have been discussing it here as our defining principle. This is the conclusion that I believe is within our reach.

---

131 Kōyama's attempt to square this particular circle is not easy to translate into convincing English. His family is not headed by a patriarch-dictator, nor does it embody the anarchy of the family as an association of volunteers. Rather, he sees it as an enduring collective bond which has respect for the differing roles and abilities of the members who compose it, and which is strong enough to cope with the alteration of these relationships over time.

132 Kōyama's use of the expression 'totalitarianism' may well refer to the condition of the 'family' under communism, where primary loyalties to the state trump the relationship between parents and children to a degree where betrayal of the parent by the child in the name of the revolution or state security would be the norm. In traditional East Asia, 'family absolutism' or father-dominated Confucianism offer other illiberal or anti-Kantian models for the family.

133 Specific or particular as in the contrast between universal and species, or between ontology-metaphysics and the special sciences.

KŌSAKA: That's all fine, but do you propose to address what we have been calling a new world order? When we say that a new stage is taking shape in the history of the world, where are we to discover the supposed 'newness' of this new order?[134] Even if we concede that this can be found to exist in traditional Japanese notions of the 'family', how do we apply this notion, with any adequate effect, to foreign peoples when there are at the same time so many tensions between different nations and peoples bringing them into conflict? Shouldn't we expect the novelty of our approach to offer a way of resolving such conflicts with the principles we are advocating? When confronting these kinds of issues, the suggestion that we merely extend the application of [essentially] domestic practices beyond our shores, or assume that the principles of our domestic life should govern political arrangements elsewhere, is to make a huge leap of reasoning. Isn't this the point that needs to be stressed here? The thrust of my questions should not obscure the fact that we share the same objectives and outlook, but the issues I have raised need to be factored into our argument so that there is an interplay between the two perspectives. Isn't this the case?

NISHITANI: Can't we think about this challenge in the light of our earlier discussion of *moralische Energie*? Contemporary Japan has assumed the burden of leadership in Greater East Asia. This is our role and, as noted before, the fact that *moralische Energie* is a living force here is the fundamental truth that matters. If we ask ourselves what is the source of this *moralische Energie*, there is probably a variety of ways of looking at the question, but fundamentally the answer is as Kōyama has articulated it: we have benefited from a kind of *Genossenschaft*, or, as we take this idea to mean in essence, a form of the family spirit. This spirit has worked with particular strength and vitality [in Japan] precisely because of the unique national polity (*kokutai*) that this country possesses, and that has influenced the whole of the nation (*kokka*). This has been the source of our [Japanese] *moralische Energie*, or at least this is how I think anyway.

As I noted before, when we become self-aware (*jikaku*) of ourselves and our essential unity as a people (*minzoku*), when this becomes the foundation of our state, then [and only then] will we be able to see the state for what it is: the manifestation of our *moralische Energie*. At the same time, it is precisely within the scope of the state that the family spirit works [its magic].[135]

---

134 This emphasis on newness is crucial because for these Kyoto School thinkers novelty is a product of history, and one of their chief objections to conventional ethics is its supposedly ahistorical, transcendent character.

135 There are striking parallels between the expressions used by Nishitani and those that Heidegger employs in his 1933 Rectoral Address; however, note that Nishitani is an advocate of subjectivity while the German philosopher is an objectivist entirely opposed to the Cartesian, Hegelian and Weberian amalgam that defines what the Kyoto School means by *shutaisei*.

For example, the reassertion of imperial authority (*taisei taikan*) that accompanied the Meiji Restoration, an event with no precedent outside Japan, stands as a remarkable manifestation of the influence of the family spirit. At the same time, the *moralische Energie* of the Japanese people (*minzoku*) revealed itself in this striking achievement. This splendid transformation (*henkaku*),[136] we may further note, provided the vehicle for the *moralische Energie* of the Japanese people (*minzoku*) to manifest itself. Via the revolution that resulted in the Restoration, this burst of *moralische Energie* was unleashed within the nation as the motive force in Japan's drive to become the great power it is today. Furthermore, this is the same *moralische Energie* that has given contemporary Japan its leadership role in Greater East Asia.

Now, when we focus our attention beyond our shores and we ask ourselves what is the nature of contemporary Japan's leadership role, the key task for this nation is to transmit our *moralische Energie* to the various peoples that compose East Asia as a region. We must seek to arouse them from their slumbers, and thus encourage their self-awakening as nations (*minzoku*). Or, to put it another way, our task is to help them nourish their capacity for subjectivity. The *moralische Energie* that has served as Japan's motive force (*gendōryoku*) must be transmitted to other nations and peoples, and thus contribute to the fostering of their native powers and inner potential for action. In this way, these peoples can set their own sails and move towards the future. From this dynamic, new ways will be discovered for Japanese *moralische Energie* itself to take yet further dramatic leaps forward. In short, this task also offers us an opportunity to develop ourselves (*jikō ikusei*) morally (*moralische*).[137] It should of course be obvious that this process is fundamentally ethical in character. Its significance is also, at the same time, political in character. It bears, in my view, the stamp of political necessity grounded in the world as it is (*genjitsu ni nezashita*). Isn't this obviously the case?

As I noted above, one of the special tasks facing East Asia as a region is the basic challenge of human development (*ningen kaihatsu*), and meeting this challenge is essential to the survival of the region as a whole. Indeed, without success on this front, Japan's own survival will remain in doubt. Thus such human development via the transmission of *moralische Energie* unites the practical politics at issue with the ethical imperative in question. Intrinsically bound together, they form a single enterprise.

It therefore follows that even if, say, one or another nation or people (*minzoku*) achieves independence, it cannot be assumed that mere independence in and of itself is sufficient, because the decision to grant independence

---

136 One of several Confucian terms for 'revolution' but with none of the French or Russian or even American revolutionary connotations. Nishitani's evocation of the 'uniqueness' of this event is, among other things, not so much Shintoist as a gesture to restrain Chinese intellectual and moral hegemony in the name of a genuine space for Japanese identity.

137 The word *moralische* is transliterated from German.

to any people or nation (*minzoku*) in particular must hang on the degree to which the content of their spirit [spirit = subjectivity, that is the capacity for self-development and self-government] has been transformed prior to independence; otherwise the entire process will end in tears (*nani mo naranai*). To gain independence in a sudden rapturous mood of self-exaltation or self-congratulation can be positively damaging. Thus, there must be a [radical] spiritual change prior to independence if what we call national self-determination is to be effective.

Moralische Energie is the essential ingredient of any such transformation. To restate the argument, the ethical foundations (*konpon*) of Greater East Asia are to be secured by the dissemination of Japanese *moralische Energie* to the various peoples of the region, and this process will help in a substantial way to enhance their respective levels of subjectivity (*seishinteki suijun*).[138] Through this superior level of spiritual self-development, an ethical relationship among these peoples can be developed (*kensetsu sare*). In this manner the region will learn to sustain itself as a pan-region [or civilization, that is, a 'world among worlds']. That is my thesis. I am assuming that the morality about which I speak will metamorphose into energy. If we think along these lines, it will become possible to make the leap between the logic, as elaborated by Kōyama, of the ethics that govern our domestic life, and the morality (*rinrisei*) that provides the ethical order for much larger regions, such as an East Asian order. Or indeed for a world order. But any such leap must also respect the continuities between these different ethical orders [if it is to be successful].

KŌSAKA: That is what I think as well.
KŌYAMA: There is one thing I want to explain here. In any discussion of the idea of the 'family', the relationship between parent and child is decisively important. When viewed from the standpoint of the parent, the ethics of the parent-child relationship turns on the upbringing of a child by a single independent 'parent' to whom the child belongs. The 'family' within which the child is raised to become an independent person is central to the ethical character [of the household]. This means that the parent-child bond involves more than the continuation of a blood relationship. However much a parent may feel that the child belongs to the parent, this tie does not mean that parental will is the be-all and end-all of the relationship. The parent is not free to abandon the child, let alone kill it. As an independent person, one day the parent will have to submit to the decisions of the child because age must yield to youth. The old will have to submit to the now-mature adult that the child has become. Parental responsibility requires that the child be nurtured to conduct itself with at least the same competence and ability as the parent, and preferably to an even higher level. But as a minimum standard, the child as person should

---

138 Literally 'spiritual level', where spirit refers to a mixture of values, motivation and skill.

not demonstrate a character that is in any way inferior to that of the parent. In this sense, the child must become the equal of the parent. This is what responsible parenting means.

This dynamic will always form an important part of the parent-child relationship; and this notion of the parent-child relationship corresponds, to some degree, with the concept of *Genossenschaft*. Beyond this, we may take one further step in our analysis to address a set of relationships that transcends even the roles of parent and child and the bond they share. What I have in mind are 'existential' (*jitsuzon-teki*) relationships of the kind one sees in the bond between husbands and wives.[139] We touched on this issue in the earlier round-table discussion when we talked about samurai society (*buke shakai*) in medieval Japan. Samurai life was strongly marked by existential relationships. Therefore today, when we speak of '*hakkō ichi-u*', it is all too easy to conjure relationships characterized by [strong] fellow feeling (*nakayoshi*); but this should not imply the mere extension of familial psychology to other contexts, because parents have other responsibilities than bringing up their children to be outstanding members of society. There must be the kind of emotional commitment one finds in existential relationships, such as the bonds of fidelity that one man pledges to another.

Kōsaka was right to remark earlier that an international order, an order characterized by relationships between independent states, will inevitably have a different nature from human society in general, and this point needs to be adequately reflected in what we are advocating. Nevertheless, if the idea of the 'family' is to have meaning, there has to be – what can one say – something of the significance one finds in some version of what I have called 'existential relationships'. At least this is what I think. What I mean by existential relationships has absolutely nothing to do with the atomism that characterizes the [formal] equality between individuals in modern (*kinsei*) societies.[140] To recap, we are talking about a category of human relationships that goes beyond the roles of parents and children, beyond the conventional understanding of the parent-child relationship, but also beyond a simple equality between individuals. No, today we require family bonds that at once embody the fundamental nurturing relationship in which the parent instructs and guides the child, and at the same time reflect the inviolable nature of the existential attachment. Isn't this what we need now? This is how I define what

---

139 Although Kōyama does not define what he means by *jitsuzon* relationships, he seems to be referring to bonds between people that are chosen freely by those involved. Parents do not choose their children and vice versa, but samurai chose their masters, and masters their retainers. Interestingly, given the conservative cast of much of Japanese society even as late as 1942, Kōyama assigns marriage to the category of existential relationships. This is consistent with the unambiguously feminist thrust of some of the arguments that follow.
140 Kōyama rejects theories such as atomism, which holds that understanding of the parts is logically prior to an understanding of the whole (as opposed to holism).

sets the ethics of the 'contemporary' fundamentally apart from the ethics of medieval and modern worlds.

14 Politics and the spirit of the family

KŌSAKA: Well, then, where does all this leave us in our attempt to define what we mean by the 'family'? Curiously, the family is the one thing that does not immediately come to mind when we talk about politics. Something sets the family proper slightly apart from the idea of the 'family spirit' which is shot through with political considerations.

KŌYAMA: That's right. That is why I have chosen to use the term 'the spirit of the family', precisely to avoid that kind of misunderstanding.

KŌSAKA: That is because the family occupies a broadly different sphere from that of politics. But despite this distinction, one says that the politics of the country (*kuni no seiji*) is informed by the spirit of the family. Not only that, we also tend to see the creation of Greater East Asia – to expand significantly the scope of the political sphere – as an extension of the spirit of the family. Because we talk in this way ... [*gap in original text*] ... what Nishitani calls the simultaneous leap between dimensions and the continuity between them. And this appears to be what it has to be. When Kōyama speaks about existential relationships (and I do take his point), I think that matter needs to conceived more in terms of *politischer Existenz*.[141] Now, I accept that there is a tendency not to link the concept of the political with that of existence, but I think these two concepts have to be considered together. When we speak of *moralische Energie*, for example, the energy that we are talking about has undeniable links with the political. And this becomes even more important when we consider the public (*oyake*) realm.

NISHITANI: Isn't this a serious issue even in contemporary Japan? On the one hand, I think it is fair to say that the spirit of the family is in lively evidence among the Japanese people, but, in contrast, on the other hand there is comparative indifference to politics. The political side [of the equation] has never quite matured. Don't you think? I don't feel a proper connection is being drawn, certainly nowadays, between domestic life and the politics of the wider sphere that includes Greater East Asia or, for that matter, the world. Indeed, until now the links between pre-existing forms of domestic politics and the family have been insufficiently cultivated. This is probably the root cause of the problem. It is particularly troubling, in my view, that the education of women has not equipped them with a greater awareness of historical reality. This is important because one can talk about the nation's *moralische Energie* without reference to women. After all, they form half of the country's population,

---

141 The phrase is transliterated from the German.

and therefore much more attention needs to be paid to their education especially when they are young.

KŌYAMA: In any case, we need to make massive improvements in the content of our political ideas today.

KŌSAKA: Yes, yes. That is absolutely right. Morality and politics have conventionally been regarded as different spheres. In much the same way that history and morality have been seen as very different things. But in both cases we need to seek to ally these spheres in a much deeper way. As an *Idee* the family, no less than politics, must be rethought in an entirely fresh manner, just as the interrelationship between these two spheres must be reconsidered.

KŌYAMA: When we speak of what we mean by the family, we must treat certain attitudes towards the past with a degree of scepticism, whether the temptation is to glorify an example of the family from one age or another or to attempt to resurrect something like the clans (*shizoku*) of antiquity. In our country, where there is an essential unity between sovereign and people (*kun-min ittai*), we cannot allow ourselves to be dominated by the pursuit of self- or group interest [at the expense of all else] of the kind as we find among such 'clans' [or other groups].[142] By contrast, what we should be celebrating is what we have been calling the spirit of the 'family'. In the struggle to renew the order of the world as well as East Asia, the social order of the Japanese state itself must be transformed in appropriate ways.[143] In short, the Japanese people themselves must cast off the old order in order to create something with the potential for total renovation. Japanese today are different from the Japanese of the past, and this means that we must become something utterly new – new [tough, disciplined and rational] enough to endure the burdens of building a new order for greater East Asia as a whole. To reshape the world, a new form of humanity is required; when this new form of human being is created, we will have in hand the means to remake the world. The task will then be achievable. This is the challenge that must never be far from our minds.

NISHITANI: Thus far I have insisted that *moralische Energie* is indeed alive and well in Japan, but at the same time one feels a great anxiety – how shall I put it? – about the state of our country at a more profound level. I don't think our culture today provides the Japanese people with a model

---

142 The language has suddenly become cautious and vague. I suspect that the literal surface meaning is adequate, but one is left with the suspicion that here again we find veiled criticism of the Tōjō clique or the more self-serving of the country's capitalist interest groups.

143 The hint here is that Japan must have a new order, but one that is consistent with the national polity (with the imperial household at its apex). Not too much should be made of the poetic, mystical and indeed elegant sound of Kōyama's adjective *fusawashii* (fitting or appropriate) in Japanese, but it can be seen to serve as a nod to the emperor, thus deflecting potential criticism that the *kokutai* is being neglected, while also suggesting that the emperor stands apart from the Tōjō clique. The Confucian gloss is once again crucial: here we have advocacy of radical change, indeed revolution, within a fixed, that is unchanging, moral cosmos.

or set of ideals, a guide or *Paradigma*,[144] if you will, for how to be human and to achieve fulfilment as a human being.

Up until the Meiji Restoration or perhaps until shortly after the Restoration, certainly no later than around 1890, the cultural paradigm which we inherited from our tradition provided a model of human fulfilment which carried conviction among us. But after that, our sense of continuity with the spiritual culture of the past was broken. As a result, one generation after another has been brought up with no [organic] link with tradition. The intelligentsia turned instead to Western culture, and a minority of them managed to discover a new model of human fulfilment. But the vast majority of the intelligentsia never got beyond superficial cultivation, the mastery of mere fragments of an imported civilization, while the general public – including women – were still less able to imbibe anything of real substance from either Japanese tradition or Western culture. In a word, the old model had broken down and a new model was nowhere to be seen. Discontinuity and disorientation were the result, and this situation remains unchanged up to the present.

It is thus my conclusion that there is a grave problem lurking beneath the surface of contemporary Japanese culture. Moreover, as if that were not enough, I am convinced that a new paradigm is not something that one just conjures out of one's head. Rather, it must be born from the depths of historical reality. But this is not something we can afford to wait for. It is by making history, and being conscious of making history while we are making it, that we can create this new cultural paradigm. Today, the Japanese must remake themselves, as Kōyama has urged, as East Asians (*Tōa ni okeru Nihonjin*) blessed with a national character specifically moulded spiritually to assume the role of regional leadership.[145]

On this point, I must confess that I have long been rather deeply pessimistic. But when I learned of the fighting spirit and self-possession displayed by the Imperial Navy at Pearl Harbor (*Hawai no kaisen*), I saw this as a ray of hope (*kōmei*). The spirit, daily discipline and training practices of the officers and men of the Imperial Navy should reach out and touch the whole nation, because we all have so much to learn from this example. As a people we can only benefit from such group discipline. We need to make its acquisition a national goal. We should learn to be tempered in this way without the outward forms of command and compliance or the excesses of stiff conformity (*katakurushii*). But in any case, a grand project of national education, training and culture is proposed. Is there a chance we can achieve it? If we can realize,

---

144 The term is transliterated from the German.
145 Literally, as 'Japanese in East Asia' and with the affirmation of Japan's leadership role: this would seem not to justify my rendering of 'the Japanese as East Asians', but the wider context of the Kyoto School's interpretation of subjectivity and moral energy implicitly anticipates the Hegelian 'moment' when the child assumes responsibility for the parent. Leader today, one day Japan will be a follower.

252 *The Standpoint of World History and Japan*

in a planned and systematic manner, the promise of this national exercise in character building and national reform, we can accomplish something never yet achieved in the entire history of the world: the fulfilment of Plato's dream.[146]

15 Ethics as the fundamental problem of co-prosperity spheres (*Großräume*)

SUZUKI: I would like to put in a word if I may ... I must acknowledge that I have only a superficial acquaintance with the field of ethics, and I have therefore contented myself with listening to your deliberations on this subject, but I would nevertheless like to try to present an impression of my feelings about what has been said. If I might attempt to summarize the main points of the argument, a set of guiding principles for any co-prosperity sphere is needed to give absolute [*zettai-sei* = non-contingent] meaning to this enterprise as only ethical principles can because, however important we judge the *moralische Energie* of a co-prosperity sphere to be as an object of historical self-awareness, this has by itself been judged insufficient. In the round, this conclusion strikes me as sound. If this is the case, however, is it entirely reasonable to expect that there will be differences between the ethical codes of the different nations that might compose any co-prosperity sphere and the new form of ethics that we think will come into play when the co-prosperity sphere is created? For anyone who is not an expert in ethics, there is inevitably a suspicion that an ethical code particular to one nation cannot be translated into an ethical code for a whole region that forms the membership of any co-prosperity sphere without provoking some form of resistance.[147]

The idea of the ethics of the family has been much mooted, and I don't really understand this idea in any detailed sense, but China, for example, has an extremely old ethical code to regulate family life. Given the well-founded expectations about the weight of Chinese tradition, what will be the likely consequences of including in a co-prosperity sphere countries such as China that possess well-established ethical codes when we face them with an alternative code that is at once of determinant character and also different from theirs? It will be very problematic if this provokes a conflict over ethical ideals and concepts (*gainen*). I have only gradually over the course of our discussions begun to understand what Kōyama means by family ethics, but I think

---

146 In essence, 'how society could be reshaped so that man might realise the best that is in him': Francis MacDonald Cornford, 'Introduction', *The Republic of Plato*, London: Oxford University Press, 1945, p. xv.
147 Suzuki's bob and weave with Confucian tradition appears to challenge the notion that his thinking as a member of the Kyoto School is founded on the *kosō* or bedrock of classical Chinese ideas, but his lengthy comment suggests, on balance, that he seeks to balance the claims of Confucian ethics with the requirements of national identity while pursuing a version of the modern that takes Confucianism as its point of departure.

that it clearly does not refer merely to the ethical code of a particular nation or people (*minzoku*). But is it really indispensable to codify an ethical framework (*gainen*) characterized by such a degree of absoluteness? That is the knot of the difficulty.

Whatever other claims may be attached to it, the ethics of a co-prosperity sphere must be defined by *das Sollen* of history (*rekishiteki tōi*).[148] This must be our point of departure in trying to conceptualize a new form of ethics. At the very least, there must be no relapse into a transcendental form of ethics or any other kind of ethics that departs from history ... However, at the same time, it is also emphatically the case that the theme that demands our closest scrutiny – perhaps the most important theme of all – is the process of our/their self-awakening to ethical consciousness. We have to be consistent on this point, because from the very outbreak of the present Great East Asia War we have insisted on the ethical or, if you will, moral character of this conflict. Furthermore, we have repeatedly asserted that if we should lose this moral quality, our struggle would, in essence, be reduced to mere conflict over natural resources and colonies. This danger must be taken to heart. As we have previously noted, our Great East Asia War has no precedent in history but if we were forced to find a struggle of comparative scale, the nearest equivalent might be the great classic wars between ancient Rome and Carthage.

Those wars were among the great conflicts of world history; but, leaving the issue of greatness aside, in defeating Carthage, Rome's moral character suffered a crucial loss. In other words, the spiritual and social traditions of ancient Rome in their hitherto essential health and soundness were eroded through the course of this struggle. Both the mind (*seishin*) and society of the traditional Romans were thus fundamentally transformed as it were in their very essence. This change is what historians call the 'Hellenization' of Rome. This is why the Punic Wars marked a turning point in the destiny of Rome. But as the material expectations from the Co-prosperity Sphere are at present manifestly so great [in this country], and because the very idea of a co-prosperity sphere derives from the urge to secure natural resources (*shigen kannen*), it is crucial that we do not follow in the tracks laid down by the Romans so many years ago. Indeed, such expectations are a dangerous illusion. This temptation is particularly damning because the goal of the present Great East Asian War is not victory but something greater that will come afterwards. This prospect becomes more obvious if we identify the purpose of our struggle as to secure [the survival of] Greater East Asia as a region, not with the goal of enhancing our own happiness but rather in the increase of our responsibilities, that is as an ethical task. If we think of our struggle in this way, if we are to wage the Great East Asian War justly, as a crusade to

---

148 Suzuki uses the term *tōi*, which as noted above is the Japanese rendering of the Kantian concept of *sollen* or *das Sollen*, that which ought to be or exist, but note the specific rejection of any transcendental aspirations for this concept of 'what ought to be' in favour of a more Hegelian or historicist definition of the term.

put the world to rights (*tadashiku*), we will have to dig deep to uncover the ethical depths of our battle.

This involves more than addressing the moral questions at issue with grave seriousness (*kinchō*). We must form what might be called an ethical framework (*rinri gaku to iu katachi*) adequate to the task we have assumed [as our responsibility]. Such feelings are only to be expected [in the light of our situation]. In addition, pressures to focus more attention on the political order needed to sustain a Greater East Asia will only grow, with a demand for policies that will shape this enterprise in an effective way (*genjitsu sarete*). But here a stern warning must be sounded: the whole project of creating a Greater East Asia region will be meaningless, that is without world-historical significance, unless the bonds that unite us as a region are moral; a political-economic union as a disguised form of colonialism will not do. Traditional notions of conventional links between one nation and another can be thought to fall into one of two categories: unity by agreement or union by force.[149] However, the nations of Greater East Asia must come together in a manner that departs from both of these strategies. We require a new form of union. As Nishitani has just argued, any Greater East Asian regionalism must be an extension of the self-awakening [to subjective agency] of the various member nations. And it is only to be expected that we [Japanese] take up the burden of helping them to achieve this. But this self-awakening must be ethical and not just political.

National self-awakening and independence as envisioned, for example, in the wake of the Treaty of Versailles, turned on the notion that national self-consciousness refers only to political independence. This idea gained force as the impact of the notion of national self-determination registered among peoples in every part of the globe. But the sounder formula is that the historical self-awakening of a people must be matched by its ethical self-awakening. Approaching the problem in this way explains why ethics represents the fundamental challenge of any co-prosperity sphere. Such are my feelings on the subject, anyway. Having hitherto given the bulk of my attention to the economic dimension of this problem, I have come via our discussions to see the issue in this new and different light.

KŌYAMA: I cannot help wondering if a form of the ethical absolute might be necessary. I know that doubt has been cast on this idea, but when I evoke the ethical absolute I in no way intend something passive and fixed or unchanging. Indeed, as we have noted above, we have judged the notion of abstracting or dehistoricizing something from the current of history to be itself unethical, and we therefore have concluded that morality

---

[149] The phrase 'unity by agreement' is transliterated from the English. While the term *kyōsei* can refer to persuasion, here the context clearly points to a sense of compulsion. See 'The Black Legend of the Kyoto School: Translating Tanabe's *The Logic of the Species*', in Williams, *Defending Japan's Pacific War*, pp. 99–105, esp. 104–5.

(*dōtoku*) must manifest itself as *moralische Energie* or *seimeiryoku*. To repeat: to dehistoricize what we call ethics is in itself anti-ethical. Attempts to maintain the outmoded old order in and of itself signal the loss of *moralische Energie*. Furthermore, what has been termed the ethics of the family represents, in almost all cases, an attempt to sustain the family system of one particular era or another, and therefore stands in opposition to *moralische Energie*. Given this expectation, none of this qualifies as what I mean by an ethical absolute. In the end, our degree of subjectivity or self-mastery is determined (*tatsu*) by our ability to shoulder the challenges (*keikō*) that world history throws at us. This means that *moralische Energie* at its most ethical is not a relative notion but rather demonstrates its claim to absolute significance while simultaneously never renouncing (*nageutsu*) life or repenting (*kuyuru*) its demands.[150] This is what the ethical absolute means. It is, ultimately, the transcendence of history within history.

SUZUKI: That is the only thing it can be.

KŌSAKA: In the light of such considerations, the family predictably comes to the fore. As for the worry that [the assertion of] something fixed and unchanging will invite misunderstanding, we certainly must exercise care here. It must be anticipated, however, that every nation [of Greater East Asia] believes that it is living a version of the ethical life by following its own customs and practices. Take the Chinese, for example, who clearly believe as a matter of conviction that they live an ethical life focused on propriety and rites (*rei*). Any direct comparison with the manners and mores of the peoples of the southern tropics (*Nanpō*) can only reveal a remarkable set of differences in values and customs. When confronted with such contrasting customs and practices, the claims of *moralische Energie* will provide a means to assess the relative strengths and weaknesses of these varying practices and to rank them. Then and only then will the superiority of Japanese *moralische Energie* be evident and convincing to all, and on the strength of this demonstration of [our effectiveness] contrasts in customs and habits will seem less important, as they must [if this collective enterprise is to succeed]. But there may be trouble unless we can devise a form of ethics capable of helping us to sustain the kind of relationships between countries (*kuni*) necessary to our project: that is, a set of ethical principles that not only is different from [those obtaining in] the past but also justifies claims to the absolute, and so a form of ethics that must steadily be fostered here at home as well. Something approaching this version

---

150 An emphatic rejection of Buddhist other-worldliness and the powers of *tariki* or 'other power' in an affirmation of the demands of life that is almost Nietzschean in its force and conviction. It confirms my suspicions that Tanabe's embrace of *zange* (repentance) towards the end of and immediately after the Pacific War was a Confucian gesture or a temporary lapse in his fundamentally Hegelian subjectivity. However, the whole question demands the closest of attention, which it has yet to receive either in Japan or elsewhere.

of the ethical absolute can – I am convinced – be realized in practice (*gutaiteki ni*).

16 Towards a new kind of Japanese

KŌYAMA: When we finally arrive at the point when we have to think about [becoming] a new kind of Japanese, what are we are really thinking about?

KŌSAKA: That is another issue we have to consider.

SUZUKI: At the very least it means that the notion advocated [recently] with such force that what was needed was merely for the Japanese to be still more Japanese-like carries no conviction.

KŌSAKA: Now that is obvious. Unless the Japanese people acquire a degree of global-mindedness (*sekai-teki fūkaku*) and become a people capable of meeting the challenge of world history – and that includes realizing the goals that are implied in this task – other peoples will not, in my view, be convinced by our moral claims.[151]

KŌYAMA: When I was in primary and secondary school, I was regularly asked by my teachers to answer this question: What does the expression '*hakkō ichi-u*' really mean? The point of the exercise was to demonstrate that this expression, in practical educational terms, refers to a pedagogic goal that involved, as a matter of necessity, imagining a [new] way of being a Japanese in the world. In other words, a specific (*gutaiteki*) type of Japanese was being offered up for discussion. Or, to turn the argument around, the point was that unless we became this new kind of Japanese, education made no sense because our ability to act effectively on the world would be impaired. Unless it teaches us to act effectively, education falls short of what it is supposed to achieve. That is the bitterly serious issue at stake here. It has always been the problem. But having said as much, what kind of ideal type [of Japanese] needs to be conceived of here? What will suffice? Some very serious thinking is required. I tried to formulate my views in a magazine article published this January entitled 'The Ideals of Contemporary Man' (*Gendai jin no rinen*), but in any case what we must have is a kind of human being who can embrace the challenge of awakening to the contemporary history-shaping mission that now presents itself to us. This human being must serve as the keystone of this project. It is essential to stress that we seek to break with the past; this new Japanese will be different from his ancestors. Narrow-minded Japanese insularity will no longer do.[152]

---

151 That is, other nations will not find persuasive Japanese's claims to the mid-twentieth-century version of a Confucian mandate of heaven. The language is exactly the same as we saw at the beginning of the second symposium. Even the same verb, *settoku*, has been used by Kōsaka.

152 The attack appears to be against the Japanese equivalent of 'Little Englanders', but with an additional implied criticism of narrow Japanese parochial chauvinism.

The creation of this new 'post-modern Japanese' (*gendai Nipponjin*) involves more than just scholarly labour. We have to think about this concept from the standpoint of the practical educator. It demands serious attention from the artist and the novelist, too. In short, today we must, as a matter of pressing national urgency, face up to the challenge of creating a new kind of Japanese, one capable of rising to the challenges of constructing an East Asian Co-prosperity Sphere.

NISHITANI: We must find that great good place (*jiban*) where the historical becomes the ethical, and the ethical, historical. Two processes are thus involved. On the one hand, we have to act without ever losing sight of insights into and awareness of historical reality; and, on the other, we have to raise the standards of human conduct to an ever higher level. This standard defines human ethics as a form of existence within this historical reality. From this process, a new form of humanity will steadily take shape and mature. Can't we conclude that?

KŌYAMA: At the same time there is another issue, one that is exceedingly important, and one that I have been widely questioned about. That is the problem of how science and the Japanese spirit can co-exist within the consciousness of this new kind of Japanese.

NISHITANI: The issue became obvious at the time of the naval battle at Hawaii.[153] That struggle was a manifestation of a seamless unity between science (*kagaku*) and spirit. Given contemporary realities, this unity represents the most authentic expression of what it is to be fully alive today; it is our most complete way of life.[154] That is what the battle showed us. One cannot begin to live in that way if one surrenders to [mutually exclusive] definitions of scientism (*kagakushugi*) and pure feeling or motivated sincerity (*seishinshugi*). Such slogans are mere words. As concepts they take us nowhere.

KŌYAMA: When I am asked about this issue, nowadays I answer it in much the same manner. Before one dismisses the argument between rationalism and the spirit [of the Japanese people] as meaningless logic-chopping, one should bring to mind the battles of Hawaii and the Malay Straits. Recall these victories. Both stand as absolutely classic examples of the successful marriage of science and [fighting] spirit, of the harmony that we can strive to achieve between reason and the Japanese spirit. So even if my arguments fail to convince proponents of the Japanese spirit, these two facts from history should be more than enough to do so. These splendid facts should be all the more convincing precisely because they are among the greatest events produced by history, because they demonstrate how

---

153 The attack on Pearl Harbor of December 1941. The Kyoto School consistently uses the term *Hawaii Kaisen* when referring to this event.
154 Because it overcomes the differences between matter and spirit, man and machine, science and humanness, Western science and Japanese identity.

harmony can be achieved between spirit and science. This means that all these dubious claims and muddled assertions that science is contrary to the Japanese spirit, or that science can be dispensed with because of the power of the Japanese fighting spirit, have been crushed by world-historical facts. These facts stand as the summits of the Japanese spirit, as the triumph of the unity of matter and spirit (*busshin ichinyo*). These facts are the handiwork of the truest of true Japanese. These are supreme examples of contemporary heroism. And that is how I have argued my case with these sceptics. These facts, in a total and compelling way, demonstrate that the fullest mobilization of the spirit requires the full mobilization of science and technology (*kagaku*).[155]

One can drive the point still closer to home, and argue that to push science to its ultimate limits is to arrive at the supreme example of the transcendence of science. I often use a pair of philosophical ideas, *ri* (reason) and *ji* or *koto* (thing), to explain my argument. When reason is pressed to its ultimate limits, reason itself is overcome, and thus takes up its place once again among the realm of things or facts, within the one absolute (*yui da hitosu no zettai*). I suspect that the fullest mobilization of science, in the way celebrated above, provides us with a classic example of the reversion of *ri* into *ji*. *Ri* and *ji* mediate one another without limit, but in the end *ri* reverts to being a single fact. It is here at this transcendent moment that one finds the Japanese spirit.

In the urge of the Japanese spirit to reject the scientific and the rational, there has always existed the opportunity to press to the ultimate, and in the end this will bring us to the perfect unity of *ri* and *ji* that occurs when all things revert to the single absolute thing (*zettai ji*). Here is to be found the [supreme] dignity of the Japanese spirit. But reason is to be respected. Even in the training (*rensei*) of the Zen monk, reason is never merely dismissed, nor is its importance denied. The Japanese spirit, and those who advocate it, should show the same kind of respect. But the greater truth is this: we must strive metaphysically to anticipate that moment when things, having been mediated by reason in unlimited fashion, without becoming reason, return to the 'absolute singularity' of the ultimate thing.

SUZUKI: Today, when so many pressing difficulties are being neglected, ethical issues must not be unwisely neglected. Morality poses the fundamental challenge. It is so overwhelming in importance that it should loom larger in our concerns than many apparently more urgent problems, including the policies being implemented in our newly occupied territories, the sorting out of currency problems, and the reorganization of the economy.

---

155 A forceful Japanese response to both Heidegger's denunciation of the alienating effects of scientific specialization and the ferocious attacks on tradition by techno-fanatics such as the Italian Futurists.

NISHITANI: On the subject of Japan's capacity for [regional] leadership, one must observe that finally leadership depends on human beings giving the lead to other human beings. No one is going to follow our lead if we reduce leadership to barking orders at people we appear to regard as inferiors because they are led and not leaders.

KŌSAKA: A number of contemporary problems are sensibly regarded as moral (*moraaru*) challenges; and they can be tackled practically if linked to our consciousness of Japan's world-historical mission. But when we do so, the issue of moral character (*dōtoku-teki fūkaku*) becomes crucial. The potential greatness of the Japanese character can be brought fully into play if we can learn to become, as it were, what we are.[156] The same will apply, to an even greater degree, when we attempt to do the same for the varied peoples who will make up the Great East Asian Co-prosperity Sphere.

As for the issue of science we were just discussing, if we can affirm the world-historical significance of science [and technology], we can at the same time moderate the previous excessive bias towards science while curbing the reactionary prejudice against it. When a new form of humanity capable of world-historical action comes into being, the challenge of science will be reconceived as the outcome of the choices made by what will be a new form of man, one possessed of a world-historical character. The analogy would be the traditional samurai ideal, which conferred a moral character on the samurai while giving him the luxury of choice (*yoyū*), the scope and unhurried freedom to be what he was.

NISHITANI: I would like to say something here even though it is completely off the subject. I think that the task of constructing a Great East Asian Co-prosperity Sphere requires far more people than Japan's present population. There are simply not enough of us. Unless our population reaches 110 million sometime soon, this is not going to work. So we need to turn to the peoples and nations of the Co-prosperity Sphere, especially those blessed with superior qualities who thus have the potential to help us build our region together. Can't we find those who could be transformed [via training and education] into Japanese, at least partially (*han-nipponjin*)?[157] Obviously this is impossible for peoples such as the Chinese and Thais, because they already possess their own distinctive histories and cultures that have given them strong inner solidarity and a sense of unity (*dōhō-teki-na kankei*). By contrast, peoples such as the Filipinos lack a [sophisticated] culture they can call their own. In any case, Filipinos

---

156 Literally, if we permeate or, better still, percolate ourselves with our profounder inner self: *mizukara jibun no naka kara shimi dasite iku ookina Nihonjin no fūkaku*.
157 Political correctness would have us bridle at the implied condescension, but having bridled one is still left with the chaos of underdevelopment and the remediable personal qualities or deficiencies that cause it.

have been spoiled by the impact of American culture. This suggests they may be resistant (*toriatsukainikui*) [to the disciplines of modern life]. On the other hand, there are peoples who appear to lack the kind of defining culture of the Chinese and the Thais but do demonstrate exactly those superior qualities needed for the task of constructing this Co-prosperity Sphere. Take, for example, the Malays. I am not very knowledgeable about Malaya but the people appear to be quite remarkable (*sōtō yūshū*) ...

SUZUKI: Perhaps the Indonesians.

NISHITANI: Yes, one hears at least that they have really superior qualities. Haushofer has described the Malays as a nation of aristocrats (*kizokuteki minzoku*). It is even said by some that Japanese blood has been mixed with Malay blood. But my suggestion is that one might educate a people of excellent qualities with the potential to become what I call 'half-Japanese' provided one starts early enough. If my second-hand knowledge can be relied upon, the Moro people in the Philippines, for example, appear to possess the kind of qualities I am speaking about.

In a similar vein, I have heard that if one educates the Takasago they become indistinguishable from the Japanese.[158] Might this be the case? And note that by 'half-Japanese' I mean someone who can take on the values and spirit of the Japanese people until they are indistinguishable from us. Such an educational approach would offer a way of making up for the lack of Japanese numbers while at the same time providing the occasion for the moral awakening of these people [as a nation] and arousing their collective moral energies. As a policy proposal is this idea too shocking? Just a bit of amateurish speculation?

KŌSAKA: I accept that one can say Japan's population is too small. But having said as much, isn't it better to say that our numbers must be increased if we are to succeed in bearing the burdens of meeting our world-historical mission? Isn't this a proper way to put the matter?

SUZUKI: I, too, think that Kōsaka might be right here.

KŌSAKA: When it comes to devising practical policies for dealing with other peoples (*ta minzoku*), one can get things very seriously wrong unless one respects the various historical stages of development of each of the nations at issue. One has to be very cautious. Because it is the moment when one assumes one's place in world history.

---

158 A group of mountain aboriginal tribes on Taiwan that had been unassimilated by the Chinese administration prior to the Sino–Japanese War (1894–95). Known in Japanese as *Takasago zoku*, they were made the object of intense acculturation by the Japanese colonial authorities, apparently with considerable success. The *Takasago hei* proved to be outstanding soldiers in the Imperial Army and have been compared to the Gurkhas who served in the British armed forces.

III Five months after Midway
The third symposium

THE PHILOSOPHY OF WORLD-HISTORICAL WARS

A round-table discussion held on the evening of 24 November 1942 at Sa-aimi Maruyama, Kyoto

Participants: Masaaki Kōsaka, Iwao Kōyama, Keiji Nishitani and Shigetaka Suzuki

Table of contents

1 The historical context of world-historical wars (*sō ryoku sen*)
2 The concept of 'world-historical wars' (*sō ryoku sen*)
3 World-historical wars (*sō ryoku sen*) and total wars (*zentai sen*)
4 World-historical wars and the concepts of war and peace
5 The importance of wars of ideas (*shisō sen*)
6 Authority (*shidō*) and persuasion in ideological struggles
7 America and systems of total war (*sō ryoku sen*)
8 Dilemmas of a creative civil society (*minkan sōi*)
9 The ideal organizational structure for waging world-historical wars
10 Creativity and innovation in world-historical wars
11 The Co-prosperity Sphere and our world-historical war
12 Co-prosperity spheres (*Großräume*) and the philosophy of the nation (*kyōei-ken to minzoku no tetsugaku*)
13 Conceiving East Asia historically (*Tōa no kannen to rekishi-kan*)
14 The contradictions of Anglo-American liberty
15 The concepts (*gainen*) of 'co-prosperity' and 'morality'
16 The world-historical foundations of the national self-defence state (*kokubō kokka*)
17 The historical necessity for co-prosperity spheres as *Großräume* (*kyōei-ken to rekishi-teki hitsuzensei*)
18 Japanese subjectivity and our qualities of leadership (*Nippon no shutai-sei to shidō-sei*)
19 The historical character of subjectivity
20 The problem of military power (*senryōku*)

21 Scholarship (*gakumon*) and military power
22 The arts and military power
23 Concentrating our powers of military resistance (*senryoku no shūchū*)

1 The historical context of world-historical wars (*sō ryoku sen*)

KŌSAKA: It might be well to start our discussions by observing that it has been almost exactly a year since we debated the meaning of 'The Standpoint of World History and Japan' in this very room. In the past twelve months, the global situation has changed enormously. In this time of turbulence, Japan's place in the world has undergone an astonishing transformation. This has provoked, of necessity, a great deal of serious reflection. Furthermore, it is also true that the fundamental cause of this vast alteration in our circumstances is the conflict we are fighting, the Great East Asian War. This, too, cannot be denied. At each and every stage of the war during the past year, the shape of history has revolutionized itself. One is thus compelled to conclude that among the forces that mould history, none rivals the power of war.

Reflecting back on the past year of conflict, I have come to appreciate the unsparing ability of war to expose the truths of historical reality. When nations go to war, things one did not suspect about the reality of history are brutally brought to light. It is as if a powerful microscope has been focused on the facts of history. These are the truths that war delivers up to us. It is probably right to conclude that history teaches us what dynamic forces truly shape our world.

Just the same, even if these lessons about history are all that war has taught, the so-called Great East Asian War, as it unfolds within the phenomenon that is 'world-historical war' (*sō ryoku sen*), has revealed a degree of change undeniably as great as the altered face of history itself. Such is the impact of the intensity of this mobilization, which has no parallel in world history. At least, this is how it seems to me. But this is also why we must reflect afresh on what is involved in fighting a world-historical war (*sō ryoku sen*). So what does it mean to fight one? Perhaps the significance of this current total war may be illustrated [in part] by thinking about the way warfare evolves from age to age, as one epoch gives way to another ... what about this, Suzuki? Might you comment on the history of war as a set of classifications [that illustrate the continuous development of different kinds of warfare]?[1]

---

1 The shift of emphasis from the indirect acknowledgement of the potential for, perhaps even the likelihood of, a Japanese defeat to the more comforting realm of academic history is perhaps understandable, given the growing doubts about the likely outcome of the war so many months after Midway. Yet the long view – and this is the perspective that dominates this round-table discussion as it draws to its stoic conclusion – captivates. What was Japan's struggle likely to mean to future generations? What was its significance in the light of the long history of human warfare that preceded it?

SUZUKI: You want me to talk about the history of war?

KŌSAKA: If you would.

SUZUKI: I must confess that I have not really spent much time studying the history of war, but I believe that much of history, indeed most of it, is in fact a product of war. As Kōsaka notes in his essay 'The Metaphysics of War', which forms part of his book *The Philosophy of the Nation*, the dynamic of history is found in war, and this is a truth that cannot be dismissed.[2] War is history's most 'vital' force.[3] Via such conflicts, history tirelessly delves [into the truth of our condition]. Yet it also becomes apparent, if one examines the matter, that the traditional historical treatments of war have tended, in my view, to fall into a more or less fixed pattern. I have come to despise this approach as unsatisfactory. Because of this dissatisfaction with the traditional history of war I have found it very difficult to arouse any enthusiasm for studying the subject.

This is not to say that there have not been classic works on the history of warfare and military tactics, but my feelings about the nature of the war take a different cast. Looking at the example of Japan's current war, I wonder if it is really possible to grasp the essence of this struggle by resorting to traditional approaches. Even if conventional methods of study allow us to understand the external dimensions of the present struggle, the old interpretations are unable to explain the defining inner essence of the war. That is my view. Furthermore, as our country is in a state of war, it is not obvious to me that any historian contemplating writing a history of the present conflict now would be serving either the war effort or scholarship.

My conclusion is that it may be time to pass the torch back to philosophy. War requires a grounding in philosophy. This defines the intellectual need of our times; this is what the age calls for. For me this stands as the defining fact of our era. This is where the challenge lies. Interestingly, the past has produced almost no philosophies of war, or certainly very few, and that is where the fascination lies. Isn't this the case?

In other words, doesn't this philosophic need represent a special, perhaps unique, feature of the present conflict? And doesn't this need distinguish this war from its predecessors? Yet when one says 'the philosophy of war', almost inevitably the idea that first comes to mind is that of philosophic reflections on war in general: that is, the philosophy of war as a kind of philosophy of history. Kōsaka's 'The Metaphysics of War' is an example of this approach: the treatment of the idea of war in general in a metaphysical manner. In this sense, I think that it is possible to conceive of a philosophy of war. But I would like to address a different aspect of the problem: the philosophic compulsion that defines contemporary warfare. In other words, my emphasis is less on the

---

2 Masaaki Kōsaka, *Minzoku no Tetsugaku*, Tokyo: Iwanami Shoten, 1942.
3 The word 'vital' is transliterated from English.

idea of war in general and more on the essence of war today. It is this essence that demands a specifically philosophic understanding; it is this essence that serves as the foundation for the problem that travels under the name 'world-historical war' (*sō ryoku sen*). This supplies the foundation (*jiban*) from which it arises. The same motivation is equally alive in current calls for a 'self-defence state' (*kokubō kokka*).[4] In any case, these are my feelings on the subject.

KŌSAKA: Who could fault this interpretation? Are we not facing an enormous and irresistible, indeed world-historical, change in our contemporary world-view? Furthermore, this change in world-view is being mediated by war itself, or at least this transformation is unfolding in a parallel movement within this global conflict. Accordingly, this conflict is also an intense struggle between world-views. In other words, this is a war of philosophies. As Kōyama has observed, within this war there is another war being fought, in this sense: that we are witnessing a war that finds its broadest context in the shift from one world order to another.

SUZUKI: I think that this very much captures the nature of the present conflict. In any case, we have to return, as Kōsaka has argued, to the examination of history itself. Certainly there are no grounds for doubting that in every age war displays a profound inward connection with the structures of the age. If one thinks of an age of pre-artillery warfare such as the medieval period, that is the age of feudalism, politics and warfare are one and the same because the social order does not distinguish between the two activities. The question of whether feudalism is an economic system or a political system has been much debated, but I think that feudalism is best understood as a military system. Indeed, unless one accepts this fact, it is almost impossible to grasp, in any strict or precise sense, what feudalism is all about.

Nevertheless, I do not think one can therefore conclude that world-historical wars or a self-defence state derive their character from an essential unity of the political-economic system and the military. Indeed, I suspect total war as a system has unique characteristics. The failure to distinguish the military aspect of society from its political-economic structure is the distinguishing feature of primitive peoples, the ancient German tribes being the most classic example. The early Romans were another. But a *Militär-staat* or a state ruled by a military clique (*gunbatsu kokka*) and a self-defence state (*kokubō kokka*)

---

4 Literally, 'national defence state' or, more expansively, a state organized and led for the purpose of protecting the country. Either way, in its consonance with the stylistics and matter of national or elite mood just noted (see Note 1), the word 'defence' in the term *kokubō kokka* now almost leaps off the page, given the stage the war effort has reached here. In an age when what are now called ministries of defence were still called ministries of war, the transmutation of Japan's Pacific struggle into a defence effort is telling.

are different things.[5] Militarism and a world-historical war (*sō ryoku sen*) are, in my view, not the same thing at all.

Take, for example, the transition in Europe from medieval to modern society: that is, very roughly speaking, the change in the organization of society from a natural or barter economy to an economy characterized by monetary exchange. With the rise of conscription and the professional soldier, warfare becomes a full-time, specialized job, and this change is, in my opinion, inevitably tied up with the transition from medieval to modern society. Similarly, in China, the dominant thesis is that the shift from medieval to modern society involved the gradual separation of the soldier from the peasant. Again, to return to Europe, the move from the modern absolute monarchies to the popular or bourgeois states from the time of the French Revolution onwards resulted in the end of the professional caste army in favour of the mass army of the nation, of the whole people. This new form of military organization was of course the direct product of the French Revolution itself. The power of the new age was probably at work in what was regarded as a shocking fact: that a trained professional army of a foreign power could be crushed by a suddenly formed army of the people. The Napoleonic Wars were a natural extension and development of this revolutionary phenomenon. This transformation was not the work of Napoleon's leadership qualities alone. Rather, I think that the society of those times bred a new type of warfare, thus emphasizing the way warfare and the times are inwardly linked.

The reasons why contemporary warfare takes the form of world-historical wars (*sō ryoku sen*), and why there are pressing demands for a national defence state system, reflect the fact that the old order, the age of the modern, is facing destruction. States based on unregulated capitalism and bourgeois class rule are doomed; and this means the modern world-view also faces destruction. What is contemporary about contemporary war arises from this transformation. Isn't this where the roots of this kind of total war (*sō ryoku sen*) lie? But to explain the appearance of the phenomenon of world-historical wars (*sō ryoku sen*) as something arising from the course of history – that is, by thinking about war itself, and not just about the history of military tactics – one must conclude that contemporary technology has reached the required stage [of development]. In other words, because the technology of warfare has developed to its current superior level, warfare necessarily takes the contemporary form that total wars (*sō ryoku sen*) have. One often hears this explanation. It may be naïve of me, who has no experience of war, but I suspect that contemporary wars cannot be explained so easily, and therefore we may need to think a little more deeply about the issue. And that means brooding on the problem in ways that reach beyond the level of mere military technology.

---

5 The term *Militär-staat* is transliterated from the German. This analysis draws a line between what the Kyoto School advocates and the realities of military clique characteristics that in retrospect seem to define governance under Tōjō.

In other words, one's analysis should not be exhausted by the argument that mere changes in tactics, weapons and the scale of warfare have made total war inevitable. Rather, we need to focus on the changes in the structure of society, in the organization of the state, and in our view of the world to explain why the present time has become the age of this unique and unprecedented form of warfare. Isn't this the truth of the matter? I feel that we should dwell on this historical inevitability when we consider the temporal character of total wars as world-historical wars.

One may conclude that as history has witnessed a great number of wars, it is right and fitting that the theme of 'world history and war' be aired. But the issue I want to address is how contemporary total wars transcend all previous ideas of conventional warfare. Or, to put it a better way, broadly speaking, it is precisely at the point where modernity has stalled that world-historical war assumes its importance: world-historical war (*sō ryoku sen*) is the overcoming of modernity [and the modern nation-state].[6]

2 The concept of 'world-historical wars' (*sō ryoku sen*)

KŌYAMA: It might be possible to think about this problem in the following way. One side of this analysis holds that today's kind of total war is unprecedented, indeed unique, in the history of warfare. The other side requires that we rethink conventional definitions of war from the standpoint of world-historical war. These two insights might be brought together, I suppose, at the point where the theory of war squares up to history in the events of the contemporary world. In the widest sense of the term, we reach a turning point when in the midst of war we, who are mindful of historical values, confront something correctly judged to be a great history-making conflict. In the [very] words [we use to describe them], [truly] historic conflicts, that is, the kind of war that has the greatest impact on history, are already linked to turning points in world-view and in the social order in the broadest sense. The Napoleonic Wars just mentioned by Suzuki were such conflicts. Until the arrival of modern times, wars were fought in medieval manner by a caste of military professionals. By contrast, modern times have seen the rise of wars sustained by the whole citizenry of a nation. In the case of Japan, the Sainan War of 1877 saw a conscripted army of the sons of peasants and townspeople defeat an army of professional samurai. This outcome made this war a turning point in modern Japanese history. In this sense, the winning side was an army of all of the people, a national force. If we interpret this Japanese conflict in this manner, [we can see that] the appearance of such modern wars on Japanese soil was rooted in the historic transition from

---

6 The expression 'overcoming modernity' derives from Hegel and his successors, including Marx. It had some currency among the Japanese intelligentsia at the time, and it was taken as the title of another famous symposium held in Tokyo in July 1942.

feudality to modernity, and thus also in a revolution in world-views. The same may be said of the war that Japan is currently fighting. It, too, finds its foundation in another revolution or turning point in world-views. Indeed, unless we grasp this shift in world-views from the modern to the contemporary, it is almost impossible to conceptualize a convincing 'ideal type' of this kind of total war.[7] This is my conviction.

If we think along these lines then, as Suzuki noted above, we will gradually shift our understanding of war from one solely focused on tactics and strategy, the mechanics of war, to [one focused on] the history of warfare. By looking at the subject more closely, we will, as a matter of necessity, learn to interpret past wars in a more comprehensive and deeper manner. We must extend our perspective a little so it reaches beyond the role of the individual in war, beyond personalities and the notion that wars are won merely on the strength of a general's personality or greatness. This applies even to the [outstanding] feudal generals. A greater depth of understanding is clearly required.

With the emergence of a new kind of war – total war (*zentai sen*) or world-historical war (*sō ryoku sen*) – during the final phase of the Great War, it became possible to revolutionize our understanding of past forms of warfare. Aspects of the question that had been surprisingly neglected became [suddenly] easier to appreciate. This is where, I think, a new beginning can be made. In other words, today we can achieve a richer understanding of warfare than was previously the case. For example, a new depth of understanding – one that draws on the idea of total war (*sō ryoku sen*) and so allows one to assess the nature of conflict from this standpoint – has become apparent. That some observers proposed this [more] sophisticated mode of interpretation from the very beginning of Japan's struggle with China is evidence of this transformation.[8]

The forms of warfare change over time, but not every era wages what can be called 'total wars' (*zentai sen*). As has been frequently observed, ancient warfare was sustained, and waged, by the whole of a community. By contrast, professional armies arose in the medieval period to replace the soldier-peasant. Then in modern times, the whole population of the nation has once again learned to shoulder the burdens of war. It cannot be denied that these forms stand as the broadest classifications of warfare. Today, it seems reasonable to conclude that contemporary warfare, that is, total war (*sō ryoku sen*), should be regarded as an expansion and development of modern warfare which, we have noted, is sustained by the entire nation working together. Furthermore, this is where, I think, one must locate the unique structure and form of today's world-historical wars (*sō ryoku sen*). But here one must also note how

---

7 'Ideal type' in the sense that Max Weber used the term: a social phenomenon stripped of its factual particulars in order to be able to talk of, for example, the 'family' in general, in contrast to a particular family. Compare Plato's notion of an ideal triangle.
8 Kōyama uses the conventional period expression *Sina Jihen* or 'China Incident'.

in one very radical way this understanding departs from the definition of 'total war' (*zentai sen*) that General Ludendorff created at the end of the last great war [the First World War].[9]

This dissent from Ludendorff's definition remains crucial to appreciating the unprecedented character of contemporary world-historical wars (*sō ryoku sen*). When thinking about today's conflict, it is dangerously misleading to assume that the conventional definition of war applies: that is, a struggle beginning with a formal declaration of war and ending in a negotiated peace agreement, returning the situation to pre-bellum conditions. I stress this point because the traditional definition remains so influential. But today's conflict began in a decisively different way, and, furthermore, I do not believe that it will follow a conventional course.

Yes, of course, as a conflict of arms the Great East Asian War may have begun on 8 December 1941,[10] but the state of total war (*sō ryoku sen*) unambiguously came into existence when economic sanctions were enforced and trade relations were broken off. In other words, conventional definitions of war and peace do not to apply either to the Great East Asian War or the China Incident (*Shina Jihen*), which began, in effect, at the same time [1937]. Or at least that is how I think these conflicts should be understood.

Thus the suspicion arises that the present conflict may not end in a negotiated settlement, like the Great War or other modern conflicts. If the current struggle assumes this new form, any peace deal may be a temporary affair, thus suggesting, I suspect, that for some years afterwards the war might begin again. But that raises the question of when the war could finally be considered concluded. There has to be a point where one side or both reach a kind of limit to the armed struggle. But even [if it has to be done] by fighting off and on, the East Asian Co-prosperity Sphere can gradually, step by step, be built. Once this regional base is created, Japan will be invincible, even if the struggle should drag on for years or even decades. Of course, the United States may work hard to consolidate (*tsukuru*) its own kind of *Großraum* (*kōiki-ken*) in the Americas. But if it were to do so, that would prove our point, and highlight the validity of Japan's solution to the problem. That solution would come into being if our opponents were to accept, by force or

---

9   The most influential definition of the expression 'absolute war' comes from the Prussian soldier and military theorist Karl von Clausewitz (1780–1831), one of Europe's most influential thinkers on war in the age of Napoleon, while the term 'total war' is credited variously to General Ludendorff (or someone on his staff) or to interwar thinkers about the changing nature of war and peace such as Carl Schmitt or Baron Julius Evola. Ludendorff's *Der Totale Krieg* was published in 1935–36, while Schmitt's essay 'Totaler Feind, totaler Krieg, totaler Staat' and Evola's 'La Guerra total' appeared in 1937. Kōyama seems to use the two terms as if they were interchangeable.
10 The international dateline made the date of the Pearl Harbor attack 7 December in Hawaii but 8 December in Japan and the Western Pacific.

otherwise, the East Asian Co-prosperity Sphere as a pillar of a new world order. This would signal our [final] victory.[11]

By contrast, it is almost impossible for the present struggle to conclude, as it were, mid-term, as the Great War was brought to an end with the Versailles Conference. The two struggles are of entirely different character. In this contrast is to be found the world-historical significance of the current war as well as its real moral meaning. In other words, our present conflict must be the occasion for a turning point in our understanding of [world] order, and, as a result, a transformation in our world-view. This is my conclusion.

To summarize: it is of course extremely natural to seek to understand the present in the light of categories derived from the past, but this current war is of an entirely novel, indeed unique, character, and this truth must be grasped. This is an absolute necessity, if we are to understand what is unfolding.

SUZUKI: Let me see if I have this right. You regard the character of the present conflict as entirely clear. It is a contest between two different [world] orders. This is, I agree, a perfectly transparent fact, and thus beyond question. Furthermore, the type of war in question is a world-historical war (*sō ryoku sen*). Or, to reverse the argument, wars fought between nations that are parts of the same order are extremely limited in their significance because the countries at war share the same character or framework of values. Thus our struggle, as a war between different orders, involves much more than the simple rise or fall of this nation or that.[12] Here we find a genuine world-historical war. Is this the way you see the present conflict?

KŌYAMA: That is correct. In contrast to the Great War, fought between the Allied and the Central Powers, the struggle now is of a [radically] different character. The true agency of war is to be located not among the ranks of the individual nations, grouped as Allied or Central Powers, but in

---

11 Defeat could be avoided only if: 1 Japan acquired the ability to hold out for a stalemate against the United States by drawing on the strengths of East Asia as a whole; or 2 Japan could claim an intellectual victory by compelling the United States to imitate Japan by strengthening its own existing 'co-prosperity sphere', thus acknowledging the logic and truth of the Japanese approach. Kōyama may be suggesting, between the lines, that although defeat is a growing possibility Japan may survive to fight again, but to do so will require the material means to hold out against America's manifestly superior power. This can be achieved only if Japan builds a co-prosperity sphere, one grounded in genuine mutual support and cooperation between the member states. Hajime Tanabe makes this point in his lecture 'On the Logic of Co-prosperity Spheres', delivered on 29 September 1942, that is, seven weeks *before* this symposium. An English translation of Tanabe's lecture can be found in David Williams, *Defending Japan's Pacific War: The Kyoto School Philosophers and Post-White Power*, London & New York: RoutledgeCurzon, 2004, 188–99. Note that Kōyama is listed among those who attended Tanabe's secret presentation to the Navy.

12 Note, once more, that the possibility of defeat in war is suggested, and the struggle's significance is being projected above and beyond such an eventuality.

'co-prosperity spheres' [*Großräume*].[13] The combatants of the Great War were all imperialist powers, all part of the same imperial world order. They all shared the same world-view. This is why a 'compromise' solution was possible to end the war. The recognition of national interests was mutual; an 'understanding' was possible. But now world-views are in conflict. As a result, compromises over uncomplicated conflicts of interests are out of court. Compromise is impossible.

SUZUKI: I now understand very well what you are saying.

NISHITANI: I am in broad agreement with this interpretation. Most previous wars, even including those that signalled historical turning points, drew their origins, so it seems, from economic and political causes, without leaving any significant impact on the sphere of culture or world-view. Former wars were largely conflicts merely between princes and governments: that is to say, their decisive characteristic was as struggles between rulers. [*Editorial break*] ... There were of course the Crusades and wars between city-states ... but as noted above, since the time of Napoleon, wars have been conflicts between national states, and this represents a new form of warfare. Nevertheless, the Great War represented only an inferior form of this new form of warfare because it was imperialistic in character, a struggle to redistribute colonies and natural resources. That was the fundamental motive, and there its novelty ended. And while the Great War did mobilize entire peoples, it was finally about economics: the main motive arises in the main from the individual economic interests of the combatants. This is why the Great War can properly be judged as an imperialist struggle and nothing more.

To repeat: the war being fought now is utterly different. While it is certainly a war between peoples, entirely different motives, positive ones, are at work. In other words, it reaches beyond the mere survival of a single nation, linking the question of national survival to the task of building co-prosperity spheres and to creating a new world order. It would be fair to conclude that wars between whole peoples may be acquiring a new meaning. The choice may be between continuing the struggle to construct a co-prosperity sphere at the risk of the survival of the nation and failing to secure the nation's survival by not waging war and not building a secure co-prosperity sphere. This is what is new about the present war.

---

13 The real suggestion in this passage, read carefully, is that Japan cannot fight, let alone win, this war on its own, and therefore that a genuine co-prosperity sphere for East Asia must be fostered as the only effective means to stave off total defeat. The paragraph as a whole offers important parallels with Carl Schmitt's wartime assessment of Wilson's 1919 counter-revolution. By destroying the post-Westphalian European order, with its shared values and rejection of discriminatory warfare, the Versailles-Geneva system made compromise impossible, because liberal imperialism in the Wilsonian mode has no room for Japanese sovereignty or a form of East Asian cultural and political autonomy that only a *Großraum* can secure. All must comply, or be made to comply, with liberal universalism.

If wars from the time of Napoleon to the Great War were inevitably linked to national (*kokumin*) and ethnic (*minzoku*) consciousness, and inevitably required the total mobilization of national strength, today's conflict demands the transformation of this national consciousness into the consciousness of a world-historical people (*kokumin*). We must see the self-awareness of a nation with achieved subjectivity (*shutaiteki kokumin*) as capable of determining an order for the whole world. This is, without question, where the fundamental condition for the radically new significance of a total war (*sō ryoku sen*) or *totale Krieg*,[14] that is *zentai sen*, originates. Facing outwards, the [world-historical] nation seeks to transform the order of the world; facing inwards, the same nation reaches down into the depths of its own self-consciousness for the motivation to pursue this transformation.

In my view the most important issue arising from this [dialectic of awareness] is the need to reflect radically on the very idea that war is an abnormal or exceptional condition.[15] Take, for example, the conventional notions of ethics and world-view. Convention holds that correct ethics and sound world-views are the products of peacetime, and that during periods of conflict these [values] are temporarily abandoned: I think that in previous conflicts this has undoubtedly been true, hence the validity of the conventional view. On the other hand, one of the special features of the current struggle is that the conflict is in no way a temporary phenomenon. Isn't this the truth about the essence of the war? In just the same way, 'life' is judged to be as our normal state while 'death' is [nothing but] the interruption of this normal state – and yet, despite this way of thinking about life and death, in reality, in life there is death; this is the essential truth of the matter. Only in death do we first come to understand the real meaning of life. In the present conflict, peace and war are one continuous condition or circumstance: hence the feeling that some profound depth has been penetrated as we reach down to the foundations [of human existence]. After all, it was Nietzsche who declared that the next centuries would be characterized by endless conflict, that mankind was entering 'the classic era of war'. The implication of this is that there is a profound bond between the antebellum and wartime phases, and that the phenomena characteristic of peacetime loom large in wartime also. In other words, war assumes its completely total character (*honto no sō ryoku sen*).[16] Furthermore, in such total struggles one must not imagine that any uncomplicated return to some '*post-bellum ante*' [is possible] when the conflict comes

---

14 The phrase *totale Krieg* is transliterated from German.
15 Nishitani uses the expression *hentaiteki genshō*, which I have chosen to translate as 'abnormal', but Carl Schmitt's notion of 'exception' comes very close to the thrust of Nishitani's point while opening up the whole discussion to the interwar German discourse and its successor, the 'war on terrorism'. For an application of Schmitt's ideas to Japan, see David Williams, 'The Japanese Evasion of Sovereignty: Article 9 and the European Canon – Hobbes, Carl Schmitt, Foucault', in Rikki Kersten and David Williams, eds, *The Left in the Shaping of Japanese Democracy*, London and New York: Routledge, 2006, pp. 42–62.
16 Nishitani uses the expression *sō ryoku sen*, rendered here only by the word 'total'.

to end. One has to accept that the peacetime elements at work within the body of war itself continue to work their influence and develop even with the return of so-called peace. It is therefore the greatest error to assume that war is some form of abnormality. And it is precisely the failure to understand this [new reality] that makes it much more difficult to sustain a fight such as the present struggle. This is as true of the economic sphere as it is of the intellectual. Indeed, this can be said of all aspects of the conflict. To dream that the post-war period will witness a return to pre-war conditions makes it impossible for us to ignore our feelings of hesitation about committing ourselves to the scale and intensity of organized effort required for this kind of war ... in contrast, those who sustain the political dimension of the struggle must understand that the form and structure of the war effort can, in my opinion at least, only be thought through on the basis of a complete acceptance of the notion that war and peace form a continuum in such struggles.[17]

3 World-historical wars (*sō ryoku sen*) and total wars (*zentai sen*)

KŌYAMA: The present conflict has developed from a 'total war' (*zentai sen*) into a 'world-historical war' (*sō ryoku sen*), thus in the end transforming our conventional understanding of war by transcending it. The present conflict cannot be understood using previous notions of war. It has surpassed all previous limits. Hitherto, concepts of war have taken battlefield struggle as their pre-eminent focus and core. The battlefield is not necessarily the decisive dimension of the present conflict because world-historical wars themselves form the decisive ingredient of the whole business.

SUZUKI: It was precisely that point that I was struck by when reading Ludendorff. His book *Der Totale Krieg* made powerful reading, especially as he experienced such bitter times as one of the more extraordinary leaders of the Great War.[18] He has a very forceful manner of expression. He is a classic stylist. The book was extremely interesting and I was very much moved by it. Nevertheless, there is a significant limitation to his work because he conceives *total wars solely from the vantage point of the battlefield.*[19]

KŌYAMA: I do not think Ludendorff's viewpoint is very useful when we try to imagine the ideal [type] of organization and structure necessary to wage a world-historical war like the one occurring now.[20]

SUZUKI: One cannot simply borrow an *Idee* from the experience of the Great War when one wants to form a proper *Idee* of the present conflict. The

---

17 Nishitani uses the expression *sensō taisei*, meaning war system or structure or organization.
18 As noted above, *Der Totale Krieg*, Ludendorff's assessment of the German effort in the First World War, appeared in 1935–36.
19 Italics in the original.
20 I think the 'ideal' Kōyama is talking about here is very close to Max Weber's notion of 'ideal type'. It is certainly a Weberian notion with which Kōyama would have been familiar.

world has changed so much since then. The work and purpose of warfare have altered. Our very subject matter has been transformed.

KŌSAKA: This repeats some of what Nishitani just observed, but I think that most previous wars have been fought with the intention of reaching a post-war settlement approximately similar, *mutatis mutandis*, to that which prevailed before the war, regardless of how badly the old equilibrium was shaking or even whether the conflict [all but] destroyed the previous order.[21] In other words, most wars are conservative in character. But today's conflict is entirely different. The fundamental thrust is towards the creation of an entirely new order. Thus, there can be no return to pre-war conditions via a peace settlement: on the contrary, something new will be born. In this sense the war is not conservative but creative or constructive (*kensetsu sure*). But this also means that this is not just a battle of arms but a total struggle.[22] While fighting, one builds [the future]; while building, one fights.

KŌYAMA: This is what is innovative about world-historical wars.

NISHITANI: Recent calls for war or construction assume these are entirely separate activities, but such urgings are misguided because they are not persuasive examples of joined-up thinking.[23]

KŌSAKA: Struggling on a single front of what is obviously a two-front war is self-defeating.

NISHITANI: The urge to see these dimensions as separate suggests a latent determination to view world-historical wars as [merely] conventional wars in the traditional sense. In reality, because such wars contain a creative or constructive dimension in their very essence, it is impossible to regard construction and fighting separately.

SUZUKI: For example, it follows therefore that if we understand the order of the nineteenth century to be an order of nation-states, then the wars of that period can be understood as consonant with that order. In other words, clashes within the nineteenth-century system of modern states were about political and economic interests, not about creating a new order of nation-states. It also follows that the peace agreements that ended those conflicts involved the preservation of the same order of nation-states. As all conflicts are settled within the same order, the order itself does not change, and that is why such wars could be satisfactorily ended

---

21 For example, the imperative of the post-Westphalian European order until its destruction in 1919 was the redressing of any dangerous imbalance in the balance of power.
22 Kōsaka is suggesting two things simultaneously. One is that there is so much at stake that the significance of the war goes beyond the practical battlefield struggle. More telling still, he is hinting that even though the battlefield struggle may be lost, the conflict is of a nature that will ensure it continues to unfold even should Japan be forced to surrender.
23 Nishitani does not use the italics and his idea is expressed much more simply and directly than my rendering here. He says that war is best regarded as but one aspect of the problem of institution-building (*kensetsu*). This is what he says, but that simple statement does not quite capture the momentous nature of the issue being discussed.

with peace treaties. However, our present conflict is a struggle to overturn the existing order – it is a conflict between different orders – and therefore it is almost inconceivable that it will end in the same manner as past wars. And [part of the reason] why it cannot end conventionally is because it involves, of necessity, an [ongoing] constructive dimension [that will outlast the armed struggle].[24]

KŌSAKA: It follows that while the idea of 'total war' or *sō ryoku sen* may have been coined in Germany, it is Japan that has put this idea [understood as 'world-historical war'] into practice. Isn't this the case?

KŌYAMA: I am entirely in agreement with all of this. It is my conviction that it is Japan that is endeavouring to fight a world-historical war in its purest form (*risō-teki*). If we think through and take to heart the supreme imperative of today's world-historical war, the [ideals of] what is called the 'Japanese way of war' (*Nippon sensō-ron*) or 'war for the emperor' (*kō-sen*) can be realized [in an unrivalled manner]. For me, a war fought for the emperor has a special meaning. Rather than attempting to determine the significance of this ideal via a transcendental or *a priori* notion such as the so-called 'Japan principle', the ideal of an imperial war must be realized by the resolute execution of the absolute imperatives that arise from today's struggle itself. This is my view anyway.[25]

SUZUKI: At all events a world-historical war is more than, for example, a struggle in which the general population is made to participate via mass conscription or the payment of war taxes. And of course it involves maximum mobilization of our most sophisticated technological and scientific resources, indeed full exploitation of all our resources and productive output. But even all of these factors taken together do not make a particular conflict a world-historical war (*sō ryoku sen*), for that term has a still profounder meaning and significance. Because such a war is historical.

The whole planet finds itself trapped in an order that is everywhere deadlocked. Therefore everything must change. The vehicle for this transformation of everything is a world-historical war. In the economic sphere, we must move from liberal capitalism to a planned economy. The structure of the state must change. The entire system must change. Our world-view must change. The entire foundations of the nineteenth century are being destroyed. These changes reflect the workings of [historical] necessity. The truth of the matter is

---

24 Like Kōyama just before him, Suzuki plays on ambiguities that allow him to imply that even if Japan loses the war and concludes, for example, an unequal peace, the struggle will not be over. But furthermore the emphasis is on the constructive dimension as the larger goal calls into question the brutal methods of the Imperial Army, most damagingly in China. The Kyoto School's vision of a regional partnership demanded that the interests of all members be served.

25 Kōyama's argument is so nuanced, bold and subversive as to defy translation. Note that Kōyama wraps his plea in the compelling idioms of sweat, struggle and intensity, as he must if his argument is to ring emotionally true in Japanese ears.

that our own war forms the centre of this storm of global transformation. And that struggle we call 'a world-historical war'. This is how I understand the challenge. The expression 'world-historical war' is shorthand for the transformation of everything. And such struggles cannot be understood merely as 'wars' or matters merely of military tactics.

NISHITANI: Pushing the argument further, one must stress the importance of not being misled by the word 'war' in the expression 'world-historical war'. It encourages too narrow an interpretation, because the current struggle is a much deeper and profounder a struggle [than mere war].

KŌSAKA: That is what I feel.

NISHITANI: As I noted earlier, world-historical wars eliminate the distinction between 'war' and 'peace'. Therefore, the distinctions conventionally drawn between military strength, the economy and culture also vanish. This is because war as a form of action becomes self-conscious, thus drawing up its powers from that deep place where all such conventional distinctions disappear. Therefore, war as the essence of our power demands a formulation that transcends the narrow scope of 'war' plain and simple, and this [transcendent] idea, the thing that follows a war, might be called [not 'peace' but] the 'post-war'.[26]

KŌSAKA: This is my 'take' on what is being said. As noted before, world-views are changing or indeed have changed. If we advance our ideas a bit, the suggestion would be that the world-view of our opponents will undergo change as well. This ideological struggle [between world-views] is part and parcel of world-historical wars. On the other hand, in another sense, the idea of a battle of ideas reduced to a propaganda war almost inevitably conjures up the idea of using special techniques or strategies to deceive a capable opponent, but this is not what I am proposing ...

SUZUKI: That is probably consistent with the line of thinking I was pursuing ...

KŌSAKA: If that is the meaning of a 'war of ideas' (*shisō sen*), we have to change it.

KŌYAMA: I suspect that the war ideals of Britain and America exhaust themselves at about that level, don't they? But if we let our ideals stop there, I don't think this will do.

Nishitani has proposed treating the notion of 'war' as a concept, and I just noted that we have now finally completed the transition from the previous total war [of 1914–18] to the world-historical war we are now fighting. The present struggle has, I think, effectively overwhelmed all the conventional

---

26 This argument may qualify as a Kyoto School response, conscious or otherwise, to ideas that developed in continental philosophy and theory from the 1930s onwards of *posthistoire* or post-philosophy or the postmodern, all of which play to the notion that history or philosophy or modernity is to be at once transcended and preserved for the future.

notions of warfare that have previously mattered. This ties in with the idea of a self-defence state (*kokubō kokka*) that has attracted so much comment of late.

The concept of a self-defence state is not the same as that of 'a nation in a state of war' (*senji kokka*) or a military state (*gunji kokka*). In the same way, world-historical wars are not mere struggles of arms. Nevertheless, having said all that, the necessity of linking a 'world-historical war' with a 'national defence state' reflects a relationship brought to the fore by the current turning point [in the war] as a trial of military strength. This situation has made the connection between these two ideas – one has merely to mention the one to evoke the other – into a paramount national concern. But it is essential to note that, even if one assumes that we have reached the stage where the military struggle has emerged as the dominant concern, it does not follow that this conflict will be followed by a new stage in which peace prevails. Much more probably, this military phase will be followed by an economic or diplomatic struggle to be fought out in a context where the battle of arms no longer occupies the foreground but in which war, as it were, forms the backdrop. Other spheres of contention may become prominent over time, the point being that how a world-historical war is contested depends on the overall objective conditions of the struggle at any particular time – and I think these will vary with circumstance. But it is from this fact of [inseparable] war and peace that concepts such as world-historical war and a national defence state arise. It is such contemporary notions that distinguish the quality of our ideas from the modern notions of warfare and the state that taint the intellectual defence of the old order proposed by Britain and America.

4 World-historical wars and the concepts of war and peace

NISHITANI: World-historical wars are obviously the products of wartime. Thus, for example, the construction of a co-prosperity sphere must be directly linked with the domestic war system if the dramatic increase in our war-making powers that is vital in any contemporary world-historical war is to be achieved. From this necessity we may conclude that any purely military struggle must also draw on the fruits of peacetime creativity and development (*kensetsu*). Or, to reverse the logic, all peacetime activity has a potential connection to wartime. The result is a contemporary version of the Japanese expression 'the arts of peace and war are one' (*bunbu itto*). But with this unity between wartime and peacetime in mind, doesn't the very term 'national defence', as reflected in notions such as 'national defence state' or 'national defence economy', sound somehow negative and narrow, especially in the context of a world-historical war? Certainly I feel that a more positive notion is required when one addresses the challenge of building (*kensetsu*) the Great East Asian Co-prosperity Sphere. The creative perspective that informs the essential nature of a world-historical war demands a more positive and comprehensive approach.

SUZUKI: I agree. These defensive notions lack the power to properly motivate and inspire.
KŌYAMA: Even during the Era of the Warring States they did not fight throughout the year.
SUZUKI: I support the idea of eliminating the distinction between war and peace. But I think that it also follows from this that we need a new concept to replace this distinction. Although I should note that some professor bawled me out when I tried to talk about this problem ... (*laughing*). Do you think it is now safe to talk about it?
KŌSAKA: You were told off? What cheek.
SUZUKI: It was not quite a telling off. More like a light kick. I thought I had explained what I was thinking well enough ... (*Everyone laughs.*)

[*Unexplained editorial deletion.*]

SUZUKI (*CONTINUING*): I was thinking about history ... or in any case about war, and the only conclusion I could come to was that war will last as long as history. War is the dynamic force that drives history. The disappearance of war, factually speaking, is absolutely unthinkable. One can only conclude from this that ideas such as 'the war to end war' are merely dreams. When one hears expressions such as this, one is left wondering what the cause of war is, and then concluding that the cause of war is peace. Among historians, Burckhardt is the one who most seriously came to grips with the problem of war. That is exactly what Burckhardt thought. In other words, the [human] condition without war is unimaginable. Not only that, war is a necessity; it is eternal. Particularly in the light of our earlier discussions about the elimination of the distinction between war and peace, isn't it reasonable to conclude that the notion that war should be waged eternally is precisely the kind of understanding that is necessary today?[27]

In general, it is held that one fights wars to win peace. This was particularly true of the Great War. It was the war fought to end all wars. That was the idea. And this ambition was embedded in the Versailles peace treaty, and became its foundation. Furthermore, this same idea opened the way to the

27 Lest one leap to the conclusion that these Kyoto School thinkers have abandoned themselves to abstract follies or become armchair militarists or Italian Futurist warmongers, the timing of these discussions makes it clear that *at one level* such abstract treatment is resorted to as a way of encouraging their readers not to despair even though the tide of the Pacific War is now running against Japan. This is the Kyoto School's way of talking publicly about battlefield realities in a manner that keeps the censor at bay. But the argument also unfolds on another level: war must be waged eternally because a liberal peace which 'means the end of all hostilities' (Kant) also implies that no state has the right to defend itself against a liberal imperium; so the only way for sovereignty to be protected is to fight until the liberal order is overturned.

arms reduction conferences that followed. It was in this manner that a war fought as war and for military reasons was transformed into a war that was fought for peace. That was the cry raised at the time. The conventional definition of war has sought the reasons for making war in ambitions for attaining peace, and has done so as a matter of [perceived] necessity. This [definition] is insufficient to our [present] needs. Doesn't this represent one of the great [conceptual] weaknesses of the conventional idea of war? The implication would be that war itself lacks definition *an sich*.[28] That is how I arrived at my idea of 'eternal war' … (*laughter*) … Now, having said this, I have been told authoritatively I shouldn't … I think the problem was that I could not get him to understand what I meant by 'eternity'. Or, to put the matter more seriously, to assert that wars will continue without limit does not really address the issue of what eternity means in this context. To say only that something continues indefinitely into the future is not in any way to justify defining it as 'eternal' [in the strict philosophic sense]. If one holds this strict position, I can only concede the point. It wasn't that I had failed to understand what eternity meant; it was that I had not understood the implications of eternity for my argument. Eternity is something deeper, more profoundly absolute. In other words, if we are really going to think about war from the standpoint of eternity, then it follows that this [the present conflict] is the last war in the absolute sense of the term. It will be decisive because this war is the last war. But what I was calling the 'last war' does not qualify as this kind of truly absolute conflict that has to be fought to achieve decisive resolution against an obstructed self-consciousness. And that is why I was scolded (*laughter*).

Putting that whole business to one side, however, I believe that the conventional claim of Anglo-Saxon propaganda that the Americans and the British are fighting a war for peace – much as they claimed they fought the Great War to resist German militarism was an attempt to [conceptually] ground war simply in the notion of peace – is not a persuasive idea. This is a concept that cannot work. It will not be any more successful than the disarmament conferences after the Great War. These conferences reflected a superficial, indeed ethically sentimental, attitude towards war. At best, these ideas reflect a certain passivity of mind. At worst, they are merely negative [denials of reality]. In order to avoid the destructiveness of war, the search was for methods [of conflict resolution] that did not require war. But one cannot prevent wars by merely limiting the weapons of war. Or, to put it more bluntly, war itself cannot be legislated out of existence, and the failure of this disarmament effort proves it. From this fiasco I conclude that the Anglo-Saxon idea of peace as a cure for war is fundamentally flawed. War cannot be prevented by arguing that it is destructive. This is the truth of war. Conflict is

---

28 Suzuki uses the term *an sich* in German and translates it into Japanese as *soku ji teki*. Despite the well-developed contrast, from Fichte to Sartre, between *an sich* ('in itself') and *für sich* ('for itself'), here the reference is closer to Kant's 'thing itself'.

unrivalled in its capacity for revealing the truths of history, as Kōsaka has argued in his essay 'The Metaphysics of War'. This is the way war should be understood. This approach encourages us to think better and more deeply about the nature of war. Might this be the case?

KŌSAKA: I think there is scope for this in what I have tried to propose. Given pause by that 'kick' you mentioned, I have been reflecting a little more carefully about what may have been unclear in my proposition. If the 'eternalization' of war meant nothing more than that, then obviously the idea had to be rejected. In the same way that the idea of eternal peace is a fiction, so there are limits to the idea of eternal war, limits arising from the realities of human nature. Nevertheless, might not the concept of war itself be understood in the light of the amended definition proposed by Suzuki, that is, not in terms of the eternalization of the conventional definition of war – definitely not that – but rather by viewing war and peace as conflicting ideas that are mutually transcending [in the Hegelian sense]: that is, as a concept incorporating a new creative and constructive dimension? How about that? At the least, this approach opens the way towards a better understanding of the shape of wars hereafter, while invalidating traditional approaches to thinking about the subject.

KŌYAMA: This may sound like a rather abrupt intervention in our argument, but isn't war, in its essence, about 'leadership' (*shidō*)? In this sense, isn't it about deciding things? Without in any way diminishing the significance of the world-historical war we are now fighting, I think it can be reduced to this idea.

SUZUKI: Explain a bit more, please.

5 The importance of wars of ideas (*shisō sen*)

KŌYAMA: If one tries to examine, for example, our current struggle as a war of ideas (*shisō sen*), things are much as treated above. Thus the character of the current conflict, its strategic essence if you will, is entirely different from the propaganda wars that were so prominent a feature of the Great War, certainly from the ideological claims that emerged from about the middle of that conflict until its conclusion. This difference arises, again as we have observed above, because the present struggle is a turning point or transition between two world-views. Furthermore, as world-views are the very stuff of ideas, such struggles [between world-views] give this ongoing conflict its fundamental nature as a 'war of ideas'. Unlike Japan, neither Britain nor the United States entered this war with so bold a purpose [as altering the order of the world in the light of a new world-view]. Nor indeed are they now fighting this war with such an end in mind. When this war finally comes to an end, whenever that is, it will reach a decisive conclusion only when the enemies of this new world order [that is implied in this new world-view], both recognize [that is, see themselves in] its novelty and are persuaded of its merits. When that recognition comes, America and Britain will have been defeated.

Now, it goes without saying that one demonstrates one's powers by defeating one's enemy on the battlefield; but the form of persuasion that matters is intellectual. In the same manner, it is not enough to convince our opponents of the rightness of our cause by waging a [successful] world-historical war. Indeed, on the domestic front, the heights of this war of ideas must be climbed, through the realms of ideas, economics, politics, education, etcetera, to demonstrate the superiority of this new order of ideas over the standpoint of its *passé* rival. Only then will we begin to be able to exploit the limitless advantages that are the inevitable fruit of world-historical wars. Or, to reverse the proposition, if we fail in the task of persuasion, this world-historical war is not winnable. In other words, it is only by transformative revolution in the realm of ideas, on both the home and the foreign front, that the genuine meaning of the current struggle will become apparent. This is the true meaning of the war of ideas that must be grasped. The goal of such a war is, of course, not to find friends among the powers that oppose us. It aims for something profounder: the transformation of enemies into friends. And how might this be possible? The answer is: by converting them, genuinely and persuasively, to our point of view. By contrast, if we aim merely for some form of relative ...

SUZUKI: On this subject, I think that is the crucial issue. To seek to persuade the enemy of the soundness of our cause does not mean deceiving him. Our foes must be convinced. That is point of wars of ideas. To persuade one's opponent is intellectually to master him.

KŌYAMA: But how is one genuinely to convince an opponent? Take the contrasting ideas of 'good' and 'evil'.[29] There is the Hinayana approach,[30] which asserts the elimination of evil as a practical impossibility. If one eliminates evil and it seems that the problem has been solved, one discovers a minute later that evil demonstrates its infinite capacity for rebirth. Evil is inexhaustible. Only the law can eradicate evil.

To make the wicked really disappear, one needs to assume the relativizing standpoint of Mahayana Buddhism,[31] from which, at it were, one looks down on 'good' and 'evil', negating evil, of course. But from this relativizing vantage one distinguishes the 'evildoer' from the 'evil' because one is able to 'lead' or 'guide' the wrongdoer [away from his mistaken path]. In order fundamentally to eliminate evil, one must assume a transcendental standpoint, that is a standpoint that rises above the conflict between good and evil, and this means

---

29 Kōyama uses the expression *sōtai*.
30 *Shōjō Bukkyō* or Buddhism of the Lesser Vehicle, a byword for narrow-mindedness in Japan.
31 By contrast, *Daijō Bukkyō* or the Buddhism of the Greater Vehicle evokes broad-mindedness.

one must agree with the Mahayana position. When one identifies 'a relationship in conflict', this involves, in the case of good and evil, a trial of 'strength'. But via such trials of strength alone it is impossible to transform the evildoer into a good person, a doer of [only] good. When the first step towards the good is taken in the struggle between good and evil, the struggle towards goodness still remains. One is left with the good of *haja* or the destruction of evil.[32] But if this struggle can be elevated to a new dimension, it becomes possible to guide the wicked. The opportunity will appear. It is at this phase that the 'evil' of the evildoer can finally be eliminated, thus allowing him to resume being a 'person' in order to be a 'good person'. This is how I view the process.

If one thinks along these lines, one can understand how it might be possible to transform an enemy into a friend, and thus completely eliminate [what is threatening in] the enemy by altering his essence. This is the standpoint at work in the notion of guidance or leadership in Mahayana Buddhism. In this connection there is no necessity to cite the example of Takuan.[33] This idea has been discussed here in Japan for centuries by a variety of people. Taking one's sword in hand, only a weapon with the power of life and death can really destroy one's opponent. It is this truth that Americans and the British are incapable of grasping. But the Japanese can, I believe, realize this high ideal. In arguing this, it is my opinion that the Japanese spirit and Japanese character can inform, as it should, the contemporary struggle of ideas that forms part of our world-historical war.

The goal of wars of ideas is to persuade one's opponent entirely of the soundness of one's position. But this goal, which is in effect the first step towards gaining mastery over one's enemy, cannot be achieved, as writers such as Clausewitz have argued, by annihilating them, for the simple reason that annihilation is not possible. Indeed, the idea of annihilation is not one of Europe's most attractive ideas.[34] By contrast, we have the fundamental idea of war that is of a kind of leadership or guidance given direction from a higher standpoint. To guide or lead a person is to move him with the essence of truth; without the truth one cannot lead because one cannot persuade. To capture the mind with the power of words and authentic insight is to persuade. Force is not the means; violence is not the answer. Accordingly, the new ideas called for today must aim to achieve more than satisfying one group or another here at home. No, these ideas must boast the power to persuade friend and foe alike. Indeed they must be able to persuade the whole world. Only if they are true can they achieve this. As if this were not enough, it also goes without saying that a group of ideas that exhibited no powers but

---

32 From the expression *haja-kenshō* or the destruction of wickedness and the establishment of righteousness.
33 Takuan (1573–1645): famous Zen master who first became a Buddhist priest of the Jōdo sect. Over a long and eventful life he acquired a national reputation for his practised virtue.
34 Kōyama describes annihilation as a 'low' idea, as in the sense of high ideals and low conduct.

the ability to satisfy some particular domestic group or interest would be utterly incapable of winning the surrender of a foe in the war of ideas.[35]

Our current world-historical war is a war of ideas. If we are to wage this great struggle, this true war, the idea of leadership [set out above] must be our most fundamental [guiding] principle. In other words, the true goal of this war is to make our opponents accept our new order by persuasion. Won't this stand as the fundamental principle that underpins the notions cited earlier of a 'holy war' or 'war for Japan' (*Nippon sensō*)? Whatever anyone else may believe, I accept this as a matter of conviction.

The issue of war and peace was raised earlier. These paired cognate ideas – war/peace or conflict/harmony – were considered apart, as separate [independent] things.[36] But the consequence of thinking in this way – establishing a rigid division between pacifism and the glorification of war – does not provide a set of ideas capable of grasping the genuine nature of conflicts either past or present. Trapped in logical [but actually simplistic] distinctions that hold that war is war and peace is peace, one misses the truths visible from a higher perspective. The so-called 'pacifist' can do nothing but despair when forced to confront the reality of war. As for the idea of eternal peace, it is something that stands outside history or must await the 'end of days'. It anticipates our arrival at the far shore after death. These ideas may be products of our brains but they have nothing to do with reality. They provide us with no way of shaping (*shidō sure*) reality as it is. The argument may be reversed. Thus the advocate of war may approach the issue in the same manner as the pacifist, and commit the same error. In other words, both sides remain at the primitive stage of binary opposites in which struggle/harmony or war/peace are in conflict as [mere] opposites between which one must choose, advocating one or the other. But if war, in its true essence, is a matter of leadership or guidance, this simplistic binary conflict is eliminated. Rather, one must see the soundness (*yoi*) of harmony (*wa*) and the 'struggle' (*sen*), that is in world-historical wars (*sen*). True harmony is not the opposite of war.[37] The greatest harmony is the Great Harmony (*Taiwa/Yamato*).[38] This is the place where

---

35 This entire paragraph may be convincingly read as an attack on the Tōjō ruling clique and its ultranationalist supporters.
36 Visions of Derrida.
37 Harmony as the (binary) opposite of conflict is a paired idea, but genuine harmony in itself is not.
38 This sentence contains so many hints and allusions as to be over-determined in its meaning. The first contrast is between domestic-grade harmony and its profoundest expression (*wa* versus *taiwa*). *Taiwa* literally means 'great harmony' as the expression occurs, for example, in *The Book of Changes* or *I Ching* (*Yi Jing*). More important, given the context, is that ancient Japan was known as *Yamato*, which came to be written in the same characters as *Taiwa*. Hence the sentence might be rendered as 'Japan is Japan' or, more suggestively, 'The greatest harmony is Japan'. One interpretation holds that Japan can only be the greatest harmony if it embodies not the virtues of aggressive war but those associated with the highest idealism of *shidō* or guidance and (moral) leadership. The *locus classicus* is again *The Analects*, Book XII, 19. See also *Mencius*, III, A. 2.

the conflict between notions of war and peace is resolved. Here is where we find that great good place where the arts of war and peace achieve their complete reconciliation [because they are transcended]. In the end, warfare is more than a military struggle. It involves a whole set of other spheres. But this is obvious only when viewed from that high vantage from which all things reveal their genuine place in the totality of things.

Faced with the issues of military struggle or war, the pacifist immediately judges them as something unethical (*han-dōgiteki*), but this is not a sound approach. If the pursuit of war is informed by genuine notions of 'leadership' and 'guidance', human struggle may acquire a moral meaning. The principle involved may not be consistent with conventions of personal ethics or the moral character of the individual (*jinkakushigi-teki rinri*) but the resulting conduct is morality in its proper sense. What do you all think of this line of argument?

KŌSAKA: I think it works. On the meaning of 'leadership' or 'guidance', I wonder if there is another way of saying what you mean. When the enemy is persuaded of the validity of our ideas [of the world], he changes his mind because he has previously found his path obstructed, and therefore he is ready to accept [another view of his circumstances]. Thus he arrives at our view, which offers a way of helping him solve his problem, and thus save himself. Indeed, I think we must see this as an occasion not for us to save him but for him to save himself. One cannot expect our foes to be persuaded by propaganda or rhetoric, but only by the truth. How could it be otherwise? The essential power of a war of ideas is to be found in the truth of a set of ideas that makes possible the salvation of human existence itself. It is in this sense that the qualities of leadership or guidance we bring to this conflict are finally about saving those we fight ... [39]

KŌYAMA: That is the real meaning of 'winning our place' in the world (*tokoro o eru*).

KŌSAKA: At the same time, the significance of the Great East Asian War must not be reduced to an act of revenge for the invasion, exploitation and oppression of the East by the nations of Europe.[40] It cannot mean just that. This would be entirely out of keeping with the great ideals of our 'war for the emperor' (*hōsen*).[41] Of course, the notion that

---

39 Thus all ideological conflicts within a national community in East Asia tend to end in re-education camps. The Confucian aims to convert the recalcitrant, not to punish or kill. Liberal imperialism, by contrast, judges its foe as essentially 'unjust': thus any act of terror may be unleashed on him to push his society to the edge of extinction (cf. 'killing a nation': Curtis LeMay's 1949 definition of total war), so as to ensure unconditional acquiescence in the liberal transformation.

40 Whatever the sins of Western imperialism, such criticism may equally be applied to the brutality of the Imperial Japanese Army. The sword of Kyoto School criticism was double-edged for those who read these pages with attention.

41 Another example of the Kyoto School criticizing Tōjō policies in the name of the highest Japanese ideals, thus seizing, or attempt to seize, control of the discourse of the war.

punishments should fit the crime has a legitimate official (*ōyake*) meaning. In any case, the word 'revenge' is used here in its narrower meaning, as in the expression, 'I take revenge for past wrongs'. By contrast, here the intent is to save one opponent from the obstructed path of evil. To kill [some] in order to save [the rest] is an insight of Buddhism of the Greater Vehicle. Isn't this the way – I for one think it is – of coming to a genuine persuasion of one's opponent?[42]

SUZUKI: This in fact is very much how I felt when I wrote the essay 'World History and the British Empire' which I included in my *The Idea of a World-historical State*.[43] While it is a fact that Britain and America have exploited East Asia, to make war on these nations in order to avenge such injuries would be mere petty-mindedness. [But] Britain is more than just Britain because it has created the Anglo-Saxon world order. This [order] is what we must fight. It is this that makes our struggle a war of [competing] orders. We are not fighting for material gain. The point of my essay was to expose the true significance of the Anglo-Saxon world order. Then, when the Great East Asian War suddenly began, and Japan simultaneously made enemies of America and Britain, I felt that a kind of [national] *karma* was subtly at work.[44] [In any case], we are not fighting against the United States and Britain, but against the Anglo-Saxon world order ...

6 Authority (*shidō*) and persuasion in ideological struggles

NISHITANI: Might this theme perhaps be broached in another way? Let me begin with something I mentioned earlier. In general it is held that world-historical wars have come into being with the development of national (*kokumin ishiki*) or ethnic consciousness (*minzoku ishiki*). But the wars that nation-states fight tend to be dominated by economic motives: to capture colonies or markets or natural resources; so if the discussion is confined solely to the nation-state (*kokumin kokka*), then wars of imperialism as a classification of warfare come into being. By contrast, the war we are now waging is not a struggle of Japan as merely one nation-state among many. Another order of significance is involved, because the war is being fought between what one might term world-historical peoples or between national popular states (*minzoku no kokka*) which can claim

---

42 Again, the relevant comparison may be the notion that Japan had to be bombed to crush its militaristic spirit, and thus make it ripe for a new liberal order. But even this democratic aspiration falls short of the generous Great Vehicle stance.
43 Suzuki Shigetaka, *Rekishi-teki Kokka no Rinen*, Tokyo: Kōbundo Shodo, 1941.
44 I think the term Suzuki uses here, *shukumei-teki*, might be more accurately rendered as 'fated' or 'destined', but because of the way Buddhism loosely frames this phase of the discussion I have used the term 'karma'. Often tough and uncompromising, Suzuki's language is now resigned, even doom-laden.

world-historical significance. In other words, our present war is best understood as a struggle between world orders.

If we accept this perspective, this interpretation will include ideas such as those just proposed by Kōyama. If the whole world, including our enemies, is to be convinced of the soundness and propriety of this new order, we must extol a sound form of morality (*tadashii dōgisei no kenyō*[45]) to enhance the persuasiveness of this intellectual system we propose to develop (*kensetsu*). This necessity applies simultaneously to Japan and to the world outside our borders. It is my view that the state in the broadest as well as the absolute sense of the term is composed of the elements of politics, economics and ethics or the general realm of spirit [in the Hegelian sense]. But these elements tend to be grasped as separate spheres. It is all too rare to find them recognized as forming a totality in which these different elements are related to one another and penetrate one another. Indeed, the state itself has only a pale self-understanding of the integrated totality that in fact defines it. And yet it has become strikingly obvious in the present conflict that the regulatory power of politics has been applied to the economic sphere, thus reflecting the state's subjective character. Furthermore, the ethical and spiritual realms have been raised over the political sphere, thus animating political action from above and within [self-consciously]. The ethical has become the subjectivity within the subject, that which should be regarded as the state's most profound essence ... the subjectivity of the state has, in the case of Japan, always been linked to the ethical as it were on a higher plane ... in any case, this essence has [finally] made itself manifest.

In such circumstances, the spiritual and the ethical assume a fundamental character: the ethical comes to reign over the political, and the political in turn comes to govern the economic. The result is unambiguous: the realms of ideas and ethics take on overwhelming importance. One consequence is that what Kōyama called 'guidance' takes on an important domestic relevance. Furthermore, the domestic dimension of the issue cannot be considered without reference to the external or the foreign. Note also that the set of ideas required – [because] they must leave our opponent with no option but to submit to their powers of persuasion – must have a character that commands universal recognition. But unless our ideas are sound in this demanding sense they will not win enthusiastic acceptance here [or anywhere else]. The short term may be different, but over the long term our ideas must be superior in this way if we are to succeed.

Within what we call 'the Great East Asian Co-prosperity Sphere', many of the peoples of our region have been deeply influenced by Anglo-American

---

45 The 'ethical character' of the Co-prosperity Sphere was exhaustively treated in the previous symposium. Furthermore, the discussants have taken great pains to exploit the ordinary sense of *dōgisei* (morality) while insisting that it means something different because higher, that is involving a potent blend of dialectical transcendence of the difference between good and evil, while also reflecting real-world success grounded in demonstrated self-mastery or subjectivity.

ideas. This intentional invasion continues even now in relentless fashion.[46] To resist and finally repel this cultural intrusion, we must foster a set of ideas of the quality just mentioned. Without a persuasive set of ideas, we will not succeed.[47] In other words, if the Japanese people are to act on the world as a world-historical people (*minzoku*), one capable of transforming the world order, we must develop from within (*uchi ni kakuritsu*) a moral and an intellectual vision (*shisō*) capable of winning the assent of the whole world, including our enemies. It goes without saying that our opponents are not, in fact, going to be that easy to persuade. Nevertheless, if our ideas carry moral conviction they will penetrate the hearts of our enemies regardless of whether they like them or not. What the heart learns will eventually speak to the mind. Such is the power of thought. And in the end, our opponent will suffer a fatal division of mind [because the mental paralysis will be inflicted from within]. Therefore, to transform the Japanese into a world-historical people, we must, as Kōyama noted earlier, cultivate a set of ideas that will truly persuade the nation itself. Our labours must be unceasing until we achieve ideas of this quality, because the Japanese people should allow themselves to be persuaded by nothing less.

KŌSAKA: Therefore when we speak and write [about this issue], we must be self-consciously aware (*jikaku*) that we are not just addressing the people of Japan, but rather, at the very least, speaking and writing to all the peoples of the co-prosperity sphere here in East Asia. If what we have to offer is not of the quality to persuade the whole of the Great East Asian Co-prosperity Sphere, it will certainly not be enough to persuade Japanese people.

KŌYAMA: In the case of wars of ideas, there is a proper sequence of stages in which such a struggle will inevitably unfold: intellectual leadership and guidance (*shisō shidō*) should first spread in the nation, then be disseminated across the Co-prosperity Sphere, then to our enemies, and finally to the whole world. Ideally, this process should occur [on all these levels] at the same time, but it is more important that the Japanese people make these changeless principles their own as a matter of intellectual conviction, otherwise the East Asian Co-prosperity Sphere as a project will fail and a new world order will not come into being. Therefore ...

KŌSAKA: These things have to be performed in a certain order.

KŌYAMA: And in the ordering of these priorities, the domestic front is pivotal.

KŌSAKA: About this matter of the order in which these plans should unfold, this is what I think. When history moves, there is a point [in space and time] from which it moves. And this point is the absolute centre of

---

46 An early approximation of what Joseph Nye would decades later call 'soft power'.
47 Nishitani says *dame*, where the nuance is not 'useless' but 'ruined'.

historical reality. It is from this point that the motion of history sends out its waves; it is from here that history is built. If one wants to speak, for example, of *moralische Energie*, this is where moral energy realizes itself. And this centre is Japan.

There is an order to [the stages of] development of moral energy. Japan must embrace the set of ideas, truths and insights that underwrite moral energy or, as noted above, the Great East Asian Co-prosperity Sphere will lack the confidence to follow.[48] This constraint applies doubly to our foes. Nor can the rest of the world be expected to be persuaded to follow [our vision unless we are convinced of it]. The whole business must be simultaneously persuasive on every front. So our responsibilities to consolidate [this vision] begin at home. This is where we find our intellectual subjectivity, and this [imperative] determines the order in which these ideas must develop.

7 America and systems of total war (*sō ryoku sen*)

KŌYAMA: Kōsaka has called upon us to save our enemy. Let's examine the case of the United States. Since the outbreak of the current European war [in 1939], America has placed itself on a war footing both economically and militarily. This mobilization has intensified with the start of the Great East Asian War. The challenge is therefore this. The United States may decide to pursue this war on the modern principles upon which it is founded: the principles of American capitalism. This means fighting this war in a manner consistent with free competition and the profit motive. Our problem has been how to respond: do we mobilize ourselves for a world-historical war, a war of total resistance, or do we try to fight this conflict in the manner of the Great War? Or do we stop at a total war system *à la Ludendorff*?[49] I think it is possible to conclude that even a nation such as the United States will find that in the end it must, as it were willy-nilly, mobilize in the manner we have described for a world-historical war. When that moment arrives, we will have won and they will have lost this pivotal contest of ideas, because our ideas offer the only practical path [to victory in such a war].

Observe the potential danger if they come to see this as a struggle between conflicting world orders, and therefore to fight their own kind of world-historical

---

48 Japan's project depends for its success on persuading other East Asians, to say nothing of Imperial Japan's wartime foes or indeed the whole world, of its virtues. Kyoto School nationalism is thus inclusive, if firmly hierarchical and top-down. Note further, however, that it is not, in the language of Ernst Nolte, narcissistic or fascistic.
49 Note that the reference to the United States is merely an excuse for Kōyama to attack Tōjō's policies, which to these Kyoto School thinkers were flawed in the Ludendorffian manner.

war. What a pity to lose in that way. After all, the United States has many natural resources and huge productive power. We must create a system of total national resistance as quickly as possible if we are to overcome their advantages. If we do this [in time], we can [still] win. But also note that if America attempts to match [the effects of] Japan's version of total war, the United States will gradually come to resemble us. On the basis of this new order, they too will consolidate their own vast *Großraum* (*kōiki-ken*). Isn't this an entirely predictable outcome? We are already seeing how the United States is using its financial and military powers to draw even South America into this *Großraum*. But if the war should drag on, I believe that it is possible that American-style free trade and democracy will suffer from internal discord. I think it is reasonable to speculate in this way because of the tensions provoked by [the slightly collectivist tendencies of[50]] Roosevelt's New Deal in the face of the traditional demands of American liberal individualism and capitalism.[51] Major trouble could be the result [in US society if America is forced to mobilize for a world-historical war].

SUZUKI: I feel the same as Kōyama. If America decides to fight a world-historical form of total war, this will mark a philosophic victory for our side. If asked why I think this, [I would say that] it is because as things stand I doubt that America is able to wage a world-historical war. In other words, to fight a world-historical war, a self-conscious awareness and a recognition of the necessity for a transformation of orders must arise from within. Without this self-conscious awareness and the recognition of this necessity, one cannot fight such a war; indeed, the very idea of engaging in a world-historical war would be beyond the conception [of most Americans]. Consequently, at the moment when America decides to create such as system out of self-conscious recognition of the need for it, at that moment it will become aware of the demands of a world-historical war. And at that instant, our victory [over America] in the contest of ideas will be assured. I suspect this kind of thinking demonstrates the paradoxical character of world-historical wars.

NISHITANI: As long as America's slogan is 'democracy', it will be all but impossible for that country to negate, in any total sense, the claims of liberty and to seek to restrain the pursuit of profit and material gain. In the end, it is very likely that any American system [of world-historical war] will be only partially realized, because to some degree acceptance (*metomeru*) of individual liberty and personal profit will persist. This implies that the ability of America to achieve a genuine total mobilization remains in doubt.

---

50 Kōyama is speaking in shorthand. This is my surmise of what he is saying.
51 By 'liberalism', Kōyama means freedom from state interference and individual liberty, or what nowadays might be called 'conservative libertarianism'.

8 Dilemmas of a creative civil society (*minkan sōi*)

NISHITANI: There is, however, a variety of dilemmas facing our country. Nowadays one often hears that the creativity of the population in general should be respected, as should their autonomy or scope for individual or private (*minkan*) initiative.[52] But our political leadership has left the process [of encouraging private initiative] half finished, thereby cheating the population of the benefits they deserve. It is not enough merely to argue for the virtues of individual creativity or private autonomy. Indeed, from the standpoint of [genuine] free speculative appropriation,[53] all that the people are left with is the residue of liberalism [the absence of certain forms of restraint or control].[54] Hegel rejected this in the name of the objective spirit, and so should we.[55] I believe that the state's powers over spheres such as the economy should be rigorously strengthened in order that the state as a whole becomes, as it must, [an administrative] system characterized by genuine clarity and efficiency [literally: clear and direct]. Without such leadership from the centre, Japan will fail to foster an effective system for sustaining our world-historical war [as a form of total resistance]. It follows that as far as autonomy and creativity are concerned, the people (*kokumin*) and the private sector as a whole will not achieve all that can be achieved unless the fundamental urges that feed so-called freedom [negative freedom only] are restrained by a web of nation-wide controls. However much a spirit of restraint is urged [on the population], unless the system functions as an integrated whole, the sense of [national] urgency will evaporate into nothing.[56] In the end, one falls into line with the occupational orientation of one job, and a feeling of passivity takes hold. This in turn encourages a return to selfishness and [mere] self-interest. Whether the momentum that keeps national needs in

---

52 Note that 'private initiative' can be read as a code word for 'free markets' and 'free enterprise'. This may explain the conspicuous place of economic controls in the discussion that follows.

53 The text seems to be incomplete. All that appears in the magazine text is 'However much one may speak of creativity and autonomy, the standpoint of free speculation (*shui-teki jiyū*)'.

54 Once the man in the street demonstrates a compelling degree of self-mastery, private initiative and creativity will make sense; until that condition is demonstrated, the state must lead from the centre to stamp out the corrupting effects of private greed and selfishness.

55 Nishitani's argument is unusual in a Japanese context only because he gives it an explicitly Hegelian gloss. The Japanese discourse on the subject of private initiative displays precise contours. For the modernizer, the question is which needs to modernize first: structures or values, institutions or spirit? For the traditionalist, the key assumption is that virtue rests with the emperor, the state and civic authority broadly. The instinctual thrust of the individual left to his own devices is towards greed and lust. Nishitani cites Hegel's objective spirit, which here serves to draw attention to the distinction between negative freedom (that is, freedom from constraint) versus positive freedom (the freedom to act in a manner consistent with progress and human potential).

56 Again the assumption is that the masses are essentially passive, and need constant urging on because they demonstrate only a weak grasp of the larger picture. In this vision of society, notions of 'leadership' and 'persuasion' take on overwhelming importance.

the forefront of the people's minds is sustained or lost depends finally on [the effectiveness of] political leadership. While it is right and proper to show respect for autonomy, it is more important that autonomy be genuinely effective and speak to the [pressing] needs of the state today.

SUZUKI: It therefore seems reasonable to conclude that the kind of consciousness that would have one merely fall in line with the war effort – and it is all too conspicuous – is not the kind of consciousness that can meet the demands of a world-historical war. Could it be that our intellectual awareness has not matured sufficiently to respond to the historic necessities of such a struggle ... ?[57]

NISHITANI: However, among businessmen and entrepreneurs, for example, there is a reasonably deep appreciation of the [seriousness of] the current situation. Isn't there? There are, of course, many people in business who lack such an appreciation but ...

SUZUKI: But there is a war on, at least to that degree they are aware. As for [the depth of] their awareness of the situation ... [58]

KŌYAMA: I suppose that by war they must be thinking, 'this is an emergency (*hijōji*)'.

NISHITANI: But if that is the case, one can go further and urge our political leaders to tackle the issue with more vigour. The public, I trust, would respond. Certainly there would be greater mindfulness of the pressing issues facing us. That is what I think ... these are just my feelings about this strategic issue of leadership.

9 The ideal organizational structure for waging world-historical wars

SUZUKI: Is there perhaps a contradiction between the spheres of ideas and politics at work here? Politics must be grounded in ideas because only with the self-conscious appropriation of ideas does effective action become possible. Political leaders need, of necessity, to be more aware of this fact.

KŌYAMA: The whole nation must embrace the ideas that inspire our world-historical struggle. Nothing matters more. One of the problems that has come to the fore is that the distinction between normality and a state of emergency has become, to some degree, less obvious. In the same manner the conventional difference, as noted earlier, between war and peace has been lost, just as the distinction between the front line and the home front has also been eroded. This is one of the distinguishing and also representative features of world-historical wars from which we may conceive their ideal structure. These features are widely accepted in defining what might be termed 'a conventional total war' (*futsū sō ryoku sen*): the

---

[57] Either something has been edited out here or Nishitani has talked across Suzuki.
[58] Either something has been edited out here or Suzuki has talked across Nishitani.

combination and fusion of the military, the economic, the diplomatic, the political and the intellectual. But there is still a problem in that it remains unclear what kind of system is required by this kind of war.

I have been giving this issue a lot of thought. The conventional view of a military struggle is one in which the spheres that are not directly involved in the fighting play a supporting role, but it seems to me hard to be precise about this distinction in practice. Take, for example, the current German U-boat campaign against merchant shipping. Is this a military struggle or economic warfare? As the German goal appears to be to prevent food shipments from reaching their opponents and thus to destroy the enemy's economic capabilities, it seems reasonable to conclude this is a kind of economic warfare. From the standpoint of those attacking these convoys and armed merchant ships, this is an impressive (*rippa*) exercise in military power pure and simple. So is this conventional military action or economic warfare? Which sphere is at issue? One is forced to conclude that it is impossible to say which sphere is secondary to the other.

Thus it is one of the distinguishing features of total wars in their new guise that the war of ideas takes on some of the functions that formerly belonged to the diplomatic sphere. In other words, one cannot really say where the intellectual sphere leaves off and the diplomatic begins, any more than one can say where the military dimension ends and the economic starts. But such perceptions do not inform Ludendorff's notion of 'total war' (*zentai sen*). The distinctive features that we have identified as central to world-historical wars are not prominent in Ludendorff's vision, because he continues to see fighting as the dominant mode with all other spheres confined to supporting roles. This reflects what I suspect are structural differences in the two types of war at issue.

Take an example from economic warfare. In order for the economic sphere to make a decisive contribution to the war effort, it is essential that capitalists and workers alike are genuinely persuaded by the ideas that underlie the new economic order. This means that a place has to be found for the sphere of ideas in the economic order, just as the military struggle has to be factored into any successful economic campaign, for example an attempt to blockade the enemy. But it also follows that while the military struggle is without question just that, the war of ideas is not identical with the diplomatic offensive. Nevertheless, I do also endorse the view that opportunities to wage a war of ideas or [to engage in] economic and diplomatic struggles arise from the war on the battlefield. But having said as much, I must repeat that when pursuing the politics of the East Asian Co-prosperity Sphere, the success of such an effort hangs critically on our confidence in the ideas that underpin the new East Asian regional order. Ideas must reinforce the whole.

If this is the case, it follows that any organizational structure designed to sustain our current world-historical war will seek to mobilize all the distinct dimensions previously noted – the military, economic, diplomatic and intellectual fronts – and unite them into a single integrated war effort (*ichi gen-teki*) that ensures that each sphere exploits the opportunities presented by the others. The standpoint of world-historical war embodied in this synthesis will then shape the direction and strategy of this struggle by defining and clarifying the political and other elements that comprise such wars. Armed in this way, we will finally arrive at a clear understanding of the genuine nature and unique features of world-historical wars.

If Clausewitz defined war 'as nothing but the pursuit of politics with the admixture of other means', then we might recast his maxim and say that while 'world-historical wars are indeed the pursuit of politics with the admixture of other means', it is also true that 'politics is the pursuit of world-historical war with the admixture of other means'. The same formulation may be applied to the military, diplomatic, intellectual and economic dimensions as well. All form essential parts of the larger whole that is world-historical war. Is this definitional formula more than a little plausible?

All this is linked, in my view, to the larger truth of our situation: we have reached the turning point in our break with the modern world-view.[59] Economic warfare offers an illustration of this transformation of our world-view. In contrast to the flawed modern economic principle according to which this aspect of human life is ruled exclusively by the drive to satisfy material wants, a world-historical war by its very nature cannot be waged merely in pursuit of the satisfaction of material desires. Quite the contrary: this economic sphere is penetrated by extra-economic influences, including the spirit of morality (*dōgi-teki seishin*). Furthermore, only the political can draw [the economic and other] such spheres into an integrated whole so that we can begin to wage a world-historical war. This insight brings us to the turning point of our current struggle. The challenge reaches beyond the transformation of the inner facts of the economy or indeed the workings of economic laws, extending to the concept of 'desire' upon which the very notion of 'economic man' rests and which forms the key assumption of modern economics.[60]

This is the idea that must alter at the turning point we are discussing. Self-negation is built into the very idea of desire as the defining characteristic of modern economic man because the whole man [is being implicitly denied; but if we can remove this centrality of desire, the whole man] will be restored to his essence.[61] The same critique applies to politics, culture and scholarship. Thus science is divided into the natural sciences and the cultural sciences (*seishin kagaku*),[62] and these sciences are further divided into narrow specialisms and so on. Each of them sets out, in identical ways, to seek out its *a priori* foundations – the path of modern science – but this is an impossible quest, given the way scholarship works.

59 The early twenty-first-century notion of a 'tipping point' in human affairs may be resonant here.
60 Here the reference is to Hegel's reading of Adam Smith.
61 This and what follows is a reprise of the Hegelian/Marxist critique of the alienation that results from the division of labour.
62 From the German *Geisteswissenschaften*.

This is where we are [scientifically] today. Furthermore, this situation arises from the internal workings of the sciences, from the laws of science itself. One result is that one can no longer distinguish science from philosophy. The latter as a field is losing its distinctive character. The epistemology that has sought to provide a methodological foundation for the sciences has become philosophy itself, rather than the sciences depending for their epistemology on philosophy, as a bamboo shoot might depend on a stake. Instead, the special sciences themselves now provide the central ideas and concepts on which philosophy is called upon to reflect.[63] Isn't this now our general situation?

In every sphere, modernity acts as an acid, breaking down [reality and the study of reality] into ever smaller units. But without the resurrection of the whole, the part itself is incapable of life, and that is why we must once more seek to unite these disparate parts into a whole. This is the situation in which, I conclude, those who work in culture, the economy, scholarship and the arts all find themselves today.

The same problem can be said to apply absolutely to the making of war. Once each soldier, as an individual, shouldered his share of the whole burden of the fighting because that work was exclusively the duty of soldiers. Nowadays the whole nation must bear the burden of war on each and every front, and this includes economic production, politics, culture and education. War is thus no longer a matter of the battlefield alone, because it now includes the battle for production and the contest of ideas. As we have noted above, the boundaries between spheres of activity, defining their range and limits, can no longer be sharply drawn. The resulting structures, as has already been pointed out, display a mutual play of influences across each and every sphere. What we call world-historical wars rest on these mixed foundations. An overarching synthesis (*kōjigen no tōitsu*),[64] directed from a commanding height and drawing into an integrated whole all these spheres, is essential if the great power of the whole is to be unleashed.

SUZUKI: I see. This is how you understand the point I have been trying to articulate: world-historical wars have the potential to overcome and replace the fundamental *a priori* assumptions of conventional war.[65]

KŌSAKA: That is, I hope, correct.[66]

---

63 The expression 'special sciences' is often associated with Martin Heidegger's distinction between ontology and the ontic sciences, the latter consisting of empirical or positivist sciences while Heidegger's ontology revives the form of being resistant to reification. The Kyoto School may be echoing Weber's critique of economic rationalization as 'an iron cage' and Husserl's doubts about science in his lectures and essays on 'The Crisis of the European Sciences'. Kōyama is making a Kyoto School rejoinder to the 'Overcoming Modernity' symposium organized by the magazine *Bungakkai* (Literary World) in July 1942.
64 Again, the Hegelian origins of this idea must be kept in mind.
65 That is, the fundamental assumptions of the *logic* of conventional war.
66 The text says 'Kōsaka' but the context suggests that the speaker here may very well be Kōyama, as he was responsible for the long comment that precedes it.

10 Creativity and innovation in world-historical wars

NISHITANI: I think we can talk about the structural issues just raised by Kōyama in this way. When the state, understood as a systemic unity or integrated whole, including all its varied dimensions (economic, political, intellectual, etc.) is set in motion, there one will find the focus (*nemoto*),[67] function, cause and dynamic that drive everything. Because this motion is creative, the structure of the state must be designed so as to maximize creativity. It is my view that because this is the truest essence of the contemporary state, this structure [best] finds its expression in the system of world-historical war. In the display and expression of creative power of the state, the fundamental truth and principles of this system of war are most fully realized.

In the current struggle, creativity, be it in production, in politics or in thought, is indispensable. Armed with such creativity, we must strive to build and then expand a [regional] base [*Großraum*] that is at once steadfast and invincible, and thus able to withstand anything an enemy nation might throw at it. At the same time, such creativity will allow us to meet the challenges of cultivating a new order capable of shouldering the great burdens of world history. An enormous creative leap is demanded. This is where our [collective] *yakudō* or *élan vital* may be brought powerfully into play.[68] This will serve and animate those things associated with what Kōyama calls 'the structure'.

In contrast, conventional natural science tends to seek a consensus of opinion within a set of *a priori* disciplinary boundaries, and thus solely within the subject at issue. Thus the economist thinks only about the *a priori* assumptions of economics, and the approach is the same within each and every field of [empirical or positivist] study. In like manner, the focus of scientific inquiry is confined to pursuit of the inner logic or rationality of [certain precisely delineated] things themselves. But the struggles of world-historical wars in

---

67 *Nemoto* here is not static, not a metaphor for a dead 'floor' or 'foundation', but rather something organic and alive, such as the root that generates the plant. The reasoning is clearly Japanese but the famous metaphor in the *Phenomenology of Spirit* on the dialectic of seed, root and plant may not be irrelevant here.
68 The French term, cited in transliteration via *furigana*, can be translated into Japanese as *seimei no yakudō*. According to the *Oxford English Dictionary*, *élan vital* is 'an intuitively perceived life-force in Bergson's philosophy; any mysterious life-force, especially one supposed to have caused the variations from which new species have emerged'. Hajime Tanabe and other members of the Kyoto School would have been intimately familiar with the thought of the most influential twentieth-century French philosopher before Sartre, but the *Oxford English Dictionary* incorrectly overemphasizes the mysterious and murky dimension of Bergson's idea and thus understates the way it gives expression to the vivid power and practical force that is crucial to acting on the real world. The notion of *élan vital* resonated strongly in the Japanese discourse of effort, enthusiasm and goal achievement. Also note that neither Shakespeare nor Nelson nor Churchill would have regarded the impact of *élan vital* on the battlefield as anything approaching murky.

their totality require something more than this [narrowly focused] kind of rationality.

In my earlier remarks, I stressed the importance of the intense rigour required if we are to put our organizations and institutions into effective objective order. The point that I was trying to make was that if our organizations are to function as efficient units, they must be united by an organizational web that is clear and effective.[69] Without this, the subjective spirit (*shukan seishin*) of the people, as individuals, cannot be raised to the level of the objective spirit. The strength of the individual will not translate [collectively] into the strength of the nation. At the same time, however, if excessive emphasis is placed on the objective character of our institutions, there is a danger that organizations will lose their capacity for self-directed action. Stability and equilibrium seek to satisfy everyone [all the relevant stakeholders] by eliminating internal contradictions.[70] But the fundamental challenge facing anyone seeking to fight a world-historical war is very different. That ambition requires not so much harmony or equilibrium within and between branches of society as one of those seemingly irrational leaps forward that should combine the best of reason and intuition in a kind of supra-rationality (*ai-risei*).

Isn't this exactly where the fundamental significance of Kōyama's 'guidance' comes into its own? Isn't this a way of explaining what we are discussing here? ... To insist, as I just mentioned, on focusing on the economy only as the economy, on politics only as politics, etc., is to fall into the logic of independent spheres. But fostering the equilibrium of individual sectors discourages the kind of risk-taking required by the process of creative destruction. To do this is to pursue the logical rationality of the [immediately] 'given' (*jitai*). It is an approach, as I see it, exactly the same as that at work in the view of the body as an organic unity. For the body to function as an integrated system requires that the unity of the various forces of which the body is composed must deal, as a system, with endless examples of disequilibrium. The body persists and grows because of the dynamic relationship between equilibrium and disequilibrium, a process in which states of disequilibrium are tirelessly turned to states of equilibrium [so that the whole process begins again]. The same lesson may be drawn concerning the economy and politics. Both types of system seek to maintain their organizational stability by balancing the various forces that form it.

This understanding of the problem assumes the existence of a kind of organic system. But this explanatory model is wholly inadequate to understand a world-historical war. If creativity is the root function and dynamic of such wars, and if we recognize the necessity for the kind of creative leaps generated by *élan vital*, the static organic model will not do. Rather, the more appropriate model calls to mind a system in which the various organs of the

---

69 Nishitani uses the expression *kammei chokusetsu* or 'concise and direct'.
70 Exactly the sort of criticism economists such as Kazuo Yoshida would make of recession-bound Japanese firms in the 1990s. See his *Heisei Fukyō no Junen-shi*, Tokyo: PHP Kenkyūjo, 1999, p. xx.

body – hands, feet, etc. – function as individual units that work with all the parts of the body in dynamic equilibrium. In other words, when the hands and feet and all the other organs of the body move or function, all the organs of the body work together to keep the body in non-static equilibrium. Doesn't this model serve our purposes better? And, of course, we are not talking about a body that is merely ambling along. This is a body running or, better still, making the kind of leaps that demand a model in whose functioning such leaps are an integral element.[71]

At the moment, the state must, as it were, run. It finds itself literally in a race with our foes. This is what it means to be caught up in any type of total war, certainly a world-historical war. As a result, this kind of action calls upon all the powers of the body, and requires the routine upsetting of the body's normal state of equilibrium because the body must be made to leap. This is not to say that when the body makes a leap it is not in equilibrium. When the body runs or jumps it must maintain equilibrium, or it will fall to the ground. But this [dynamic] equilibrium fundamentally negates passive equilibrium. It raises equilibrium to a higher plane.[72] This is something of what I meant when I spoke earlier of the rationality at work within irrationality. Thus, in a state of ordinary equilibrium, a system has to be in equilibrium to begin to move at all. My point is that, within this kind of equilibrium, there must emerge the power to deny this [static] equilibrium. And within this movement, and via this movement, [dynamic] equilibrium is established. Thus disequilibrium within itself houses the capacity to re-establish a state of equilibrium. Or rather, to put it another way, in order to negate [a static state of] equilibrium, movement requires a state of equilibrium. Just as when one tries to stand or run, a higher form of equilibrium comes into play. In other words, equilibrium does not come first; motion does. Equilibrium arises from within action. Although the concept of equilibrium tends to signify a system at rest, what I refer to as a higher form of equilibrium is equilibrium in motion or, perhaps better still, what might be called the equilibrium of the leap. In any case, it is a motion that frustrates assumptions of rationality – that is, what I think of as subjective motion – and requires us to conceive of a form of rationality that is contained within irrationality. It is from here that one can begin to imagine the nature of genuine creativity. This suggests to me that when one thinks about organization and the balance and stability of powers in politics or the economy or other spheres of life, one's ideas [of the world] will prove simply inadequate to the case, particularly in attempting to address phenomena such as world-historical wars, unless one is prepared to consider the notions argued for here. Surely this is the case.

---

71 The long-winded grapple with the idea of equilibrium that begins with this paragraph may appear to be belabouring a scientific point. It may reflect the Kyoto School's determination to wrest control of the discourse on Japan's war policy and conduct – including the use of organic metaphors – from both the Tōjō clique and the ultra-right.
72 Physically and conceptually. The analysis is rooted in Hegel's dialectical approach to nature.

It is at this point that I think the relationship between such phenomena and the general notions of 'leadership' (*shidō*) and 'guidance' (*shidō sure*) comes into play. As I noted earlier, I understand the state to be the function of three dimensions: the economic, the political, and the ethical or intellectual. These three dimensions are ordered in a hierarchy in which the economy is governed by the political, and the political is informed and regulated by the ethical and by ideas. This [hierarchy] gives expression to the state as subjectivity. With ethics and thought as their foundation, these three dimensions take shape as an integrating power that defines the central essence of the contemporary state. It is at this point that the state can begin to acquire the degree of unity and integration that allows it to act in and on the world.

At the same time, as I just noted, this idea of the state as a dynamic system capable of taking [creative] leaps proceeds from the notion that politics regulates the economy, and that this form of politics is in turn governed by morality and thought: the spiritual realm [of Hegel]. For example, when the body takes a leap it is not only the body that is involved. It is the spirit that moves the body. In other words, there has to be subjectivity. It is the subject [agent] that makes the decision to leap. The body then concentrates its strength, and the jump is made. This simile can be seen to illustrate the point made earlier about the relationship between leadership and the subjectivity of states or nations today. In other words, what I want to say is that leadership should have creative leaps that focus our entire strength as its main goal and purpose. Leadership must direct our *élan*.

This is a bit off the subject, but what gives rise to these ideas was something I read before – I am pretty sure it was in *The History of Japan*[73] – about Hideyoshi.[74] Apparently, as soon as Hideyoshi learned of the assassination of Nobunaga, he turned back with two trusted retainers only to set off suddenly, entirely on his own, leaving his followers to catch up with him. Then, when he had gathered his entire force, he fought the battle of Yamazaki. This is how the spark of inspiration motivated Hideyoshi. It reminds one of the Ch'in period [*c.*221–206 BCE] in ancient China or the civil strife during the Jōkyū period [1219–21 CE] period in medieval Japan. It is when one dashes off alone, making one's followers chase, trying to catch up. It is at such moments that one seizes the opportunity presented by the historical occasion (*toki o eru*), but this is also the moment when true rationality [reason as the setting and

---

73 Nishitani is very likely referring to one of the 22 volumes of *Nihon Gaishi* (1827), a history by Rai San-yō of Japan from the Shogunate of Yoritomo (1192) to the victory of Ieyasu Tokugawa at Sekigahara in 1600.
74 Hideyoshi Toyotomi (1536–98): general and politician; one of the greatest military figures of Japanese history. The story Nishitani recounts is one of those telling incidents in the haze of marches and counter-marches, assassinations and near-assassinations, fanatical loyalty and wretched betrayal, bitter defeats and astonishing victories that characterized what the British political historian S.E. Finer called 'Japan's War of the Roses'. The incident with Mōri and co. was more complicated than Nishitani's take on it here suggests.

achieving of goals] is acted on and thus realized.[75] Waiting until one's forces have assembled and then setting off is normal rational behaviour; but allowing normal time to set the tempo of battle is not really the most effective (*hontō no gōrisei*) mode of waging war. By contrast, there is a profound kind of rationality at work when a general such as Hideyoshi or Nobunaga boldly seizes an opportunity that has suddenly appeared. Rationality – that kind of rationality within irrationality I mentioned above – is part of the leaping creativity that I include within the notion of 'leadership' – and that notion is nothing other than the kind of leadership exhibited on the occasions cited by commanders such as Hideyoshi. Think of the strategy of 'leading from the front' where one leaps forward, convinced that one's troops are in place and ready to march, and when one knows that the one thing one must not do is to look back …

KŌYAMA: I agree with the idea that world-historical wars are creative. Such struggles foster situations which necessitate innovation that otherwise might not arise on the battlefield, in the economic struggle, in the war of ideas or in the war of diplomacy, regarded as separate and distinct spheres of action. The supreme imperative of world-historical wars as struggles of total resistance is the generation of an infinity of 'plus alpha', of that creative extra that is found within such wars as part and parcel of their very nature. One endlessly produces a new version of oneself, and this is the active source of the unlimited 'creative extra' just mentioned. This is the categorical imperative of world-historical wars. It is here one finds one's *élan*, that vital force that transcends logic.

Such creativity cannot, obviously, be totally irrational, but it must embody a deeper and higher kind of rationality. Thus, if you will, 'rational irrationality' moves towards ever newer forms of innovation by concentrating the totality of the strength of the system. Such a system will be one pregnant with openness to the opportunities for its constituent parts to serve the whole, and one informed by a rationality that seeks disequilibrium from within equilibrium, including what Nishitani called the kind of analysis that continually breaks the problem down into smaller dimensions. This kind of rationality and analytical logic is what is called for.[76] On this point, I am entirely in agreement with Nishitani's position. The challenge is to be found in the content of this hyper-rationality (*ai-risei*). I suspect that perhaps it might be termed 'synthesizing' or 'organizational' reason. There are the Buddhist ideas in the Tendai

---

75 Judging *guru* in *toki o guru* is a variant of *eru* as in the expression *tokoro o eru*. But while *toki* usually refers to time, given the context and Nishitani's inverted commas around *toki* I have rendered it as 'opportunity', as the expression *toki o eru* normally refers to opportunities that chance or the time provides.
76 Note the resolute refusal of these Kyoto thinkers to abandon the claims and dignity of reason in the face of the press of war, patriotism or the Japanese Zen-inspired distaste for logic-chopping.

and Kegon schools of *ichi soku issai; issai soku ichi* and *ichi soku ta; ta soku ichi*, or 'the one *qua* the many' and 'the many *qua* the one'. This is the logic of the history of the last days of the Law (*mappō engi*).

For us moderns raised in a civilization based on differential logic (*bunbetsu ronri*), this kind of Buddhist logic is graspable in a general way but remains difficult to understand. Somehow it suggests the world of speculative logic, one removed from historical reality. But [when we are] confronted with the nature of world-historical wars, somehow there seems to be a precise fit between this Buddhist logic and the logic of historical reality. In fact, somehow it seems that philosophic logic, using schools of thought such as Mahayana Buddhism, is able to explain what the eyes cannot deny as facts that have now appeared before us but otherwise are difficult to explain. Whether one calls it institutional or synthesizing logic, we have to move towards something like this if we are to embrace fresh ideas. This is necessary. I have deliberately proposed the notion of 'the institutional universal' (*soshikiteki fuhen*) to paint a contrast with the established notions of concrete universal and abstract universal. This logic departs from the analytical logic of modern civilization, but the times are calling for a set of structural principles that can furnish [our] new world-view. This is how I approach the issue.

NISHITANI: So that is it. Compared to this, what I just spoke of would appear to vanish [as a problem]: compared to the Tendai school it is more like *makujiki* [direct] in Zen. It is a kind of [radical] simplification.

KŌSAKA: *Makujiki*?

NISHITANI: Yes, *makujiki* as in the expression *matsujigura ni sare*, to depart straight away, forthrightly – to depart four-square.

11 The Co-prosperity Sphere and our world-historical war

KŌYAMA: Nowadays total wars are often described as 'total wars of national resistance' (*kokka sō ryoku sen*), but I have doubts about this term. A genuine world-historical war must reach beyond the scale of a single nation or state and become a war to create and defend a co-prosperity sphere (*kyōeiken sō ryoku sen*).

KŌSAKA: That's right.

KŌYAMA: At the moment, because Japan is bearing the burden of fighting the Great East Asian War, the impression is given that this country alone boasts a total war system (*sō ryoku sen taisei*). But in reality this country cannot sustain even a national war of total resistance (*Nippon no kokka sō ryoku sen*) without mobilizing the resources and the labour power of the Co-Prosperity Sphere as a whole. This is why transport [within the Co-prosperity Sphere] has become such a pressing issue. But if the organizational structure that is conventionally linked with the phrase 'Japan's total war system' can be transformed into the genuine article, then the expression will become *Kyōeiken Sō ryoku sen* or War for the Co-prosperity Sphere, and be all the more accurate.[77]

All the constituent peoples of the East Asian Co-Prosperity Sphere must share their respective burdens, reflecting their relative capacities, in waging this world-historical war. In the manner mentioned earlier in connection with the structure of such an effort, we need to organize our war-making system on a regional basis, with Japan playing the central role. This needs to be done as a matter of urgency. In this way, the Co-prosperity Sphere can come to play its full role in this struggle. If this can be achieved, we will be able to resist [the advance of] the United States even if America's total war system mobilizes all of North and South America. Because East Asia can provide Japan with an almost unlimited advantage (*mugen no purasu*) in this struggle, we will never be defeated even if the war should drag on for centuries, let alone decades. Such is the promise of East Asia. Given this potential, the task of properly organizing the region must be addressed without delay. We need to shift from a war of total resistance fought by Japan alone to one waged by the whole of the Co-Prosperity Sphere.[78] When this is achieved, and only when it is achieved, will the present struggle become a turning point in world history and thus a world-historical war.

KŌSAKA: I am in entire agreement with this.
KŌYAMA: If, therefore, we can wage this kind of co-prosperity sphere war of total resistance (*kyōeiken sō ryoku sen*), it follows that there can be no colonies and no exploitation [of our neighbours, by anyone].[79] In such ideals, our world-historical war may claim its unique character. If this kind of war, in the true sense we have defined it, can be sustained, the principles of a new order, one reflecting a higher plane of morality and thus transcending the old order with its foundations in profit and gain, will be realized.

12 Co-prosperity spheres [*Großräume*] and the philosophy of the nation (*kyōei-ken to minzoku no tetsugaku*)

NISHITANI: Let me return to a theme I addressed in our previous symposium: how to wage a world-historical war fought to establish and sustain a

---

77 Generically, the Great East Asian Co-prosperity Sphere is a *Großraum*. The successful creation of such a sphere affirms the polycentric nature of the globe. Hegel and Schmitt are constantly hovering presences throughout this argument, as are Presidents Monroe and Wilson.
78 In his secret lecture ('On the Logic of Co-prosperity Spheres') to the Navy with Kōyama six weeks earlier, Tanabe had insisted that co-prosperity spheres must involve willing participation (and all this implies about fair and decent treatment by Japan), but had gone on to insist that in the normal evolution of things nations other than Japan – China being the most obvious candidate – might be expected to assume the role of leadership within the sphere after Japan
79 Kōyama's striking declaration must qualify as the boldest statement found in any of the three symposia, and the severest criticism of Tōjō's policies, for the Kyoto School is asserting that colonial exploitation is an option open neither to the West nor to Japan.

co-prosperity sphere [and in turn be sustained by such a *Großraum*]. Given this imperative, we must hope that it is possible (*kūsō ja nai*) that the totality of the various peoples found within the Greater East Asian Co-prosperity Sphere can be transformed, through an intense programme of education and training, into Japanese [in their levels of subjective effectiveness and rational self-mastery] – that is, that they can be Japanized (*Nipponjin-ka*). As Kōyama observed in his book *The Philosophy of the Nation*, nations (*minzoku*) make history, but history makes nations. The peoples that make up nations possess a flexible circumference, a floating dimension that is neither fixed nor totally defined; through the historical process such peoples can be welded into something with a more or less uniform national identity. Take the example of Korea, which may in fact be rather different from most other cases. Even so, if we accept the widely held proposition that 'the Korean people' is a fixed immutable idea, it is also true that the present demands something more from such fixed identities.

When we contemplate, one by one, how the various examples of individual 'nations' have congealed into self-sustaining entities, this vantage (*tachiba*) allows one to conceive the [modern] notion of national self-determination.[80] But the current imposition of conscription on the 'Korean nation' (*Chōsen minzoku*) means that in terms of subjectivity – and this refers to Korean subjectivity in the whole of its substance [and reality] – Korean subjectivity may be effectively absorbed into [a large transnational concept of] Japanese subjectivity. Therefore one may conclude that the concept embodied in a small nation has in effect been subsumed into a larger [more powerful] idea.[81] And this suggests that we might reasonably conclude that two peoples – the Yamato people[82] and the Korean people – have in some sense become something new: the Japanese nation (*Nippon minzoku*).[83] From this it follows that the expanded and altered notion of the peoples of the Japanese Empire (*Nippon minzoku*) might come to include, again through the process of education, the

---

80 That includes, at least in theory, self-determination for the Korean people as well if the plans for the Co-prosperity Sphere should falter.
81 'Concept' here in the sense of the living historical shaping or power of an idea.
82 *Yamato* is the traditional name for the Japanese, like the Han in the expression 'Han Chinese'. The expression embodies the biological notion of a shared heritage (all Japanese are in this sense related 'by blood'), and *Yamato minzoku* has often been rendered in less than careful usage as 'the Japanese race' in English. Strictly speaking, the Japanese are not a race.
83 Here the Kyoto School is giving metaphysical blessing to the proposal of the Japanese Governor's Office of Korea that intermarriage between Japanese subjects and Korean colonials be encouraged because only by creating a new imperial people could the Japanese Empire have any chance of surviving into the future as a vital historical force. Note that such a policy would spell the death of any notion of Japanese 'racial' or ethnic purity. Here is another example of the unsuspected liberal dimension of the wartime Kyoto School's proposals.

peoples of the southern tropics and the high deserts [of North-East Asia]. Isn't this possible?

In any case the larger point is that the notion of nation (*minzoku*) – and this applies to the people in Japan and in Korea or elsewhere – has to be conceived in much broader terms, on a scale much larger than then the conventional conception of *minzoku* (nation or people). This is what I think is required now.

KŌSAKA: That is what I think, too. I suspect that previous ideas of the nation/people (*minzoku*) have been too narrowly conceived. Although a people may live and act within history, those peoples who do not act historically stand, strictly speaking, apart from history; they are peoples without a history. They qualify as nothing more than 'peoples in a state of nature'. When one speaks of national self-determination, this is the condition in which all such peoples find themselves.[84] Today, however, to foster a co-prosperity sphere for East Asia demands something so new and radically different that the traditional definition of a *minzoku* is incapable of meeting the challenge. The times demand that the nation be theorized in a new way, and the transcendence of narrow nationalism must find expression in this kind of theory.[85] It is my belief that the Korean nation (*Chōsen minzoku*) can achieve a genuine historical character within a revamped and expanded notion (*kōgi*) of the [imperial] Japanese nation (*Nippon minzoku*).[86] And can't the same conclusion be applied to the idea of the state itself? As in the case of a united Europe, the organization of a co-prosperity sphere that seeks to unite the states of East Asia with Japan at the centre in a Great East Asian Co-prosperity Sphere requires that the whole idea of separate national independence be abandoned.[87] The state itself must be entirely rethought afresh from the standpoint of a co-prosperity sphere. This suggests a return to the traditional Eastern conception of the state.[88]

---

84 In these cases the call for national self-determination is empty because the people are manifestly unready to assume the burden of making history.
85 Once again, Kyoto School ambiguity cuts more than one way. On the surface, other potential members of the Great East Asian Co-Prosperity Sphere are being asked to shed their nationalist egoism in favour of the greater good. Below the surface, the Kyoto School intend that this call to transcend narrow nationalistic sentiment and conduct should apply equally to Imperial Japan.
86 Either Kōsaka has suddenly become more mindful of the censor or he is suggesting that the word *minzoku* must be redefined in a way that sheds the narrow nationalist colour of the term *Nippon minzoku* – as, indeed, is suggested in the next sentence.
87 The Kyoto School renounces the nation-state idea in favour of Schmitt's *Großraum*. When read alongside Tanabe's lecture on the philosophy of co-prosperity spheres, this observation endorses pooled sovereignty for all East Asian nations, including Japan.
88 An astonishing proposal to return to the traditional Chinese concept of East and North-East Asia as a collection of semi-independent peoples caught in orbit around a cultural centre that gives the entire region coherence and order.

NISHITANI: Kōyama is arguing that peoples are state-forming (*kokka-keisei-teki*). In my book, I insist on much the same thing; but today peoples are state-forming and, at the same time, co-prosperity forming.

KŌSAKA: Rather than being the independent entity as it is conceived of in Europe, the nation has to be primordially mediated.[89] I think this process can be called 'state formation'.

KŌYAMA: I thought of directing this question to Kōsaka, but do you see evidence of the trend or even the will to state-building action, in the modern Western sense of the term, among the nations (*minzoku*) of the Orient, whether Buddhist or Islamic, such as China, India or the countries of the Middle East (*Nishi A*)?

KŌSAKA: No, I don't think you see the same kind of nationalist drive (*kokka iyoku*) in the Orient. We find, I suspect, the most problematic manifestation of this drive among the comparatively new states in Europe. They stand at the brink of change. This drive takes a very different cast in China. For one thing, the Chinese state, as a state, lacks distinct boundaries.[90] Thus China tends to stand apart from the conventional struggle between modern states over boundaries. The Chinese concept of the state as a state is totally different. A struggle against intruding barbarians in no way qualifies as a war between [modern] states. Because the Chinese traditionally refuse to recognize proper boundaries between nations [of nominally equal status], while one can speak of the 'state' of China in fact the notion of *tenka* ('all under heaven') applies to but a single entity. There is, by definition, only one *tenka*. One might describe China as a *tenka kokka*: the only state under heaven. Even in Japan, when the notion of 'all nations under one roof' (*hakkō no ichi-u*) is reverently evoked, meaning the 'family' (*ie*), it goes without saying that this does not refer to 'the family' in any narrow sense.[91] The stress is on the 'roof' as a covering [rather than the idea of other nations being subordinate].

KŌYAMA: I think that the essential thrust of the [Chinese] experience is different from the state-building impulse of the nations (*minzoku*) of modern Europe. It might be better to understand the Chinese impulse as having been towards *tenka-keisei-teki* (as in 'an-all-under-heaven' or 'cosmos-forming' process). Certainly it is different from the kind of national consciousness one sees in Europe, which has not been the experience in East Asia yet. In one sense one can say that a dimension of the state[-building

---

89 The title of the first two volumes of Nishitani's complete works is *Kongenteki Shutaisei no Tetsugaku* (The Philosophy of Primordial Subjectivity).
90 Another ambiguous comment. China's lack of clear boundaries makes its periphery vulnerable to imperialist ambitions on the part of the great powers. The difficulty is compounded by the fact that the Chinese Republic was, at the time, the uncertain heir to the territorial legacy of the Manchu dynasty, and ethnically speaking the Manchu were not Chinese.
91 *Hakkō no ichi-u* is translated conventionally but not literally as 'all eight corners of the world under one roof'.

process] is present, but the concept of state boundaries is not accepted in the way associated with the idea of the [modern] European state. While I think one might conclude that there has been an impulse towards something like a state, or at least an umbrella-like, state-like notion such as 'all under heaven', if East Asia sticks to tradition events are likely to unfold in a particular direction. In any future effort to move towards state formation or an association of nations, East Asia is not likely to experience state building as a natural phenomenon for some time, certainly when compared to the region building one sees in Europe. The contrast remains sharp.

KŌSAKA: I, too, am in agreement with this assessment. A co-prosperity sphere for East Asia is not something that has been conceived in somebody's head. Rather, it emerged in a kind of spontaneous fashion. It is a manifestation of the latent Oriental urge towards state building. And this probably allows us to think of this development as reflecting the workings of a kind of historical necessity.

NISHITANI: When one speaks of peoples or nations (*minzoku*) in the contemporary world, one may think of the nation as a clear expression of national consciousness (*minzoku ishiki*), as appears to characterize the peoples of Europe, but in the case of the nations of the East the meaning of the term 'nation' (*minzoku*) is different. Even today European-style national consciousness can still not be found among many of the peoples of the Orient, and this is probably a good thing from the standpoint of attempting to construct a Great East Asian Co-prosperity Sphere. In order to foster a co-prosperity sphere among the nations of East Asia, certainly from the standpoint of Japan ...

KŌYAMA: As Suzuki noted earlier, the [central] problem facing us is whether or not state formation in the European manner provides the proper and best model for such an enterprise [outside Europe]. Let's think, for example, about the Philippines, Thailand and Burma in the light of the theory of the European state. When one considers the problem of modern state formation in the light of the world-historical facts of the European experience – an order of states based on winners and losers, that unleashed the Great War and made the present war inevitable – I think one wants to persuade others of the importance, indeed the necessity, of fostering a co-prosperity sphere.

KŌSAKA: Modern European civilization has given birth to a host of disasters and tragedies. And it now finds its future path blocked. In this sense one can describe the modern European state as a tragedy. Certainly the tragic trajectory of the European state is the one thing that must be avoided when building modern states in East Asia. It appears that China wants to construct a state in the European manner, and therefore it is essential that the Chinese people reflect deeply about the possible consequences of repeating the European error and reconsider their approach.

NISHITANI: They have been profoundly influenced by British and American ideas of national self-determination ...

KŌSAKA: Yes, they have. And not only China.
NISHITANI: They must replace this with a different system of ideas.
KŌSAKA: That is absolutely right.

13 Conceiving East Asia historically (*Tōa no kannen to rekishi-kan*)

SUZUKI: Doesn't this confront us with the problem of historical interpretation or how to view history? In other words, what is at issue in my view is the overcoming of the 'stages of development' theory of history as well as the theory of evolutionary relay hierarchy.[92] And why is this? Because these theories hold that the whole world is governed by the same set of laws of historical development experienced by Europe. The assumption is that as Europe has hitherto followed a set of stages of development, the rest of the world must follow suit. Thus the non-European world finds itself somewhere part-way down the path already trail-blazed by Europe. In all this, a theoretical primacy is accordingly assigned to Europe, and on this basis (*kongen*) not only is the rest of the world judged to be backward vis-à-vis Europe, but it follows that progress is, by definition, what non-Europeans struggle to do in order to climb up the developmental ladder built by Europe. This is in essence what the law of progress and the laws of world history signify. This is the European view of world history, and it governs how world history is understood in general. This intellectual hegemony provides the compulsion for East Asians to devise their own standpoint from which to judge history, because without our own standpoint East Asia will be unable to transform history.

Take, for example, the stages of economic development thesis, [which traces a progression] from the domestic economy of the medieval period to the city economies of the early modern period, from such civic economies to national economies, and thence to a [unified] world economy. A series of fixed stages is implied, and this is to be followed in an equally fixed order. The development of the state traces the same pattern: thus the state evolves from the primitive state of tribal societies to the feudal state, and thence to the monarchy, and [thence to] the nation state (*kokumin kokka*).[93] What will come next is uncertain, but the notion of a particular set of stages to be followed in a particular order is widely accepted as an article of faith. The assumption is that peoples that have hitherto lacked nation-states, such as the peoples of

---

92 Also known as 'convergent evolution', this theory attempts to explain how independent species acquire similar characteristics via the evolutionary process. It is used here as an analogy rather than as a strict scientific theory.
93 The conventional rendering of 'nation-state' is *kokumin kokka*, but the expression in Japanese both affirms a strong state in the positive Hegelian sense and approaches the Latin American notion of a 'national popular state' in ways that do not apply to the expression in English.

East Asia, must necessarily follow the European pattern, and that this [in turn] must necessarily result in the embrace of the idea of national self-determination for the peoples involved. The challenge is to overcome this interpretation of history because it all but precludes the possibility of solving [the national question] with a new East Asian order.[94] Not only that, this understanding of history is a philosophical obstruction standing in the way of [the progress of] Europe itself. Overcoming this view of history may pose the greatest challenge of all.

Formidable difficulties will certainly result if the nations of East Asia – the Chinese and other peoples – try to create nation-states based on the same principles as those we find in Europe in their quest for self-consciousness. The [national] self-consciousness of Europe is not East Asian. Nor does the application of the idea to East Asian reality qualify as the work of world-historical consciousness. A new idea of world history has the power to overcome this kind of national self-assertion. This, too, provides another motivation for the study of world history (*sekaishi-gaku*). Does all of this, in fact, return us to the priority of overturning the conventional Western paradigm of stages of development? What do you think?

KŌSAKA: When did the idea of evolutionary relay emerge?

SUZUKI: In broad terms, it is a nineteenth-century idea. In other words, defeating this historical interpretation requires us to overcome the nineteenth century, that is, to overcome modernity.

KŌYAMA: This idea had a major impact on German historiography.

SUZUKI: And in France as well. Note also that the idea of progress largely originated in France. It was in France that an extraordinary form of humanism gained currency under the banner of the *esprit d'humanité*. There is also the impact of a version of the idea of evolution [to be considered]. The net result is a problem of world-historical interpretation (*rekishi-kan*).

KŌYAMA: A world-historical view has to become a convincing understanding of world history.

SUZUKI: In fact, even in Europe there has been an effort to overcome the [social] implications of the idea of evolutionary relay. Thus, from the 1920s, theories of the plurality of history began to appear. Huizinga's theory of historical morphology is an example of this trend. So is Dobbish's explanation of the transition from 'a natural [barter] economy to a money economy'. These pluralistic interpretations of history come quite close to the ideas proposed by Kōyama. But, in any case, it is a fact beyond doubt that even within Europe itself nineteenth-century ideas such as progress and stages of development are being dismissed as

---

94 Here, as before, the Japanese expression is *rekishikan*, literally 'historical view' or more awkwardly 'history' as a parallel concept to 'world-view' (*sekaikan*). So the Japanese nuance is stronger and more theoretically rigorous than the English expression 'view of history'.

intellectual dead ends. The settling of accounts suggests that these ideas can no longer explain Europe even to itself. This is even truer of the rest of the world.

As for Kōyama's theory of [world-historical] pluralism, I cannot say that I do not have some questions. Having set out some of them in print, I see a number still to be addressed. But the splendid achievement of Kōyama's theory that I would like to recognize is this: he has effectively demolished the implicit hierarchy [Europe above the rest] that underpins the theory of stages of development, thus securing the theoretical foundations for the creation and nurturing by the rest of the world of principles [of social existence] uniquely suited to the different regions of the planet. This is enormously important, and this accomplishment transcends any fine points of academic scepticism.

14 The contradictions of Anglo-American liberty

KŌYAMA: Last year Churchill and Roosevelt jointly proclaimed the 'Atlantic Charter'. This declaration reaffirmed the principles of national self-determination and open markets, and [promulgated] a version of the Open Door Policy [reduction of trade barriers and freer access to raw materials]. In other words, the Atlantic Charter offers not the slightest advance on the ruling ideas of a now *passé* old order. We have no easy way of assessing its possible impact as propaganda. But we can note that such an overt stress on the importance of national self-determination inevitably raises the question of colonial-style imperialism. In other words, there is a stark contradiction between national self-determination and imperialism at the very heart of this statement. Note that these contradictory movements can trace their historical roots to the same source: modern Europe. This is a manifest fact and truth of history beyond denial or evasion. So if we see the Atlantic Charter as an attempt to obscure this truth, this failure can be found in its apparent suggestion that the future belongs not to colonial imperialism and global domination (*kenryoku shihai*) but to national self-determination alone.[95]

The logic of this assessment [embodied in the Atlantic Charter] is simply indefensible, as is immediately obvious to even the meanest intelligence.[96] It may be an agreeable-sounding slogan designed to elicit easy applause, but in fact it is without substance. It has no basis in the facts of modern history. Consider the meaning of words such as 'freedom' and 'equality', and you will

---

95 Beyond the 'contradictions' of Anglo-American liberty, the objection is to the claim to viability of the nation-state itself as it existed pre-1919 in the post-1919 era of liberal imperialism and the *Großraum* response.
96 Leaving aside the contradictions inherent in the Atlantic Charter, Tōjō's policies in China and South-East Asia are also the target here.

see my point. If one advocates freedom in the [strict doctrinaire] liberal sense, a commitment to free competition and a refusal to intervene [to protect the weak] follows. Laissez-faire means the strong are free to triumph over the weak in an act of dog-eat-dog carnage. The result follows as night follows day: equality is sacrificed so the strong may rule. Thus any principle of freedom so enunciated allows one to sit comfortably with the contradiction between national determination and colonial imperialism, but in fact one slogan depends on an abstract form of ethics while the other hangs on the brutal fact of domination by force. To fail to understand this is to have no feeling for the truth. The contradictions of the Atlantic Charter as an expression of modern thought are spectacularly clear, and I think one should be able to persuade the world that from the standpoint of the theory and the facts of modern history, this stance is nothing more than can be expected from the [old] order that started this war.

Yes, it is true that the first part of the Atlantic Charter assures the rest of world that neither Britain nor America has any further territorial ambitions. Closer to the end of the Charter one finds the commitment to open markets and freer trade. But one is forced to ask oneself: who closed their markets to the world in the first place? Having conquered vast tracts of the globe, America and Britain now seek to play the innocent. Thus does the robber put on a brazen face ...

KŌSAKA: That's the way it is!
KŌYAMA: One must not ridicule people by assuming they are blind ... but in a war of ideas the fundamental strategy must seek to do more than just identify the contradictions in the world-view of one's opponents. One has to offer a fresh set of moral principles.[97]
NISHITANI: I am afraid that the Americans and British are assuming that their colonies are not yet ready for independence, that they have not yet reached this stage of [politically mature] development, and therefore that London and Washington will have to look after them until they are mature enough for self-government. But this does not mean that the colonies are not to be exploited in the meantime. Therein lies the contradiction. The intention is to deceive. The contrast with Japan, entrusted as we are with almost the whole burden of historical necessity, is unambiguous and telling.

Japan's role is to help foster national awakening of the nations of East Asia, and to help nurture a co-prosperity sphere that meets the needs of all the peoples of our region. That is our mission, to be carried out by seeking to lead and to guide them in a positive way.[98] This is what we must seek to do.

97 Once again, criticism of the Atlantic Charter can be read as a tilt at Tōjō and his policies.
98 By contrast, Tōjō can hardly be seen to be leading the region in a 'positive' way: thus Nishitani transforms one of the most hackneyed of Japanese expressions, *seikyokuteki*, into a slap at government policy.

By contrast, this quality of leadership and guidance has no place in the Anglo-American democratic approach to national self-determination. On the contrary, any degree of genuine national self-awakening would be very problematic for them. The commitment to national self-determination is a ploy, nothing more than an empty slogan. Under the banner of democracy, the colonial powers remain in charge of the colonies in question until they are [considered] ready for independence, while in the meantime ensuring that these colonies are materially exploited via a series of hidden policies designed to keep them in thrall to the metropolitan power [now and later]. This strategy lies at the heart of Anglo-American commitment to 'democracy'. Moreover, whatever they intend or do not intend, they are trapped by historical necessity in this bitter form of hypocrisy.

KŌYAMA: That is manifestly the case.
KŌSAKA: Modern Europe has been shaped by contradictions built into the very fabric and structure of its political system. The most potent source of Europe's sickness is to be found in its divided moral sense or, to put the point still more strongly, the outright collapse of the moral confidence of Europe itself.[99] All too often people conclude that it is the ideals of liberty and individualism that most readily characterize [the essence of] modern Europe. This is not only a simplification but also neglects the fact that among all the achievements of modern Europe none matters more, at least in my view, than the creation of the modern state. This invention is in no way inferior to those other great European creations machine civilization, capitalism, the Reformation and modern science. And my claim can be sustained in the face of the obviously complex and mutually reinforcing nature of these achievements. From the very outset of the Renaissance, the impact of popular ethnic nationalism (*minzokushugi*) and statism (*kokkashugi*) were evident. This does not mean that the influence of the ideas of freedom, equality and humanity was an illusion. Quite the contrary: the widely held view that these ideals exerted enormous influence on the Renaissance is correct. But we must not forget that such benevolent forces were merely the other side of the coin, the binary inversions of nationalism, absolutism and statism. This view – that each manifest virtue has had a manifest price – has been relatively neglected [in the assessments of the pros and cons of European civilization]. Indeed, Europeans seem to be utterly oblivious to the implied contradiction. Such obliviousness reflects a radical failure of reflection. Certainly Europeans have not thought through this political issue with anything approaching the kind of seriousness it demands, which is precisely why we must.

---

99 *Jinrintai* (or *jinrisei*) is the Japanese for *Sittlichkeit* or (customary) morality.

This failure of reflection explains Europe's moral sickness, its state of moral collapse. It is also the root cause of Europe's fundamentally mistaken attitude towards the Orient.[100] In other words, while Europeans lecture the rest of the world on the ideals of liberty, equality and fraternity as well as on the [supposed] virtues of national self-determination, such rhetoric only serves to make easier prey out of the victims of European imperialism and aggression.

The interesting thing here is that this fatal (*zettai-teki*) rupture in Europe's moral condition appears to feed the radical divide within the European mind between individualism and totalitarianism. And this is having practical impact on the world outside Europe. Thus, when Europe uses its power to act on the world, while simultaneously proclaiming the rhetoric of humanism, this force takes on an extremely aggressive form. The net result is that such humanism provides an all too perfect kind of camouflage for such aggression. This is the dangerous contradiction at work in the Western approach to the rest of the world we must warn about.[101] Don't you think?

KŌYAMA: We have to appreciate that the fundamental contradiction at work here derives from the way that humanism as a creation of modern Europe is really a form of self-love [parading as universalism].[102]

KŌSAKA: This is the contradiction of humanism. This is what happens when you make man the measure of all things.[103]

NISHITANI: This thing we call modern democracy, its standpoint, if you will, begins with the affirmation of a selfish form of liberty. This has, I suspect, formed its core. So however much the value of equality is asserted as a kind of contract [between members of society], the doctrine of equality serves only as a form of [mild] restraint on the otherwise unlimited assertion of selfishness and self-gratification (*yokubō*). At no point is the individual's right to pursue selfish desires called into question or denied. Thus we arrive at the first contradiction within European thought: the [unequal] contest between equality and individual

---

100 Kōsaka's criticism is over-determined. Europe's moral failure reflects simultaneously the impact of post-Christian nihilism and the duplicitous exploitation of liberal morality to bolster a decaying European imperialist order and to justify liberal imperialism in tandem with the rise of America's global hegemony. Criticism of the takeover of Manchuria in Lord Lytton's report of 1932 was the final legal blow to Japan's support for the post-1919 Versailles-Geneva order.

101 Another implicit critique of the conduct of the Imperial Army and Tōjō's policies in China and South-East Asia.

102 This needs to be set against Karl Löwith's remarks in his 'Afterword to the Japanese Reader', in *Martin Heidegger and European Nihilism*, that the Japanese unwillingness to tolerate 'immoderate criticism of themselves or others' is rooted in a form of 'self-love'.

103 The Japanese text should be understood as it is written: nevertheless it anticipates Heidegger's (late) dismissal of Nazism as a pernicious form of humanism. For a more detailed treatment of this controversy, see my *Defending Japan's Pacific War*, pp. 139–40.

freedom. Reproduce this contest at the level of the state and nation (*minzoku*) and modern democracy is the result.[104] Thus in the advocacy of the modern democratic state we find a fundamental contradiction between the assertion that each and every country should enjoy such liberty and autonomy and the unrestrained pursuit of national interests and material desires by one's own nation [at the expense of weaker nations].

KŌYAMA: And here one finds the roots of the ideas we are criticizing. Granted, we have treated this as a problem in the previous symposia [*possible editorial gap*] ... in other words, this set of ideas assumes that agency exists in an already perfected form, be that the individual or the nation (*minzoku*). This stands as the fundamental assumption of the philosophy of individualism, as a theory of liberty and equality, and the source of its fundamental misunderstanding of the world. This assumption ignores the truth about mankind as it is. The same ability to act in and on the world is not shared by all. One has to earn one's place in the world by self-mastery; this capacity is not God-given. It cannot be assumed. Or, to put it another way, to think that everybody is equal in this way is to surrender to an abstract notion that has no purchase on reality. This Western approach ends where the real struggle begins. The necessary task of winning a genuine place in the world is thus occluded. Because there is no notion of 'place' [or rank] in this web of ideas, the significance of the idea of a 'place' is lost from view. When this happens, the necessary challenge that confronts each and every human being, [the call] to make history, is also lost from view. Furthermore, because this approach begins with an ideal that, as a premise, has no relationship whatever with reality, it entirely lacks any practical power to shape and guide reality in a moral way. It leaves the conflict between ethics and power, ideals and reality totally unresolved. And furthermore it seeks to impose such abstractions on relations between nationalities in the attempt to extract some sort of international system or order from this vortex of theoretical failure. This, to repeat, is to compound the error because the original assumption, with its tangle of abstractions and flawed ideas, has proceeded from the brain as a pure [untested] conception. This 'truth' (*dōgi*) offers no foundations upon which to erect a peaceful world order. The manifest simplicity of the error involved – and it is an obvious one – makes one wonder if the Anglo-American mind has departed from its senses (*general laughter*).[105]

NISHITANI: One may evoke ideals such as 'freedom' and 'equality' but at root such ideas are grounded in the pursuit of desire and self-gratification

---

104 The pursuit of happiness, in the American tradition, falls under censure here.
105 This is the laughter not of derision but of intellectual embarrassment on behalf of one's opponents.

(*yokubō*). What we have here is not freedom and equality as such but freedom and equality from the standpoint of desire ... [106]

KŌYAMA: Desire cannot, in the end, bed down with freedom and equality.

NISHITANI: If one does not violate the freedom of others, if one acknowledges the equality of others, then one is in a position to recognize the right to self-determination of other 'nations' (*minzoku*). This situation of mutual recognition of the liberty of others would permit the emergence of a plausible world order. But such an order would not call into radical question any self-serving desires and tendencies towards self-gratification among either individuals or nations. Indeed, a domestic or international order based on the idea that my desires and ambitions serve to limit those of my neighbour and vice versa would only intensify those desires on all sides. This highlights the truth that such mutual recognition of the freedom of others hangs on the idea of human beings as content-free abstractions. In the absence of any reference to genuine agency, one ends up insisting on formal equality between two 'human beings' who are in fact nothing but ciphers or imagined beings. Any would-be domestic or international order ruled by such notions of equality and freedom would lack any substance and would therefore be purely formal in character. Worse still it would be a formality and nothing else. Only mutual [respect for] our freedoms can guarantee the freedom to pursue what we desire. Nevertheless, the notion that one must recognize the freedom of others tends to become something abstract and meaningless when applied to relationships between 'human beings' or 'peoples'. It really refers only to equality between individuals seen as 'human beings' in the abstract: hence my stress on the merely formal character of such notions of equality. One has merely to look beneath the coin inscribed with formal declarations of freedom and equality to reveal a realm of ever greater treachery where the lust for power is unrestrained and the strong devour the weak. And this is the realm of Anglo-Saxon global economic hegemony and colonialist exploitation. Yet, because they have proclaimed their commitment to an order based on freedom and equality, this pretence serves to silence those who would resist the injustice of Anglo-Saxon economic domination. If, out of necessity, one is then forced to resort to armed resistance, one is labelled an 'aggressor nation'. In other words, an order based on 'freedom and equality' turns out to be the perfect strategy for sustaining their global economic hegemony. The way the League of Nations has become the puppet of the British may be the outstanding example of this phenomenon. In this way, equality as a formal principle can become in reality a formidable weapon for protecting global inequality. The ideal and

---

106 Only a decade earlier, Alexandre Kojève had celebrated Hegel as the 'the philosopher of desire' in Paris. Vulnerable to Confucian suspicion of individualism, the Kyoto thinker concedes that equality must trump desire, even if one man's version of happiness is another's vision of hell.

the reality work together. And this is what I meant when earlier I spoke of the 'hypocrisy' of democracy.

KŌYAMA: The history of modern Europe in and of itself, certainly in terms of the pursuit of desire and material gain, has denied a proper existence to other individuals and peoples. Lacking a principle that goes much further than the pursuit of profit or material gain, it has thus made a decent life and livelihood for humanity and the world impossible. Isn't this the truth that the trajectory of modern Europe has necessarily brought us to? And one of the facts that has been revealed by our current struggle is a higher moral principle than [the] mere [pursuit of] profit.

15 The concepts (*gainen*) of 'co-prosperity' and 'morality'

NISHITANI: From this vantage it becomes necessary to define what we mean when we use the term 'co-prosperity'.

KŌYAMA: There is an awkwardness here, but I believe one should understand *kyōei* (co-prosperity) as something to be to be allied with *dōgi eiyo* (pride in being moral).

NISHITANI: What do you mean by *eiyo*?

KŌSAKA: *Eiyo* means being proud of being principled. In other words, taking pride in what we are doing or moral pride. One might also use the word *kōei* (honour) as well.

NISHITANI: Of course. I understand now what you want to say. It is worth noting in this connection that in English *kyōei* tends to be rendered as 'co-prosperity', and thereby the Japanese nuance of the word *kyōei* is inevitably lost: it becomes but a pale version of the Japanese original if we fall back on the fundamental American emphasis on the term 'prosperity' with its obvious stress on the economic at the expense of everything else.[107] Indeed the danger, and it is a grave one, is that the high ideals expressed in the term *kyōei* will be displaced in favour of the [merely] economic [business and money making]. Granted, economic strength plays a vital role in the current struggle. It is terribly important. And this means that the economic development of the nations that belong to the co-prosperity sphere is a crucial consideration; but more is at stake than the American priorities of money making and economic advantage. We have to think about the question in this way lest the moral dimension ...

---

107 The term *kyōei* in Japanese, from which the English expression 'co-prosperity' is derived, consists of two Chinese characters. *Kyō* means 'together' or 'shared'; this is the source of the 'co' in co-prosperity'. But *ei* in Japanese is the *on-yomi* or Chinese reading of the Chinese character that also carries the *kun* or Japanese reading *sakae*, and this can mean 'prosperity' but also 'honour', 'glory', 'splendour' or ' brilliance'; hence Nishitani's complaint about the nuance lost in the English rendering.

KŌYAMA: And that is why we need an idea such as moral pride.

NISHITANI: There is something I remembered when Huizinga's name came up before. In his book *In the Shadow of Tomorrow*, he offers an analysis of the present (that is the present as of 1935 when the book appeared) in which he explains what he sees as the various signs of danger and decline in European culture. Then in his concluding chapter he proposes remedies for these problems, and in particular he calls for what he terms a new 'asceticism' in order to achieve a kind of spiritual cleansing of the whole culture. This task can only be successfully undertaken by human beings who themselves have already undergone this spiritual cleansing.

If the asceticism of the ancients involved a withdrawal from the world, the new asceticism urges us towards the overcoming of ourselves (*jikō o kokufuku sure*).[108] Such an overcoming would mean that what we call *Leben* must be allied with death. At least, this is what I remember Huizinga saying. I have thought the same thing for some time, and found it interesting to discover that Huizinga is of the same mind about this question. This new asceticism or moral cleansing is becoming a problem of great practical importance today.

Let's take an everyday commonplace example. We are currently at war. Almost every facet of our lives is regulated or controlled. When liberalism confronts this kind of situation, all it feels is the discomfort of the restraints imposed by the narrowing of the scope of freedom. Restraints on the pursuit of profit fuel similar emotions. But we see this [constraint] is something more than the price of necessity. Rather, we embrace it positively as our duty, and we pursue it with ever greater rigour and determination. And this is where the new transformation of values must begin.[109]

The negation of profit making and pleasure seeking can give birth to an awareness of higher values, much higher ones. The general public of the whole nation (*kokumin ippan*) must share in this moral awakening. This is what I believe. If this can be achieved, a new standpoint for humanity, a new standpoint for spiritual cleansing, the very things we must have, will manifest itself among us.[110] Without this transformation, the sense of confinement and restriction that results from [wartime] regulation ends in something reduced and negative: a mere 'minus'. And the longer it lasts, the more likely it is that it will result in a withering away of the soul itself. But also note that any

---

108 The apparent similarity to Nietzsche's idea of the 'superman', someone who has overcome himself, may not be accidental. Nietzsche was Nishitani's favourite German author, and *Thus Spake Zarathustra* his favourite Nietzschean text. See the new translation by Graham Parkes of Nietzsche's masterpiece, published by Oxford University Press (New York) in 2006.
109 Again, Nishitani sounds what seems to be a very Nietzschean note.
110 The language bears uncanny resemblance to the idiom of Heidegger's 1933 Rectoral Address.

scheme to provide temporary diversions, in the form of amusements of one kind or another, from the burdens of war represents a policy failure because it falls so obviously between stools.

The fundamental move towards building a [proper] way of life in wartime starts with the transformation of the privations of war into something positive and uplifting. It is here that a first step can be taken towards the creation of a new kind of human being, and thus a new standpoint [from which to conceive and organize such a life], that is, a way of life that transcends the distinction between war and peace.

In fact, the spirit that Huizinga sees at work in a life that is allied with death is already making its presence felt in Japan today. There has been a revival of old samurai virtues as set forth in works such as *Hagakure*.[111] And from such roots a robust way of living can grow and flourish. But nothing that qualifies as the great cultural spirit that Huizinga believes must define this programme for a new age seems to be taking shape here. We must nurture something truly great that transcends the divide between war and peace, that therefore sees these two defining aspects of life as a unity driven by a common current. If I am right to argue in this way, I would also note that Japan has produced this kind of spiritual greatness in the past. It was certainly evident in the way the Tokugawa Period transformed the ethos of the samurai into the ever-deepening amalgam of the warrior arts and the civilized arts (*bun-bu itto*) that not only transformed our lives and culture but gave them definition and shape. And this makes it all the more interesting that during the disturbances of the Meiji Restoration, this same amalgam of the arts of war and peace made people then so intensely alive and aware of life's possibilities. Meiji as a manifestation of the standpoint of humanity (*ningen*) about which I have been speaking is an utterly arresting phenomenon.

The philosophy that simultaneously cultivates the spirit of the warrior within the civilian and civilizes the fighter with the virtues of the scholar must be brought to life once more today. This is the spirit that overcomes the difference between war and peace, and that allows one to stay the course, unmoved and unchanging, through all the fluctuations of life. We need to develop a culture that reaches all the way back to the cult of learning to die in the manner set out in the *Hagakure* (*Hagakure no shi*). In this way the fierce passionate spirit that bursts to the surface during an emergency, all ardour and intensity, is not lost even during the otherwise placid normalcy of peacetime. In this way the civilized values of the arts may be blended with the readiness and skills of the warrior, thus forming a unity of mind and nature in

---

111 The title given to the so-called 'book of the samurai' dictated by Tsunetomo Yamamoto (1659–1719). In introducing this observation, Nishitani uses the expression 'Bushido' or the 'Way of the Warrior', a set of medieval Zen doctrines for the samurai that displayed a stark and stoic realism about the manner and meaning of death, in the field or at one's own hand.

which the flame of passion burns in an otherwise perfect calm.[112] This is the truth that must be affirmed now. And this need can be met by the kind of cultural work of moral and spiritual cleansing that Huizinga terms 'the new asceticism'. Does this not constitute the point of departure for the spiritual transcendence – and it would be a fundamental one – of the [limitations of] the Anglo-Saxon lifestyle of money making (prosperity) and selfish individualism (the ideology of democracy)?[113]

KŌYAMA: I am in entire agreement with all of that.

16 The world-historical foundations of the national self-defence state (*kokubō kokka*)

SUZUKI: I find that the idea of a new asceticism very attractive. I have not read Huizinga's book ... but to hark back to the idea developed earlier about eliminating the gap between the values of war and of peace, I am convinced that we do need a new concept of warfare that transcends this conventional distinction. To say as much is to face up to the problem of clarifying what is meant by the concept of 'the national self-defence state'. I suspect that this idea requires some considered specific attention. The notion of 'national self-defence state' first came into prominence, somewhat noisily, during the China Incident, [even though], regardless of the history of the term itself, calls for a new organization of the state had been conspicuous for some time before that. But the question before us [now] is what should serve as the theoretical foundations for the idea that travels under the name 'national self-defence state'? How is this idea best understood? What makes it a proper idea ... ?

NISHITANI: The reasons why the notion of the 'national self-defence state' became an object of public awareness are the consequence of quite specific historical conditions. The decisive factor is something we have previously discussed at length: the collapse of the distinction between war and peace, the fact that present war began to take shape under what were effectively peacetime conditions ...

SUZUKI: Of course one agrees with that, but it does not follow that historical conditions being favourable to the idea of a national self-defence state is sufficient alone to explain the appearance of the concept. The obvious

---

112 *Resshi*, literally 'the ardent warrior', means 'patriot' or 'hero' in Japanese, emotional intensity being the positive expression of two cardinal virtues – sincerity and effort. But Nishitani's comments play on the total self-control of the warrior, the perfect inner stillness of his spirit, while he is caught up in the ferocity of battle. Finally, there is the implicit notion that the core attributes of inner Japanese feeling, its cultural validity and truth, are immune to the fortunes of the current war, will outlast defeat, and perhaps one day will reverse its effects. The passionate intensity and tireless effort that drove the post-war Japanese miracle is being predicted here, just as Nishitani's 'reading' of the Japanese national character will be confirmed by the unfolding of economic fact between 1955 and 1990.

113 Nishitani uses the expression *demokurashii no shisō*, which I have rendered here as 'the ideology of democracy'.

link between this idea and the phenomenon of total war must not lead one to conclude that a war like this would [necessarily] give birth to such an idea. Something with such profound roots in the [world-]historical process – and this process of development continues even now – has been given a special intensity and weight by the war. At least, this is how we might want to think about it. In short, all I am saying is that the idea is not the product of a temporary military emergency but rather refers to the workings of something far more profound, something essential rather than transient ...

KŌYAMA: I do not disagree with this analysis. The idea of a 'national defence state' has a historical character consistent with your notion of the 'historical state' (*rekishi-teki kokka*). And as an idea it has absolutely nothing to do with the transient or the accidental. Its historical character derives from a fundamental turning point: the passing of the old order, the end of the order of the modern state and the modern world. Note the fact that it has proven impossible to maintain the Anglo-Saxon order in continental Europe. As this order has collapsed on the continent, the urge to create, 'to will' a new order, to bring it into being, has gained force.[114] But it is equally true that the Anglo-Saxons have in response sought to bring the full weight of their reserves of wealth and power into play to crush this determination to construct a new [post-modern] order. And it is because of this counter-offensive that a defensive position must be erected [in East Asia][115] in order to counter this [Anglo-Saxon] offensive, and thus to allow us to overturn the old order by defeating it.

As we have clearly arrived at this stage [in the conflict] it is obvious that a national self-defence state is essential.[116] And this reality unites this struggle to overturn the existing order with our current struggle understood as a war

---

114 The reference to the rise of fascism and the expansion of German power in continental Europe is obvious, while the expression 'to will' can be seen to echo Heidegger's Rectoral Address. The reference to *bōgyo* may also suggest interest in the notion of 'Fortress Europe' once Germany had been decisively defeated in North Africa and on the Eastern Front at Stalingrad. But what is remarkable about this passage is that neither Hitler, nor the Third Reich, nor yet the alliance with Germany and Italy is mentioned. In fact there is no reference to Germany and Italy as Japan's allies anywhere in these three symposia. Many Navy officers disapproved of Japan's tripartite pact with Nazi Germany and Fascist Italy, and the wording here suggests that the Kyoto School also disapproved. The silence on the Third Reich in 1942 is striking.
115 Kōyama uses the term *bōgyo*; however, 'Fortress Europe' as translated into Japanese literally means a defensive position.
116 Have the events of Midway as well as Stalingrad and El Alamein been factored into this realistic assessment of Japan's military position? The idea of 'a national self-defence state' is usually dated from the 1930s, when it was used to urge Japan to gird its loins and better mobilize its economy for a war of expansion against Republican China, but by November 1942 it had assumed an entirely new meaning. The Kyoto School's definition of the Great East Asian War as a world-historical conflict or a war of total resistance suggests that while these thinkers conceded that the war was probably lost, they still believed that the old European order was doomed. Eventually East Asians would be their own masters.

of total resistance (*sō ryoku sen*).[117] Nevertheless, just as a war of total resistance must also be a struggle fought by the whole Co-prosperity Sphere, the main purpose of any national self-defence state must be the construction [and development] of the Co-Prosperity Sphere. Indeed, the national defence state, the war of total resistance and the Co-prosperity Sphere must become three things in one: a trinity, if you like.

NISHITANI: Don't you perhaps think that the name 'national self-defence state' is excessive, a bit over the top? Isn't it really?

SUZUKI: That is indeed how I sort of feel about it. Perhaps we can think about it in this way. As I spelled out in *The Idea of the World-historical State*, if one dwells only on the most conspicuous contemporary forces, one might conclude that politics – or, more precisely, political power – is very much to the fore at the moment. There is an extraordinary emphasis on the power of politics, the stronger the better, to solve problems. And if one asks oneself why this might be the case, the answer is that the historical situation encourages one to take this view. The most obvious example of a problem for which a strong form of politics offers a solution is the business of overcoming class divisions. Demands for forceful political action are fuelled by fears of the crisis that class warfare would provoke. Hence the call for a power that transcends the divisiveness of class struggle, and such calls have without question resulted in the strengthening of the powers of the state (although they constitute only one factor among others that contribute to an explanation of this change).

But the larger point is this. Notwithstanding this pronounced stress on enhancing the powers of the state, I remain unconvinced that politics, however robust, offers a solution to each and every problem we face now. Nevertheless, this belief in the ability of political action to solve problems forms the intellectual or ideological foundation for the growth of the powers of the state everywhere. And in broad terms the result is this: the state is burdened with the challenge of an urge to transcend the merely political. Today the weight and scope of this challenge are becoming ever greater. State claims to political and legal existence, in the strict meaning of these ideas, are no longer in and of themselves satisfying. Today's states need to embody sociological and philosophical existence.[118] This represents a radical new form of the state, and it is becoming ubiquitous.

---

117 Here, once again, the meaning of the term *sō ryoku sen* is ambiguous, moving around like water in a partially filled glass that is being shaken. The nuance of the usage here is closer to 'total war' or the conventional rendering 'all-out war', but as both of these terms have been completely rejected by the symposia participants on numerous occasions, I have employed 'war of total resistance' as opposed to a 'war for world history' or a 'world-historical war'.

118 The first substantial chapter of *The Logic of the Species*, Hajime Tanabe's monumental magnum opus from the mid-1930s, is entitled the 'philosophy of social existence'. There Tanabe rejects the traditional notion of philosophical anthropology in favour of a 'philosophical sociology'.

Where once in Europe, the Church, the universities and the enterprise were entrusted with a broad set of social roles, today the state has been reabsorbing all these functions. And more is at stake in this change than the mere expansion of the authority and sovereignty (*shuken*) of the state. The state is altering in its very essence. In other words, we are witnessing the historical transition from the modern to the contemporary state. This transformation explains why the state needs to demonstrate an intellectual or theoretical or ideological coherence that was previously not expected of it. This furthermore explains why such states have to engage in the struggle of ideas long before they need to, or are able to, resort to armed conflict. In the same way, economic struggle will precede the state's resort to war. It is this early stage, not later, that witnesses the initial appearance of the 'national self-defence state'. And this means one must reject out of hand the notion that the national self-defence state is merely an exercise in the intense mobilization of a nation's powers to fight wars. In others words, the national self-defence state is not is some reactionary rebirth of old-fashioned militarism in more sophisticated dress. Quite the contrary: the national self-defence state begins with and is grounded in the struggle of ideas and economic competition between nations. Isn't this what the expression really means? Isn't this the stage [of development] at which the Japanese state finds itself now? The true sophistication of the Japanese state now is to be found in the struggle to foster our co-prosperity sphere. This demonstrates how far we have advanced.

Even more telling is the fact that this is a global phenomenon. In other words, states everywhere are caught in a momentous transition.[119] Note also the impressive manner in which the current phase of state development, the one embodied in the national self-defence state, captures exactly what our historical awareness demands of the times. Consciousness and reality find themselves in rare accord.

The British historian Christopher Dawson argues a similar case. Communist and other totalitarian states have assumed a global offensive based on their new-style state powers, and in response the states of the old order have been placed on the defensive. And this means we are approaching a critical fork in the road. The crucial act of national self-re-examination confronts us with the question: what kind of state is Japan? We have to decide this for ourselves.

One must understand that there is no likelihood whatever of the democracies converting to communism or totalitarianism. Certainly in the case of Great Britain there are powerful historical, cultural and intellectual reasons why the British will never abandon democracy. But the salient point is this: the very principles of democracy allow democratic states to create formidably

---

119 This claim that the Japanese national self-defence state is a universal idea, and therefore in the eyes of the Kyoto School has greater validity than some narrow nativist vision of the Japanese state, suggests an intellectual approach remarkably close to that of the great secularizing jurist Tatsukichi Minobe. For a fuller development of this comparison with Tanabe, see Williams, *Defending Japan's Pacific War*, pp. 110–11.

powerful systems of government. Indeed, in extreme cases the concentration of power [and the mobilization of the society] is so comprehensive, so complete, that one can imagine a kind of 'democratic totalitarianism'.[120] In this context, it is possible to see such mobilized democratic states as [exemplifying] a kind of 'national self-defence state'. Britain and America could change in this way. In some ways they are already doing so. Indeed, to fight this war, they must. Reality, in my judgement, means there is no alternative.

To repeat: the rise of the national self-defence state is not a uniquely Japanese phenomenon; it is a global phenomenon. The same challenge confronts all serious states. And, to drive the point home, one must once again insist that national self-defence states are not merely the product of wartime necessity. In other words, the sequence of cause and effect does not begin with the start of war, continuing as the burdens of fighting a war mount and so the state begins to focus its energies under the guise of a national self-defence state. If anything, the sequence is the reverse. The transformation of history, the world-historical moment, reveals a new vision of the state and its essence, and a set of principles that reflect that essence as revealed at this world-historical turning point, thus making the [creation of the] national self-defence state a natural and inevitable stage in the unfolding of historical reality. Wars of world-historical significance are then fought to bring about the changes envisioned. History, not the temporary exigencies of warfare, is in the driving seat. Isn't this the real logic of the thing?

KŌYAMA: We need a concept that allows us to draw a categorical distinction between the idea of the national self-defence state, understood in this way, and a conventional military state (*gunji kokka*) or a state merely at war (*senji kokka*) or, if you will, in 'a state of emergency'.

SUZUKI: It follows from this that 'national defence' (*kokubō*) as an idea anticipates reality. It is not a product of reality that waits upon events and developments. It has a more general [metaphysical or philosophical] character; it is not a factual example but a category that shapes historical fact and reality.

NISHITANI: The kind of 'totalitarian democracy' discussed by Dawson is, in my view, a development that proceeds from an intellectual standpoint. The concept comes first.

SUZUKI: What is one to think about this? Finally, I think there is a point of substance here. In Great Britain, a coalition of national unity has been

---

120 The term 'totalitarianism' in Suzuki's usage refers as much to totality of scale, as in the expressions 'total mobilization' or 'total war', as it does to authoritarian totalitarianism. In this sense Suzuki's line of thought approaches that of the German nationalist thinker Ernst Jünger, who argued in his essay 'Totale Mobilization' that democracies are better able to mobilize the whole of the population than class-ridden modern feudal states such as Imperial Germany or the Austro-Hungarian Empire under the Habsburgs. See Williams, *Defending Japan's Pacific War*, pp. 11–12.

created and seems set to persist well into the future, and this in itself is inconsistent with the normal workings of the British constitution.[121] In the United States, the expansion of President Roosevelt's powers under the New Deal programme has been the stuff of severe constitutional controversy.[122] Indeed, his three successive elections to the presidency are in themselves a radical departure from the normal democratic state [state = central government] practice. The pressures of the moment have transformed the formerly unthinkable into reality. Dawson and others are thus suggesting that Britain is in the process of abandoning the nineteenth-century tradition of continental European (*tairiku*) liberalism in favour of its own brand of democratic statist nationalism.[123] In this manner, the British are finding their own way of fostering a [genuinely] twentieth-century state via the rediscovery of their own unique pre-nineteenth-century tradition.[124]

NISHITANI: The new form of statehood demanded by the times, by the transition from the present to the future, cannot be achieved by the kind of fusion one finds in totalitarian democracies. The genuine innovation is always something that is new already, that is spiritually [in the Hegelian sense] prepared.[125] There must be a third way: not democracy and not totalitarianism, nor some hybrid fusion of the two. The third way must possess its own unique spirit because without this unique spirit it will not be new. And my conclusion is that this new spirit has manifested itself in our Japan because it embodies the new standpoint of the kind of new state that history demands. This new standpoint incorporates what Suzuki calls 'the national self-defence state' and this indeed is to a significant degree a universal phenomenon. But Japan's position within this universal trend represents a breakthrough that is just that much more advanced, and thus qualifies as a general or universal trend …

---

121 If one assumes that Suzuki's understanding of British politics is sound, he may be referring to the suspension of the normal contest between 'His Majesty's Government' and 'the loyal Opposition'. A subtle issue is the supremacy of the British cabinet in parliament, a doctrine with roots in Britain's pre-democratic tradition of monarchic absolutism. Carl Schmitt forcefully reminded twentieth-century democrats that while the concept of 'liberal democracy' makes these two different notions work in tandem, in fact democratic legitimacy and liberal legitimacy are, in essence, different things. Roosevelt's wartime powers in 1942, no less than the powers assumed by George W. Bush after 11 September 2001, illustrate the lesson.
122 The immediate issue to which Suzuki is referring may be the president's growing war powers, but the attempt by his Administration to 'pack' the Supreme Court so that it ceased to stand in the way of New Deal programmes provoked constitutional controversy of the first order.
123 Suzuki used the term 'ultranationalism' (*kokusui-teki dentō*), which tends to refer to popular ethnic nationalism (and not only in Japan) rather than to statism, but, in the context, I think that he means 'statism' (*kokkashugi*).
124 Curiously, Suzuki is less persuasive about Churchill's government but strikingly clairvoyant about the Blair 'presidential' subversion of Whitehall and parliament sixty years later.
125 Nishitani uses the expression 'the spirit itself'. Here, as in Hegel and elsewhere in nineteenth-century German philosophy, the spiritual is the opposite of the mutely material.

SUZUKI: That's the point, this breakthrough to the future. It is as Kōyama just mentioned in his insistence on a co-prosperity sphere as a creative programme of construction that provides an example of the [indispensable] horizon for this advance into the future.

NISHITANI: This is the shape that reality is actually taking. For example, totalitarianism is confining itself to the challenges of one nation and one nation alone.[126] It takes as its point of departure the problems of a single society, but this [focus] alone is not enough to stand as the organizing principle for a new world order. As long as communism remains focused on class [and therefore class struggle], it cannot provide a theoretical framework for the required [universal] principle.[127] As the nation-state (*kokka*) is the subject (*shutai*) that moves history, Russia's contribution to the advance of history is as a state, and only as a state. Because Japan has assumed the standpoint that accepts that the state is the subject that makes history, because it has rejected communism and embraced a concept of the state that seeks universal significance (*sekai-sei*), this country offers the third way (*dai san no tachiba*) that the world is so desperately seeking.

17 The historical necessity for co-prosperity spheres as *Großräume* (*kyōei-ken to rekishi-teki hitsuzensei*)

KŌYAMA: There is nothing here with which I can take issue. Indeed, I am entirely in agreement. But it does occur to me that there are issues we may still need to address. For example, might we ponder why the kinds of new ideas we are discussing are appearing at exactly the same moment as the opportunity to realize them? The suggestion would be that temporal necessity, the relationship between this principle and the course of history [literally 'historical trends'], unfolds in a matter not that dissimilar from breathing in and breathing out. Indeed, this dynamic of ideas and opportunity, thought and action, drives the whole process.

The self-defence state and the co-prosperity sphere are in essence nothing less than the obverse and reverse of the coin of a world-historical turning point. Furthermore, this new principle itself must be grounded in a new set of moral principles. This point has not been problematic in our discussion so far. The issue I want to focus on [now] is that such developments must be

---

126 Stalin's 'socialism in one country' falls into this category no less than the obsessive nationalism of Nazi Germany or the singular focus on the state of Italian Fascism.
127 Suzuki's point only seems strained. Communism does propose a theoretical solution to the divisions of society in the triumph of the working classes. Post-bourgeois society would be a post-conflict society. But Suzuki rejects this notion. Part of the reason may be the conservative Japanese horror at the prospect of class conflict. Another is the suspicion that the Soviet Union will always act in its own national interest, and therefore Communism directed from Moscow will never genuinely serve the interests of a universal movement.

understood as arising from time itself, and not, therefore, a matter of accidental ahistorical 'when' and 'wherefore'. Such [developmental] manifestations or flowerings arise, have their roots, so to speak, in the previous stage of history and arrive in the present as a trend. Such trends take their shape from and work in tandem with the historical conditions that give them birth, but the answer they suggest is not included in the question. And it is here that my problem appears.

As was noted earlier, the self-defence state is a direct response to the covert counter-offensive against the globe's newly emerging powers by the Anglo-Saxon powers who seek to frustrate the will to create a new order.[128] This resistance has provoked the response. However, when we seek to create a new order of co-prosperity spheres or *Großräume* (*kōiki-ken*), to meet the need that previous notions of the state and economy cannot address, this effort must be understood as arising from historical necessity, and not as a manifestation of the mere subjective selfishness and egoism one associates with the traditional state.[129] This necessity is grounded in history, in world-historical conditions that have arisen since the end of the Great War. These new conditions have struck at the heart of our imperative need for military security and economic prosperity, and our identity as a civilization (*bunmei jō, keizai jō gunji jō*). Or, to reverse the perspective, one can assert that the need for a new world order of the kind embodied in concepts such as that of the co-prosperity sphere simply did not exist a century or two ago. Unlike now, the conditions simply did not apply. Take, for example, the contemporary importance of certain 'strategic resources'.[130] The existence of such resources, and the need to have access to them within one's own territory, provide a persuasive practical definition of where *Großräume* (*kōiki-ken*) will draw their boundaries. Such constraints, among other factors, effectively define the geographic scope of such pan-regions. Although a product of the current stage of a globalizing economy, co-prosperity spheres reflect history's need for a new and different set of principles of economic organization, one that breaks with the body of ideas that underwrite conventional global trade. There is much talk of the divide between 'have' and 'have not' economies, but this is a mere symptom of a larger transition. Because the 'have' economies control so much

---

128 *Shinsetsujō no ishii.* Compare this usage with Heidegger's 'will to the future'.
129 A defence of the necessity for imperial expansion based on the insight, widespread at the time – even Hitler's *Mein Kampf* mentions it – that the great powers of the future would possess a continental-scale homeland upon which to base their defence and expansion. Russia and the United States provided the key examples then, just as China, India and perhaps Brazil do today. Given the Pacific War context of this symposium, the Kyoto School thinkers are focusing attention on the imperative for Japan of matching America's 48 contiguous states as the indispensable strategic homeland and base for the post-1945 consolidation of America's unipolar global hegemony.
130 Petroleum would be the example that would occur to most Japanese reading this symposium in January 1943, but Japan's fundamental lack of basic 'modern' natural resources, both energy- and production-related, would play on the minds of all readers at the time.

power, they can intimidate lesser powers with what appear, at first glance, to be wholly peaceful means. Thus an opponent of the old order has to contend with the ability of the established powers to impose an economic blockade, as we saw in the case of the Allies in the last war.[131] The unmistakable impression is that the established order is so powerful that it can see off challenges to its authority without resorting to violent means. But this strategy is vulnerable because it depends on the Allied ability to nurture and sustain a wide coalition [of conflicting interests], as we saw in the last war.

For 'have not' nations, those that seek to challenge the old order, the strategy that must be pursued in the face of this overwhelming power is the construction of an enduring fortress or defensive position, and it is at this point that the notion of 'self-defence state' comes into its own. In other words, a national self-defence state as a pan-regional defence zone (*kokubō kūkan*) must include within the borders of its *Großraum* sufficient territory to ensure economic self-sufficiency. Anything less than such a creation, and national security will not be assured. But this *Großraum* cannot succeed if it is nothing more than a colonial empire.[132] The 'have-not' powers must not attempt to establish their own version of the imperialist colonial order of the past. That would be worse than intolerance. Why? Because the colonialist approach is now doomed in both fact and principle, as the historical fate of imperialism since the last war demonstrates.[133] In terms of principles, we need to take one step higher and achieve something truly new. Only when these various conditions start to be met on all fronts will the co-prosperity sphere as a moral order come into being.

Just before the outbreak of the current European conflict [September 1939], I think it was Chamberlain who declared that the Rhine was Britain's 'lifeline' (*seimeisen*).[134] Even earlier, Japan had announced to the world that Manchuria was our 'lifeline'. Both observations offer early objective evidence of

---

131 The victims were Imperial Germany and Austria-Hungary. However, note also that by 1942 the threat was emerging of a blockade of Japan, and by the time the symposia appeared in book form in the spring of 1943 it was on its way to becoming a reality.

132 Here is more criticism of Tōjō's policies, veiled but damning, couched within a denial of the efficacy and morality of European imperialism. The lesson that Japan's wartime regime did not learn, but which the United States had long since mastered through its interventions in and domination of Central and South America, can be summed up in the strategy of 'base imperialism': a hegemony founded not on direct rule or colonies but on protectorates and military alliances undergirded by a global network of military installations.

133 An undoubted reference to the growth of anti-colonial feeling across the colonized world, from the Philippines to Egypt; perhaps also an oblique reference to nationalist self-assertion in China and Korea. Note that Kōyama does not say that '*European* imperialism' is doomed or *passé*, but makes this claim of imperialism itself, including therefore, in principle, Japanese imperialism as well.

134 Or it may have been an earlier British prime minister, Stanley Baldwin, who in 1934 observed in a speech before the House of Commons: 'When you think about the defence of England you no longer think of the chalk cliffs of Dover. You think of the Rhine. That is where our frontier lies.'

the inability of the modern state as conventionally conceived to meet the challenges posed by the contemporary world. In other words, these military and economic challenges, as they arise from the very nature and limitations of modern civilization, are bursting the confines of the conventional modern state, forcing the revision of traditional borders that have hitherto defined its sovereignty.[135] Now, it is true that nation-states (*minzoku kokka*) find themselves trapped within the boundaries of modern states; but historical necessity pushes such states to expand these borders into order to form a national self-defence state. This is particularly true of 'have-not' nations because they must assume the form of a national self-defence state [if they are to survive]. Once they take the next step down this road, such 'have not' states find themselves at a crucial stage [of historical development] in which the national self-defence state expands beyond its [inherited modern] boundaries and begins to evolve into a *Großraum*. This process of state development by stages reflects, in my view, the workings of a form of historical necessity. This phenomenon should be understood as arising from the completion [and exhaustion] of modernity, and therefore the transition from modernity into something contemporary, the phase of human history that comes after the modern.[136]

The historical situation, thus described, is entirely the work of objective, that is, from a human point of view, passive factors. They might be termed 'chance causes' (*kikaiin*). But to establish a principle of action capable of shouldering, and thus exploiting, these passive factors, we must devise a set of moral principles that is unique to our circumstances. This does not mean that this positive morality of action will not, as the occasion demands, exploit the apparently unrelated accidents of history, those gifts of heaven, that appear in the course of the historical process. Quite the contrary: the genuine power to move history begins to manifest itself only when our positive actions work in harness with the opportunities presented by 'chance causes', objective historical conditions and the atmospherics of the *Zeitgeist* (*reikishiteki fuenki*).

This point matters because our place in the sun will be won when we develop a moral perspective that transcends the pursuit of mere profit and [material] satisfaction that dominates [the ideology of] the Anglo-Saxons. The construction of a genuinely moral order will advance by synthesizing and supplementing this objective [literally, 'passive'] aspect of the challenge. It follows therefore, in my view, that we must proceed to think deeply about the true nature of world history, confident that our moment in the sun will reflect the historical nature of our unique set of positive principles of effective human action.

SUZUKI: It is certainly a fact that the germ of the notion of the *Großraum* or *kōeki-ken* first appeared in a clearly defined form as an economic idea in

---

135 The Kyoto School analysis is sound, but only if one understands that Japan did end up as part of America's *Großraum* in the Pacific.
136 One of the earliest elaborations of the idea that would later travel under the term 'postmodern', as reflected in Naoki Sakae's translation of *gendai* as 'the time after the modern'.

response to the perceived need for much greater living space among the 'have-not' nations. As a concept, an economic *Großraum* assumes an entirely different character from the notion of economic blocs that one finds among 'have' nations such as Great Britain. The latter is merely a strategy for pursuing and maintaining economic privileges, and thus it qualifies neither as a national self-defence state nor as living space, that is a large extension of territory as space judged indispensable to national [or state] survival. Economic blocs among 'have' nations are in essence strategies for coping with the world depression or ways of defending the old capitalist order against fresh economic pressures. But the fact that the idea of the *Großraum* first emerged out of a need to find space sufficient for economic survival suggests that the root of the problem can be linked directly to the limits of modernity. It follows, therefore, as night follows day that building such economic survival zones will involve the creation of a new economic order. But even then the results may still not qualify as the final or highest stage[137] in the consolidation of a genuinely new world order.[138] Indeed, this stress on the economic reflects the limits (*teimei*) of the principle of modernity itself. It points to the need for the new order to reflect a new order of the spirit.[139] This must be ...

KŌYAMA: This new moral principle cannot be shaped from the modern obsession with the pursuit of profit. That dimension or aspect of life is insufficient to this need; but it may provide the contest or conflicted context (*katto no naka kara*) from which can emerge ... (*Kōyama turns towards Kōsaka.*) Didn't Kant insist in his epistemology that that an idea emerges with experience rather than proceeds from it or something like that ... what did Kant say?

KŌSAKA: Ah, yes, the quotation goes as follows [*the German is in the original*]: all understanding (*ninshiki*) arises with experience (*mit der Erfahrung anhebt*) but even so, it does not follow that all understanding arises from experience [alone] (*aus der Erfahrung entspringt*).[140] In contrast to

---

137 The usage mimics that of Marxism-Leninism in which imperialism, for example, is described as the final and highest stage of capitalism. Such borrowings imply a fundamental rejection of Marxist conclusions but demonstrate yet again the depth of the Kyoto School's attention to Marxism and the impact of Marxist language on the discourse of wartime Japanese philosophy.

138 The key word here is 'world'. In Kyoto School usage, the term 'world', as in the expression 'world order', refers to a planet-wide order in which non-Europeans exercise a genuine subjectivity, that is the power to shape world history without dependence on Europe or the West.

139 Again, the term 'spirit' is German (*Geist*), with its specific meaning as embodying subjectivity and the *Zeitgeist*.

140 Quotation from the opening of Kant's *Critique of Pure Reason*: 'Daß alle unsere Erkenntnis mit der Erfahrung anfange, daran ist kein Zweifel ... Wenn aber gleich alle unsere Erkenntnis mit der Erfahrung anhebt, so entspringt sie darum doch nicht eben alle aus der Erfahrung', or, in Norman Kemp Smith's translation, 'There can be no doubt that our knowledge begins with experience ... it does not follow that it all arises from experience'.

anheben, the idea of *entspringen* is intended. In other words, whatever may arise solely from empirical foundations, the understanding that results are determined, in essence, by experience alone. Whatever may arise from the facts of empiricism, that ground cannot provide the origins (*gensen*) of *entspringen*. Or at least that is what I think Kant is trying to argue.

18 Japanese subjectivity and our qualities of leadership (*Nippon no shutai-sei to shidō-sei*)

SUZUKI: The causes of the current conflict can be found within the very nature of the world.[141] There we find the foundations for our present struggle, regarded as a struggle to fulfil a world-historical mission that reaches beyond the scale and scope of Japan to the world itself. The building of a new order for East Asia is not, ultimately, a task that Japan has assumed for itself; it is one that the world has, as it were, imposed on Japan.[142]

NISHITANI: But this coin has an obverse side because we know that the awareness (*jikaku*) of this new world standpoint has unfolded here in Japan itself, thus making this country the global point of self-awareness for this new world.[143]

KŌSAKA: That's the thing.

SUZUKI: Armed with this self-consciousness, Japan must awaken the world. Isn't that right? This, of course, requires that Japan must raise itself, entirely with its own powers, to this new level of consciousness; but this project cannot end there, because Japan has [then] to help awaken the whole world to this new level of consciousness and self-awareness. That is the important thing. It therefore follows that our world-historical mission requires Japan to be more than just a vehicle or means for the manifestation of objective truths only unselfconsciously grasped. For authentic self-consciousness to be achieved, it must be indisputably subjective self-awareness. This is the taxing formula that governs world-historical consciousness.

KŌSAKA: It is a fact that numerous nations have felt it necessary, in varying degrees, to build a self-defence state. This is a global trend. But when one speaks of Japan's national defence state (*kokubō kokka*) one is talking about something different in essence. The word 'breakthrough' (*tsuki*

---

141 See gloss on the term 'world' in Note 138.
142 Suzuki is not evoking the world as in the expression 'world opinion' but rather the constitution of the world that moves and shapes humanity and at the same time is moved and shaped by action on a world scale, both geographically and, in temporal terms, world-historically.
143 All the Hegelian conceits – self-awareness, historical consciousness, world-historical peoples and recognition of the other – are engaged here. But furthermore, the idea of a 'point', as in the expression *jikakuten*, within a universe of possibility harks back to the fundamental metaphysical assumptions of the Kyoto School about the nature of the cosmos.

nukeru) was mentioned earlier: Japan's version of a national defence state must obviously be just that much greater a breakthrough. We have to make that essential leap into another dimension that is wholly new ... This is where Japan's subjective creativity as a nation must come into play.[144] But when we insist that all of this is a historical necessity for Japan, this recognition also demands that we grasp the profound truths to be drawn from the depths of the Japanese past.[145] When one attempts to grasp the problem from this vantage, the crucial horizon comes into view. Thus, if we want to speak responsibly about what form a specifically Japanese national defence state should take today, our conception must break with the general notion of a self-defence state found elsewhere. In other words, care must be exercised to avoid a simple, and therefore tempting, mixture of the flawed general model with the essence of the superior form of the national defence state that we seek to realize here. Thus we must set out with precision the essential structure of such a state as a matter of necessity. And we must work hard to make this distinction obvious [to all]. Furthermore, several questions must be answered. For example, how has this process been mediated by the development of Japanese subjectivity during our long history as a nation? How has Japan's past prepared the way for this country's contemporary world-historical leadership role? Finally, where should one locate the sources of Japanese creativity today? We need to produce considered responses to such questions, and Japan itself will benefit from what we discover.

The search for the answers will be revealed by examining our long history as a nation, both the continuities of [our] tradition and the internalization of external influences, that is 'the world'. At each and every point in our considerations, the font and foundation remains Japanese history. More recently, the building of the Great East Asian Co-Prosperity Sphere has become our [world-historical] goal. The successful pursuit of this goal in turn necessitates the creation of a new world order. The one is indispensable to the other.

NISHITANI: In other words, the role of Japanese subjectivity in the contemporary world arises from the confluence or tangency between the principle of

---

144 That is, subjective as the active history-forming power of the nation-state as actor, as an agent of change. Hegelian subjectivity is in essence a doctrine of agency for the Kyoto School.

145 Compare this interplay of 'future' and 'past' via the metaphor of depth in Heidegger's 'The Self-Assertion of the German University'. The sentence has been recast by adding a grammatical subject that 'recognizes' and 'understands'. Note that in Japanese or German such sentences take on a certain power when they give an objective cast to a feature or dynamic of the historical world. But when translated into English, such modes of expression can become a ghostly gobbledegook precisely because of the absence of an explicit actor or thinker.

self-awareness that has arisen here and the demand for a new order as it reflects the needs of the world itself.

SUZUKI: The world as it stands is flawed; it is caught in a web of contradictions. Modernity, as revealed by the whole history of the modern world, is trapped in a dead end of its own making. Europe's second great war [from 1939 onwards] has been caused by the failed path of Europe itself. The roots of the Great East Asian War can also be traced to Europe's obstructed path. One factor is the contradictions within European life. Another is Europe's contradiction-ridden relationship with the rest of the world. I think the following conclusion will stand. It is inconceivable to me that Japan's subjectivity will not be recognized in the course of the current conflict. Quite the contrary: the world will be compelled to extend this recognition because the world-historical necessity that lies behind the present war is itself a product of the same world that radically contradicts Europe's place in it. The recognition of Japan's subjectivity will come.[146] This is beyond doubt.

This in turn brings us to Kōyama's insistence on the plurality of worlds or the multipolar nature of the globe (*tagensei*). Some time ago I wrote an essay in which I questioned some of the ideas that Kōyama aired.[147] At the time, my friends responded to this essay in a variety of ways, both favourably and critically. Among the criticisms, the suggestion was made that Japanese subjectivity, from Kōyama's standpoint, was under-theorized.[148] This was a key insight. And this is exactly the point we must address, as I noted on an earlier occasion during these discussions. It is my conviction that the theoretical understanding of Japanese subjectivity can be best achieved by deeper reflection on the idea of the plurality of worlds. Nevertheless, when one turns to the issue of Japan's leadership in the world, the issue becomes more complicated. In a 'multi-polar world', or a world characterized by a plurality of worlds [worlds = civilizations], India has a natural place. So does China. There is a variety of other nations/regions/civilizations that qualify as 'worlds'.[149] But Japan has the power to exercise the kind of leadership that is not true of these other worlds. So a classificatory system that merely catalogues this plurality of worlds can provide neither a convincing explanation, nor a theoretical grounding, for Japan's specific gifts for regional and global leadership.

KŌYAMA: The classification or mere listing in a table of the different civilizations scattered across the planet will not remedy the theoretical weaknesses

---

146 Japan will win Hegelian recognition because of what it achieves on the stage of world history.
147 The source is not mentioned but it is almost certainly Suzuki's article in the January 1941 issue of the magazine *Risō*.
148 Literally: 'it required theoretically better-grounded foundations.'
149 All that follows is largely a response to and an elaboration of Kōsaka's original notion of *rekishi-teki sekai* or historical worlds.

that have been identified, and when I formulated my stance I was under no illusion that it would. The key concern is the subjective difference between civilizations. A self-consciousness derived from a unipolar conception of the world will never be able to account for the plurality of worlds in this sense, and I argued against any simplistic insistence on unipolarity in favour of the plurality of worlds [as a fact of history] with this in mind.[150] World history should be looked at in plural terms [because Europe is not the world]. This is what I stressed. But I urged particular attention to this multipolar nature of the past as a world-historical development in order to criticize cyclical theories of culture (*junkan-setsu*) [as we find in Frobenius].[151] Therefore in no way do my views fall into the conventional theory or practice of classificatory pluralism. In this way, I tried to call in question the notion that different cultures' centres have merely co-existed [without reference to the philosophy of world history or Hegelian subjectivity].[152] This was to break with the conventional theory of a multipolar world.

But I was similarly convinced that the school of cultural classification, with its implicit hierarchy between and among different cultural centres or civilizations, was somehow linked to the theory of world history. And this provoked criticism of my interpretation because it appeared not to allow for Japan's attainment of genuine subjectivity and appeared to stop at the theory of co-existence of different civilizations [without allowing for differences between different cultures in terms of their relative subjectivity, but more importantly without giving scope for changes in the hierarchical relationship between different cultures].

However, even a cursory reading of my new book, *The Philosophy of World History*, will, I believe, eliminate the grounds for this kind of misunderstanding.[153] Those who have until recently been keen to repudiate the whole notion

---

150 Thus challenging Hegel's assumption of modern Europe's singular command of subjectivity, and thereby also its claim to be sole maker of authentic world history. Hegel's stance is reaffirmed empirically in Max Weber's 'Author's Introduction' to the English translation of *The Protestant Ethic and the Spirit of Capitalism*.
151 Kōyama rejects cyclical theories of culture for two unstated reasons: 1 his implicit endorsement of linear theories of history (if not cyclical, it must be linear); and 2 his support for the idea of progress. Japan's modernizing take-off effectively endorses and requires both ideas. But one translation quandary leads to an expanded and more nuanced appreciation of Kōyama's dismissal of cyclical theories. His treatment of Frobenius's concept of *Kulturkreislauflehre* in *Sekai-shi no Tetsugaku* comes to mind.
152 Kōyama concedes that the modern world is a European creation – a fact that has made the world effectively unipolar – but asserts that Japan's emergence as an authentic subjective power spells the end of such unipolarity. Nevertheless, the fact that China or India or any other non-European civilizations exist as civilizations or worlds does not mean that they possess the subjective capacity to reshape their own spheres, let alone the world. In 1942, there were the West and Japan, and they alone qualified as Hegelian world history-shaping peoples or civilizations.
153 *Sekai-shi no Tetsugaku*, Tokyo: Iwanani Shoten, 1942.

of world history have been forced by the events of 8 December 1941 suddenly to confront its importance. But they insist that Japan now be held up as the sole beneficiary of a new unipolar view of world history, and indeed claim because of their sudden conversion to the world-historical school that Japan's subjectivity will not be properly recognized by anything less. At least, this appears to be what some people think. Of course, my intention in writing about this theme has been to stress the importance of Japan's subjective self-mastery; but I do not accept that Japan has some kind of monopoly over subjectivity. I disagree as a consequence with those who are attempting to assert a new unipolar scheme into the interpretation of contemporary world history. My idea is that ... [154]

There is no question that now as never before Japan is subjectively shaping (*shidōteki ni*) world history. We ourselves have taken up the burden of transforming the world order, acting as the spear-point and avant-garde of world history. And these shaping powers have rapidly begun to come into their own since 8 December 1941. But the road to this moment can be traced back deep into the past. Take the Great East Asian War that started four years earlier with the outbreak of the Sino–Japanese War or the 'China Incident' (*Sina Jihen*). The China Incident can in turn be linked to the Manchurian Incident [1931], while the origins of that affair reach back even further into the past.

History is the obscure story, starting even before the present China Incident, of how Japan learned to exercise the kind of subjective leadership that has now come to the fore in the Great East Asian War [from December 1941]. The truth of this claim had already been demonstrated by the Russo–Japanese War [1904–05]. That great Japanese victory served as a powerful stimulus to nationalist feelings and awareness in India, the Islamic world and elsewhere. It confirmed, by the display of effective action, Japan's potential to assume its role as the leader of the peoples of Asia and as the spokesman for Asia as a whole to the outside world. The reason was simple: Japan showed itself to be the only non-European power capable of resisting and defeating European imperialism.

If one takes the story back still further, one can see, at least in my view, the Meiji Restoration and the success of its programme of modernization as a kind of resistance [because prophetic] both to Euro-American hegemony over

---

154 It is extremely rare for a symposium speaker to drop an idea mid-stream unless he is being interrupted by someone else attempting to comment. The suggestion is that either Kōyama stopped himself mid-stream or that what he said was so sensitive that the editors at *Chūō Kōron* decided to delete it. Either way, the editors chose to begin the next set of comments by Kōyama with a new paragraph. My reading of the balance of Kōyama's comments suggests that something important has happened because the tone here shifts towards a conventional assertion of Japanese nationalism, even occasionally becoming jingoistic, rather than couched in the ironic and critical ambiguities and double meanings that one finds throughout the text before this point. Perhaps one of the other participants in the discussion signalled the need to resort to conventional patriotic spirit lest the censors take offence. Whether this is true or not I cannot say with confidence, but the tone and language in the following passage is inconsistent with what precedes and largely follows it.

East Asia and to the consolidation of the West's global order. Since the Meiji Restoration Japan has learned, in sometimes magnificent fashion, how to make what might be called 'Japan's world history' (*Nippon no sekai-shi*). With the restoration of the monarchy's powers in 1868, Japan's national polity (*kokutai*) shone forth with unprecedented brilliance. Thus, if one seeks to locate the sources of Japan's subjective capabilities, one need look no further than our national polity. Nevertheless, it is also true that Japan has only begun to act in world-historical fashion since the Meiji Restoration, and with this conclusion who can disagree?[155]

Whatever else one might want to claim, Europe has stood at the heart of modern world history. But that truth explains precisely why we are fighting Europe's global order. From the Muromachi Period [1392–1573], Japan sustained an expansive drive southwards. This development of a position overseas for the country might have continued but for the self-imposed isolation of the Tokugawa Period [1600–1868]. If this enterprise had been allowed to continue during those centuries, our place in the modern world would have been completely different. We would have achieved a much greater degree of self-mastery, of subjectivity. Our leadership role in the world would have been much more prominent. But because of the isolation of the Tokugawa Period, this expansion did not take place, and the world evolved, without challenge, from a condition of exclusively European domination of the planet to a joint global hegemony shared between the United States and Europe. But this condition contributed in turn to the emergence of Japanese subjectivity. It is precisely this Euro-American co-domination of the world that has made it essential that Japan come to exercise the leadership role it is now exhibiting. This was of course just one of the conditions that prepared for Japan's emergence on the world scene. The foundations of Japanese subjectivity are to be found in the Japanese spirit of our national polity. This is what I have explained in my new book, and to anyone who reads it my position is obvious. But this does not mean that Japanese subjectivity can be understood ahistorically, as if it had no relationship with or roots in the historical process.[156]

As I noted above, if we are to be faithful to the supreme moral imperative that commands us to fight the war we are now waging, we must be able to lead [the world]. And this means facing up resolutely to the demands of moral leadership. We must strive for higher things. Then [and only then] will our struggle qualify as a 'holy war', as 'a struggle for Japan' (*Nippon sensō*).

---

155 The note of defiance and the implied reference to unnamed critics suggests that the speaker feels himself to be under distinct pressure to speak something less than his mind; but Kōyama was stubborn and gave ground to his opponents with great difficulty.

156 My view is that something is amiss in the text here. Kōyama has become defensive, not vis-à-vis the other participants with whom he is discussing Japanese subjectivity, but towards his critics and the Imperial Army censors. He is in retreat, but still refuses to yield his fundamental point: that Japan must be understood historically, not mythically, the repeated references to the *kokutai* or national essence notwithstanding.

And to achieve that, what must be done? There must be an unmistakable air of truth about our war ideals. This truth must be of an order that the rest of the world cannot deny because it will be manifestly compelling as the truth. After all, the Japanese state has already lasted 2,600 years. Our eternal glory has been promised by the steadfast spirit of the gods. Japan's truth is the truth of our national polity. This embodies the highest civilized and martial virtue, this object of supreme reverence, and it is here that we stand and take our place in the world. That is how this truth is revealed to the world, in direct and un-ignorable fashion. No matter how much authority is handed over to the men and horses of the generals, there is no way that the leaders of mere barbarians will triumph over our emperor. Even without martial authority, the Imperial Throne will never quake because it is peerless in all the world. This is a manifestation of the transcendent truth of the Imperial Institution, a truth that transcends the merely martial. Because Japan's war has truth written on its banner, even if we are not perfect in every aspect, we will still mobilize our every strength. That is our unshakable conviction. If Japan's [moral] leadership in this struggle can reach ever greater heights, we will win this war. The outcome is not in doubt. It cannot be. In the end, our enemies will concede the greatness of our ideals. This is because of the truth that is Japan. But in arguing as much, I am being neither abstract nor ahistorical. The method I adhere to is that which matches [the greatness of] Japanese history itself.

SUZUKI: On the question of Japan's truth, I am in entire agreement. But I remain of the view that it is not some academic quibble to insist that Japan's truth must of necessity be identical with world-historical principles, that any 'Japan principle' is at the same time a universal or world (*sekai-teki*) truth. Our foundations, therefore, are not Japanese alone. This highlights the depth of our insight, the significance, in fact, of our belief that it is Japan's unique role – because only we are capable of performing it – to foster a new order for East Asia. This is what makes Japanese leadership so critical today.

The demand for a new East Asian order means more than the liberation of the oppressed and requires more than giving freedom to those hitherto unfree. Its significance reaches beyond liberation in terms of conventional liberal thought. Nor does this new order seek to foster [a mere formal] equality between nations through what, to use some extreme language, might be called the international or interstate equivalent of class war. It is none of these things. Japan's true significance, its historical importance, derives from the fact that this nation – although it has kept and will keep its freedom and independence, and although it [uniquely among the non-Western powers] achieved a formidable status within the old international order – that, despite all these things, Japan insists now and will go on insisting that a new order be created despite the impressive fist this country made of the previous but now defunct old order.[157] All of this qualifies as historical significance of the first order. The result is that Japan's grounds for [global and regional] leadership have had to be recognized both at home and abroad.[158] The peoples of East Asia must reflect on and reconsider their posture (*hansei*) towards this truth; indeed, the whole world must. And of course this necessary act of reflection must be undertaken by the Japanese people as well.[159]

At the same time, we must dwell on the one truth underwriting Japan's gift and capacity for leadership that is most ready to hand and therefore most compelling: the fact of Japan's successful programme of 'modernization' (*kindai*). As was noted in our previous discussions, continental East Asia experienced antiquity but not modernity. China's achievement during its ancient period was of the highest order, one that reached beyond even that of Western antiquity.[160] Nevertheless, however superb the accomplishments of what we now call 'Chinese antiquity', modernization has eluded contemporary China. Or, to put the point bluntly, among all the peoples of East Asia, the Japanese alone have achieved modernity. Furthermore, the ongoing project of Japanese modernization is opening a new chapter in the history of our entire region. This is a historical fact that is in my view beyond denial.

From this fact, one can make the following observation. The stage achieved by world-historical Europe produced, via its expansion around the globe, by this act of mediation, the very world-historical condition that now encompasses the whole planet. But by doing so, Europe's system (*kōzō*) of global hegemony invited its own destruction. In response to the [irresistible] global trend that is modern world history, Japan picked up and mastered itself, achieved [genuine] subjectivity and joined this [European] world order, and in the process remade itself as a modern nation. Thus Japan did not follow China's path of allowing itself to be battered by this globalizing force through

---

157 This transcendent quality assumes special meaning in the Kyoto School reworking of the Hegelian conceit of progressive self-consciousness as a driving force that enables the Japanese state to take that creative leap up the evolutionary scale, that is to metamorphose in a single step from a crawling insect into a butterfly, or, in Hegel's famous metaphor, from a seed into an oak.
158 The word 'recognized' here carries a double meaning. The first is the conventional sense of acceptance by the international community, and particularly by the leading Western nations, of the fact of Japanese power. The second is the Hegelian sense of recognition, in which 'the Other' serves as a mirror in which a national self-consciousness learns to appreciate the scale of its achievements – an appreciation that can only be secured by the recognition of the 'Other'.
159 The 'reflection' is richly over-determined here.
160 This Kyoto School conceit is not shared by any of the Europeans thinkers who figure most prominently in Japanese writings on the subject, despite the deepening appreciation of Eastern thought that registers in the reflections of Schopenhauer, Nietzsche and Heidegger himself. Note also that such outspoken praise of China's past achievements during the sixth year of full-scale war between China and Japan would have brought no joy to the Imperial Army censors. It was not what they wanted to read in one of wartime Japan's most influential organs of informed opinion.

bungling its own programme of modernization. Or, to put the matter yet another way, China failed itself, and thus fell into a semi-colonized condition. By contrast, Japan made a success of the modern world and did not allow itself to become a semi-colonized victim of European power, but rather actively and subjectively modernized itself. Indeed, wasn't it precisely because Japan passed through the trial of modernization that it created for itself the occasion and opportunity to demonstrate our subjectivity?[161] Granted, there are those who dismiss Japanese modernization as an act of mere imitation of Europe and America; but it was much more than just imitation. As I argued in the previous symposium in this series, mere imitation does not result in genuine subjectivity. It is a completely different order of achievement. Self-mastery cannot be brought to fruition by copying.

So how has the multicentred world that Kōyama has described been transformed into a single unified system (*ichigen-teki sekai*), into a world made by world history (*sekai-shi-teki sekai*)? This act of unification or globalization has not been accomplished by a gentle synthesis or by acts of international cultural and economic exchange between equals, but by the expansion of European civilization, the 'European world' in Kōyama's usage, across the face of the planet. I think this is an obvious historical fact. It forms the central trunk in the genealogy of modern world history. But to acknowledge this fact is in no way to deny the contemporary reality of Japanese subjectivity. Does Japan's subjectivity not meet the standards of something decisively superior to the mere ideal of multiple uniqueness?[162] To proclaim this superiority is to reject emphatically any suggestion that the concept of 'Japanese subjectivity' is a contradiction in terms.[163] What do you all think?

KŌYAMA: This is exactly the point I stressed in my article 'Moral Energy and What Drives the Making of History' ('*Rekishi no Suishin Ryoku to*

---

161 Here the target of Kyoto School criticism is not poor China, tormented by all the great powers and most particularly by Imperial Japan, but rather those ultranationalists and members of the Japan Romantic School who had insisted, to Suzuki's irritation, that Japan's modernization was a mistake and a sickness in the 'Overcoming Modernity' symposium only four months before.

162 Suzuki is a consistent opponent *avant la lettre* of the post-1945 notion that all civilizations are equal because they are, ultimately, all 'civilizations'. This cultural relativism cannot account for the superiority of European civilization over the rest of the contemporary world nor allow one to theorize, as we would now say, Japan's huge success after 1868 that at once closed the gap between Japan and the modern West and opened up a gap between the relatively underdeveloped state of China and the colonized state of India. Here Suzuki is the unflinching ally of the author of *The Protestant Ethic and the Spirit of Capitalism* and the uncompromising foe of latter-day 'postcolonial political correctness'. He wants the non-European world not to be patronized by Western politeness but to be respected for its genuine achievements.

163 Again, Suzuki is offering a sharp rebuke to ultranationalist critics of the Kyoto School, who insisted that the idea of 'subjectivity' was a Western standard of national and civilized success that should not be, indeed could not be, applied to the 'Land of the Gods'. On this subject, Suzuki's logic is tellingly close to that of the liberal constitutionalist Tatsukichi Minobe.

Dōtoku Seimeiryoku'), which appeared in the pages of *Chūō Kōron*. I returned to this theme in my recent book mentioned above, *The Philosophy of World History*. The Japanese adoption of the things of Europe is of an entirely different character from the phenomenon of Europeanization that occurs when undeveloped peoples encounter a superior civilization. On this point, [one is tempted to say] all foreigners have been entirely mistaken, and indeed so have a great number of Japanese. In fact many of them still are. It is precisely because Japan already possessed its own form of subjectivity that it was able to import selectively and freely the products and ideas of Europe. This is why Japan was able to create a modern state. This distinguishes us from India and China. The view articulated by writers such as Lin Yutang that Japan became great by merely imitating Europe and America is yet another example of the Chinese refusal to understand [and acknowledge] what Japan has accomplished.[164] This benighted view holds that this country did not become great by virtue of things Japanese; it became formidable by one-sided borrowing from the West. This judgement is a cardinal error, as we made clear in the previous symposium in this series.

In mounting a defence of Japanese subjectivity there can be no resort to atemporal arguments: rather, the case must be argued entirely as a matter of demonstrated subjectivity or the ability to act within history.[165] An ahistorical concept of Japanese subjectivity is no subjectivity at all. It reduces agency to something like an [passive] objective 'idea' or form.[166] Many people find this point really difficult to grasp. Japan's subjectivity today is a consequence of this country's successful programme of modernization. This Japanese subjectivity, which is the product of the achievement of modernity, is grounded in a moral subjectivity that differs from that of Europe. This difference has

---

164 Lin Yutan (1895–1976): celebrated Chinese writer and translator who won an international reputation via his writings in English. He was nominated for the Nobel Prize several times.
165 Another uncompromising rejection of the nativist and imperialist insistence that Japan is the Land of the Gods, exterior to human history because located in a kind of superior spiritual dimension outside time. This will stand as a recantation of Kōyama's earlier apparent moment of panic or caution. The contrast is so sharp that one wonders whether a police officer had suddenly appeared at the symposium earlier and had now left. The censors would have to be dealt with later, but Kōyama's earlier lapse into the undiluted language of *Kokutai* and the Japanese way has been abandoned here.
166 Kōyama uses the Greek word *idea* which is conventionally translated into Latin as *forma*. He is referring to Platonic forms such as the perfect triangle which exist nowhere in nature. Kōyama thereby slyly hints that proponents of ahistorical subjectivity can be understood as advocates of an inappropriate Greek (i.e. foreign or non-Japanese) notion, thus deflecting criticism that Kōyama himself has committed lese-majesty by calling into question Japan's divine status. But the other point, which matters more to the substance of Kōyama's thesis, is that Japanese subjectivity or national self-mastery or potency as a real world actor is empirically, that is factually, true. It is not a religious myth, nor does it depend for the proof of its validity on religious dogma.

produced Japan's current opportunity for a 'moment in the sun' (*toki o ette*). We ourselves have demonstrated a truth that will stand for ever. It is history that provides the arena where such truths must be tested to be proven. But the act of demonstrating such truths in history is not a matter of wilful opportunism. One cannot do it on random impulse. It is necessary to seize the day [when the right moment comes], and the day to be seized is now.

KŌSAKA: I think the argument that Suzuki has just made is unquestionably correct. The foundations for Japan's status as a [literally] leading power — that is, a power capable of contemporary leadership in a world-historical sense — lie in the fact that Japan made modernity, in the proper European sense, its own, and thus became an active and effective participant in that European world order. This involvement has furthermore been genuinely subjective — we chose to do it — not, as in the case of China, as a result of being dragged into the system willy-nilly by Western traction. Thus, in pronounced contrast to China's situation, Japan has, by virtue of its demonstrated position as a leading power of the age, been able to move from strength to strength, from our prestigious rank within the old order to our new mission of constructing a world order. What we have achieved already will enable us to achieve still more. In broad terms, this is how I interpret Suzuki's analysis which, in my view, was brilliant. What is beyond question is that the present old order must be negated (*hitei sarenakereba naranai*). But to say as much is not to argue that the old order was always and entirely without its own truth. Any one-sided argument that insists the old order lacked [world-historical] plausibility as a global system cannot be regarded as serious. Take the example of modern science. This in no way qualifies as a 'summary error'. Quite the contrary: modern science has continued its advance well into the contemporary age, and more innovation must be wrung from it in the future.[167] Indeed, without the sciences, our Great East Asian War as a project cannot be brought to completion. Doesn't this prove the truth of claims for the history-shaping powers of modern science? Making the truth of science our own has been an indispensable dimension of Japan's positive acceptance of, involvement in and participation (*sanka sure*) in the modern world. But the Japanese commitment to the sciences has not obliterated our awareness of their limitations. This ability to balance the strengths and weaknesses of sciences, to judge them, exploit them and not be overawed by them, derives from the spiritual confidence of Japanese tradition. It is precisely by virtue of our active embrace of modernity that we have cultivated the truth of history in which we negate modernity by mediating it.

---

167 The point is that although science is quintessentially a modern development, its virtues are so great that the Kyoto School affirms its importance, despite all the distinctions repeatedly drawn by these four thinkers between *kindai* (the modern) and *gendai* ('the time after the modern') in favour of the latter.

Isn't this the case? What do you all think? I suspect that this dynamic captures the significance and challenge of Japan's unique place [in a post-modernizing world] but ...

NISHITANI: Agreed. The cardinal insight at issue here is that Japan has achieved what the world regards as a genuine form of modernity; but beyond this we are arguing that Japan has [been able to] become modern because it experienced a form of antiquity that provided the foundations for this modern achievement. Or, to reverse the proposition, the success of Japan's antiquity made possible our modern success. This is the paradoxical truth that counts.[168]

SUZUKI: In what sense does that ...

NISHITANI: What I mean to say is that Japan was able to modernize, as Kōyama noted earlier, because it avoided colonization by virtue of the success of the Meiji Restoration. The colonial threat was seen off because we were able to make so rapid a transformation from a feudal to a modern state through the Meiji reforms. I have also proposed elsewhere, I think in a magazine [ed. note: *Bungakkai*], that this is one of the consequences of the effectiveness (*chikara*) of Japanese *moralische Energie*. This power, as manifested economically and militarily since 1868, has in turn allowed us to absorb the culture and civilization of Europe and thus sustain our drive to become, as the slogan has it, a rich country and a strong one. By contrast, the Chinese proved unable to match this Japanese success because of their conviction that their country remained the centre of the world [regardless of the European challenge]. The unbending conviction that Chinese civilization *is* civilization conspired against precisely the form of mental flexibility that Japan has displayed throughout this period. But how did Japan cultivate a form of subjectivity with this high degree of flexibility? If one reflects on how our consciousness has escaped the limitations of China's rigid notion of civilized superiority, I think one can conclude that its roots can be traced back to the origins of our nation. Something vital has been there from the outset. It characterizes the Japanese way of life (*kokutai*).This power has manifested itself remarkably since the decision to return the hands of government to the emperor in our struggle to expel the [Western] barbarians and revere the Imperial House. I would conclude that the fundamental spirit behind the decision to restore imperial rule inspires the Japanese system of world-historical war that dominates our thoughts today.

One can develop this notion [of flexibility] further. The power to absorb and make any and every foreign thing one's own has been crucial to national

---

168 This is more than a truism or empty assertion because of the Kyoto School argument that the Philippines, for example, cannot simply modernize at will because it lacks the backbone and discipline of an authentic and therefore enabling form of pre-modernity: what Nishitani terms *kodai* or antiquity.

self-definition – call it the Japanese way – since antiquity, indeed from the very founding of the nation.[169] Thus this spirit has been continually refined and developed since antiquity – indeed, from even earlier, as is often observed; and this fundamental impulse has remained vital through medieval and modern times when other nations have managed to lose their originary spirit. This spirit combines extraordinary flexibility with unshakable confidence in our culture. It is much as Kōyama said earlier: the wars of the remotest past were total wars. This spirit of total mobilized resistance has informed the whole of our history from its very inception. It was on display during our resistance to the Mongol invasions as it was in the restoration of imperial rule in 1868. If you would allow me to amplify a point developed earlier in our discussions, this idea links directly to the notion that the Japanese state [literally, national family] stands on the principle of the family.

In other words, Japan has been able to modernize precisely because it has been animated by this spirit from the most distant past down to the present. Other nations have not manifested the same kind of continuity over so long a period. In the final analysis, resilient flexibility and adaptability [of mind] is what defines the Japanese spirit. It is what makes us special, in my view, among the nations of the world.

In this sense, we might say that the standpoint of the democratic state (*kokka*) ultimately rests on the individual (*kojin*). In Hegelian terms, the *shukanteki seishin* or subjective spirit of the individual is the keystone.[170] In contrast, the objective spirit (*kyakukanteki seishin*) provides the ground for the totalitarian state. Even communism falls into the category of the objective spirit, broadly defined, because class is a form of *Gesellschaft*.[171] By contrast, in the case of Japan the state embodies more than just the objective spirit because – I think it can be put this way – the objective spirit is rather an expression or manifestation (*hyōgen*) of the *zettai seishin* [*absoluter Geist* or absolute spirit] at work beneath. Why? Because the standpoint of the absolute spirit has been at work inside the very notion of the objective spirit from the outset [of this developmental process].

At the same time, the demands of this absolute spirit provide and secure the foundations (*konpon*) for the contemporary demand for what we call 'a new world order'. It is a call from the depths, the *basso profundo* of contemporary world history, which summons us to act. This is what I meant when I concluded earlier that the intellectual breakthrough that characterizes Japan's [world-historical] standpoint must soar above the breakthroughs of

---

169 Antiquity or *kodai-shi* is traditionally associated in the study of Japan's past with the arrival of literacy from mainland China. Pre-history refers to what went before.
170 Arguably the most complicated use of a single German term in the entirety of *The Standpoint of World History and Japan*. The difference between *shukanteki* and *shutaiteki* is decisive. The former is closer to the English use of the word 'subjective' when we refer to a 'subjective impression' or 'that is just being subjective' (that is, a personal opinion regardless of reality).
171 Transliterated from the German as *furigana*.

the other nations of the world. Today world history is crying out to Japan; it calls to us. This is how I interpret the expression 'everything under one roof' (*hakkō no ichi-u*).

19 The historical character of subjectivity

KŌYAMA: I am entirely in agreement. No criticism occurs to me. But we should take note of the fact that many people, when hearing such observations, may be left with the mistaken impression that Japan lacks its own form of [genuine] subjectivity. Hardly any of these doubters have written what might be called proper history, be it world history or Japanese history. As a result they may be uncertain what to say about our ideas [because they have no grounding in the rigours of historical research]. They don't seem to understand what is at stake. They evoke the mantra 'subjectivity, subjectivity' but seem to think that subjectivity is some kind of eternal idea entirely alien to the course of history. As a consequence they fall back on a pre-historical understanding of the world. Then, when confronted with an analysis of contemporary Japan based on a genuine understanding of the past, they retreat to an intellectual position that allows them no purchase on historical reality. Only temporality – awareness of time at the expense of [allegiance to] eternal ideas untouched by time – has given the Japanese people the chance to seize the day (*toki o eru*). The construction and creation of history as a path requires a course of action. Mere organic evolution or passive development cannot perform the required job of work. This approach to the past provides no standpoint from which to assume the responsibilities of subjectivity and take on the burdens of making (*kensetsu*) history. An eternal truth has no history. Ideas are not historical [in this sense]. As an idea, neither liberty nor equality nor, for that matter, absolute spirit has a history. History cannot therefore be grasped with either Greek or German philosophy, [not] even [with] Hegel's philosophy of absolute spirit. The truth of history can be found only in 'time'. But just as we say that history exists only in time, so the future is a history that has not yet occurred. To occur in time is to begin in time, and thus to set time in motion. It is at this point that history intersects with eternity. It is at that juncture and place that one 'finds' history. This is the point from which history unfolds. When we say that Japan must seize the day, it is towards this frontier that we must move.

For time to begin it must be born. If, at the beginning of heaven and earth, God created time, human beings found themselves in this created time – when God created human beings, a new age was set in motion. This marked the launch of history. And in this way we achieve a connection with eternity through the creation of time. Human beings became linked to God. With the human beginnings of time, history was created; but it is also true that evil had a necessary place in the human world created by God. History was conceived as a history in which moral energy would negate this evil. But in opposing God, this evil shares with God the same will to desire, the desire for eternity, and that will is also the will to negate history. Thus history does not begin with the creation of heaven and earth, or with the creation of Nature, but rather it begins with the birth of man, or more precisely with the birth of the person who commits evil. It is my view that history starts at the specific point when the energy behind the natural justice of the universe manifests itself in the act of negating evil – and this provides the foundation that links the divine to moral energy. Because what one describes as the evil of history is nothing more than the eternal but futile exercise of the will; one sets one's heart on the spiritual (*seishin*), but this should be regarded as nothing more than the inertia of history. It is in opposition to this eternal but futile exercise of the will that moral energy manifests itself. This energy is not satisfied with an eternity of empty desire. On the contrary, it seeks out history. Nevertheless, moral energy is linked to the divine because its very foundations are to be found in the truth of eternity.

This constitutes the final challenge that has philosophically taxed religious-minded consciousness since antiquity, in both the East and the West ... the divine as the eternal absolute does not reveal itself as merely the eternal absolute. The God that existed before the creation of the world was a God in waiting, a God not yet (*imada kami de wa nai*). This God ceased to wait when the world was born, when man was born, when the evil of the human world that resists God was born. In other words, God manifests himself by the negation of that which would deny him. In this way, God becomes God. And God's truth is manifested through the actions of human beings because such actions are the means through which the evil and darkness that turn against God are negated. Therefore human action has a divine source; it comes from God. Whether one calls it 'moral energy' or 'the spark of the natural justice of the universe' or 'the sincerity of the heart', in any case, there is a mystery at work here because God becomes true God, manifests this eternal absoluteness, via, of all things, the relativizing standpoint of history itself. This is where one encounters the mystery of how God becomes God. Just as the Bodhisattva cannot answer our prayers without becoming Amida and thus secure salvation for the people, and just as the believer cannot achieve enlightenment unless Gautama performs his life of penance, so humanity cannot be saved unless Christ dies on the cross. This essential mystery has thus assumed a variety of forms in different faiths.

The absolute is not just the brilliance of the light. If that were the case, light would not be light. Light shines because there is darkness. Light reveals itself as light only when there is a patch of darkness to illuminate. The same thing applies to the truth of eternity. The truth manifests itself as the truth in the face of falsehood and evil. It is along this divide that truth finds its vehicle in an authentic means: the means employed by the truth make those means truthful (*shinjitsu hōben/hōben shinjitsu*). The paradox is circular: only by confronting evil and destroying it does the absolute begin to assume its truth as the absolute. Such action is the responsibility of the human beings whom God has created, and it is through these means that the absoluteness of God, his truth, is made incarnate. This is what, for me, history means. In other words, Japan's truth has existed throughout the eternity of the past (*eien no mukashi kara*). Japanese history can be properly described as the proven path of the truth. However, to realize this genuineness of this eternal truth, it must be manifested – the day must be seized – both within the sphere of our national history and within the sphere of world history. The paradoxical fact of the matter may be this: that it is only when, in the course of our history, people start to forget the true meaning of our national polity that its eternal truthfulness becomes manifest. When Britain and America go down to unprincipled defeat, Japan's claim to eternal truth will be demonstrated.[172] This we will achieve with the divine strength with which our creator has imbued us. This is the historic mission of the Japanese people. And this is why we must possess genuine subjectivity. Japanese subjectivity finds itself in world history. Thus it has always been. But it can only be authentically realized when we start to seize the day. And this [imperative] defines Japan's world-historical significance and mission today, a challenge and an opportunity not previously witnessed in the entirety of our past. Have I grasped the profound issue at stake here?

NISHITANI: This is how I express it. (*Turning to Kōyama*) To borrow your phrase, Japan bears the burden of something true … the weight of the truth. This truth has been there from the start. But even though it has been part of our history from the beginning, this does not mean that we should boast that this makes us peerless among the nations of the world. This is a burden we should bear in silence, because such decorum is proper and fitting for the task. Form is of the essence here. True subjectivity involves taking up this burden, bearing it responsibly, as often and for as long as the task demands, whenever and wherever it is required. To bear the burden of the truth is to take responsibility for it. It means that we must all assume this burden of responsibility, towards our country, our ancestors and our descendants. To bear this burden is what subjectivity is all about. Indeed it is subjectivity.

SUZUKI: That is entirely clear and, I think, wholly correct, but what I am trying to say is this: if we are mindful of the momentous stage in world history at which we find ourselves today, we must call into question the very notion that the relationship between 'Japan' and 'the world' is solely

---

172 This claim is in effect over-determined in Kōyama's mind because it draws simultaneously on the central claims and dogmas of Shinto, Confucianism and Buddhism, all cast in the language of Hegel (with Ranke between the lines): for simplicity's sake, we may note only the assumption that Anglo-American defeat would spell the lapse of their moral mandate to run the world.

and completely about a confrontation between us and the world. The idea of genuine Japanese subjectivity must mean that this nation is part and parcel of the wider world. Those who insist that Japanese subjectivity, to be authentic and convincing, requires that we occupy some space entirely apart from the rest of the world, indeed that Japanese subjectivity is unthinkable unless Japan is completely apart, are wrong. This sort of narrow thinking utterly frustrates any practical hopes of Japan exercising proper leadership in the world ...

NISHITANI: Or, to reverse the [flawed] logic, these people want to us believe that outside Japan the world does not exist.

SUZUKI: That's right. That is what I wanted to say.

20 The problem of military power (*senryōku*)

KŌYAMA: World-historical wars (*sō ryoku sen*), to return to something that has become an important issue for us, are more than the sum of their conventional parts.[173] Such wars demand an utterly new form of creative force. This power gushes forth like a fountain, and reaches beyond the military, political/diplomatic and economic as well as the intellectual or ideological spheres, taken individually or together. To harness this power is the supreme mission and categorical imperative (*shijō-meirei*) of any genuine world-historical war.[174] If this is true, relying on economic power alone – material, resources and productive capacity – will not suffice, and in any case Britain and America possess these in such abundance that we cannot win relying on material means alone. But by total mobilization of all our powers (*sō ryoku*), it may be possible to withstand such superior resources.[175] Or, to put the issue more realistically, if the gap [in material capabilities] is as great as one assumes, we have no chance of defeating our enemies in a conventional total war today. Therefore, while we must, of course, squeeze the maximum from our productive powers as they stand, only by adding something especially effective to this equation can we hope to bridge the gap between us and our opponents. It is this extra dimension that we must foster. This is what we must have.

---

173 By this point in the conflict, Japan's only hope was for a stalemate ending in an armistice such as concluded the Great War. The first of the battles for the Coral Sea (May 1942) offered a slight hope for this outcome, but Nishitani and his colleagues, with their excellent Navy connections, knew as they spoke that the Japanese war effort was doomed. The ambiguities of this section all but disappear when read in this light.

174 The term *shijō-meirei* here may mean nothing more than the conventional usage implies – 'supreme mission'. But these are philosophers discussing philosophy: the crowning moment of this section is the evocation of Nishida's idea of 'absolute nothingness', and the other meaning of *shijō-meirei* is a central building block of Nishida's system (Hegelian self-consciousness is another). Accordingly, the Kantian reading may be relevant here.

175 An etymologically decisive moment. Kōyama sets out *sō* and *ryoku* as two words, making *sō* a noun, not an adjective, and thus rendering the meaning 'all our powers' not 'all-out war'.

In other words, it will not suffice that the Japanese commit themselves emotionally to this struggle to the same degree as the British and the Americans. Merely to match their levels of motivation is insufficient. Indeed, we will be in trouble if that is all we achieve. No, the demand of the hour is that the Japanese, and I mean all of us, as an entire people together, embrace and surrender to the truth that *this moment* is indeed a turning point [in world history], and therefore that we are fighting, in effect, *to make history turn*. Then, armed with this insight into the stakes at issue, we can mobilize the entirety of our abilities and capacities, forcing them to higher and higher levels. This is what necessity demands of us ... because the consequences will be so grave if we falter in our convictions, in the philosophy of our national ideals.

This suggests that to enhance our material capabilities we must mobilize our spiritual powers, seeking a synthesis of the material and the spiritual so that they become as one. In this way, we can foster our true capacity for total resistance. And thus we will become capable of continually renewing the 'plus alpha' of the power that we require.[176]

The implication would be that the current war will mark the first time that the powers of the spirit and the material (*busshitsu*), morale and materiel, will become as one, as indeed they must if we are to win. Military strength, conventionally understood, is greatly influenced by the spiritual or psychological dimension we term 'martial morale'.[177] When the military strength of two contending forces is roughly the same, neither is likely to achieve victory over the other. But if one has superior morale, it will triumph. So the decisive factor here is not the organization or composition of one's armed forces. These factors alone are never decisive on the battlefield, and in the case of the present struggle the armed forces of the two sides display a remarkably similar character. The armies and navies are structured in roughly the same ways. What distinguishes the two sides is the American belief that the side that can boast the greater productive powers and mobilize the larger army and navy will inevitably win. But I think, and this I believe is the general Japanese view, that the integration of superior morale with productive power can generate formidable creative power which can [still] be brought to bear on this struggle.

SUZUKI: This explains why productive power, in the economic sense, has obviously come to the fore in the present conflict but also why, at the same time, productive power as the embodiment of morale has assumed

---

176 Kōyama says *atarashii purasu*, literally 'the new plus (factor)', but in post-war Japanese the equivalent and much more widely used term is the algebraic expression 'plus alpha', which captures exactly what Kōyama means in a way that most Western students of Japanese and all Japanese themselves will immediately grasp.

177 Kōyama uses the expression *shiki*, which is sometimes rendered in English as 'martial spirit' but which actually means 'the energy or spirit of the samurai'; so on the page many Japanese readers might have viewed the term as a conventional evocation of the way of the warrior, but 'morale' is the determinate rubric.

equal importance. The realm of the economy as well as that of the psyche must make us more effective.[178] In other words, we are talking about the creative spirit. Isn't this in fact what Kōyama is referring to when he speaks of the unlimited gains that the spirit of creativity may generate? Doesn't this insight allow us to begin to address this subject with confidence for the first time?

The very idea of a world-historical war is inconceivable without sustained creativity [and inventiveness] of the highest level. But boosting such creativity involves more than the mere intensification of our feelings, moral or otherwise. Mere expansion of the moral realm is not enough to achieve such gains. Straining at the thing [as is the Japanese temptation] is not enough.[179] Those of us involved in scholarship must pursue this higher standard of creativity with all of our abilities. Our research can enhance our intellectual powers [as a nation].[180] None of this means that there can be any slackening in the tensing of our moral resources, in our determination [to resist]. We are, after all, at war. As the expression has it, 100 million Japanese hearts must beat as one. But the welling up of our feelings is not enough to meet the challenge facing us.[181] It is not a solution. Rather, it is just one more aspect of the larger breakthrough we must strive to achieve. That will demand intellectual labour of an unrivalled order.[182] [*Break in the text*] ... This mobilization of the mind is just as important as the enhanced production and expansion of the economy that are being so noisily advocated; the life of the spirit is vital because the depths within this interiority of the human being that the spirit can plumb are so rich. In other words, the rise of the scientific spirit ... [183]

KŌYAMA: All reflection and scholarship must be grounded in philosophic (*shisō*) conviction, and therefore ...

---

178 The word 'productive' in this sense is cited in English.
179 The verb has been partially obscured on the relevant page of *Chūō Kōron*. It appears to be *kinchō*, to strain at.
180 That is, 'spirit' in the German sense of *Geist* as the powers of the non-material realm, including 'morale', but not the English sense of the realm of ghosts and saints.
181 An audacious challenge to one of the mantras of Japanese wartime motivation and national feeling, just as the war had turned decisively against Japan. The apoplexy provoked by such a remark among the military authorities must have been audible across Tokyo through the shut windows at Chūō Kōron-sha.
182 In other words, mere sloganeering will not win the war; and this means that, if they have any sense, the military censors, to say nothing of the ultra-right, should stop attacking the Kyoto School and accept that these demonstrated powers of reflection should be harnessed to the war effort rather than persecuted.
183 The term 'scientific' refers to *Wissenschaft*, the German term that covers not only the natural sciences but all intellectual disciplines. Suzuki uses the term *gakumon*, which is normally translated as 'scholarship', but the last thing Suzuki is talking about is pedantry or research as such. Comparison with Heidegger's criticism in his Rectoral Address of scholarly absent-mindedness and intellectual lack of focus may be relevant here.

SUZUKI: Such convictions must demonstrate an objective weight. It is therefore not just a question of whether you or I benefit from such convictions; the whole population, all of our people, must benefit from them as well.

KŌSAKA: This is where, in my view, the ambitions and necessity of the Greater East Asian Co-prosperity Sphere figure as a problem of logic.[184] The point was made reasonably clear in the second symposium in this series when we discussed the historical and ethical character of the Greater East Asian Co-Prosperity Sphere. Success in the project to build such a sphere demands that we become, via this struggle, ever clearer and more persuasive, in logical terms. Or, to put it another way, numbers and organization are vital, but the essence of the matter is logic.[185] Without this logical foundation, no organization can exert a compelling claim to genuine objectivity.[186] Without feeding this need, our efforts cannot become the focus of secure belief or intellectual conviction, certainly not at the profoundest level. If we are to underwrite our daily economic and political lives with sound beliefs, especially when we consider the overarching nature of the Greater East Asian Co-prosperity Sphere taken as a whole, we must be able to assume, as matter of conviction, the logicality of the enterprise. If, as Kōyama just remarked, it is crucial that the form of world-historical wars be governed by a logic that integrates all the relevant branches [of Japanese life] and sets them to work in harness, I think that the logic of place (*basho no ronri*) qualifies as the logic we require for the success of a Greater East Asian Co-prosperity Sphere.[187] This is the logic that helps us to identify and thus to locate the place (*tokoro*) we seek in order to win a place (*tokoro o eru*) for ourselves as a nation in the world.[188] Such is the idea I would like to propose.

---

184 Another twist in the elaborate discourse over the logic of social existence inaugurated with the early parts of Tanabe's *The Logic of the Species*.
185 That is, the whole business must be underpinned by a metaphysical system, an ontology disciplined by propositional logic.
186 This objectivity may refer to the Hegelian notion of active existence rather than inert fact.
187 In a non-complex way, Nishida's idea of *basho* can be compared with Plato's notion of *topos* or Aristotle's idea of *hypokeimenon*. Take, for example, Viglielmo's definition of *basho*: 'place is the substratum within which all forms become actualized'. The point would be that co-prosperity spheres, like tables or societies, would belong to one place or another. But for the reasons elaborated in all three symposia, the co-prosperity sphere is the singular means of world-historical transformation, a form of forms. Furthermore, as the highest institutional embodiment of Japanese subjectivity, it must reflect the supreme embodiment of the national self-consciousness and at the same time be recognized by the world as such. Finally, the Kyoto School holds that this metaphysical totality embodies, at some level, the architecture of Nishida's thought, a set of insights that transcends European metaphysics. The fly in the ointment of this moment of Japanese philosophical expansiveness is the test embodied in Hegelian (and Weberian) subjectivity and the rationalization of institutional forms and conduct.
188 *Tokoro* here serves as another term for *basho*.

The ethics of the Greater East Asia Co-Prosperity Sphere is the ethics of the place as the space (*tokoro*) we seek to gain when we evoke the idea of winning a place [in the sun]. It is the ethics of place (*basho no rinri*). It is proper to understand this logic in the same manner as we grasp the logic of place (*basho*). To gain such a 'place' is to return us to 'the logic of the place'. The two logics are the same.[189]

To the degree that something is planned by a subject, such subjectivity when expressed is mutually mediated by the logic of the mediation of place (*basho-teki baikai*).[190] Naturally, mediation is exercised through a core or centre. In the case of the mediation of the Great East Asian Co-prosperity Sphere, Japan forms this centre. All subjectivity is concentrated in this centre, is given expression through and by this centre. All organization leadership is exercised from and by this centre.[191] One can safely conclude that the logic of world history guarantees the objectivity of these claims. The matters of conviction about which Suzuki has spoken must demonstrate their objective character in this manner. Such an expectation is both right and inevitable. How could it be otherwise? That at least is my surmise. Of course, it goes without saying that the historical, ethical and logical character of this enterprise forms an indivisible unity, but when we turn to the task of building a new world, when our moment arrives to realize this task, the logic of the matter, what we call 'the logic of world history', comes to the fore. To realize or act out the ethics that applies to such situations requires the mediation of this logic. Isn't that right?

NISHITANI: For me the logic at issue here is a special form of logic, one inescapably shot through with subjectivity. This [greater] logic demands the unity of logic and ethics, objectivity and subjectivity. Such a unity might usefully be described as seamless. A moment ago when I stressed how the [degree of] creativity demanded by a system of total resistance emerges from the material or objective preparation for such a struggle (*kyakutaiteki no seibi*), this is what I meant ... [*unexplained break in the text*]. Just focusing on the inner workings of the state for a moment, let us consider the domestic front. There are three key dimensions of the problem if we take the state, as I mentioned earlier, as functioning on three different levels: the economic, the military and the ethical. One of the strategic considerations of wars of total resistance is precisely that stage at which economic power and productivity make the indispensable

---

189 Viglielmo's definition of 'place' as 'the substratum within which all forms become actualized' is again relevant here: Nishida Kitarō, *The Encyclopedia of Philosophy*, vol. 5, p. 519.
190 A Kyoto School reworking of the original Kantian insight that all objectivity must finally be consistent with the human agency that of necessity can understand it, and therefore can shape it.
191 Such assertions are not expressions of bombast or self-exaltation but mere statements of fact. In 1942, Japan is the only East Asian society that has demonstrated incontestably the powers of rational self-mastery that define subjectivity in the Hegelian and Weberian modes.

leap to a higher dimension [as we have been discussing]. It is precisely because we need to make such a leap now more than ever that effective political power (*seijiryoku*) must be brought to bear in a systematic way on the workings of the economy. Without such intervention in the economy, I fear that the kind of leap in Japanese productivity we are hoping for will not be achievable.

Such a programme of political action must be grounded in certain truths to be effective. Of necessity, politics must be founded on a formidable degree of awareness and self-consciousness [in the Hegelian sense] of the responsibilities of leadership. But this in turn means that the political sphere and the exercise of political power must be suffused with the proper ethical spirit – one that reflects, as I noted above, an idea of the Japanese nation-state (*kokka*) that embodies the principle of total [ethical] renewal of the world (*sekai isshin*). As was discussed in the round-table discussion previous to this one, Japanese moral energy – a moral energy properly defined by two principles: *shutaisei* [rational self-mastery] and the genuine 'newness' of a new world order – must be mobilized from within the mind, the consciousness and values, of our political leaders.[192] In this manner, our economic strength, political power and spiritual vitality (*seishin ryoku*) may reinforce one another [and thus form a kind of unity in which mind and body, the psychological and the physical, morale and materiel, become one].[193] The expression that was used earlier, 'mind and matter', is suggestive, for isn't the very notion of the state making mind and matter work together fundamental to the kind of mobilization required for waging world-historical wars? How else can we bring to life the unity of purpose that will allow us to expand our productive powers, to make our political leadership more tenacious and cohesive, and to make our ethics even more a matter of conviction?

Recently there has much talk about the moral dimension of economic life. If one intends to preserve the profit principle, there has to be some form of engagement with ethical conduct. In the case of Japan, one speaks of [a need for] corporate or popular self-control or restraint [on consumption] but these calls do not appear to be very effective (*kōka ga nai*). The reason why such policies are ineffectual is because the public is given the impression that such moralizing is just a means to another end. The Japanese people have the impression that the ethical spirit (*rinri seishin*) is something abstract, without practical consequence. Such sermonizing therefore conspires against public awareness of the fact that proper ethics, that profound and formidable force, has the power to move and shape the nation and the world by virtue of its

---

192 Nishitani refers only to 'the new world order' but, in Japan as elsewhere in Confucian East Asia, such new-ness refers not to novelty, something merely different from what existed before, but a genuine innovation in which the impracticality of a defeated past is supplanted by a new regime that has been tested and found effective, that is practical.

193 Nishitani uses the single expression *busshin ichinyo*, conventionally rendered as the unity of matter and mind.

powers of self-awareness. Such trivializing of the moral should be resisted as a national imperative. It robs us as a nation-state (*kokka*) of our greatness of spirit and energy. Those responsible for the political affairs of this country need to give this issue the consideration it deserves.

Because moral rhetoric appears to do nothing to harness the pursuit of profit [for national ends], the government (*seiji*) is finally incapable of galvanizing the economy from within. In short, the spirit of the nation cannot be transformed into reality-altering practice. It is incapable of becoming an objective force. The spirit of the state (*kokka seishin*) falls short of the objective spirit. This is not to say that 'self-restraint' [on consumption, etc.] is not desirable, but it is to insist that effective restraint, that is self-discipline, is a natural product of the cultivation of genuine [productive] power; and the state is capable of achieving this when [and only when] it seeks the perfect unity of mind and matter noted above, in which authentic forms of economic power, political leadership and spiritual vitality come together as one.

KŌYAMA: I am entirely in agreement. We are talking about *moralische Energie*.
KŌSAKA: This requires intensive pursuit of the logical.
KŌYAMA: Nishitani has called for a new synthesis of the economic, the political and the ethical, but even if this is achieved, we have to seek a new idea [of the world], one that departs from modern notions of economics, labour and technology. Take the economic sphere, for example. Hitherto, economics has been thought to operate exclusively on the level of desire and greed. As was discussed earlier, economics as we conceive it today cannot function in this way. In the broadest sense, economics is about cultivating the individual, and this means raising the sphere of economics to a higher level. At least, that is the hope. This also implies that the organization of the economy has to be redesigned. The idea of work or, if you will, labour service tends immediately to conjure up an image of arduous activity, or rather the difficult choice of discomfort, even suffering, over enjoyment. But this suggests that work should not be conceived solely in terms of desire or greed. We have to reconsider work in a manner that lifts this concept to a better plane, even if it is just one step higher. Our notions of civilization and technology reveal the same need. This furthermore means that the notion of realizing the ego via the subjugation of nature is no longer tolerable. This is because such a definition of the self or the ego reduces it to nothing more than economic greed and desire.

The problem is very much as Ninomiya Sontoku and others have conceived it.[194] All these things – the economic, labour and technology – must all be

---

194 Ninomiya Sontoku (1787–1856): practical thinker and agricultural reformer. Emphasized the dignity and morally improving qualities of work while developing fresh understanding of techniques and ideas such as compound interest to improve the lives of ordinary people. A much admired figure in the Japanese tradition: attractive, frugal and humane.

brought to bear on a single task: the nurturing of a human being. This goal is beyond the reach of a definition of the economic that is confined entirely to the fulfilment of desire and the feeding of mere greed. Rather, we must turn to a broader definition of the economic, one that qualifies in the broadest sense as the 'moral'. By beginning afresh in this way, we can transform the idea of desire in such a way that it can once more be made to serve life. This is the new ideal we need to develop. This is one of the projects that the modern history of the world has left unresolved, and it is the one that Japanese people must by all means labour to solve. It is my conviction that the world-historical war we are now fighting provides the test of whether we can or cannot meet this challenge. How it can be met in concrete terms is beyond my ability to say, but I am in no doubt that the solution will manifest itself as an expression of moral energy. It should arise from that unity of matter and spirit, of heart and the things of the world, that we noted earlier. The whole of reality will as a result be penetrated by a world-view anchored in a unified morality that nourishes revitalized notions of labour, education, culture and economy. The result will be an entirely new creation, something utterly distinct from modernity. This innovation will come into being as a fruit of this world-historical war. This is why we must all feed on moral energy, and why we must cultivate it with utter intensity. This is essential. Only a moral vantage will allow us to exploit desire in a genuinely effective way. We must find a place, one that is right and fitting, for [the potency of] desire. This is where [moral] leadership and guidance find their deepest meaning and significance.

KŌSAKA: My suspicion is that hitherto this notion of leadership has referred to the application of external pressure or leadership 'from above'. Where this style of leadership has been pursued most vigorously, a huge gap between the leader and the led has been assumed, as we see in places such as Germany today. This is not what we are advocating. A genuinely Japanese form of leadership takes a very different form. It does not place our leaders in some vastly superior position over the rest of us, but rather it seeks to motivate [each person] from within. It is a form of leadership consistent, as was just mentioned, with the logic of place. It is leadership that accepts the burden of world-historical responsibility.

NISHITANI: The power of morality comes from the strength and capabilities of the individual.[195] This is the fundamental truth at issue here. But it is equally the case that this power also requires a genuinely effective objective [institutional] form. This [alone] can give effect to the power of morality and provide it with an organizing framework sufficient to our needs.

---

195 Nishitani's sentence is tighter but purposefully abstract: *Tsumari dōgiryoku to iu mono ga shutaiteki na chikari de*. Note that the idea of *shutai* (the subject) allows Nishitani to address the positive contribution of individuals to society without evoking the negative qualities that pre-war Japan almost always assigned to the terms *kojin* and *kokinshugi* (the individual and individualism). In his web draft, Heisig renders this passage from Nishitani as 'That is, ethical strength is a subjective strength'.

Only an approach of this kind allows one even to start down the path towards organizational effectiveness, the institutional equivalent of the perfect union of mind and matter. This provides the exact fit between object and subject that defines [effective] leadership as an aspect of the subjectivity of the state, where the state is understood to be the crucial embodiment of the agency that acts on history. This objective dimension of the problem is what Kōyama calls its 'logical' aspect. He refers to it as 'leadership from within'. But if the objective conditions are not sufficiently prepared, if, for example, workers in an organization are merely ordered to be efficient – an order in and of itself not a bad thing – the desired dramatic effect will not be achieved.[196]

KŌYAMA: This is of course the case. This mobilization has to consist of something more than merely urging oneself onwards with one's own voice. It has to be objectively embodied in an organization or institution, one grounded in a totally new morality. But it does not follow that one should in turn raise the cry 'organization, organization' and rush to erect a complicated system that results in an ill-considered mishmash. That would be truly pointless. To bring a modern touch to solving this problem ... what might it be called? ... the positivist idea of scientific laws in order to nurture a flawed form of equilibrium ... this would also be wrong.[197] Any attempt to embrace universal forms of organization must be consistent with the mission of cultivating and sustaining the best kind of creativity.[198] And such an approach will probably have moral energy as its foundation. But the pursuit of a new moral energy with the intensity it demands will not even begin to be successful unless we can give objective form to the organization of our world-historical war as our supreme vocation, and this in turn requires precisely the kind of structure that will work frictionlessly with the grain of reality as it is. This will guarantee that such an organizational system can in fact be realized, as it were, objectively.[199] But [merely] advocating the pursuit of this form of moral

---

196 In effect, Nishitani is giving a metaphysical gloss to one of the commonplaces of post-war human resource management philosophy, but the point is that such insights were comparatively rare in the official discourse of wartime Japan, which was preachy and obsessed with willpower, an emotionally satisfying but organizationally ineffectual blend of *gambaru* and *gaman*. A closer Japanese example is not the motivational policies of moral suasion that Sheldon Garon beautifully describes in *Molding Japanese Minds: The State in Everyday Life* (Princeton, NJ: Princeton University Press, 1997), but rather the 'rationalization campaigns' sustained by the Ministry of Commerce and Industry and later the Ministry of Munitions, described in Chalmers Johnson's *MITI and the Japanese Miracle: The Growth of Industrial Policy, 1925–1975* (Stanford: Stanford University Press, 1982).
197 This is an attack not on the natural sciences but on economics, particularly in its unreconstructed orthodox liberal phase prior to the Wall Street Crash.
198 Visible hands rather than the invisible hand; moral sentiments rather than market logic.
199 This is an uncompromising rejection of indulgent nationalist emotionalism in favour of the rigours of rationality and rationalization in the Weberian sense; more Harvard Business School than Ikki Kita or the ethos of the *kamikaze* pilot.

energy will come to nothing unless we have a proper method to hand. Method is the essence of the problem.

My view, as expressed when the matter was raised during the first symposium in this series (when we discussed subjective responsibility), remains unchanged: there is one effective means for driving home the importance of this system of responsibility. In simple terms, we have to reinforce our [collective and individual] sense of responsibility. A system of organization that is objectively effective is one in which each and every one of us takes full responsibility for his performance. This is essential. Any organization where the scope of responsibility is narrowly defined only by the [immediate] task of the individual and his private interest ends up being an organization where no one takes responsibility [for the whole]. This [flawed] approach is the child of modern democracy.[200] Does this make sense? To repeat, the essence of my case is this: unless one is prepared to stake the whole of one's existence [on the common task], until one sees [the need to] take responsibility for one's own task and every other that needs to be done, with this kind of seriousness, and ensures that this seriousness penetrates every dimension of one's organization, the very idea of 'organization' [that is, putting a body of people into effective order] is meaningless.[201]

But – and this is the key issue – if one thinks about how to inculcate this sense of responsibility, one conclusion irresistibly follows: subjective responsibility must be freely assumed; it must be the product of individual initiative. To take individual responsibility and to assume this burden freely means, by definition, that one must not be controlled by others.[202] This does not mean that orders do not have to be followed in the various departments and sections of an organization, but it does require that when orders are given, the individual in question freely assumes responsibility for carrying out these orders. The exercise of responsibility begins in freedom; not the other way around. It is precisely because freedom forms the foundation and point of departure for effective action that to blame others for one's own failings, to seek as it were to 'pass the buck', is entirely unacceptable.[203]

200 Kōyama's argument might have been stronger if he had targeted Anglo-American capitalism rather than modern democracy. The singular focus on job specialization and demarcation would after the war all but destroy the ability of the British shipbuilding industry to compete globally. For a cogent analysis of the dilemma of individual versus shared responsibility in the workplace, see Kazuo Yoshida's *Heisei no Fūkyō: Jūnen-shi*, Tokyo: PHP Kenkyūjo, 2001.
201 That is to say, it will not stave off national defeat for Japan. A veiled criticism of Tōjō's approach to the organization of Japan's war effort, as is made clear in the comments that follow.
202 Here is a wartime anticipation of the post-war philosophies of autonomy and subjectivity proposed by the political thinker Masao Maruyama and the economic historian Hisao Ōtsuka, hailed by the *Japan Times* on their deaths in the same year as the intellectual pillars of post-war Japanese democracy.
203 With one stroke of the sword, Kōyama cuts through the conventional Japanese complexities involved with 'taking (official) responsibility' for institutional failings. This sentence might have been penned by the Austro-American business school guru Peter Drucker.

Or [to put the matter philosophically], the great good place where others cannot constrain our freedom to act responsibly is the realm of nothingness (*mu*).[204] In other words, the pursuit of genuine responsibility brings us face to face with absolute nothingness. With this encounter, we begin to transcend the limits of the ego and achieve a state of non-self (*muga*).[205] The pretensions of the ego, of the 'I', dissolve in the waters of absolute nothingness totally and irreversibly. To take genuine responsibility for our actions in any complete sense necessarily demands that we transcend the 'self' (*muga ni naru*). As the proverb has it, 'Man proposes; God disposes'.[206] The same is true when we seek to act justly, when we realize justice by taking on responsibility. To the degree that human beings are given direction by subjective responsibility, we will bear the burden of the mandate of heaven (*tenmei*). This does not mean that God acts and the mandate of heaven is fulfilled only when we fold our arms and do nothing. Quite the contrary. We ourselves are indispensable to the realization of the mandate of heaven, because it is we who act and no one else. But this does not imply that it is merely the 'I' who acts because we are forced to do this or that. I believe that one acts justly precisely because justice is at stake. We are compelled to act morally [by virtue of an absolute standard outside ourselves]. Isn't this the fundamental circumstance [and constraint] that confronts us when we act in a genuinely moral way? However much we may rely on the ego or the self, thus exhausting its energies, when we undertake a task, inevitably motivation [because entirely grounded in the self] ebbs away, and with it [the effectiveness of] the action itself.[207] The selfish heart may boast of its virtuousness, but its virtue can never manifest itself in proper conduct. Perfect moral behaviour is, in my view, always the product of the non-self, the selfless self.[208] It is in this manner that we assume the standpoint of subjective

---

204 The link is pure Kyoto School. Here is Nishitani's indispensable gloss: 'Each of us is one of the focal points of the world's awareness. In giving birth to an infinite number of such focal points of self-awareness, the world reflects itself through them and becomes creative in the process ... That we exist as self-conscious individuals independent from one another, and that we live and act as such, is the world's reflection of itself in us as its foci of self-awareness. We are what Leibniz called "the living mirrors of the universe".' Keiji Nishitani, *Nishida Kitarō*, trans. Yamamoto Seisaku and James W. Heisig, Berkeley: University of California Press, 1991, p. 36.
205 One aspect of this form of *muga* is the non-selfish self capable of taking responsibility without blaming others for his own failures.
206 The Chinese proverb Kōyama evokes is rendered in Japanese as *Hitogara o tsukushite, tenmei o matsu* ('When you seek to make a man endeavour, wait for orders from on high').
207 Lest we regard this as mere pro-group sentiment or collective anti-individualism or a surrender by Kōyama to the clichéd rejection of 'selfish individualism' of pre-war Japanese thought, recall the superhuman strength of the mother set on saving her children (or her piano) from a fire, or the unstinting capacity for sacrifice of soldiers in combat when risking all to rescue a fallen comrade. Kōyama is giving a metaphysical gloss to the surge of adrenalin that even play or sport naturally provokes.
208 The two Japanese expressions that Kōyama uses here are *muga* and *mushi*, the latter being conventionally rendered into English as 'unselfishness', but the Chinese character or *kanji* that leaps off the Japanese page is *mu* (the 'less' in 'egoless', the 'nothing' in 'nothingness'), as in *mu no tetsugauku*.

responsibility,[209] in which the perfection of the self as an agent culminates inevitably in the transformation, or retranslation, of the self into the non-self.

The perfection of selfless conduct is accomplished in genuine action: the actions of the self become in fact the actions of the non-self. I think we can attain this state in the daily struggle of our lives. Or, to rephrase my point, the culmination of the power of the self is to be found in the power of the other. I think this is a necessary truth; it must be so. If this assertion is correct, it opens the door to the perfection of the power of the other *qua* the power of the self, and the power of the self *qua* the power of the other. In this way, what we call 'the power of the self' comes into its own. But the power of the self [in this sense] is not the action of the [limited or unextended] self but rather becomes absolute action, the purest form of conduct.

It is furthermore my view that the Japanese people are already realizing this paradoxical vision with unresisting, because uncomplicated, simplicity. Logically speaking, this paradox cannot be understood rationally because the power of the non-self *qua* the power of the self and vice versa is a complete contradiction of logic. But this contradiction is not a hopeless one. If we unresistingly surrender to the sincerest part of our feelings – cultivating them, burnishing them – they will manifest the truth.

Doesn't this aspiration define what is classically meant by being Japanese? And I mean 'You! Yes, you Japanese!' I am talking about the kind of people who draw sustenance from the national past and find the source of their existence in the pages of history. At the same time these people embody the very same community to whom we can appeal with the traditional norms embodied in what we think of as the ideal Japanese. My sense is that this kind of person is somehow able to transcend mere logic-chopping rationality in reaching out for the uplands of unspoilt feeling. I am talking about the [intensity of] sentiment that arises from absolute loyalty such as one might experience with particular force when one is with one's lord facing death, and finds oneself overcome with the emotion that one would freely sacrifice oneself in his place.[210] We are talking of that sense of total responsibility in which one unresistingly offers up one's existence to fate, be it life or death, for one's lord, the kind of feeling that culminates in the extinction of separate identities and the complete identification of one's being with one's lord in death.[211]

---

209 Here is the other foundational meaning (*Grund*) of the expression of '*tachiba*' or 'standpoint' as the fundamental ordering idea of all three symposia.

210 Kōyama uses the word *taikun* (the origin of our word 'tycoon'), which can mean 'sovereign'; however, given the intimate nature of the kind of death evoked, be it on the battlefield or the deathbed, the word 'lord' seems more appropriate.

211 The register of feeling here, of the dissolution of the ego, is captured, admittedly in a different key, by Wagner's celebration of *Liebestod* (love-death): 'No longer Tristan, no longer Brundhilde.' A cultural link may be found in the homoeroticism that characterized some samurai bonding, but the greater theme is the mystery of losing one's sense of self in 'the Other' or the moment or the task.

Today, we might say that such feelings are expressed in the death cry of the soldier: 'Long live the Emperor!' Isn't this appeal of the purest heart to be found in the language of the absolute that is voiced at the final moment when one has expended all one's energy and soul in the struggle to carry out one's duties to the end?[212] Here one achieves the fullest form of subjective responsibility. Just as we find it said in the teachings of Zen and the Buddha that the power of the other and the self are locked in struggle, so the culmination of self-fullness is to be found in non-self-fullness, just as the ego ends in non-ego: self-power *qua* other-power and other-power *qua* self-power stand as perfect identities. There can be neither religion nor the absolute nor any such notion based on self-power alone. This much should be obvious.[213] Nevertheless, it is equally true that other-power does not manifest itself by chance; but genuine Japanese sentiment offers, among others, one such occasion for its expression. For me, it seems that Western civilization represents an excessive triumph of the ego and the powers of the self, while the Indian and Chinese civilizations embrace to excess the non-self and the heart that appreciates the truth beyond the mere self (*teinen*). But Japanese tradition stands slightly apart from these two extremes, and the reason is that the spirit of ego *qua* non-ego has prevented the domination of either extreme. As a result, non-ego has emerged from the tireless application of the idea of authentic responsibility and intense embrace of the standpoint of responsible subjectivity. Today, encouraged once more, these feelings are to be put to the test.

NISHITANI: The non-self you just mentioned is what I spoke of before as a new *ascesis* or disciplining of the self.[214] I have of course also spoken of the subjectivity of the non-self (*muga no shutaisei*), but … That each individual serving in his post has to abandon the ego in order to fulfil his responsibilities is obvious and follows as a matter of course. But this approach needs to be complemented by another that incorporates the objective facts involved and treats organizations as objective phenomena [not just the accumulative effect of individual assertion or will]. Both dimensions of the problem must be addressed if our world-historical war is to benefit to the maximum degree required. Maximizing this benefit as an act of [sustained] creativity makes the 'all' in wars of all of our powers and capacities (*sō ryoku sen*) or world-historical wars possible. This organizational objectivity helps to define what we mean by the objectivity of the state (*kokka*). When we speak about sacrificing our egos when doing our jobs or performing the duties of whatever post we are assigned,

---

212 There is an implied reference to the Confucian notion of suicide when loss in battle signals the collapse of the moral world for which one is fighting. In such circumstances one does not want to survive to serve heaven's new mandate. All that has commanded one's loyalty has been destroyed. The moral trial is consummated.
213 Oh good (DW).
214 Nishitani uses the term transliterated from the nineteenth-century Greek.

the important gains to be achieved by this sacrifice will be greater still if and only if we address the organizational dimension of the challenge.

From the standpoint of the state as a whole, it is not enough to tell people to focus all their efforts just on their jobs and occupations. The more important thing is that a national system or organization of work should coordinate and unify all [war-related] occupations from above. In this way, the self-nullifying, because generous, spirit of the workplace can make a formidable contribution to the national cause. Everything else is rhetoric. Without a state vision and focus, all talk of work as national service ends up encouraging no more than the minimum expected. Worse still, it offers verbal cover to protect [the selfish] pursuit of one's own private interests. No work will be able to rise above the level of the *durchschnittlich* unless it exploits jointly the strength of the individual and the collective.[215] Only when the subjective and objective dimensions of the task interpenetrate and thoroughly reinforce each other can the massive potential of a world-historical war emerge. In all this it is vital for those in positions of leadership to carry out their own responsibilities meticulously. But perhaps more than anything else, responsible subjectivity, as referred to earlier, must contribute to ensuring that the objective nature of this system is at once clear, obvious and compelling to every Japanese. The darkness, in Kōyama's expression, is within us all. The term is suggestive. Think of the sense of the 'dark dealings' (*yami*) of the black market. On this matter of darkness, I remember reading in a newspaper that today such black markets have recently taken on an increasingly organized character. If that is the case, we need an organized 'light' to overcome this organized darkness.

KŌYAMA: Lest our deliberations conclude with a variety of theoretical elaborations, what finally must be done in a practical way if we are [to stave off defeat and] to achieve a victory in our war of total resistance? There is no merit in engaging in mere discourse (*rikutsu*) about the problem. Rather, we must constantly think of ways to generate the ever-renewing 'plus alpha' that forms the categorical imperative of such wars ... if we can achieve this, then the best possible organization of our efforts becomes that more likely.[216] About this, I entertain no doubts. But note also that if this effort is spoiled by flawed reasoning and destructive criticism, the net result will be negative.

NISHITANI: Nietzsche once noted that people ordinarily think that a good cause makes a war holy. In other words, if the aims of a war are worthy

---

215 The word *durchschnittlich* is transliterated from the German for 'average'.
216 Kōyama says 'win' but the entire thrust of this final part of this symposium, including the concluding evocation of the spirit of hopeless resistance that inspired the Spartans at Thermopylae (480 BCE), suggests that he really means 'stave off defeat' or 'fight to a standstill' or 'eventually triumph in a later round of this eternal struggle'. This is what I have translated as 'the best possible organization of our efforts'.

or its motivations are good, then a holy war it is. But in fact, according to Nietzsche, it is a good war that makes a cause good. I found this argument stimulating ... For example, the usual way of thinking would say that the aim of the present war is, as noted before, to set up a new world order or construct a Greater East Asian Co-Prosperity Sphere, and it is these goals that make this war holy. The common assumption is that an aim gives value to an activity. But it is also possible to look at things more subjectively (*shutaiteki*). According to this view, the goodness of an activity would manifest itself, as it were, in the goodness of the aim. It seems to me that this latter way of thinking better grasps the meaning of the present war ... For even in the case of constructing a Greater East Asia, it is not just a matter of focusing entirely on the outcome of the process. To do so would be to give primary value to the 'conceptualization' of the project, and thereby to run the danger of foundering in the 'conceptual' [as opposed to the actual practical achievements].

It is better to make our starting point this question: observing the war being waged, examining the actual facts about the act of warfare involved, how sound and decent is the spirit that is emerging from this activity? It is not just a matter of a good cause, but of the goodness that shines forth from those who shoulder that cause actively and embody it in their own persons. This is where the real good cause lies ... Well, that's the idea, anyway, because otherwise the subjective essence of war (*shutai-teki-na honshitsu*) does not really come to the fore. So the question is not about pursuing a good cause but rather turns on the challenge of how we can become a nation of people who strive to realize in our actions the virtue of our cause.

Conjure up the spectacle of a great nation at war. For a nation to be great, its political leadership must reflect that greatness. It must be great, too. Consistent with this greatness, this nation's leaders will take a stand or intellectual position based on a clear and deep insight into the direction that world history ought to take. These leaders will be fired by moral spirit, and thus inspire their nation through inspired leadership. The people will in turn act in concert with the nation's leadership by absorbing this same spirit. Any war waged by such a nation and its people will qualify as an example of what Nietzsche called a 'good war'. Certainly things follow when the subjects who wage wars can draw on a set of profound insights into world history. When such a nation or people tries to become what it is in potential, to actualize itself, in war, this is a nation that has the potential to infuse fresh vitality and new spirit into world history. Only from this lofty standpoint can the waging of war be a 'good cause'. If a nation or a people does not have such a high moral standpoint and just claims to have a great cause, this is no more than arrogance. In essence, our standpoint as a nation must be high and deep and broad. Thus I find suggestive the idea that a good war sanctifies its intended cause. Particularly in the case of our present war of total resistance, a struggle in which not only economic issues but also spiritual forces are significantly involved, Nietzsche's idea merits close attention and thought.

21 Scholarship (*gakumon*) and military power

SUZUKI: The contribution of the realm of the mind or spirit [to this struggle] can be deepened by the methods of scholarship. As noted earlier, whatever else it is, knowledge is power.[217] For me, this issue has a special poignancy because it is the study of world history that confronts us with this challenge. We have all acknowledged that the Great East Asian War is a world-historical struggle, but this is not only a matter of the scale of the conflict or indeed our awareness of what is at stake in the outcome of this war. No, a more fundamental significance must be assigned to this struggle. Whatever drama is captured by the expression 'world-historical', this term is better understood as a call to reflection.[218] We must make the term bear a fuller and a more profound significance than it is conventionally accorded. I therefore intend to speak about the mission of scholarship. As a struggle to transform the order of the world, the Great East Asian War strikes at the fundamentals of mental outlook. I see my scholarly vocation as a student of history in terms of the challenge to give expression to the profound significance of what we call the 'world-historical' in its essence as true thought.[219]

The goal of the present struggle is starkly obvious. As our country has proclaimed at home and abroad, we are fighting to create a new order in East Asia. In other words, this is a war not for national gain but for a new order [ing of human affairs in our region]. This is a struggle between different [world] orders. Conflicts of this kind inevitably are sustained as they must be by one fixed notion of order, but such notions or concepts of order can finally be reduced to a view of history. Without necessarily being self-serving, I believe that the current struggle takes its meaning from the conflict of historical interpretations that arises from our conviction and understanding of history. In short, the transformation of [our regional] order arises from historical necessity while the Anglo-American view of history finds itself unable to recognize the necessity for this change. If in the end we should win and establish a new order in East Asia, this would represent the triumph of our interpretation of history (*rekishi-kan*).

---

217 *Sore ga chikari da.*
218 Suzuki uses the word *hansei*, which can mean just 'reflection', as in 'to think about [something]', but often carries the nuance of rethinking an error, a negative result or even bad conduct. Suzuki may have thought the ambiguity was pregnant here, given the occasion and Japan's slide into defeat.
219 Suzuki uses the word *shisōsei*, which conjures up Valéry's use of the term *une pensée* in his poem *Le Cimetière marin*.

Granted, our current struggle is grounded in the confidence we have in our conviction that this transformation of [our regional] order is driven by historical necessity. Nevertheless, the historical necessity at work here is of a particular kind, as Kōyama makes clear in his new book, because it remains necessity regardless of whatever we Japanese or the Anglo-Saxons want or think, that is whether we feel we must have this change or whether others do not want it.[220] It is a kind of necessity that all must [finally] recognize and yield to. The significance of the historical necessity we are talking about reaches beyond the subjective expression of mere [nationalist] feeling or excitement: rather, it is something profound that demands clarification through deep scholarly analysis [and reflection]. Here the orientating powers of the university can lend spiritual depth to the matter.[221] In facing up to this challenge as a practising historian, I feel a poignant challenge sharper than any other.

If historians take the world-historical fact of the Great East Asian War as an object of scholarly perusal, they come under pressure from the realities of the conflict to rethink their ideas about history. There are two dynamics at work here. It is as Kōsaka has argued: via history our understanding comes to mediate our existence; and, at the same time, caught up in the contemporary realities of world history, scholarship itself acquires a new depth and profundity. Furthermore, I think it can also be argued that in fact it is not just the study of history that it influenced in this way: the problem affects all fields of scholarship. This in the end is what happens to all knowledge when world history comes to dominate our horizon.

NISHITANI: I see your point. If a thought goes no further than feeling, then when it is expressed in words it is all too quickly transformed into a theoretical mantra or concept (*kannen*). But while ideas may originally emerge from something vital and alive, when they become 'concepts' they are forced into a 'form' that conspires to block the development of genuine thinking.[222] They lose their strength to move our hearts. This has its dangers (*kiken*).[223]

---

220 The book in question is Iwao Kōyama's *Sekai-shi no Tetsugaku* (The Philosophy of World History), published in Tokyo by Iwanani Shoten in 1942.
221 Here, as is so often the case in these symposia, the Japanese word 'spirit' cuts two ways: it can resonate with the national obsession with the Japanese 'spirit', but also clearly alludes to the German meaning of *Geist*, which draws a distinction between the merely material world and its human opposite. English connotations of the supernatural, whether the 'spirits' and 'ghosts' of the occult or the 'Holy Spirit' of Christianity, have, as noted above, no relevance here.
222 A paraphrase of the historicist attack on eternal ideas, or a nod to Heidegger's critique of Western philosophy since Plato or, more likely, a mobilization of Nishida's dissent from philosophic and logical formalism in the European tradition.
223 'Danger' seems the wrong word here but the ultranationalist and official assault on 'dangerous ideas' (*kiken shisō*) may be playing on Nishitani's mind.

SUZUKI: No, what we need is not some form of rigid abstraction but rather the deepening of scholarly insight within and in response to the dynamic flux of historical reality; that is the thing.

KŌSAKA: What power makes world-historical wars possible? What allows one to fight one? Of course, a form of rational organization completely free of all ambiguity is essential. So is a style of leadership that can animate such an organization. But none of these practical requirements, whatever else one might say, excuses scholars from the necessity of deepening the scope of our labours as scholars in order to make our contribution to the war effort. This is our responsibility. As for the question of what kind of power defines our world-historical war, [the answer merits an overarching metaphor because] the larger truth at issue is this: because the power that sustains a genuine world-historical war is the fruit of Japanese subjectivity, and furthermore because it bears the stamp of world-historical necessity, all our efforts must draw their direction and orientation from the vast surging current of the world, drawing as it does on the plurality of worlds that makes the world, and which in turn forms part of the great river of world history, the depths of which serve as the source of this power and which give it its huge creative thrust. Is it not Japan's supreme task to animate and give direction to this world-historical trend? Isn't the huge significance of all this to be found here? In any case, it is my passionate belief that all the powers (*sō ryoku*) of world history need to be mobilized afresh and given a new home, and then all this strength we will have drawn from history can be put to maximum practical use in the greatest number of ways possible, because it should be. I believe that this necessary task must be the work of Japanese hands. Here the key agency is of course our subjectivity, itself the product of thousands of years of Japanese history and our experience of the power of history itself. The goal would then be to ally these national gifts with the living force of the whole of the world's past, mobilizing all this today, in pursuit of Japan's world-historical mission, an effort to which we must lend our voices in vigorous support. In this we can rely on the protection of Japan's countless and endlessly varied gods to sustain us in this effort; but also note that in this Japanese conception of world history, even the history of classical Greece, for example, is not something foreign or separate. We are heirs to it all. Thus it is possible, indeed more than possible, for the truth, courage and beauty of the ancient Greeks, reconceived afresh, to form part of the historical horizon of Japan itself. By such exercises in imaginative reconstruction, we can locate Japan's place (*tokoro*) in the totality of the world produced by the past. Thus, in the world-historical world of the present, ancient Greece is not some alien planet or civilization. Everything is grist to the mills of Japanese subjectivity as its concentrates the energies of the world and gives them focus. The ambition must be to bring out the potential in everything. By mediating all the powers of world history (*sekaishi-teki sō ryoku*), our true war-making capability can be brought to the fore. As for those who are puzzled by or critical of my studying ancient Greek philosophy today, one can only conclude that they have failed to understand what form the necessity that drives and transforms world history assumes [and the world-historical scope of consciousness required by this great task].

Let us proceed to examine the issue from the point about how one cultivates creativity of the spirit. If one grasps the true character of the arts properly, that is, not just conceptually, it becomes obvious that they have an unrivalled capacity to reveal the truth of reality, to shape it and make its powers manifest. The consequence is [of] compelling [significance], because true beauty has helped to give meaning to history and to affirm its value ... [*gap in original*] ... authentic grasp of anything of the order of great art is to expose oneself to the utter clarity of the transforming mission of world-historical war.[224] So we must seek to exploit fully the total power (*sōryoku*) otherwise hidden within the realm of the spirit that is scholarship and the arts. Hence my conclusion: the spirit may contribute to the organization of all our powers as a manifestation of world-historical power; they foam forth outwards from within a world history that is true.[225]

22 The arts and military power

NISHITANI: I feel the same. Even Nietzsche talks of feeling the whole history of humanity as one's own history. As the subject of art has come up, I recall the proscription against imprisoning things – the arts being especially vulnerable – in 'concepts' in the sense we just referred to. But the main point is to move the hearts of people and touch their essence. For instance, take the poem of Ishikawa Takuboku that contains the line: 'Quiet before the mountains of my home town, I am so grateful that these mountains are here!'[226] Such lyrics reveal affection for one's native place. Sentiments aroused by such poetry, if they speak to the occasion, can inspire feelings of gratitude towards one's country or give expression to love for one's family. Or take Akahiko's words: 'It is still cold though the ice is melting, and the waves capture the shadows of the March moon.'[227]

---

224 Kōsaka's point does not translate easily into English, and clearly part of his argument is designed to fend off critics of the professional study of philosophy (especially non-Japanese philosophy), but a relevant comparison is the role of the Parthenon in giving expression to, while also confirming, the powers of the classical Athenian *polis*. The whole enterprise made Athenians more Athenian, thus enhancing their sense of confidence, their identity and, yes, their powers. It was, as Thucydides affirms, no mere artistic ornament.
225 World history is understood in its Hegelian sense, not as the totality of empirical facts or developments in the past but as only those movements and achievements that qualify as revolutionary advances or breakthroughs in the history of the planet.
226 Takuboku Ishikawa (1886–1912): popular Japanese poet.
227 Possibly Shimagi Akahiko (1876–1926), another much admired *tanka* poet.

Somehow the suggestiveness of this poignant vision of crystal clear light, or what have you, finally touches one deeply. If the scholar is so affected, he should let it infuse his labours at his desk; if the soldier is so touched, let it animate his spirit on the battlefield. Somehow this marvellous sensation must colour the totality of how we live in the world. It must not be lost even though the poet directly evokes none of these worlds: not scholarship, nor military service, nor indeed the state itself (*kokka*) ... [but] even in these other spheres the authentic arts have their place and meaning. Even if we ask of the arts only that they deepen our truest feelings as a people and a nation (*kokumin*) while elevating us all to a kind of nobility of spirit, this, too, would be good. Here we would find another indispensable means to cultivate, in an authentic manner, the spiritual powers that characterize world-historical wars. Don't you think so?

Music is another branch of the arts where this is true. Take the example of Beethoven, who has attracted a passionate following among students and other young Japanese today. This is a splendid development in our culture. Just how profoundly such music enhances our capacity as individuals to feel the purest forms of *pathos* is probably impossible to say.[228] But to negate our potential for *pathos* is to bar the way to the deepest [and most genuine] of our human sentiments. The celebration of the histrionic strain in heroism is finally tendentious and vain.

SUZUKI: Musing on this theme, I have just recalled something somebody once said to me. We met when I was a child during the Russo–Japanese War. There was a song at the time whose lyrics included the lines: 'I went because even the neighbour's horse would have gone to the front if called to the colours.' I listened to the story as a tale about how a simple child's heart responded enthusiastically to the war, but I can't help thinking that we need marching songs now that move us as they moved the innocent child I was in response to that song. I remember it. Both the lyrics and the music were admittedly sentimental but it possessed the power of simplicity. The naïve feeling of 'Father, you were strong' is somehow rather different.

NISHITANI: There has been a great deal of excited chat about symbols and concepts of late, but if one considers the magnitude of the impact that music and the like have on the human spirit, these things may have to be taken more seriously. In *The Republic* Plato treats music as something of consequence, and Confucius speaks of 'ritual music' which puts music on a par with ritual. If we learn to give proper weight to the relationship between politics and music, we may find that the ancients arrived at this profundity of insight long ago.

KŌYAMA: 'The Light of the Firefly' seems to have recently become an object of some controversy.

---

228 The word *pathos* is transliterated from the Greek.

KŌSAKA: About that, the issue is not that a folk song of an enemy country is popular here. Rather, there is a deeper and more troubling problem at root here. Don't you think so?

23 Concentrating our powers of military resistance (*senryoku no shūchū*)

KŌYAMA: Apropos world-historical wars, I suspect a few points remain that merit our attention, including the broad question of what form a world-historical war will take at this stage of world-historical development.[229] Of course, we are not privy to the practical details essential to addressing the specifics of this question,[230] but as our deliberations began with the larger issue of the ideal organizational structure for fighting world-historical wars, I suspect there is still scope for a useful discussion of this theme. I take the view that the supreme imperative of world-historical wars is to create that extra measure of enhanced performance that may prove decisive to any victory in such a struggle. If I may borrow one of Nishitani's expressions, the contrasting approach involves us in merely trying to sustain a degree of 'rational equilibrium' among the various sectors [of the national war effort].[231] This would mean continuing to assign equal priority to all the sectors engaged in waging this form of total war, sectors we might note that have already benefited from liberal 'equal shares for all' (*sōbana*) generosity by the state.

The truth of the situation [requires an approach that] is very different, and indeed I suspect that the current approach will not achieve the level of creativity demanded by this epic struggle. Furthermore, looking at the issue from the standpoint of an educator, I would argue that we need to think about the long-term implications of what we are doing in the classroom. The figures for production have to be calculated with an eye to the long term as well.

---

229 The word 'development' has been added by the translator. Kōyama says only *reikishiteki dankai* (historical stage).
230 Less than two months earlier, Hajime Tanabe observed, in his secret lecture on the nature of co-prosperity spheres to Tōjō's opponents in the Imperial Navy: 'Today I would like to talk about the structures of co-prosperity spheres, touching, in a very formal way, that is only abstractly, on the logical dimension at issue. I take this approach because I have no concrete knowledge of the problems posed by co-prosperity spheres, and therefore what I have to say will be of a very general character.' The tone, content and even some of the language (e.g. *risōteki kōzō-ron*) offer close parallels with the remarks here of Kōyama, who was present when Tanabe delivered his talk. The suggestion would be that the contributors to *The Standpoint of World History and Japan* and *The Ōshima Memos* worked and thought in tandem. For the full text of Tanabe's remarks, see 'On the Logic of Co-prosperity Spheres', in Williams, *Defending Japan's Pacific War*, pp. 188–99.
231 Kōyama uses the term 'equilibrium', but the context and his subsequent remarks lead one to suspect that a better rendering might be 'routine'. In the follow paragraph or two, *kinkō* will be translated, where appropriate, as 'routine'.

364 *The Standpoint of World History and Japan*

Certainly everyday, routine thinking will not generate the kind of *élan* and creativity that this kind of war demands.

As I noted above, world-historical wars totally integrate each and every section of society into a comprehensive whole (*issoku issai*), and therefore a logic quite distinct from conventional analytical logic (*bunseki ronri-sei*) is involved. Or, to put the matter in the form of a question: what happens when one sector begins to set the pace for the rest? The issue then becomes how to prioritize the national effort and resources vis-à-vis the whole. This forces one to distinguish between those sectors that are more deserving of such largesse and those that are not. Furthermore, because such determinations have to be made in response to the objective circumstances thrown up by the evolving character of our world-historical war, we cannot look to the ideal structure for the answers. For a solution, one should turn to what might be termed the *Dynamik* of a world-historical war.[232]

An example may be relevant here. Since 8 December 1941, the military sector has burst forth in a blaze of fireworks and all other sectors have rallied to support this effort. That situation still prevails today. In reality, ever since the fighting began, the military sphere has predictably set the pace. The surprise attack on Hawaii in order to destroy the Pacific Fleet required a precise assessment of Japan's capacity to sustain a total war. I think the military operation was stupendous (*subarashii*), but the larger conclusion is this: to give priority to the military struggle at this stage of the conflict, indeed, to concentrate the whole of one's effort in this way, is from the vantage of world-historical war, a form of total war, a strategic necessity. And therefore in any national mobilization of all of our powers, abilities and resources as a state (*kokka sōryoku*), there may arise an obvious and irresistible need to trim the budget, resources and manpower for other sectors. Such sacrifices are inevitable because, pushed to its limits, the policy of prioritizing all sectors may result in denying Japan the very thing we seek most: victory in this world-historical war.[233]

If we accept this argument as sound, we must seek that creative leap that any war of total resistance demands, and it follows from this that we cannot think in terms of organizing the sectors that sustain such an effort in terms of routine and equivalent treatment. I have in mind such examples of modern thinking as equilibrium theory in economics or the balance of power in diplomatic relations. Earlier in our discussions Nishitani mentioned the idea of organic forms of organization, and this brings to mind relevant examples from physics, biology or, for that matter, democracy.[234] In any case, all such

---

232 The word *Dynamik* is transliterated from the German.
233 These comments should be read in the light of the fact that at this point Kōyama was attached as a civilian adviser to the Navy Ministry, and was involved in the secret seminars that form the content of *The Ōshima Memos*. The ambiguities and veiled nature of this argument suggests a covert message which is unclear. For more information about this struggle, see Chapter 10.
234 In mentioning democracy, Kōyama may be thinking of Montesquieu's theory of checks and balances.

approaches tend to be antithetical to innovation; but in the circumstances of today's struggle it is precisely the principle of [maximum] creativity that must be embraced. This is because equilibrium and routine, even if occasionally upset, are never going to give birth to that decisive improvement [in performance], that essential 'plus alpha'.[235] Struggles of total resistance demand the perfect union of matter and mind. The mental half of this equation, the spirit if you will, has to be given an opportunity to display its powers. If mere calculation suggests that two sides are equal in their fighting capacity, the prospects of victory recede accordingly. But if the 'plus alpha' effect can be brought into play, victory may follow. It may even pry open the door to success for an apparently weaker side over a more powerful opponent. Unless this were true, the humbling of great powers in the past would have been impossible. Such victories are a product of the creativity that war inspires, and this is as true of the contests of world-historical wars as of those of any other kind of war. Indeed, such conflicts inspire the kind of supreme genius in war that is inconceivable to a mind governed by the mediocre rationality that defines routine.

KŌSAKA: I think what Kōyama is saying makes sense. The creativity of war is beyond the reach of such rationality. It is literally unimaginable. But can one say, therefore, that the higher reason with which history makes its leaps won't mediate this [kind of creativity]? Surely this isn't the case. Reason may hold back all of its powers (because we have held back its powers), but absolute reason may still come into play just in time to deliver just the degree of success required. After all, this is the [same] reason that creates history. And what we mean by this falls under Kōyama's rubric of 'the supreme genius in war'.

One can even take the air strikes on Hawaii as an example. These appeared to be what they unmistakably were: a carefully executed surprise attack. But interwoven into this instant in time was a final, almost desperate, act of unambiguous self-sacrifice unto death. This was, of course, not how this event was thought of at the time. Rather, the operation was correctly judged to be the product of the most careful planning and rigorous training. But it was also a moment of inspired creativity occasioned by the unavoidable necessity that is the Great East Asian War. This explains why the whole episode resonated so deeply in our hearts:[236] because it involved an authentic act of self-sacrifice.

---

235 As before, Kōyama uses the expression *purasu* or 'plus', but this appears to carry a meaning similar to the post-war Japanese mathematical cliché of 'plus alpha'.
236 One may disagree profoundly with Kōsaka's analysis and still appreciate that his is the most compelling gloss of the subsequently widely criticized mood of exultation with which so many thoughtful Japanese greeted the outbreak of war in the Pacific. It suggests that Yoshimi Takeuchi's often-cited criticism of the paper-thin difference between support for and opposition to the Pacific War in Japan was misplaced and superficial.

I had always been troubled by the business in China. This is because the Great East Asian War as a whole has to be resolved rationally. This was consistent with my understanding of world[-historical] reason, which I took to include the ability to respond to the sudden shifts in historical circumstances and to judge them correctly. I was forced to accept this dimension of reason's power for the first time when this act of sacrifice was made. At the same time I also entertained the more tough-minded notion that if one could defeat one's opponent, one might manage to escape death. The point was to maintain one's sense of balance in these shifting circumstances. On the one hand, there is the spirit of self-sacrifice, but at the same time one had to remain soberly prudent when responding to the creative breakthroughs of the historical process. Such care has been integral to the Great East Asian War as whole, and it has been, of necessity, mediated by reason. The more one sees the war as a form of constructive creation (*kensetsu*), the more one accepts that this process must be governed by planning and rational calculation. This is what I am saying. This is consistent with what I heard on my Chinese travels: the way we treat [our occupied territories] must be entirely rethought. This is what people were insisting on. This imperative applies not only to China; it is necessary here in Japan itself. Isn't this the case?

To bring the totality of our powers into play, we must have a system capable of exercising these powers. This requires, I would say, a most formidable kind of reason. I lay great emphasis on the role of reason because I believe a proper sense of balance must govern any application of such total power. This balance must be mediated by its calculability (*keikukusei*), which will tell one which sector or sphere must be favoured and which must be judged to be lower priority [in the execution of policy and the application of resources]. To cut to the essence of the matter, this is not the business of slaughter, of just killing one's opponent and thereby utterly neglecting his life and needs: rather, one must ensure that growth follows the knife (*koroso koto in yotte ikasu*). A negative form of mediation is at work here. Others may be allowed to progress while the self [including ourselves] may be sacrificed. Well, in any case ... this is what I mean by the necessity of reason. Unless we follow this course, discord will emerge at home. This may take a severe toll, and our ability to wage a total war may be compromised. Of course, there is no other option but to drag along those who fail to grasp this truth no matter how well and how often one explains to them. But either way I believe the essential truth of the matter can only be perceived in depth by grasping the whole.

SUZUKI: It is well to understand reason as divided into analytical reason and reason as the force that moves [history]. This higher form of reason – let us call it 'absolute reason' – can be well understood. But it is entirely mistaken to assume that the power of the totality (*sō ryoku*) should be understood as consisting of only the harmonious balancing of forces or the work of routine equilibrium. Quite the contrary: the power of the totality is exactly as we have described it: something entirely different from routine and easy compromise. Harmonious equilibrium (*chōwa*) is a product of the analytical logic of modernity, and as such is to be totally rejected when judged from the standpoint we have assumed.[237] In face of such doctrines, we can do no other. Indeed, theories of world-historical wars understood as wars of total resistance have been devised precisely to overcome the social, economic and political paralysis (*ikizumari*) caused by such complacent ideas. Rather, the situation is as I described it at the start of these discussions: our world-historical war has come into being to open the door to the future. To bring about that tomorrow, history [as a planetary force] will transform modern notions of the [modern] state, society, the economy and culture, taken together as a world-view, when – and only when – they are completely overturned. It is to demolish such notions that world-historical wars are waged. To pretend otherwise and proceed in a manner consistent with the pre-existing harmony of the powers that be as an act of principle is simply meaningless. On the contrary, the irresistible logic demands principles consistent with the fullest mobilization of our strengths and capabilities. By this I am not referring to the logic of [effective] policy making but the logic of history. By their very nature world-historical wars embody and facilitate history's turning points. This is why the structure of such wars demands the fullest mobilization of our powers consistent with the overarching priorities of history. State policy must reflect this truth.

This affirms the truth of what we have affirmed repeatedly in this discussion: dynamism rather than equilibrium must rule this mobilization in the implementation of the clearest priorities and the most effective modes of action.[238] Thus, the expectation is that a new spirit of creativity – and by 'spirit' I mean something that merits the name 'spirit'[239] – has to be born. This is a cardinal point. It is the power of this spirit we are talking about when we insist that the spirit is indispensable to any total mobilization of our other strengths, abilities and potential. A world-historical war must therefore have such a spiritual underpinning, but by this we emphatically do not mean some ancillary 'spiritual' aspect or dimension as a mere supplement to conventional routine reasoning and analysis.

---

237 Although he does not specify, Suzuki as an economic historian appears to be attacking ideas such as natural equilibrium in liberal economics, as this doctrine was formulated by Adam Smith, David Ricardo and John Stuart Mill, and natural order theories such as proposed by Herbert Spencer.
238 This time the term 'dynamism' is transliterated not from the German but from the English.
239 Given that the speaker is Suzuki, it may be reasonable to conclude that by 'spirit' he is referring not so much to the ideal of *Nippon no seishin*, as to Max Weber's notion of *Geist* as in *The Protestant Ethic and the Spirit of Capitalism*.

NISHITANI: Gosh, if everyone shared that view, I suppose I'd feel very gratified about all this. It is much the same thing I have urged before about creative *élan* being the indispensable foundation of any attempt to wage a successful world-historical war, and I have been disappointed that in general this [argument] has been overlooked [in the larger debate over the war]. With the approach of war, different aspects of the challenge have come into view. For example, the need to marshal our energies and resources, and then to organize them in order to concentrate them properly and promptly, will be all but impossible to meet unless we grasp the problem from the standpoint of the dynamic of a proper system of total mobilization (*sō ryoku sen*). Once again, the task of setting priorities and sticking to them raises its ugly head. For me, this is why one must insist that in any effective system of world-historical war, the organization of leadership and decision-making in particular must be clear and uncomplicated. Nothing would be more damaging to the national cause in these demanding times than the organizational problems that would arise from a divided or ineffective leadership. Such a condition would violate the very essence of the contemporary state. Each branch of society has its own particular standpoint, but such factors as tradition, custom and conventional practice, as well as the impact of social roles and amour propre or 'face', can sap morale and deflect our energies. For this reason it is essential that all branches of society assume the general standpoint of the nation to overcome such deleterious influences in order to ensure that the kind of spirited vitality (*kihaku*) demanded by this enormous struggle can be brought to bear, forcefully and effectively, on our historic labours. Without such resolute clarity of intent, the dangers of inconstancy and confusion of purpose will overwhelm us. This is why I have frequently urged that a national committee of state be created to bring together a handful of top people representing the three or four obviously pre-eminent parts or sectors of society, the commanding heights, if you will, in order to discuss and formulate a consensus that would genuinely reflect the supreme needs of this nation, as judged from the grandest and most sober perspective. In a word, the ambition would be for the nation and people in their entirety to adopt the posture of sacrifice unto death in the service of this great hour in our history. In the encounter between the highest seriousness of both sides that characterizes the present, the most fitting posture is to be found in our willingness to surrender to the claims of ambitious sacrifice in a wager of the highest stakes in which one may win all only by risking all.

This is a dynamic stance, one that will feed and foster innovative *élan*. This is how I understand what Suzuki meant by the creative spirit. Faced with the challenges of our times, one must not hesitate before the great task out of respect for conventions, the sensitivities of 'face' or private material interest. The psychological danger is that if we succeed too easily as first, we may become overconfident, even complacent, but as soon as things start going even a little badly, we may lose our nerve and allow a mood of defeatism to take over.[240]

Nowadays people talk of 'making the impossible possible'. As I said earlier, such sentiment can fan bolder creativity and more radical innovation. To take as one's basis only what has been received from the past and to think only with inherited ideas is to constrict unduly the scope of what we can achieve. It makes all sorts of things all but impossible. The very idea of taking this great but necessary gamble becomes unimaginable. In the very posture of ambitious sacrifice I cited earlier there is an element of 'letting go' [of one's ego, one's very life] that is absolutely indispensable if one is to make the impossible possible. Since ancient times those who have vanquished great opponents, as the Greeks did the Persians, hungrily embraced such soaring sacrifice and thus made the impossible victory possible. Think of the classic Japanese example I mentioned earlier: the great Nobunaga. The battle in the seas of Hawaii has reawakened this spirit. This will enable us, indeed the nation as a whole, in every sphere and branch, to exhaust our every resource in this supreme struggle. Isn't that what makes a world-historical war a war of all our powers?

---

240 A Japanese or particularistic twist on one of the pivotal universal patterns of Confucian behaviour that derive from *toku* and the mandate of heaven. Or, to put it another way, think of the predictable national response to the tumultuous seven months from Pearl Harbor to Midway.

Index

ABCD encirclement 180, 180n165
absolute nothingness *(zettai mu)* 149
absolute war 268n9
Abu Ghraib 62
academic history, shift to realm of 262n1
Acton of Aldenham, Baron John 36
agreement, unity by 254n149
Aihara, Setsuko 134n62
Aihara, Shinsaku 20, 21
air bombardment, potential for 71
Akahiko, Shimagi 361, 361n226
al-Qaeda 77
Alberto-Culver 85
Althusserian Marxism 185n10
Amani-Oshima, US occupation of 71
America: Civil War (1861–65) 76; East Asian domination by 233n112; hegemony of xxvi, 27, 75–76; hegemony of, 'base imperialism' and 324n132; mobilization of, reference to 287, 287n49; moral-universalism of 53–54; Occupation of Japan 99; Pacific co-prosperity sphere of 325n135; pursuit of happiness, tradition of 311n104; rise in power of 7; strategic interest of 57
America, explanations of 175–77; Kōsaka 176, 177; Kōyama 176; Nishitani 176, 177; Suzuki 175–76, 176–77
America and systems of total war *(sō ryoku sen)* 287–88; Co-Prosperity Sphere, persuasive requirements of ambition for 287n48; 'conservative libertarianism' in language of Kōyama 288n51; free trade and democracy, American style 288; Great East Asian War 287; *Großraum,* vision of 288; Kōyama 287; New Deal, collectivist tendencies of 288; Nishitani 288; Suzuki 288
The Analects of Confucius 31, 33, 96, 181n167, 282n38
Anglo-American capitalism 352n200
Anglo-American defeat, assumption of 342, 342n172
Anglo-American liberty, contradictions of 307–13; Anglo-American democratic approach to national self-determination 309; Atlantic Charter, contradictory aspects of 307–8; customary morality *(jinrintai)* 309n99; East Asia, national awakening in, Japan's role in 308; freedom, contradictory aspects of 307–8; Kōsaka 308, 309, 310; Kōyama 307, 308, 309, 310, 311, 313; moral sickness in Europe 310; Nishitani 308, 310–11, 311–12, 312–13; pursuit of happiness, American tradition of 311n104
Anglo-Japanese Alliance 151
annihilation: description of 281n34; medieval theory of wars of 61
anti-colonial feeling, growth of 324n133
'anti-establishment' establishment 31
anti-war liberalism 64
appeasement, opposition to 73
Aquinas, St Thomas 65, 66n8, 142n80
architecture and interior design 161n115
Aristotle xxviii, 54, 133n58, 204n54, 336n166, 346n87
Arnold, Matthew 132n54
art and artistic forms, history of 151
arts and military power 361–63; Ishikawa, Takuboku 361; Kōsaka 363; Kōyama 362; music 362; Nishitani 361–62; Suzuki 362

Asada, Sadao 78n2, 78n6, 78n7, 78n10
Asahi, Heigo 103
asceticism of the ancients 314
Asia, national awakenings in 117
astronomical terminology, use of 206n63–64
asymmetric warfare 71–72
Athenian *polis* 361n224
Atlantic Charter 307n96, 308n97; contradictory aspects of 307–8
St Augustine 65
Austria-Hungary, victims of 324n131
authority *(shidō)* and persuasion in ideological struggles 284–87; Co-Prosperity Sphere, 'ethical character' of 285n45; ethics, fundamental character of 285; Great East Asian Co-Prosperity Sphere 285–86; 'guidance' 285; Kōsaka 286–87; Kōyama 286; language of Suzuki, resignation in 284n43–44; Nishitani 284–85; spirituality, fundamental character of 285
autonomy and subjectivity, anticipation of post-war philosophies of 352n202
average *(durchschnittlich)*, rising above 356

Badiou, Alain 195n36
Baldwin, Stanley 324n134
Barthes, Roland 22, 32, 101, 105n16
Bergson, Henri 294n68
Bertolucci, Bernardo 25
Bismarck, Otto von xxxiii
Bix, Herbert P. xviii, 46, 105n7
Black Legend of Kyoto School 254n149
Blair, Tony 321n124
The Book of Changes (I Ching) xviii, 29, 33n1, 282n38
Borgia, Caesar 145
Borradori, Giovanna 29
Brandenberg, Arnold Otto Erich 113n16
Briand, Aristide 60, 61
British Empire 225–26; Economic Conference 212n80
Buddhism 15, 19, 20, 21, 31, 32, 53, 60, 85; Buddhist categories 32; *Daijō Bukkyō* (Buddhism of the Greater Vehicle) 280n31, 284n42; discourse of factual dialectics *(jitsusōron)* 236; introduction to Japan of 154–55; in Kyoto School xxiii; other-worldliness of, rejection of 255n150; *Shōjō Bukkyō* (Buddhism of the Lesser Vehicle) 280n30; Zen doctrines 315n111
Bullock, Alan 215n85
Bungakkai (Literary World) 103
Burckhardt, Jacob 142n79
Buruma, Ian 60, 66n4
Bush, George W. 62, 99, 321n121
Bushido ('Way of the Warrior') 315n111
Butterfield, Herbert xxii, 35, 50n2, 51n19, 51n28

Calichman, Richard F. xviv, 33n5
The Cambridge History of Japan (Hata, I.) 75
capitalism 122n35; Anglo-American capitalism 352n200; consumer capitalism 85; *The Spirit of Capitalism* 330n150, 335n162, 367n239
Carthage, Roman moral character at 253
Catholicism 85, 147, 148n92, 157n109
Central Intelligence Agency (CIA) 62, 64
Chakrabarty, Dipesh 118n27
Chang, Iris 59, 60, 61, 65n2
Chiang Kai-shek 104, 219n88
China: ancient achievements of 334, 334n160; borders of, lack of clarity on 303n90; East and North-East Asia, traditional Chinese concept of 302n88; economic power of 57; historiography, successes and limitations of 39; military atrocities of Japan in 233n110; morality in 198–99, 198n44, 199–200, 200n45; narratives of 'other people' centred on 227n103; philosophy of history, rejection of 38; Shina (Sanskrit-Latinate term), Kyoto thinkers use of 198n43
Chippendale, Heian xxviii–xxx
Chou dynasty 97
Christianity 147n90; Atlanticism of Spain, Mediterranean Catholicism and 148n92
Chronicle of the Direct Descent of Divine Sovereigns 179n164
Chronicles of Japan (720 CE) 152n99, 237n119
chronology: factions xlv; patterns xlv; phase I; rise of Tōjō faction and origin on Yonai-Kyoto 'brains trust' xlvi–xlvii; phase II; resistance to Tōjō's policies – Yonai faction and genesis of *Chūō* transcripts and

Ōshima Memos xlvii–xlix; phase III; Yonai-Kyoto School faction and decline of Tōjō government xlix–lii; respect for 41
Chūō Kōron xvii, xxi, xxii, xxiii, xxiv, xxx, xxxi, xxxiii, liii, 40, 41, 42, 43, 44, 45, 50–51n16, 50n15, 331n154, 336, 345n179, 345n181; archive, text of texts 94–95; discussions 7, 11, 20–21, 23, 27, 30, 37–38, 39, 41, 43, 55, 64, 82, 90, 102; prophetic character of xxv; symposia 4, 15, 16–17, 18, 19, 20, 22, 29–33, 45, 54, 83, 84, 90, 95; transcripts 3, 7, 16, 22, 32, 35, 36, 37, 38, 43, 44, 45, 55, 56, 69, 95
Chūō Kōron symposia, Confucian form and language of 29–33; 'anti-establishment' establishment 31; Buddhist categories 32; Confucianism of Kyoto School 31–33; discussion in groups, East Asian practice of 32–33; 'logic of place,' Nishida's keystone concept 32; minds, meeting of 30–31; mutual commitment to each other 30; vision, sharing of 30; world order, plea for remaking of 30–31
Churchill, Winston S. 75, 321n124
The City of God (Augustine) 65
Classifications of Culture (Kōyama, I.) 20
Clausewitz, Karl von xxxii, 16, 268n9; ideal organizational structure for waging world-historical wars 292
Cleary, Thomas 93, 104n3
Clemenceau, Georges xxxiii
closed economic zones, formation of 215–16
'co-prosperity' and 'morality,' concepts *(gainen)* of 313–16; asceticism of the ancients 314; co-prosperity *(kyōei)*, derivation of 313n107; *Hagakure (Hagakure no shi)* 315–16; Kōsaka 313; Kōyama 313, 314, 316; Nishitani 313, 314; profit making and pleasure seeking, negation of 314; samurai inheritance 315
Co-Prosperity Sphere 269n11, 270n13, 300n77, 301n80, 302n85; ambition for, persuasive requirements of 287n48; 'ethical character' of 285n45; world-historical war and 299–300
co-prosperity spheres as *Großräume (kyōei-ken to rekishi-teki hitsuzensei)*, historical necessity for 322–27; Kōsaka 326–27; Kōyama 322, 326; Suzuki 325–26
co-prosperity spheres *(Großräume)* and the philosophy of the nation *(kyōei-ken to minzoku no tetsugaku)* 300–305; Chinese borders, lack of clarity on 303n90; colonial exploitation, Kōyama declaration on 300n79; East and North-East Asia, traditional Chinese concept of 302n88; Great East Asian Co-Prosperity Sphere 300n77, 301; *hakkō no ichi-u* (all eight corners of the world under one roof) 303n91; Korean people, self-determination for 301n80; Kōsaka 302, 303, 304, 305; Kōyama 303–4, 305; logic of 300n78, 302n87; national self-determination 302n84; pooled sovereignty, endorsement of 302n87
coffee shops, sexual encounters in 172n153
colonial exploitation, Kōyama declaration on 300n79
Columbus, Christopher 77; European Renaissance and modern history 146
compulsion, powers of 98
Comte, Auguste 210n75
concept of world-historical wars *(sō ryoku sen)* 266–72; East Asian Co-Prosperity Sphere 268–69; ethnic consciousness, wars linked to 271; Great East Asian War 268; *hentaiteki genshō* (abnormal or exceptional) 271n15; Kōyama 266–67, 269–70; national consciousness, wars linked to 271; Nishitani 270; Suzuki 269, 270; total war *(zentai sen)*, emergence of 267; warfare, changes over time in forms of 267–68
conflict, continuity of 273n22, 274n24–25
Confucian ethics 196n40
Confucian happy endings 86
Confucian interregna 93–94, 101, 102
Confucian obligation to comply 86–87
Confucian pacifism 45, 63–64, 84, 89–90
Confucian psychology 74
Confucian resistance xx
Confucian revolutions xxv–xxvi, 97–99, 99–101; American Occupation of

Japan 99; *Bungakkai* (Literary World) 103; *Chūō Kōron* archive, text of texts 94–95; compulsion, powers of 98; Confucianism, nationalism and 97; conspiracy theories 100; counter-elites, challenge by 96–97; elites, governance by 96; Greater East Asian Co-Prosperity Sphere 95; hour of the blade 101–2; International Military Tribunal of the Far East (IMTFE) 100; interregna 93–94, 101, 102; language of 'right' and 'left,' domestication of 99; liberal political analysis, East Asian realities and 99; liberal scholarship on modern history 97–98; liberalism and failure to win 'hearts and minds' 102–4; making sense of 97–99; Meiji Restoration rejection of Tokugawa values 98; Nogi, suicide of 101–2; Overcoming Modernity symposium 103; pacific democracy, embrace of 97; Pax Americana 101; Peace Preservation Law (1925) 96; persuasion, goal of 98; Post-Meiji Confucian Revolution 101, 104; reconstruction *(kaizō)*, call for (post-First World War) 102; regime change and 96; revolutionary nationalism, rise of 99; Russo–Japanese War 101, 102; Taishō democracy, Western enthusiasm for 104; Taishō experiment 98; timing and form in 99–101; violent transformations in Japanese politics 97–98; war-as-revolution factionalism 97; war decision, 'total' mobilization and 103–4; warriors, Confucian suspicion of 98–99

Confucian tipping points 80–91, 167, 167n129, 292n59; Alberto-Culver 85; Confucian happy endings 86; Confucian obligation to comply 86–87; Confucianism 80–91, 167, 167n129, 292n59; consensus, achievement of 86–87; consensus, legitimate authority and 87; consumer capitalism 85; criticism, job of 87–88; cultural domination 85; East Asian way 80–83; ethnic identity, defence of 87; experience (first-hand) *vs.* armchair moralism 83–85; financial crisis 85; Greater East Asian Co-prosperity Sphere 90, 91; knowledge, conditions of possibility of 87–88; Kyoto School, Kōji Eizawa's criticism of 89–91; Marxist *tenkō* 88–89; *mission civilisatrice* 85; moral unanimity 86; national history, Confucian pacifism in field of 89–90; Post-Meiji Confucian Revolution 81, 82, 89; revisionism 37–39; web-based virtuality 85–86; Western individualism, embrace of 86

Confucianism xvii, 4, 5, 7, 18, 19, 20, 21, 22, 24–25, 30, 31–33, 38, 39, 41, 42, 45–46, 47, 53, 55, 60, 63, 64, 95, 96, 105n18, 125n38, 149n95, 158n111, 166n128; decisive importance to political reflections of Kyoto School xxv; of Kyoto School 31–33; loyalties, resolution of ethical dilemma of division of 214n82; mandate of heaven 256n151; morality infused with practicality in 197n41; national identity, Suzuki's balancing claims of ethics with requirements of 252n147; nationalism and 97; nationalism and aggressive militarism, resistance to 139, 139n68; recalcitrant, conversion of 283n39; suicide, Confucian notion of 355n212; transformation *(henkaku)* 246, 246n136

conscience: inflamation of 59–61; wages of 61–62
consciousness *(ishiki)* 203n50
consensus: achievement of 86–87; legitimate authority and 87
'conservative libertarianism' in language of Kōyama 288n51
conservative philosophies 225n99
conspiracy theories 100
Constitution of Japan, Article 9 of xxiv, 64
consumer capitalism 85
contemporary Japan and the world 178–81; 'culture,' reflection on use of term 178; Kōsaka 178–79, 180, 181; Kōyama 179–80, 181; Nishitani 180–81; Suzuki 179, 180; world-historical necessity 178–79
contemporary life, crisis of 130
convergent evolution 305n92
Cornford, Francis MacDonald 252n146
cosmopolitan individualism 156n105
cosmos, fundamental assumptions about nature of 327n143
counter-elites, challenge by 96–97
Counter-Reformation 146

counter-revolution, principles of 26
creative civil society *(minkan sōi)*, dilemmas of 289–90; free speculation *(shui-teki jiyū)* 289n53; Kōyama 290; Nishitani 289–90; passivity of masses, assumption of 289n56; 'private initiative,' use of term 289n52; speculative appropriation 289; Suzuki 290
creativity and innovation in world-historical wars 294–99; East Asian Co-Prosperity Sphere 300; *élan vital* (life-force) 294, 294n68, 295–96; equilibrium, idea of 296, 296n71; guidance, leadership and 295, 297; Kōsaka 299; Kōyama 298; Mahayana Buddhism 299; *nemoto* (focus) 294n67; *Nihon Gaishi* (Rai San-yō) 297n73; Nishitani 294, 299, 300–301, 303, 304, 305; rationality of creativity 298–99; *toki o eru* (opportunity presented by historical occasion) 297–98, 298n75
criticism, job of 87–88
Critique of Pure Reason (Kant, I.) 326n140
Croce, Benedetto 189n26
crown colonies 226n101
Crusades 146
Cuban Missile Crisis (1962) 78
culture: cultural domination 85; Eurocentric cultural assumptions 65; European culture, universal validity of 121; Meiji Restoration, cultural revolution and 125; reflection on use of term 178; rejection of cyclical theories of 330n151; self-transparency, Japanese culture and 204n52
Cumming, John 215n85
customary morality *(jinrintai)* 309n99
cyber-warfare 77

Dalai Lama 104
Dawson, Christopher 119n29
de Bary, William 93, 104n2
defeat, avoidance of 269n11
Defending Japan's Pacific War (Williams, D.) 49
Defoe, Daniel 150n96
democracy 97, 103, 137, 215, 235, 309, 310–11, 319, 352, 364; *demokurashii no shisō* (ideology of democracy) 316, 316n113; free trade and, American style 288; 'hypocrisy' of 313;

institutions of 85; Taishō democracy 41, 104; 'totalitarian democracy' 320, 321
Derrida, Jacques 46, 51n18, 60, 282n36
Dessauer, Friedrich 131n52
determine *(kettei)* 184n6
Die Deutsche Genossenschaftrecht (Gierke, O.F. von) 239n124
developmental progress, concept of 127–28
Dewey, John 189n26
Dilthey, Wilhelm 110n4
division of labor, alienation resulting from 292n61
Dopsch, Alfons 128n42
Dore, Ron 105n15
Dostoevsky, Fyodor 132n55
Drucker, Peter 352n203
The Dynamic of World History (Kōyama, I.) 21

East Asia: discussion in groups, East Asian practice of 32–33; East and North-East Asia, traditional Chinese concept of 302n88; East Asian way 80–83; Great East Asia War 253–54; ideological conflict, re-education and 283n39; Japanese in 251n145; nation-states in, creation of 306; national awakening in, Japan's role in 308; new form of ethics for 184–85
East Asia, conception historically of *(tōa no kannen to rekishi-kan)* 305–7; economic development thesis, stages of 305; Kōsaka 306; Kōyama 306; pluralism (world-historical), Kōyama's theory of 307; Suzuki 305, 306–7
East Asian Co-Prosperity Sphere xxix, xxxi, 220, 291, 300; proposals for xviii
East Asian Co-Prosperity Sphere, ethical and historical character of (second symposium, 4 March, 1942): ethics as fundamental problem of co-prosperity spheres *(Großräume)* 252–56; ethics of nation *(minzoku)*, ethics of world and 213–24; ethics of the family *(ie)* 237–49; ethics of war and ethical wars 231–34; ethics *(rinri)* of historical turning points, birth of world-historical consciousness *(jikaku)* and 193–95; Greater East Asia as region of nations *(minzoku ken)* 225–29; history and ethics 183–86; Japan and

China *(Nippon to Shina)* 201–11; Japanese, towards new kind of 256–60; methodological approaches to world history *(sekai-shi no hōhō)* 189–93; politics and spirit of family 249–52; politics of philosopher-kings/ sages *(kentetsu)* 234–37; Ranke or Hegel: empirical world history *vs.* the philosophy of world history 186–88; Western ethics and Eastern ethics 229–31; world-historical peoples *(minzoku)* and the ethical *(rinrisei)* 195–201; world history and *Großräume (kōiki ken)* 211–13

economics: attack on 351n197; development thesis, stages of 305; economic regionalism 56–57; economic warfare 291, 292; of scale 69–70

Eden, Anthony 75

Edo period 39; ethics of the family *(ie)* 238–39; individuals, problem of our awareness as 140

Eisenhower, Dwight D. 75

Eizawa, Kōji 89–91, 92n14

El Alamein, battle of 317n116

élan vital (life-force) 294, 294n68, 295–96

elites, governance by 96

Emperor Hirohito 36, 74

L'Empire de signe (Barthes, R.) 101

equality between individuals, ideal of 242

equilibrium, idea of 296, 296n71

'Eternal Peace' (Kant, I.) 243n130

'eternal war,' idea of 278

'Eternity, History, Action' (Tanabe, H.) 20

ethics: ethical rules, challenge of formation of 242–43; fundamental character of 285; philosophy and 190n27–28

'Ethics and Logic' (Tanabe, H.) 21

ethics as fundamental problem of co-prosperity spheres *(Großräume)* 252–56; Carthage, Roman moral character at 253; ethics of the family, idea of 252–53; Great East Asia War 253–54; Greater East Asian regionalism 253–54; Kōsaka 255–56; Kōyama 254–55; *moralische Energie*, loss of 255; national self-awakening 254; Suzuki 252, 255; Versailles Treaty 254

ethics as power: liberal navalism 11–13; liberal unease 8–9; new world order 9–11

ethics of nation *(minzoku)*, ethics of world and 213–24; closed economic zones, formation of 215–16; East Asian Co-Prosperity Sphere 220; *Großräume (kōiki-ken)* 219; Japan and Germany, ideological divergence between 222; Kōsaka 216, 217, 218, 219, 221, 223, 224; Kōyama 219, 223, 224; League of Nations 221; Manchuria, Japan's relationship with 221; Manchurian Incident 220; *moralische Energie*, national possession of 215; *moralische Energie*, programme of action 218; nation-states, shaping of 217–18; Nishitani 213–14, 218, 221–22, 223–24; political awareness 224; *rinen* (ideas as concepts) 221; Suzuki 216–17, 218, 219, 222–23; Versailles Treaty, unfairness of 219–20

ethics of the family *(ie)* 237–49, 252–53; East Asian Co-Prosperity Sphere 241; Edo period 238–39; equality between individuals, ideal of 242; ethical rules, challenge of formation of 242–43; existential relationships 248–49; family, human ethics and 239; family as ideal type 243–44; *Genossenshaft*, Gierke's idea of 239, 240, 244, 245, 248; harmonious totality *(zentai)* 243; human development *(ningen kaihatsu)*, challenge of 246; imperial authority *(taisei taikan)* 246; independence, spirit and 246–47; Kōsaka 241, 245, 247, 248–49; Kōyama 237–38, 240, 242, 247–48; *moralische Energie*, ethics and 245–46, 247; Nishitani 240–41, 245; parent-child relationship, family and 243, 248; rationality, false clarity of 243; samurai society 238, 248; self-awakening as nations *(minzoku)*, encouragement of 246; society, rules for regulation of 244; state, organization of 238

ethics of war and ethical wars 231–34; human development 233–34; Kōsaka 231, 232–33, 234; Nishitani 233; Suzuki 231, 232, 233

ethics *(rinri)* of historical turning points, birth of world-historical

consciousness *(jikaku)* and 193–95; Kōsaka 194–95; Kōyama 193–94; Nishitani 195; Suzuki 194
ethnic consciousness, wars linked to 271
ethnic identity, defence of 87
Eurocentric cultural assumptions 65
Europe: culture of, universal validity of 121; excellence of, provocation of 17–18; 'Fortress Europe' 117; liberty and individualism in modern Europe 137; moral sickness in 310; nations and peoples of 226; order in, post-Westphalian 270n13, 273n21; trasition from medieval to modern society 265
European civilization, defining qualities of 122–23; Kōsaka 123; Kōyama 122, 123; Nishitani 122–23
European Orientalism xxiii–xxiv
European reflections on unity of Europe 119–20; Kōsaka 119, 120; Nishitani 119; Suzuki 119, 120
European Renaissance and modern history 141–48; Columbus, Christopher 146; Counter-Reformation 146; Crusades 146; Henry the Navigator 146; Kōsaka 144–46, 148; New World, Europe and 146; Nishitani 142–43, 144, 146; Ottomans 145, 148; Peasants' Revolt in Germany 144; Protestant Reformation 142, 144; Spain, mediating role of 148; Suzuki 141–42, 143–44, 146, 147
European sense of crisis, Japanese world-historical consciousness and 115–19; Asia, national awakenings in 117; 'Fortress Europe' 117; Kōsaka 118; Kōyama 116, 118, 119; Nishitani 115–16, 117, 118; Suzuki 116, 117, 118
European sense of superiority 120–22; European culture, universal validity of 121; Kōyama 120, 121; Nishitani 120–21, 122; Suzuki 120, 121–22
European Union (EU) 241n127
Evola, Baron Julius 268n9
existential relationships 248–49
expansion as means of survival 55–56
experience: experience (first-hand) *vs.* arm-chair moralism 83–85; importance of 138–39

fact and opinion 35–37
Falklands War (1982) 75

family: human ethics and 239; as ideal type 243–44; parent-child relationship 243, 248
fascism, rise of 317n114
feudal society: individuals, problem of our awareness as 136; religious spirit of 124
Fichte, Johann Gottlieb 194n35, 278n28
Fichte (Mutai, R.) 20
financial crisis 85
Finer, S.E. 98, 105n5, 297n74
First World War, Japanese losses in 75
Fitzgerald, Frances 92n11
Foucault, Michel 80, 87–88, 91n3
France: fall of (1940) xxxii; Third Republic in 166n125
free speculation *(shui-teki jiyū)* 289n53
free trade and democracy, American style 288
freedom: contradictory aspects of 307–8; individual consciousness in pre-modern Japan and 136
Friedman, Thomas 8, 16
Frobenius, Leo 171n148, 330n151
Fukuyama, Francis 85, 92n10

Garon, Sheldon xviii, 351n196
'The Genealogy of World History' (Mutai, R.) 21
Genossenshaft, Gierke's idea of 239, 240, 244, 245, 248
genuine reform *(kakushin)* 112
geographical assumptions of Kyoto School 68–69
geopolitics and Kyoto School 15–17
Gierke, Otto Friedrich von 239n124
Gilson, Etienne 142n80
Gladwell, Malcolm 80, 91n1, 91n5
global community, hierarchy of 228–29
Goethe, Johann Wolfgang von 185n9
Goldhagen, Daniel Jonah 46, 59, 65n1
Goldstein, D.M. and Dillon, K.V. 7n3
An Inquiry into the Good (Nishida, K.) 19
Goto-Jones, Christopher 49
Great East Asian War xxxii, 253–54, 317n116; America and systems of total war *(sō ryoku sen)* 287; concept of world-historical wars *(sō ryoku sen)* 268; historical context of world-historical wars *(sō ryoku sen)* 262; Japan and China *(Nippon to Shina)* 206

Great Harmony *(Taiwa/Yamato)*
282–83, 282n38
great power status, modern Japanese
state and 53–54
The Great Powers (Aihara, S.) 20
Greater East Asia as region of nations
(minzoku ken) 225–29; British
Empire 225–26; Europe, nations and
peoples of 226; global community,
hierarchy of 228–29; individual
freedom, concept of 229; international
bodies, voting in 228; Kōsaka 227–28,
229; Kōyama 228; laissez-faire
liberalism, doctrine of 228; *moralische
Energie,* moral leadership and 229;
Nishitani 226, 229; practical needs of,
fit between governance by
philosopher-kings and 236–37,
237n118; Suzuki 225, 227
Greater East Asian Co-Prosperity
Sphere 40, 43; authority *(shidō)* and
persuasion in ideological struggles
285–86; co-prosperity spheres
(Großräume) and the philosophy of
the nation *(kyōei-ken to minzoku no
tetsugaku)* 300n77, 301; Confucian
revolutions 95; Confucian tipping
points 90, 91; Greater East Asian
regionalism 253–54; Tōjō's decision
for war, rejection of 55–56; world
history and *Großräume (kōiki ken)*
213
Großräume (kōiki-ken): America and
systems of total war *(sō ryoku sen)*
288; concept of xxvi; ethics of nation
(minzoku), ethics of world and 219;
Kyoto School 69–70; Tōjō's decision
for war, rejection of 54, 55–56, 57
group dynamics 73–74
Guantanamo Bay 62
'guidance': authority *(shidō)* and
persuasion in ideological struggles
285; leadership and 295, 297

Hagakure (Hagakure no shi) 315–16
haja-kenshō (destruction of wickedness)
281n32
hakkō no ichi-u (all eight corners of the
world under one roof) 303n91
hakuai (love of humanity) 230n104
Hanazawa, Hidefumi 42, 50n10
Hannibal 70
happiness and hell, visions of 312n106
harmonious totality *(zentai)* 243

harmony: as binary opposite of conflict
282n37; consensus and 74
Hata, Ikuhiko 75, 78n11
Hatanaka, Shigeo 44
Hatten Dankai-setsu 128n43
Hauriou, Maurice 27, 65
Hegel, Georg W.F. xxxi, 5–6, 16, 17, 19,
20, 54, 110n4, 111n6, 133n58, 147n91,
150n96, 169n146, 179n161, 179n163,
180n166, 185n12, 187n22, 189n25,
204n54, 210n73, 266n6, 300n77;
Anerkennung (recognition), use of
term 207n66; engagement with
conceits of 327n143; idealism of
185n14; idealism of, Kōyama's
criticism of 113n14; *Lectures on
World History* 196n38; matter and
spirit, distinction between 202n47;
nature, dialectical approach to
296n72; objective spirit of 289n55;
Phenomenology of Spirit 196n38,
207n66, 294n67; *Philosophy of
History* 196n37; private initiative,
argument on 289n55; reading of
Adam Smith, reference to 292n60;
subjectivity, assumption of modern
European command of, challenge to
330n150; subjectivity of 255n150;
world history understood in terms of
Hegelian philosophy 361n225
Hegel (Kōyama, I.) 20
hegemonic leadership 55
Heidegger, Martin xvii–xviii, 60, 63,
66n12, 130n49, 132n53, 161n116,
161n118, 184n5, 187n22, 196n39,
245n135, 258n155, 314n110, 317n114,
334n160; critique of Western
philosophy since Plato 359n222;
Nazism, dismissal (late) of 310n103;
ontology and the ontic sciences,
distinction between 293n63; 'Self-
Assertion of the German University,'
interplay of 'future' and 'past' and
328n145; 'will to the future' 323n128
'Heidegger and Japanese Fascism'
(Parkes, G.) 49
Heisig, James W. 350n195, 353n204
Henry the Navigator 146
hentaiteki genshō (abnormal or
exceptional) 271n15
historical context of world-historical
wars *(sō ryoku sen)* 262–66; Europe,
transition from medieval to modern
society 265; Great East Asian War

262; Kōsaka 262, 263, 264;
metaphysics of war 263–64;
militarism, military state and 264–65;
national defence state system, pressing
need for 265; philosophy, war and
requirement for grounding in 263;
Suzuki 263–64
The Historical World (Kōsaka, M.) 20
historicism, Japanese history and,
challenges of teaching 148–51;
absolute nothingness *(zettai mu)* 149;
Anglo-Japanese Alliance 151; art and
artistic forms, history of 151;
historicism, exploitation of full
potential of 149; Kōsaka 148–49,
149–50, 151; Nishitani 148, 150, 151;
Suzuki 149, 150–51
historicism, problem of 133–35;
individual consciousness,
responsibility and 135; Kōsaka 134;
Kōyama 134, 135; modern world, role
of ideas in 135; Nishitani 134; Suzuki
133, 134
history: academic history, shift to realm
of 262n1; art and artistic forms,
history of 151; direction of 130n46;
distinction between study and
philosophy of 114n17; historical spirit
of the nation *(minzoku)* 132;
historical view *(rekishikan)* 306n94;
historical world, Kōsaka's idea of
158n110, 329n149; history-forming
power of nation-state as actor
328n144; ideas and 188n24; Kyoto
School, historical perspective of 5–6;
novelty as product of 245n134;
subjective movement of 167, 167n131;
textual history, facts on pages of
39–44; transcendence of limits of its
own time 187n20
history and ethics 183–86; East Asia,
new form of ethics for 184–85;
Eastern morality 183; Kōsaka 183;
moral posture *(taidō)* 183; *moralische
Energie,* display of 183, 185; morality,
traditional approach to 184; Suzuki
185–86
history in the East *(Tōyō),* concept of
126–28; developmental progress,
concept of 127–28; Kōsaka 126–27;
Kōyama 127, 128; Nishitani 127–28;
Suzuki 126, 128
Hitler, Adolf 9, 59, 99, 168n137,
220n90, 224n96, 317n114

Ho Chi Minh 82, 97, 166n128
Hobbes, Thomas 16
Hölderlin, J.C.F. 164n124
Holocaust 59
Hosoya, Chihiro 100, 105n11
Howard, Michael 10
Huizinga, Johan 143n81
Hull, Cordell 13, 74, 89
Hull Note (1941) 10, 42
human development *(ningen kaihatsu):*
challenge of, ethics of the family and
246; ethics of war and ethical wars
233–34
humanist philosophy 130n49
Husserl, Edmund 23–24, 232n109

I Ching see Book of Changes
The Idea of the Historical State
(Suzuki, S.) 20–21
'The Idea of World History'
(Kōyama, I.) 20
The Idea of World History (Suzuki, S.
and Aihara, S.) 21
ideal organizational structure for waging
world-historical wars 290–93;
Clausewitz, Karl von 292; East Asian
Co-Prosperity Sphere 291; economic
warfare 291, 292; integrated war effort
(ichi gen-teki) 291–92; Kōsaka 293;
Kōyama 290–91; military struggle,
conventional view on 291; modernity,
action of 293; morality, economic
warfare and spirit of 292; sciences,
division of 292–93; Suzuki 290, 293;
total wars, wars of ideas and 291
'ideal type,' Weberian use of term 267n7,
272n20
ideas as concepts *(rinen)* 188n24, 210,
221, 222, 225, 227, 241
The Ideas of the Kyoto School (Ōhashi,
R., ed.) 48–49, 51n23
ideological conflict, re-education and
283n39
Ihara, Saikaku 123n37
imperial authority *(taisei taikan)*
246
imperial expansion, defence of 323n129
Imperial Germany, victims of 324n131
Imperial Japan, great powers and 6–7
Imperial Japanese Army, brutality of
283n40
Imperial Navy xlii–xliii; at Pearl Harbor
(Hawai no kaisen), fighting spirit of
251; war options of 40–41

imperialism 205n55; Japan and China *(Nippon to Shina)* 207–9
independence, spirit and 246–47
individual consciousness, responsibility and 135
individual freedom, concept of 229
individuals, problem of our awareness as 135–41; Edo period 140; experience, importance of 138–39; feudal society 136; freedom and individual consciousness in pre-modern Japan 136; Kōsaka 139, 140; Kōyama 135–37, 137–38, 139–40, 141; liberty and individualism in modern Europe 137; moral conduct 136; Nishitani 138–39, 141; Osaka Castle, siege of 140; samurai rules of conduct 136; self-actualizing subjectivity *(shutaisei no jihatsusei)* 137; Suzuki 137, 138; trust and loyalty in social relations 137; warrior society 136
institution-building *(kensetsu)* 273n23
integrated war effort *(ichi gen-teki)* 291–92
intellectual persuasion, importance of 280
intermarriage between Koreans and Japanese, blessing for 301n83
international bodies, voting in 228
international law: Japanese expansion and 210n72; moral revolution in 27–28
International Military Tribunal of the Far East (IMTFE) 59, 62, 100
International Monetary Fund (IMF) 23
interregna *see* Confucian interregna
Introduction to the Philosophy of History (Kōsaka, M.) 21
Inwood, Michael 188n24, 207n66
Ishida, Mikinosuke 159n113
Ishikawa, Major Kanji 68
Ishikawa, Takuboku 361

Jacques, Martin 85, 92n9
James, William 31
Japan and China *(Nippon to Shina)* 201–11; Great East Asian War 206; imperialism 207–9; Kōsaka 202, 203, 204, 206, 209, 210–11; Kōyama 201, 202, 203, 205, 211; Lansing-Ishii Accord (1917) 209–10; Manchukuo 209; Marco Polo Bridge Incident 210; Nishitani 201–2, 203, 204–5, 206;

Russo–Japanese War 209; Sino–Japanese War 209; Suzuki 202, 204, 206–7, 209–10, 211
Japan and Germany, ideological divergence between 222
Japan and the Enemies of Open Political Science (Williams, D.) 33n6
Japan Forum 48, 49
Japan Romantic School, ultranationalists within 335n161
Japan studies 59–65; Abu Ghraib 62; annihilation, medieval theory of wars of 61; anti-war liberalism 64; Central Intelligence Agency (CIA) 62, 64; *The City of God* (Augustine) 65; Confucian pacifism 60, 63–64; conscience, wages of 61–62; conscience inflamation of 59–61; Constitution of Japan, Article 9 of 64; empirical research 60; Eurocentric cultural assumptions 65; Guantanamo Bay 62; Holocaust 59; International Military Tribunal of the Far East (IMTFE) 59, 62; Kellog-Briand Pact 60, 63, 64; liberal imperialism, ethics of 63; moral dilemmas 60; moral history 60–61; moral reform, post Versailles international public law and 62–63, 64; moral relativism 63; Moral Revolution (1914–45) 59–60; Orientalism 63; pacifism in academe 60–61; righteousness, forces of 61–62; Tōjō, war criminal? 62–63, 65; violence, enforcement of liberal norms with 64–65; Voltaire, Westphalian reticence of 64–65; Wars of Religion, sectarian strife of 65; Westphalian system 62, 65
Japanese, towards new kind of 256–60; Kōsaka 256, 259, 260; Kōyama 256, 257–58; Nishitani 257, 259–60; postmodern Japanese *(gendai Nipponjin)*, creation of 257; science, issue of 259; single absolute thing *(zettai ji)*, reversion to 258; Suzuki 256, 258, 260
Japanese Naval Academy, Kōyama's lecture to 42–43
Japanese subjectivity and qualities of leadership *(Nippon no shutai-sei to shidō-sei)* 327–40; Kōsaka 327–28, 337–38; Kōyama 329–30, 335–36; Nishitani 327, 328–29, 338; Suzuki 327, 329, 333, 338

380 Index

Japanese surrender, Confucian expectations and 39
Japan's Agenda and World History (Kōyama, I.) 21
Jihen ('struggle' or 'incident') 179, 179n162
Johnson, Chalmers 69, 78n1, 351n196
Jünger, Ernst xxxii, 320n120
Just and Unjust Wars (Walzer, M.) 63
just war, theory of 47

kan'i bureaucracy 153, 153n101
Kant, Immanuel (and Kantian tradition) 17, 19, 20, 23, 24, 25, 27, 54, 65, 110n4, 191n30, 277n27, 278n28, 326n139, 343n174; *Critique of Pure Reason* 326n140; 'Eternal Peace,' essay on 243n130; Metaphysics of Morals 243n130; objectivity, Kantian insight on 347n190; Reich der Zwecke 243n130; *Sollen* (that which ought to be), concept of 219n87, 241n126, 253n148
Katō, Admiral Kanji 72–73
Katō, Admiral Tomosaburō 73, 96
Keene, Donald 93, 104n2
Kellog-Briand Pact (1928) xxiv, 8, 9, 60, 63, 64
Kellogg, Frank B. 60
Kelsen, Hans 215n85
Kennedy, John F. (and administration of) 77–78
Kersten, Rikki 66n9, 91n6, 271n15
Keynes, John Maynard 9
Kierkegaard, Søren 132n55, 161n122
Kita, Ikki 100, 102, 351n199
knowledge, conditions of possibility of 87–88
kodai-shi (antiquity) 338n168, 339n169
Kojève, Alexandre 312n106
kokumin kokka (nation-state) 305n93
Konoe, Prince Fumimaro 24, 57, 88–89, 94
Korean kingdoms, Japanese absorption of 153–54
Korean people, self-determination for 301n80
Kōsaka, Masaaki xli, xlii, xliii, 5, 6, 15, 16, 17, 19, 20, 21, 29, 30, 38, 44, 56, 109, 182, 261; America, explanations of 176, 177; Anglo-American liberty, contradictions of 308, 309, 310; arts and military power 363; authority *(shidō)* and persuasion in ideological struggles 286–87; 'co-prosperity' and 'morality,' concepts *(gainen)* of 313; Co-Prosperity Sphere and our world-historical war 299, 300; co-prosperity spheres as *Großräume (kyōei-ken to rekishi-teki hitsuzensei)*, historical necessity for 326–27; co-prosperity spheres *(Großräume)* and the philosophy of the nation *(kyōei-ken to minzoku no tetsugaku)* 302, 303, 304, 305; conflict, continuity of 273n22; contemporary Japan and the world 178–79, 180, 181; creativity and innovation in world-historical wars 299; East Asia, conception historically of *(tōa no kannen to rekishi-kan)* 306; ethics as fundamental problem of co-prosperity spheres *(Großräume)* 255–56; ethics of nation *(minzoku)*, ethics of world and 216, 217, 218, 219, 221, 223, 224; ethics of the family *(ie)* 241, 245, 247, 248–49; ethics of war and ethical wars 231, 232–33, 234; ethics *(rinri)* of historical turning points, birth of world-historical consciousness *(jikaku)* and 194–95; European civilization, defining qualities of 123; European reflections on unity of Europe 119, 120; European Renaissance and modern history 144–46, 148; European sense of crisis, Japanese world-historical consciousness and 118; Greater East Asia as region of nations *(minzoku ken)* 227–28, 229; historical context of world-historical wars *(sō ryoku sen)* 262, 263, 264; historicism, Japanese history and, challenges of teaching 148–49, 149–50, 151; historicism, problem of 134; history and ethics 183; history in the East *(Tōyō)*, concept of 126–27; ideal organizational structure for waging world-historical wars 293; *idee* (German) and *rinen* (Japanese), use of words 227n102; individuals, problem of our awareness as 139, 140; Japan and China *(Nippon to Shina)* 202, 203, 204, 206, 209, 210–11; Japanese, towards new kind of 256, 259, 260; Japanese subjectivity and qualities of leadership *(Nippon no shutai-sei to shidō-sei)* 327–28, 337–38;

mechanized civilization, problem of 132–33; methodological approaches to world history *(sekai-shi no hōhō)* 190, 191, 192; military power, problem of *(senryōku)* 346–47, 349, 350; military resistance, concentration of powers of *(senryoku no shūchū)* 365; modernity, notion Japan has experienced two kinds of 126; moral failure of Europe, critical overdetermination of 310n100; morality or ethics, reference to 231n107; Pacific war, Japanese exultation at outbreak of 365n236; philosophy and reality 162, 163, 164; politics and spirit of family 249, 250; politics of philosopher-kings/sages *(kentetsu)* 236–37; race, nation, people *(shuzoku, minzoku, kokumin)* 169, 170–71, 172; scholarship *(gakumon)* and military power 360–61; stages of development, criticism of theory of 129; urban life, problems of 173, 175; wars of ideas *(shisō sen)*, importance of 283; Western ethics and Eastern ethics 229–30; world-historical peoples *(minzoku)* and the ethical *(rinrisei)* 197, 198, 199, 200; world-historical war, transforming mission of 361, 361n224; world-historical wars and concepts of war and peace 277, 279; world-historical wars *(sō ryoku sen)* and total wars *(zentai sen)* 273, 274, 275; world history, philosophers vs. historians on 114, 115; world history, viewing Japanese history from standpoint of 154; world history and *Großräume (kōiki ken)* 211–12, 213; world history and morality *(moraru)* 167–68, 169; world history as method 155, 157, 158–59, 160–61; world history the problem of our era, reasons why 110–11, 112–13

Kōyama, Iwao xli, xlii, xliii, 5, 16, 17, 19, 20, 21, 29, 30, 39, 41, 42–43, 44, 89–90, 101, 109, 182, 261; America, explanations of 176; America and systems of total war *(sō ryoku sen)* 287; Anglo-American liberty, contradictions of 307, 308, 309, 310, 311, 313; annihilation, description of 281n34; arts and military power 362; *atarashii purasu* (new plus factor), use of term 344n176; atomism, rejection of 248n140; authority *(shidō)* and persuasion in ideological struggles 286; 'co-prosperity' and 'morality,' concepts *(gainen)* of 313, 314, 316; Co-Prosperity Sphere and our world-historical war 299–300; co-prosperity spheres as *Großräume (kyōei-ken to rekishi-teki hitsuzensei)*, historical necessity for 322, 326; co-prosperity spheres *(Großräume)* and the philosophy of the nation *(kyōei-ken to minzoku no tetsugaku)* 303–4, 305; concept of world-historical wars *(sō ryoku sen)* 266–67, 269–70; conflict, continuity of 274n24–25; 'conservative libertarianism' in language of 288n51; contemporary Japan and the world 179–80, 181; creative civil society *(minkan sōi)*, dilemmas of 290; creativity and innovation in world-historical wars 298; culture, rejection of cyclical theories of 330n151; democracy, challenge to modern aspects of 352n200; East Asia, conception historically of *(tōa no kannen to rekishi-kan)* 306; equilibrium, use of term 363n231; ethics as fundamental problem of co-prosperity spheres *(Großräume)* 254–55; ethics of nation *(minzoku)*, ethics of world and 219, 223, 224; ethics of the family *(ie)* 237–38, 240, 242, 247–48; ethics *(rinri)* of historical turning points, birth of world-historical consciousness *(jikaku)* and 193–94; European civilization, defining qualities of 122, 123; European sense of crisis, Japanese world-historical consciousness and 116, 118, 119; European sense of superiority 120, 121; 'Fortress Europe,' use of term 317n115; Greater East Asia as region of nations *(minzoku ken)* 228; historicism, problem of 134, 135; history in the East *(Tōyō)*, concept of 127, 128; idea, use of the term 336n166; 'ideal' and Weber's notion of 'ideal type' 272n20; ideal organizational structure for waging world-historical wars 290–91; individuals, problem of our awareness as 135–37, 137–38, 139–40, 141; institutional failings, taking (official)

responsibility for 352n203; Japan and China *(Nippon to Shina)* 201, 202, 203, 205, 211; Japanese, towards new kind of 256, 257–58; Japanese subjectivity and qualities of leadership *(Nippon no shutai-sei to shidō-sei)* 329–30, 335–36; mechanized civilization, problem of 131, 132; methodological approaches to world history *(sekai-shi no hōhō)* 192–93; military power, problem of *(senryōku)* 343, 345, 349, 351–52, 356; military resistance, concentration of powers of *(senryoku no shūchū)* 363; modern world as European creation, acceptance of 330n152, 332; modernity, notion Japan has experienced two kinds of 123–25, 125–26; national polity, requirement for *fusawashii* (fitting or appropriate) new order in 250n143; national self-defence state *(kokubō kokka)*, world-historical foundations of 317, 320; national self-mastery, Japanese potency as real world actor and 336n166; Navy Ministry, attachment as civilian adviser to 364n233; organization of efforts to 'fight to a standstill' 356n216; philosophy and reality 161–62, 163, 164, 165–66; politics and spirit of family 249, 250; politics of philosopher-kings/sages *(kentetsu)* 234–35, 236, 237; race, nation, people *(shuzoku, minzoku, kokumin)* 169–70, 171, 172; relationships 248n139; *Sekai-shi no Tetsugaku* 210n73, 330n153, 359n220; *shiki* (energy of the samurai), use of term 344n177; stages of development, criticism of theory of 129, 130; stubborn quality of argument of 332n155, 332n156; subjectivity, historical character of 340; taikun (lord), use of term 354n210; tone shift in comments of, significance of 331n154, 332n156, 336n165; urban life, problems of 172, 173, 174, 175; wars of ideas *(shisō sen)*, importance of 279–80, 283–84; Western ethics and Eastern ethics 230; world-historical peoples *(minzoku)* and the ethical *(rinrisei)* 199–200; world-historical wars and concepts of war and peace 277, 279; world-historical wars *(sō ryoku sen)* and total wars *(zentai sen)* 272, 273, 274, 275; world historiography, use of term 205n58; world history, philosophers vs. historians on 115; world history, viewing Japanese history from standpoint of 152–54, 154–55; world history and *Großräume (kōiki ken)* 212; world history and morality *(moraru)* 166, 167, 168, 169; world history as method 156, 157, 158, 159, 160, 161; world history the problem of our era, reasons why 113–14
Kuhn, Thomas xxiv, xxi
Kuki, Shūzū 49
Kyoto School xvii, xx–xxiii, xliii–xliv; air bombardment, potential for 71; al-Qaeda 77; Amani-Oshima, US occupation of 71; American Civil War (1861–65) 76; American hegemony 75–76; appeasement, opposition to 73; asymmetric warfare 71–72; Black Legend of 254n149; Buddhism in xxiii; *Chūō Kōron* discussions and 20–21; Confucianism of 31–33; contest with Tōjō regime 42; cosmos, fundamental assumptions about nature of 327n143; Cuban Missile Crisis (1962) 78; cyber-warfare 77; East Asian Co-Prosperity Sphere, proposals for xviii; economics of scale 69–70; European excellence, provocation of 17–18; expressions used in wartime by, overthrow of xxvi; Falklands War (1982) 75; First World War, Japanese losses in 75; flowering of philosophy of 48–49; genesis of classical School 18–20; geographical assumptions of 68–69; geopolitics and 15–17; grand strategy, construction of 69–70; *Großraum*, vision of 69–70; group dynamics 73–74; harmony, consensus and 74; historical perspective of 5–6, 37–39; Imperial Navy and, links between 41; intermarriage between Koreans and Japanese, blessing for 301n83; Kōji Eizawa's criticism of 89–91; liberal imperium, abstraction and continuity of fight against 277n27; Masaichi Niimi and war scenarios 71–72; metaphysical position of 205n59; Miki's links with 43–44; Monroe Doctrine 76–77; oceanic mastery

76–77; organizational realities 74–75; panic and despair (1941) 72–76; pooled sovereignty, endorsement of 302n87; prophetic nature of meditations xxvi; rejection of liberal imperialism 23–24; Russo-Japanese War 68, 76; September 11 attacks on US 77; strategic position of Japan, realities of 70–71; strategic remedy endorsed by 72; thinker as grand strategist 68–78; Tsushima, naval triumph at (1905) 76; Versailles-Geneva-Washington system 74–75; victory at sea, Japanese vision of 76; war, terminological precision about nature of xxxii–xxxiii; Westphalian system 75
The Kyoto School and the Japanese Navy (Ōhashi, R.) 48

Lacan, Jacques 32
laissez-faire liberalism, doctrine of 228
Land of the Gods, Japan as 335n163, 336n165
language: of 'right' and 'left,' domestication of 99; of Suzuki, resignation in 284n43–44
Lansing-Ishii Accord (1917) 209–10
The Last Emperor (Bernardo Bertolucci film) 25
Lauterpacht, Hersch 65
League of Nations xxiv, 8, 9, 16, 56, 64, 114, 192, 221, 221n91, 312
Lectures on World History (Hegel, G.W. F.) 196n38
Lee, Homer 72, 78n9
The Left in the Shaping of Japanese Democracy (Kersten, R. and Williams, D., eds.) 66n9, 91n6, 271n15
Lehman Brothers 85
Leibnitz, Gottfried Wilhelm 353n204
LeMay, Curtis 283n39
Leonard, Mark 105n19
Leyton, Walter, Lord Leyton 56
liberal history xxi; exhaustion of xviii, xxvi, 46–48; Protestantism in xxiii
liberal imperialism 3, 6–7, 10, 11, 12, 13, 18, 22–23, 24, 25, 26, 27, 28, 283n39; abstraction and continuity of fight against 277n27; ethics of 63; Kyoto School rejection of 23–24
liberal navalism 11–13

liberal revolution, changes wrought by 27
liberal scholarship on modern history 97–98
liberalism 22–24; American hegemony, liberal imperialism and 23; anti-war liberalism 64; failure to win 'hearts and minds' 102–4; laissez-faire liberalism, doctrine of 228; liberal imperialism, pillars of 23; liberal unease, ethics as power and 8–9; moral universalism and liberal imperialism 23; neo-liberalism 23; political analysis, East Asian realities and 99
Liebestod (love-death), Wagner's celebration of 354n211
Lincoln, Abraham xxxiii, 76
literacy, pre-historic as pre-literate 128n41
Lloyd George, David xxxiii
logic of co-prosperity spheres *(Großräume)* 300n78, 302n87
'The Logic of National Ontology' (Tanabe, H.) 20
'logic of place,' Nishida's keystone concept 32
The Logic of the Species (Tanabe, H.) 17, 18, 19, 20, 45, 54, 133n58, 254n149, 318n118, 346n184
Löwith, Karl 87–88, 92n12, 122n36, 139n70, 310n102
loyalties, resolution of ethical dilemma of division of 214n82
Ludendorff, Erich von xxxii–xxxiii, 16, 268n9, 272n18, 287n49
Lytton Report (1932) 310n100

McAlister, John T. 22, 80, 91n4, 92n7, 93, 97, 104n1, 105n4, 105n21
MacArthur, Douglas 97, 101
Machiavelli, Niccoló 16, 145
McPherson, James M. 78n12
Mahan, Alfred Thayer xxvi, 11
Mahayana Buddhism 21; creativity and innovation in world-historical wars 299; wars of ideas *(shisō sen)*, importance of 280–81
Manchu ancestral lands 203n49
Manchu dynasty 64, 303n90
Manchukuo 78n1, 209, 213
Manchuria xli, 310n100; Japan's relationship with 221
Manchurian Incident (1931) xviii, 220

384 Index

Manchurian Railway *(Mantetsu)* 209n70
mandate of heaven 256n151
Manyōshū (Tachibana no Moroe) 140, 140n74
Mao Ze Dong 97
Marco Polo Bridge Incident 210
Marcus Aurelius 60
Marcuse, Herbert 63, 66n12
Martin Heidegger and European Nihilism (Löwith, K.) 92n12, 122n36, 310n102
Marx, Karl 54, 180n166, 187n21, 266n6; realism of 185n14
Marxism (and neo-Marxism) 19, 39, 46, 48–49, 204n54; consciousness *(ishiki)* 203n50; impact on political thinking 172n152; Marxist *tenkō* 88–89
Marxism-Leninism 326n137
Masako, Hōjō 140n71
Massignon, Louis xxiii–xxiv
Massis, Henri 116n21
mechanized civilization, problem of 130–33; contemporary life, crisis of 130; historical spirit of the nation *(minzoku)* 132; Kōsaka 132–33; Kōyama 131, 132; modernity, material civilization and spirit of mankind 130; Nishitani 130–31, 131–32; Suzuki 130, 131, 132; total war, mechanistic civilization and 133
medieval Japan, romantic figures of 140n72
Meiji consensus 82, 85
Meiji era 30, 39, 41, 53, 54, 55–56, 89, 94, 99, 102, 103; failings and limitations of 1868 project 119n28
Meiji project, ambitions of 53
Meiji Restoration 39, 69, 81, 82, 98; cultural revolution and 125; Kōyama's perspective on 39; politics and spirit of family 251; rejection of Tokugawa values 98
Mein Kampf (Hitler, A.) 120n32, 323n129
Meinecke, Friedrich 191n31
Mencius 15, 96, 282n38
Mencken, H.L. 9
metaphysical position of Kyoto School 205n59
Metaphysics of Morals (Kant, I.) 243n130
metaphysics of war 263–64

methodological approaches to world history *(sekai-shi no hōhō)* 189–93; Kōsaka 190, 191, 192; Kōyama 192–93; Nishitani 190–91, 193; Suzuki 189–90, 191, 193
Middle Ages, strife between kings and princes in 157n109
Midway, events of battle at 317n116
Miki, Kiyoshi 19, 20, 29, 43–44, 50n13
militarism, military state and 264–65
military position of Japan, assessment of 317n116
military power, problem of *(senryōku)* 343–58; Kōsaka 346–47, 349, 350; Kōyama 343, 345, 349, 351–52, 356; Nishitani 347–48, 350–51, 355–56, 356–57; Suzuki 344–45, 346
military resistance, concentration of powers of *(senryoku no shūchū)* 363–69; Kōsaka 365; Kōyama 363; Nishitani 368; Suzuki 366–67
military state *(militär-staat)* 265n5, 276, 320
military struggle, conventional view on 291
Mill, John Stuart 367n237
Miller, Edward S. 13n4
Minama (Gaya), destruction of authority in 152–53
minds, meeting of 30–31
Minear, Richard H. 105n12
Minobe, Tatsukichi 319n119, 335n163
mission civilisatrice 55, 85
Mitchell, Richard H. 50n14
MITI and the Japanese Miracle (Johnson, C.) 69, 78n1, 351n196
modernity: action of 293; material civilization and spirit of mankind 130; modern world, role of ideas in 135; overcoming modernity 266n6
modernity, notion Japan has experienced two kinds of 123–26; feudal period, religious spirit of 124; Kōsaka 126; Kōyama 123–25, 125–26; Meiji Restoration, cultural revolution and 125; Nishitani 125; samurai inheritance 124; Suzuki 126; Tokugawa peace 124
modernization, programme for 53
'moment,' idea in Japanese Hegelian context 212n79
monarchic absolutism, British tradition of 321n121
Monroe, James 300n77

Monroe Doctrine (1823) 10, 13, 76–77
Montaigne, Michel de 132n56
Montesquieu, Charles-Louis de Secondat, Baron de 364n234
moral conduct 136
moral dilemmas 60
moral history 35–37, 60–61
moral judgement, contagion of 48
moral posture *(taidō)* 183
moral reform, post Versailles international public law and 62–63, 64
moral relativism 63
Moral Revolution (1914–45) xxiv, xxx, 59–60
moral sickness in Europe 310
moral unanimity 86
moralische Energie: display of 183, 185; ethics and 230, 245–46, 247; loss of 255; moral leadership and 229; national possession of 215; programme of action 218
morality: customary morality *(jinrintai)* 309n99; Eastern morality 183, 183n3; economic warfare and spirit of 292; infused with practicality in Confucianism 197n41; moral posture *(taidō)* 184n7; traditional approach to 184
Mori, Tetsurō 42
Morley, James W. 105n15
Moroe, Tachibana no 140n74
Mosse, George L. 99, 105n8
Moulding Japanese Minds (Garon, S.) 351n196
Münzer, Thomas 144n82
Murasaki, Shikibu xxix
Mus, Paul xxiii–xxiv, 22, 80, 83–85, 91n4, 92n7, 93, 97, 104n1, 105n4, 105n21, 214n81
Musashi, Miyamoto 104n3
music 362
Mussolini, Benito 99
Mutai, Risaku 20, 21
mutual commitment 30
Myth (Kōsaka, M.) 20

Nagumo, Admiral Chūichi 77
Naitō, Konan 208n68
Nakamura, Kenjirō 44
Napoleon Buonaparte xxxiii, 268n9
nation-state *(kokumin kokka)* 305n93, 307n95; in East Asia, creation of 306; pre-1919 world order and 221n91;

shaping of 217–18; transcendence of 54–57
national consciousness, wars linked to 271
national consensus, urge to foster 38
national defence state 264n4; system of, pressing need for 265
national education, project for 251–52
national history, Confucian pacifism in field of 89–90
national identity 155n103; Suzuki's balancing claims of ethics with requirements of 252n147
national self-awakening 254
national self-defence state *(kokubō kokka)*, world-historical foundations of 316–22; Kōyama 317, 320; national self-defence state, claim of universality for 319n119; Nishitani 316, 318, 320, 321, 322; Suzuki 316–17, 318, 320–21, 322
national self-determination 302n84
national self-improvement, idea of progress and 236n117
nationalism 207n67; aggressive militarism and, resistance to 139, 139n68
nationalist emotionalism, rejection of 351n199
Nazi Germany 31, 180n165, 317n114, 322n126
nemoto (focus) 294, 294n67
neo-Marxism 46, 48, 49
New Deal, collectivist tendencies of 288
New World, Europe and 146
new world order: ethics as power and 9–11; principles of 42
Nhu, Madame 104
Nichira (Official in Kudera, proponent of abandonment of conscription) 153, 153n100
Nicholas of Cusa 145n84
Nietzsche, Friedrich xxiii, 19, 20, 29, 167n133, 187n22, 255n150, 271, 314n108, 334n160
Nihilism (Nishitani, K.) 19, 131n51, 134n61
Nihon Gaishi (Rai San-yō) 297n73
Niimi, Commander Masaichi and war scenarios 71–72
Nishi, Amane xviii
Nishida, Kitarō xli–xlii, xliii, 17, 18, 19, 20, 21, 30, 32, 42,

45, 94, 130n49, 133n59, 141n77, 185n10, 189n26; *basho,* idea of 346n187

Nishitani, Keiji xli, xlii, xliii, 5, 16, 17, 19, 20, 21, 29, 30, 44, 50n9, 78n4, 109, 182, 261; America, explanations of 176, 177; America and systems of total war *(sō ryoku sen)* 288; Anglo-American liberty, contradictions of 308, 310–11, 311–12, 312–13; arts and military power 361–62; *ascesis* (disciplining of the self) 355; authority *(shidō)* and persuasion in ideological struggles 284–85; 'co-prosperity' and 'morality,' concepts *(gainen)* of 313, 314; concept of world-historical wars *(sō ryoku sen)* 270; consciousness *(ishiki)* 203n50; contemporary Japan and the world 180–81; creative civil society *(minkan sōi),* dilemmas of 289–90; creativity and innovation in world-historical wars 294, 299, 300–301, 303, 304, 305; dangerous ideas *(kiken shisō),* thoughts about 359n223; ethics of nation *(minzoku),* ethics of world and 213–14, 218, 221–22, 223–24; ethics of the family *(ie)* 240–41, 245; ethics of war and ethical wars 233; ethics *(rinri)* of historical turning points, birth of world-historical consciousness *(jikaku)* and 195; European civilization, defining qualities of 122–23; European reflections on unity of Europe 119; European Renaissance and modern history 142–43, 144, 146; European sense of crisis, Japanese world-historical consciousness and 115–16, 117, 118; European sense of superiority 120–21, 122; focal points of self-awareness, world awareness and 353n204; Greater East Asia as region of nations *(minzoku ken)* 226, 229; *hentaiteki genshō* (abnormal or exceptional) 271n15; historicism, Japanese history and, challenges of teaching 148, 150, 151; historicism, problem of 134; history in the East *(Tōyō),* concept of 127–28; individuals, problem of our awareness as 138–39, 141; institution-building *(kensetsu),* on war and 273n23; Japan and China *(Nippon to Shina)* 201–2, 203, 204–5, 206; Japanese, towards new kind of 257, 259–60; Japanese subjectivity and qualities of leadership *(Nippon no shutai-sei to shidō-sei)* 327, 328–29, 338; mechanized civilization, problem of 130–31, 131–32; methodological approaches to world history *(sekai-shi no hōhō)* 190–91, 193; military power, problem of *(senryōku)* 347–48, 350–51, 355–56, 356–57; military resistance, concentration of powers of *(senryoku no shūchū)* 368; modernity, notion Japan has experienced two kinds of 125; national self-defence state *(kokubō kokka),* world-historical foundations of 316, 318, 320, 321, 322; 'new world order,' reference to 348n192; Nietzsche, favorite German author for 314n108; philosophy and reality 163, 164; philosophy of post-war human resource management, insight on 351n196; politics and spirit of family 249–50, 250–51; politics of philosopher-kings/sages *(kentetsu)* 236, 237; private initiative, argument on 289n55; race, nation, people *(shuzoku, minzoku, kokumin)* 170, 171, 172; scholarship *(gakumon)* and military power 359; society, on positive contribution of individuals to 350n195; 'spirit itself,' use of term 321n125; subjectivity, historical character of 342, 343; unity of matter and mind *(busshin ichinyo),* use of term 348n193; urban life, problems of 172, 173, 175; warrior characteristics *(resshi),* comments on 316n112; Western ethics and Eastern ethics 230–31; world-historical peoples *(minzoku)* and the ethical *(rinrisei)* 196–97, 197–98; world-historical wars and concepts of war and peace 276; world-historical wars *(sō ryoku sen)* and total wars *(zentai sen)* 273, 275–76; world history, philosophers *vs.* historians on 115; world history and morality *(moraru)* 167, 168, 169; world history as method 156–57, 157–58, 159, 160, 161

Nogi, General Count Maresuke 101–2

Nolte, Ernst 99, 105n9, 287n48

Nye, Joseph S. 85, 92n8, 286n46

Obama, Barack (and administration of) 57
oceanic mastery 76–77
Ōhashi, Ryōsuke 21n3, 31, 44–46, 48, 50n7, 51n17, 58n1, 89, 92n13
Ōkawa, Shūmei 100
Okinawa 27
opinion, fact and 35–37
organizational realities 74–75
Oriental ethics, nature of 230
Orientalism xviii, 63; Asianism and 117n23; Orientalist rigour 36; *see also* European Orientalism
O'Rourke, Ronald 79n14
Osaka Castle, siege of 140
Ōshima, Yasumasa xxxii, xlii, xliv, 40, 41, 45–46, 50–51n16, xxxivn1
The Ōshima Memos xxxiii, 21, 33n4, 40, 41, 44, 46, 47, 48, 50n7, 55, 58n1, 69, 92n13, 363n230, 364n233
Ōtsuka, Hisao 116n22
Ottomans 145, 148
Ōuchi, Tsutomu 105n15
outsiders *(tabibito)* 173n154
Overcoming Modernity symposium 21, 31, 33n5, 103, 266n6, 293n63, 335n161

pacific democracy, embrace of 97
'Pacific War,' use of term xxxi–xxxii
pacifism in academe 60–61
Paglia, Camille 35, 49, 50n3
pan-interventionism 26–27
panic and dispair (1941) 72–76
parent-child relationship, family and 243, 248
Parkes, Graham 35, 48–49, 50n1, 51n20, 51n25–27, 134n62, 139n69, 314n108
parochial chauvinism, implied criticism of 256n152
Parry, Admiral Sir William E. 97
Pascal, Blaise 132n56
passivity of masses, assumption of 289n56
Pax Americana 26, 101
Peace Preservation Law (1925) 96
Pearl Harbor, attack on (December 1941) xxxi, 6, 251, 257n153, 268n10
Peasants' Revolt in Germany 144
Petrarca, Francisco 145n85
petroleum, Japanese lack of resources 323n130
Phenomenology of Spirit (Hegel, G.W.F.) 196n38, 207n66, 294n67

Philippines, modernization of 338n168
philology, rejection of scientific approach to 35–36
philosopher-kings 235–36
Philosophic Anthropology (Kōyama, I.) 20
philosophy: autonomy and subjectivity, anticipation of post-war philosophies of 352n202; conservative philosophies 225n99; ethics and 190n27–28; humanist philosophy 130n49; 'moment,' idea in Japanese Hegelian context 212n79; orientating aspect of 112n12; philosophical conceptualization, power of 189n25; 'philosophical sociology' 318n118; post-philosophy, *posthistoire* or the postmodern, ideas of 275n26; *tokushu-kagaku* and 115n19; 'value philosophy' 167–68; verities in, unchanging nature of 190n27; war and requirement for grounding in 263; of world history 186n13
philosophy and reality 161–66; Kōsaka 162, 163, 164; Kōyama 161–62, 163, 164, 165–66; Nishitani 163, 164; Suzuki 161, 162–63, 164–65
The Philosophy of History and Political Philosophy (Kōsaka, M.) 20
Philosophy of History (Hegel, G.W.F.) 196n37
The Philosophy of History (Miki, K.) 19, 20
'On the Philosophy of History' (Nishida, K.) 20
The Philosophy of Primordial Subjectivity (Nishitani, K.) 20, 303n89
The Philosophy of the Nation (Kōsaka, M.) 21
The Philosophy of World History (Kōyama, I.) 21
'The Philosophy of World History' (Nishitani, K.) 21
Pincus, Leslie 49
Plato 16, 204n54, 336n166, 346n187, 359n222
pluralism (world-historical), Kōyama's theory of 307
Pol Pot 105n18
political correctness 259n157
Political Theology (Schmitt, C.) 26
politics: decisive importance to political reflections of Kyoto School xxv; national polity, requirement for new

order consistent with 250n143; political awareness 224
politics and spirit of family 249–52; Imperial Navy at Pearl Harbor *(Hawai no kaisen)*, fighting spirit of 251; Kōsaka 249, 250; Kōyama 249, 250; Meiji Restoration 251; national education, project for 251–52; Nishitani 249–50, 250–51
politics of philosopher-kings/sages *(kentetsu)* 234–37; Buddhist discourse of factual dialectics *(jitsusōron)* 236; Kōsaka 236–37; Kōyama 234–35, 236, 237; Nishitani 236, 237; philosopher-kings 235–36; Seventeen-Article Constitution 235–36
Pollack, Martyn P. 66n13
pooled sovereignty, endorsement of 302n87
positivist history 115n18
post-liberal history 35–37, 47, 48
Post-Meiji Confucian Revolution xxii, 95–97; Confucian revolutions 101, 104; Confucian tipping points 81, 82, 89; revisionism 41
post-philosophy, *posthistoire* or the postmodern, ideas of 275n26
postmodernism 325n136; postmodern Japanese *(gendai Nipponjin)*, creation of 257
powers: imbalance in 211n76; *sō ryoku* (all our powers), etymological decisiveness in 343n175
Prester John 147, 147n89
'private initiative,' use of term 289n52
The Problem of Japanese Culture (Nishida, K.) 20
profit making and pleasure seeking, negation of 314
prophetic nature of Kyoto School meditations xxvi
The Protestant Ethic (Weber, M.) 330n150, 335n162, 367n239
Protestant Reformation 142, 144
Provincializing Europe (Chakrabarty, D.) 118n27
psychology 202n47
purpose, purity of 138, 138n66
pursuit of happiness, American tradition of 311n104
'The Putative Fascism of the Kyoto School and the Political Correctness of the Modern Academy' (Parkes, G.) 48, 49

race, nation, people *(shuzoku, minzoku, kokumin)* 169–72; Kōsaka 169, 170–71, 172; Kōyama 169–70, 171, 172; Nishitani 170, 171, 172; Suzuki 170, 171
racism, qualification of term 220n90
Ranke, Leopold von xxxi, 6, 16, 44, 111n7, 116n21, 166n128, 187n23, 189n25; historians, Suzuki's dissent from ideas on duty of 186n17
Ranke and the Study of World History (Suzuki, S.) 20
Ranke or Hegel: empirical world history vs. the philosophy of world history 186–88; Kōsaka's perspective 188; Suzuki's perspective 186–88
rationality: of creativity 298–99; false clarity of 243; rational self-mastery, Japanese demonstration of 347n191
realism: global orders and 25–28; realist history 47
recalcitrant, Confucian conversion of 283n39
'recognition,' double meaning for 334n158
reconstruction *(kaizō)*, call for (post-First World War) 102
Regan, Ronald 75
regime change, Confucian revolutions and 96
regional stability, establishment of Japan as force for 153
Reich der Zwecke (Kant, I.) 243n130
Reischauer, E.O. and Fairbank, J.K. 15, 21n2
Religion and Nothingness (Nishitani, K.) 19
Renan, Ernest xxvii, 35
research standards, decay of 46–47
revisionism 35–49; Chinese historiography, successes and limitations of 39; Chinese philosophy of history, rejection of 38; chronology, respect for 41; Confucian tipping points 37–39; exhaustion, evidence of 49; fact and opinion 35–37; Greater Asian Co-Prosperity Sphere 40, 43; *The Ideas of the Kyoto School* (Ōhashi, R., ed.) 48–49, 51n23; Imperial Navy, war options of 40–41; *Japan Forum* 49; Japanese Naval Academy, Kōyama's lecture to 42–43; Japanese surrender, Confucian expectations and 39; just war, theory

of 47; Kyoto School, contest with Tōjō regime 42; Kyoto School, flowering of philosophy of 48–49; Kyoto School, historical perspective of 37–39; Kyoto School, Imperial Navy and, links between 41; Kyoto School, Miki's links with 43–44; liberal history, exhaustion of 46–48; Meiji Restoration, Kōyama's perspective on 39; moral history 35–37; moral judgement, contagion of 48; national consensus, urge to foster 38; neo-Marxism 46, 48, 49; New World Order, Principles of 42; Ōhashi's discovery 44–46; opinion, fact and 35–37; Orientalist rigour 36; orthodoxy, world-view and 35–36; philology, rejection of scientific approach to 35–36; post-liberal history 35–37, 47, 48; Post-Meiji Confucian Revolution 41; 'The Putative Fascism of the Kyoto School and the Political Correctness of the Modern Academy' (Parkes, G.) 48–49; realist history 47; research standards, decay of 46–47; textual history, facts on pages of 39–44; Versailles-Geneva-Washington 41; Washington, 'Shidehara appeasement' of 41–42
revolutionary nationalism, rise of 99
Ricardo, David 367n237
Rickert, Heinrich 110n3, 168n135
righteousness, forces of 61–62
Roosevelt, Franklin D. (and administration of) 10, 13, 46, 57, 62, 73, 75, 321n121; war powers of 321n122
Roosevelt, Theodore 11, 12
Rudmin, Floyd W. 78n8
Russo-Japanese War: Confucian revolutions 101, 102; Japan and China *(Nippon to Shina)* 209; Kyoto School 68, 76

Said, Edward W. 50n4, 116n20
Saionji, Baron Kimmochi 118n26
Sakae, Naoki 325n136
samurai: absolute fact of life or death for 136, 136n63, 137n65; relationship with master 137, 137n65; rules of conduct 136; samurai society 238, 248; *shiki* (energy of the samurai), Kōyama's use of term 344n177; Yamamoto's 'book of the samurai' 315n111
samurai inheritance: 'co-prosperity' and 'morality,' concepts *(gainen)* of 315; modernity, notion Japan has experienced two kinds of 124
Sansom, G.B. 174n156
Sartre, Jean-Paul 278n28, 294n68
Scelle, George 65
Schelling, Friedrich W.J. 110n4
Schiller, Friedrich 168n136
Schleiermacher, Friedrich D.E. 110n4
Schmitt, Carl xvii–xviii, xxii, 7n2, 8, 16, 22, 26, 27, 43, 50n11, 56, 57, 63, 66n14, 69–70, 77, 78n5, 79n13, 145n87, 211n78, 268n9, 270n13, 271n15, 300n77, 302n87; 'liberal democracy,' concept of 321n121; sovereignty and international law, reflections on xxvi
scholarship *(gakumon)* and military power 358–61; Kōsaka 360–61; Nishitani 359; Suzuki 358, 360
Schopenhauer, Arthur 334n160
sciences: development of 337n167; division of 292–93; issue of 259; scientific analysis, rejection of 155; scientific *(Wissenschaft)*, terminology of 345, 345n185; 'special sciences,' associations of expression 293n63
Sekai-kan to Kokka-kan 179n160
Sekai-shi no Tetsugaku (Kōyama, I.) 210n73, 330n153, 359n220
self-actualizing subjectivity *(shutaisei no jihatsusei)* 137
self-awakening as nations *(minzoku)*, encouragement of 246
self-criticism, self examination and 111
self-defence state, concept of 276
self-mastery 289n54
self-transparency: lack of, self-limitation of 193n33; self-assessment and *(jikaku)* 112n10
Sen no Rikyū (master of the tea ceremony) 160n114
'Senji Ninshiki no Kichō' (Miki, K.) 43
September 11 attacks on US 77
Sereny, Gitta 65n3
Sergi, Giuseppe 170n147
Seventeen-Article Constitution 234, 235–36
Shidehara, Kijūrō 41–42, 75, 96
Shimamura, Toratarō 19, 21, 176n157

Shintoism 53
Shōwa Kenkyū-kai (Sho-wa Research Association) 94
Shōwa period 82, 88, 119n28
shukanteki seishin (subjective spirit) 339, 339n170
Sibree, J. 196n37
Siegfried, André 177n158
single absolute thing *(zettai ji)*, reversion to 258
Sino-American 'co-dominion,' paving way towards 57
Sino-Japanese War 209
sloganeering 345, 345n182
Slotkin, Richard 76, 78n12
Smith, Adam 292n60, 367n237
Smith, Norman Kemp 326n140
'The Social Ontological Structure of Logic' (Tanabe, H.) 20
society, rules for regulation of 244
Sombart, Werner 116n22
Sontoku, Ninomiya 349n194
Soseki, Natsumei 102
Sources of Japanese Tradition (Tsunoda, R., de Bary, W.T. and Keene, D., eds.) 99, 100, 104n2, 105n6, 105n10
sovereignty: pooling of 231n105; of states 52
Soviet Union 12, 56, 62, 77, 322n127; Communism in, fall of 6
Soyinka, Wole 171n148
Spain, mediating role of 148
speculative appropriation 289
Speer, Albert 59, 65n3
Spencer, Herbert 367n237
Spengler, Oswald 113n15
'spirit' *(Geist)*, non-material powers and 345n180, 359n221, 367n239
The Spirit of Capitalism (Weber, M.) 330n150, 335n162, 367n239
'On the Spirit of *Hakkō no Ichiu*' (Kōyama, I.) 21, 43
spirit *(seishin)*, spiritual values as 202n47
spirituality, fundamental character of 285
St Bartholomew's Day massacre (1572) 3
'On *Staatsräson*' (Nishida, K.) 20
stages of development, criticism of theory of 128–30; Kōsaka 129; Kōyama 129, 130; Suzuki 128–29
Stalin, Josef 322n126
Stalingrad, battle of 317n116

Standpoint of World History and Japan 5–6, 40, 43, 44, 111n6–7, 113n15, 156n106, 183n1, 207n65, 262, 339n170, 363n230
state: organzation of 238; as political community, new approach to 54–55
statism *(kokkashugi)* 207n67
Steiner, Gary 122n36
Steiner, George 161n119
Stephanson, Anders 7n1
Stimson Doctrine (1938) 10
strategic position of Japan, realities of 70–71
The Structure of Scientific Revolutions (Kuhn, T.) xxi
subjectivity: autonomy and subjectivity, anticipation of post-war philosophies of 352n202; significance of notion of xxvi; subjective movement of history 167, 167n131; *Zeitgeist* and 326n139
subjectivity, historical character of 340–43; Kōyama 340; Nishitani 342, 343; Suzuki 342–43
Sudō, Shinji 50n8
Sui dynasty (c.581–618) 154
suicide, Confucian notion of 355n212
supreme mission *(shijō-meirei)* 343n174
Suzuki, Shigetaka xxx, xlii, xliv, 5, 16, 17, 19, 20, 21, 29, 30, 38, 43, 44, 69, 80, 103, 109, 182, 261, 284n43–44; America, explanations of 175–76, 176–77; America and systems of total war *(sō ryoku sen)* 288; arts and military power 362; British politics, understanding of 321n121; on civilizations, notion of 335n162; co-prosperity spheres as *Großräume (kyōei-ken to rekishi-teki hitsuzensei)*, historical necessity for 325–26; Communism and divisions in society, thoughts on 322n127; concept of world-historical wars *(sō ryoku sen)* 269, 270; conflict, continuity of 274n24; contemporary Japan and the world 179, 180; creative civil society *(minkan sōi)*, dilemmas of 290; *do-toku-teki-na seimeiryoku* (Japanese variation of *moralische Energie*) 196n40; East Asia, conception historically of *(tōa no kannen to rekishi-kan)* 305, 306–7; ethics as fundamental problem of co-prosperity spheres *(Großräume)* 252, 255; ethics of nation *(minzoku)*, ethics of world

and 216–17, 218, 219, 222–23; ethics of war and ethical wars 231, 232, 233; ethics *(rinri)* of historical turning points, birth of world-historical consciousness *(jikaku)* and 194; European reflections on unity of Europe 119, 120; European Renaissance and modern history 141–42, 143–44, 146, 147; European sense of crisis, Japanese world-historical consciousness and 116, 117, 118; European sense of superiority 120, 121–22; Greater East Asia as region of nations *(minzoku ken)* 225, 227; historical context of world-historical wars *(sō ryoku sen)* 263–64; historicism, Japanese history and, challenges of teaching 149, 150–51; historicism, problem of 133, 134; history and ethics 185–86; history in the East *(Tōyō)*, concept of 126, 128; history's transcendence of limits of its own time 187n20; ideal organizational structure for waging world-historical wars 290, 293; individuals, problem of our awareness as 137, 138; Japan and China *(Nippon to Shina)* 202, 204, 206–7, 209–10, 211; Japanese, towards new kind of 256, 258, 260; Japanese subjectivity and qualities of leadership *(Nippon no shutai-sei to shidō-sei)* 327, 329, 333, 338; language of, resignation in 284n43–44; liberal economics, attack on natural equilibrium in 367n237; mechanized civilization, problem of 130, 131, 132; methodological approaches to world history *(sekai-shi no hōhō)* 189–90, 191, 193; military power, problem of *(senryōku)* 344–45, 346; military resistance, concentration of powers of *(senryoku no shūchū)* 366–67; modernity, notion Japan has experienced two kinds of 126; nation state, extension of atomic critique on 225n99; national identity, balancing claims of Confucian ethics with requirements of 252n147; national self-defence state *(kokubō kokka)*, world-historical foundations of 316–17, 318, 320–21, 322; philosophy and reality 161, 162–63, 164–65; practical necessity *(jissenteki hitsuzensei)*, triplet of meanings for 185n10; race, nation, people *(shuzoku, minzoku, kokumin)* 170, 171; reflection *(hansei)*, use of term 358n218; scholarship *(gakumon)* and military power 358, 360; self-transparency, Japanese culture and 204n52; *an sich,* translation of term 278n28; stages of development, criticism of theory of 128–29; subjectivity, assumption of modern European command of, challenge to 335n163; subjectivity, historical character of 342–43; *tōi* (Japanese rendering of Kantian concept of *sollen*), use of term 253n148; 'totalitarianism,' use of term 320n120; 'ultranationalism,' use of term 321n123; urban life, problems of 173–74, 175; wars of ideas *(shisō sen),* importance of 280, 284; world-historical conflicts 231n106; world-historical peoples, irony in critique of Hegel's concept 196n38; world-historical peoples *(minzoku)* and the ethical *(rinrisei)* 195–96, 199; world-historical wars and concepts of war and peace 277, 279; world-historical wars *(sō ryoku sen)* and total wars *(zentai sen)* 272–73, 273–74, 275; world history, philosophers *vs.* historians on 114–15; world history and *Großräume (kōiki ken)* 212–13; world history as method 157, 160; world history the problem of our era, reasons why 111–12, 113; world scale movements, evocation of 327n142

Taishi, Shotoku 234–35, 234n115
Taishō democracy, Western enthusiasm for 104
Taishō era 41, 82, 94, 98, 103–4
Taishō experiment 98
Taiwan, mountain aboriginal tribes in 260n158
Takagi, Admiral Sōkichi xli, xlii–xliii
Takahashi, Tetsuya 60–61
Takeda, Hiroko 61, 66n7
Takeuchi, Yoshimi 44, 365n236
Takuan (Zen master) 281n33
Takuboku, Ishikawa 361, 361n226
Tamamoto, Tsunetome 315n111
Tanabe, Hajime xli–xlii, xliii, 17, 18, 19, 20, 21, 30, 45, 52, 54, 55, 58n1, 60,

392   Index

61, 66n5, 133n58–59, 222n95, 238n121, 254n149, 255n150, 269n11, 294n68, 300n78, 302n87, 318n118; on co-prosperity spheres 363n230
techno-fascism 258n155
Teschke, Benno xxiv, 7n2, 22
textual history, facts on pages of 39–44
Thatcher, Margaret 75
thaumazin, Greek idea of 161n120
The Theory of Social Ontology (Mutai, R.) 20
Thermopylae, Spartan '300' at 148n94
thinker as grand strategist 68–78
Thomas, Dylan 168n137
Thucydides 361n224
Thus Spake Zarathustra (Nietzsche, F.) 314n108
timing and form in Confucian revolutions 99–101
Tōgō, Heihachirō 71
Tōjō, Hideki (and governent of) xvii, xx, xxi, xxii, 10, 21, 30, 40, 42, 54, 57, 62, 65, 70, 72, 75, 84, 88, 89, 94, 95–97, 99, 101, 103, 137n64; China and South-East Asia, policies in 307n96, 308n98, 310n101; military conduct, criticism of 204n51; policies of, veiled criticism of 324n132, 352n201; ruling clique and ultranationalist supporters, attack on 282n35; veiled criticism of clique in cautious language 250n142; war criminal? 62–63, 65
Tōjō's decision for war, rejection of 52–57; America, moral-universalism of 53–54; American strategic interest 57; China, economic power of 57; economic regionalism 56–57; expansion as means of survival 55–56; great power status, modern Japanese state and 53–54; Greater East Asian Co-Prosperity Sphere 55–56; *Großraum*, vision of 54, 55–56, 57; hegemonic leadership 55; Meiji project, ambitions of 53; modernization, programme for 53; nation-state, transcendence of 54–57; Sino-American 'co-dominion,' paving way towards 57; sovereignty of states 52; state as political community, new approach to 54–55; Westphalian system 56; world order, hostile and liberal 53
toki o eru (opportunity presented by historical occasion) 297–98, 298n75

Tokugawa, Ieyasu 98, 297n73
Tokugawa Shogunate 53, 81, 98; compulsory attendance of vassals at court 174n156; peace of 124
tokushu-kagaku and philosophy 115n19
Tolstoy, Leo 132n55
Tōsaka, Jun 19
total war *(zentai sen)*: emergence of 267; mechanistic civilization and 133; wars of ideas and 291
totalitarianism xxxii, 91, 136, 141, 220, 221, 230, 244, 310, 319, 320, 320n120, 321, 322
transcendence: of limits of its own time 187n20; special meaning of 334n157
transformation *(henkaku)* 246, 246n136
Transubstantiation, doctrine of xxviii
Trevelyan, George Macaulay 8, 10, 64
Troeltsch, Ernst 112n11, 133n60
Truman, Harry S. (and administration of) xxiv–xxv, 25, 46, 62, 97
trust and loyalty in social relations 137
truth in history, conflict and 278–79
Tsunoda, Ryusaku 93, 104n2
Tsushima, naval triumph at (1905) 76

Ujigawa River, battles at 140n73
United States *see* America
unity, transcendent unity of contrasting ideas 141n76
universal moralism, resurrection of 26–27
urban life, problems of 172–75; Kōsaka 173, 175; Kōyama 172, 173, 174, 175; Nishitani 172, 173, 175; Suzuki 173–74, 175

Valéry, Paul 120n31, 358n219
validation *(urazukeru)* of ethics 230
The Valor of Ignorance (Lee, H.) 72
'value philosophy' 167–68
Versailles, Treaty of (1919) xxiv, 3, 26; ethics as fundamental problem of co-prosperity spheres *(Großräume)* 254; German resentment after 27, 219n89; unfairness of 219–20; Versailles-Geneva system and 221n91, 270n13, 310n100
Versailles-Geneva-Washington system 26, 41, 74–75
Vico, Giambattista xxxi, 133n58
victory at sea, Japanese vision of 76
Viglielmo, Valdo H. 346n187, 347n189

violence: enforcement of liberal norms with 64–65; violent transformations in Japanese politics 97–98
visible hands 351n198
vision, sharing of 30
Voltaire 66n13, 167n133; Westphalian reticence of 64–65

Wagner, Richard 354n211
Waley, Arthur xxviii–xxix
Walker, David 215n85
Wall Street Crash 351n197
Walzer, Michael 62–63, 66n11
Wang-ming Ng 33n1
Wannsee Conference on 'Final Solution' policies 209n69
'War on Terror' xxiv, xxv, 64, 271n15
warfare: changes over time in forms of 267–68; effort of Japan, doomed nature of 343n173; terminological precision about nature of xxxii–xxxiii; war-as-revolution factionalism 97; war decision, 'total' mobilization and 103–4; war of total resistance *(sō ryoku sen)* 318n117
warrior society 136; Confucian suspicion of warriors 98–99
wars of ideas *(shisō sen)*, importance of 279–84; annihilation, description of 281n34; goal of wars of ideas 281–82; Great Harmony *(Taiwa/Yamato)* 282–83, 282n38; *haja-kenshō* (destruction of wickedness) 281n32; intellectual persuasion, importance of 280; Kōsaka 283; Kōyama 279–80, 283–84; Mahayana Buddhism 280–81; Suzuki 280, 284
Wars of Religion, sectarian strife of 65
wartime motivation, challenge to 345, 345n181
Watsuji, Tetsurō 19, 141n78
web-based virtuality 85–86
Weber, Max 25, 46–47, 122n34, 266n6, 272n20, 330n150, 335n162, 351n199, 367n239; economic rationalization, critique of 293n63; *The Protestant Ethic* 330n150, 335n162, 367n239; *The Spirit of Capitalism* 330n150, 335n162, 367n239
Western ethics and Eastern ethics 229–31; Kōsaka 229–30; Kōyama 230; *moralische Energie*, ethics and 230; Nishitani 230–31; Oriental ethics,

nature of 230; validation *(urazukeru)* of ethics 230
Western individualism, embrace of 86
Westphalia, Treaty of (1648) 3
Westphalian system xviii, xxiv, 4, 8, 53, 56, 60, 62, 63, 65, 69, 75; Japan studies 62, 65; Kyoto School 75; Tōjō's decision for war, rejection of 56
Williams, David 51n22–24, 58n1, 66n9, 78n9, 91n6, 105n20, 133n58, 238n121, 254n149, 269n11, 310n103, 319n119, 320n120
Wilson, Woodrow 3, 6, 8, 9–10, 11, 12, 16, 24, 26–27, 47, 57, 61–62, 63, 65, 69, 100, 225n98, 270n13, 300n77; assault on Westphalian system (1919) xxiv; counter-revolution of xviii, 3, 9, 10, 26, 27, 53, 62, 70, 100, 270; war to end all wars, notion of xxxiii
Wolin, Richard 122n36
Woodings, R.B. 215n85
workplace responsibilities 352n200
world-historical necessity 178–79
world-historical peoples *(minzoku)* and the ethical *(rinrisei)* 195–201; Kōsaka 197, 198, 199, 200; Kōyama 199–200; Nishitani 196–97, 197–98; Suzuki 195–96, 199
'The World Historical View of History' (Suzuki, S.) 21
world historical war *(sō ryoku sen)* xxx–xxxiv
world-historical wars, philosophy of (third symposium, 24 November, 1942): America and systems of total war *(sō ryoku sen)* 287–88; Anglo-American liberty, contradictions of 307–13; arts and military power 361–63; authority *(shidō)* and persuasion in ideological struggles 284–87; 'co-prosperity' and 'morality,' concepts *(gainen)* of 313–16; Co-Prosperity Sphere and our world-historical war 299–300; co-prosperity spheres as *Großräume (kyōei-ken to rekishi-teki hitsuzensei)*, historical necessity for 322–27; co-prosperity spheres *(Großräume)* and the philosophy of the nation *(kyōei-ken to minzoku no tetsugaku)* 300–305; concept of 'world-historical wars' *(sō ryoku sen)* 266–72; creative civil society *(minkan sōi)*, dilemmas of

289–90; creativity and innovation in world-historical wars 294–99; East Asia, conception historically of *(tōa no kannen to rekishi-kan)* 305–7; historical context of world-historical wars (so-ryoku sen) 262–66; ideal organizational structure for waging world-historical wars 290–93; Japanese subjectivity and qualities of leadership *(Nippon no shutai-sei to shidō-sei)* 327–40; military power, problem of *(senryōku)* 343–58; military resistance, concentration of powers of *(senryoku no shūchū)* 363–69; national self-defence state *(kokubō kokka)*, world-historical foundations of 316–22; scholarship *(gakumon)* and military power 358–61; subjectivity, historical character of 340–43; wars of ideas *(shisō sen)*, importance of 279–84; world-historical wars and concepts of war and peace 276–79; world-historical wars *(sō ryoku sen)* and total wars *(zentai sen)* 272–76

world-historical wars and concepts of war and peace 276–79; 'eternal war,' idea of 278; Kōsaka 277, 279; Kōyama 277, 279; liberal imperium, abstraction and continuity of fight against 277n27; Nishitani 276; Suzuki 277, 279; truth in history, conflict and 278–79

world-historical wars *(sō ryoku sen)* and total wars *(zentai sen)* 272–76; conflict, continuity of 273n22, 274n24–25; 'ideal' and Weber's notion of 'ideal type' 272n20; institution-building *(kensetsu)*, on war and 273n23; Kōsaka 273, 274, 275; Kōyama 272, 273, 274, 275; Nishitani 273, 275–76; post-philosophy, *posthistoire* or the postmodern, ideas of 275n26; self-defence state, concept of 276; Suzuki 272–73, 273–74, 275

world history: embrace of 110–11; Europe and idea of 111–12; philosophy of 186n13

world history, philosophers *vs.* historians on 114–15; Kōsaka 114, 115; Kōyama 115; Nishitani 115; Suzuki 114–15

world history, viewing Japanese history from standpoint of 152–55; Buddhism, introduction of 154–55; Korean kingdoms, Japanese absorption of 153–54; Kōsaka 154; Kōyama 152–54, 154–55; Minama (Gaya), destruction of authority in 152–53; regional stability, establishment of Japan as force for 153; scientific analysis, rejection of 155; Sui dynasty (c.581–618) 154

world history and *Großräume (kōiki ken)* 211–13; Greater East Asian Co-Prosperity Sphere 213; Kōsaka 211–12, 213; Kōyama 212; Suzuki 212–13

world history and Japan, standpoint of (first symposium, 26 November, 1941): America, explanations of 175–77; contemporary Japan and the world 178–81; European civilization, defining qualities of 122–23; European reflections on unity of Europe 119–20; European Renaissance and modern history 141–48; European sense of crisis, Japanese world-historical consciousness and 115–19; European sense of superiority 120–22; historicism, Japanese history and, challenges of teaching 148–51; historicism, problem of 133–35; history in the East *(Tōyō)*, concept of 126–28; individuals, problem of our awareness as 135–41; mechanized civilization, problem of 130–33; modernity, notion Japan has experienced two kinds of 123–26; philosophy and reality 161–66; race, nation, people *(shuzoku, minzoku, kokumin)* 169–72; stages of development, criticism of theory of 128–30; urban life, problems of 172–75; world history, philosophers *vs.* historians on 114–15; world history, viewing Japanese history from standpoint of 152–55; world history and morality *(moraru)* 166–69; world history as method 155–61; world history the problem of our era, reasons why 110–14

world history and morality *(moraru)* 166–69; Kōsaka 167–68, 169; Kōyama 166, 167, 168, 169; Nishitani 167, 168, 169

world history as method 155–61; Kōsaka 155, 157, 158–59, 160–61; Kōyama 156, 157, 158, 159, 160, 161; Nishitani 156–57, 157–58, 159, 160, 161; Suzuki 157, 160
world history the problem of our era, reasons why 110–14; genuine reform *(kakushin)* 112; Kōsaka 110–11, 112–13; Kōyama 113–14; Suzuki 111–12, 113; world history, embrace of 110–11; world history, Europe and idea of 111–12
world order 326, 326n138, 327n141; hostile and liberal 53; plea for remaking of 30–31
Worldviews and Views of the State (Nishitani, K.) 20

Xavier, St. Francis 147n90

Yamamoto, Admiral Isoruko xlii
Yamamoto, Isoroku 71
Yamamoto, Seisaku 353n204
Yamamoto, Yūzō 183n1, 184
Yamashita, General Tomoyuki 62
Yamato (traditional name for Japanese) 301n82
Yanō, Jinichi 209n71
Yonai, Admiral Mitsomasa xli, 40–41, 41–42, 46, 54, 55, 69, 70, 72, 97
Yoritomo Shogunate 297n73
Yoshida, Kazuo 352n200
Yusa, Michiko xli
Yūshoku Jinshu no Sensen 118n25
Yutan, Lin 336n164

Zen Buddhism 15, 21, 31, 32
Zen no Kenkyū (Nishida, K.) 17, 18
Žižek, Slavoj 195n36, 204n52
Zschimmer, Eberhard 131n52